T0181683

Logic Programming

Logic Programming

Proceedings of the 1999 International Conference on Logic Programming

edited by Danny De Schreye

The MIT Press
Cambridge, Massachusetts
London, England

ISSN 1061-0464
ISBN 978-0-262-54104-6 (pb. : alk. paper)

Contents

Program Committee

The Association for Logic Programming

The Association for Logic Programming (ALP) was founded in 1986. In addition to the ICLP'99 conference being held in Las Cruces, New Mexico, USA, from November 29 to December 4, 1999, the ALP has sponsored International Conferences and Symposia in Melbourne (1987), Seattle (1988), Lisbon (1989), Cleveland (1989), Jerusalem (1990), Austin (1990), Paris (1991), San Diego (1991), Washington D.C. (1992), Budapest (1993), Vancouver (1993), Santa Margherita Ligure (1994), Ithaca, New York (1994), Kanagawa (1995), Portland, Oregon (1995), Bad Honnef (1996), Leuven (1997), Port Jefferson, New York (1997), and Manchester, United Kingdom (1998). The proceedings of all these meetings are published by The MIT Press.

The Association sponsors workshops, contributes support to other meetings related to logic programming, and provides limited support for attendance at its sponsored conferences and workshops by participants in financial need. Members receive the Association's newsletter quarterly and can subscribe to the *Journal of Logic Programming* at a reduced rate.

The affairs of the Association are overseen by the Executive Council. Current members are Philippe Codognet, Veronica Dahl, Danny De Schreye, Joxan Jaffar, Catuscia Palamidessi, Peter Stuckey, and Peter Szeredi; Association President: Krzysztof Apt; and Past President: David Scott Warren. The current officers of the Association are: Robert Kowalski, Secretary; Francesca Toni, Treasurer and Conference Budget Auditor; Veronica Dahl, Conference Coordinator; and Patricia Hill, Newsletter Editor.

Further information about the Association may be obtained from:

Cheryl Anderson-Deakin
ALP Administrative Secretary
ICSTM, DOC
180 Queen's Gate
London SW7 2BZ

Tel: +44 (171) 594 8226
Fax: +44 (171) 589 1552
e-mail: alp@doc.ic.ac.uk

Series Foreword

The logic programming approach to computing investigates the use of logic as a programming language and explores computational models based on controlled deduction.

The field of logic programming has seen a tremendous growth in the last several years, both in depth and in scope. This growth is reflected in the number of articles, journals, theses, books, workshops, and conferences devoted to the subject. The MIT Press Series in Logic Programming was created to accommodate this development and to nurture it. It is dedicated to the publication of high-quality textbooks, monographs, collections, and proceedings in logic programming.

Ehud Shapiro
The Weizmann Institute of Science
Rehovot, Israel

Preface

This volume contains the papers presented at ICLP'99, the Sixteenth International Conference on Logic Programming, held in Las Cruces, New Mexico, from November 29 to December 4, 1999. The conference is primarily sponsored by the Association for Logic Programming.

There were 88 papers submitted to this conference. The program committee selected 35 papers from them to appear in this volume. In addition, there were 4 invited talks by Ken Bowen, Vladimir Lifschitz, Fernando Pereira, and Bernhard Thalheim, and 3 tutorials by Manuel Hermenegildo, Ken Kahn, and Peter Van Roy. Frank Harary was the banquet speaker.

The conference was organized in a theme-based fashion, with invited sessions, regular sessions, and workshops following the main research streams in logic programming. The conference also contained a poster session, offering a wider view of the active research in logic programming. One-page abstracts of these posters appear in this volume. Other events were the open poster session, providing an open forum for researchers active in the field, and the Prolog programming competition.

Many people contributed to the conference and to this volume. I want to thank the authors of the submitted papers. The quality of the work submitted to this conference was very high. I much regret that there were many papers reporting on significant work that the programming committee could not accept for this volume in their present form. I thank the members of the program committee and the many referees for their thorough evaluations. In particular, I want to thank Dale Miller and Catuscia Palamidessi for continuing their electronic discussions on submitted papers until a few hours before Catuscia gave birth to their child. My best wishes for a most wonderful future to Nadia Alexandra Miller.

I thank Gopal Gupta, the general conference chair, for his enthusiasm and his continuous support and help. I thank Andy King for the poster coordination, Enrico Pontelli for the workshop coordination and for maintaining the web pages, Michael Leuschel and C. R. Ramakrishnan for publicity work, Vladimiro Sassone for providing his software for electronic handling of submissions and program committee interaction, Nikolay Pelov for continuous support on adapting and using this system, and Bart Demoen for organizing the open poster session and the Prolog programming competition and for much local support.

I thank Monique, Fardou, and Armel for putting up with a husband and a father who was more of a zombie-at-home than usual.

Danny De Schreye

Referees

Jose Alferes
Ilies Alouini
Maria Alpuente
Jean-Marc Andreoli
Sergio Antoy
Roberto Bagnara
Pedro Barahona
Steve Barker
Natashia Boland
Sven-Erik Bornscheuer
Stefan Brass
Gerhard Brewka
Krysia Broda
Kai Bruennler
Maurice Bruynooghe
Francisco Bueno
Michele Bugliesi
Jo Calder
Manuel Carro
Barbara Catania
Augusto Celentano
Serenella Cerrito
Iliano Cervesato
Weidong Chen
Eric de la Clergerie
Nicoletta Cocco
Michael Codish
Marco Comini
Agostino Cortesi
Michael Covington
Carlos Viegas Damasio
Gabriel David
Hendrik Decker
Giorgio Delzanno
Marc Denecker
Yves Deville
Agostino Dovier
Thomas Eiter
Maarten van Emden

Jesper Eskilson
Sandro Etalle
Francois Fages
Alfred Fent
Jose Alberto Fernandez
M. C. F. Ferreira
Manuel Vilares Ferro
Gilberto File
Peter Flach
Maurizio Gabbrielli
Bjorn Gamback
Alejandro J. Garcia
Michael Gelfond
Yan Georget
Fosca Giannotti
Parke Godfrey
Roberta Gori
Mustapha Hadim
James Harland
Warwick Harvey
Pat Hill
Joshua Hodas
Chris Hogger
Christian Holzbaur
Jacob Howe
Gerda Janssens
Bharat Jayaraman
Yvonne Kalinke
Michael Kohlhase
Robert Kowalski
Per Kreuger
Frank Kriwaczek
Yves Lesperance
Francesca Levi
Renwei Li
Vladimir Lifschitz
Anne Liret
Pedro Lopez-Garcia
Salvador Lucas

Victor Marek
Julio Marino
Kim Marriott
Bern Martens
Viviana Mascardi
Maria Chiara Meo
Luis Monteiro
Chris Moss
Tobias Mueller
Gopalan Nadathur
Lee Naish
Ilkka Niemela
Catuscia Palamidessi
Alessandra Di Pierro
Inna Pivkina
Enrico Pontelli
Konstantin Popov
Fred Popowich
German Puebla
Alexander Rabinovich
Horst Reichel
Olivier Ridoux
Stephen Rochefort
Vitor J. R. Rocio
Francesca Rossi
Salvatore Ruggieri
Paul Sabatier
Konstantinos Sagonas
Patrick Saint-Dizier
Antonino Salibra
Taisuke Sato
Fredric Saubion
Torsten Schaub
Christian Schulte
Dietmar Seipel
Marek Sergot
Guillermo Simari
Jan-Georg Smaus
Zoltan Somogyi

Referees (continued)

Invited Talks

Declarative Programming for a Messy World

Fernando Pereira
AT&T Labs – Research
A247, Shannon Laboratory, 180 Park Avenue
Florham Park, NJ 07932, USA

Programming emerged from the tidy world of tabular data, logic, and artificial languages associated with formalized scientific and business disciplines. In contrast with this idealized realm, real-world data is highly variable, its interpretation is often ambiguous, and uncertainty tinges any inferences drawn from it. Now, advances in data storage, transmission and encoding have brought the messiness of real-world data into the digital world in the form of digitized signals, speech and images, and natural language text. Researchers from many different areas and backgrounds have been drawn to this wealth of messy data and developed many techniques and systems for analyzing, selecting and transforming it, including speech recognizers, image classifiers and indexers, video trackers, search engines, text information-extraction systems, biological sequence matchers and classifiers, multimedia indexers and abstracters, and data mining systems.

Research on processing messy data has drawn upon and contributed to a wide range of disciplines – approximate matching algorithms, statistics, signal processing, information theory, pattern recognition, machine learning – to find ways of accommodating variability, disambiguating ambiguous situations, and ranking the plausibility of alternative answers. However, this extraordinary cross-fertilization has not occurred with respect to programming languages and systems. While application-specific languages like S and MATLAB are very convenient for expressing the mathematical core of many signal processing, pattern recognition, statistical and machine learning algorithms used for drawing inferences from messy data, they offer no systematic means for expressing the relationships between those inferences and actual data transformations. Other application-specific languages like Perl provide useful primitives for transforming textual data, but they offer no help in dealing with ambiguity and combination of uncertain evidence. Furthermore, large-scale processing of messy data requires a much more efficient integration of inference and data transformation steps than is typically possible in those application-specific languages.

Nevertheless, several recent developments show that ideas from declarative programming languages and their implementation have a potentially very valuable role to play in systems for processing messy data. In each case, the expressions of a language denote (sets of) possible expression values with associated weights of evidence, and the denotational semantics of

4

the language combines sets of alternative values and their weights of evidence according to appropriate rules for evidence combination, for instance the laws of probability.

The first example, which I will discuss in most detail, is a library for defining and combining weighted finite-state transductions that attempts to do for speech recognition what lex and yacc did for programming language compilation [3, 4]. The objects of the library, implemented as weighted finite-state transducers, generalize regular expressions to weighted input-output relations that can be composed as well as combined using the standard regular operations union, concatenation and Kleene closure. The theory of rational power series provides the semantic foundation for the library. Different choices of weight algebra (a semiring) lead to different methods of evidence combination, but powerful optimization algorithms, which generalize classical determinization and minimization, are applicable independently of the choice of semiring. Implementation techniques based on tabulation and lazy evaluation are play also a crucial role in the efficiency of the library.

The second example is WHIRL, a system that combines deductive database and information retrieval techniques to answer queries over Web-derived tables in which join fields may have to be approximately matched [1]. The main semantic idea in WHIRL is to assign weights to answer substitutions that represent the degree of textual similarity between variables involved in approximate matches. Efficient search techniques from information retrieval and artificial intelligence are used to generate substitutions in best-first order, ensuring that the answers for which there is most evidence can be found efficiently.

The third example shows how graphical models and belief network ideas from artificial intelligence and statistics can be extended to a rich class of stochastic single-assignment programs [2]. Many special purpose formalisms for probabilistic inference, such as probabilistic grammars and object-oriented belief networks, are special cases of this language. Furthermore, these ideas suggest how to extend the finite-state formalism of the first example into a richer pattern-matching and transformation language.

While all of these examples are based on intuitively related semantic and computational intuitions, much remains to make those connections rigorous and to distill the semantic and implementation ideas in them into their elementary constituents. Only then will we be able to recombine those elements into a family of general declarative computational abstractions for managing variability, ambiguity, and uncertainty, following when possible the lead of constraint programming.

References

[1] William W. Cohen. Integration of heterogeneous databases without common domains using queries based on textual similarity. In *Proceedings of*

ACM SIGMOD-98, 1998.

[2] Daphne Koller, David McAllester, and Avi Pfeffer. Effective Bayesian inference for stochastic programs. In *Proceedings of the 14th National Conference on Artificial Intelligence (AAAI)*, 1997.

[3] Mehryar Mohri, Fernando Pereira, and Michael Riley. A rational design for a weighted finite-state transducer library. In *WIA '97: Proceedings of the Workshop on Implementing Automata*. Springer-Verlag, 1997.

[4] Fernando Pereira and Michael Riley. Speech recognition by composition of weighted finite automata. In Emmanuel Roche and Yves Schabes, editors, *Finite-State Language Processing*, pages 431–453. MIT Press, Cambridge, Massachusetts, 1997.

Logics and Database Modeling

Bernhard Thalheim
Computer Science Institute,
Brandenburg University of Technology at Cottbus,
PostBox 101344, D-03013 CottbusUniversity
thalheim@informatik.tu-cottbus.de

Abstract

Database modeling approaches are applications of methods developed in discrete mathematics, mathematical logics and algebra. They have been developed in separate from research performed in the logics community. Only during the last years an integration of results can be observed. Research on logics, logic programming can highly contribute to database technology and database modeling in special. Integration can be based on declarative database models such as the entity-relationship model. This papers surveys in brief some of the starting points for common research of both communities.

1 Background

Database literature and teaching is divided into at least two branches: applications and their formal treatment and database theory. The first branch uses database theory mainly on the basis of results obtained until the mid-80ies. For computer engineers, logics and algebra becomes more and more a 'Terra incognita'. There are already statements that database theory research is 'dead on its feet'[1]. However, database theory, database application formalization and database applications have gained from logics and discrete mathematics more than it is acknowledged.

From the other side, database research and research on logics has still a small overlap. The logics basis of database research is known to a certain extent. Database research could gain a lot from logics research if their common root is better known and used. A large number of results obtained in logics can be directly applied to databases. This possibility is based on the declarative way of specifying properties of database applications.

Database modeling is one application area of logics. Declarative database models such as the entity-relationship model can be investigated on the basis of results developed in logics. In this paper we demonstrate the similarity of research in both areas and show how results obtained in one area can be generalized to the other area.

---

[1] M. Stonebraker, ICDE, Vienna 1993

1.1 Database Modeling

The problem of database design can be stated as follows:
Design the logical and physical structure of a database in a given database management system (or for a database paradigm), so that it contains all the information required by the user and required for the efficient behavior of the whole information system for all users. Furthermore, specify the database application processes and the user interaction.

The implicit goals of database design are:

- to meet all the information (contextual) requirements of the entire spectrum of users in a given application area;
- to provide a "natural" and easy-to-understand structuring of the information content;
- to preserve the designers entire semantic information for a later redesign;
- to achieve all the processing requirements and also a high degree of efficiency in processing;
- to achieve logical independence of query and transaction formulation on this level;
- to provide a simple and easily to comprehend user interface family.

While on the one hand the input to the process is informal and sometimes fuzzy, the final output of the database design is a database definition with formal syntax, including qualitative and quantitative decisions related to problems of physical design such as physical placement, indexing and the organization of data.

1.2 Database Models

Database design is based on one or more database models. Often design is restricted to structural aspects. Static semantics which is based on static integrity constraints is sparsely used. Processes are then specified after implementing structures. Behavior of processes can be specified by dynamic integrity constraints. In a late stage, interfaces are developed. Due to this orientation the depth of the theoretical basis is different as shown in the following table:

	Used in practice	Theoretical background
Structures	well done	well developed
Static semantics	partially used	well developed
Processes	somehow done	parts and pieces
Dynamic semantics	some parts	some parts and tiny pieces
Interfaces	intuitive	nothing

Database design requires consistent and well-integrated development of structures, processes *and* interfaces. We will demonstrate below that extended entity-relationship models allow to handle all three aspects. Before introducing ER models we discuss first object-orientation.

Object-oriented database models have been developed in order to over-come the impedance mismatch between languages for specification of structural aspects and languages for the specification of behavioral aspects. So far, no standard approach is known to object-orientation. *Objects* are handled in databases systems and specified on the basis of database models. They can own an *object identifier*, are structurally characterized by *values* and *references* to other objects and can posses their own *methods*, i.e.

$$o = (i, \{v\}, \{ref\}, \{meth\})$$

The value characterization is bound to a *structure* of the type T which is already defined. Characterizing properties of objects are described by *attributes* which form the structure of the object. Objects also have a *specific semantics* and a *general semantics*. The properties describe the *behavior* of objects. Objects which have the same structure, the same general semantics and the same operators are collected in *classes*. The structure, the operations and the semantics of a class are represented by *types* $T = (S, O, \Sigma)$. In this case, the modeling of objects includes the association of objects with classes C and their corresponding value type T and reference type R. Therefore, after classification the structure of objects is represented by

$$o = (i, \{(C, T, v)\}, \{(C, R, ref)\}, \{(T, meth)\})$$

The recognized design methodologies vary in the scale of information modeled in the types. If objects in the classes can be distinguished by their values, then the identifiers can be omitted and we use *value-oriented modeling*. If this is not the case, we use an *object-oriented approach*. In the object-oriented approach, different approaches can be distinguished. If all objects are identifiable by their value types or by references to identifiable objects, then the database is called *value-representable*. In this case, the database can also be modeled by the *value-oriented* approach, and a mapping from the value-representable scheme to a value-oriented scheme can be generated. If the database is not value-representable, then we have to use object identifiers. In this case either the identifier handling should be made public or else the databases cannot be updated and maintained. Therefore, value-representable databases are of special interest. Thus, we can distinguish database models as displayed in Figure 1.

Database specifications are defined over **type systems**. For each type the *generic operations insert, delete* and *update* for the basic treatment of object insertion, object deletion and object update into classes. The *multi-layer architecture* allows descriptive management of the database. In this approach we can separate the internal (physical or logical) layer from the conceptual layer and the last from the external layer which is used to define user interfaces of the database. Database semantics is usually based on model-theoretic treatment. Furthermore, the query treatment is based on the *closed-world assumption*.

9

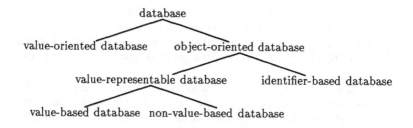

Figure 1: Classification of Database Models

It has been shown in [1, 9] that the concept of the object identifier can only be treated on the basis of higher-order epistemic and intuitionistic logics. Furthermore, identification by identifiers is different from identification by queries, equational logics and other identification methods. For this reason, the concept of the object identifier is far more complex than wanted and cannot be consistently and equivalently treated in database systems. Furthermore, methods can be generically derived from types only in the case if all objects are value-representable. Value-representable cyclic type systems require topos semantics[10] what is usually too complex to be handled in database systems. It can be shown that value-representable, non-cyclic type systems can be represented by value-oriented models.

The entity-relationship model has been extended to the higher-order entity-relationship model (HERM)[11]. HERM is a set-theoretic based, declarative model which objects are value-oriented. For this reason, object identifiers are omitted.

1.3 Inductive Type Construction

Induction has shown to be an efficient and simple process of definition and reasoning that determines enumerable sets of finite structures reachable from an initial base case. Induction has been used for Hilbert-type definitions in the following sense:

- The initiality condition determines base elements.

- The iteration condition allows new elements to be constructed from initial elements using constructors. Additionally correctness criteria may be applied to the constructors.

- The minimality condition restricts the set to be constructed that only elements so constructed are definable.

Induction is based on the *minimality principle*: everything is forbidden that is not allowed.

A *type constructor* is a function from types to a new type. The constructor can be supplemented with a *selector* for retrieval (such as *Select*) and *update functions* (such as *Insert*, *Delete*, and *Update*) for value mapping from the new type to the component types or to the new type, with correctness criteria and rules for validation, with default rules, with one or more user representations, and with a physical representation or properties of the physical representation.

Typical constructors used for database definition are the *set*, *tuple*, *list* and *multiset* constructors. For instance, the set type is based on another type and uses algebra of operations such as union, intersection and complement. The retrieval function can be viewed in a straightforward manner as having a predicate parameter. The update functions such as *Insert*, *Delete* are defined as expressions of the set algebra. The user representation is using the braces $\{,\}$. The type constructors define type systems on basic data schemes, i.e. a collection of constructed data sets. In some database models, the type constructors are based on pointer semantics.

General operations on type systems can be defined by *structural recursion*. Given a types T, T' and a collection type C^T on T (e.g. set of values of type T, bags, lists) and operations such as generalized union $\cup_{C^T}$, generalized intersection $\cap_{C^T}$, and generalized empty elements $\emptyset_{C^T}$ on C^T. Given further an element h_0 on T' and two functions defined on the types

$$h_1 \quad : \quad T \to T' \qquad\qquad h_2 \quad : \quad T' \times T' \to T' \quad .$$

Then we define the structural recursion by insert presentation for R^t on T as follows

$$srec_{h_0,h_1,h_2}(\emptyset_{C^T}) \;=\; h_0$$
$$srec_{h_0,h_1,h_2}(\{\!|s|\!\}) \;=\; h_1(s) \qquad \text{for singleton collections } \{\!|s|\!\}$$
$$srec_{h_0,h_1,h_2}(\{\!|s|\!\} \cup_{C^T} R^t) \;=\; h_2(h_1(s), srec_{h_0,h_1,h_2}(R^t))$$
$$\text{iff } \{\!|s|\!\} \cap_{C^T} R^t = \emptyset_{C^T} \;.$$

All operations of the relational database model and of other declarative database models can be defined by structural recursion. Structural recursion is also limited in expressive power. Nondeterministic while tuple-generating programs (or object generating programs) cannot be expressed.

Another very useful modeling construct is *naming*. Each concept and each concept class has a name. These names can be used for the definition of further types.

1.4 Overview on the Paper

The paper is oriented towards a logics community. For this reason, all classical definitions are omitted. They can be found in any textbook on mathematical logics or books on logic programming etc. such as [4, 7, 8].

The entity-relationship model is the main declarative and powerful database model. The model has attracted a large number of researchers. Results discussed in this paper *without* reference are taken from [11] where the theory of the entity-relationship models has been summarized and compiled and a large bibliography has been collected. The collection [3] surveys different ER-oriented modeling approaches.

The main aim of the paper is to give a survey on results obtained for the entity-relationship model.

2 The Extended Entity-Relationship Model

In this section we partially define an extension of the entity-relationship model, the higher-level entity-relationship model (HERM). The model has maximal expressiveness compared with value-based database models.

2.1 Specification of Static and Dynamic Components

The entity-relationship model uses basic (or atomic) data types such as INT, $STRING$, $DATE$, etc. the null type $\perp$ (value not existing). Using type constructors for tuples, finite (multi-)sets and lists and union we construct more complex types based on standard set semantics:

$$t = b \mid (a_1 : t_1, \ldots, a_n : t_n) \mid \{t'\} \mid \langle t' \rangle \mid [t'] \mid (a_1 : t_1) \cup \ldots \cup (a_n : t_n)$$

These types will be used to describe the domains of (nested) attributes.

Attributes allow to conceptually abstract from describing values. Associated data types provide the possible values. We use a set of *names* $\mathcal{N} = \mathcal{N}_0 \cup \mathcal{N}_c$ for attributes such as *address, street, city, name, first_name, destination, trip_course* etc. Elements from $\mathcal{N}_0$ are called atomic attributes. Each atomic attribute is associated with a atomic type $dom(A)$.
Nested attributes are inductively constructed from simpler or atomic attributes by the iteration condition:
For already constructed nested attributes $X, X_1, \ldots, X_n$ and new attributes $Y, Y_1, \ldots, Y_m$ the sequences

$$Y(X_1, \ldots, X_n), \ Y\{X\}, \ Y\langle X \rangle, \ Y[X], \ Y((Y_1 : X_1) \cup \ldots \cup (Y_n : X_n))$$

are tuple-valued, set-valued, list-valued, multiset-valued and union-valued nested attributes.
Associated complex types are defined by the attribute structure. In the logical calculus below we use only tuple-valued and set-valued attributes. The calculus can similarly be extended.

For all types we use set semantics based on the basic type assignment.

Entity Types (or *level-0-types*) $E = (attr(E))$ are defined by a set $attr(E)$ of nested attributes. A subset X of attributes can be used for identification. This subset is called key of E. In this case we consider only those classes which objects can be distinguished by their values on X.

Relationship Types (or *level-(i + 1)-types*) $R = (comp(R), attr(R))$ are defined by a tuple $comp(R)$ of component types at levels $\leq i$ with at least one level-i-type component and a set $attr(R)$ of nested attributes. We use set semantics with expanded components under the restriction that $comp(R)$ forms a key of R. Unary relationship types with $|comp(R)| = 1$ are subtypes.

Clusters (also level-i-types) $C = C_1 \oplus \ldots \oplus C_k$ are defined by a list $\langle C_1, \ldots, C_k \rangle$ of entity or relationship types or clusters (components). The

12

maximal level of components defines level i. We set semantics (union) or equivalent pointer semantics.

Corresponding classes of a type T are denoted by T^C. $\mathcal{R}(T)$ is the set of all classes of T. Basic type assignment is equivalent to pointer semantics with *value representability*.

The usual graphical representation of the extended ER model is a labeled directed acyclic graph. Entity types are denoted graphically by rectangles. Relationship types are graphically represented by diamonds with arrows to their components. Attributes are denoted by strings and attached to the types by lines. Key components are underlined.

A HERM scheme S is a set $\{R_1,...R_m\}$ of types of level $0,...,k$ which is closed, i.e. each set element has either no components (entity type) or only components from $\{R_1,...R_m\}$.

An example of a HERM diagram is displayed in Figure 2.

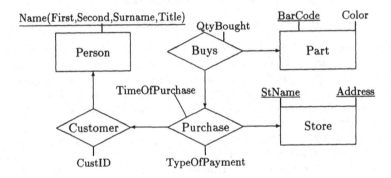

Figure 2: A Customer-Relationship Diagram

A person can be customer. People are identified by their names. Customers have an additional customer identification. A store is characterized by its name and address. For each purchase a customer can buy several parts. Addresses and names can be more complex than displayed in the diagram. The diagram is used for representing types. For instance, in our example the relationship type *Purchase* is defined by

Purchase = (Customer, Store, { TimeOfPurchase, TypeOfPayment }) .

Since customers are persons purchases are identified by the name of the person and the name and the address of the store.

Based on the construction principles of the extended ER model we can introduce the HERM algebra. In general, for a HERM scheme S the set $Rec(S)$ of all expressions definable by structural recursion can be defined. Since this set is too large, we use only some specific simple operations:

- Set-operations such as $\cap, \cup, \backslash$ for intersection, union and difference of sets over the same types and the cartesian product $\times$ of sets are de-

13

fined in the algebra.

- The projection $T^C[T']$ of sets T^C over a type T to a subtype T' of T restricts the objects in T^C to components of T'. Identical objects are taken once.
  The selection $\sigma_\alpha(T^C)$ is used to select those elements of T^C which satisfy the condition α.

- A type mapping $h_1 : T \to T'$, can be extended by structural recursion to comprehensions $ext(h_1)(T^C)$ for the union function $h_2 = \cup_{T'}$ and the null element h_0 of T'.
  Typical comprehensions are nesting ν and unnesting μ. The first operation is the application of the set constructor to a subtype of the given type. The later is the deconstruction of a set construction. Renaming, structure destroying operations, reordering are comprehensions.

The join operation $\bowtie$ is definable by the cartesian product, the selection of those tuples of the result which are equal on common components and the projection to the set of components of the two types.

The algebraic operations can be used to define *queries* on the scheme. For instance, the query   *Who buys products from Safeway ?*   is specified by the expression

$(Person^C \bowtie Customer^C \bowtie Purchase^C \bowtie \sigma_{\text{StName="Safeway"}}(Store^C))[Name]$.

Database management is based on the assumption that the internal management can be based on the logical and physical schema, the database application development can be based on the conceptual schema and the management of interaction can be based on external schemata. Conceptual schemata can be specified on the basis of the entity-relationship model. The conceptual schema is mapped to logical and physical schemata. External schemata are derived from the conceptual schema. For this reason, they can be mapped to specific functionality of the database engine. External schemata are specified by *views*. If we use the HERM then views are expressions of the HERM algebra. We can define algebraic expressions for views. Then for database management by relational database systems, views and algebraic expressions are mapped to families of relational views and families of relational expressions.

Data warehouse, internet or OLAP (online analytical processing) applications are specifiable on the basis of HERM views extended by algebraic expressions on views.

2.2   Logical Language and Calculus

Since HERM database schemes are acyclic and types are strictly hierarchical we can construct a many-sorted logical language by generalizing the concept of variables.

Given a HERM scheme S. Let $\mathcal{N}_S$ the set of all names used in S including type names. A sort is defined for each name from $\mathcal{N}_S$. The sort sets are constructed according to the type construction in which the name has been used. Entity and relationship types are associated with predicate variables. The logical language uses type expansion for representation of relationship types. We can used key-based expansion or full expansion. Full expansion uses all components of the component type. Key-based expansion uses only key components. If all names are different in S then we can use lower-case strings for variable names. If this is not the case then we use a dot notation similar to the record notation in programming languages.

For instance, the entity type *Person* is associated with the unary predicate variable

person (name(first,second,surname,title)) .

The relationship type *Purchase* is associated with the predicate variable

purchase(customer(person(name(first,second,surname,title)),ID),
          store(name,address),typeOfPurchase, timeOfPurchase) .

The HERM predicate logic is inductively constructed in the same way as the predicate logic. Instead of simple variables we use structured variables.

This language enables us to specify restriction on the scheme. for instance, the formula

part(barCode,color) ∧ part(barCode,color') → color = color'

expresses that the same part with the same ID cannot have different color, i.e. parts can be identified by their bar code.

Queries can be expressed in a similar way. The query above is expressed by the logic program

q(x) ← purchase(customer(person(x),_),store("Safeway",_),_,_) .

Logic programs are more expressive than the algebra since recursion can be expressed by a program. A large variety of results has been obtained for *deductive databases* (see for instance [2]), i.e. databases schemata extended by logical formulas. Sophisticated query evaluation strategies can be applied for optimization of database behavior. Logic programs can also be used for defining database views or OLAP schemata. Since logic programs are integrated into HERM the query and view management facilities of deductive databases are incorporated. Since HERM schemata are hierarchical stratification and layering is also applicable to HERM query processing.

We can also specify behavior of a database over lifetime. A database is modified by an action or more general by a transaction. Basic actions are queries or conditional manipulation operations. Manipulation operations such as *insert, delete, update* are defined in the HERM algebra. Conditions enable us to restrict the impact of manipulation operations. Actions are parallel programs inductively defined over basic actions. Transactions are used to restrict actions to those which do not validate integrity of the database. In general, they are constructed similar to actions. However, the state of a database is changed after performing a transaction only if specified integrity constraints remain to be valid.

Database behavior can be specified on the basis of states. Given a HERM scheme $S = \{R_1, ... R_m\}$. A *state* is the set of classes $\{R_1^C, ... R_m^C\}$ with $R_i^C \in \mathcal{R}(R_i)$, $1 \leq i \leq m$ which satisfies certain restrictions Σ. Let us denote by $\mathcal{R}(S)$ the set of all states on S. For the first step let us assume that $\Sigma = \emptyset$.

A transition system on S is a pair $\mathcal{TS} = (\mathcal{S}, \{\xrightarrow{a} | \ a \in \mathcal{L}\})$ where $\mathcal{S}$ is a non-empty set of state variables, $\mathcal{L}$ is a non-empty set (of labels), and for each $a \in \mathcal{L}$ $\xrightarrow{a} \subseteq \mathcal{S} \times (\mathcal{S} \cup \{\infty\})$.
State variables are interpreted by states from from $\mathcal{R}(S)$. Transitions are interpreted by transactions on S.
Database lifetime is specified on the basis of paths on $\mathcal{TS}$. A *path* π through a transition system is a finite or ω length sequence of the form $s_0 \xrightarrow{a_1} s_1 \xrightarrow{a_2} ....$ The length of a path is its number of transitions.

For the transition system $\mathcal{TS}$ we can introduce now a *temporal dynamic database logic* [6] using the quantifiers $\forall_f$ (always in the future)), $\forall_p$ (always in the past) $\exists_f$ (sometimes in the future), $\exists_p$ (sometimes in the past).

Dynamic database logic has not attracted a lot of research except [5] . For this reason, we mainly discuss the introduced HERM logic in this paper.

2.3   Co-Inductive Types and Interaction Modeling

Interaction is based on observation far more complex than what can be modeled by inductive types. Recently introduced approaches [12] allow modeling of interaction on the basis of co-induction and an observation paradigm: observing already constructed elements.

Co-Induction is a stronger form of definition and reasoning for non-enumerable sets of infinite structures. It requires stronger creation principles and as shown in [12] extends mathematical modeling power from inductively definable processes to observation processes for interaction. The initiality condition is eliminated. The direction of iteration is reversed, i.e. instead of construction we use destruction of composite structures into progressively more primitive ones.

Co-induction and *abduction* support the *maximality principle*: everything is allowed that is not forbidden. Instead of that, the minimality principle requires that user interfaces are specified such that all exceptions are specified or derivable from the specification. In this case, the number of exceptions is combinatorically exploding.

3   Database Semantics

We extend now HERM schemes to schemata by adding integrity constraints to the scheme. In Figure 3 different classical integrity constraints are distinguished in HERM:

static integrity constraints (for the representation of the semantics for all possible instances of the database) and

dynamic integrity constraints (for the representation of the behavior of the
database during its lifetime, e.g. the correctness of sequences for states
of the database).

Static integrity constraints can be put into classes according to their func-

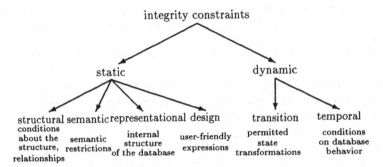

integrity constraints

static   dynamic

structural semantic representational design   transition   temporal
conditions
about the   semantic   internal   user-friendly   permitted   conditions
structure,   restrictions structure   expressions   state   on database
relationships   of the database   transformations   behavior

Figure 3: The Classification of Integrity Constraints

tion in the scheme:
1. structural dependencies, i.e. dependencies which are in reality used for
   the database design and which express conditions of the structure, e.g.
   inclusion, exclusion, functional dependencies;
2. semantic dependencies, i.e. dependencies which are in reality used for
   database design and are semantic restrictions, e.g. functional, multivalued dependencies;
3. representation dependencies, i.e. dependencies which are used for representing or implementing the database, e.g. inclusion, join, tuple-
   generating dependencies;
4. design dependencies, i.e. dependencies which can be used to create
   a user-friendly schema design, e.g. general functional and generalized
   functional dependencies.

It can be proved that these constraints can be used in dynamic integrity
constraints. Dynamic integrity constraints are useful for the maintenance
of the database system. At present, there is no general framework for the
utilization of dynamic integrity constraints. There are several proposals for
treating functional dependencies and transition constraints. Dynamic integrity constraints can be classified according to their functionality:
1. transition constraints, i.e. constraints which restrict the application of
   database operations and database state transformations, e.g. pre- and
   postconditions for update operations;
2. temporal formulas, i.e. constraints on state sequences.

Transition constraints can be specified on HERM-database paths with a
length of 2.

17

3.1 Static Integrity Constraints

Static integrity constraints on HERM schemes $S = \{R_1, ...R_m\}$ define a function C from $\mathcal{R}(R_1) \times \mathcal{R}(R_2) \times ... \times \mathcal{R}(R_m)$ to { *true, false* }. The set $SAT(S, C)$ is a subset of the cartesian product of classes on R_i which elements are evaluated by C to *true*.

The set of integrity constraints introduced for ER models is very rich, e.g.

functional dependencies $X \to Y$ stating that if objects are equal on X then they are equal on Y too,

inclusion constraints $e \subseteq e'$ stating that the set obtained by applying the algebraic expression e is a subset of that obtained by e',

cardinality constraints $comp(e, e') = (m, n)$ stating for an algebraic expression e and a subexpression e' of e that elements of the set obtained by application of e' appear in the set obtained by application of e at least m times and at most n times (for instance, the cardinality constraint *card(owns,Person)* = (1,4) states that a persons owns between one and four cars),

multivalued dependencies $X \to Y|Z$ stating that if two objects are equal on X then another object of the class can be constructed by shuffle product from the two on X.

The set of integrity constraints is very rich. Some classes are axiomatizable (e.g. functional and full multivalued dependencies), other are not axiomatizable (e.g. cardinality constraints restricted to classes for e). The implication problem is decidable for some classes (e.g. functional dependencies) and undecidable for others (e.g. functional and inclusion dependencies).

Some classes of integrity constraints (e.g. functional and full multivalued dependencies) have an equivalent representation by propositional formulas. In this case their treatment is very simple.

The logical treatment of integrity constraints might not coincide with the meaning applied by users. For illustrating this consider cardinality constraints in Figure 3.1. Classically lookup semantics has been used for cardi-

Figure 4: The Meaning of Cardinality Constraints

nality constraints, i.e. in the example, a person owns none, one or two cars. Lookup constraints turned out not to be generalizable to relationship types with more than 2 component types. For this reason, participation interpretation is more appropriate. Furthermore, the cardinality constraints might be interpreted in different ways:

1. *Strong interpretation*: There are cars which are not owned by somebody and also cars which have two owners.

2. *Logical interpretation*: Cars are owned by nobody or by one or by two persons.

3. *Deontic interpretation*: A car is normally owned by nobody or up to 2 persons.

The different interpretation lead to different logical systems which different operational support

Database practice has led to several doubtful beliefs:

The **completeness assumption** in database design has been used for restructuring and optimizing applications. It requires that all integrity constraints valid in the schema are implied by those already specified. The task of design is to develop complete sets of constraints.

Normalization (restructuring) aims in deriving structures which have a simple operation support and maintenance. Normalization is a form of optimization. The **local restructuring assumption** supposes that optimization by restructuring can be applied locally.

The **equal importance assumption** presupposes that all constraints have the same importance for the database application.

The **static specification assumption** postulates that the set of static integrity constraints does not change over time. In this case, exceptional states overwhelm specifications.

The belief that **applications have usually simple sets of constraints** can be used in some applications. In most cases, however, the size of minimal sets of integrity constraints is exponential in size of components.

Missing, inapplicable, computed and incorrect values are mixed by the **null value representation**. Later computations become incorrect or are not interpretable.

3.2 Dynamic Integrity Constraints

Static integrity constraints can be enforced in three different ways:

1. We derive transition constraints and maintain those constraints by restricting the applicability of operations.

2. Operations are refined to such operations which invariants imply the static integrity constraint.

3. We check the validity of constraints after performing a transaction and in the case of invalidation go back to the state the database was before the transaction.

One approach widely accepted in the database community is the rule triggering approach. Active database schemata and maintenance has been based on rule triggering systems. However, rule triggering requires beside confluence and termination also that the system has the required behavior. If we consider the system $C_1 \subseteq C_2$, $C_1 \subseteq C_3$, $C_2 \| C_3$ of class inclusion constraints then application of rule triggering approaches to the operation $insert_{C_1}$ nondeterministically derives one of the operations $delete_{C_3} delete_{C_2} delete_{C_1}$ or $insert_{C_3} delete_{C_2} delete_{C_1}$ or $insert_{C_2} delete_{C_3} delete_{C_1}$ which are all wrong.

The greatest consistent specialization of the operation is *fail*[11].

Integrity maintenance is still an open problem. Approaches recently developed on description logics and abductive reasoning can be generalized to management of layered constraint maintenance systems for ER schemata. Instead of the "all-or-nothing" approach used for transaction management integrity maintenance can be based on obligations and permissions. Transaction management is based on the pessimistic assumption that integrity constraints have to be valid at any time and integrity maintenance has to be done immediately.

Abduction can be applied to reasoning on problematic structures and on causes for integrity fault.

4   Concluding Remarks on Research Gaps

Declarative database models such as the entity-relationship model are widely applied in applications. The following difficult problems are still unsolved although methods developed for logic programming can be used for their solution:

- *Satisfiability of constraint sets*: Database constraints can conflict or contradict. Dependencies, i.e. constraints that are valid in the empty database and domain-invariant, are satisfiable. Sets of cardinality constraints can be unsatisfiable.

- *Flexible management of static constraints*: Constraints can be of different meaning and importance. Integrity constraint maintenance should consider these differences and be more flexible.

- *Treatment of implicit constraints*: Database models have their own implicit correctness conditions. Modeling constraints and restrictions are different from constraints specified for an application. Thus, treatment should be different.

- *State-based process specification*: Several process languages have been used for parts of behavior description. There is currently no consistent theory for handling such specification although the situation calculus can be good basis for treatment of dynamic specifications.

- *Parallel execution* of database programs is the normal case of database operating. Program logics can be applied to modeling of such processes.

- *Unsafety of raw data*: Database operating is currently based on the assumption that all data are correct. However data might be insecure, unprecise, aggregated, (currently) not available etc. Evaluation programs need to distinguish such data.

- *Support for integrity modeling*: The database application modeling is a step-wise construction procedure with refinement, revision similar to theory development. Heuristics and design principles are necessary.

- *Schema equivalence*: Although schema equivalence in undecidable and not axiomatizable reasoning on the equivalence of different schemata is required whenever several developers are specifying, extending or refining schemata.
- *Integration of interaction*: Schemata are developed based on inductive approaches. Interaction is based on co-induction and abduction. Thus, the two paradigms should be integrated for applications development.
- *Considering sets of real-world constraints*: Constraint theory is currently based on classes of real-world constraints. However, classification by constraint classes is far too general. Instead of that, behavior pattern for dependency sets can be used.

Application of logic programming to database technology has been mainly based on deductive databases or knowledge bases. In this case, databases are treated on a proof-theoretic approach. These results have gained the maturity for getting applied in real world applications. However, logics research can be applied to other problems as well. Areas of logics which can be applied in database theory and technology include the following but are not restricted to these areas:

- *Integration of theories*: Schemata can be understood as theories. The meta-theory on theories developed in the last 50 years can be extended to database handling, integration and mapping.
- *Gentzen etc. calculus*: Static integrity constraints have mainly be considered on the basis of Hilbert-type calculus. Join dependencies have been axiomatized by a Gentzen calculus. Non-axiomatizability by Hilbert-type calculi does not imply non-axiomatizability by other calculi.
- *Non-monotonic reasoning*: Database behavior is not monotonic. It is state-dependent. Semantical constraints can be changed depending on the state.
- *Deontic, modal and dynamic logics*: Integrity maintenance is currently based on the (strong) logic interpretation of constraints although it is known that constraints have different meaning and pragmatics.
- *Knowledge theory*: Federated databases can be understood as knowledge islands what eases the database integration problem.
- *Situation logics:*: State are used in the situation calculus. In this calculus, transactions and active database behavior has been considered. It seems possible to express database behavior in situation logics.

Acknowledgement

I am thankful to Danny De Schreye and the ICLP'99 PC for the invitation since writing this survey has already been an aim for several years and has been delayed for several reasons. Due to the PC invitation the review has been written at the end.

References

[1] C. Beeri, B. Thalheim, Identification as a Primitive of Database Models. *7th Int. Workshop 'Foundations of Models and Languages for Data and Objects' FoM-LaDO'98* (Eds. T. Polle, T. Ripke, K.-D. Schewe), Kluwer Acad. Publ., London 1998, 19-36.

[2] S. Ceri, G. Gottlob, A. Tanca, *Logic programming and databases.* Springer 1990.

[3] P.P. Chen, J. Akoka, H. Kangassalo, B. Thalheim, *Conceptual modeling: current issues and future directions.* LNCS 1565, Springer, 1998.

[4] H. Gallaire and J. Minker, *Logic and databases.* Plenum Press, New York, 1978.

[5] U.W. Lipeck, *Dynamic integrity of databases.* Informatik-Fachberichte 209, Springer, Heidelberg, 1989.

[6] U.W. Lipeck and B. Thalheim (eds), *Modeling database dynamics.* Springer Workshops in Computing, Heidelberg, 1993.

[7] G. Metakides and A. Nerode, *Principles of logic programming.* Elsevier Publ., Amsterdam, 1996.

[8] J. Minker (ed.), *Foundations of deductive databases and logic programming.* Morgan Kaufman, Los Altos, 1988.

[9] K.-D. Schewe, *The specification of data-intensive application systems.* Advanced PhD, TU Cottbus, 1994.

[10] K.-D. Schewe and B. Thalheim, A generalization of Dijkstra's calculus to typed program specifications. *Proc. FCT'99,* Iasi, Romania, 1999.

[11] B. Thalheim, *Fundamentals of the entity-relationship model.* Springer Publ., Heidelberg, 1999.

[12] P. Wegner and D. Goldin, Interaction as a framework for modeling. In [3] pp. 243 - 257.

Adventures in the Prolog Trade

Ken Bowen
Applied Logic Systems, Inc.
PO Box 400175
Cambridge, MA 02140
ken@als.com

Summary
The speaker has spent the past 15 years as a vendor of Prolog systems and services. The talk will describe some of his experiences, primarily focusing on applications encountered.

Answer Set Planning

Vladimir Lifschitz
University of Texas
Austin, TX 78712, USA
vl@cs.utexas.edu

Abstract

In "answer set programming," solutions to a problem are represented by answer sets, and not by answer substitutions produced in response to a query, as in conventional logic programming. Instead of Prolog, answer set programming uses software systems capable of computing answer sets. This paper is about applications of this idea to planning.

1 Introduction

Over the years, the declarative semantics of negation as failure has attracted the attention of many researchers. Take the one-line program

$$p \leftarrow not \ q. \tag{1}$$

Given this program, a logic programming system is expected to answer *yes* to query p. Can we explain why—without referring to query evaluation procedures, in declarative terms?

Each of many existing theories of negation as failure answers this question in its own way. One can say, for instance, that p logically follows from the "completion" of this program [1]; or that p is true in its "well-founded model" [22]; or that p belongs to its "answer set" [7].

For some logic programs, theories of negation as failure do not describe a *yes*-part of the set of ground queries as definitely as they do for program (1). There may be a "gray area" where neither *yes* nor *no* would be an appropriate answer. This happens, for instance, for the program consisting of two rules

$$\begin{aligned} p &\leftarrow not \ q, \\ q &\leftarrow not \ p. \end{aligned} \tag{2}$$

The completion of (2) does not entail p, but it does not entail the negation of p either. The truth value assigned to p in the well-founded model of (2) is neither *true* nor *false*; it is *undefined*. Furthermore, (2) has two answer sets. One of them is $\{p\}$; it suggests that p should be viewed as a *yes*-query. But the second answer set $\{q\}$ suggests that that would be incorrect. The situation with query q is similar. Both p and q are in the gray area of program (2). Accordingly, the evaluation of these queries by SLDNF resolution would not terminate.

One might think that programs with large gray areas are pretty much useless. But such programs play an important part in the work of the proponents of *answer set programming*[1] [14, 16] who represent solutions to a problem by answer sets, and not by answer substitutions produced in response to a query, as in conventional logic programming. Instead of Prolog, answer set programming requires a software system capable of computing answer sets. Four such systems were demonstrated at the Workshop on Logic-Based AI held in June of 1999 in Washington, DC: SMODELS, DLV, DERES and CCALC.[2] Their creators keep learning from each other and from the experience accumulated by users, and the performance of the systems keeps improving with every new release.

Two examples of answer set programming are given in Section 3 below. A potentially important application of this programming style is described in [19]. Answer set programming has been also used as a planning method, which is the main subject of this paper.

2 Answer Sets

First we will we review the definition of an answer set. Consider a set of propositional symbols, called *atoms*. A *literal* is an expression of the form A or $\neg A$, where A is an atom. (We call the symbol $\neg$ "classical negation," to distinguish it from the symbol *not* used for negation as failure.[3]) A *rule element* is an expression of the form L or *not* L, where L is a literal. A *rule* is an ordered pair

$$Head \leftarrow Body \qquad (3)$$

where *Head* and *Body* are finite sets of rule elements. If

$$Head = \{L_1, \ldots, L_k, not\ L_{k+1}, \ldots, not\ L_l\}$$

and

$$Body = \{L_{l+1}, \ldots, L_m, not\ L_{m+1}, \ldots, not\ L_n\}$$

$(n \geq m \geq l \geq k \geq 0)$ then we will write (3) as

$$L_1; \ldots; L_k; not\ L_{k+1}; \ldots; not\ L_l \leftarrow L_{l+1}, \ldots, L_m, not\ L_{m+1}, \ldots, not\ L_n. \qquad (4)$$

A rule (3) is a *constraint* if $Head = \emptyset$. A *program* is a set of rules.

The notion of an answer set is defined first for programs that do not contain negation as failure ($l = k$ and $n = m$ in every rule (4) of the program). Let Π be such a program, and let X be a consistent set of literals.[4] We say that X is *closed* under Π if, for every rule (3) in Π, $Head \cap X \neq \emptyset$ whenever $Body \subseteq X$. We say that X is an *answer set* for Π if X is minimal among the sets closed under Π (relative to set inclusion).

For instance, the program

$$p; q \leftarrow$$
$$\neg r \leftarrow p \qquad (5)$$

has two answer sets: $\{p, \neg r\}$ and $\{q\}$. If we add the constraint

$$\leftarrow q$$

to (5), we will get a program whose only answer set is $\{p, \neg r\}$.

The last example illustrates a general property of constraints: adding a constraint to a program affects its collection of answer sets by eliminating the answer sets that "violate" this constraint. This is true for programs with negation as failure also.

To extend the definition of an answer set to programs with negation as failure, take any program Π, and let X be a consistent set of literals. The *reduct* Π^X of Π relative to X is the set of rules

$$L_1; \ldots; L_k \leftarrow L_{l+1}, \ldots, L_m$$

for all rules (4) in Π such that X contains all the literals $L_{k+1}, \ldots, L_l$ but does not contain any of $L_{m+1}, \ldots, L_n$. Thus Π^X is a program without negation as failure. We say that X is an *answer set* for Π if X is an answer set for Π^X.

For instance, the reduct of (1) relative to $\{p\}$ consists of one rule $p \leftarrow$. Since set $\{p\}$ is an answer set for this reduct, it is an answer set for (1). The reduct of (1) relative to $\{p, q\}$ is the empty set. Since set $\{p, q\}$ is not an answer set for this reduct, it is not an answer set for (1).

3   Programming with Answer Sets

As an example, we will show how answer set programming can be used to find all Hamiltonian cycles in a given finite directed graph G. To this end, we will turn G into a program whose answer sets correspond to the Hamiltonian cycles in G. (The program is reproduced, with minor changes, from [14].)

Let the vertices of G be $0, \ldots, n$. The set of atoms of the program consists of the expressions $in(u, v)$ for all edges $\langle u, v \rangle$ of G and the expressions $reachable(u)$ for all vertices u. The first group of rules is

$$in(u, v); \neg in(u, v) \leftarrow \tag{6}$$

for all edges $\langle u, v \rangle$. The answer sets for this part of the program are in a 1–1 correspondence with the subsets of the edges of G: an answer set X corresponds to the subset $\{\langle u, v \rangle \ : \ in(u, v) \in X\}$. We will now add constraints that eliminate all subsets other than the Hamiltonian cycles.

This is done in two steps. First, the constraints

$$\leftarrow in(u, v), in(u, w) \tag{7}$$

for all edges $\langle u, v \rangle$ and $\langle u, w \rangle$ with $v \neq w$ and the constraints

$$\leftarrow in(u, w), in(v, w) \tag{8}$$

```
                          1            2
       1    2             2            1
     -------            -----        -----
```

Figure 1: Configurations of blocks for $n = 2$

for all edges $\langle u, w \rangle$ and $\langle v, w \rangle$ with $u \neq v$ are added. These constraints prohibit edges with a common endpoint. It remains to ensure that, by starting at 0 and following the *in*-edges, one can visit all vertices of G and come back to 0. To this end, we define

$$
\begin{aligned}
reachable(u) &\leftarrow in(0, u) \\
reachable(v) &\leftarrow reachable(u), in(u, v)
\end{aligned}
\tag{9}
$$

and add the constraints

$$
\leftarrow not\ reachable(u).
\tag{10}
$$

Our second example is a favorite toy world of AI researchers—the blocks world. Each of n blocks can be somewhere on the table or on top of exactly one other block. Each block can have at most one other block immediately on top of it. Figure 1 shows all possible configurations of blocks for $n = 2$. If $n = 3$, the number of possible configurations is 13. How to find all possible configurations?

The answer sets for program (11) below correspond to the possible configurations of a given set of blocks. The range of the "block variables" b, b', b'' consists of the names of blocks; the range of the "location variables" l, l' includes both the names of blocks and the symbol *table*.

$$
\begin{aligned}
&on(b, l); \neg on(b, l) \leftarrow \\
&\leftarrow on(b, l), on(b, l') &&(l \neq l') \\
&\leftarrow on(b, b''), on(b', b'') &&(b \neq b') \\
&supported(b) \leftarrow on(b, table) \\
&supported(b) \leftarrow supported(b'), on(b, b') \\
&\leftarrow not\ supported(b)
\end{aligned}
\tag{11}
$$

4 Systems DLV and SMODELS

We will now briefly describe some possibilities of two of the systems mentioned in the introduction. System DLV computes answer sets for finite programs without negation as failure in the heads of rules ($l = k$ in every rule (4) of the program). For instance, given the input file

```
p :- not q.
q :- not p.
```

it will return the answer sets for program (2). Given the input file

```
p; q.
-r :- p.
```

it will return the answer sets for program (5). Schematic rules with variables can be used to specify sets of rules obtained by instantiation. Variables are assumed to range over the object constants used in the program (function symbols are not allowed in the current version), and "built-in" predicates can be used to express restrictions on the values of variables. For instance, program (6)–(10) can be turned into an input for DLV as follows:

```
in(U,V); -in(U,V) :- edge(U,V).

:- in(U,V), in(U,W), V!=W.
:- in(U,W), in(V,W), U!=V.

reachable(U) :- in(0,U).
reachable(V) :- reachable(U), in(U,V).

:- not reachable(U), #int(U).
```

Appended to this should be the description of graph G in the form of a definition of edge/2. Built-in predicate #int/1 expresses membership in an initial segment of nonnegative integers; the length of the segment is specified on the command line when DLV is invoked.

The input language of system SMODELS is less expressive in that the program is supposed to be nondisjunctive (besides $l = k$, $k \leq 1$ in every rule (4) is required). Also, the current version of SMODELS does not support classical negation.[5]

For some purposes, the unavailability of disjunctive rules is an essential limitation. But a disjunctive rule of the form

$$p; \neg p \leftarrow$$

can be always replaced by a pair of rules similar to (2):

$$p \leftarrow not\ \neg p,$$
$$\neg p \leftarrow not\ p$$

(see [3]). Furthermore, the use of classical negation can be always avoided, because a negative literal $\neg p$ can be replaced by a new atom p' provided that the constraint

$$\leftarrow p, p' \tag{12}$$

is added to the program. Using these two tricks, programs (6)–(10) and (11) can be turned into programs containing neither ; nor $\neg$ (in these two cases, adding constraints (12) is not even necessary). Then SMODELS can be used

Initial state: Goal:

```
                                   3    6
      1    3    5                  2    5
      2    4    6                  1    4
    ----------------             ---------
```

Figure 2: A planning problem in the blocks world

instead of DLV to find Hamiltonian cycles and configurations of blocks. Actually, SMODELS allows the user to specify such modified programs in a concise way, without introducing the new atoms explicitly. The same can be done with the planning program discussed in Section 5.

5   Planning

In a planning problem, we look for a sequence of actions that leads from a given initial state to a given goal state.[6] Turning one configuration of blocks into another (Figure 2) is a planning problem. We will use this example here to illustrate some ideas of answer set planning.

To specify a planning problem completely, we need to say which actions are allowed in a plan. When a block is "clear" (there is nothing on top of it), we assume that it can be placed on top of any tower of blocks or on the table. Thus moving a block located in the middle of a tower, along with everything on top of it, is prohibited. This is because we think of moving performed by a robot that grasps blocks from above.

To make the blocks world more interesting, let us assume that the robot has two grippers that can move blocks independently. For instance, in the initial state shown in Figure 2, blocks 1 and 3 can be moved concurrently. Since a block can be moved only when it is clear, moving blocks 1 and 2 concurrently is impossible. (That would require a better synchronization between the grippers than the robot is supposed to have.) Besides, we assume that the robot is unable to move b onto b' if b' is being moved also. Even with these restrictions, the planning problem above can be solved in 3 steps:

1. Place blocks 1 and 3 on the table.
2. Place block 2 on block 1 and block 5 on block 4.
3. Place block 3 on block 2 and block 6 on block 5.

Research on planning has two components: representation (design of declarative languages for specifying planning problems) and search (design of planning algorithms).

An important class of planning algorithms is based on the idea of reducing a planning problem to the problem of finding a satisfying interpretation for a set of propositional formulas. This is known as satisfiability planning [9]. The latest satisfiability planning system created by the inventors of this method is available at `http://www.research.att.com/~kautz/` `blackbox` . Answer set planning differs from satisfiability planning in that it uses logic programming rules instead of propositional formulas. An important advantage of answer set planning is that the representation of properties of actions is easier when logic programs are used instead of classical logic, in view of the nonmonotonic character of negation as failure.[7]

The idea of answer set planning is due to Subrahmanian and Zaniolo [20], and the results of computational experiments that use SMODELS to compute answer sets are reported in [2, 16]. The logic programming representation of the blocks world below follows [3] and is based on some of the ideas of [15, 21, 10, 11].

The key element of answer set planning is the representation of a dynamic domain such as the blocks world in the form of a "history program"—a program whose answer sets represent possible "histories," or evolutions of the system, over a fixed time interval. In the next section we show how to write such a program for the blocks world. The answer sets for that program represent possible evolutions of the blocks world over the time interval $0, \ldots, T$ for a fixed positive integer T. A history of the blocks world is characterized by the truth values of atoms of two kinds: $on(b, l, t)$ ("block b is on location l at time t") and $move(b, l, t)$ ("block b is moved to location l between times t and $t + 1$"). Here b ranges over blocks and l ranges over locations, as in Section 3; the time variable t ranges over the time instants $0, \ldots, T$, except that the atoms $move(b, l, t)$ are introduced only for $t \neq T$.

When such a program is available, we can find a plan of length T that solves a given planning problem, or establish that there is no such plan, in the following way. The history program is extended by the constraints representing the initial state and the goal state of the problem. In the example above, $T = 3$ and the constraints are

$$\begin{aligned} &\leftarrow not\ on(1, 2, 0)\\ &\leftarrow not\ on(2, table, 0)\\ &\leftarrow not\ on(3, 4, 0) \end{aligned} \qquad (13)$$

$$\ldots$$

$$\begin{aligned} &\leftarrow not\ on(1, table, 3)\\ &\leftarrow not\ on(2, 1, 3)\\ &\leftarrow not\ on(3, 2, 3) \end{aligned} \qquad (14)$$

$$\ldots$$

The answer sets for the extended program correspond to the plans of length T that lead from the initial state to the goal state. A planner would invoke a system for computing answer sets to find an answer set X for the extended program, and then return the list of all atoms in X that represent actions (in the case of the blocks world, the atoms beginning with $move$).

To find a plan consisting of the smallest possible number of steps, the planner would invoke a system for computing answer sets several times, with different values of T, using binary search if desired. (A similar process is used in satisfiability planning.)

6 A History Program for the Blocks World

Since actions in the blocks world domain are deterministic, a history is completely defined by its starting point—the truth values of atoms $on(b, l, 0)$—and the actions that have been executed—the truth values of $move(b, l, t)$. We begin the construction of the history program by allowing these atoms to have arbitrary values:

$$on(b, l, 0); \neg on(b, l, 0) \leftarrow , \qquad (15)$$

$$move(b, l, t); \neg move(b, l, t) \leftarrow \qquad (t \neq T). \qquad (16)$$

Some of the other rules will encode what we know about the effects of moving blocks by characterizing the truth values of the atoms $on(b, l, t)$ with $t \neq 0$. We will also have rules expressing what we know about the executability of actions and about possible configurations of blocks.

The main rule tells us that moving a block b onto a location l causes b to be on l:

$$on(b, l, t + 1) \leftarrow move(b, l, t) \qquad (t \neq T). \qquad (17)$$

But this is not all that needs to be said about the configuration of blocks at time $t + 1$. Two things are still missing.

First, we need to say that the blocks that are not being moved remain where they were. In other words, we need to solve the frame problem for the blocks world. This can be done by postulating

$$on(b, l, t + 1) \leftarrow on(b, l, t), not \ \neg on(b, l, t + 1) \qquad (t \neq T). \qquad (18)$$

The idea of this solution to the frame problem goes back to [17].

Second, we need to ensure that when a block is moved to a new location, it disappears from the old one. An elegant way to do this does not even mention moving blocks. We can use the rule

$$\neg on(b, l, t) \leftarrow on(b, l', t) \qquad (l \neq l') \qquad (19)$$

which is similar to the second line of (11), except that now on has a time argument, and that this rule is not a constraint.[8]

The history program includes also the constraints expressing the assumptions about the executability of $move$ stated in Section 5. A block can be moved only when it is clear:

$$\leftarrow move(b, l, t), on(b', b, t) \qquad (t \neq T) \qquad (20)$$

and when the target is not moving:

$$\leftarrow move(b, b', t), move(b', l, t) \qquad (t \neq T). \qquad (21)$$

The robot has only two grippers:

$$\leftarrow move(b, l, t), move(b', l', t), move(b'', l'', t)$$
$$(\langle b, l \rangle \neq \langle b', l' \rangle, \ \langle b, l \rangle \neq \langle b'', l'' \rangle, \ \langle b', l' \rangle \neq \langle b'', l'' \rangle, \ t \neq T). \qquad (22)$$

Finally, the history program includes the last two of the three constraints on possible configurations of blocks from (11), applied to every time instant:

$$\leftarrow on(b, b'', t), on(b', b'', t) \qquad (b \neq b'), \qquad (23)$$

$$supported(b, t) \leftarrow on(b, table, t)$$
$$supported(b, t) \leftarrow supported(b', t), on(b, b', t) \qquad (24)$$
$$\leftarrow not\ supported(b, t).$$

There is no need to include the counterpart (26) of the first of those constraints, because we have already included a "stronger" rule (19).

History program (15)–(24) can be used to solve planning problems in the blocks world as described at the end of the previous section.[9] Information on the performance of several answer set solvers on a few planning problems in the blocks world can be found at http://www.cs.utexas.edu/users/esra/experiments/experiments.html .

7 Expressiveness

As a formalism for representing properties of actions, logic programming is remarkably expressive. Here are three examples of how it handles relatively complex cases—all of them are beyond the expressive capabilites of the classical STRIPS language [5].

Conditional Effects. After toggling a switch, the light in the room is on if it was off before, and the other way around:

$$light\text{-}on(t+1) \leftarrow toggle(t), \neg light\text{-}on(t),$$
$$\neg light\text{-}on(t+1) \leftarrow toggle(t), light\text{-}on(t).$$

Implicit Effects. When I walk to another place, this action indirectly affects the locations of the objects that I have in my pockets. Any other action that changes my location—running, or riding a bus, or driving a car—has the same implicit effect. Describing implicit effects of actions is known as the "ramification problem." In logic programming, we can solve the ramification problem by writing rules that do not mention actions, such as (19) or

$$at(x, l, t) \leftarrow at(I, l, t), in\text{-}my\text{-}pocket(x, t).$$

Implicit Preconditions. Rules of the history program above specify three cases when moving blocks is impossible: when the block to be moved is not clear (20), when the target is a block that is being moved (21), and when more than two blocks are being moved at once (22). Is it possible, in the initial state shown in Figure 2, to place block 1 on top of block 6? That would not violate any of the three explicitly stated preconditions. Nevertheless, the answer is no, unless block 5, which was initially on top of block 6, is being moved at the same time. This fact is a consequence of constraint (23): two blocks cannot be located on top of the same block.

The expressiveness of logic programming as a language for describing actions is illustrated also by the fact that any definite action description in action language $\mathcal{C}$ [8] can be translated into logic programming [11].

8   Why Answer Sets?

In the introduction, the notion of an answer set was mentioned as one of three mathematical concepts that can be used to give a declarative meaning to negation as failure, the other two being completion and the well-founded model. Can any of the other two concepts serve as a basis for a logic programming style similar to answer set programming?

The well-founded model classifies ground queries into three groups: true, false, and undefined. It is useful as a specification for query answering systems that are similar to Prolog but have better termination properties, such as XSB (http://www.cs.sunysb.edu/~sbprolog/xsb-page.html). Given program (2), and either p or q as a query, such a system can be expected to terminate and return the answer *undefined*. But the information about a program provided by its well-founded model does not seem to be adequate for anything similar to answer set programming. It does not allow us, for instance, to distinguish between programs (2) and

$$
\begin{aligned}
p &\leftarrow not\ p, \\
q &\leftarrow not\ q
\end{aligned}
\tag{25}
$$

—both have the same well-founded model. The answer set approach to negation as failure recognizes a big difference between the two programs: the latter has no answer sets.

With the completion semantics, the situation is different. The definition of completion is not applicable to disjunctive programs, nor to programs with two kinds of negation. But, as discussed at the end of Section 4, these are not very severe limitations. In particular, classical negation can be always eliminated at the cost of adding new atoms and constraints (12). Also, completion has a counterpart defined for programs with classical negation— "literal completion."[10]

Consider a finite nondisjunctive program Π without classical negation, such as (2). For simplicity, assume also that Π does not contain constraints.

Two basic facts are known about the relationship between the answer sets for Π and the models of the completion of Π (see [4]). If we identify an interpretation in the sense of classical logic with the set of atoms that are true in that interpretation then

- every answer set for Π is a model of the completion of Π, and

- if Π is tight[11] then, conversely, every model of the completion of Π is an answer set for Π.

For instance, program (2) is tight, and its answer sets are the models of its completion $p \equiv q$. Program (25) is tight also; its completion $p \equiv \neg p$, $q \equiv \neg q$ is inconsistent.

It follows that answer sets for a tight program can be computed by finding models of its completion. This is, essentially, how CCALC (see Introduction) operates when used to find answer sets for a logic program. It forms the (literal) completion of the given program Π and submits the result to a propositional solver. Thus CCALC can be used to find answer sets for Π only if Π is tight, or if we know in some other way that every model of the completion of Π is an answer set. For such programs, "completion programming" differs from answer set programming only in that it uses a different computational mechanism for computing answer sets.

On the other hand, if the completion of a program has a model that is not an answer set then this model is usually "unwanted"—it does not reflect the intended meaning of the program. This is the case, actually, for all three examples of answer set programming given in this paper. Generally, the completion of (the result of eliminating disjunctive rules and classical negation from) program (6)–(10) has models that do not correspond to Hamiltonian paths. The completion of (11) has models that do not correspond to valid configurations of blocks. The completion of the history program from Section 6 has models that do not correspond to possible evolutions of the blocks world. In this sense, "completion programming" is not a good idea.

It is interesting that, in each of the last two examples, a small modification of the part of the program that involves *supported* would help us get rid of the unwanted models of completion. In the case of the history program, it is sufficient to replace (24) by the rules

$$above(b, l, t) \leftarrow on(b, l, t)$$
$$above(b, l, t) \leftarrow above(b, b', t), above(b', l, t)$$
$$\leftarrow above(b, b, t)$$
$$\leftarrow not \; above(b, table, t).$$

Although the resulting program is not tight, every model of its completion is an answer set (Norman McCain and Hudson Turner, personal communication). This modification may be helpful when CCALC is used for planning in the blocks world.

Acknowledgements

This report is an outcome of many enjoyable discussions with Esra Erdem, Michael Gelfond, Nicola Leone, Victor Marek, Norman McCain, Ilkka Niemelä, Teodor Przymusinski, Miroslaw Truszczyński and Hudson Turner. This work was partially supported by National Science Foundation under grant IIS-9732744.

Notes

1. Answer set programming is also known as "stable model programming." The term "stable model" was used in place of "answer set" in a preliminary publication on the answer set semantics [6]. That old terminology stems from the view that a rule in logic programming is merely a clause in the sense of classical logic, with one of its positive literals designated as the "head." If so, we can talk about models of a logic program in the sense of classical logic, and a semantics of negation as failure can be defined by specifying an additional condition on models—"stability." For instance, program (1), according to this view, is simply the disjunction $p \vee q$ written in the logic programming notation. The usual truth table for disjunction shows that this formula has 3 models: $\{p\}$, $\{q\}$ and $\{p, q\}$. The first model is "stable"; the other two are not.

This view does not extend, however, to programs with two kinds of negation that are defined in [7] and are used in this paper. It is better to think of *inference rules*, rather than clauses, as the classical logic counterpart of logic programming rules. A rule with negation as failure is similar to a default in the sense of [17] which combines an inference rule with a list of "justifications." This is actually more than an analogy: there is a precise relationship between answer sets for programs and extensions for default theories [13, 7].

2. See

```
http://www.tcs.hut.fi/Software/smodels/
http://www.dbai.tuwien.ac.at/proj/dlv/
http://www.cs.engr.uky.edu/~lpnmr/DeReS.html
http://www.cs.utexas.edu/users/mccain/cc
```

3. Some authors call the second kind of negation "strong" or "explicit." It is natural to think of this negation as "taken from classical logic" in connection with the relationship between logic programs and default theories mentioned at the end of Note 1. Generally, the conclusion of a default is a formula of classical logic. If we require that the conclusion be a literal, and limit the syntactic form of the other parts of a default (prerequisite and justifications) in a similar way, we will arrive at the class of defaults corresponding to nondisjunctive logic programs.

4. Some expositions of the answer set semantics allow answer sets to be inconsistent, but different papers treat this case in different ways. It is best to eliminate inconsistent answer sets altogether.

5. On the other hand, SMODELS permits function symbols in schematic rules, which is often convenient. System CCALC permits function symbols as well. The problem with the use of function symbols in answer set programming is that it can make the set of ground atoms infinite. The user of a system for computing answer sets should be careful not to provide an input that has an infinite answer set—such a set cannot be returned as output!

6. More generally, a planning problem may involve a set of initial conditions instead of a specific initial state, and a set of goal conditions instead of a specific goal state. Instead of a sequence of actions, we may be looking for a "strategy" built from actions using conditional operators and loops.

7. In fact, the emergence of formal nonmonotonic reasoning twenty years ago was motivated to a large degree by the need to solve a knowledge representation problem related to properties of actions—the frame problem. A history of attempts to solve the frame problem, in their relation to nonmonotonic logics and logic programming, is described in [18].

8. The difference between (19) and the constraint

$$\leftarrow on(b, l', t), on(b, l, t) \qquad (l \neq l') \qquad (26)$$

is similar to the difference between "ramification constraints" and "qualification constraints" in the sense of [12].

9. In the extended program described at the end of Section 5, the part consisting of disjunctive rules (15) and constraints (13) can be equivalently replaced by the initial conditions represented as facts:

$$on(1, 2, 0) \leftarrow$$
$$on(2, table, 0) \leftarrow$$
$$on(3, 4, 0) \leftarrow$$
$$\cdots$$

More importantly, the program can be further extended by constraints that limit the set of executable sequences of actions without changing the class of solvable planning programs. In this way, domain-dependent control information can be conveyed to the answer set solver, which may help it find a solution faster. For instance, we can tell the solver that *if a block and all blocks under it are in their final positions then that block should not be moved* by adding a constraint that makes such a move impossible.

10. Literal completion was defined for a language of causal theories in [15] and extended to nondisjunctive logic programs in [11]. It does not introduce new atoms. The models of the literal completion of a program are

similar to its *complete* answer sets—those that contain one element of every complementary pair of literals.

11. We say that Π is *tight* if there exists a function λ from atoms to ordinals such that, for every rule

$$A_0 \leftarrow A_1, \ldots, A_m, not\ A_{m+1}, \ldots, not\ A_n$$

in Π,

$$\lambda(A_1), \ldots, \lambda(A_m) < \lambda(A_0).$$

This condition does not impose any restrictions on $A_{m+1}, \ldots, A_n$. In [4], such programs are called "positive-order-consistent."

References

[1] Keith Clark. Negation as failure. In Herve Gallaire and Jack Minker, editors, *Logic and Data Bases*, pages 293–322. Plenum Press, New York, 1978.

[2] Yannis Dimopoulos, Bernhard Nebel, and Jana Koehler. Encoding planning problems in non-monotonic logic programs. In *Proc. European Conf. on Planning 1997*, pages 169–181, 1997.

[3] Esra Erdem and Vladimir Lifschitz. Transformations of logic programs related to causality and planning. In *Logic Programming and Nonmonotonic Reasoning: Proc. Fifth Int'l Conf.*, 1999. To appear.

[4] François Fages. Consistency of Clark's completion and existence of stable models. *Journal of Methods of Logic in Computer Science*, 1:51–60, 1994.

[5] Richard Fikes and Nils Nilsson. STRIPS: A new approach to the application of theorem proving to problem solving. *Artificial Intelligence*, 2(3–4):189–208, 1971.

[6] Michael Gelfond and Vladimir Lifschitz. The stable model semantics for logic programming. In Robert Kowalski and Kenneth Bowen, editors, *Logic Programming: Proc. Fifth Int'l Conf. and Symp.*, pages 1070–1080, 1988.

[7] Michael Gelfond and Vladimir Lifschitz. Classical negation in logic programs and disjunctive databases. *New Generation Computing*, 9:365–385, 1991.

[8] Enrico Giunchiglia and Vladimir Lifschitz. An action language based on causal explanation: Preliminary report. In *Proc. AAAI-98*, pages 623–630, 1998.

[9] Henry Kautz and Bart Selman. Planning as satisfiability. In *Proc. ECAI-92*, pages 359–363, 1992.

[10] Vladimir Lifschitz. Action languages, answer sets and planning. In *The Logic Programming Paradigm: a 25-Year Perspective*, pages 357–373. Springer Verlag, 1999.

[11] Vladimir Lifschitz and Hudson Turner. Representing transition systems by logic programs. In *Logic Programming and Non-monotonic Reasoning: Proc. Fifth Int'l Conf.*, 1999. To appear.

[12] Fangzhen Lin and Raymond Reiter. State constraints revisited. *Journal of Logic and Computation*, 4:655–678, 1994.

[13] Victor Marek and Mirosław Truszczyński. Stable semantics for logic programs and default theories. In *Proc. North American Conf. on Logic Programming*, pages 243–256, 1989.

[14] Victor Marek and Mirosław Truszczyński. Stable models and an alternative logic programming paradigm. In *The Logic Programming Paradigm: a 25-Year Perspective*, pages 375–398. Springer Verlag, 1999.

[15] Norman McCain and Hudson Turner. Causal theories of action and change. In *Proc. AAAI-97*, pages 460–465, 1997.

[16] Ilkka Niemelä. Logic programs with stable model semantics as a constraint programming paradigm. *Annals of Mathematics and Artificial Intelligence*, 1999.

[17] Raymond Reiter. A logic for default reasoning. *Artificial Intelligence*, 13:81–132, 1980.

[18] Murray Shanahan. *Solving the Frame Problem: A Mathematical Investigation of the Common Sense Law of Inertia*. MIT Press, 1997.

[19] Timo Soininen and Ilkka Niemelä. Developing a declarative rule language for applications in product configuration. In Gopal Gupta, editor, *Proc. First Int'l Workshop on Practical Aspects of Declarative Languages (Lecture Notes in Computer Science 1551)*, pages 305–319. Springer-Verlag, 1998.

[20] V.S. Subrahmanian and Carlo Zaniolo. Relating stable models and AI planning domains. In *Proc. ICLP-95*, 1995.

[21] Hudson Turner. Representing actions in logic programs and default theories: a situation calculus approach. *Journal of Logic Programming*, 31:245–298, 1997.

[22] Allen Van Gelder, Kenneth Ross, and John Schlipf. The well-founded semantics for general logic programs. *Journal of ACM*, pages 620–650, 1990.

Logic Programming in Oz
with Mozart

Peter Van Roy
Université catholique de Louvain
B-1348 Louvain-la-Neuve, Belgium
pvr@info.ucl.ac.be

This short tutorial explains how to do Prolog-style logic programming in Oz. We give programming examples that can be run interactively on the Mozart system, which implements Oz. The Oz language is the result of a decade of research into programming based on logic. The Oz computation model subsumes both search-based logic programming and committed-choice (concurrent) logic programming with deep guards. Furthermore, Oz provides new abilities, such as first-class top levels and constant-time merge, that exist in neither of its ancestors. We show two of the Oz interactive graphic tools, namely the Browser and the Explorer, which are useful for developing and running logic programs. We conclude by explaining why logic programming is just a prelude to the real strengths of Oz, namely constraint programming and distributed programming. In these two areas, Oz is equal to or better than any other system existing in the world today. For example, for compute-intensive constraint problems Oz provides parallel search engines that can be used transparently, i.e., without changing the problem specification.

1 Introduction

The Oz language makes it easy to write efficient, declarative logic programs that combine the advantages of search-based logic and constraint languages (such as Prolog, CHIP, and cc(FD) [16, 7]) and committed-choice (concurrent) logic languages (including flat languages such as Parlog, FCP, and FGHC, but also deep languages such as Concurrent Prolog and GHC [14]). Furthermore, Oz provides powerful new programming techniques that are not possible in either language family.

This tutorial explains the basic ideas of Oz by means of small examples that run on Mozart, a recently-released system that efficiently implements the latest version of Oz, also known as Oz 3 [8]. Mozart has an easy-to-use interactive user interface based on Emacs. We suggest that you download the Mozart system and try the examples at the keyboard. Only a few basic keyboard commands are needed to use

Mozart interactively; see the Oz tutorial for more information [4].

The purpose of this tutorial is to be an entry point into the Oz universe for people with some Prolog experience. We assume that you understand the basic concepts of Prolog and that you have written or understood some small Prolog programs. We show that the step from Prolog to Oz is not hard at all, and we try to explain some of the vastly more general and powerful operations that are possible in Oz.

This tutorial focuses on logic programming for general-purpose applications that require manipulating structured data according to logical rules, i.e., applications such as rule-based expert systems or compilers. The Oz support for logic programming just scratches the surface of the real strengths of Oz, which are constraint programming and distributed programming. It is not the purpose of this tutorial to investigate these two areas, but we invite the interested reader to look at them. There exist excellent tutorials on constraint programming in Oz, e.g., with finite domains [13], with finite sets of integers [9], and for natural language processing [3]. There also exists a tutorial on distributed programming in Oz [18].

This tutorial is structured as follows. Section 2 shows how to do deterministic logic programming in Oz, i.e., sequential logic programming without search. This section also presents the Browser, a graphic tool for examining data structures. Then Section 3 extends this to nondeterministic logic programming, i.e., including search. This section also explains how to use first-class top levels, and it presents the Explorer, a graphic tool for interactive exploration of the search tree. Section 4 shows how to do committed-choice logic programming in Oz. Then Section 5 shows how search-based and committed-choice logic programming are combined. Section 6 summarizes the logic programming support in the Oz kernel language. Section 7 gives some glimpses into constraints and distribution in Oz. Finally, Section 8 concludes and gives perspectives on future developments.

2 Deterministic Logic Programming

Oz supports deterministic logic programming with three statements: **if**, **case**, and **cond**. The following example defines an Append predicate that can be used to append two lists:

```
declare
proc {Append L1 L2 L3}
   case L1
   of nil then L2=L3
   [] X|M1 then L3=X|{Append M1 L2}
   end
end
```

This example introduces two important syntactic short-cuts of Oz. In a **case** statement, variables in the branches of the case (like x and M1) are declared implicitly and their scope covers one branch of the case. Any procedure, e.g., Append, can be syntactically used as a function. The procedure's last argument is the function's output and is syntactically hidden.

This definition looks very much like a standard functional definition of append, but it is in fact much more general. The definition has a precise logical semantics in addition to its operational semantics. The logical semantics are:

$$\forall l_1, l_2, l_3 : \text{append}(l_1, l_2, l_3) \leftrightarrow$$
$$l_1 = \text{nil} \land l_2 = l_3 \lor$$
$$\exists x, m_1, m_3 : l_1 = x|m_1 \land l_3 = x|m_3 \land \text{append}(m_1, l_2, m_3)$$

The operational semantics of the **case** statement are as follows. The **case** statement waits until its input is sufficiently instantiated to decide that one branch succeeds and all previous branches fail. If all branches fail then it takes the else branch or raises an exception if there is none. For Append this means that L1 must be bound to a list. If L1 has an unbound tail, then execution blocks until the tail is bound.

Variable declaration and variable scope are defined quite differently in Oz and Prolog. In Prolog, both declaration and scope are defined *implicitly* through the clausal syntax. Namely, variables in the head are universal over the whole clause and new variables in the body are existential over the whole clause body. In Oz, declaration and scope are defined *explicitly*. The scope is restricted to the statement in which the declaration occurs. This is important because Oz is fully compositional (all statements can be nested). Oz has syntactic support to make the explicit declarations less verbose.

2.1 The Browser

Here's one way to execute Append and display the result:

```
declare A in
{Append [1 2 3] [4 5 6] A}
{Browse A}
```

which can also be written as follows:

```
{Browse {Append [1 2 3] [4 5 6]}}
```

This uses the same syntactic short-cut as the definition of Append. Note that elements of Oz lists are not separated by commas as in Prolog. This code displays the output of Append in the *Browser*, a graphic tool for examining data structures and observing their evolution [10]. The Browser is fully concurrent and it can display any number of data

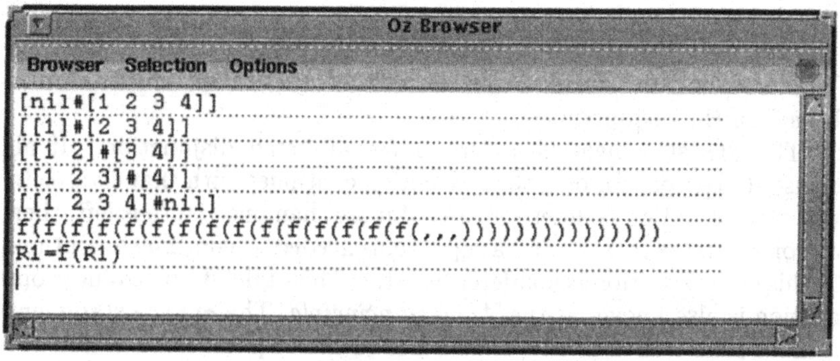

Figure 1: Screen shot of the Oz Browser.

structures simultaneously (see Figure 1). The display of a data structure containing unbound variables is updated when one of the variables is bound. The Browser has options to let it either ignore sharing or display sharing. In the second case, shared subterms (including cycles) are displayed only once.

Figure 1 gives a screen shot of a Browser window that shows the five solutions of a nondeterministic append (see next section) as well as two displays of:

```
declare X in {Browse X=f(X)}
```

The first displays x as a tree, stopping at the default depth limit of 15. The second displays x as a minimal graph, which makes all cycles and sharing explicit. You can set up the Browser to display the minimal graph by selecting Display Parameters in the Options menu.

3 Nondeterministic Logic Programming

Oz supports nondeterministic logic programming through two concepts: disjunctions (**dis** and **choice**) and first-class top levels. The **dis** and **choice** disjunctions do a don't-know choice, i.e., they can be used for search.

Let's write a nondeterministic version of append, i.e., one that can be used with many call patterns, similar to Prolog's:

```
declare
proc {FullAppend L1 L2 L3}
    dis L1=nil L2=L3
    [] X M1 M3 in
        L1=X|M1 L3=X|M3 {FullAppend M1 L2 M3}
```

```
   end
end
```

The "X M1 M3 **in**" declares new variables X, M1, and M3 for the second branch of the disjunction.

The **dis** statement is a determinacy-directed disjunction. If all clauses fail except for one, then execution continues with that clause. In this case execution is deterministic. If more than one clause is left, then a choice point is created and a top level is needed to continue execution. In this case execution is nondeterministic. This style of constraint propagation is also known as the *Andorra principle*. The **choice** statement is more primitive than **dis**; it generates a choice point immediately for all its clauses without checking if any clauses fail.

Both Append and FullAppend have exactly the same logical semantics. They differ only in their operational semantics. If used inside a top level, FullAppend gives results in cases where Append blocks.

3.1 First-Class Top Levels

The definition of FullAppend can be executed immediately, if used in a purely deterministic way:

```
{Browse {FullAppend [1 2] [3 4]}}    % Shows [1 2 3 4]
```

But the definition blocks if used nondeterministically:

```
{Browse {FullAppend X Y [1 2 3 4]}}    % Blocks
```

To get an answer, you need to execute the nondeterministic call in a top level. Here's how to create a top level with a given query:

```
declare
proc {Q A}
   X Y
in
   {FullAppend X Y [1 2 3 4]} A=X#Y
end
S={New Search.object script(Q)}
```

This defines a new procedure Q (the query) and a new object S (the top level) of class Search.object. The Search.object class is part of the Search module [2]. The class makes it possible to create any number of top levels. The top levels are accessed like objects, can run concurrently, and can be passed as arguments and stored in data structures. We say the top levels are *first class*. Each top level is initialized with a query. The query is entered as a one-argument procedure called a *script*. In this example, procedure Q contains the query. The procedure's output is A, i.e., the pair X#Y.

Creating a top level can be written more concisely as:

```
declare
S={New Search.object script(
   proc {$ A} X#Y=A in {FullAppend X Y [1 2 3 4]} end)}
```

This exploits two syntactic short-cuts. First, the "$" is a nesting marker that implicitly declares the variable Q. Second, putting an equation left of **in** implicitly declares all variables of the equation's left-hand side. That is, "X#Y=A **in**" declares X and Y, creates the pair X#Y, and unifies the pair with A.

You can get answers one by one by calling s as follows:

```
{Browse {S next($)}}
```

Each call {S next($)} gives a new answer. As before, the "$" is a nesting marker that implicitly declares a variable. The next method of object s is used to get the next answer. This is similar to the semicolon ";" in an interactive Prolog session. It is not identical, since the next must be called to get the first answer.

How do we know when there are no more answers? In a very simple way: each answer A is returned as a one-element list [A]. When there are no more answers, then nil is returned. So repeatedly asking for answers displays:

```
[nil#[1 2 3 4]]
[[1]#[2 3 4]]
[[1 2]#[3 4]]
[[1 2 3]#[4]]
[[1 2 3 4]#nil]
nil
```

There are five answers, from nil#[1 2 3 4] to [1 2 3 4]#nil. All further requests for answers give nil.

We conclude the discussion of top levels with a few random remarks:

- Creating a new top level is very cheap; you should not hesitate to do so for each query.

- A program can consist of deterministic and nondeterministic predicates used together in any way. A top level script can call such a program; this is possible because both deterministic and nondeterministic predicates have logical semantics. Of course, only the nondeterministic predicates can create choice points.

- It is easy to add information to an existing top level while it is active. It suffices for the script to have an external reference, i.e., to have a reference to something outside of the top level.

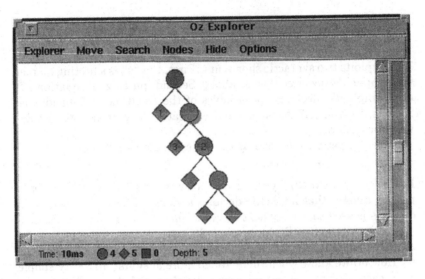

Figure 2: Screen shot of the Oz Explorer.

3.2 The Explorer

In addition to first-class top levels, another way to execute a logic program is by means of the *Explorer*, a graphic tool for interactive exploration of the search tree [12]. The Explorer was designed for constraint programming applications, but it is also very useful for logic programming. Here we show only a very small part of what the Explorer can do. To go further, we suggest that you try out the Mozart constraint demos with the Explorer.

The Explorer is an object that is given a script. Let's do this with the same FullAppend query as in the previous section:

```
{Explorer.object script(
  proc {$ A} X#Y=A in {FullAppend X Y [1 2 3 4]} end)}
```

This opens a window that displays the search tree. Initially, just the root is displayed, as a gray circle. The circle means that the root has a choice point. The gray color means that the choice point is not fully explored. It is in fact completely unexplored.

Select the root by clicking on it, and press "n" (Next Solution, in the Search menu). This adds a green diamond[1], which corresponds to one solution. Double-clicking on the green diamond numbers the diamond (here it is 1) and displays the number and the solution in the Browser,

---

[1]The exact color depends on your screen; sometimes it is blue-green.

that is, `1#(nil#[1 2 3 4])`.

Now select the root again and press "a" (All Solutions, in the Search menu). This displays the tree in Figure 2. Each subtree's root node is a purple circle, which means that it is a fully explored choice point. Double-clicking on any node numbers the node and also displays what's known about the solution at that node. For example, double-clicking on node 2 displays `2#((1|2|_)#_)` and double-clicking on node 3 displays `3#([1]#[2 3 4])`.

4   Committed-Choice Logic Programming

A logic program in Oz can have multiple threads that bind shared variables. If predicates are defined only with **case**, **if**, and **cond**, then this is exactly committed-choice logic programming. The **case** and **if** statements are special cases of **cond**, which does a general don't-care choice, i.e., if the guard of any branch succeeds then execution can commit to that branch and discard all the others.

Here is a simple example of a producer-consumer program with flow control:

```
declare
proc {Producer N L}
   case L of X|Ls then X=N {Producer N+1 Ls}
   else skip end
end

fun {Consumer N L A}
   if N>0 then X L1 in L=X|L1 {Consumer N-1 L1 A+X}
   else A end
end
```

The producer generates a list L of consecutive increasing integers. The consumer sums the N first elements of L. The consumer asks for the next element by binding the list tail to a new list pair. The producer waits until the list is bound before generating the next element. Producer and consumer therefore run in lock step. A possible call is:

```
local L S in % Variable declaration
   thread {Producer 0 L} end
   thread S={Consumer 100000 L 0} end
   {Browse S}
end
```

The producer and consumer each runs in its own thread. The producer generates the list `[0 1 2 3 ...` and the consumer sums the list's first 100000 elements. The main thread immediately displays an unbound variable and later updates the display to `4999950000` when the consumer terminates.

Because only **case** and **if** are used, both the producer and the consumer have a precise logical semantics as well as an operational semantics. (This is not true for **cond** unless its conditions are mutually exclusive.) The **if** statement has the logical semantics $(c \wedge t) \vee (\neg c \wedge e)$ where c is the boolean condition, t is derived from the then part, and e is derived from the else part. The **if** statement has the following operational semantics. It waits until enough information exists to decide the truth or falsity of its boolean condition. At that point, it executes its then or else part.

5 Nondeterministic Concurrent Logic Programming

If a logic program has only a single thread and uses the **dis** statement to express nondeterminism, then its behavior is exactly like that of a Prolog program where the Prolog system is modified to do clause selection according to the Andorra principle. However, because of concurrency and first-class top levels, Oz lets you do much more. For example, let's say you have two sequential logic programs. There is a design choice when running them, i.e., whether to put them in the same top level or in different top levels:

- If the programs are independent, e.g., two independent queries to a database, then they should be run in different top levels. This ensures that each program gets a fair share of the processing power and that no wasted work is done.

- If the programs are dependent, i.e., they are cooperating to solve one problem, then it is often best to run them in the same top level. This ensures that they can share information. Fairness of each program is not important in this case. Rather, it is the progress made by *both programs considered together* that is important.

The second technique, dependent programs that cooperate, is not often used in logic programming, but it is very important for constraint programming. In Oz, a typical real-life constraint problem has hundreds, thousands, or even more active threads. Each thread observes the store and attempts to add information concurrently with the other threads. We call such a thread a *propagator* if it only adds correct information, i.e., it never creates a choice point [13, 15]. Propagators are implemented very efficiently in Oz and together with spaces they are the foundation of the Oz constraint programming model. Oz provides propagators for many complex constraints on the three constraint domains of finite domains, finite sets, and rational trees.

⟨S⟩ ::= ⟨C⟩

| if ⟨C⟩ then ⟨S1⟩ else ⟨S2⟩ end

| case X
   of $f1(l11:Y11$ ... $l1m:Y1m)$ then ⟨B1⟩
   ...
   [] $fn(ln1:Yn1$ ... $lnm:Ynm)$ then ⟨Bn⟩
   else ⟨S⟩ end

| cond
      ⟨G1⟩ then ⟨B1⟩ [] ... [] ⟨Gn⟩ then ⟨Bn⟩
   else ⟨S⟩ end

| dis
      ⟨G1⟩ then ⟨B1⟩ [] ... [] ⟨Gn⟩ then ⟨Bn⟩
   end

| choice ⟨S1⟩ [] ... [] ⟨Sn⟩ end

| ⟨Spaces⟩

Figure 3: Oz kernel support for logic programming.

6 Oz Kernel Support for Logic Programming

The full Oz language is defined in terms of a kernel language. The complete kernel language includes cells (explicit state), procedures, and threads in addition to logic programming support (see [19]). Figure 3 shows just the logic programming support. In this figure, ⟨C⟩ denotes a basic constraint, i.e., a constraint that is completely expressed in the store, ⟨G⟩, ⟨B⟩, and ⟨S⟩ denote statements (the first two are called guard and body), and ⟨Spaces⟩ denotes the support for computation spaces. Previous sections have explained part of the Oz support for logic programming, namely: (1) the don't-care disjunctive statements **if**, **case**, and **cond** (see Sections 2 and 4) and (2) the don't-know disjunctive statements **dis** and **choice** (see Section 3). The guards in the **cond** and **dis** statements can be arbitrary computations. If a guard is more than just a basic constraint, then we say that it is a *deep* guard. The then parts of a **dis** statement are optional. An omitted then part behaves as if it were "**then skip**", where **skip** is a statement that does nothing.

First-class top levels are not primitive. They are implemented in Oz through the *computation space* abstraction, which is outside the scope of this tutorial (see [11]). Computation spaces fully support deep guard execution, i.e., they can be nested to any level. Computation spaces interact with don't-know disjunctions to allow easy and efficient programming within Oz of arbitrary search strategies that work for arbitrary constraint domains. Most of the commonly-used search strategies are provided as library modules (see the Search module [2]). These modules include also some more unusual strategies, such as limited discrepancy search and saturation search, that are sometimes useful.

7 Constraints and Distribution

Up to now, we have explained how to write Prolog-style logic programs in Oz and how Oz extends what you can do in Prolog. But all this is just a warm-up exercise. Oz was never intended to be just a Prolog substitute. The main power of Oz is in constraint programming and distributed programming.

We summarize what the current Mozart release implements for distributed programming [6, 18]. Mozart completely separates the aspects of language semantics and distribution structure. The Oz semantics of all language entities are independent of their distribution structure. Furthermore, the network operations of the language entities are predictable, allowing efficient distributed applications to be written. These capabilities are implemented by means of a network layer that contains a distributed algorithm for each type of language entity, as well as distributed garbage collection [19, 5, 1]. Mozart has primitives for fully open computing, i.e., it is possible for independently-written applications that share no common ancestral information (such as an IDL definition) to connect and fruitfully interact. Finally, Mozart provides failure-detection primitives that allow building non-trivial fault tolerance abstractions within the language [17].

The constraint and distribution abilities of Oz can be combined. For example, the `search` module implements a parallel search engine that is very useful for compute-intensive constraint problems [2]. The search engine is initialized by giving it a list of machine names and a script. The parallelism is completely transparent, i.e., the problem is specified without any knowledge of whether it is executed in parallel or not. The same script can be used with a top level, with the Explorer, and with a parallel search engine.

8 Conclusions and Perspectives

This tutorial gives an elementary introduction to doing logic programming in Oz. Along the way, we introduce first-class top levels, concurrency, and the Browser and Explorer tools. We explain how search-based and committed-choice logic programming with deep guards are integrated, and we outline how the logic programming support smoothly ties in to constraint programming.

Current active research topics in Oz include constraint programming for natural language processing, constraint debugging, fault tolerant and secure distributed execution, open computing architectures, and support for environments with limited computational resources.

Acknowledgements

The author thanks Denys Duchier, Seif Haridi, and Christian Schulte for their helpful comments on drafts of this paper. The author also thanks all the other contributors and developers of the Mozart system, of whose abilities this tutorial only gives the faintest echo. This research is partly financed by the Walloon Region of Belgium.

References

[1] Iliès Alouini and Peter Van Roy. Le protocole réparti de Distributed Oz (in French). In *Colloque Francophone sur l'Ingénierie des Protocoles (CFIP 99)*, pages 283–298, April 1999.

[2] Denys Duchier, Leif Kornstaedt, Tobias Müller, Christian Schulte, and Peter Van Roy. System modules. Technical report, 1999. In Mozart documentation, available at http://www.mozart-oz.org.

[3] Claire Gardent, Joachim Niehren, and Denys Duchier. Oz for natural language processing. Technical report, University of the Saarland, Saarbrücken, Germany, 1999.

[4] Seif Haridi and Nils Franzén. Tutorial of Oz. Technical report, 1999. In Mozart documentation, available at http://www.mozart-oz.org.

[5] Seif Haridi, Peter Van Roy, Per Brand, Michael Mehl, Ralf Scheidhauer, and Gert Smolka. Efficient logic variables for distributed computing. *ACM Transactions on Programming Languages and Systems*, 2000. To appear.

[6] Seif Haridi, Peter Van Roy, Per Brand, and Christian Schulte. Programming languages for distributed applications. *New Generation Computing*, 16(3):223–261, May 1998.

[7] Joxan Jaffar and Michael Maher. Constraint logic programming: A survey. *J. Log. Prog.*, 19/20:503–581, May/July 1994.

[8] Mozart Consortium. The Mozart programming system (Oz 3), January 1999. Available at http://www.mozart-oz.org.

[9] Tobias Müller. Problem solving with finite set constraints in Oz. A tutorial. Technical report, 1999. In Mozart documentation, available at http://www.mozart-oz.org.

[10] Konstantin Popov. The Oz Browser. Technical report, 1999. In Mozart documentation, available at http://www.mozart-oz.org.

[11] Christian Schulte. Programming constraint inference engines. In Gert Smolka, editor, *Proceedings of the 3rd International Conference on Principles and Practice of Constraint Programming*, volume 1330 of *Lecture Notes in Computer Science*, pages 519–533, Schloß Hagenberg, Austria, October 1997. Springer-Verlag.

[12] Christian Schulte. Oz Explorer–Visual constraint programming support. Technical report, 1999. In Mozart documentation, available at http://www.mozart-oz.org.

[13] Christian Schulte and Gert Smolka. Finite domain constraint programming in Oz. A tutorial. Technical report, 1999. In Mozart documentation, available at http://www.mozart-oz.org.

[14] Ehud Shapiro. The family of concurrent logic programming languages. *ACM Computing Surveys*, 21(3):413–510, September 1989.

[15] Gert Smolka. Problem solving with constraints and programming. *ACM Computing Surveys*, 28(4es), December 1996. Electronic Section.

[16] Leon Sterling and Ehud Shapiro. *The Art of Prolog–Advanced Programming Techniques*. Series in Logic Programming. MIT Press, 1986.

[17] Peter Van Roy. On the separation of aspects in distributed programming: Application to distribution structure and fault tolerance in Mozart. In *International Workshop on Parallel and Distributed Computing for Symbolic and Irregular Applications (PDSIA 99)*, Tohoku University, Sendai, Japan, July 1999.

[18] Peter Van Roy, Seif Haridi, and Per Brand. Distributed programming in Mozart – A tutorial introduction. Technical report, 1999. In Mozart documentation, available at http://www.mozart-oz.org.

[19] Peter Van Roy, Seif Haridi, Per Brand, Gert Smolka, Michael Mehl, and Ralf Scheidhauer. Mobile objects in Distributed Oz. *ACM Transactions on Programming Languages and Systems*, 19(5):804–851, September 1997.

Program Analysis, Debugging, and Optimization Using the Ciao System Preprocessor[1]

Manuel V. Hermenegildo
Francisco Bueno
Germán Puebla
Pedro López
{herme,bueno,german,pedro}@fi.upm.es
School of Computer Science, T.U. Madrid (UPM)

Abstract

We present a tutorial overview of Ciaopp, the Ciao system preprocessor. Ciao is a public-domain, next-generation logic programming system, which subsumes ISO-Prolog and is specifically designed to a) be highly extensible via libraries and b) support modular program analysis, debugging, and optimization. The latter tasks are performed in an integrated fashion by Ciaopp. Ciaopp uses modular, incremental abstract interpretation to infer properties of program predicates and literals, including types, variable instantiation properties (including modes), non-failure, determinacy, bounds on computational cost, bounds on sizes of terms in the program, etc. Using such analysis information, Ciaopp can find errors at compile-time in programs and/or perform partial verification. Ciaopp checks how programs call system libraries and also any assertions present in the program or in other modules used by the program. These assertions are also used to generate documentation automatically. Ciaopp also uses analysis information to perform program transformations and optimizations such as multiple abstract specialization, parallelization (including granularity control), and optimization of run-time tests for properties which cannot be checked completely at compile-time. We illustrate "hands-on" the use of Ciaopp in all these tasks. By design, Ciaopp is a generic tool, which can be easily tailored to perform these and other tasks for different LP and CLP dialects.

Keywords: Global Analysis, Debugging, Verification, Parallelization, Optimization, Partial Evaluation, Multiple Specialization, Abstract Interpretation.

[1] We would like to thank the members of the ICLP'99 Program Committee for their kind invitation to present this tutorial. The CIAO system is a collaborative effort of members of several institutions, including UPM, U.Melbourne, Monash U., U.Arizona, Linköping U., NMSU, K.U.Leuven, Bristol U., and Ben-Gurion U. The system documentation and related publications contain more specific credits. The development of Ciaopp has been funded in part by ESPRIT project "DiSCiPl" and CICYT project "ELLA".

1 The Ciao Program Development System

Ciao [14] is a public-domain,[2] next-generation logic programming environment. It is intended at the same time as a robust public-domain ISO-Prolog implementation supporting programming in the large and in the small, and as an experimentation workbench for new logic programming technology. The Ciao environment includes an enhanced version of the interactive shell found in most Prolog systems, a standalone compiler, a powerful preprocessor/debugger, a script interpreter, an automatic documentation generator, a rich interface to the emacs editor, and some program visualization tools.

The Ciao system has been specifically designed to be highly extensible and to support modular program analysis, debugging, and optimization. The language includes a simple kernel with a robust module system, on top of which extensions are added via libraries. These libraries are generally normal Ciao modules which provide run-time support predicates (including attributed variable handling code) and compile-time support such as operator declarations and macro expansions. The latter are all local to the modules which import the library. The Ciao libraries currently support the full ISO-Prolog standard, several constraint domains, functional and higher order programming, concurrent and distributed programming, Internet programming, objects, persistence, database access, rich interfaces to other languages (such as C, tcl/tk, and Java), etc.

The Ciao compilation process is conceptually divided into two levels. The *low-level compiler*, Ciaoc, itself a Ciao application, is in charge of producing object code for each module, and linking the object code into executables. This compilation is performed automatically and incrementally, in the sense that only necessary modules whose source code has changed are recompiled when a module is used. Ciaoc generates executables which are small and of performance which is competitive with state-of-the-art bytecoded systems.[3] At a higher level, the *preprocessor*, Ciaopp, performs modular, incremental global program analysis based on abstract interpretation [4] to infer information on the program. This information is applied in a novel way to aid the program development and debugging process, as well as in the more traditional areas of program transformation and optimization. By design, Ciaopp is a generic tool, which can be easily tailored to perform these and other tasks for different LP and CLP dialects.

In the following, we present an overview of Ciaopp at work. Our aim is to present not the techniques used by Ciaopp, but instead the main functionalities of the system in a tutorial way, by means of examples. However, we do provide references where the interested reader can find more details on the actual techniques used.[4] Section 2 presents Ciaopp at work performing

---

[2]The ciao system is available from http://www.clip.dia.fi.upm.es.

[3]In addition, the *script processor*, allows executing *scripts* written in Prolog [13].

[4]Space limitations prevent us from providing a complete set of references to related work on the many topics touched upon in the paper. Thus, we only provide the references

```
:- module(qsort, [qsort/2], [assertions]).
:- use_module(compare,[geq/2,lt/2]).

qsort([X|L],R) :-
        partition(L,X,L1,L2),
        qsort(L2,R2), qsort(L1,R1),
        append(R1,[X|R2],R).
qsort([],[]).

partition([],_B,[],[]).
partition([E|R],C,[E|Left1],Right):-
        lt(E,C),  partition(R,C,Left1,Right).
partition([E|R],C,Left,[E|Right1]):-
        geq(E,C), partition(R,C,Left,Right1).

append([],Ys,Ys).
append([X|Xs],Ys,[X|Zs]):- append(Xs,Ys,Zs).
```

Figure 1: A modular qsort program.

program analysis, while Section 3 does the same for program debugging and validation and Section 4 for program transformation and optimization.

2   Static Analysis and Program Assertions

The fundamental functionality behind Ciaopp is static program analysis. For this task Ciaopp uses the PLAI abstract interpreter [18, 2], its CLP [11] and incremental [15, 22] versions, and adaptations of Gallagher's regular type analysis [8]. The system includes several abstract domains and can infer information on basic properties such as moded types, definiteness, freeness, and grounding dependencies, as well as on more complex properties such as determinacy, non-failure, bounds on term sizes, and bounds on computational cost. Ciaopp implements several techniques for dealing with "difficult" language features (such as side-effects, meta-programming, higher-order, etc.) and as a result can for example deal safely with arbitrary ISO-Prolog programs [1]. A unified language of assertions [1, 19] is used to express the results of analysis, to provide input to the analyzer, and, as we will see later, to provide program specifications for debugging and validation.

Modular Static Analysis Basics: Ciaopp takes advantage of modular program structure to perform more precise and efficient, incremental analysis [1]. Consider the program in Figure 1, defining a module which exports the qsort predicate and imports predicates geq and lt from module compare. During the analysis of this program, Ciaopp will take advantage of the fact that the only predicate that can be called from outside is the exported predicate qsort. This allows Ciaopp to infer more precise information than if it had to consider that all predicates may be called in any possible way (as would be true had this been a simple "user" file instead of a

---

most directly related to Ciaopp, which are typically our own work. We ask the reader to kindly forgive this. The publications referenced do contain comprehensive references to related work.

module). Also, assume that the compare module has already been analyzed. This allows Ciaopp to be more efficient, since it will use the information obtained for geq and lt during analysis of compare instead of reanalyzing them. Assuming that geq and lt have a similar binding behavior as the standard comparison predicates, a mode and independence analysis ("sharing+freeness") of the module using Ciaopp yields the following results:

```
:- true pred qsort(A,B)
        : mshare([[A],[A,B],[B]])
        => mshare([[A,B]]).
:- true pred partition(A,B,C,D)
        : ( var(C), var(D), mshare([[A],[A,B],[B],[C],[D]]) )
        => ( ground(A), ground(C), ground(D), mshare([[B]]) ).
:- true pred append(A,B,C)
        : ( ground(A), mshare([[B],[B,C],[C]]) )
        => ( ground(A), mshare([[B,C]]) ).
```

These *assertions* express, for example, that the third and fourth arguments of partition have "output mode": when partition is called (:) they are free unaliased variables and they are ground on success (=>). Also, append is used in a mode in which the first argument is input (i.e., ground on call). Also, upon success the arguments of qsort will share all variables (if any).

Assertions and Properties: The above output is given in the form of *assertions*. Assertions are a means of specifying *properties* which are (or should be) true of a given predicate, predicate argument, and/or *program point*. If an assertion has been proved to be true it has a prefix true – like the ones above. Assertions can also be used to provide information to the analyzer in order to increase its precision or to describe predicates which have not been coded yet during program development. These assertions have a trust prefix [1]. For example, if we commented out the use_module/2 declaration in Figure 1, we could describe the mode of the (now missing) geq and lt predicates to the analyzer for example as follows:

```
:- trust pred geq(X,Y) => ( ground(X), ground(Y) ).
:- trust pred lt(X,Y)  => ( ground(X), ground(Y) ).
```

Finally, assertions with a check prefix can be used to specify the *intended* semantics of the program, which can then be used in debugging and/or validation [19, 20], as we will see in Section 3. The same assertions are also used to generate documentation automatically [17].

Assertions refer to certain program points. The true pred assertions above specify in a combined way properties of both the entry (i.e., upon calling) and exit (i.e., upon success) points of *all calls* to the predicate. It is also possible to express properties which hold at points between clause literals. The following is a fragment of the output produced by Ciaopp for the program in Figure 1 when information is requested at this level:

```
qsort([X|L],R) :-
   true((ground(X),ground(L),var(R),var(L1),var(L2),var(R2), ...
   partition(L,X,L1,L2),
   true((ground(X),ground(L),ground(L1),ground(L2),var(R),var(R2), ...
   qsort(L2,R2), ...
```

In Ciaopp properties are just predicates, which may be builtin or user defined. For example, the property var used in the above examples is the standard builtin predicate to check for a free variable. The same applies to ground and mshare. The properties used by an analysis in its output (such as var, ground, and mshare for the previous mode analysis) are said to be *native* for that particular analysis. The system requires that a logic program (or system builtin) exist defining each property, that it be marked as such with a prop declaration, and that it be visible to the module in which the property is used (needed, for example, if a run-time test needs to be performed –see later). Properties defined in a module can be exported as any other predicate. For example:

```
:- prop list/1.
list([]).
list([_|L]) :- list(L).
```

defines the property "list". A list is an instance of a very useful class of user-defined properties called regular types, which is simply a syntactically restricted class of logic programs. We can mark this fact by stating ":- regtype list/1." instead of ":- prop list/1." (this can be done automatically). The definition above can be included in a user program or, alternatively, it can be imported from a system library, e.g.:

```
:- use_module(library(lists),[list/1]).
```

Type Analysis: Ciaopp can infer (parametric) types for programs both at the predicate level and at the literal level. The output for Figure 1 at the predicate level, assuming that we have imported the lists library, is:

```
:- true pred qsort(A,B)
        : ( term(A), term(B) )
        => ( list(A), list(B) ).
:- true pred partition(A,B,C,D)
        : ( term(A), term(B), term(C), term(D) )
        => ( list(A), term(B), list(C), list(D) ).
:- true pred append(A,B,C)
        : ( list(A), list1(B,term), term(C) )
        => ( list(A), list1(B,term), list1(C,term) ).
```

where term is any term and prop list1 is defined in library(lists) as:

```
:- regtype list1(L,T) # "@var{L} is a list of at least one @var{T}'s."
list1([X|R],T) :- T(X), list(R,T).
:- regtype list(L,T) # "@var{L} is a list of @var{T}'s."
list([],_T).
list([X|L],T) :- T(X), list(L).
```

We can use entry assertions [1] (essentially, "trust calls" assertions) to specify a restricted class of calls to the module entry points as acceptable:

```
:- entry qsort(A,B) : (list(A, num), var(B)).
```

This informs the analyzer that in all external calls to qsort, the first argument will be a list of numbers and the second a free variable. Note the use of builtin properties (i.e., defined in modules which are loaded by default, such as var, num, list, etc.). Note also that properties natively understood by different analysis domains can be combined in the same assertion. This assertion will aid goal-dependent analyses obtain more accurate information. For example, it allows the type analysis to obtain the following, more precise information:

```
:- true pred qsort(A,B)
        : ( list(A,num), term(B) )
        => ( list(A,num), list(B,num) ).
:- true pred partition(A,B,C,D)
        : ( list(A,num), num(B), term(C), term(D) )
        => ( list(A,num), num(B), list(C,num), list(D,num) ).
:- true pred append(A,B,C)
        : ( list(A,num), list1(B,num), term(C) )
        => ( list(A,num), list1(B,num), list1(C,num) ).
```

Non-failure and Determinacy Analysis: Ciaopp includes a non-failure analysis, based on [6], which can detect procedures and goals that can be guaranteed not to fail, i.e., to produce at least one solution or not terminate. It also can detect predicates that are "covered", i.e., such that for any input (included in the calling type of the predicate), there is at least one clause whose "test" (head unification and body builtins) succeeds. Ciaopp also includes a determinacy analysis which can detect predicates which produce at most one solution, or predicates whose clause tests are disjoint, even if they are not fully deterministic (because they call other predicates which are nondeterministic). For example, the result of these analyses for Figure 1 includes the following assertion:

```
:- true pred qsort(A,B)
        : ( list(A,num), var(B) ) => ( list(A,num), list(B,num) )
        + ( not_fail, covered, is_det, disjoint ).
```

(The + field in **pred** assertions can contain a conjunction of computational properties which are global to the predicate.)

Size, Cost, and Termination Analysis: Ciaopp can also infer lower and upper bounds on the sizes of terms and the computational cost of predicates [5, 7]. The cost bounds are expressed as functions on the sizes of the input arguments and yield the number of resolution steps. Various measures are used for the "size" of an input, such as list-length, term-size, term-depth, integer-value, etc. Note that obtaining a non-infinite upper bound on cost also implies proving *termination* of the predicate.

As an example, the following assertion is part of the output of the upper bounds analysis:

```
:- true pred append(A,B,C)
        : ( list(A,num), list1(B,num), var(C) )
        => ( list(A,num), list1(B,num), list1(C,num),
             upper_size(A,length(A)), upper_size(B,length(B)),
             upper_size(C,length(B)+length(A)) )
        + upper_time(length(A)+1).
```

Note that in this example the size measure used is list length. The assertion `upper_size(C,length(B)+length(A)` means that an (upper) bound on the size of the third argument of append/3 is the sum of the sizes of the first and second arguments. The inferred upper bound on computational steps is the length of the first argument of append/3.

The following is the output of the lower-bounds analysis:

```
:- true pred append(A,B,C)
        : ( list(A,num), list1(B,num), var(C) )
        => ( list(A,num), list1(B,num), list1(C,num),
             lower_size(A,length(A)), lower_size(B,length(B)),
             lower_size(C,length(B)+length(A)) )
        + ( not_fail, covered, lower_time(length(A)+1) ).
```

The lower-bounds analysis uses information from the non-failure analysis, without which a trivial lower bound of 0 would be derived.

Decidability, Approximations, and Safety: As a final note on the analyses, it should be pointed out that since most of the properties being inferred are in general undecidable at compile-time, the inference technique used, abstract interpretation, is necessarily *approximate*, i.e., possibly imprecise. On the other hand, such approximations are also always guaranteed to be safe, in the sense that (modulo bugs, of course) they are never *incorrect*.

```
:- module(qsort, [qsort/2], [assertions]).

qsort([X|L],R) :-
     partition(L,L1,X,L2),
     qsort(L2,R2), qsort(L1,R1),
     append(R2,[x|R1],R).
qsort([],[]).

partition([],_B,[],[]).
partition([e|R],C,[E|Left1],Right):-
        E < C, !, partition(R,C,Left1,Right).
partition([E|R],C,Left,[E|Right1]):-
        E >= C,   partition(R,C,Left,Right1).

append([],X,X).
append([H|X],Y,[H|Z]):- append(X,Y,Z).
```

Figure 2: A tentative qsort program.

3   Program Debugging and Assertion Validation

Within Ciaopp, global analysis is not only used to infer program properties, but also to detect classes of errors at compile-time which go well beyond the usual syntactic checks. Errors can be detected in conventional programs or, alternatively, assertions can be added to such programs stating intended program properties, and which can then be validated or falsified, in the latter case detecting an error.

Static Debugging: The idea of using analysis information for debugging comes naturally after observing analysis outputs for erroneous programs. Consider the program in Figure 2. The result of regular type analysis for this program includes the following code:

```
:- true pred qsort(A,B)
        : ( term(A), term(B) )
        => ( list(A,t113), list(B,^x) ).

:- regtype t113/1.
t113(A) :- arithexpression(A).
t113([]).
t113([A|B]) :- arithexpression(A), list(B,t113).
t113(e).
```

where `arithexpression` is a library property which describes arithmetic expressions and list(B,^x) means "a list of x's." A new name (t113) is given to one of the inferred types, and its definition included, because no definition of this type was found visible to the module. In any case, the information inferred does not seem compatible with a correct definition of qsort, which clearly points to a bug in the program.

Ciaopp includes a number of facilities to help in the debugging task beyond manual inspection of the analyzer output. For example, Ciaopp can find incompatibilities between the ways in which program predicates are called and their definitions. It can also detect incompatibilities between the way library predicates are called and their intended mode of use, expressed in the form of assertions in the libraries themselves. In order to use these capabilities, we add to the program the same declaration of its intended use of previous examples:

```
:- entry qsort(A,B) : (list(A, num), var(B)).
```

Turning on compile-time error checking and selecting type and mode analysis produces the following messages:

```
WARNING: Literal partition(L,L1,X,L2) at qsort/2/1/1 does not succeed!
ERROR: Predicate E>=C at partition/4/3/1 is not called as expected:
       Called:   num>=var
       Expected: arithexpression>=arithexpression
```

where `qsort/2/1/1` stands for the first literal in the first clause of `qsort` and `partition/4/3/1` stands for the first literal in the third clause of `partition`.

The first message warns that all calls to `partition` will fail, something normally not intended (e.g., in our case). The second message indicates a wrong call to a builtin predicate, which is an obvious error. This error has been detected by comparing the mode information obtained by global analysis, which at the corresponding program point indicates that E is a free variable, with the assertion:

```
:- check calls A<B (arithexpression(A), arithexpression(B)).
```

which is present in the default builtins module, and which implies that the two arguments to `</2` should be ground. The message signals a compile-time, or *abstract*, incorrectness symptom [3], indicating that the program does not satisfy the specification given (that of the builtin predicates, in this case). Checking the indicated call to `partition` and inspecting its arguments we detect that in the definition of `qsort`, `partition` is called with the second and third arguments in reversed order – the correct call is `partition(L,X,L1,L2)`.

After correcting this bug, we proceed to perform another round of compile-time checking, which produces the following message:

```
WARNING: Clause 'partition/4/2' is incompatible with its call type
        Head:       partition([e|R],C,[E|Left1],Right)
        Call Type:  partition(list(num),num,var,var)
```

This time the error is in the second clause of `partition`. Checking this clause we see that in the first argument of the head there is an e which should be E instead. Compile-time checking of the program with this bug corrected does not produce any further warning or error messages.

Validation of User Assertions: In order to be more confident about our program, we add to it the following check assertions:[5]

```
:- calls qsort(A,B) : list(A, num).                           % A1
:- success qsort(A,B)  => (ground(B), sorted_num_list(B)).    % A2
:- calls partition(A,B,C,D) : (ground(A), ground(B)).         % A3
:- success partition(A,B,C,D) => (list(C, num),ground(D)).    % A4
:- calls append(A,B,C) : (list(A,num),list(B,num)).           % A5

:- prop sorted_num_list/1.
sorted_num_list([]).
sorted_num_list([X]):- number(X).
sorted_num_list([X,Y|Z]):-
        number(X), number(Y), X<Y, sorted_num_list([Y|Z]).
```

where we also use a new property, `sorted_num_list`, defined in the module itself. These assertions provide a partial specification of the program. They can be seen as integrity constraints: if their properties do not hold, the

---

[5]The `check` prefix is assumed when no prefix is given, as in the example shown.

program is incorrect. `Calls` assertions specify properties of all calls to a predicate, while `success` assertions specify properties of exit points for all calls to a predicate. Properties of successes can be restricted to apply only to calls satisfying certain properties upon entry by adding a : field to `success` assertions (see [19]).

Ciaopp can *check* the assertions above, by comparing them with the assertions inferred by analysis (see [3, 20] for details), producing:

```
:- checked calls qsort(A,B) : list(A,num).                          %A1
:- check success qsort(A,B) => sorted_num_list(B).                  %A2
:- checked calls partition(A,B,C,D) : (ground(A),ground(B)).        %A3
:- checked success partition(A,B,C,D) => (list(C,num),ground(D) ).%A4
:- false calls append(A,B,C) : ( list(A,num), list(B,num) ).        %A5
```

Assertion A5 has been detected to be false. This indicates a violation of the specification given, which is also flagged by Ciaopp as follows:

```
ERROR: (lns 22-23) false calls assertion:
  :- calls append(A,B,C) : list(A,num),list(B,num)
        Called append(list(^x),[^x|list(^x)],var)
```

The error is now in the call `append(R2,[x|R1],R)` in `qsort` (x instead of X). From the rest of the output we can conclude that the rest of the specification has been partially validated: assertions A1, A3, and A4 have been detected to hold, but it was not possible to prove statically assertion A2, which has remained with `check` status. Ciaopp can, on request, introduce run-time tests in the program which will call the definition of `sorted_num_list` at the appropriate times. Note that A2 has been simplified, and this is because the mode analysis has determined that on success the second argument of `qsort` is ground, and thus this does not have to be checked at run-time. On the other hand the analyses used in our session (types and modes) do not provide enough information to prove that the output of `qsort` is a *sorted* list of numbers, since this is not a native property of the analyses being used. While this property could be captured by including a more refined domain (such as constrained types), it is interesting to see what happens with the analyses selected for the example.[6]

Dynamic Debugging with Run-time Checks: Assuming that we stay with the analyses selected previously, the following step in the development process is to compile the program obtained above with the "generate run-time checks" option. In the current implementation of Ciaopp we obtain the following code for predicate `qsort` (the code for `partition` and `append` remain the same as there is no other assertion left to check):

```
qsort(A,B) :-
        new_qsort(A,B),
        postc([ qsort(C,D) : true => sorted(D) ], qsort(A,B)).
```

---

[6]Not that while property `sorted_num_list` cannot be proved with only (over approximations) of mode and regular type information, it may be possible to prove that it does *not* hold (an example of how properties which are not natively understood by the analysis can also be useful for detecting bugs at compile-time): while the regular type analysis cannot capture perfectly the property `sorted_num_list`, it can still approximate it (by analyzing the definition) as `list(B, num)`. If type analysis for the program were to generate a type for B not compatible with `list(B, num)`, then a definite error symptom would be detected.

```
new_qsort([X|L],R) :-
      partition(L,X,L1,L2),
      qsort(L2,R2), qsort(L1,R1),
      append(R2,[X|R1],R).
new_qsort([],[]).
```

where postc is the library predicate in charge of checking postconditions of predicates. If we now run the program with run-time checks in order to sort, say, the list [1,2], the Ciao system generates the following error message:

```
?- qsort([1,2],L).
ERROR: for Goal qsort([1,2],[2,1])
Precondition: true holds, but
Postcondition: sorted_num_list([2,1]) does not.

L = [2,1] ?
```

Clearly, there is a problem with qsort, since [2,1] is not the result of ordering [1,2] in ascending order. This is a (now, run-time, or *concrete*) incorrectness symptom, which can be used as the starting point of diagnosis. The result of such diagnosis should indicate that the call to append (where R1 and R2 have been swapped) is the cause of the error and that the right definition of predicate qsort is the one in Figure 1.

4 Source Program Optimization

We now turn our attention to the program optimizations that are available in Ciaopp. These include abstract specialization, parallelization (including granularity control), and multiple program specialization. All of them are performed as source to source transformations of the program. In most of them static analysis is instrumental, or, at least, beneficial.

Abstract Specialization: Program specialization optimizes programs for known values (substitutions) of the input. It is often the case that the set of possible input values is unknown, or this set is infinite. However, a form of specialization can still be performed in such cases by means of abstract interpretation, specialization then being with respect to abstract values, rather than concrete ones. Such abstract values represent a (possibly infinite) set of concrete values. For example, consider the definition of the property sorted_num_list/1, and assume that regular type analysis has produced:

```
:- true pred sorted(A) : list(A,num) => list(A,num).
```

Abstract specialization can use this information to optimize the code into:

```
sorted_num_list([]).
sorted_num_list([_]).
sorted_num_list([X,Y|Z]):- X<Y, sorted_num_list([Y|Z]).
```

which is clearly more efficient because no number tests are executed. The optimization above is based on "abstractly executing" the number literals to the value true. The notion of *abstract executability* [23, 12] can reduce some literals to true, fail, or a set of primitives (typically, unifications) based on the information available from abstract interpretation.

Ciaopp can also apply abstract specialization in the optimization of programs with dynamic scheduling (e.g., using delay declarations) [21]. The transformations simplify the conditions on the *delay declarations* and also move delayed literals later in the rule body, leading to substantial performance improvement. This is used by Ciaopp, for example, when supporting complex computation models, such as Andorra-style execution [14].

62

Parallelization: Another application of global analysis in Ciaopp is in automatic program parallelization [2]. It is also performed as a source-to-source transformation, in which the input program is *annotated* with parallel expressions. A number of heuristic parallelization algorithms are available, which guarantee certain no-slowdown properties [16] for the parallelized programs. We consider again the program of Figure 1. A possible parallelization (obtained in this case with the "MEL" annotator) is:

```
qsort([X|L],R) :-
        partition(L,X,L1,L2),
        ( indep([[L1,L2]]) -> qsort(L2,R2) & qsort(L1,R1)
                            ; qsort(L2,R2), qsort(L1,R1) ),
        append(R1,[X|R2],R).
```

which indicates that, provided that L1 and L2 do not have variables in common (at execution time), then the recursive calls can be run in parallel. Given the information inferred by, e.g., the mode and independence analysis (see Section 2), where L1 and L2 are ground after `partition` (and therefore do not share variables) the annotator yields instead:

```
qsort([X|L],R) :-
        partition(L,X,L1,L2),
        qsort(L2,R2) & qsort(L1,R1),
        append(R1,[X|R2],R).
```

which is much more efficient since it has no run-time test.

Granularity Control: Another application of the information produced by the Ciaopp analyzers, in this case the cost analysis, is to perform run-time task granularity control [10] of parallelized code. Such parallel code can be the output of the process mentioned above or code parallelized manually.

In general, this run-time granularity control process involves computing sizes of terms involved in granularity control, evaluating cost functions, and comparing the result with a threshold[7] to decide for parallel or sequential execution. Optimizations to this general process include cost function simplification and improved term size computation, both of which are illustrated in the following example.

Consider again the qsort program in Figure 1. We use Ciaopp to perform a transformation for granularity control, using the analysis information of type, sharing+freeness, and upper bound cost analysis, and taking as input the parallelized code obtained in the previous section. Ciaopp adds a clause "qsort(_1,_2) :- g_qsort(_1,_2)." (to preserve the original entry point) and produces g_qsort/2, the version of qsort/2 that performs granularity control (s_qsort/2 is the sequential version):

```
g_qsort([X|L],R) :-
        partition_o3_4(L,X,L1,L2,_2,_1),
        ( _1>7 -> (_2>7 -> g_qsort(L2,R2) & g_qsort(L1,R1)
                         ; g_qsort(L2,R2), s_qsort(L1,R1))
                ; (_2>7 -> s_qsort(L2,R2), g_qsort(L1,R1)
                         ; s_qsort(L2,R2), s_qsort(L1,R1))),
        append(R1,[X|R2],R).
g_qsort([],[]).
```

---

[7]This threshold can be determined experimentally for each parallel system, by taking the average value resulting from several runs.

Note that if the lengths of the two input lists to the qsort program are greater than a threshold (a list length of 7 in this case) then versions which continue performing granularity control are executed in parallel. Otherwise, the two recursive calls are executed sequentially. The executed version of each of such calls depends on its grain size: if the length of its input list is not greater than the threshold then a sequential version which does not perform granularity control is executed. This is based on the detection of a recursive invariant: in subsequent recursions this goal will not produce tasks with input sizes greater than the threshold, and thus, for all of them, execution should be performed sequentially and, obviously, no granularity control is needed.

In general, the evaluation of the condition to decide which predicate versions are executed will require the computation of cost functions and a comparison with a cost threshold (measured in units of computation). However, in this example a test simplification has been performed, so that the input size is simply compared against a size threshold, and thus the cost function for qsort does not need to be evaluated.[8] Predicate partition_o3_4/6:

```
partition_o3_4([],_B,[],[],0,0).
partition_o3_4([E|R],C,[E|Left1],Right,_1,_2) :-
      E<C, partition_o3_4(R,C,Left1,Right,_3,_2), _1 is _3+1.
partition_o3_4([E|R],C,Left,[E|Right1],_1,_2) :-
      E>=C, partition_o3_4(R,C,Left,Right1,_1,_3), _2 is _3+1.
```

is the transformed version of partition/4, which "on the fly" computes the sizes of its third and fourth arguments (the automatically generated variables _1 and _2 represent these sizes respectively) [9].

Multiple Specialization: Sometimes a procedure has different uses within a program, i.e. it is called from different places in the program with different (abstract) input values. In principle, (abstract) program specialization is then allowable only if the optimization is applicable to all uses of the predicate. However, it is possible that in several different uses the input values allow different and incompatible optimizations and then none of them can take place. In Ciaopp this problem is overcome by means of "multiple program specialization" where different versions of the predicate are generated for each use. Each version is then optimized for the particular subset of input values with which it is to be used. The abstract multiple specialization technique used in Ciaopp [24] has the advantage that it can be incorporated with little or no modification of some existing abstract interpreters, provided they are *multivariant* (PLAI and similar frameworks have this property).

This specialization can be used for example to improve automatic parallelization in those cases where run-time tests are included in the resulting program. In such cases, a good number of run-time tests may be eliminated and invariants extracted automatically from loops, resulting generally in lower overheads and in several cases in increased speedups. We consider automatic parallelization of a program for matrix multiplication using the same analysis and parallelization algorithms as the qsort example used before. This program is automatically parallelized without tests if we provide

---

[8]This size threshold will obviously be different if the cost function is.

the analyzer (by means of an **entry** declaration) with accurate information on the expected modes of use of the program. However, in the interesting case in which the user does not provide such declaration, the code generated contains a large number of run-time tests. We include below the code for predicate `multiply` which multiplies a matrix by a vector:

```
multiply([],_,[]).
multiply([V0|Rest],V1,[Result|Others]) :-
    (ground(V1),
     indep([[V0,Rest],[V0,Others],[Rest,Result],[Result,Others]]) ->
        vmul(V0,V1,Result) & multiply(Rest,V1,Others)
    ;   vmul(V0,V1,Result), multiply(Rest,V1,Others)).
```

Four independence tests and one groundness test have to be executed prior to executing in parallel the calls in the body of the recursive clause of `multiply`. However, abstract multiple specialization generates four versions of the predicate `multiply` which correspond to the different ways this predicate may be called (basically, depending on whether the tests succeed or not). Of these four variants, the most optimized one is:

```
multiply3([],_,[]).
multiply3([V0|Rest],V1,[Result|Others]) :-
    (indep([[Result,Others]]) ->
        vmul(V0,V1,Result) & multiply3(Rest,V1,Others)
    ;   vmul(V0,V1,Result), multiply3(Rest,V1,Others)).
```

where the groundness test and three out of the four independence tests have been eliminated. Note also that the recursive calls to `multiply` use the optimized version `multiply3`. Thus, execution of matrix multiplication with the expected mode (the only one which will succeed in Prolog) will be quickly directed to the optimized versions of the predicates and iterate on them. This is because the specializer has been able to detect this optimization as an invariant of the loop. The complete code for this example can be found in [24]. The multiple specialization implemented incorporates a minimization algorithm which keeps in the final program as few versions as possible while not losing opportunities for optimization. For example, eight versions of predicate `vmul` (for vector multiplication) would be generated if no minimizations were performed. However, as multiple versions do not allow further optimization, only one version is present in the final program.

In the context of Ciaopp we have also studied the relationship between abstract multiple specialization, abstract interpretation, and partial evaluation. Abstract specialization exploits the information obtained by multivariant abstract interpretation where information about values of variables is propagated by simulating program execution and performing fixpoint computations for recursive calls. In contrast, traditional partial evaluators (mainly) use unfolding for both propagating values of variables and transforming the program. It is known that abstract interpretation is a better technique for propagating success values than unfolding. However, the program transformations induced by unfolding may lead to important optimizations which are not directly achievable in the existing frameworks for multiple specialization based on abstract interpretation. In [25] we present a specialization framework which integrates the better information propagation of abstract interpretation with the powerful program transformations performed by partial evaluation.

References

[1] F. Bueno, D. Cabeza, M. Hermenegildo, and G. Puebla. Global Analysis of Standard Prolog Programs. In *European Symposium on Programming*, number 1058 in LNCS, pages 108–124, Sweden, April 1996. Springer-Verlag.

[2] F. Bueno, M. García de la Banda, and M. Hermenegildo. Effectiveness of Abstract Interpretation in Automatic Parallelization: A Case Study in Logic Programming. *ACM Transactions on Programming Languages and Systems*, 1999. In Press.

[3] F. Bueno, P. Deransart, W. Drabent, G. Ferrand, M. Hermenegildo, J. Maluszynski, and G. Puebla. On the Role of Semantic Approximations in Validation and Diagnosis of Constraint Logic Programs. In *Proc. of the 3rd. Int'l Workshop on Automated Debugging–AADEBUG'97*, pages 155–170, Linkoping, Sweden, May 1997. U. of Linkoping Press. Available from ftp://clip.dia.fi.upm.es/pub/papers/aadebug_discipldeliv.ps.gz.

[4] P. Cousot and R. Cousot. Abstract Interpretation: a Unified Lattice Model for Static Analysis of Programs by Construction or Approximation of Fixpoints. In *Fourth ACM Symposium on Principles of Programming Languages*, pages 238–252, 1977.

[5] S. K. Debray, P. López García, M. Hermenegildo, and N.-W. Lin. Estimating the Computational Cost of Logic Programs. In *Static Analysis Symposium, SAS'94*, number 864 in LNCS, pages 255–265, Namur, Belgium, September 1994. Springer-Verlag.

[6] S. K. Debray, P. López García, and M. Hermenegildo. Non-Failure Analysis for Logic Programs. In *1997 International Conference on Logic Programming*, pages 48–62, Cambridge, MA, June 1997. MIT Press.

[7] S. K. Debray, P. López-García, M. Hermenegildo, and N.-W. Lin. Lower Bound Cost Estimation for Logic Programs. In *1997 International Logic Programming Symposium*, pages 291–305. MIT Press, Cambridge, MA, October 1997.

[8] J.P. Gallagher and D.A. de Waal. Fast and precise regular approximations of logic programs. In Pascal Van Hentenryck, editor, *Proc. of the 11th International Conference on Logic Programming*, pages 599–613. MIT Press, 1994.

[9] P. López García and M. Hermenegildo. Efficient Term Size Computation for Granularity Control. In *International Conference on Logic Programming*, pages 647–661, Cambridge, MA, June 1995. MIT Pres.

[10] P. López García, M. Hermenegildo, and S. K. Debray. A Methodology for Granularity Based Control of Parallelism in Logic Programs. *J. of Symbolic Computation, Special Issue on Parallel Symbolic Computation*, 22:715–734, 1996.

[11] M. García de la Banda, M. Hermenegildo, M. Bruynooghe, V. Dumortier, G. Janssens, and W. Simoens. Global Analysis of Constraint Logic Programs. *ACM Trans. on Programming Languages and Systems*, 18(5):564–615, 1996.

[12] F. Giannotti and M. Hermenegildo. A Technique for Recursive Invariance Detection and Selective Program Specialization. In *Proc. 3rd. Int'l Symposium on Programming Language Implementation and Logic Programming*, number 528 in LNCS, pages 323–335. Springer-Verlag, August 1991.

[13] M. Hermenegildo. Writing "Shell Scripts" in SICStus Prolog, April 1996. Available from http://www.clip.dia.fi.upm.es/. Posting in comp.lang.prolog.

[14] M. Hermenegildo, F. Bueno, D. Cabeza, M. García de la Banda, P. López, and G. Puebla. The CIAO Multi-Dialect Compiler and System: An Experimentation Workbench for Future (C)LP Systems. In *Parallelism and Implementation of Logic and Constraint Logic Programming*. Nova Science, Commack, NY, USA, April 1999.

[15] M. Hermenegildo, G. Puebla, K. Marriott, and P. Stuckey. Incremental Analysis of Logic Programs. In *International Conference on Logic Programming*, pages 797–811. MIT Press, June 1995.

[16] M. Hermenegildo and F. Rossi. Strict and Non-Strict Independent And-Parallelism in Logic Programs: Correctness, Efficiency, and Compile-Time Conditions. *Journal of Logic Programming*, 22(1):1–45, 1995.

[17] M. Hermenegildo and The CLIP Group. An Automatic Documentation Generator for (C)LP – Reference Manual. The CIAO System Documentation Series – TR CLIP5/97.1, Facultad de Informática, UPM, August 1997.

[18] K. Muthukumar and M. Hermenegildo. Compile-time Derivation of Variable Dependency Using Abstract Interpretation. *Journal of Logic Programming*, 13(2/3):315–347, July 1992.

[19] G. Puebla, F. Bueno, and M. Hermenegildo. An Assertion Language for Debugging of Constraint Logic Programs. In *ILPS'97 WS on Tools and Environments for (C)LP*, October 1997. ftp://clip.dia.fi.upm.es/pub/papers/assert_lang_tr_discipldeliv.ps.gz.

[20] G. Puebla, F. Bueno, and M. Hermenegildo. A Framework for Assertion-based Debugging in Constraint Logic Programming. In *Logic-based Program Synthesis and Transformation (LOPSTR'99)*, Venezia, Italy, September 1999.

[21] G. Puebla, M. García de la Banda, K. Marriott, and P. Stuckey. Optimization of Logic Programs with Dynamic Scheduling. In *1997 International Conference on Logic Programming*, pages 93–107, Cambridge, MA, June 1997. MIT Press.

[22] G. Puebla and M. Hermenegildo. Optimized Algorithms for the Incremental Analysis of Logic Programs. In *International Static Analysis Symposium*, number 1145 in LNCS, pages 270–284. Springer-Verlag, September 1996.

[23] G. Puebla and M. Hermenegildo. Abstract Specialization and its Application to Program Parallelization. In J. Gallagher, editor, *VI International Workshop on Logic Program Synthesis and Transformation*, number 1207 in LNCS, pages 169–186. Springer-Verlag, 1997.

[24] G. Puebla and M. Hermenegildo. Abstract Multiple Specialization and its Application to Program Parallelization. *J. of Logic Programming. Special Issue on Synthesis, Transformation and Analysis of Logic Programs*, 1999. In press.

[25] G. Puebla, M. Hermenegildo, and J. Gallagher. An Integration of Partial Evaluation in a Generic Abstract Interpretation Framework. In O Danvy, editor, *ACM SIGPLAN Workshop on Partial Evaluation and Semantics-Based Program Manipulation (PEPM'99)*, number NS-99-1 in BRISC Series, pages 75–85. University of Aarhus, Denmark, January 1999.

From Prolog and Zelda to ToonTalk

Ken Kahn
Animated Programs
49 Fay Avenue, San Carlos, CA 94070, USA
kenkahn@toontalk.com

Abstract

ToonTalk looks like a video game. This is not surprising since its design and user interface were strongly influenced by games like *The Legend of Zelda: A Link to the Past* and *Robot Odyssey*. What may be more surprising is that ToonTalk is a programming language and environment based upon ideas that have evolved from Prolog over a period of nearly twenty years.

ToonTalk is a synthesis of ideas from concurrent constraint programming, video games, and programming languages for children. In the spirit of Logo [3], ToonTalk is an attempt to take the best ideas in computer science and make them accessible to children. When Logo was designed over thirty years ago, the best programming language ideas could be found in the Lisp language. The design of ToonTalk is based upon the belief that the best programming language ideas can be found in concurrent logic programming and concurrent constraint programming languages like Janus, Linear Janus, FGHC, Vulcan, DOC, AKL, and Oz [4,5,6]. These languages, in turn, borrow heavily from earlier languages like Concurrent Prolog and Parlog that in turn grew out of research on Prolog.

While these languages have many desirable aspects – they are powerful, elegant, theoretically well grounded, and expressive – they are not generally considered easy to learn. If it takes substantial time and effort for computer scientists to understand one of these languages, then how can one hope to make the underlying ideas accessible to young school children?

An answer lies with video games. Many of these games present a large and complex world with many kinds of objects and possible actions. And yet, children as young as 4 years old learn to master these game worlds without help. The fundamental idea underlying ToonTalk is that a game world can be created in which the objects and actions map directly onto programming language constructs. In ToonTalk, a clause becomes a robot, a term or tuple becomes a box, a number becomes a pad, and so on. The act of putting a box and a team of robots into a truck becomes a way of expressing a process spawn or procedure call. The act of dropping a number pad on another number pad becomes a way of expressing an arithmetic operation. And so on.

1   Concretizations

Concretizations are mappings between programming language abstractions and tangible objects. The idea is to preserve the semantics while providing a concrete analog for each computational abstraction. Ideally, the concrete analog should be a familiar object with widely known properties – e.g. boxes are good for holding things. Furthermore, these mappings work best when they fit together in a consistent theme – in the case of ToonTalk, a modern city was used. The ToonTalk concretizations are summarized in Table 1.

The ToonTalk programmer starts off flying her helicopter over a nearly empty city. When she lands she is followed by Tooly the Toolbox, which contains the essential building blocks and tools for programming. After entering a house, she can sit down and begin to train robots to work on boxes. She can then arrange for teams of robots to work in different houses, communicating by giving birds items to deliver to their nests.

Computational Abstraction	ToonTalk Concretization
computation	city
process	house
clause	robots
guard	contents of thought bubble
body	actions taught to robot
tuples or terms	boxes
comparison tests	scales
process spawning	loaded trucks
process termination	bombs
constants	numbers, text, and pictures
channel transmit capabilities (tellers)	birds
channel receive capabilities (askers)	nests
program storage	notebooks

Table 1 - ToonTalk Concretizations

A logic program is typically a collection of clauses. In concurrent logic programming languages the clause consists of a guard that specifies the preconditions for running the clause and a body that specifies what actions should be taken. In ToonTalk the guard corresponds to the box (i.e. tuple) that a robot is thinking about, which is displayed in the thought bubble of the robot. ToonTalk programmers understand that a robot will not work on a box unless it matches the box in his thought bubble. Matching is understood in visual terms. A robot is happy with boxes that have more detail than the one in his thought bubble, but he will not accept a box if something is in a hole of a thought bubble box and something else is in the corresponding location. The only exception to this is if there is a nest in the corresponding location. A nest is the "ask" or read part of a variable. As with concurrent logic programming languages in this situation the arguments are insufficiently specified and the process is suspended. The "story" for ToonTalk programmers is that if a robot is expecting something and finds a nest instead, he does not give up. Instead he waits for a bird to come and cover her nest with something. If she covers her nest with the right kind of thing, the robot will wake up and start working.

The behavior of a robot is specified by the training he gets from the programmer. This training corresponds to defining the body of a clause. The possible actions are

- **sending a message** by giving a box or pad to a bird,
- **spawning a new process** by dropping a box and a team of robots into a truck (which drives off to build a new house),
- **performing simple primitive operations** such as addition or multiplication by building a stack of numbers (which are combined by a small mouse with a big hammer),
- **copying an item** by using a magician's wand,
- **terminating a process** by setting off a bomb, and
- **changing a tuple** by taking items out of compartments of a box and dropping in new ones.

These correspond to the permissible actions of a concurrent logic programming agent or process. The last one may appear to introduce mutable data structures into the language, which are known to introduce complexity into parallel programs and make it difficult to provide a simple, clean semantics for the language. In fact, though, since boxes are copied and not shared, this is not the case. An apparently destructive operation on a private copy is semantically equivalent to constructing the resulting state from scratch. But a destructive operation is often a more convenient or direct kind of expression.

When the user controls the robot to perform these actions, she is acting upon concrete values. This has much in common with keyboard macro programming and programming by example [2,7]. The hard problem for programming by example systems is how to abstract the example to introduce variables for generality. ToonTalk does no induction or learning. Instead the user explicitly abstracts a program fragment by removing detail from the thought bubble. The preconditions are thus relaxed. The actions in the body are general since they have been recorded with respect to which compartment of the box was acted upon, not what items happened to occupy the box.

2 The *Append* predicate – an detailed example

Let us consider the classic *append* predicate of Prolog and concurrent logic programming. The programmer starts by connecting boxes together to construct sample input to the procedure. The box in Figure 1 corresponds to the arguments in the call *append([a,b],[c],X)*. (The labels *List1*, *List2*, and *Both* are just annotations.)

Figure 1 – Sample input to Append

The programmer then gives the box to a fresh robot, illustrated in Figure 2A, and enters the robot's thoughts. As she does so, she stops controlling her persona and begins to control the robot, illustrated in Figure 2B. She starts by having the robot take the box out of the first hole and set it down.

A   **B**

Figure 2 – Starting to train a robot to append lists

The program at this point corresponds to the following program fragment:

```
append(Arg1, Arg2, Arg3) :-
  Arg1 = [X1 | X2],
  X1 = a,
  X2 = [X3 | X4],
  X3 = b,
  X4 = [],
  Arg2 = [X5 | X6],
  X5 = c,
  X6 = [],
  Arg3 = $bird(Answer) | // guard is generated from the box in Step A
  Floor1 = Arg1, // from Step B
```

She then removes and puts the rest of the list back (step C), takes out a new nest to create a new asker/teller pair and drops the nest in the empty hole (step D), gives the box to the original bird in the box (step E), the bird then flies way and when she returns the programmer vacuums her up (step F), and drops the

71

bird that hatched from the nest in the hole (step G), and exits the robot's thoughts and labels him "App" (step H). Since she exited the robot's thoughts without setting off a bomb, the robot will repeatedly do what he was trained to do so long as the box continues to match the box in his thought bubble.

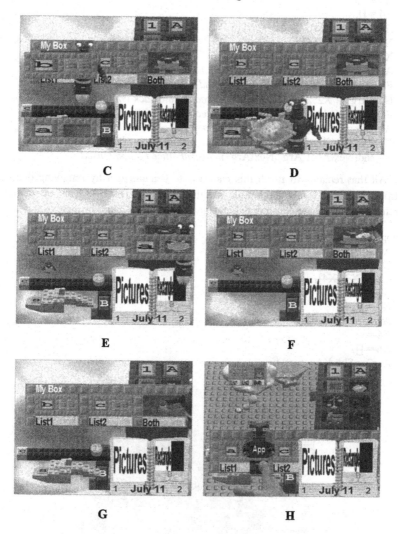

C

D

E

F

G

H

Figure 3 – Completing the recursive Append clause

The training of the robot is now complete and the corresponding program is:

```
append(Arg1, Arg2, Arg3) :-
 Arg1 = [X1 | X2],
 X1 = a,
 X2 = [X3 | X4],
 X3 = b,
 X4 = [],
 Arg2 = [X5 | X6],
 X5 = c,
 X6 = [],
 Arg3 = $bird(Answer) | // guard from the box given to the robot (step A)
 Floor1 = Arg1, // put contents of second hole on the floor (step B)
 NextArg1 = X2, // move contents of second hole back (step C)
 Floor2 = [X1 | Nest1], // drop nest in second hole (step D)
 Answer = Floor2, // give box to bird (step E)
 NextArg3 = $bird(Nest1), // replace old bird with new bird (steps F and G)
 append(NextArg1,Arg2,NextArg3). // recur since no bomb used
```

All that remains to finish this clause is to generalize it by removing details from the robot's thought bubble as illustrated in Figure 4. This effectively removes some of the constraints in the guard so that the guard becomes

```
append(Arg1, Arg2, Arg3) :-
 Arg1 = [X1 | X2],
 X1 = a,
 X2 = [X3 | X4],
 X3 = b,
 X4 = [],
 Arg2 = [X5 | X6],
 X5 = c,
 X6 = [],
 Arg3 = $bird(Answer) |
```

Figure 4 – The Append clause generalized (Step I)

After simplifying the clause by substitutions we obtain

```
append([X|Y],Z,$bird(Answer)) :-true |
  Answer = [X|Nest1],
  append(Y,Z,$bird(Nest1)).
```

The programmer is now ready to define the base or termination clause. She gives the *App* robot the box and watches him execute two iterations before changing his box so that it no longer matches his thought bubble box as displayed in Figure 5K. The first hole of the box has a box with no holes (like [] in Prolog) while in the corresponding position in the thought bubble there is a box with two holes. The robot has filled the nest with the equivalent of the list [a, b | X].

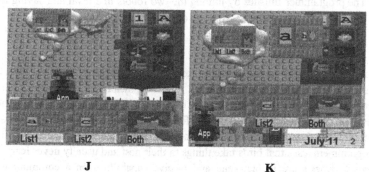

J   K

Figure 5 – Running the Append robot to generate the base case

The programmer gives the box to a new robot (step L) and trains him to grasp the box in the second hole and to give it to the bird (step M). Since in ToonTalk robots are implicitly recursive, she next overrides this default by taking a bomb and setting it off (step N). She then exits the thought bubble and removes the box in the second hole in the box in the robot's thought bubble. The resulting clause is

```
append(Arg1, Arg2, Arg3) :-
  Arg1 = [],
  Arg3 = $bird(Answer) | // from thought bubble box
  Answer = Arg2 // give bird contents of the second hole (step L)
    . // set off bomb(step M)
```

L   M   N

Figure 6 – Training another robot to terminate the computation

The programmer finishes by joining the two robots in a team and saving them in her notebook for future use. She can optionally add comments to the robots.

3 Discussion

ToonTalk is a new way of creating, testing, and debugging programs. One can think of ToonTalk as a very unusual animated syntax for a concurrent logic programming language and an integrated programming development environment that exploits the unique features of the syntax. Program elements can be learned and understood solely as ToonTalk "game" elements. ToonTalk programmers learn that birds take things to their nest and usually never learn that birds and nests are in fact send and receive capabilities on a communication channel. They can work out how their programs should behave by manipulating concrete sample values and only later abstracting their programs for generality. Simply watching their robots at work often is enough to understand a program or see a bug and how to fix it. This aspect of ToonTalk is a form of algorithm animation [1].

But a more global perspective often is necessary for a full understanding of a parallel algorithm. Inspired by the work of Shapiro on systolic programming in Concurrent Prolog [6], ToonTalk supports the ability to see the entire process structure of a computation. The programmer need only stand up, walk to her helicopter, and fly above the city as a computation runs. She sees houses being built (processes spawn), birds flying between houses (communications), and houses blowing up (process termination).

The default layout of the houses in a computation is that houses are built as close as possible to the house containing the robot that initiated the construction. One can override this default and create computations where stacks, trees, or grids of processes are laid out as houses that form lines, trees, or rectangular areas. The programmer can pan and zoom in and out of the unfolding computation by flying her helicopter around and up and down.

The process of designing an animated syntax for a concurrent logic programming language was not trouble free. Guards in ToonTalk are limited to what can be expressed as a pictorial matching process. Negation (e.g. a "not equal" predicate) could have been expressed by introducing some kind of visual convention such as a circle with a diagonal line through it. But this would have added too much complexity. Instead, ToonTalk was designed so that teams of robots work sequentially. If the first robot of a team fails to match, then the robot directly behind him tries to match. This means negation can be expressed by the failure of previous robots to match. This diverges from the usual indeterminate committed choice clause selection of concurrent logic programming languages. In ToonTalk if there is insufficient information to decide the match the entire team suspends. This means that you can express the classic "merge" predicate of concurrent logic programming. Since ToonTalk communication channels (birds and nests) support many-to-one, one-to-many, and many-to-many communication this is not a critical shortcoming. Note that ToonTalk could be enhanced to have two kinds of teams: sequential and committed choice.

The earliest version of ToonTalk provided graphics, animation, and sound libraries via a message-sending interface in keeping with the spirit of concurrent logic programming. Testing with children and adults who were not computer scientists or software professionals revealed that this kind of interface is difficult to understand and master. The process of constructing a message and giving it to the correct bird in order to make a sound or move a picture was too indirect for most users.

To alleviate this problem a direct interface was provided based on the metaphors of remote controls and sensors. Some data objects are active in that they are repeatedly updated automatically. And some data objects when changed make a change to a corresponding element in a graphics or sound library. For example, a sensor for the width of a picture always displays the current width of the picture. If the sensor is changed, then the width of the picture changes accordingly. Children as young as 6 years old master these kinds of sensors and remote controls. But in a limited way, these constructs introduce shared mutable state to a concurrent programming system. To minimize the dangers of race conditions, sensors and remote controls in ToonTalk were limited to work in a very local fashion. But these constructs are a blemish from a theoretical point of view on the attempt to making concurrent logic programming widely accessible.

The computation model underlying ToonTalk is a concurrent logic programming language. Could other animated game-like worlds be constructed that matched other programming languages? It would probably be very difficult to construct a ToonTalk-like world for large complex languages, especially those that rely upon side effects to shared data like Java or C++. It would probably be much easier to make a ToonTalk-like world for other logic programming or constraint languages. For example, choice points could be "concretized" by splitting the ToonTalk city into multiple copies. A copy would be created whenever more than one robot in a team matches a box. The copies of the world would initially differ only by the choice of which of the matching robots gets to run. Cities that run into failure would just go away.

ToonTalk includes a Java applet generator. Anything built inside of ToonTalk can be exported as an applet that can run in a browser. Effort was expended to make the generated Java source code as readable as possible. A similar capability could be added to ToonTalk to produce source code in a concurrent logic programming language. The sample code presented here for the ToonTalk *Append* robots could have been automatically generated. Such a generator might provide a very nice "bridge" between the playful, game-like, child-oriented world of ToonTalk and the computer science underlying logic and constraint programming.

Acknowledgements

I am very grateful for the help, advice and support I have received from many people during the design and building of ToonTalk. In particular David Kahn, Mary Dalrymple, and Markus Fromherz deserve special thanks for all their help. Big thanks go to Ruth Peterson and her 4th grade class at Encinal School in Menlo Park, California where ToonTalk testing has been proceeding since 1995. And I am very thankful to the hundreds of beta testers throughout the world who have provided invaluable bug reports, comments, and suggestions.

References

[1] Marc H. Brown. *Algorithm Animation*. The MIT Press, 1987.

[2] Allen Cypher, Daniel C. Halbert, David Kurlander, and Henry Lieberman, editors. *Watch What I Do: Programming by Demonstration*, The MIT Press, August 1993.

[3] Seymour Papert. *Mindstorms: Children, Computers, and Powerful Ideas*. Basic Books, New York, 1980.

[4] Vijay A. Saraswat. *Concurrent constraint programming languages*. Doctoral Dissertation Award and Logic Programming Series. The MIT Press, 1993.

[5] Vijay A. Saraswat, Kenneth Kahn, and Jacob Levy. Janus--A step towards distributed constraint programming. In *Proceedings of the North American Logic Programming Conference*. The MIT Press, October 1990.

[6] Ehud Shapiro. The family of concurrent logic programming languages. *ACM Computing Surveys*, 1989.

[7] David Smith, *Pygmalion: A Creative Programming Environment*, Stanford University Computer Science Technical Report STAN-CS-75-499, June 1975.

Contributed Papers

Disjunctive Logic Programs with Inheritance

Francesco Buccafurri
DIMET – Universitá di Reggio Calabria
89100, Reggio Calabria, Italia
bucca@ns.ing.unirc.it

Wolfgang Faber, Nicola Leone
Institut für Informationssysteme E184/2
Technische Universität Wien
1040 Vienna, Austria
{faber,leone}@dbai.tuwien.ac.at

Abstract

The paper proposes a new knowledge representation language, called DLP$^<$, which extends disjunctive logic programming (with strong negation) by inheritance. The addition of inheritance enhances the knowledge modeling features of the language providing a natural representation of default reasoning with exceptions.

A declarative model-theoretic semantics of DLP$^<$ is provided, which is shown to generalize the answer set semantics of disjunctive logic programs.

The knowledge modeling features of the language are illustrated by encoding classical nonmonotonic problems in DLP$^<$.

The complexity of DLP$^<$ is analyzed, proving that inheritance does not cause any computational overhead, as reasoning in DLP$^<$ has exactly the same complexity as reasoning in disjunctive logic programming. This is confirmed by the existence of an efficient translation from DLP$^<$ to plain disjunctive logic programming. Using this translation, an advanced KR system supporting the DLP$^<$ language has been implemented on top of the dlv system.

1 Introduction

Disjunctive logic programs are logic programs where disjunction is allowed in the heads of the rules and (NAF) negation may occur in the bodies of the rules. Such programs are now widely recognized as a valuable tool for knowledge representation and commonsense reasoning [5, 18, 13]. One of the attractions of disjunctive logic programming is its ability to naturally model incomplete knowledge [5, 18]. The need to differentiate atoms, which are false because of the failure to prove them true (NAF, or CWA negation), from atoms the falsity of which is explicitly provable, led to extend disjunctive logic programs by strong negation [13]. Strong negation, permitted also in the rules' heads, further enhances the knowledge modeling features of the language, and its usefulness is widely acknowledged in the literature [1, 5, 16, 2, 26, 3]. However, it does not allow to represent default reasoning with exceptions in a direct and natural way. Indeed, to render a default rule r *defeasible*, r must be equipped by an extra negative literal, which "blocks" inferences from r for abnormal instances [14]. For instance, to encode the famous NMR example stating that birds *normally* fly while penguins do not fly, one should write the rule $fly(X) \leftarrow bird(X), \; not \; \neg fly(X)$ along with the fact $\neg fly(penguin)$.[1]

This paper proposes an extension of disjunctive logic programming by inheritance, called DLP$^<$. The addition of inheritance enhances the knowledge modeling features of the language. Possible conflicts are solved in favour of the rules which are "more specific" according to the inheritance hierarchy. This way, a direct and natural representation of default reasoning with exceptions is achieved (e.g., defeasible rules do not need to be equipped with extra literals as above – see section 4).

The main contribution of the paper are the following.

- We formally define the DLP$^<$ language, providing a declarative model theoretic semantics of DLP$^<$, which is shown to generalize the answer set semantics of [13].

- We illustrate the knowledge modeling features of the language by encoding classical nonmonotonic problems in DLP$^<$. Interestingly, DLP$^<$ supplies a natural representation also of frame axioms.

- We analyze the computational complexity of reasoning over DLP$^<$ programs. Importantly, while inheritance enhances the knowledge modeling ability of disjunctive logic programming, it does not cause any computational overhead, as reasoning in DLP$^<$ has exactly the same complexity as reasoning in disjunctive logic programming.

- We compare DLP$^<$ to related works proposed in the literature. In particular, we evidentiate the differences between DLP$^<$ and Disjunctive Ordered Logic ($\mathcal{DOL}$) [7]; we point out the relation to the answer set semantics of [13]; we compare DLP$^<$ with prioritized disjunctive logic programs [26], and analyze its relationships to inheritance networks [28] and to updates of logic programs.

- We implement a DLP$^<$ system. To this end, we first design an efficient translation from DLP$^<$ to plain disjunctive logic programming. Then, using this translation, we implement a DLP$^<$ evaluator on top

---

[1]*not* and $\neg$ denote the weak negation symbol and the strong negation symbol, respectively.

of the `dlv` system [11]. The system prototype can be freely retrieved from [12]. To the best of our knowledge, this is the first fully operational system supporting a prioritized disjunctive logic programming language.

The long version of this paper, containing proofs of all theorems, further DLP$^<$ encoding, and details can be retrieved from the above mentioned web page.

2 Syntax of DLP$^<$

Let the following disjoint sets be given: a set $\mathcal{V}$ of *variables*, a set Π of *predicates*, a set Λ of *constants*, and a finite partially ordered set of symbols $(\mathcal{O}, <)$, where $\mathcal{O}$ is a set of strings, called *object identifiers*, and $<$ is a strict partial order (i.e., the relation $<$ is: (i) irreflexive – $c \not< c$ $\forall c \in \mathcal{O}$, and (ii) transitive – $a < b \wedge b < c \Rightarrow a < c$ $\forall a, b, c \in \mathcal{O}$).

A *term* is either a constant in Λ or a variable in $\mathcal{V}$ (note that function symbols are not considered in this paper).

An *atom* is a construct of the form $a(t_1, ..., t_n)$, where a is a *predicate* of arity n in Π and $t_1, ..., t_n$ are terms.

A *literal* is either a *positive literal* p or a *negative literal* $\neg p$, where p is an atom ($\neg$ is the *strong negation* symbol). Two literals are *complementary* if they are of the form p and $\neg p$, for some atom p.

Given a literal L, $\neg.L$ denotes its complementary literal. Accordingly, given a set A of literals, $\neg.A$ denotes the set $\{\neg.L \mid L \in A\}$.

A *rule* r is an expression of the form:

$$a_1 \vee \cdots \vee a_n \leftarrow b_1, \cdots, b_k, not\ b_{k+1}, \cdots, not\ b_m, \qquad n \geq 1,\ m \geq 0$$

where $a_1, \cdots, a_n, b_1, \cdots, b_m$ are literals, and *not* is the *negation as failure* symbol. The disjunction $a_1 \vee \cdots \vee a_n$ is the *head* of r, while the conjunction $b_1, ..., b_k, not\ b_{k+1}, ..., not\ b_m$ is the *body* of r. $b_1, ..., b_k$ is called the *positive part* of the body of r and $not\ b_{k+1}, ..., not\ b_m$ is called the *NAF (negation as failure) part* of the body of r. We often denote the sets of literals appearing in the head, in the positive part of the body, and in the NAF part of the body of a rule r by $Head(r)$, $Body^+(r)$, and $Body^-(r)$, respectively.

An *object* o is a pair $\langle oid(o), \Sigma(o) \rangle$, where $oid(o)$ is an object identifier in $\mathcal{O}$ and $\Sigma(o)$ is a (possibly empty) set of rules.

A *knowledge base* on $\mathcal{O}$ is a set of objects, one for each element of $\mathcal{O}$.

Given a knowledge base $\mathcal{K}$ and an object identifier $o \in \mathcal{O}$, the DLP$^<$ *program for o (on $\mathcal{K}$)* is the set of objects $\mathcal{P} = \{(o', \Sigma(o')) \in \mathcal{K} \mid o = o'\ \text{or}\ o < o'\}$.

The relation $<$ induces a partial order on $\mathcal{P}$ in the obvious way, that is, given $o_i = (oid(o_i), \Sigma(o_i))$ and $o_j = (oid(o_j), \Sigma(o_j))$, $o_i < o_j$ iff $oid(o_i) < oid(o_j)$ (read "o_i is more specific than o_j").

A term, an atom, a literal, a rule, or program is *ground* if no variable appears in it.

Informally, a knowledge base can be viewed as a set of *objects* embedding the definition of their properties specified through disjunctive logic rules, organized in a IS-A (inheritance) hierarchy (induced by the relation $<$). A program $\mathcal{P}$ for an object o on a knowledge base $\mathcal{K}$ consists of the portion of $\mathcal{K}$ "seen" from o looking up in the IS-A hierarchy. Thanks to the inheritance mechanism, $\mathcal{P}$ incorporates the knowledge explicitly defined for o plus the knowledge inherited from the higher objects.

If a knowledge base admits a *bottom* element (i.e., an object less than all the other objects, by the relation $<$), we usually refer to the knowledge base as "program", since it is equal to the program for the bottom element.

Moreover, we represent the transitive-reduction of the relation $<$ on the objects.[2] In order to represent the membership of a pair of objects (resp., object identifiers) (o_2, o_1) to the transitive-reduction of $<$ we use the notation $o_2 : o_1$, and say that o_2 is a *sub-object* of o_1.

Example 1 Consider the following program $\mathcal{P}$:

$$o_1 \quad \{\, a \vee \neg b \leftarrow c, not\ d \,\}$$
$$o_2 : o_1 \,\{\, b \leftarrow \quad \neg a \vee c \leftarrow \quad c \leftarrow b \,\}$$

$\mathcal{P}$ consists of two objects o_1 and o_2. o_2 is a sub-object of o_1. According to the convention illustrated above, the knowledge base on which $\mathcal{P}$ is defined coincides with $\mathcal{P}$, and the object for which $\mathcal{P}$ is defined is o_2 (the bottom object). ∎

3   Semantics of DLP$^<$

In this section we assume that a knowledge base $\mathcal{K}$ is given and an object o has been fixed. Let $\mathcal{P}$ be the DLP$^<$ program for o on $\mathcal{K}$. The *Universe* $U_{\mathcal{P}}$ of $\mathcal{P}$ is the set of all constants appearing in the rules. The *Base* $B_{\mathcal{P}}$ of $\mathcal{P}$ is the set of all possible ground literals constructible from the predicates appearing in the rules of $\mathcal{P}$ and the constants occurring in $U_{\mathcal{P}}$. Note that, unlike in traditional logic programming the Base of a DLP$^<$ program contains both positive and negative literals. Given a rule r occurring in $\mathcal{P}$, a *ground instance* of r is a rule obtained from r by replacing every variable X in r by $\sigma(r)$, where σ is a mapping from the variables occurring in r to the constants in $U_{\mathcal{P}}$. We denote by $ground(\mathcal{P})$ the (finite) multiset of all instances of the rules occurring in $\mathcal{P}$. The reason why $ground(\mathcal{P})$ is a multiset is that a rule may appear in several different objects of $\mathcal{P}$, and we require the respective ground instances be distinct. Hence, we can define a function obj_of from ground instance of rules in $ground(\mathcal{P})$ onto the set $\mathcal{O}$ of the object identifiers, associating with a ground instance $\bar{r}$ of r the (unique) object of r.

A subset of ground literals in $B_{\mathcal{P}}$ is said to be *consistent* if no pair of complementary literals is in it. An *interpretation* I is a consistent subset

---

[2](a, b) is in the transitive-reduction of $<$ iff $a < b$ and there is no c such that $a < c$ and $c < b$.

of $B_{\mathcal{P}}$. Given an interpretation $I \subseteq B_{\mathcal{P}}$, a ground literal (either positive or negative) L is *true* w.r.t. I if $L \in I$ holds. L is *false* w.r.t. I otherwise.

Given a rule $r \in ground(\mathcal{P})$, the head of r is *true* in I if at least one literal of the head is true w.r.t I. The body of r is *true* in I if: (i) every literal in $Body^+(r)$ is true w.r.t. I, and (ii) every literal in $Body^-(r)$ is false w.r.t. I. Rule r is *satisfied* in I if either the head of r is true in I or the body of r is not true in I.

Two ground rules r_1 and r_2 are *conflicting on L* if $L \in Head(r_1)$ and $\neg.L \in Head(r_2)$.

Next we introduce the concept of a *model* for a DLP$^<$-program. Unlike in traditional logic programming, the notion of satisfiability of rules is not sufficient for this goal, as it does not take into account the presence of explicit contradictions. Hence, we first present some preliminary definitions.

Definition 1 For an interpretation I, two conflicting ground rules $r_1, r_2 \in ground(\mathcal{P})$, such that $L \in Head(r_2)$, we say that r_1 *overrides* r_2 on L in I if: 1) $obj\_of(r_1) < obj\_of(r_2)$, 2) $\neg.L \in I$, and 3) the body of r_2 is true in I.

A rule $r \in ground(\mathcal{P})$ is *overridden in I* if for each $L \in Head(r)$ there exists $r_1 \in ground(\mathcal{P})$ such that r_1 overrides r on L in I. ∎

Intuitively, the notion of overriding allows us to solve conflicts arising between rules with complementary heads. For instance, suppose that both a and $\neg a$ are derivable in I from rules r and r', respectively. If r is more specific than r' in the inheritance hierarchy, then r' is overruled, meaning that a should be preferred to $\neg a$ because it is derivable from a more trustable rule.

Example 2 Consider the program $\mathcal{P}$ of Example 1. Let $I = \{\neg a, b, c\}$ be an interpretation. Rule $\neg a \vee c \leftarrow$ in the object o_2 overrides rule $a \vee \neg b \leftarrow c, not\ d$ in o_1 on the literal a in I. Moreover, rule $b \leftarrow$ in o_2 overrides rule $a \vee \neg b \leftarrow c, not\ d$ in o_1 on the literal $\neg b$ in I. Thus, the rule $a \vee \neg b \leftarrow c, not\ d$ in o_1 is overridden in I. ∎

Definition 2 Let I be an interpretation for $\mathcal{P}$. I is a *model for $\mathcal{P}$* if every rule in $ground(\mathcal{P})$ is satisfied or overridden in I. I is a *minimal model for $\mathcal{P}$* if no (proper) subset of I is a model for $\mathcal{P}$. ∎

Definition 3 Given an interpretation I for $\mathcal{P}$, the *reduction of $\mathcal{P}$ w.r.t. I*, denoted by $G_I(\mathcal{P})$, is the set of rules obtained from $ground(\mathcal{P})$ by 1) removing every rule overridden in I, 2) removing every rule r such that $Body^-(r) \cap I \neq \emptyset$, 3) removing the NAF part from the bodies of the remaining rules. ∎

Example 3 Consider the program $\mathcal{P}$ of Example 1. Let I be the interpretation $\{\neg a, b, c\}$. As shown in Example 2, rule $a \vee \neg b \leftarrow c, not\ d$ is overridden in I. Thus, $G_I(\mathcal{P})$ is the set of rules $\{\neg a \vee c \leftarrow, b \leftarrow, c \leftarrow b\}$. Consider now the interpretation $M = \{a, b, c\}$. It is easy to see that $G_M(\mathcal{P}) = \{a \vee \neg b \leftarrow c, \neg a \vee c \leftarrow, b \leftarrow, c \leftarrow b\}$. ∎

We observe that the reduction of a program is simply a set of ground rules. Given a set S of ground rules, we denote by $pos(S)$ the positive disjunctive program (called the *positive version of S*), obtained from S by considering each negative literal $\neg p(\bar{X})$ as a positive one with predicate symbol $\neg p$.

Definition 4 Let M be a model for $\mathcal{P}$. We say that M is a *(DLP$^<$-)answer set* for $\mathcal{P}$ if M is a minimal model of the positive version $pos(G_M(\mathcal{P}))$ of $G_M(\mathcal{P})$. ∎

Example 4 Consider the program $\mathcal{P}$ of Example 1:

It is easy to see that the interpretation I of Example 3 is not an answer set for $\mathcal{P}$. Indeed, although I is a model for $pos(G_I(\mathcal{P}))$ it is not minimal, since the interpretation $\{b, c\}$ is a model for $pos(G_I(\mathcal{P}))$, too. Note that the interpretation $I' = \{b, c\}$ is not an answer set for $\mathcal{P}$ either, because $G_{I'}(\mathcal{P}) = \{a \vee \neg b \leftarrow c, \neg a \vee c \leftarrow, b \leftarrow, c \leftarrow b\}$, and I' is not a model for $pos(G_{I'}(\mathcal{P}))$, since the rule $a \vee \neg b \leftarrow c$ is not satisfied in I'.

On the other hand, the interpretation M of Example 3 is an answer set for $\mathcal{P}$, since M is a minimal model for $pos(G_M(\mathcal{P}))$. Moreover, it can be easily realized that M is the only answer set for $\mathcal{P}$. ∎

4 Knowledge Representation with DLP$^<$

In this section, we present a number of examples which illustrate how knowledge can be represented using DLP$^<$. To start, we show the DLP$^<$ encoding of a classical example of nonmonotonic reasoning.

Example 5 Consider the following program $\mathcal{P}$ with $\mathcal{O}(\mathcal{P})$ consisting of three objects *bird*, *penguin* and *tweety*, such that *penguin* is a sub-object of *bird* and *tweety* is a sub-object of *penguin*:

$$
\begin{array}{ll}
bird & \{\ flies \leftarrow\ \} \\
penguin : bird & \{\ \neg flies \leftarrow\ \} \\
tweety : penguin & \{\ \}
\end{array}
$$

Unlike in traditional logic programming, our language supports two types of negation, that is *strong negation* and *negation as failure*. Strong negation is useful to express negative pieces of information under the complete information assumption. Hence, a negative fact (by strong negation) is true only if it is explicitly derived from the rules of the program. As a consequence, the head of rules may contain also such negative literals and rules can be conflicting on some literals. According to the inheritance principles, the ordering relationship between objects can help us to assign different levels of reliability to the rules, allowing us to solve possible conflicts. For instance, in our example, the contradicting conclusion *tweety both flies and does not fly* seems to be entailed from the program (as *tweety* is a *penguin* and *penguins* are *birds*, both *flies* and ¬*flies* can be derived from the rules of the program). However, this is not the case. Indeed, the "lower" rule ¬*flies* ← specified in the object *penguin* is considered as a sort of refinement to the first general rule, and thus the meaning of the program is rather clear: *tweety does not fly*, as tweety is a penguin. That is, ¬*flies* ← is preferred to the default rule *flies* ← as the hierarchy explicitly states the specificity of the former. Intuitively, there is no doubt that $M = \{\neg flies\}$ is the only reasonable conclusion. ∎

The next example, from the field of database authorizations, combines the use of both weak and strong negation.

Example 6 Consider the following knowledge base representing a set of security specification about a simple *part-of* hierarchy of objects.

o_1 $\{$ $r_1 :$ *authorize(bob)* ← *not authorize(ann)*

          $r_2 :$ *authorize(ann)* ∨ *authorize(tom)* ← *not* ¬*authorize(alice)* $\}$

$o_2 : o_1$ $\{$ $r_3 :$ ¬*authorize(alice)* ← $\}$

$o_3 : o_1$ $\{$ $r_4 :$ ¬*authorize(bob)* ← $\}$

Objects o_2 is part-of the object o_1 as well as o_3 is part-of o_1. Access authorizations to objects are specified by rules with head predicate *authorize* and subjects to which authorizations are granted appear as arguments. Strong negation is utilized to encode negative authorizations that represent explicit denials. Negation as failure is used to specify the absence of authorization (either positive or negative). Inheritance implements the automatic propagation of authorizations from an object to all its sub-objects. The overriding mechanism allows us to represent exceptions: for instance, if an object o inherits a positive authorization but a denial for the same subject is specified in o, then the negative authorization prevails on the positive one.

     Consider the program $\mathcal{P}_{o_2} = \{(o_1, \{r_1, r_2\}), (o_2, \{r_3\})\}$ for the object o_2 on the above knowledge base. This program defines the access control for the object o_2. Thanks to the inheritance mechanism, authorizations specified for the object o_1, to which o_2 belongs, are propagated also to o_2. It consists of rules r_1, r_2 (inherited from o_1) and r_3. Rule r_1 states that *bob* is authorized to access object o_2 provided that no authorization for *ann* to access o_2 exists. Rule r_2 authorizes either *ann* or *tom* to access o_2 provided that no denial for *alice* to access o_2 is derived. Finally, rule r_3 defines a denial for *alice* to access object o_2. Due to the absence of the authorization for *ann*, the authorization to *bob* of accessing the object o_2 is derived (by rule r_1). Further, the explicit denial to access the object o_2 for *alice* (rule r_3) allows to derive neither authorization for *ann* nor for *tom* (by rule r_2). Hence, the only answer set of this program is $\{authorize(bob), \neg authorize(alice)\}$.

     Consider now the program $\mathcal{P}_{o_3} = \{(o_1, \{r_1, r_2\}), (o_3, \{r_4\})\}$ for the object o_3. Rule r_4 defines a denial for *bob* to access object o_3. The authorization for *bob* (defined by rule r_1) is no longer derived. Indeed, even if rule r_1 allows to derive such an authorization due to the absence of authorizations for *ann*, it is overridden by the explicit denial (rule r_4) defined in the object o_3 (i.e., at a more specific level). The body of rule r_2 inherited from o_1 is true for this program since no denial for alice can be derived, and it entails a mutual exclusive access to object o_3 for *ann* and *tom* (note that no other head contains *authorize(ann)* or *authorize(bob)*). The program $\mathcal{P}_{o_3}$ has two answer sets, namely $\{authorize(ann), \neg authorize(bob)\}$ and $\{authorize(tom), \neg authorize(bob)\}$ representing two alternative authorization sets utilizable to grant the access to the object o_3. ∎

Solving the Frame Problem

The frame problem has first been addressed by McCarthy and Hayes [22], and in the meantime a lot of research has been conducted to overcome it (see e.g. [27] for a survey).

In short, the frame problem arises in planning, when actions and fluents are specified: An action affects some of the fluents, but all unrelated fluents should remain as they are. In most formulations using classical logic, one must specify for every pair of actions and unrelated fluents that the fluent remains unchanged. Clearly this is an undesirable overhead, since with n actions and m fluents, $n \times m$ clauses might have to be specified.

Instead, it would be nice to be able to specify for each fluent that it *"normally remains valid"* and that only actions which explicitly entail the contrary can change them.

Indeed, this goal can be achieved in a very elegant way using DLP$^<$: One object contains the rules which specify *inertia* (the fact that fluents normally do not change). Another object inherits from it and specifies the actions and the effects of actions — in this way a very natural, straightforward and effective representation is achieved, which avoids the frame problem.

Example 7 As an example we show how the famous Yale Shooting Problem, which is due to Hanks and McDermott [15], can be represented and solved with DLP$^<$:

The scenario involves an individual (or in a less violent version a turkey), who can be shot with a gun. There are two fluents, *alive* and *loaded*, which intuitively mean that the individual is alive and that the gun is loaded, respectively. There are three actions, *load*, *wait* and *shoot*. Loading has the effect that the gun is loaded afterwards, shooting with the loaded gun has the effect that the individual is no longer alive afterwards (and also that the gun is unloaded, but this not really important), and waiting has no effects. It is also known that initially the individual is alive, and that first the gun is loaded, and after waiting, the gun is shot with. The question is: Which fluents hold after these actions and between them?

In our encoding, the *inertia* object contains the defaults for the fluents, the *domain* object additionally specifies the effects of actions, while the *yale* object encodes the problem instance including the time framework.[3]

$$inertia \ \{ \quad alive(T1) \leftarrow alive(T), next(T,T1)$$
$$\neg alive(T1) \leftarrow \neg alive(T), next(T,T1)$$
$$loaded(T1) \leftarrow loaded(T), next(T,T1)$$
$$\neg loaded(T1) \leftarrow \neg loaded(T), next(T,T1)\}$$
$$domain : inertia \ \{ \quad loaded(T1) \leftarrow load(T), next(T,T1)$$
$$\neg loaded(T1) \leftarrow shoot(T), loaded(T), next(T,T1)$$
$$\neg alive(T1) \leftarrow shoot(T), loaded(T), next(T,T1)\}$$
$$yale : domain \ \{ \quad load(0) \leftarrow \quad wait(1) \leftarrow \quad shoot(2) \leftarrow \quad alive(0) \leftarrow$$
$$next(0,1) \leftarrow \quad next(1,2) \leftarrow \quad next(2,3) \leftarrow \}$$

The only answer set for this program contains, besides the facts of the *yale* object, *loaded*(1), *loaded*(2), *alive*(0), *alive*(1), *alive*(2) and ¬*loaded*(3), ¬*alive*(3). That is, the individual is alive until the shoot action is taken, and no longer alive afterwards, and the gun is loaded between loading and shooting. ∎

We want to point out that this formalism is equally suited for solving problems which involve finding a plan (i.e. a sequence of actions), rather than determining the effects of a given plan as in the Yale Shooting Problem: You have to add a rule $action(T) \lor \neg action(T) \leftarrow next(T,T1)$ for every action, and you have to specify the goal state by a query, e.g. ¬*alive*(3), ¬*loaded*(3)?[4]. The complete DLP$^<$ encoding of a planning example is shown in the full version of this paper that can be retrieved from [12].

5 Computational Complexity

As for the classical nonmonotonic formalisms [20, 19, 25], two important decision problems, corresponding to two different reasoning tasks, arise in DLP$^<$:

(Brave Reasoning) Given a DLP$^<$ program $\mathcal{P}$ and a ground literal L, decide whether there exists an answer set M for $\mathcal{P}$ such that L is true w.r.t. M.

(Cautious Reasoning) Given a DLP$^<$ program $\mathcal{P}$ and a ground literal L, decide whether L is true in all answer sets for $\mathcal{P}$.

We next prove that the complexity of reasoning in DLP$^<$ is exactly the same as in traditional disjunctive logic programming. That is, inheritance comes for free, as the addition of inheritance does not cause any computational overhead. We consider the propositional case, i.e., we consider ground DLP$^<$ programs.

---

[3]With our prototype the more convenient builtins of dlv can be used instead.

[4]This is a dlv language feature which (for this example) is equivalent to the rules $h \leftarrow \neg alive(3), \neg loaded(3)$ and $i \leftarrow not\ h, not\ i$, meaning that only answer sets containing ¬*alive*(3) and ¬*loaded*(3) should be considered.

Lemma 5.1 *Given a ground* DLP$^<$ *program* $\mathcal{P}$ *and an interpretation* M *for* $\mathcal{P}$, *deciding whether* M *is an answer set for* $\mathcal{P}$ *is in* coNP.

Proof. We check in NP that M <u>is not</u> an answer set of $\mathcal{P}$ as follows. Guess a subset I of M, and verify that: (1) M is not a model for $pos(G_M(\mathcal{P}))$, or (2) I is a model for $pos(G_M(\mathcal{P}))$ and $I \subset M$. The construction of $pos(G_M(\mathcal{P}))$ (see Definition 3) is feasible in polynomial time, and the tasks (1) and (2) are clearly tractable. Thus, deciding whether M is not an answer set for $\mathcal{P}$ is in NP, and, consequently, deciding whether M is an answer set for $\mathcal{P}$ is in coNP. ∎

Theorem 5.2 *Brave Reasoning on* DLP$^<$ *programs is* Σ_2^P-*complete.*

Proof. Given a ground DLP$^<$ program $\mathcal{P}$ and a ground literal L, we verify that L is a brave consequence of $\mathcal{P}$ as follows. Guess a set $M \subseteq B_\mathcal{P}$ of ground literals, check that (1) M is an answer set for $\mathcal{P}$, and (2) L is true w.r.t. M. Task (2) is clearly polynomial; while (1) is in coNP, by virtue of Lemma 5.1. The problem therefore lies in Σ_2^P.

Σ_2^P-hardness follows from Theorem 6.1 and the results in [8, 9]. ∎

Theorem 5.3 *Cautious Reasoning on* DLP$^<$ *programs is* Π_2^P-*complete.*

Proof. Given a ground DLP$^<$ program $\mathcal{P}$ and a ground literal L, we verify that L is not a cautious consequence of $\mathcal{P}$ as follows. Guess a set $M \subseteq B_\mathcal{P}$ of ground literals, check that (1) M is an answer set for $\mathcal{P}$, and (2) L is not true w.r.t. M. Task (2) is clearly polynomial; while (1) is in coNP, by virtue of Lemma 5.1. Therefore, the complement of cautious reasoning is in Σ_2^P, and cautious reasoning is in Π_2^P.

Π_2^P-hardness follows from Theorem 6.1 and the results in [8, 9]. ∎

6 Related Work

6.1 Answer Set Semantics

Answer set semantics, proposed by Gelfond and Lifschitz in [13], is the most widely acknowledged semantics for disjunctive logic programs with strong negation. For this reason, while defining the semantics of our language, we took care of ensuring full agreement with answer set semantics (on inheritance-free programs).

Theorem 6.1 *Let* $\mathcal{P}$ *be a* DLP$^<$ *program consisting of a single object* $o = \langle oid(o), \Sigma(o) \rangle$: *Then,* M *is an answer set of* $\mathcal{P}$ *if and only if it is a consistent answer set of* $\Sigma(o)$ *(according with [13]).*

6.2 Disjunctive Ordered Logic

Disjunctive Ordered Logic ($\mathcal{DOL}$) is an extension of Disjunctive Logic Programming with strong negation and inheritance (without default negation) proposed in [7]. The DLP$^<$ language incorporates some ideas taken from $\mathcal{DOL}$. However, the two languages are very different in several respects. Most importantly, unlike with DLP$^<$, even if a program belongs to the common fragment of $\mathcal{DOL}$ and of the language of [13] (i.e., it contains neither inheritance nor default negation), $\mathcal{DOL}$ semantics is completely different from answer set semantics, because of a different way of handling contradictions.[5] In short, we observe the following differences between $\mathcal{DOL}$ and DLP$^<$:

- $\mathcal{DOL}$ does not include default negation *not*, while DLP$^<$ includes it.

- $\mathcal{DOL}$ and DLP$^<$ have different semantics on the common fragment. Consider a program $\mathcal{P}$ consisting of a single object $o = \langle oid(o), \Sigma(o) \rangle$, where $\Sigma(o) = \{p \leftarrow; \quad \neg p \leftarrow\}$. Then, according with $\mathcal{DOL}$, the semantics of $\mathcal{P}$ is given by two models, namely, $\{p\}$ and $\{\neg p\}$. On the contrary, $\mathcal{P}$ has no answer set according with DLP$^<$ semantics.

- DLP$^<$ generalizes (consistent) answer set semantics to disjunctive logic programs with inheritance; while $\mathcal{DOL}$ does not generalize it.

6.3 Prioritized Logic Programs

DLP$^<$ can be also seen as an attempt to handle priorities in disjunctive logic programs (the lower the object in the inheritance hierarchy, the higher the priority of its rules).

There are several works on preference handling in logic programming [6, 14, 23, 16, 24, 26]. However, we are aware of only one previous work on priorities in <u>disjunctive</u> programs, namely, the paper by Sakama and Inoue [26]. This interesting work can be seen as an extension of answer set semantics to deal with priorities. Comparing the two works, under the viewpoint of priority handling, we observe the following:

- On priority free programs, the two languages yield essentially the same semantics, as they generalize answer set semantics and consistent answer set semantics, respectively.

- In [26], priorities are defined among <u>literals</u>, while priorities concern program's <u>rules</u> in DLP$^<$.

- The different kind of priorities (on rules vs. literals) and the way how they are dealt with in the two approaches, imply different complexity in the respective reasonings. Indeed, from the simulation of abductive reasoning in the language of [26], and the complexity results on abduction derived in [10], it follows that brave reasoning is Σ_3^P-complete

---

[5] Actually, this was a main motivation for the authors to look for a different language.

for the language of [26]. On the contrary, brave reasoning is "only" Σ_2^P-complete in DLP$^{<6}$.

A comparative analysis of the various approaches to the treatment of preferences in ($\vee$-free) logic programming has been carried out in [6].

6.4 Inheritance Networks

From a different perspective, the objects of a DLP$^<$ program can also be seen as the nodes of an inheritance network.

We next show that DLP$^<$ satisfies the basic semantic principles which are required for inheritance networks in [28].

[28] constitutes a fundamental attempt to present a formal mathematical theory of multiple inheritance with exceptions. The starting point of this work is the consideration that an intuitively acceptable semantics for inheritance must satisfy two basic requirements:

1. Being able to reason with redundant statements, and

2. not making unjustified choices in ambiguous situations.

Touretzky illustrates this intuition by means of two basic examples.

The former requirement is presented by means of the *Royal Elephant* example, in which we have the following knowledge: "Elephants are gray.", "Royal elephants are elephants.", "Royal elephants are not gray.", "Clyde is a royal elephant.", "Clyde is an elephant."

The last statement is clearly redundant; however, since it is consistent with the others there is no reason to rule it out. Touretzky shows that an intuitive semantics should be able to recognize that Clyde is not gray, while many systems fail in this task.

Touretzky's second principle is shown by the *Nixon diamond* example, , in which the following is known: "Republicans are not pacifists.", "Quakers are pacifists.", "Nixon is both a Republican and a quaker."

According to our approach, he claims that a good semantics should draw no conclusion about the question whether Nixon is a *pacifist*.

The proposed solution for the problems above is based on a topological relation, called *inferential distance ordering*, stating that an individual A is "nearer" to B than to C iff A has an inference path *through* B to C. If A is "nearer" to B than to C, then as far as A is concerned, information coming from B must be preferred w.r.t. information coming from C. Therefore, since Clyde is "nearer" to royal elephant than to elephant, he states that Clyde is not gray. On the contrary no conclusion is taken on Nixon, as there is not any relationship between *quaker* and *republican*.

The semantics of DLP$^<$ fully agrees with the intuition underlying the *inferential distance ordering*.

---

[6]We refer to the complexity in the propositional case here.

Example 8 Let us represent the Royal Elephant example in our framework:

$$elephant \qquad\qquad\qquad\qquad \{gray \leftarrow\}$$
$$royal\_elephant : elephant \qquad \{\neg gray \leftarrow\}$$
$$clyde : elephant,\ royal\_elephant \quad \{\ \}$$

The only answer set of the above DLP$^<$ program is $\{\neg gray\}$.

The Nixon Diamond example can be expressed in our language as follows:

$$republican \qquad\qquad\qquad \{pacifist \leftarrow\}$$
$$quaker \qquad\qquad\qquad\quad \{\neg pacifist \leftarrow\}$$
$$nixon : republican,\ quaker \quad \{\ \}$$

This DLP$^<$ program has no answer set, and therefore no conclusion is drawn.

6.5 Updates in Logic Programs

The definition of the semantics of updates in logic programs is another topic where DLP$^<$ could potentially be applied. Roughly, a simple formulation of the problem is: given a ($\vee$-free) logic program P and a sequence $U_1, \cdots, U_n$ of successive updates (insertion/deletion of ground atoms), determine what is or is not true in the end. Expressing the insertion (deletion) of an atom A by the rule $A \leftarrow (\neg A \leftarrow)$, we can represent this problem by a DLP$^<$ knowledge base $\{\langle t_0, P\rangle, \langle t_1, \{U_1\}\rangle, \cdots, \langle t_n, \{U_n\}\rangle\}$ (t_i intuitively represents the instant of time when the update U_i has been executed), where $t_n < \cdots < t_0$. The answer sets of the program for t_k can be taken as the semantics of the execution of $U_1, \cdots, U_k$ on P. For instance, given the logic program $P = \{a \leftarrow b, not\ c\}$ and the updates $U_1 = \{b \leftarrow\}$, $U_2 = \{c \leftarrow\}$, $U_3 = \{\neg b \leftarrow\}$, we build the DLP$^<$ program

$$t_0 \qquad \{\ a \leftarrow b, c, not\ d\ \}$$
$$t_1 : t_0 \quad \{\ b \leftarrow\ \}$$
$$t_2 : t_1 \quad \{\ c \leftarrow\ \}$$
$$t_3 : t_2 \quad \{\ \neg b \leftarrow\ \}.$$

The answer set $\{a, b, c\}$ of the program for t_2 gives the semantics of the execution of U_1 and U_2 on P; while the answer set $\{c\}$ of the program for t_3 expresses the semantics of the execution of U_1, U_2 and U_3 on P in the given order.

The semantics of updates obtained in this way is very similar to the approach adopted for the ULL language in [17]. Further investigations are needed on this topic to see whether DLP$^<$ can represent update problems in more general settings like those treated in [21] and in [4].

7 Implementation Issues

We have implemented a fully operational prototype supporting the DLP$^<$ language on top of the disjunctive logic programming system dlv [11]. To this end, we have defined a rewriting function π which translates a DLP$^<$

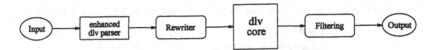

Figure 1: Flow diagram of the prototype.

program $\mathcal{P}$ in an equivalent plain disjunctive logic program $\pi(\mathcal{P})$ (with strong negation, but without inheritance), the (consistent) answer sets of $\pi(\mathcal{P})$ correspond to the answer sets of $\mathcal{P}$ and vice versa. For space limitation, we cannot show the rewriting technique here; full details on the translation algorithm along with the formal proof of its correctness are provided in the long version of the paper which can be retrieved from the web [12].

A schematic visualisation of its architecture is shown in Figure 1. First of all, we have extended the dlv parser to incorporate the DLP$^<$ syntax. In this way, all the advanced features of dlv (e.g. bounded integer arithmetics, comparison builtins, etc.) are also available with DLP$^<$. The *Rewriter* module implements the translation function π mentioned above. Once the rewritten version $\pi(\mathcal{P})$ of $\mathcal{P}$ is generated, its answer sets are then computed using the dlv core. Before the output is shown to the user, a suitable filtering function is applied in order to strip the internal predicates (which are added by the rewriting function π) from the output.

On the webpage [12] the prototype is described in detail, and binary versions are available for different platforms.

Acknowledgements

The idea of representing inertia in planning problems in a higher object is due to Axel Polleres. This work was partially supported by FWF (Austrian Science Funds) under the projects P11580-MAT and Z29-INF.

References

[1] Alferes, J., Pereira, L.M., On Logic Program Semantics with Two Kinds of Negation *Proc. of JICSLP 1992*, pp. 574-588

[2] Alferes, J., Pereira, L.M., Przymusinski, T.C., Strong and Explicit Negation in Non-Monotonic Reasoning and Logic Programming, *Proc. of JELIA 1996*, pp. 143-163

[3] Alferes, J., Pereira, L.M., Przymusinski, T.C., 'Classical' Negation in Nonmonotonic Reasoning and Logic Programming, *Journal of Automated Reasoning* 20(1), 1998, pp. 107-142.

[4] Alferes, J., Leite, J.A., Pereira, L.M., Przymusinska, H., Przymusinski, T.C., Dynamic Logic Programming, *Proc. KR'98*, Morgan Kaufmann, 1998.

[5] Baral, C., Gelfond, M. Logic Programming and Knowledge Representation *Journal of Logic Programming*, Vol. 19/20, May/July 1994, pp. 73-148.

[6] Brewka, G., Eiter, T., Preferred Answer Sets for Extended Logic Programs, *Proc. KR'98*, Morgan Kaufmann, 1998.

[7] Buccafurri, F., Leone, N., Rullo, P., Disjunctive Ordered Logic: Semantics and Expressiveness, *Proc. KR'98*, Morgan Kaufmann, 1998.

[8] Eiter, T., Gottlob, G., On the Computational Cost of Disjunctive Logic Programming: Propositional Case. *Annals of Mathematics and Artificial Intelligence*, 1995.

[9] Eiter, T., Gottlob, G., and Mannila, H., Disjunctive Datalog, *ACM Transactions on Database Systems*, 22(3), September, 1997.

[10] Eiter, T., Gottlob, G., Leone, N., Abduction From Logic Programs: Semantics and Complexity. *Theoretical Computer Science* 189(1-2), pp. 129–177, 1997.

[11] Eiter, T., Leone, N., Mateis, C., Pfeifer, G., and Scarcello, F., The Knowledge Representation System dlv: Progress Report, Comparisons, and Benchmarks, *Proc. KR'98*, Morgan Kaufmann, 1998.

[12] Faber, W., The DLP< Homepage: www.dbai.tuwien.ac.at/proj/dlv/inheritance/

[13] Gelfond, M., and Lifschitz, V., Classical Negation in Logic Programs and Disjunctive Databases. *New Generation Computing*, 9:365-385, 1991.

[14] Gelfond, M. and Son, T.C., Reasoning with Prioritized Defaults, *Proc. of LPKR'97*, Port Jefferson, New York, October 1997.

[15] Hanks, S., McDermott, D., Nonmonotonic Logic and Temporal Projection, *Artificial Intelligence*, 33:379–412, 1987.

[16] Kowalski, R.A., Sadri, F., Logic Programs with Exceptions, *Proc. of 7th ICLP*, Jerusalem, 1990, pp. 598-616.

[17] Leone, N., Palopoli, L., Romeo, M., A Language for Updating Logic Programs, *Journal of Logic Programming*, 23(1), 1995, pp. 1–61.

[18] Lobo, J., Minker, J., and Rajasekar, A., *Foundations of Disjunctive Logic Programming*. MIT Press, Cambridge, MA, 1992.

[19] Marek, W., Truszczyński, M., Modal logic for default reasoning, *Annals of Mathematics and Artificial Intelligence*, 1, 1990, pp. 275-302.

[20] Marek, W., Truszczyński, M., Autoepistemic Logic, *Journal of the ACM*, 38, 3, 1991, pp. 518-619.

[21] Marek, W., Truszczyński, M., Revisions Specifications by means of Programs, *Proc. JELIA'94*, Sringer, LNAI 838, 1994, pp. 122–136.

[22] McCarthy, J., Hayes, P. J., Some Philosophical Problems from the Standpoint of Artificial Intelligence, in *Machine Intelligence 4*, pp. 463–502, 1969.

[23] Nute, D., Defeasible Logic. In D. Gabbay, C. Hogger, and J. Robinson, editors, *Handbook of Logic in Artificial Intelligence and Logic Programming*, volume III, pages 353–395. Clarendon Press, Oxford, 1994.

[24] Pradhan, S., and Minker, J., Combining Datalog Databases Using Priorities. *International Journal of Cooperative Intelligent Systems*, 1996.

[25] Reiter, R., A Logic for Default Reasoning, *Artificial Intelligence*, vol.13, pp. 81-132, 1980.

[26] Sakama, C., Inoue, K., Representing priorities in logic programs, *Proc. JICSLP'96* MIT Press, 1996, pp. 82–96.

[27] Shanahan, M., *Solving the Frame Problem: A Mathematical Investigation of the Common Sense Law of Inertia*, MIT Press, 1997.

[28] Touretzky, D.S., *The Mathematics of Inheritance Systems*, Pitman London, 1986.

Event, Property and Hierarchy in Order-Sorted Logic

Ken Kaneiwa, Satoshi Tojo
School of Information Science
Japan Advanced Institute of Science and Technology
Tatsunokuchi, Ishikawa 923-1292, Japan
{kaneiwa,tojo}@jaist.ac.jp

Abstract

Knowledge representation in logics, even in the order-sorted logic that includes a
sort hierarchy, tends to lose the conciseness and the nuances of natural language.
If we could construct a logic that includes both predicates and terms as classes in
the hierarchies, it would be very useful for connecting general knowledge to specific
knowledge. Although there are actually logics that are equipped with such a predicate hierarchy, they are built by logical implication and they cause the problem
of predicate unification between different argument structures. In this paper, we
present a logic language with a class hierarchy of predicates, where in the unification
of predicates we devise a mechanism for deriving superordinate predicates in the
hierarchy and for quantifying supplementary arguments. The arguments are quantified differently, depending on whether a predicate is interpreted as an occurrence
of an event or a universal property. Thus, we include the distinction between events
and properties in predicates and present a logic language that can flexibly relate
predicates with different argument structures. We formalize the logic language both
by syntax and semantics, and develop the inference system.

1. Introduction

The goal of knowledge representation is not to put statements to be executed in
order into a computer system, but to describe declarative knowledge in the real
world. However, the logic language that is often applied to represent knowledge
is unable to express the various nuances of natural language. In order to realize
correct inferences in logic language, we need devices to describe more complicated
expressions.

In working on this problem, many logic languages have been investigated from
the viewpoints of knowledge representation and the rational reasoning. Amongst
these languages, there seem to be two approaches to knowledge representation.
One is typed logic programming [5], including order-sorted logic [13, 14, 4, 11].
LOGIN [1], LIFE [2], F-logic [6] and $\mathcal{Q}\mathcal{U}\mathcal{I}\mathcal{X}\mathcal{O}\mathcal{T}\varepsilon$ [15, 16] are inference systems with
such type notions. They introduce class hierarchies together with feature struc-
tures, where a term represents a set of objects. New HELIC-II [10, 9], developed
as a legal reasoning system, introduces H-terms (based on Ψ-terms in LOGIN) that
consist of verb-type and and noun-type symbols. The other approach is the temporal reasoning [3, 8, 12] that considers various aspects of an eventuality. Allen [3]
distinguished between event, property, and process in English sentences, and so did
McDermott [8] between fact and event.

We consider defining both predicates and terms as classes in the hierarchies. In order to do this, we amalgamate the above two approaches, and attribute both predicate hierarchy and event/property distinction to the issue of proper quantification of classes.

The objective of this paper is to propose a logic language which has two extensions as follows:

- Class-hierarchy of predicates (as well as sorted terms), together with an inference mechanism which is independent of argument structures;

- Distinction between event and property in predicate interpretation with the appropriate unification/ resolution mechanism.

We develop an inference system that includes substitution, quantification and supplementation of arguments, to realize the above specifications.

The paper is arranged as follows. Section 2 contains preliminaries about order-sorted logic and Ψ-terms [1]. Section 3 discusses the problem using examples. In Section 4, we illustrate how we introduce our extensions into order-sorted logic. In Section 5, we formalize the syntax and the semantics of the proposed logic. In Section 6, we define the logic programming based on this logic. Finally in Section 7, we give our conclusions and discuss future works.

2. Preliminaries

In this section, we state the notation of order-sorted logic, especially for Ψ-terms in LOGIN. S is a set of *sorts*, and the sorts are ordered by a subsort relation $\sqsubseteq_S$ ($\subseteq S \times S$). A hierarchy of sorts is a pair $(S, \sqsubseteq_S)$ of the set S and a subsort relation $\sqsubseteq_S$, containing the greatest sort $\top$ and the least $\bot$.

We can declare that *apple* and *orange* are subsorts of *fruit* as below.

$apple \sqsubseteq_S fruit$

$orange \sqsubseteq_S fruit$

A *sorted term* t_s is a term t of sort s. A variable x of a sort s is written as

$x: s$

which is called a *sorted variable*.

Aït-Kaci [1] proposes a notation, called Ψ-terms, based on sorted terms in order-sorted logic. A Ψ-term accompanies a sorted term $x: s$ with a *feature structure* written by a sequent of pairs of an attribute label and its value. The Ψ terms with feature structures represent more detailed information than simple sorted terms. For instance, the Ψ-term corresponding to 'red sour apples' is as below where *color* and *taste* are attribute labels and *red* and *sour* are their values, respectively.

$x: apple[color \rightarrow y: red, taste \rightarrow z: sour]$

Since the meaning of a Ψ-term is narrowed by the succeeding feature structure, the sorted term $x: apple$ is a more abstract expression than the Ψ term $x: apple[color \rightarrow y: red, taste \rightarrow z: sour]$. Note that $x: apple$ shows 'apples' and $x: apple[color \rightarrow y: red, taste \rightarrow z: sour]$ shows 'red sour apples'.

LOGIN has been developed as a logic programming language where PROLOG's arguments are replaced by Ψ-terms. For a predicate p, attribute labels $l_{11}, ..., l_{nk}$, Ψ-terms $t_{11}, ..., t_{nk}$, and variables $x_1: s_1, ..., x_k: s_k$, a fact is written in LOGIN as:

$$p(x_1: s_1[l_{11} \rightarrow t_{11}, ..., l_{n1} \rightarrow t_{n1}], ..., x_k: s_k[l_{1k} \rightarrow t_{1k}, ..., l_{nk} \rightarrow l_{nk}]).$$

Thus, it can express the relation of the concepts as complex objects.

Although we can translate Ψ-terms into the form of first order logic without sorted terms, we cannot directly represent knowledge by them. Sorted expressions(sorted terms or Ψ-terms) do not only retain the meaning of the original knowledge, but also represent the form simply. For example, the assertion describes an expression of 'John, who is a twenty years old man, is walking' as below.

$$walk(x: John[age \rightarrow y: twenty\_years, sex \rightarrow z: male]).$$

For the sake of simplicity, we use a sort *John* as a singleton instead of a constant.

In [1], Aït-Kaci contended that the inference by unification of sorted terms was more efficient than by resolution processes. In Section 4 and Section 5, we will extend the expression based on the Ψ-term explained above.

3. Motivation

In this section, we shall discuss examples that raise the questions of knowledge representation using Ψ-terms.

Example 1: A Hierarchy of Predicates

We now consider that superordinate predicates are derived from subordinate ones in the hierarchy of predicates. That is, the abstract expression of predicate can be inferred from the concrete expression.

In the hierarchy of predicates in Fig. 1 we expect the following results of an inference. Suppose a fact `hit(x:John)` holds, then the superordinate predicate `illegal_act` can be derived from the predicate `hit` from the direction (1) in Fig. 1. However, the first query 'Did John do an illegal act against Mary?' will give the answer no. It is certain that John hit somebody but not that John hit Mary. Thus, the second query 'Did John do an illegal act against somebody?' will yield yes.

```
hit(x:John).
?-illegal_act(x:John, y:Mary).
no.
?-illegal_act(x:John, y:person).
yes.
```

This exemplifies the case of a derivation of predicate higher in the hierarchy of predicates with more arguments than the predicate representing the fact. To make the inference above, we have to supplement the arguments existing only in `illegal_act` and not existing in `hit`. In addition, we have to take account of the quantification of the supplemented arguments. When the second argument `y:person` is interpreted as all persons, the answer to second query may be no. However the interpretation does not fit with what we expect, so that `y:person` should be interpreted as a `person(somebody)`.

Similarly, assuming a predicate `illegal_act` with fewer arguments than the predicate in a fact `steal(x:John, y:Mary)`, in the direction (2) in Fig. 1 the derivation of the following query results in yes. The answer is plausible because a fact `steal(x:John, y:Mary)` implies `illegal_act(x:John)` as more abstract information.

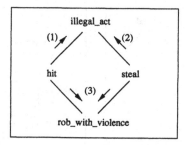

Figure 1: A hierarchy of predicates

```
steal(x:John, y:Mary).
?-illegal_act(x:John).
yes.
```

Additionally, the predicate `rob_with_violence` as the conjunction of `hit` and `steal` will be derived from the two predicates (on (3) in Fig. 1). That is, by the facts `hit(x:John, y:Mary)` and `steal(x:John, z:wallet)` in an incident John's robbing with violence holds and then the query 'Did John steal Mary's wallet using robbery with violence?' will yield `yes`.

```
hit(x:John, y:Mary).
steal(x:John, z:wallet).
?-rob_with_violence(x:John, y:Mary, z:wallet).
yes.
```

Example 2: Event and Property Interpretations

Interpreting a predicate from a natural language assertion can result in the reasoning process having a different direction, depending on the interpretation. Using a predicate in knowledge representation, there are two roles for the predicate, these being *event* and *property* [3, 8]. In the example of the sort hierarchy in Fig. 2, we consider the assertion `fly(x:bird)`. This is ambiguous because the term can be interpreted in two ways.

The fact `fly(x:bird)`, when interpreted as an event, states that a bird is flying. The fact entails that an animal is flying so that the query `?-fly(x:animal)` results in `yes`. However the fact does not state that a penguin is flying, and the answer to query `?-fly(x:penguin)` is no as follows.

Interpretation 1: A bird is flying.

```
fly(x:bird).
?-fly(x:animal).
yes.
?-fly(x:penguin).
no.
?-move(x:animal).
yes.
```

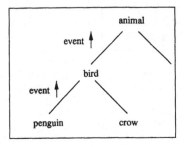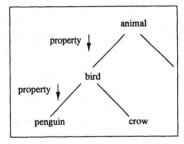

Figure 2: The inference by event and property

The assertion `fly(x:bird)` as an event can be used to deduce the superordinate
terms. For example, `animal` is one of the superordinate terms of `bird` as in Fig 2. In
contrast, the fact `fly(x:bird)` which is interpreted as a property, states that birds
have the property of flight. If birds have this property, then penguins should have
the same property. Thus, the query `?-fly(x:penguin)` will have the answer yes.
However since the information does not imply that all animals have the property of
flight, the following answer for query `?-fly(x:animal)` will yield no.

Interpretation 2: Birds have the property of flight.

```
fly(x:bird).
?-fly(x:animal).
no.
?-fly(x:penguin).
yes.
?-move(x:animal).
no.
```

Fig. 2 demonstrates that the subordinate terms inherit the property from superordinate terms. Namely, a conclusion `fly(x:penguin)` can be inferred from the fact
`fly(x:bird)` by an inheritance to the subordinate term `x:penguin`. If an assertion does not distinguish between event and property, then we cannot deal with
inferences using the two kinds of directions in the hierarchy.

The problems of the above two examples we have seen suggest the necessity of
both hierarchies of sorts(terms) and predicates and the distinction of a predicate
(event or property).

4. Event, Property and Hierarchy

In order to realize the inference in the previous section, we introduce the hierarchy
and the event/property distinction in predicates.

4.1. A hierarchy of predicates

We would like to realize a hierarchy of predicates, independent of the hierarchy of
sorts (terms). A hierarchy of predicates is built by a binary relation $\sqsubseteq_P$ of predicate

symbols that is a partial order, e.g. for any predicates p_1, p_2, $p_1 \sqsubseteq_P p_2$ means that p_2 is a superordinate predicate of p_1 and that p_1 is a subordinate predicate of p_2.

Normally, a relation in the hierarchy of predicates is expressed by the implication symbol, used in first order logic, as an ISA-relation. The following example will illustrate a rule that *move* is a superordinate predicate of *fly* using the logical implication.

$$fly(X) \rightarrow move(X)$$

The implication infers that if *fly(a)* holds, then *move(a)* does.

However, such rules do not completely represent the relation between predicates in the hierarchy. The problem is that each superordinate/subordinate predicate has its own unique argument structure, and that there may be a difference between them. For example, suppose there are predicates *explain* and *talk*. Both predicates have two arguments and are written like:

$$explain(x: John, y: book)$$
$$talk(x: John, z: Mary)$$

In this case, the first argument of both predicates is same, whereas the second arguments are different. The role of both first arguments is agent, and the role of the second argument in *explain* is object but in *talk* is coagent. Therefore, the second argument cannot be unified between *explain* and *talk* when these predicates are in the relation $\sqsubseteq_P$ in the hierarchy of predicates. If we were to stick to semantics by logical implication, we may have to write several rules to associate arguments in the premise with those in the conclusion (e.g. $p(X,Y) \rightarrow q(X,Y)$, $p(X,Y) \rightarrow q(Y,X)$, $p(X,X) \rightarrow q(X,X), ...$). In particular, they would become more complicated as the number of predicates in the hierarchy increased.

Suppose that

$$explain \sqsubseteq_P talk$$

is declared, then to fill the gap between the argument structures of predicates, we need to complement missing arguments by adding and deleting some of them. How do we obtain the information for the argument structures of predicates? We use *argument labels* to render arguments roles. Note that these differ from the attribute labels in Ψ-terms shown in Section 2. Argument labels *agt, obj* and so on, which are written like

$$explain(\underline{agt} \Rightarrow x: John, \underline{obj} \Rightarrow y: book)$$

uniquely represent the argument roles to build an argument structure. In this example *agt* is an argument label 'agent' and *obj* is an argument label 'object'. This notation would be able to treat the query

$$?\text{-}talk(agt \Rightarrow x: person, coagt \Rightarrow y: person)$$

where the fact

$$explain(agt \Rightarrow x: John, obj \Rightarrow y: book)$$

is given, in the following way.

$$explain(agt \Rightarrow x\colon John, obj \Rightarrow y\colon book)$$
$$\downarrow(1) \text{ derivation of the superordinate predicate}$$
$$talk(agt \Rightarrow x\colon John, obj \Rightarrow y\colon book)$$
$$\downarrow(2) \text{ deletion of an argument}$$
$$talk(agt \Rightarrow x\colon John)$$
$$\downarrow(3) \text{ addition of an argument}$$
$$talk(agt \Rightarrow x\colon John, coagt \Rightarrow z\colon person)$$
$$\downarrow(4) \text{ substitution of the sort}$$
$$talk(agt \Rightarrow x\colon person, coagt \Rightarrow z\colon person)$$

By (1), the predicate *talk* is derived from the subordinate predicate *explain*. (2) deletes the argument $obj \Rightarrow y\colon book$ that is a surplus argument in predicate *talk*. (3) adds the argument $coagt \Rightarrow z\colon person$ that is deficient in the arguments of the predicate *talk*. Finally, (4) substitutes $agt \Rightarrow x\colon person$ for the first argument $agt \Rightarrow x\colon John$.

For (2) and (3), each argument label gives a scope to the argument. Let *SCP* be a function from the set of argument labels to the set of sorts. For argument labels *agt,obj*, if we define $SCP(agt) = person$ and $SCP(obj) = thing$, then the sorts *person* and *thing* indicate the scope of *agt* and *obj*. In the supplementation of arguments, the addition and deletion of arguments depend on the argument structure, and the value of the added argument is supplied from the scope of the argument indicated by the argument label.

4.2. Predicates as Event and Property

Predicate symbols can be used to represent features or states of objects. For example, $walk(x\colon John)$ means that John is walking, and $red(y\colon apple)$ means that an apple is red. However, predicates in these assertions may not have a consistent usage. That is, the predicate in $walk(x\colon John)$ implies an event and the predicate in $red(y\colon apple)$ implies a property. As a result, the inference in the hierarchy can give rise to erroneous unification for the two kinds of usage. Also the single predicate *walk* may have two kinds of interpretation as the event 'is walking' and the property 'can walk'.

We need to present reasoning for each predicate either as an event or a property with different notation and need to define the relevant unification. The distinction is whether an assertion is interpreted as an occurrence of an event, or as a property of objects. We define two aspects of predicates as follows.

Definition 4.1 (Two aspects of a predicate). *For any predicate p_i there are the predicate p_i as event and the predicate $p_i^{\sharp}$ as property.*

We alter terms, which are based on Ψ-terms, to distinguish between an existential notation and a universal notation for the sorted domain, e.g. *bird* denotes all birds and $x\colon bird$ denotes a bird. Thus, examples of an assertion defined as event and as a property are given below:

Event assertion: The predicate as event expresses that there is a fact or there is an occurrence of such an event. The argument of the predicate is limited to an object, so that the following assertion is interpreted as 'A bird is flying'.

$$fly(x\colon bird) \simeq \exists x \; fly\_as\_event(x\colon bird)$$

Property assertion: The predicate as property expresses an attribute of objects. The argument is universal in the set of objects within a sort, so that the following form means 'All birds have the property of flight'.

$$fly^\S(bird) \simeq \forall x \; fly\_as\_property(x\!:\!bird)$$

Moreover, the two aspects of a predicate naturally cause a difference in inferences. If the predicate is an event, then the added argument should be one occurrence of an object corresponding to one event. If the predicate is a property, then the added argument should not be a unique object but a global feature of that sort. Therefore, if we add a term $x\!:\!s$ to a predicate interpreted as event, the term will denote an object within sort s; if we add a term s to a predicate interpreted as property, it will denote all objects in sort s.

For example, the supplementation of arguments can be distinguished as follows.

Predicate as event:
$$hit(agt \Rightarrow x\!:\!John)$$
$$\Downarrow \text{ addition of an argument}$$
$$hit(agt \Rightarrow x\!:\!John, coagt \Rightarrow \underline{y\!:\!person})$$
(John hit a person.)

Predicate as property:
$$hit^\S(agt \Rightarrow x\!:\!John)$$
$$\Downarrow \text{ addition of an argument}$$
$$hit^\S(agt \Rightarrow x\!:\!John, coagt \Rightarrow \underline{person})$$
(John has the property of hitting every person.)

The scope of the argument label $coagt$ can determine the sort $person$ of terms added to the predicates hit and $hit^\S$. In this case, $y\!:\!person$ is added to the predicate as event, and $person$ is added to the predicate as property.

5. An Order-Sorted Logic with Event, Property and Hierarchy

In this section, we formalize an order-sorted logic which adopts a hierarchy of predicates and a distinction between event and property.

5.1. Signature

We now revise the order-sorted logics and the Ψ-term in [7, 4, 1].

Definition 5.1 (Signature). *A signature for logic with order-sorts is $\Sigma = (S, P, LP)$ if*

(1) $(S, \sqsubseteq_S)$ *is a partially ordered set of sort symbols with the greatest sort $\top$ and the least $\bot$.*

(2) $(P, \sqsubseteq_P)$ *is a partially ordered set of predicate symbols.*

(3) LP *is a set of argument labels of predicates.*

(4) SCP *is a function from LP to S.*

(5) ARG *is a function from P to 2^{LP}.*

$SCP(l)$ denotes a sort as the scope of an argument label l. $ARG(p)$ indicates a set of argument labels as the unique argument structure of a predicate p. We use ‖ to indicate that the predicate is read as a property, where the predicate $p^{\parallel}$ is called a *property predicate* and the predicate p without it is called an *event predicate*. The set P of predicates can be extended as follows: $P^+ = P \cup \{p^{\parallel}|p \in P\}$. In the latter sections, all our signatures will be the extended signature $\Sigma = (S, P^+, LP)$.

5.2. Syntax

A language L of signature Σ contains the following: the family $V = \{V_s|s \in S\}$ of variables where $V_s(= \{v_1 : s, \ v_2 : s, ...\})$ is all the variables of sort s, the set LS of attribute labels and the propositional operations$(\lor, \neg)$.

We define the expressions of L: *terms* and *formulas*.

Definition 5.2 (Terms). *Given a language L of signature Σ, the set TERM of terms is defined by:*

(1) *A sort s and a sorted variable $x: s$ are atomic terms of sort s.*

(2) *If t_0 is an atomic term of sort s, $t_1, ..., t_n$ are terms without variable and $l_1, ..., l_n$ are attribute labels, then $t_0[l_1 \to t_1, ..., l_n \to t_n]$ is a term of sort s.*

We say that a term t of sort s is a term of argument label l if s and $SCP(l)$ are in the subsort relation, namely, $(s, SCP(l)) \in \sqsubseteq s$.

Definition 5.3 (Formulas). *Given a language L of a signature Σ, the set FORM of formulas is defined by:*

(1) *If $t_1, ..., t_n$ are terms of $l_1, ..., l_n$ and p is a predicate where $ARG(p) = \{l_1, ..., l_n\}$, then $p(l_1 \Rightarrow t_1, ..., l_n \Rightarrow t_n)$ is the atomic formula for an event predicate.*

If $t_1, ..., t_n$ are terms of $l_1, ..., l_n$ and $p^{\parallel}$ is a predicate where $ARG(p) = \{l_1, ..., l_n\}$, then $p^{\parallel}(l_1 \Rightarrow t_1, ..., l_n \Rightarrow t_n)$ is the atomic formula for a property predicate.

(2) *If A and B are formulas, then $\neg A$ and $A \lor B$ are formulas.*

5.3. Semantics

For a language L of signature Σ, a structure is a pair $T = (U, [\![\ ]\!])$ (a universe U and an interpretation $[\![\ ]\!]$.) For each attribute label l_i in LS, $[\![l_i]\!]$ is a function from U to U. An interpretation of sorts is defined by $[\![\ ]\!] : (S, \sqsubseteq s) \to (U, \subseteq)$ where $[\![\top]\!] = U$ and $[\![\bot]\!] = \phi$.

Definition 5.4 (Interpretation). *Given a family $\alpha = \{\alpha_s : V_s \to [\![s]\!] | s \in S\}$ of variable assignments, an interpretation $[\![\ ]\!]$ of terms and atomic formulas is defined by:*

(1) $[\![s]\!]_\alpha = [\![s]\!]$, $[\![x : s]\!]_\alpha = \{\alpha_s(x : s)\}$.

(2) $[\![t_0[l_1 \to t_1, ..., l_n \to t_n]]\!]_\alpha = \{x \in [\![t_0]\!]_\alpha | \exists y_1 \in [\![t_1]\!]_\alpha, ..., \exists y_n \in [\![t_n]\!]_\alpha, [\![l_1]\!](x) = y_1, ..., [\![l_n]\!](x) = y_n\}$.

(3) $[\![\varphi]\!] \subseteq X_p$,
$[\![\varphi(l_1 \Rightarrow t_1, ..., l_n \Rightarrow t_n)]\!]_\alpha = 1$ *iff* $\{f \in X_p | \forall l_i \in ARG(p), f(l_i) \in [\![t_i]\!]_\alpha\} \subseteq [\![\varphi]\!]$

where φ is an event predicate p or a property predicate $p^{\natural}$ and $X_p = \{f \in (ARG(p) \rightarrow U) | \forall l \in ARG(p), f(l) \in [\![SCP(l)]\!]\}$.

By this definition, the ordering of arguments in a predicate does not alter the interpretation of the atomic formula. For example, formulas

$$p(l_1 \Rightarrow t_1, l_2 \Rightarrow t_2) \text{ and } p(l_2 \Rightarrow t_2, l_1 \Rightarrow t_1)$$

are regarded as semantically identical. As an argument is a term of a sort, that is, interpreted as a subset of U, a predicate has to be interpreted as the relation of the subsets.

I^{σ} or $I^{\sigma\natural}$ is an interpretation of the supplementation of predicate arguments distinguished between event and property.

Definition 5.5 (Interpretation of supplementation of arguments). For p, $p^{\natural}, q \in P^{+}$, let be $l_j \in ARG(p) \cap ARG(q)$ and $r_k \in ARG(q) - ARG(p)$. An interpretation $(I^{\sigma}_{q/p}$ or $I^{\sigma\natural}_{q/p})$ of supplementation of arguments is defined by:

- $I^{\sigma}_{q/p}([\![p]\!]) = \{g \in (ARG(q) \rightarrow U) | \forall f \in F_i, g(l_j) = f(l_j), g(r_k) = \alpha_k(x_k{:}s_k)\}$

- $I^{\sigma\natural}_{q/p}([\![p^{\natural}]\!]) = \{g \in (ARG(q) \rightarrow U) | \forall f \in F_i, g(l_j) = f(l_j), g(r_k) \in [\![s_k]\!]\}$

where $s_k = SCP(r_k)$ and $\alpha_k{:} V_{s_k} \rightarrow [\![s_k]\!]$.

The subscript q/p of $I^{\sigma}_{q/p}$ and $I^{\sigma\natural}_{q/p}$ means a translation from an interpretation of the predicate p into the predicate q. Accordingly, we can say $I^{\sigma}_{q/p}([\![p]\!]) \subseteq X_q$ where $X_q = \{f \in (ARG(q) \rightarrow U) | \forall l \in ARG(q), f(l) \in [\![SCP(l)]\!]\}$.

Next we will give an interpretation of hierarchy of predicates.

Definition 5.6 (Hierarchy of predicates). Given the set P of predicates and a subpredicate relation $\sqsubseteq_P$, a hierarchy of predicates is a pair $(P, \sqsubseteq_P)$, which is interpreted by:

$$[\![\ ]\!] : (P, \sqsubseteq_P) \rightarrow (2^{X_P}, I^{\sigma}, I^{\sigma^{\natural}}, \subseteq)$$

where $X_p = \{f \in (ARG(p) \rightarrow U) | \forall l \in ARG(p), f(l) \in [\![SCP(l)]\!]\}$ and $X_P = \bigcup_{p \in P} X_p$.

We define the one-step subordinate relation $\sqsubseteq^1_P = \{(p_i, p_j) \in \sqsubseteq_P | i \neq j, (p_i, r), (r, p_j) \notin \sqsubseteq_P\}$. For any predicates p_i in the hierarchy of predicates, the interpretation $[\![\ ]\!]$ of subpredicate relation $\sqsubseteq_P$ satisfies the following conditions.

(1) If $p_1 \sqsubseteq_P p_2$, then $I^{\sigma}_{p_2/p_1}([\![p_1]\!]) \subseteq [\![p_2]\!]$ and $I^{\sigma\natural}_{p_2/p_1}([\![p^{\natural}_1]\!]) \subseteq [\![p^{\natural}_2]\!]$

(2) If $p_0 \sqsubseteq_P p_1, ..., p_0 \sqsubseteq_P p_n (n > 1)$,
    then $\bigcap^n_{i=1}[I^{\sigma}_{p_0/p_i}([\![p_i]\!])] \subseteq [\![p_0]\!]$ and $\bigcap^n_{i=1}[I^{\sigma\natural}_{p_0/p_i}([\![p^{\natural}_i]\!])] \subseteq [\![p^{\natural}_0]\!]$

where $p_1, ..., p_n$ are all predicates such that $p_0 \sqsubseteq^1_P p_i$.

Definition 5.7 (Satisfaction relation). Let T be a structure and F a formula. The satisfaction relation $T \models F$ is defined by:

(1) $T \models \varphi(l_1 \Rightarrow t_1, ..., l_n \Rightarrow t_n) \Leftrightarrow$ for some family α of variable assignments,
    $[\![\varphi(l_1 \Rightarrow t_1, ..., l_n \Rightarrow t_n)]\!]_{\alpha} = 1$

(2) $T \models A \vee B \Leftrightarrow T \models A$ *or* $T \models B$

(3) $T \models \neg A \Leftrightarrow T \not\models A$

For every formula $F \in \Gamma$, we write $T \models \Gamma$ (T is a model of Γ) if $T \models F$. We say that Γ is *satisfiable* if it has a model. Otherwise, we say that Γ is *unsatisfiable* if it has no models.

6. Logic Programming

We define a logic programming that includes a definition of our extended order-sorted language.

Definition 6.1 (Program). *Let* $\neg L_1, ..., \neg L_n$ *be negative literals and* L *be a positive literal. A program clause is* $L \vee \neg L_1 \vee ... \vee \neg L_n$. *The general form of program clause is written as:* $R_i : L \leftarrow L_1, ..., L_n$.

Let $p, p' \in P$ and $s, s' \in S$. HS_i is the declaration of a subsort relation and HP_j the declaration of a subpredicate relation as follows.

$HS_i : s \sqsubseteq_S s'$,

$HP_j : p \sqsubseteq_P p'$.

A program $\mathcal{P}$ *is a finite set of program clauses, declarations of a subsort relation and declarations of a subpredicate relation.*

$$\mathcal{P} = \{R_1, ..., R_n, HS_1, ..., HS_k, HP_1, ..., HP_m\}$$

A goal clause is $\neg L_1 \vee ... \vee \neg L_n$. The form of goal clause is written as: $\leftarrow L_1, ..., L_n$. The substitution of sorted terms depends on whether the literals with the terms are positive or negative in the clause. *Atts*(called *attributes*) is a finite sequence of pairs of attribute labels and terms $l_1 \rightarrow t_1, ..., l_k \rightarrow t_k (k \geq 0)$.

Definition 6.2 (Substitution). *Given a program* $\mathcal{P}$ *and a goal clause* G, *for* $x: s_i \in V_{s_i}$, $y: s_j \in V_{s_j}$, $s_i, s_j \in S$, *a substitution* θ *is a function from TERM to TERM defined as one of the following by the rules:*

(1) $x: s_i[Atts] \overset{\theta}{\Longrightarrow} s_i[Atts]$,

(2) $s_i[Atts] \overset{\theta}{\Longrightarrow} s_j[Atts]$ *where* $(s_i \sqsubseteq_S s_j) \in \mathcal{P}$,

(3) $x: s_i[Atts] \overset{\theta}{\Longrightarrow} y: s_j[Atts]$ *where* $(s_j \sqsubseteq_S s_i) \in \mathcal{P}$,

(4) $x: s_i[Atts] \overset{\theta}{\Longrightarrow} x: s_i[Atts, l_{k+1} \rightarrow t_{k+1}]$ *where* $l_{k+1} \rightarrow t_{k+1}$ *does not occur in the Atts.*

Let $\varphi(l_1 \Rightarrow t_1, ..., l_m \Rightarrow t_m), L_1, ..., L_n$ be atomic formulas and θ a substitution. $\theta\varphi(l_1 \Rightarrow t_1, ..., l_m \Rightarrow t_m)$ and $\theta(L_1, ..., L_n)$ are defined by:

- $\theta\varphi(l_1 \Rightarrow t_1, ..., l_m \Rightarrow t_m) = \varphi(l_1 \Rightarrow \theta t_1, ..., l_m \Rightarrow \theta t_m)$ where θt_i is a term of l_i,

- $\theta(L_1, ..., L_n) = \theta L_1, ..., \theta L_n$.

Let A and B be expressions. A substitution θ is a unifier of A and B if $\theta A = B$. *Args*(called *arguments*) is a finite sequence of pairs of argument labels and terms $l_1 \Rightarrow t_1, ..., l_m \Rightarrow t_m (m > 0)$. $FORM_0 (\subset FORM)$ is the set of atomic formulas, and

$$FORM_0^* = \{\varphi(l_1 \Rightarrow t_1, ..., l_n \Rightarrow t_n) | \{l_1, ..., l_n\} \in 2^{LP}, \varphi \in P^+, t_i \in TERM\}$$

is the set of atomic formulas that is expanded by all argument structures including illegal ones (e.g. $p(l_1 \Rightarrow t_1, l_1 \Rightarrow t_2)$ is illegal when $ARG(p) \neq \{l_1, l_2\}$).

Definition 6.3 (Supplementation of arguments). *Given an atomic formula A, a supplementation σ of predicate arguments, that is a function from $FORM_0^*$ to $FORM_0$, is defined by:*

$$\sigma(A) = ADD^m(DEL^n(A))$$

where ADD^m is a composition of m-functions of ADD and DEL^n a composition of n-functions of DEL and therefore m is the least number such that $ADD^m = ADD^{m+1}(m > 0)$ and n the least number such that $DEL^n = DEL^{n+1}(n > 0)$. For $l \in LP$, $\varphi \in P^+$, $s \in S$, $x: s \in V_s$ and $t \in TERM$, an addition ADD of arguments is

$$ADD(\varphi(Args)) = \begin{cases} \varphi(Args, l \Rightarrow x: s) & \text{if } \varphi = p \text{ and } \exists l \in A, \\ \varphi(Args, l \Rightarrow s) & \text{if } \varphi = p^\sharp \text{ and } \exists l \in A, \\ \varphi(Args) & \text{otherwise,} \end{cases}$$

where $A = \{l \in ARG(p) | l \Rightarrow t \notin Args\}$ and $SCP(l) = s$. And a deletion DEL of arguments is

$$DEL(\varphi(Args, l \Rightarrow t)) = \begin{cases} \varphi(Args) & \text{if } l \notin ARG(\varphi) \text{ and} \\ & (\varphi = p^\sharp, t = v: s) \text{ or} \\ & (\varphi = p, t = s), \\ \varphi(Args, l \Rightarrow t) & \text{if } B - ARG(\varphi) = \phi, \end{cases}$$

where $B = \{l_i | l_i \Rightarrow t_i \in (Args \cup \{l \Rightarrow t\})\}$ and $SCP(l) = s$.

We define the inference rules in the logic programming that are applied to derivations. LS and LS' are finite sequences of positive literals, L is a positive literal.

Definition 6.4 (Inference rules). *Let θ be a substitution and σ a supplementation of arguments. Inference rules are written as follows:*

$$\frac{\leftarrow LS', L \quad L \leftarrow LS}{\leftarrow LS, LS'} \ (RP) \qquad \frac{\leftarrow LS}{\leftarrow \theta LS} \ (Sub)$$

$$\frac{p_1 \sqsubseteq_P p_2 \quad \leftarrow LS, p_2(Args)}{\leftarrow LS, \sigma(p_1(Args))} \ (Spec1)$$

$$\frac{p_1 \sqsubseteq_P p_2 \quad \leftarrow LS, p_2^\sharp(Args)}{\leftarrow LS, \sigma(p_1^\sharp(Args))} \ (Spec2)$$

$$\frac{p_0 \sqsubseteq_P p_1 \quad \cdots \quad p_0 \sqsubseteq_P p_n \quad \leftarrow LS, p_0(Args)}{\leftarrow LS, \sigma(p_1(Args)), ..., \sigma(p_n(Args))} \ (Gen1)$$

$$\frac{p_0 \sqsubseteq_P p_1 \quad \cdots \quad p_0 \sqsubseteq_P p_n \quad \leftarrow LS, p_0^\sharp(Args)}{\leftarrow LS, \sigma(p_1^\sharp(Args)), ..., \sigma(p_n^\sharp(Args))} \ (Gen2)$$

if σ is properly applied in each of $(Spec1)$, $(Spec2)$, $(Gen1)$ and $(Gen2)$, where $p_1, ..., p_n(n > 1)$ are all predicates such that $p_0 \sqsubseteq_P^1 p_i$ in $(Gen1)$ and $(Gen2)$.

We write $\Gamma \models F$ (F is a consequence of Γ) if every model of Γ is a model of a formula F.

$$\mathcal{P}_1 = \{\text{rob\_with\_violence} \sqsubseteq_P \text{hit}, \quad \text{rob\_with\_violence} \sqsubseteq_P \text{steal},$$

$$\text{hit} \sqsubseteq_P \text{illegalact}, \quad \text{steal} \sqsubseteq_P \text{illegalact}, \quad \text{wallet} \sqsubseteq_S \text{thing},$$

$$\text{John} \sqsubseteq_S \text{person}, \quad \text{Mary} \sqsubseteq_S \text{person},$$

$$\text{hit}(\text{agt} \Rightarrow \text{x:John}, \text{coagt} \Rightarrow \text{y:Mary}),$$

$$\text{steal}(\text{agt} \Rightarrow \text{x:John}, \text{obj} \Rightarrow \text{w:wallet}) \qquad\qquad \}$$

$$\mathcal{P}_2 = \{\text{fly} \sqsubseteq_P \text{move}, \quad\quad \text{walk} \sqsubseteq_P \text{move},$$

$$\text{bird} \sqsubseteq_S \text{animal}, \quad \text{penguin} \sqsubseteq_S \text{bird}, \quad \text{crow} \sqsubseteq_S \text{bird},$$

$$\text{fly}(\text{sbj} \Rightarrow \text{x: bird}),$$

$$\text{fly}^{\sharp}(\text{sbj} \Rightarrow \text{bird}) \qquad\qquad\qquad\qquad \}$$

Figure 3: The programs for examples

Theorem 6.1. *The conclusion C' of each inference rule of definition 6.4 is a consequence of its premise $\{C_1, C_2\}$ or $\{C\}$. That is, $\{C_1, C_2\} \models C'$ or $\{C\} \models C'$.*

Definition 6.5 (Derivation). *From a program $\mathcal{P}$ and a goal G ($\mathcal{P} \cup \{G\}$), a goal G' is obtained from G using one of the inference rules. We write $\mathcal{P} \cup \{G\} \vdash_{LP} G'$ to indicate the derivation.*

Given $\mathcal{P} \cup \{G\}$, we can construct a signature $\Sigma_{\mathcal{P} \cup \{G\}}$ where $s, s' \in S$, $p, p' \in P$, $(s, s') \in \sqsubseteq_S$ and $(p, p') \in \sqsubseteq_P$ for every $s \sqsubseteq_S s', p \sqsubseteq_P p' \in \mathcal{P}$.

Let T be a structure of $\Sigma_{\mathcal{P} \cup \{G\}}$,

$$T \models_{LP} \mathcal{P} \cup \{G\} \text{ iff } T \models C_i \text{ for every clause } C_i \in \mathcal{P} \cup \{G\}.$$

We say that T is a model of program $\mathcal{P} \cup \{G\}$. We write $\mathcal{P} \cup \{G\} \models_{LP} C$ (C is a consequence of program $\mathcal{P} \cup \{G\}$) if every model of program $\mathcal{P} \cup \{G\}$ is a model of a clause C.

A *refutation* is to derive the empty clause $\square$ from $\mathcal{P} \cup \{G\}$.

Theorem 6.2 (Soundness of refutation). $\mathcal{P} \cup \{G\} \vdash_{LP} \square \Rightarrow \mathcal{P} \cup \{G\} \models_{LP} \square$

Let us look at the refutation processes from the examples we have seen in Section 3. The programs $\mathcal{P}_1$ for the example 1 and $\mathcal{P}_2$ for the example 2 are shown in Fig. 3. From a goal

$$?\text{-}rob\_with\_violence(agt \Rightarrow x: John)$$

and $\mathcal{P}_1$, the refutation process is described in Fig. 4.

In the same way, from a goal

$$?\text{-}move(sbj \Rightarrow y: animal)$$

and $\mathcal{P}_2$, the refutation succeeds as in Fig. 5.

On the other hand, another goal

$$?\text{-}move^{\sharp}(sbj \Rightarrow y: animal)$$

and $\mathcal{P}_2$ cannot derive the empty clause and the refutation fails.

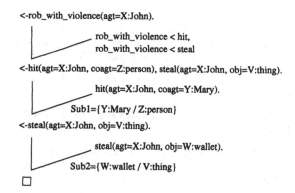

Figure 4: A refutation process 1

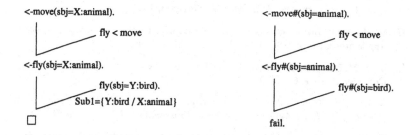

Figure 5: Refutation processes 2

7. Conclusions and Future Work

We have presented an order-sorted logic for knowledge representation, which enables us to describe the hierarchies of both predicates and terms inherent in natural language. We have developed the new logic programming language using SICStus Prolog^{TM} ver.3.0, and have shown that the language properly solves the examples shown in Section 3.

In this language, we can write database statements, disregarding the argument structures of other predicates. The most advantageous point of our system is the mechanism of argument supplementation to unify predicates with different argument structures. It allows us to write hierarchical relations between predicates flexibly and concisely. Also, we can precisely distinguish *event* from *property* as two different aspects of a predicate. In addition, our logic programming language provides unification/ resolution mechanisms that fit human reasoning.

Thus far, we have considered making order-sorted logic closer to the semantics of natural language. In addition to the event/property distinction, we are now tackling the inclusion of the proper treatment of negation in the predicate/sort hierarchy. Although this work seems to be difficult, we contend that such notions are significant in representing knowledge naturally and precisely.

References

[1] H. Ait-Kaci and R. Nasr. Login: A logic programming language with built-in inheritance. *Journal of Logic Programming*, pages 185–215, 1986.

[2] H. Ait-Kaci and A. Podelski. Towards a meaning of life. *Journal of Logic Programming*, pages 195–234, 1993.

[3] J. F. Allen. Towards a general theory of action and time. *Artificial Intelligence*, 23:123–154, 1984.

[4] C. Beiercle, U. Hedtsuck, U. Pletat, P.H. Schmit, and J. Siekmann. An order-sorted logic for knowledge representation systems. *Artificial Intelligence*, 55:149–191, 1992.

[5] P. M. Hill and R. W. Topor. A semantics for typed logic programs. In F. Pfenning, editor, *Types in Logic Programming*. MIT Press, 1992.

[6] M. Kifer, G. Lausen, and J. Wu. Logical foundations of object-oriented and frame-based languages. *J. ACM*, 42(4):741–843, 1995.

[7] M. Manzano. Introduction to many-sorted logic. In *Many-sorted Logic and its Applications*, pages 3–86. John Wiley and Sons, 1993.

[8] D. V. McDermott. A temporal logic for reasoning about processes and plans. *Cognitive Science*, 6:101–155, 1982.

[9] K. Nitta, S. Tojo, and et al. Knowledge representation of new helic II. In *Workshop on Legal Application of Logic Programming,ICLP '94*, 1994.

[10] K. Nitta, S. Wong, and Y. Ohtake. A computational model for trial reasoning. In *Proc. 4th Int. Conf. on AI and Law, Amsterdam*, 1993.

[11] M. Schmidt-Schauss. *Computational Aspects of an Order-Sorted Logic with Term Declarations*. Springer-Verlag, 1989.

[12] Y. Shoham. *Reasoning about Change*. The MIT Press, 1988.

[13] C. Walter. A mechanical solution of schuber's steamroller by many-sorted resolution. *Artificial Intelligence*, 26(2):217–224, 1985.

[14] C. Walter. Many-sorted unification. *Journal of the Association for Computing Machinery*, 35:1, 1988.

[15] H. Yasukawa, H. Tsuda, and K. Yokota. Objects properies and modules in *Quixote*. In *Proc. FGCS'92*, pages 257–268, 1992.

[16] K. Yokota. *Quixote:A Constraint Based Approach to a Deductive Object-Oriented Database*. PhD thesis, 1994.

Temporal Probabilistic Logic Programs

Alex Dekhtyar
University of Maryland
dekhtyar@cs.umd.edu

Michael I. Dekhtyar
Tver State University
Michael.Dekhtyar@tversu.ru

V.S. Subrahmanian
University of Maryland
vs@cs.umd.edu

August 13, 1999

Abstract

There are many applications where the precise time at which an event will occur (or has occurred) is uncertain. Temporal probabilistic logic programs (TPLPs) allow a programmer to express knowledge about such events. In this paper, we develop a model theory, fixpoint theory, and proof theory for TPLPs, and show that the fixpoint theory may be used to enumerate consequences of a TPLP in a sound and complete manner. Likewise the proof theory provides a sound and complete inference system. Last, but not least, we provide complexity results for TPLPs, showing in particular, that reasonable classes of TPLPs have polynomial data complexity.

1 Introduction

There are a vast number of applications where uncertainty and time are indelibly intertwined. For example, the US Postal Service (USPS) as well as most commercial shippers have detailed statistics on how long shipments take to reach their destinations. Likewise, we are working on a Viennese historical land deed application where the precise time at which certain properties passed from one owner to another is also highly uncertain. Historical radio carbon dating methods are yet another source of uncertainty, providing approximate information about when a piece was created.

Logical reasoning in situations involving temporal uncertainty is definitely important. For example, an individual querying the USPS express mail tracking system may want to know when he can expect his package to be delivered today — he may then choose to stay home during the period when the probability of delivery seems very high, and leave a note authorizing the delivery official to leave the package by the door at other times.

In this paper, we propose the concept of a *Temporal Probabilistic Logic Program* (or TPLP for short). We define the syntax of TPLPs and provide a formal model theoretic and fixpoint semantics that are shown to coincide. We then develop polynomial time bottom-up, sound and complete fixpoint computation algorithms. Then we present a "brute force" sound and complete proof procedure. Though this procedure is inefficient, it is transparent and easy to understand. Subsequently, a more sophisticated proof procedure that manipulates succinct representations of temporal-probabilistic information had been developed, but is omitted from this paper due to space restrictions.

2 Temporal Probabilistic Programs: Syntax

Let L be a language generated by finitely many constant and predicate symbols. We assume that L has no ordinary function symbols, but it may contain *annotation function* symbols for a fixed family of functions. Annotation function symbols are split into two disjoint sets of *probabilistic annotated functions* and *temporal annotated functions*. If p is an n-ary predicate symbol and $a_1, \ldots, a_n$ are either constants or variables, then $p(a_1, \ldots, a_n)$ is called a *simple event atom*. When all the a_i's are constants, $p(a_1, \ldots, a_n)$ is said to be *ground*. We use B_L to denote the set of ground simple event atoms. A calendar τ is any initial segment of the set of natural numbers: $\tau = \{1, \ldots, t_{max}\}$ for some t_{max}. We will denote such calendar $\tau = [1, t_{max}]$.

Definition 1 *Let* $A_1, \ldots A_k$ *all be simple event atoms. Then* $A_1 \wedge \ldots \wedge A_k$ *and* $A_1 \vee \ldots \vee A_k$ *are called* compound event atoms. *Simple event atoms and* compound event atoms *are both* event atoms.

Definition 2 *A probabilistic annotation function* f_p *of arity* n *is a total function* $f_p : [0,1]^n \longrightarrow [0,1]$.
A temporal annotation function f_t *of arity* n *is a total function* $f_t : \tau^n \longrightarrow \tau$

We assume that associated with each *annotation function* is a body of terminating software code implementing that function.

We also assume that all variable symbols from L are partitioned into three classes. We call one class *object variables* and this class contains the regular first order logic variable symbols. The second and third classes of variable symbols, *probabilistic annotation variables* and *temporal annotation variables* will contain variable symbols that range over the interval $[0,1]$ and over calendar τ respectively. These variables can appear only inside *annotation items*, which are defined below:

Definition 3 *An* annotation item δ *based on a set of constants* $\hat{C}$, *a set of variables* $\hat{V}$ *and a set of* annotation functions $\hat{\mathcal{F}}$ *is either (a) a constant* $\alpha \in \hat{C}$; (b) a variable $v \in \hat{V}$; or (c) an expression of the form $f(\delta_1, \ldots, \delta_k)$ where $\delta_1, \ldots, \delta_k$ are all annotation items based on $\langle \hat{C}, \hat{V}, \hat{\mathcal{F}} \rangle$ and $f \in \hat{\mathcal{F}}$ is a k-ary function symbol.

In this paper, we consider two types of annotation items: *probabilistic annotation items* and *temporal annotation items*. Both are defined below.

Definition 4 *A probabilistic annotation item* δ *is an annotation item based on the set of constants in the* $[0,1]$ *interval, and on the sets of probabilistic annotation variables and probabilistic annotation functions of* L.

A temporal annotation item δ *is an annotation atom based on the set of all constants from* τ, *and on the sets of temporal annotation variables and temporal annotation functions from* L.

Definition 5 *A temporal constraint* $c = c(y, y_1, \ldots, y_k)$ *with* independent variables $y_1, \ldots y_k$ *and* dependent variable y *is one of the following:*

- Let λ be a temporal annotation item with $y_1, \ldots y_k$ being its only variable symbols. Then y *op* λ where $op \in \{=, <, >, \leq, \geq, \neq\}$ is a temporal constraint.

- Let λ_1 and λ_2 be temporal annotation items that contain only variables $y_1, \ldots y_k$. Then $y : \lambda_1 \sim \lambda_2$ is a temporal constraint.

- Let c_1 and c_2 be temporal constraints with the same dependent variable. Then $c_1 \wedge c_2$, $c_1 \vee c_2$ and $\neg c_1$ are temporal constraints.

A temporal constraint c is called *ground* if it contains no independent variables.

We will slightly abuse notation and sometimes write t instead of constraints $y = t$ and $y : t \sim t$.

Definition 6 *Let $c = c(y)$ be a ground temporal constraint. The* solution set *of c, denoted $sol(c)$ is defined as follows:*

1. c is atomic. $sol(c)$ is determined by the following table:

Case	$sol(C)$		Case	$sol(C)$
$y \leq t$	$\{x \in \tau \mid x \leq t\}$		$y \neq t$	$\{x \in \tau \mid x \neq t\}$
$y < t$	$\{x \in \tau \mid x < t\}$		$y > t$	$\{x \in \tau \mid x > t\}$
$y = t$	$\{t\}$		$y : t \sim t'$	$\{x \in \tau \mid x \geq t \wedge x \leq t'\}$

2. If $c = c_1 \wedge c_2$, $c_1 \vee c_2$ or $\neg c_1$ then $sol(c)$ is defined as $sol(c_1) \cap sol(c_2)$, $sol(c_1) \cup sol(c_2)$ and $\tau - sol(c_1)$ respectively.

We can expand the definition of a solution set to non-ground temporal constraints by postulating that the solution of a constraint is a mapping from ground substitutions to sets of timepoints which has to agree with the solution sets for ground temporal constraints.

Definition 7 *Let $c = c(y, y_1, \ldots y_k)$ be a (non-ground) temporal constraint. We define $sol(c(y, y_1, \ldots, y_k))$ as a function $sol(c) : \tau^k \longrightarrow 2^\tau$ such that $(\forall (a_1, \ldots a_k) \in \tau^k)(sol(c)(a_1, \ldots, a_k) = sol(c(y, a_1, \ldots, a_k))$.*

Definition 8 *A* probabilistic weight function *w associated with a subset T of calendar τ is a function $w : T \longrightarrow [0, 1]$.*

If $c = c(y, y_1, \ldots, y_k)$ is a temporal constraint, a generalized probabilistic weight function *ω_c is defined as a function that takes as arguments (i) a substitution $\bar{a} = (a_1, \ldots, a_k)$ of values for $y_1, \ldots y_k$ and (ii) a timepoint $t \in \tau$ and returns a number between 0 and 1. We only require that if $\omega_c(\bar{a}, t) \neq 0$, then $t \in sol(c(t, a_1, \ldots, a_k))$.*

The intuition underlying the above definition is as follows. Consider a constraint $c = c(y, y_1, \ldots, y_k)$ and let $\bar{a}$ be a vector of k time points. and let $\theta = [y_1, \ldots, y_k]/\bar{a}$. Then $c\theta$ determines a set of time points, viz. those that make c true by making an assignment to the dependent variable y. A probabilistic weight function assigns a probability to each time point in this set.

Example 1 *For instance, consider the temporal constraint $c = c(y, y_1, y_2)$ of the form $2 \leq y \wedge y \leq y_1 \wedge y_1 \leq y_2 \wedge y_2 \leq 4$. When we set $y_1 = y_2 = 4$, i.e. $\bar{a} = (4, 4)$, this constraint determines the set of time points $\{2, 3, 4\}$. A probabilistic weight function $\omega_c(\bar{a}, t)$ may associate the respective values $1, 1, 0.5$ with these time points.*

We will use probabilistic weight functions as follows. Now suppose we consider a formula A, and suppose we want to say that A is true with probability $\omega_c(\bar{a}, t)$ at any time t which is a solution of c. Then this means that A is true with 100% probability at times 2 and 3 and 50% probability at time 4.

Notice that if temporal constraint c is *ground* then any generalized probabilistic weight function ω_c is reduced to a simple probabilistic weight function defined on $sol(c)$. In this case, as no independent variables are present in c, we will write $\omega_c(y)$ and not distinguish between it and the simple weight function.

Let $c(y, y_1, \ldots, y_k)$ be a temporal constraint such that $(\forall (a_1, \ldots, a_k) \in \tau^k)$ $(|sol(c(y, a_1, \ldots, a_k))| = 1)$. We will denote by $\sharp$ the generalized probabilistic weight function ω_c, such that $\omega_c(t, a_1, \ldots a_k) = 1$ iff $t = sol(c)(a_1, \ldots, a_k)$. This defines $\sharp$ to be a *universal identity* weight function.

Also, we will sometimes specify the weight function in the form of a set $\{v_1, \ldots, v_k\}$ of values. We can do this when we know that the $|sol(c)| = k$. For example, if $c(y) = y : 3 \sim 5$, a weight function ω_c can be represented as $\{0.5, 1, 0\}$. This will mean $\omega_c(3) = 0.5, \omega_c(4) = 1, \omega_c(5) = 0$.

Definition 9 *A temporal probabilistic annotation is a quadruple $\langle c, l, u, \omega_c \rangle$ where c is a temporal constraint, l and u are probabilistic annotation items and ω_c is a generalized probabilistic weight function.*

Definition 10 *Let $F = A_1 * \ldots * A_k$ be an event atom $(* \in \{\vee, \wedge\})$ and $\mu = \langle c, l, u, \omega_c \rangle$ be a tp-annotation. Then $F : \mu$ is a tp-annotated basic formula or just an* annotated basic formula.

Intuitively when F is ground, $F : \langle c, l, u, \omega_c \rangle$ represents the fact that the events described by F happened at a point in $sol(c)$ with a probability in the interval $[l, u]$ and that the probability that these events occured at a particular timepoint $t \in sol(c)$ is given by the weight function ω_c.

Definition 11 *Let $A : \mu, F_1 : \mu_1, \ldots F_m : \mu_m$ be tp-annotated basic formulas, $A \in B_L$. Then $A : \mu \longleftarrow F_1 : \mu_1 \wedge \ldots \wedge F_m : \mu_m$ is called a* temporal probabilistic clause *or a tp-clause.*

Definition 12 *A temporal probabilistic program (tp-program) is a finite set of tp-clauses. If P is a tp-program, we let $ground(P)$ denote the set of all ground instances of rules of P.*

Example 2 Let $\tau = [0, \ldots 30]$. Consider the following ground tp-program:

```
arrived(Item,Place): [y : 3 ∼ 5, 0.5, 0.8, {0.5, 0.3, 0.2}] ⟵
          sent(Item,Place): [y = 1, 0.9, 1, ♯].
arrived(Item,Place): [y : 6 ∼ 8, 0.2, 0.4, {0.75, 0, 0.25}] ⟵
          sent(Item,Place): [y = 1, 0.9, 1, ♯].
arrived(Item,paris): [y : 3 ∼ 4, 0.5, 0.9, {0.6, 0.4}] ⟵
          sent(Item,paris): [y = 1, 0.95, 1, ♯]∧
          express_mail(Item): [y = 1, 1, 1, ♯].
sent(shoes,rome): [y = 1, 1, 1, ♯] ⟵ .
sent(letter,paris): [y = 1, 1, 1, ♯] ⟵ .
express_mail(letter,paris): [y = 1, 1, 1, ♯] ⟵ .
```

This program represents a small part of a deductive database of some company that deals with projected arrivals of the packages shipped by the company. First two rules of the program provide the information on the probability distribution of the arrival time of an arbitrary package sent to any place. The third rule gives some extra information about the arrival time of packages sent to Paris via express-mail. Three facts about shipments complete this simple program.

3 Temporal Probabilistic Programs: Model Theory and Fixpoint Semantics

3.1 Model Theory

In this section we introduce the model theory of tp-programs.

Definition 13 (Thread) *A thread is a function* $th : B_L \to 2^\tau$.

Intuitively, a thread th contains information about the times when *each* event occurs. It specifies one possible way events could occur in time. If for some ground event atom A, $th(A) = \emptyset$, we interpret it as meaning that the event associated with A does not occur in thread th at all. The notion of TP-world below says that we may not know which of several possible threads actually describes the occurrence of events over time.

Definition 14 *A TP-world M is a pair $M = \langle TH, p \rangle$ where $TH = \{th\}$ is a set of threads and $p : TH \to [0,1]$ is a probability distribution function such that* $\sum_{th \in TH} p(th) \leq 1$ [1].

Here, TH represents a set of possible ways events could occur, while p specifies the probability of each thread. Given a TP-world M, we may specify the probability of a formula via the following definition.

Definition 15 *Suppose $M = \langle TH, p \rangle$ is a TP-world and $A \in B_L$. The probability $p_M(A, t)$ that the event denoted by A occurred at time t according to the TP-model M is defined as follows:*

$$p_M(A, t) = \sum_{th \in TH, th(A) \ni t} p(th).$$

If $F = A_1 \wedge \ldots \wedge A_k$ and $G = A_1 \vee \ldots \vee A_k$ are ground compound event atoms, then $p_M(F, t)$ and $p_M(G, t)$ are definable as:

$$p_M(F, t) = \sum_{th \in TH, th(A_1) \ni t, \ldots, th(A_k) \ni t} p(th).$$

$$p_M(G, t) = \sum_{th \in TH, (\exists i \in \{1, \ldots k\})(th(A_i) \ni t)} p(th).$$

The above definition specifies the probability of a formula being true at a given point in time. We can extend this to define the probability that a formula is true at some (possibly more than one) time point in a solution of a ground temporal constraint c.

Definition 16 *If $M = \langle TH, p \rangle$ is a TP-world, $F = A_1 \wedge \ldots \wedge A_k$ and $G = A_1 \vee \ldots \vee A_k$ are event atoms, and $c = c(y)$ is a ground temporal constraint, then $p_M(F, c)$ is defined as:*

$$p_M(F, c) = \sum_{th \in TH, th(A_1) \cap \ldots \cap th(A_k) \cap sol(c) \neq \emptyset} p(th).$$

$$p_M(G, c) = \sum_{th \in TH, (\exists i \in \{1, \ldots k\})(th(A_i) \cap sol(c) \neq \emptyset)} p(th).$$

---

[1] If the sum is equal to 1 we can talk about a *complete distribution*, otherwise the distribution is *incomplete*.

We are now in position to define satisfaction for *ground formulas*.

Definition 17 (Satisfaction) *Let* $M = \langle TH, p \rangle$ *be a TP-world.*

- $M \models F : [c, l, u, \omega_c]$, *where* $c = c(y)$ **iff**

  - $p_M(F, c) \in [l, u]$
  - $(\forall t \in sol(c)) p_M(F, t) \in [\omega_c(t) \cdot l, \omega_c(t) \cdot u]$.

- $M \models F_1 : \mu_1 \wedge \ldots \wedge F_k$ **iff** $\forall i \in \{1, \ldots k\} M \models F_i : \mu_i$.

- $M \models F : \mu \longleftarrow F_1 : \mu_1 \wedge \ldots \wedge F_k$ **iff** *either* $M \models F : \mu$ *or* $M \not\models F_1 : \mu_1 \wedge \ldots \wedge F_k$.

A TP-world M is called a model of a tp-program P ($M \models P$) iff $(\forall r \in P)(M \models r)$. A tp-program P is consistent if it has a model.

As usual we say that $F : \mu$ is a consequence of P ($P \models F : \mu$) iff for every model M of P, it is the case that $M \models F : \mu$.

Example 3 *Picking up from where we left off in Example 2, consider the following TP-world M which consists of two tp-threads th_1 and th_2, defined as follows:*

$th_1(sent(letter,paris)) = \{1, 3, 7\}$
$th_1(express\_mail(letter,paris)) = \{1, 7\}$
$th_1(arrived(letter, paris)) = \{3, 6, 8\}$
$th_2(sent(letter,paris)) = \{1\}$
$th_2(express\_mail(letter,paris)) = \{1\}$
$th_2(arrived(letter, paris)) = \{4\}$

The probability distribution p is: $p(th_1) = 0.6$ and $p(th_2) = 0.4$.

The first thread states that three letters had been sent to Paris on dates 1, 3 and 7, two of them (on dates 1 and 7) had been sent via express mail, and that the letters arrived in Paris on dates 3, 6 and 8 respectively. The second thread has information that only one letter to Paris had been sent (on date 1), via express-mail and arrived to Paris on date 4.

We see that according to M, the probability that the letter arrived in Paris on date 3 is 0.6 and the probability that it arrived on date 4 is 0.4.

3.2 Fixpoint Semantics

We now provide a fixpoint procedure to compute the *semantics* of tp-programs. The fixpoint procedure maps certain structures called tp-interpretations to tp-interpretations — in order to define tp-interpretations, we need to define some intermediate structures called tp-piles and tp-sets below.

Definition 18 *Let F be a ground event atom, $t \in \tau$ be a timepoint and $[l, u] \subseteq [0, 1]$. Then the quadruple (F, t, l, u) is called a tp-tuple.*

A collection (multiset) of tp-tuples is called a TP-pile. If R is a TP-pile we will use $R[F, t]$ to denote the set $\{(F, t, \_, \_) \in R\}$. If for each pair F, t the size of $R[F, t]$ is at most 1, then we call R a TP-set.

Intuitively, each tp-tuple contains information about the probability of an event associated with F (which can be compound) at timepoint t. A TP-pile is an arbitrary collection of such information. In a TP-pile there may be two or more tp-tuples that have information about the probability of some event F at some time t.

A TP-set R is complete iff $(\forall F)(\forall t)(R[F, t] \neq \emptyset)$. On non-complete TP-sets, we define a *completion* operation *compl* as follows: $compl(R) = R \cup \{(F, t, 0, 1) | R[F, t] = \emptyset\}$. Clearly for each TP-set R there is a uniquely defined completion of it. **Therefore without loss of generality from now on we will consider only *complete TP-sets*.** We define the satisfaction by such sets as follows:

Definition 19 *Let R be a TP-set and $F : [c, l, u, \omega_c]$ be an event atom where $c = c(y, y_1, \ldots, y_k)$ is a temporal constraint.*

- *R satisfies $F : [c, l, u, \omega_c]$ ($R \models F : [c, l, u, \omega_c]$) iff for all $\bar{a} = (a_1, \ldots, a_k) \in \tau^k$ such that $sol(c)(\bar{a}) \neq \emptyset$ and for all $t \in sol(c)(\bar{a})$ there exists such interval $[l_t, u_t]$ that*

  - *$(F, t, l_t, u_t) \in R$*
  - *$[l_t, u_t] \subseteq [\omega_c(\bar{a}, t) \cdot l, \omega_c(\bar{a}, t) \cdot u]$*

- *$R \models F_1 : [c_1, l_1, u_1, \omega_{c_1}] \wedge \ldots \wedge F_n : [c_n, l_n, u_n, \omega_{c_n}]$ iff $(\forall i \in \{1, \ldots n\})R \models F_i : [c_i, l_i, u_i, \omega_{c_i}]$*

- *$R \models F : [c, l, u, \omega] \longleftarrow F_1 : [c_1, l_1, u_1, \omega_1] \wedge \ldots \wedge F_n : [c_n, l_n, u_n, \omega_n]$ iff $R \models F : [c, l, u, \omega_c]$ or $R \not\models F_1 : [c_1, l_1, u_1, \omega_{c_1}] \wedge \ldots \wedge F_n : [c_n, l_n, u_n, \omega_{c_n}]$*

- *R satisfies a tp-program P ($R \models P$) iff R satisfies every clause in P.*

A TP-interpretation is a TP-set that satisfies certain simple axioms. It will turn out that these axioms are exactly "right" from the point of view of making our fixpoint procedure compute the notion of logical consequence associated with tp-programs.

Definition 20 *A TP-set R is called a TP-interpretation iff the following conditions hold:*

- Conjunctive ignorance.
  $(\forall F = A_1 \wedge \ldots \wedge A_k, G = B_1 \wedge \ldots \wedge B_m)(\forall t \in \tau)((F, t, l_1, u_1) \in R \wedge (G, t, l_2, u_2) \in R) \Rightarrow (R \models (F \wedge G) : [t, \max(0, l_1 + l_2 - 1), min(u_1, u_2), \sharp])$

- Disjunctive ignorance.
  $(\forall F = A_1 \vee \ldots \vee A_k, G = B_1 \vee \ldots \vee B_m)(\forall t \in \tau)((F, t, l_1, u_1) \in R \wedge (G, t, l_2, u_2) \in R) \Rightarrow (R \models (F \vee G) : [t, max(l_1, l_2), min(1, u_1 + u_2), \sharp])$

If *nothing is known about the relationship between the events*, then the intervals $[\max(0, l_1 + l_2 - 1), min(u_1, u_2)]$ and $[max(l_1, l_2), min(1, u_1 + u_2)]$ represent the intervals in which the probability of conjunction and disjunction (respectively) of two events with probability intervals $[l_1, u_1]$ and $[l_2, u_2]$ will lie, if *nothing is known about the relationship between the events*.

In order to define a fixpoint operator, we first define an intermediate operator T_P^* which when applied to a TP-interpretation produces a TP-pile. The operator T_P corrects the result of T_P^* to make it a $TP - interpretation$. In the definition of T_P^* we will employ the $\oplus$ notation defined below to "split" a compound event atom.

Definition 21 *Let $F = F_1 * \ldots * F_n$, $G = G_1 * \ldots * G_k$ ($k > 0$), $H = H_1 * \ldots * H_m$ ($m > 0$) where $* \in \{\wedge, \vee\}$. We write $G \oplus H = F$ iff:*
(a) $\{G_1, \ldots, G_k\} \cup \{H_1, \ldots, H_m\} = \{F_1, \ldots, F_n\}$ and
(b) $\{G_1, \ldots, G_k\} \cap \{H_1, \ldots, H_m\} = \emptyset$.

Definition 22 *Let P be a tp-program.*

- *Let $F = A$ be an atom of B_L. Let $t \in \tau$*

$T_P^*(R)(A, t) = \{(A, t, l, u) | (\exists r \in ground(P))$
$(r = A : [c, l', u', \omega_c] \longleftarrow Body; R \models Body;$
$t \in sol(c)$ and $[l, u] = [\omega_c(t) \cdot l', \omega_c(t) \cdot u'])\}$

- *Let $F = A_1 \wedge \ldots \wedge A_k$.*

$T_P^*(R)(F, t) = \{(F, t, l, u) | (\exists H, G)$
$(F \equiv H \oplus G; (H, t, l_1, u_1), (G, t, l_2, u_2) \in R$
and $[l, u] = [\max(0, l_1 + l_2 - 1), \min(u_1, u_2)])\}$

- *Let $F = A_1 \vee \ldots \vee A_k$.*

$T_P^*(R)(F, t) = \{(F, t, l, u) | (\exists H, G)$
$(F \equiv H \oplus G; (H, t, l_1, u_1), (G, t, l_2, u_2) \in R$
and $[l, u] = [\max(l_1, l_2), \min(1, u_1 + u_2)])\}$

We may now extend the definition of T_P^* to map tp-interpretations to tp-interpretations.

Definition 23 *Let P be a tp-program. We define operator T_P as follows: $T_P(R)(F, t) = (F, t, l, u)$, where $[l, u] = \cap\{[l', u'] | (F, t, l', u') \in T_P^*(R)(F, t)\}$.*

In order to describe the fixpoint procedure based on the operators described above, we need to introduce an ordering on TP-interpretations, and prove that T_P operator is monotonic w.r.t. this order.

Definition 24 *Let R and S be two TP-sets. We say that $R \leq S$ **iff** for every F and $t \in \tau$ if $(F, t, l, u) \in R$ and $(F, t, l', u') \in S$ then $[l, u] \supseteq [l', u']$.*

The following statement shows that the set $\mathcal{R}_{B_L}$ of all TP-interpretations for the formulas constructed out of atoms of B_L forms a complete lattice.

Lemma 1 $\langle \mathcal{R}_{B_L}, \leq \rangle$ *is a complete lattice.* [2]

The following result states that out T_P operator is monotonic.

Theorem 1 *Let $R \leq S$ and let P be a TP-program. Then $T_P(R) \leq T_P(S)$.*

The following definition specifies how we might iteratively apply the T_P operator.

Definition 25 *Let P be a tp-program.*

- $T_P^0 = \perp = compl(\emptyset)$

- $T_P^{i+1} = T_P(T_P^i)$

- $T_P^\lambda = \cap_{i \leq \lambda}(T_P^i)$

The following theorem is important. It shows that T_P has a least fixpoint, $lfp(T_P)$, and that this least fixpoint precisely captures the model-theoretic notion of logical consequence associated with tp-programs. Thus, iterative application of the T_P operator yields all ground event atoms that are logical consequences of P.

Theorem 2   *1. $R \models P$ iff $T_P(R) \leq R$*

2. $lfp(T_P) \models P$

3. $(\forall F)(P \models F : [c, l, u, \omega_c]$, where $c = c(y, y_1, \ldots y_k)$ iff
$(\forall \bar{a} \in \tau^k)(sol(c)(\bar{a}) \neq \emptyset) \Rightarrow (\forall t \in sol(c)(\bar{a}))(\exists l_t, u_t)((F, t, l_t, u_t) \in lfp(T_P) \wedge$
$[l_t, u_t] \subseteq [\omega_c(\bar{a}, t) \cdot l, \omega_c(\bar{a}, t) \cdot u])))$.

---

[2] The bottom element of the lattice, representing total lack of knowledge will be the TP-set $\perp = \{(F, t, 0, 1)\}$ for all $t \in \tau$ and all ground event atoms F. The top element of the lattice, representing absolute contradictory knowledge will be the TP-set $\top = \{(F, t, 1, 0)\}$.

4 Fixpoint Computation and Entailment Problem (Ground Case)

In this section, we develop algorithms and associated complexity results for computation of the fixpoint of a ground tp-program, checking its consistency, and query answering. To simplify time bounds, we assume that elementary problems such as checking "$t \in sol(c)$" and computing $\omega_c(\bar{a}, t)$ can be done in constant time[3] , and enumeration of $sol(c)$ can be done in time linear w.r.t. $|sol(c)|$.

For any TP-set (TP-interpretation) R, let $atoms(R) = \{(A, t, l, u) \in R, A$ is a simple event atom\}. Let P be a ground tp-program over the set of ground simple event atoms $\{A_1, ..., A_N\}$ and the calendar $\tau = [0, t_{\max}]$. Let us denote $lfp(T_P)$ by R_P. The following lemma shows that R_P can be easily defined by $atoms(R_P)$.

Lemma 2 *For all $t \in \tau$ and all ground compound event atoms F*

- *if $F = A_1 \wedge ... \wedge A_k$ and for each $1 \le i \le k$ $(A_i, t, l_i, u_i) \in atoms(R_P)$ then $(F, t, l, u) \in R_P$, for $l = l_1 + ... + l_k + 1 - k$ and $u = \min\{u_1, ..., u_k\}$;*

- *if $F = A_1 \vee ... \vee A_k$. and for each $1 \le i \le k$ $(A_i, t, l_i, u_i) \in atoms(R_P)$ then $(F, t, l, u) \in R_P$, for $l = \max\{l_1, ..., l_k\}$ and $u = \min\{1, u_1 + ... + u_k\}$.*

This lemma allows to propose an efficient algorithm to construct $atoms(R_P)$ for the ground case. This algorithm will also check the consistency of tp-programs. Let P be a ground tp-program over the set $B_L = \{A_1, ..., A_N\}$ and let $\{F_1, ..., F_s\}$ be the set of all compound event atoms included in clauses of P. **Algorithm LFP-atoms.**
Input: a ground tp-program P.
Output: $atoms(R_P)$.
BEGIN (algorithm)
1. $OLD := \emptyset$; $NEW := \emptyset$;
2. FOR $i = 1$ TO N DO
   FOR EACH $t \in \tau$ DO
   $NEW := NEW \cup \{(A_i, t, 0, 1)\}$;
3. FOR $j = 1$ TO s DO
   FOR EACH $t \in \tau$ DO
   $NEW := NEW \cup \{(F_j, t, 0, 1)\}$;
4. WHILE $OLD \ne NEW$ DO
   BEGIN
   $OLD := NEW$;
   5. FOR EACH $r = A : [c, l, u, \omega_c] \leftarrow Body \in P$ such that $OLD \models Body$ DO
      6. FOR EACH $t \in sol(c)$ DO
      BEGIN
      LET $(A, t, l', u') \in NEW$;
      $l_1 := \max(l', \omega_c(t) * l)$;
      $u_1 := \min(u', \omega_c(t) * u)$;
      IF $u_1 < l_1$ THEN RETURN $\emptyset$;
      $NEW := (NEW \setminus \{(A, t, l, u)\}) \cup \{(A, t, l_1, u_1)\}$;
      $P := P \setminus \{r\}$
      END;

---

[3]We do this to make our complexity results independent of issues such as the implementation of the ω_c functions. We can then factor the complexity of computing $\omega(\bar{a}, t)$ back into our complexity estimate if needed. It should be noted that for ground programs, on which we are concentrating in this section the assumption that $\omega_c(t)$ can be computed in constant time quite reasonable.

7. FOR $j = 1$ TO s DO
8. FOR EACH $t \in \tau$ DO
   BEGIN
   LET $F_j = B_1^j * \ldots * B_k^j$ AND FOR EACH $1 \leq p \leq k$ $(B_p^j, t, l_p^j, u_p^j) \in NEW$
   IF $* = \wedge$ THEN BEGIN
      $l := l_1^j + \ldots + l_k^j + 1 - k;$ $u := \min\{u_1^j, \ldots, u_k^j\}$ END
   ELSE BEGIN $\{* = \vee\}$
      $l := \max\{l_1^j, \ldots, l_k^j\};$ $u := \min\{1, u_1^j + \ldots + u_k^j\}$ END;
   $NEW := (NEW \setminus \{(F_j, t, \_, \_)\}) \cup \{(F_j, t, l, u)\}$
   END;
   END;
9. RETURN $atoms(NEW)$
END.

The following theorem shows that algorithm **LFP-atoms** is a correct way of checking P for inconsistency and (if P is consistent) of computing the least fixpoint of T_P for simple event atoms. It also establishes the polynomial time complexity of the algorithm. The proof of this result uses lemma 2.

Theorem 3 *Let P be any ground tp-program and let P contain m clauses. Let $|P|$ be the size of P (under some standard encoding). Then **Algorithm LFP-atoms** returns $\emptyset$ iff P is inconsistent. If P is consistent then it computes $atoms(R_P)$ in time $O(m \cdot |P| \cdot t_{max})$.*

Now we consider the entailment problem: given a tp-program P and a ground query G, check whether $P \models G$. Our queries will be conjunctions of annotated basic formulas of the form $F : [c, l, u, \omega_c]$ where F is ground. One way to answer such queries is to add F to the list of compound events $\{F_1, \ldots, F_s\}$ of P, run algorithm **LFP-atoms**, and after it terminates check the values (F, t, l, u) for all $t \in sol(c)$. A better way, however, is to use a preprocessing step on which algorithm **LFP-atoms** is run once to obtain $atoms(R_P)$, and then to answer to queries using the following simple algorithm.
    Algorithm Simple query.
Input: set $atoms(R_P)$ and a simple query $F : [c, l, u, \omega_c]$.
Output: "YES" if $P \models F : [c, l, u, \omega_c]$, otherwise "NO".
BEGIN (algorithm)
   LET $F = B_1 * \ldots * B_k$
   FOR EACH $t \in sol(c)$ DO
   BEGIN   LET FOR EACH $1 \leq p \leq k$ $(B_p, t, l_p, u_p) \in atoms(R_P)$;
      IF $* = \wedge$ THEN BEGIN
        $L := l_1 + \ldots + l_k + 1 - k;$ $U := \min\{u_1, \ldots, u_k\}$ END
      ELSE BEGIN $\{* = \vee\}$
        $L := \max\{l_1, \ldots, l_k\};$ $U := \min\{1, u_1 + \ldots + u_k\}$ END;
      IF $(L < l * \omega_c(t))$ OR $(U > u * \omega_c(t))$
      THEN RETURN "NO"
   END
   RETURN "YES"
END.

The following theorem shows that after polynomial time preprocessing, the entailment problem can be solved in linear time.

Theorem 4 *(1) Algorithm **Simple query** gives a correct answer to any simple query of the form $F : [c, l, u, \omega_c]$ in time $O(|F| + |sol(c)|)$.*

119

(2) There exists an algorithm which given the set atoms(R_P) answers to any query G of the form $F_1 : [c_1, l_1, u_1, \omega_1] \wedge ... \wedge F_n[c_n, l_n, u_n, \omega_n]$ in time linear of $(|G| + \sum_{i=1}^{n} |sol(c_i)|)$.

5 Proof Procedure

Below we present a basic proof procedure for temporal probabilistic programs. It is quite inefficient, because it requires the resolution to be always performed for the event atoms annotated by single timepoints, which means that more complex temporal constraints are forcefully "broken down". Nevertheless, this procedure is quite easy to understand and serves as a starting point for a more efficient and sophiscitated proof procedure which had also been developed. Unfortunately, the space limitaions disallow us to include the second proof procedure here.

5.1 Unification

If $*$ is either $\wedge$ or $\vee$, then we say that two event atoms $A_1*...*A_k$ and $B_1*...*B_m$ are unifiable iff there is a substitution θ such that $\{A_1\theta, ..., A_k\theta\} = \{B_1\theta, ..., B_m\theta\}$. This notion of unification was introduced in [23] and it was proved that though most general unifiers are not necessarily unique, a corresponding notion of a *maximally general unifier* (max-gu) exists. For space reasons, we do not go into details of this here.

5.2 A Basic (Inefficient) Proof Procedure

In this section, we describe how we can expand a tp-program P into a program called its *closure*. This closure may then be used to define a resolution based proof procedure.

Definition 26 (Explosions) *Let $F : [c, l, u, \omega_c]$ be a ground formula. The explosion of $F : [c, l, u, \omega_c]$, denoted $\mathcal{E}(F : [c, l, u, \omega_c])$, is defined as $\{F : [t, \omega_c(t) \cdot l, \omega_c(t) \cdot u, \sharp]|t \in sol(c)\}$. The exploded basic formula for $F : [c, l, u, \omega_c]$, denoted $\mathcal{E}_\mathcal{F}(F : [c, l, u, \omega_c])$, is $\bigwedge_{t \in sol(c)} F : [t, \omega_c(t) \cdot l, \omega_c(t) \cdot u, \sharp]$.*
Let $r = F : [c, l, u, \omega_c] \longleftarrow Body$ be a tp-clause. Then the explosion of r, denoted $\mathcal{E}(r)$, is defined as $\{F : [t, \omega_c(c, t) \cdot l, \omega_c(c, t) \cdot u, \sharp] \longleftarrow Body|t \in sol(c)\}$.
If P is a tp-program, then the explosion of P, denoted $\mathcal{E}(P)$, is defined as $\{\mathcal{E}(r)|r \in P\}$

The explosion operation explicitly enumerates the probabilities of an event at all time points associated with a constraint. (As this set of time points can potentially be very large, we use the term explosion to describe this operation). Using this, we can now define the timepoint-based closure of program P.

Definition 27 (Timepoint-based Closure) *Let P be a tp-program.*
•$REDUN(P) = \mathcal{E}(P) \cup \{F : [t, 0, 1, \sharp] \longleftarrow |F \in B_L; t \in \tau\}$
• *We define the closure of P (denoted $TCL(P)$) iteratively:*

1. *$TCL^0(P) = REDUN(P)$*

2. *To construct $TCL^{i+1}(P)$ given $TCL^i(P)$ apply the following rules to all possible pairs of elements of $TCL^i(P)$:*

- Clarification rule:

If clauses $F : [t, l, u, \sharp] \longleftarrow Body$ *and* $F' : [t, l', u', \sharp] \longleftarrow Body'$ *are in* $TCL^i(P)$ *and* F *and* F' *are unifiable via max-gu* Θ, *add the clause* $(F : [t, \max(l, l'), \min(u, u'), \sharp] \longleftarrow Body \wedge Body')\Theta$ *to* $TCL^{i+1}(P)$.

- $\wedge$-composition rule:

If clauses $F : [t, l, u, \sharp] \longleftarrow Body$ *and* $F' : [t, l', u', \sharp] \longleftarrow Body'$ *are in* $TCL^i(P)$, $F = A_1 \wedge \ldots \wedge A_k$ *and* $G = B_1 \wedge \ldots \wedge B_m$ $(k, m \geq 1)$, *add the clause* $(F \wedge G) : [t, \max(0, l + l' - 1), \min(u, u'), \sharp] \longleftarrow Body \wedge Body'$ *to* $TCL^{i+1}(P)$.

- $\vee$-composition rule:

If clauses $F : [t, l, u, \sharp] \longleftarrow Body$ *and* $F' : [t, l', u', \sharp] \longleftarrow Body'$ *are in* $TCL^i(P)$, $F = A_1 \vee \ldots \vee A_k$ *and* $G = B_1 \vee \ldots \vee B_m$ $(k, m \geq 1)$, *add the clause* $(F \vee G) : [t, \max(l, l'), \min(u + u', 1), \sharp] \longleftarrow Body \wedge Body'$ *to* $TCL^{i+1}(P)$.

3. $TCL(P) = \cup_{i \geq 0} TCL^i(P)$.

Lemma 3 *For every clause* $r \in TCL(P)$, $P \models r$.

Note that the syntax of $TCL(P)$ is somewhat different from the syntax of P, as we allow the rules in $TCL(P)$ to have non-atomic heads. However this extension is supported by our definitions of satisfaction on TP-models (def. 17) and TP-sets (def. 19). We are now ready to proceed with the resolution procedure.

Definition 28 *A tp-query is an expression of the form* $\exists(H_1 : [c_1, l_1, u_1] \wedge \ldots \wedge H_n : [c_n, l_n, u_n])$. *The* explosion *of a tp-query* Q, *denoted* $\mathcal{E}_{\mathcal{F}}(Q)$ *is an expression of the form:* $\bigwedge_{i=1}^{n} \mathcal{E}_{\mathcal{F}}(H_i : [c, l_i, u_i, \omega_c])$

In other words, the explosion of a tp-query is a conjunction of the explosions of all basic formulas in the query.

Definition 29 *Let* Q *be a query and let* $\mathcal{E}_{\mathcal{F}}(Q) = F_1 : [t_1, l_1, u_1, \sharp] \wedge \ldots F_n : [t_n, l_n, u_n, \sharp]$. *Let* $r \equiv G : [t, l, u, \sharp] \longleftarrow G_1 : \mu_1 \wedge \ldots G_k : \mu_k \in TCL(P)$ *and* G *be unifiable with* F_i *via max-gu* Θ. *Then*

$$\exists((F_1 : [t_1, l_1, u_1, \sharp] \wedge \ldots \wedge F_{i-1} : [t_{i-1}, l_{i-1}, u_{i-1}, \sharp] \wedge \mathcal{E}_{\mathcal{F}}(G_1 : \mu_k) \wedge \ldots \wedge \mathcal{E}_{\mathcal{F}}(G_k : \mu_k) \wedge$$

$$F_{i+1} : [t_{i+1}, l_{i+1}, u_{i+1}, \sharp] \wedge \ldots \wedge F_n : [t_n, l_n, u_n, \sharp])\Theta)$$

is a tp-resolvent of r *and* Q *iff* $[l, u] \subseteq [l_i, u_i]$.

Definition 30 *Let* $Q \equiv \exists(F_1 : \mu_1 \wedge \ldots \wedge F_n : \mu_n)$ *be an initial query, and* P *a tp-program. A* tp-deduction *of* Q *from* P *is a sequence* $< Q_1, r_1, \Theta_1 > \ldots < Q_s, r_s, \Theta_s > \ldots$ *where,* $Q_1 = \mathcal{E}_{\mathcal{F}}(Q)$, *for all* $i \geq 1$, r_i *is a renamed version of a clause in* $TCL(P)$, *and* Q_{i+1} *is a tp-resolvent of* Q_i *and* r_i *via max-gu* Θ_i. *A* tp-refutation *of* Q *from* P *is a finite tp-deduction* $< Q_1, r_1, \Theta_1 > \ldots < Q_s, r_s, \Theta_s >$ *where, the tp-resolvent of* Q_s *and* r_s *via* Θ_s *is the empty query.* $\Theta_1 \ldots \Theta_r$ *is called the* computed answer substitution.

The following theorem states that our first proof procedure is sound and complete.

Theorem 5 *[Soundness/Completeness of tp-refutation]*
1. Let P be a tp-program, and Q be an initial query. If there exists a tp-refutation of $Q \equiv \exists (F_1 : \mu_1 \wedge \ldots \wedge F_n : \mu_n)$ from P with the answer substitution Θ then $P \models \forall ((F_1 : \mu_1 \wedge \ldots \wedge F_n : \mu_n)\Theta)$.
2. Let P be a consistent tp-program and Q be a query. Then, if $P \models Q$ then there exists a tp-refutation of Q' from P.

6 Related Work

To date, there has been no work on temporal probabilistic logic programming that we are aware of — hence, we compare our work with work on probabilistic logic programming, and with logics of probability and time.

In addition to the authors' works, probabilistic logic programs were studied by Thone *et al.*[25], and Lakshmanan [17] who showed how different probabilistic dependencies can be encoded into logic programs. Kiessling's group [14, 25] and Lukasiewicz [21] made important contributions to bottom up computations of logic programs. The work reported in this paper may be viewed as an extension of the above works (as well as [23, 24, 2, 4]) to handle temporal-probabilistic information. In addition to the model theory, we have developed both bottom up fixpoint computation algorithms and alternative proof procedures for TPLPs.

Lehmann and Shelah [19] and Hart and Sharir [11] were among the first to integrate time and probability. Kanazawa also studied the integration of probability and time with a view to developing efficient planning algorithms [12]. Their main interest is in how probabilities of facts and events change over time., Haddawy [10] develops a logic for reasoning about actions, probabilities, and time using an interval time model. Our framework is different from theirs in that (i) we allow arbitrary distributions in our syntax, (ii) we provide a fixpoint theory, (iii) we provide and manipulate constraint based representations of time, and (iv) we provide constraint based proof procedures and complexity results for the "Horn clause like" fragment of this logic.

Dubois and his colleagues [5] have studied the integration of uncertainty and time – they extend the well-known possibilistic logic theory to a "timed possibilistic logic." This logic associates, with each formula of possibilistic logic, a set of time points reflecting the times at which the formula has a given possibilistic truth value. However, this framework is not probabilistic.

Last but not least, our use of possible worlds models was inspired by the work of Fagin and Halpern ([7],[9]), in which similar in spirit models had been introduced for probabilistic nontemporal logics.

7 Conclusions

In this paper, we have defined temporal probabilistic (tp-) logic programs that allow us to reason about instantaneous events in a probabilistic environment, We have provided a formal syntax and model theory for tp-programs, developed a fixpoint theory that is equivalent to the model theory and developed sound and complete bottom up computation procedures for entailment. We also developed a sound and complete proof procedure for tp-programs which supports a resolution based query processing for tp-programs.

Acknowledgments

The work of the second author had been partially supported by Russian Fundamental Studies Foundation (Grants 97-01-00973). The other authors were supported by the Army Research Office under Grants DAAH-04-95-10174, DAAH-04-96-10297, and DAAH04-96-1-0398, by the Army Research Laboratory under contract number DAAL01-97-K0135, by an NSF Young Investigator award IRI-93-57756, and by a TASC/DARPA grant J09301S98061.

References

[1] M. Baudinet. (1992)*A Simple Proof Of The Completeness Of Temporal Logic Programming*, in Intensional Logics and Programming (eds. L.G. del Cerro, M. Pentonen), pp 51-83, Clarendon Press, 1992.

[2] A. Dekhtyar and V.S. Subrahmanian. (1998) *Hybrid Probabilistic Logic Programs*, accepted to Journal of Logic Programming, Feb. 1999. Early version in Proc. 1997 Intl. Conf. on Logic Programming (ed. L. Naish), MIT Press.

[3] A. Dekhtyar, R.Ross and V.S. Subrahmanian. (1998) *Probabilistic Temporal Databases, I: Algebra*, available as University of Maryland tech report CS-TR-3987

[4] M. Dekhtyar, A. Dekhtyar and V.S. Subrahmanian. (1998) *Hybrid Probabilistic Programs: Algorithms and Complexity*, accepted to Uncertainty in AI'99, extended version available as University of Maryland tech. report CS-TR-3969.

[5] D. Dubois, J. Lang and H. Prade. (1991) *Timed Possibilistic Logic*, Fundamenta Informaticae, XV, pps 211–234.

[6] C. Dyreson and R. Snodgrass. (1998) *Supporting Valid-Time Indeterminacy*, ACM Transactions on Database Systems, Vol. 23, Nr. 1, pps 1—57.

[7] R Fagin, J.Halpern, Uncertainty, belief, and probability, Computational Intelligence 7, 1991, pp. 160-173

[8] R. Fagin,J. Halpern, N. Megiddo, A logic for reasoning about probabilities, Information and Computation 87:1,2, 1990, pp. 78-128

[9] R. Fagin, J. Halpern, Reasoning about knowledge and probability, Journal of the ACM 41:2, 1994, pp. 340-367

[10] P. Haddawy. (1991) *Representing Plans under Uncertainty: A Logic of Time, Chance and Action*, Ph.D. Thesis. Available as University of Illinois Tech. Report UIUCDCS-R-91-1719.

[11] S. Hart and M. Sharir. (1986) *Probabilistic propositional temporal logic*, Information and Control, 70:97–155.

[12] K. Kanazawa. (1991) *A Logic and Time Nets for Probabilistic Inference*, AAAI-91, pps 360–365.

[13] S. Kraus and D. Lehmann. (1988) *Knowledge, Belief and Time*, Theoretical Computer Science 58, pp 155-174.

[14] W. Kiessling, H. Thone and U. Guntzer. (1992) *Database Support for Problematic Knowledge*, Proc. EDBT-92, pps 421–436, Springer LNCS Vol. 580.

[15] V.S. Lakshmanan, N. Leone, R. Ross and V.S. Subrahmanian. ProbView: A Flexible Probabilistic Database System. ACM TRANSACTIONS ON DATABASE SYSTEMS, Vol. 22, Nr. 3, pps 419–469, Sep. 1997.

[16] V.S. Lakshmanan and F. Sadri. (1994) *Modeling Uncertainty in Deductive Databases*, Proc. Int. Conf. on Database Expert Systems and Applications, (DEXA'94), September 7-9, 1994, Athens, Greece, Lecture Notes in Computer Science, Vol. 856, Springer (1994), pp. 724-733.

[17] V.S. Lakshmanan and F. Sadri. (1994) *Probabilistic Deductive Databases*, Proc. Int. Logic Programming Symp., (ILPS'94), November 1994, Ithaca, NY, MIT Press.

[18] V.S. Lakshmanan and N. Shiri. (1997) *A Parametric Approach with Deductive Databases with Uncertainty*, accepted for publication in IEEE Transactions on Knowledge and Data Engineering.

[19] D. Lehmann and S. Shelah. (1982) *Reasoning about Time and Chance*, Information and Control, 53, pps 165–198.

[20] T. Lukasiewicz. (1998) *Probabilistic Logic Programming*, in Procs. 13th biennial European Conference on Artificial Intelligence, pps 388-392, Brighton, UK, August 1998.

[21] T. Lukasiewicz. (1998) *Magic Inference Rules for Probabilistic Deduction under Taxonomic Knowledge*, Proceedings of the 14th Conference on Uncertainty in Artificial Intelligence, pps 354-361, Madison, Wisconsin, USA, July 1998.

[22] J.W. Lloyd. (1987) *Foundations of Logic Programming*, Springer.

[23] R. Ng and V.S. Subrahmanian. (1993) Probabilistic Logic Programming, INFORMATION AND COMPUTATION, 101, 2, pps 150–201, 1993.

[24] R. Ng and V.S. Subrahmanian.(1993) A Semantical Framework for Supporting Subjective and Conditional Probabilities in Deductive Databases, JOURNAL OF AUTOMATED REASONING, 10, 2, pps 191–235, 1993.

[25] H. Thone, W. Kiessling and U. Guntzer. (1995) *On Cautious Probabilistic Inference and Default Detachment*, Annals of Operations Research, 55, pps 195–224.

An Optimized Prolog Encoding of Typed Feature Structures

Gerald Penn
SFB 340
Kl. Wilhelmstr. 113
72074 Tübingen, Germany
gpenn@sfs.nphil.uni-tuebingen.de

Abstract

A new Prolog-term-encoding of typed feature structures, a data structure commonly used for natural language processing, is presented that, in many significant cases, allows for faster unification in Prolog implementations of feature-structure-based natural language processing systems, e.g., ALE ([5]). It remains general enough, however, to handle the full range of signatures characterized in [3], a common reference on typed feature logics for computational linguistics, and HPSG ([19]), a common linguistic theory based on typed feature structures. A logical and empirical comparison is drawn with several alternative encodings.

1   Introduction: Typed Feature Structures

Typed feature structures (TFSs, [3]) are like the record structures found in many programming languages, or the "frames" that are used in artificial intelligence. They are collections of pairs of attributes and values along with a semantic type, that characterize or classify an object for the purposes of some computation. Feature structures of many varieties have enjoyed a wide use in linguistics over the past 30 years, and at every level of linguistic reasoning (syntax, phonology, etc.). The main reasons for their popularity are: (1) their support for named reference of attributes, in contrast to the exclusively positional reference provided by Prolog terms and (2) the inclusional polymorphism provided by their type system. The former allows for terse descriptions of very large structures; and the latter provides an additional means of classifying the kinds of (linguistic) knowledge represented by those structures.

When programming with TFSs, one must define the types and features available to structures ahead of time by specifying a *type signature*, consisting of a partial order of types (*type hierarchy*) and a set of *appropriateness conditions* that constrains features to take values on all and only feature structures of particular "appropriate" types, and only values that are themselves of a certain type (*value restrictions*). A sample type signature is shown

125

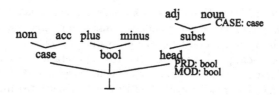

Figure 1: A sample type signature.

in Figure 1.[1] All feature structures of type *head* must have values for all and only the features PREDICATIVE (PRD) and MODIFIER (MOD), with values of at least type *bool(ean)*. Subtypes *inherit* their supertypes' appropriate features, so that *noun* also has PRD and MOD values, in addition to a value for CASE. The feature logic of [3] is, in fact, distinguished from other feature logics by its very strict interpretation of appropriateness conditions. This strict interpretation allows for more efficient processing with TFSs because, for every type, the exact set of these appropriate features that can and must occur with feature structures of that type can be computed at compile-time. TFSs can, in fact, be viewed as a conservative extension of Prolog terms in which, for any single type, the feature structures of that type have a fixed arity; but the arity of a feature structure can be augmented as its type promotes to a more specific subtype. Such is the case for a *subst*-typed FS that promotes to *noun*, thereby acquiring a value for CASE, restricted to at least *case*.

Appropriateness is related, although not identical to the use of arity constraints in the LIFE/Half-Life and Oz systems ([1, 18, 22]). Crucially, feature-based linguistic theories, notably Head-driven Phrase Structure Grammar (HPSG, [19]), either explicitly or implicitly observe the constrained arity property embodied in appropriateness conditions, whereas their restricted use of features cannot be encoded by LIFE/Oz-style arity constraints without substantial rewriting of the type signatures involved.

Appropriateness also allows us to encode typed feature structures as Prolog terms efficiently. Arity augmentation and subtyping are the two major sources of complexity when encoding TFSs as Prolog terms. This paper presents a collection of methods to address both sources by reducing the former to a graph coloring problem, and by presenting for the latter what is, to the author's knowledge, the first algorithm for finding an optimal flat first-order-term encoding of any finite meet semi-lattice of types, and an approximate solution that can be derived in cubic time in the number of types from a transitively closed adjacency representation of the semi-lattice. An empirical comparison of these to previous work as well as other encodings that are available using the extra functionality provided by the library(atts) library of SICStus Prolog is also presented.

---

[1]In keeping with the choice of notation in [3], ⊥ will stand for the most general type, and supertypes are depicted below their subtypes. In that setting, the unification of two types corresponds to their join, where it exists, and is undefined otherwise.

The value of Prolog encoding stems from the value of using Prolog itself. Most systems based on TFSs rely on a few standard means of search in order to solve problems in natural language processing — some subset of Prolog-like SLD resolution, parsing and content-driven generation. All of these have been extensively researched within Prolog; and, in the case of SLD resolution, current commercial implementations of Prolog have benefited from a 15 year history of optimizations to WAM compilation technology. There have been a few abstract machines proposed directly for TFSs, e.g., [6], implemented as described in [14], and [23]; but these inevitably rely on a recapitulation of that history for their own optimization. With the arguable exception of the unification operation itself, any additional innovations made in the course of their development are probably better applied to WAM optimization itself, given the nearly identical requirements of the two communities and research programs. The approach to arity augmentation presented here, however, would be equally useful to custom-abstract-machine-based approaches; and the present approach to subtyping essentially brings Prolog-based implementations in line with the bit-vector encodings for type unification used in many abstract machines stemming from the influential paper ([2]) on that subject.

2 Subtyping

In this section, we consider type signatures without features — just type hierarchies. Carpenter ([3]) requires type hierarchies to be finite meet semi-lattices. When two TFSs are unified, their types must unify. In a finite meet semi-lattice, every consistent pair of types, t_1, t_2 has a unique join, $t_1 \sqcup t_2$, which corresponds to type unification.

Here, we take a "Prolog encoding" to mean one in which the only operation necessary for FS unification at run-time is Prolog unification of the corresponding terms. That excludes other "Prolog representations," such as the representation of feature structures in ALE, a logic programming language based on TFSs, which requires a dereferencing operation and table look-up at run-time ([4]), as well as the representation given in [12], which because of its slightly different interpretation of appropriateness conditions, requires the maintenance of extra constraints on the side in the worst case. The actual construction of any Prolog encoding can be performed at compile-time.

2.1 Previous Work: Tree Encodings

The first work to consider Prolog encodings of arbitrary meet semi-lattices was presented in [16], although no general encoding algorithm was presented. Previous work, dating back to [7], concerned a restricted subset of semi-lattices that admit a Prolog *tree encoding*, i.e., an encoding by terms in which no variable is used more than once. These and other logical-term-encoding approaches are systematically presented in [11].

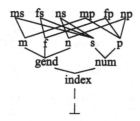

Figure 2: A type hierarchy with full-product multiple inheritance.

[16] was also the first to characterize the general encoding problem for-mally: the search for a function from a type hierarchy to a set (of Prolog terms) that is:

1. injective, i.e., no term encodes more than one type,

2. homomorphic with respect to unification, i.e., unification in the encod-ing corresponds to unification in the type hierarchy, and

3. zero preserving, i.e., failure of unification in the type hierarchy corre-sponds to failure of unification in the encoding.

What is now regarded as the most efficient tree-encoding algorithm was first presented in [15] as a general encoding algorithm for systemic networks. All systemic networks are tree-encodable because the "multiple inheritance" that they effectively provide is always a full product of two or more sub-networks. The ProFIT system ([8, 9, 10]), another TFS-based system, first adapted this encoding to a subset of type hierarchies expressed in a more traditional ISA-link form. The ALEP system ([21]) used essentially the same encoding for its TFS-like records.

Mellish's encoding ([15]) exploits the restricted inheritance provided by systemic networks to represent a type with a term that, using subterms, represents the path(s) taken to reach that type from the root. In Figure 1, the representation of *head* would be head(_); that of *subst*, head(subst(_)); and that of *noun*, head(subst(noun)). The noun subterm does not require a variable argument because *noun* is maximally specific.[2]

To represent multiple inheritance, the tree-based encoding uses multiple argument positions to represent the different paths that lead to a single type. In Figure 2, any pair of *gend* and *num* subtypes can intersect. So *index*'s term contains two argument positions, one for *gend* and one for *num*. The representations of *gend*, *s* and *ms* are index(gend(_),_), index(_,num(s)) and index(gend(m),num(s)), respectively.

Tree-based encoding does not work for arbitrary finite meet semi-lattices, as proven in [16, 17]. Figure 3, for example, represents a simple classification

---

[2]In practice, an extra variable argument is necessary to distinguish feature values that are variants from feature values that are extensionally identical, because the logic of typed feature structures is intensional. These are systematically ignored here.

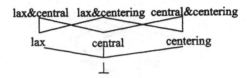

Figure 3: A type hierarchy with no tree encoding.

of vowels, taken from [13] (and cited in [16]). There are vowels that have any pair of the three properties, *lax*, *central* and *centering*; but there are no vowels that have all three at once. This has no tree encoding because separate argument positions for *lax*, *central* and *centering* would entail the consistency of *lax* with *central&centering*, for example.

ProFIT dealt with this limitation simply by restricting its type hierarchies to exclude all counter-examples. Specifically, it allowed for two kinds of declarations:

$Super > [Sub_1, Sub_2, \ldots, Sub_n]$.

$Super > [Sub_{1,1}, \ldots, Sub_{1,n_1}] * \ldots * [Sub_{m,1}, \ldots, Sub_{m,n_m}]$.

The first implicitly declares $Sub_1, \ldots, Sub_n$ to be mutually exclusive, i.e., no multiple inheritance. The second declares *multi-dimensional inheritance*, essentially restricting multiple inheritance to the full products of types in different dimensions attainable in systemic networks. All possible combinations of dimensions must be possible in such hierarchies, so again, Figure 3 cannot occur. We could declare the subhierarchy rooted at *index* in Figure 2 as:

$index > [gend] * [num]$.

$gend > [m, f, n]$.

$num > [s, p]$.

The maximally specific types, *ms,fs* etc., are implicitly encoded by the intersection of their *gend* and *num* subtypes.

2.2   Flat-Term Encoding

The present work attempts to improve on tree encodings in terms of both coverage and speed. With regard to coverage, the methods presented here both work for arbitrary finite meet semi-lattices. With regard to speed, they are both *flat-term encodings*, i.e., a term whose substructures are all reachable from the root by a path of length at most 1. Because first-order terms are of fixed arities, unification of a variable with a flat term can be compiled into a primitive recursive loop that compilers can unwind off-line. Unification of nested compound terms, however, typically involves some amount of pointer chasing on the heap before the actual addresses can be passed to the unifier.

Thus, with all other things being equal, "broader beats deeper," i.e., two flat terms with n arguments can be unified more quickly than two terms of

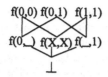

$$f(0,0) \quad f(0,1) \quad f(1,1)$$

$$f(0,\_) \quad f(X,X) \quad f(\_,1)$$

$$\bot$$

Figure 4: A flat-term encoding of Figure 3.

arity one, with subterms nested n levels deep. A tree encoding of a type hierarchy has terms whose depths are bounded by the maximum length of any subtype chain in the hierarchy, although with (limited) multiple or multi-dimensional inheritance, more than one path of that depth may be created; and in the case of true multiple inheritance (in the cases where the encoding works), some duplication of structure may be necessary at the ends of the paths. Flat-term encodings do not require redundant structure, but, in the *best* case, have arities equal to the length of the maximum subtype chain in the hierarchy — multiple inheritance can force it to be wider. In cases where both are applicable, it is an empirical question as to whether the speed-up from flatness outweighs the fact that very general types in a tree encoding have smaller term sizes.

Mellish ([16, 17]) proved (non-constructively) that while not all finite meet semi-lattices admit tree encodings, they do all admit flat-term encodings. While this encoding can instantiate arguments only to constants, it can also use individual variables in more than one argument position. A flat-term encoding of Figure 3 is given in Figure 4.

Mellish also showed ([15]) that what is now known as *Colmerauer's method* can be used to encode systemic networks using flat terms of arity $n+1$, where n is the number of possible property assignments allowed for by the network. The first argument is always 0, the last argument is always 1, and every assignment is assigned a pair of arguments in between. Every description that excludes an assignment numbered i is represented by a term whose ith and $i+1$st arguments are bound to a common term. If there are 5 possible assignments, then we use a term of arity 6 as follows ([15]):

```
            1       2       3       4       5
            |       |       |       |       |
f(0,        -,      -,      X,      X,      1)   (excludes assignment 4)
f(0,        0,      -,      X,      X,      1)   (excludes 1 and 4)
f(0,        X,      X,      X,      1,      1)   (excludes 2, 3, and 5)
```

The number of possible assignments is, in the worst case, exponential in the number of properties in the systemic network; so this method is not practical for encoding systemic networks, because it can yield terms with exponentially large arities.

Fall ([11, p. 94]) observed that Colmerauer's method could be used for unification-preserving encodings of arbitrary ordered sets, but mistakenly assumed that the method yielded exponential-sized terms for that task as well. It is exponential for systemic networks because systemic networks can, in some cases, provide exponentially compact encodings of possible assignments. For the case of an enumerated set of assignments, the method yields linear-sized terms. Colmerauer, in fact, had originally used his method for computing arbitrary set intersections. ProFIT used this encoding in the same spirit for finite domains, i.e., flat type hierarchies with no appropriate features. We now consider a method that makes optimal use of Colmerauer's method with meet semi-lattices, a subcase of ordered sets.

2.2.1   Method 1: Colmerauer's method for meet semi-lattices

The first observation we can make is that meet semi-lattices can be decomposed into *modules*, pieces whose types can never unify:

Definition 1 *Given a type hierarchy, $\langle T, \sqsubseteq \rangle$, the set of modules of $\langle T, \sqsubseteq \rangle$ is the finest partition of $T - \{\bot\}$, $M_1, \ldots M_m$, such that:*

1. *each M_i is upward-closed (w.r.t subsumption), and*

2. *if t_i and t_j are unifiable, then they belong to the same module*

Figure 1, for example, has three modules, one each rooted at *case*, *bool*, and *head*. In general, a module might not have a unique least type. Figure 3 has one module, for example. Modularizing in this fashion can be performed as the first step to any encoding strategy, because the modules can be encoded separately. The definition of module above can be generalized in order to develop hybrid tree-based / flat-term-based encodings as well, although for brevity, this will not be considered further here. Without loss of generality, we can now consider only type hierarchies that have one module with no least type. As in a tree encoding, $\bot$ can be represented by a Prolog variable; and if there is a least type in a module, then it can be represented by a term with a unique variable in every argument, i.e., the most general term of that functor and arity.

Definition 2 *Given a type hierarchy, $\langle T, \sqsubseteq \rangle$, a type, $t \in T$, is meet reducible iff there are distinct types $u, v \in T$ not equal to t such that the meet of u and v, $u \sqcap v = t$ (and dually for join reducible types). The meet irreducible types of T are all types in T except the meet reducible types.*

Proposition 1 *The meet irreducible types of a type hierarchy are precisely the maximally specific types and the types with one immediate subtype.*

Proposition 2 *Every type hierarchy has a flat-term encoding with an arity equal to the number of meet irreducible types plus 1.*
Proof: Use Colmerauer's method on the set of meet irreducible types. Every type in the meet semi-lattice can be represented by the set of meet irreducible types that it subsumes. Maximally specific types only unify with

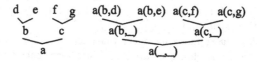

Figure 5: A binary tree and its optimal flat-term encoding.

themselves. All other types can then be characterized by the maximally specific types that they subsume except the types with one immediate subtype, which would be characterized by the same maximally specific subtypes as that immediate subtype. Those types are meet irreducible as well, however, and so are distinguished by their own occurrence in the representation.

One of the algorithms in [2] achieves essentially the same encoding, but for bit vectors. Finding the set of meet irreducible types takes at most cubic time — the time it takes to test all u and v for meets given a transitively closed adjacency representation of subsumption.

This method yields an optimal encoding in the sense that no encoding that uses Colmerauer's method can result in terms with a smaller arity than the number of meet irreducible types plus 1 ([11]). Arity is the relevant measure since extra argument constants in the encoding come comparatively cheaply, and multiple occurrences of individual variables does not make unification slower. In general, however, this method does not yield an optimal flat-term encoding overall. Figure 5 shows a binary tree module, which has no join reducible types. No binary trees have types with only one immediate subtype, so the number of meet irreducible elements is the number of maximally specific types, or half the total number of types. It can be proven, however, that the flat-term encoding of smallest arity for a binary tree, in fact for any module without join reducible types, is equal to the length of its longest subtype chain, which for binary trees, is equal to the logarithm of the total number of types. That encoding is shown in Figure 5.

What is the smallest arity required for arbitrary meet semi-lattices?

2.2.2 Method 2: Parametrized Search for an Optimal Encoding

A flat-term encoding is characterized by a choice of functor for the term (which is irrelevant, provided every module has one unique functor), a choice of arity of the term, and a choice of constants to instantiate some of the arguments of the term.

The set of first-order terms can be characterized as a meet semi-lattice in its own right, called the lattice of Generalized Atomic Formulae (GAF, [20]). We only need the sublattice of flat terms, GAF_1; and for a given module, only those flat terms of the same principal functor (which can remain implicit) and arity, a, with argument constants, 0 through some k, $GAF_{1,k}^a$. This is finite. Subsumption in this sublattice should be familiar to anyone who has used Prolog — in $GAF_{1,1}^2$, for example $f(\_,\_)$ is the most general term, $f(\_,1) \sqsubseteq_{GAF} f(1,1)$, $f(1,\_) \sqsubseteq_{GAF} f(1,1)$ and the term with the same variable in both positions, $f(X,X) \sqsubseteq_{GAF} f(1,1)$.[3]

The fact that *every* finite meet semi-lattice has a Colmerauer-style encoding means that our choice of arity in a flat-term encoding never needs to be greater than the number of meet irreducible types of a module plus 1. There are other constraints on arity that can be proven as well (the proofs are omitted here for brevity):

Definition 3 *Given type hierarchy, $\langle T, \sqsubseteq \rangle$ and type $t \in T$, the information level of t, $\delta_T(t)$, is the length of the longest subtype chain from $\perp$ to t.*

We can implicitly order our types into a sequence t_i, such that if $i < j$ then $\delta_T(t_i) \le \delta_T(t_j)$, with $\perp$ as t_1. We can also extend δ to flat-term encodings, thinking of them as meet semi-lattices, $GAF_{1,k}^a$.

Proposition 3 *Let $\bar{T}$ be a flat-term encoding of T and $\bar{t}$ be the term corresponding to $t \in T$ in $\bar{T}$. Then:*

1. *For any t, $\delta_{\bar{T}}(\bar{t}) \ge \delta_T(t)$.*

2. *If $\bar{t}_1 \sqcup \bar{t}_2 = \bar{t}_3$, then $\delta_{\bar{T}}(\bar{t}_3) = \delta_{\bar{T}}(\bar{t}_1) + \delta_{\bar{T}}(\bar{t}_2) - \delta_{\bar{T}}(\bar{t}_1 \sqcap \bar{t}_2) \le \delta_{\bar{T}}(\bar{t}_1) + \delta_{\bar{T}}(\bar{t}_2)$.*

3. *For any t, its supertype branching factor $\sigma(t) \le 2^{\delta_T(t)} - 1$.*

The arity of the terms in a module's encoding must be constant, so (1) implies that that arity must be at least as large as the length of the longest subtype chain in T, since the type at the end of that chain must be encoded by a term of at least that arity. This lower bound can always be attained if there are no join reducible types. (2) says that the δ-value of the result of unification in a unification-preserving encoding cannot exceed the sum of its operands' δ-values — since we are not requiring our encodings to be meet-preserving, we might not know the value of $\delta_{\bar{T}}(\bar{t}_1 \sqcap \bar{t}_2)$. This means that join reducible types can, in general, force an encoding to have greater arity to allow for higher δ-values of two supertypes so that there will be enough "room" for their join. (3) essentially documents the same effect as a result of the bound on the number of terms that can possibly subsume a Prolog term of a given arity.

The choice of constants for instantiation of arguments is also bounded as a function of arity:

Proposition 4 *In a type hierarchy, T, if there is a flat-term encoding of arity a, there is a flat-term encoding of arity a that uses no more than $a \cdot max(T)$ constants, where $max(T)$ is the number of maximally specific types in T.*

---

[3] We will not consider terms $f(X, Y)$ with $X \ne Y$, although Prologs with inequations would allow us to use these in encodings as well.

	⊥	lax	cl	cng	lax& cl	lax& cng	cl& cng
⊥	1	1	1	1	1	1	1
lax	0	1	0	0	1	1	0
cl	0	0	1	0	1	0	1
cng	0	0·	0	1	0	1	1
lax&cl	0	0	0	0	1	0	0
lax&cng	0	0	0	0	0	1	0
cl&cng	0	0	0	0	0	0	1

Figure 6: The subsumption matrix for Figure 3.

Proof: Because flat-term encodings preserve unification, they also preserve subsumption, so a constant used in any term is reflected in the same argument position of the encoding of some maximally specific type. There are $a \cdot \max(T)$ such positions. Of course, a Colmerauer-style encoding only uses two constants, 0 and 1.

The net result of these constraints is that there is a finite space of parameters — arity and number of constants — through which we can search for an optimal encoding, provided that we have a uniform representation of encodings through which to search. That representation can be achieved by looking at a different characterization of the algebras we are trying to encode, and relating them to the Prolog terms eligible to participate in our encodings.

Definition 4 *Given a type hierarchy, $\langle T, \sqsubseteq \rangle$, the subsumption matrix of $\langle T, \sqsubseteq \rangle$, S, is a $|T| \times |T|$ boolean matrix where S_{ij} is 1 if $t_i \sqsubseteq t_j$.*

Subsumption matrices can be computed by building a matrix of the reflexively closed immediate subsumption relation that a programmer defines, and then multiplying the matrix by itself until it reaches a fixed point, thus computing the transitive closure ([2]). A subsumption matrix uniquely characterizes a finite meet semi-lattice's behavior with respect to unification, since joins are completely determined by subsumption. In fact, as observed in [2], each row can be used as an encoding of the type labelling t, with unification corresponding to component-wise AND. The subsumption matrix of Figure 3 is shown in Figure 6.

For a fixed a and k, $GAF^a_{1,k}$ has a fixed subsumption matrix. With this view of finite meet semi-lattices, finding a flat-term encoding of one with a subsumption matrix S amounts to finding the right rows and columns of a GAF lattice that will behave like S:

Proposition 5 *Every flat-term encoding of a type hierarchy with subsumption matrix, S, uniquely corresponds to a selection matrix, P, such that:*

1. *$P \cdot GAF^a_{1,k} \cdot P^T = S$, for some arity, a, some maximum constant, k, and*

2. the rows (and columns) selected by P are closed under component-wise AND in $GAF_{1,k}^a$.

An optimal flat-term encoding is one with the least arity a for which such a P exists.

The fact that we are using selection matrices — matrices with exactly one 1 in any row and no more than one 1 in any column, means that we satisfy the injectivity condition of [16] (see Section 2.1, this paper). The first condition given here means that it satisfies Mellish's homomorphism condition — the terms corresponding to the rows and columns in $GAF_{1,k}^a$ preserve unification because they have the same subsumption matrix. The second condition is necessary to ensure Mellish's zero-preservation condition — it could be that we threw out the row of a term that is the unification of two terms that we included. There is no trace of it because we also threw out its column, and no trace appears in S if the two corresponding types were not unifiable. We want Prolog unification to fail when unification in T fails, however.

We can thus reduce the search for an encoding to a search for a selection matrix over a finite space of parameters: arity, ranging from 0 to the number of meet irreducible types, and number of constants, ranging from 0 to $a \cdot \max(T)$. S is no ordinary matrix, furthermore. If we break it into submatrices $A_{i,j}$ for rows of types with $\delta = i$ and columns of types with $\delta = j$, then for all i, j, $A_{i,i}$ is an identity matrix, and $A_{i,j}$ is a zero matrix when $i < j$. Due to the constraints mentioned above, we can consider the problem, to a great extent, independently by information level when solving for P. The general problem is, of course, still horrendously expensive. Even small parts of finding the optimal flat-term encoding are known to be NP-complete ([11]).

3 Features

Once we add features, we need to accommodate their values in the encoding, including possibly circular structures, which reduce straightforwardly to circular Prolog terms. Carpenter ([3]) proves that some type signatures inherently require dynamic type checking, which Prolog encodings, as defined here, cannot do. For most applications, only statically typable signatures are necessary, although it is possible to implement the non-statically typable ones using the functionality of an enhanced Prolog such as SICStus's `library(atts)`, which allows for hooks to unification. Using this library as a means of encoding TFSs is considered in the evaluation.

Tree-based encodings can add extra arguments at subterms where features are introduced. A TFS of type *noun*, from Figure 1, would be encoded as `head(subst(noun(case(nom)),plus,plus))`, where the two `plus` values are for the PRD and MOD features introduced by *head*. The logic of [3] allows subtypes to refine the value restrictions on features introduced by their supertypes, and for feature introduction at joins. ProFIT's declaration language allows for neither of these; but a tree encoding is compatible with them, in principle.

An alternative is to encode all of the feature values of a module as extra arguments at the top level of the subtype encoding. This again appeals to the wisdom, "broader beats deeper," particularly since feature values are themselves encoded TFSs. It has the additional advantage that binding a variable to a feature value, another very common operation, can in many cases be compiled out to a very efficient **arg/3** call in Prolog run-time code, where the tree-based encoding would require a more expensive term traversal. It also has the same empirical caveat as with subtype encoding — that empirical domains that make reference to a large number of TFSs with types more general than types that introduce features may still perform better with the tree encoding, because they avoid the extra unused feature positions.

How many extra argument positions do we need for a module's encoding? The naive answer is the number of features introduced in that module. It is possible to do better:

Definition 5 *The* feature graph, $G(M)$ *of module M, is an undirected graph whose vertices correspond to the features introduced in M, and in which there is an edge, (F, G), iff F and G are appropriate to a common type in M.*

Proposition 6 *The least number of argument positions required for the features of M in a flat encoding is the least N for which $G(M)$ is N-colorable.*

The positions correspond to the colors. This is related to using graph coloring in compiler design for register allocation. In Figure 1, the features PRD, MOD, and CASE form a graph that is at best 3-colorable, because they are all appropriate to the common type, *noun*.

4   Evaluation

The alternatives presented here have been evaluated on the task of tabulation-based parsing with two English grammars using the same 11 sentences chosen on the basis of the size of their substring tables,[4] which loosely correlates with processing difficulty. Measurements were made on a dual-250-MHz SPARC Ultra 450 with 512 MB of RAM.

The first, on which Figure 7 is based, is the HPSG grammar distributed with the ALE system, a straightforward encoding of the first five chapters of [19], and a common benchmark for logic programming with TFSs. It has 162 types and 37 features, which decompose into a large number of small modules, each having at worst 5-colorable feature graphs. All modules but two are free of join reducible types, which means that they are optimally tree-encodable; but the two, lists and sets, are heavily used within the grammar. The top alternative depicted is the performance of a naive encoding

---

[4]The size ranges from 13 to 8551 edges with the HPSG grammar, and from 14 to 199 edges with the Bell Labs grammar.

of typed feature structures using the SICStus Prolog attributed variables library, where the type is represented as the value of an extra feature defined on every structure. The second uses the same library but with one attribute for every "color" of feature as described above, rather than for every feature. This takes advantage of the high modularity of the grammar. The third uses undocumented SICStus internal predicates to manipulate those attributes directly in order to exploit the existence of appropriateness conditions. The fourth is not a proper Prolog encoding — it uses a Prolog data structure that must be dereferenced before unification. This result was obtained from ALE 3.2. Both the third and the fourth use the exact feature arity of every type for its representation, so no coloring is needed. For non-statically typable modules, these two are the best alternatives available. The advantage of the third is that it can be used together with Prolog-term-encoded static modules because of the availability of the verify_attributes/3 unification hook for attributed variables.

The last three are proper Prolog term encodings as elaborated upon here. The fifth was obtained from ProFIT 1.54 with its tree encoding method — the list and set modules are tree encodable. The last two use an optimal tree encoding on modules with no join reducible types. These are so easy to detect and the encoding is so quickly derived that no other choice makes sense. The sixth was obtained using the approximate method presented in Section 2.2.1 on the two other modules, but without feature graph coloring. The seventh uses the optimal method presented in Section 2.2.2 with feature coloring. The sixth and seventh bound the performance of the four possible permutations of encoding method with feature coloring; and, as can be seen, it makes very little difference. For this grammar, a completely polynomial approximation is worthwhile.

The second grammar (Figure 8) is a categorial grammar from Bell Labs encoded in typed feature logic, designed to have similar coverage to the ALE HPSG grammar. It has a total of 209 types and 27 features. It has only five modules, however, with the largest containing 119 of the types, including 88 meet-irreducible types, but having an optimal encoding of arity 6 — in fact, there is only one join-reducible type in it. Another module has 17 of the features, with a 6-colorable feature graph. The Bell Labs grammar is much faster than the HPSG grammar; but within its performance, feature coloring can be seen to be of more significance. Optimal type encoding is of great significance — even dereferencing is better than Colmerauer's method here.

5   Conclusion

Two methods have been presented to encode arbitrary type signatures as flat Prolog terms, which provides an improvement in speed over other general representation methods, and a competitive performance with tree encoding, in addition to its more general applicability. A few of the results, such as the graph-coloring reduction and the selection matrix reduction, are

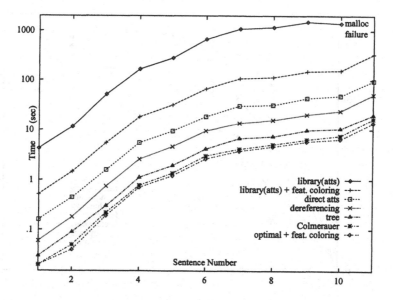

Figure 7: Evaluation on the ALE HPSG grammar.

independently of some theoretical interest.

What remains now is to find heuristic methods that, for linguistically prevalent type signatures, can constrain the compile-time parametric search for optimal flat-term type encodings; and to conduct a wider empirical comparison than can be attempted in this paper to find hybrid encodings best suited to the realistic processing needs of the knowledge representation and linguistics communities.

References

[1] H. Aït-Kaći. An introduction to LIFE — programming with logic, inheritance, functions and equations. In D. Miller, editor, *Proceedings of the International Symposium on Logic Programming*, pages 52–68. MIT Press, 1993.

[2] H. Aït-Kaći, R. Boyer, P. Lincoln, and R. Nasr. Efficient implementation of lattice operations. *TOPLAS*, (11-1-1989), 1989.

[3] B. Carpenter. *The Logic of Typed Feature Structures*. Cambridge, 1992.

[4] B. Carpenter and G. Penn. Compiling typed attribute-value logic grammars. In H. Bunt and M. Tomita, editors, *Recent Advances in Parsing Technologies*. Kluwer, 1996.

[5] B. Carpenter and G. Penn. *ALE 3.2 User's Manual*, May 1999. Available from the ALE Homepage: http://www.sfs.nphil.uni-tuebingen.de/~gpenn/ale.html.

[6] B. Carpenter and Y. Qu. An abstract machine architecture for typed attribute-value grammars. In *Proceedings of the 4th International Workshop on Parsing Technology*, 1995.

[7] V. Dahl. Un systeme deductif d'interrogation de banques de donnes en espagnol. Technical report, Groupe d'Intelligence Artificielle, Université de Marseille-Luminy, 1977.

[8] G. Erbach. Multi-dimensional inheritance. In *Proceedings of KONVENS 94*. Springer, 1994.

[9] G. Erbach. Profit: Prolog with features, inheritance and templates. In *Proceedings of EACL '95*, 1995.

138

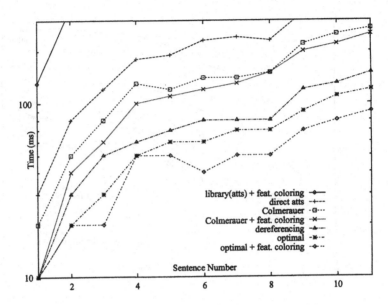

Figure 8: Evaluation on the Bell Labs Categorial Grammar.

[10] G. Erbach. *Bottom-Up Earley Deduction for Preference-Driven Natural Language Processing.* PhD thesis, Universität des Saarlandes, 1996.

[11] A. Fall. *Reasoning with Taxonomies.* PhD thesis, Simon Fraser University, 1996.

[12] D. Gerdemann. Term encoding of typed feature structures. In *Proceedings of the 4th International Workshop on Parsing Technologies*, pages 89–97, 1995.

[13] R. A. Hudson. Systemic generative grammar. In M. A. K. Halliday and J. R. Martin, editors, *Readings in Systemic Linguistics.* Batsford Academic, 1981.

[14] T. Makino, K. Torisawa, and J. Tsuji. LiLFeS — practical unification-based programming system for typed feature structures. In *COLING/ACL '98*, 1998.

[15] C. Mellish. Implementing systemic classification by unification. *Computational Linguistics*, 14(1):40–51, 1988.

[16] C. Mellish. Graph-encodable description spaces. Technical report, University of Edinburgh, 1991. DYANA Deliverable R3.2B.

[17] C. Mellish. Term-encodable description spaces. In D.R. Brough, editor, *Logic Programming: New Frontiers*, pages 189–207. Kluwer, 1992.

[18] R. Meyer, B. Dumant, and P. Van Roy. The Half-Life 0.1 system. Technical report, 1994. Available from http://www.info.ucl.ac.be/people/PVR/halflife.html.

[19] C. Pollard and I. Sag. *Head-driven Phrase Structure Grammar.* Chicago, 1994.

[20] J.C. Reynolds. Transformational systems and the algebraic structure of atomic formulas. In B. Meltzer and D. Michie, editors, *Machine Intelligence 5.* Edinburgh, 1970.

[21] N.K. Simpkins and M. Groenendijk. Multiple inheritance. Technical Report ALEP-1.3, Cray Systems, August 1994.

[22] P. Van Roy, M. Mehl, and R. Scheidhauer. Integrating efficient records into concurrent constraint programming. In *8th International Symposium on Programming Languages, Implementations, Logics, and Programs (PLILP 96)*, pages 438–453, 1996.

[23] S. Wintner. *An Abstract Machine for Unification Grammars with Applications to an HPSG Grammar for Hebrew.* PhD thesis, Technion, 1997.

A generic approach to monitor program executions

Erwan Jahier, Mireille Ducassé
IRISA/INSA, Campus Universitaire de Beaulieu,
F-35042 RENNES Cedex - France
jahier@irisa.fr, ducasse@irisa.fr

Abstract

Monitoring requires to gather data about executions. The monitoring functionalities currently available are built on top of ad hoc instrumentations. Most of them are implemented at low-level; in any case they require an in-depth knowledge of the system to instrument. The best people to implement these instrumentations are generally the implementors of the compiler. They, however, cannot decide which data to gather. Indeed, hundreds of variants can be useful and only end-users know what they want.

In this article, we propose a primitive which enables users to easily specify what to monitor. It is built on top of the tracer of the Mercury compiler. We illustrate how to use this primitive on two different kinds of monitoring. Firstly, we implement monitors that collect various kinds of statistics; each of them is well-known, the novelty is that users can get exactly the variants they need. Secondly, we define two notions of test coverage for logic programs and show how to measure coverage rates with our primitive. To our knowledge no definition of test coverage exist for logic programming so far. Each example is only a few lines of Mercury. Measurements show that the performance of the primitive on the above examples is acceptable for an execution of several millions of trace events. Our primitive, although simple, lays the foundation for a generic and powerful monitoring environment.

1   Introduction

A *program execution monitor* is a system that oversees the dynamic runtime behavior of a program. Monitors are generally implemented by ad hoc instrumentations of source [6, 13, 17], medium or low level [14] code. Those instrumentations are not technically very difficult, but they always require a significant programming effort. Low (assembler) or medium (abstract machine) level instrumentations require an in-depth knowledge of the system to instrument. They typically can be done by the language compiler implementors who, however, cannot envisage all the possible functionalities users may need. An alternative to low-level instrumentation is source level instrumentation (see for example how runtime behavior information can be extracted by source-to-source transformation for ML [17, 13] or Prolog [6]). Such instrumentations can be tricky for casual users; furthermore, for certain new declarative programming language like Mercury, they may even be impossible. Indeed, in Mercury, the declarative semantics is simple and well defined, but the operational semantics is implicit and complex. For example, the compiler reorders the goals according to its needs and the input-outputs can be made only in deterministic predicates.

On the other hand, the difficult task of instrumenting the code to extract runtime information has already been done for the debugger (when available). Indeed, debuggers, which help users to locate faults in programs are based on tracers which restore a relatively complete image of the operational semantics of the underlying language.

Therefore, we propose in this article a high level primitive built on top of an execution trace that allows users to easily and efficiently collect information about program executions. This primitive, called `collect`, is a kind of `fold` (metacall) which operates on the trace. We have implemented it on top of the Mercury trace. Measurements show acceptable performances for an execution of several million of events. Our primitive, although simple, lays the foundation for a generic and powerful monitoring environment.

Another marginal contribution of the article is to define two notions of test coverage for logic programs. To our knowledge no definition of test coverage exists for logic programming so far.

Section 2 gives a quick overview of the Mercury language and of the information delivered by the tracer. Section 3 specifies the *collect* primitive and briefly describes its implementation. Section 4, illustrates the use of *collect* to implement four monitors that collect various kinds of statistics; a monitor that counts the number of predicate calls, a monitor that counts the number of events at each port, a monitor that counts the number of events at each depth and a monitor that collects the solutions generated by a set of predicates. Each of them is well-known, the novelty is that users can get exactly the variants they need. Section 5 defines two concepts of test coverage for logic programs, namely predicate and goal coverage, and shows how those coverage rates can be performed with the *collect* primitive. Section 6 discusses performance issues. Section 7 presents related work.

2 A quick outlook of Mercury

2.1 The Mercury language

Mercury [15] is a purely declarative, logical and functional programming language. The principal difference with Prolog is that Mercury has strong type, mode and determinism systems; Mercury syntax allows functions and high order terms. Another major difference is that there are no side effects. Even the inputs/outputs are managed in a declarative way; the "state of the world" is passed in argument of all the deterministic predicates which make inputs/outputs (i.e. such inputs/outputs cannot be made in predicates which can fail).

```
:- pred append(list(T), list(T), list(T)).
:- mode append(in, in, out) is det.
:- mode append(in, in, in) is semidet.    % implied
:- mode append(in, out, in) is semidet.
:- mode append(out, out, in) is multi.
append([], Ys, Ys).
append([X | Xs], Ys, [X | Zs]) :-
        append(Xs, Ys, Zs).
```

Figure 1: The Mercury predicate append/3

Figure 1 shows the Mercury code of the append/3 predicate. In Mercury, users need to define the type of the predicate (:- pred append(...)) and the different modes it can be called with (:- mode append(...) is ...). A *mode* declaration of a predicate states a mode for every argument of the predicate and a determinism. A Mercury *procedure* is characterized by a predicate and a mode. The determinism markers of Mercury are: det for procedure which have exactly 1 solution, semidet for those which have 0 or 1 solution, nondet for those which have any number of solutions, multi for those which have at least 1 solution, failure for those that have no solution and erroneous for those which lead to a runtime error. The compiler will generate a different code for each procedure. It is important to note that subgoals can be reordered.

Even if it means renaming some predicates, we can suppose that there is only one mode per predicate; hence we will use the terms predicate or procedure inter-changeably in the rest of the article.

2.2 The Mercury trace

A *trace* is a sequence of events. An *event* is a tuple of event attributes. An *event attribute* is an elementary piece of information that can be extracted from the current state of any particular point of the program execution. A trace can be seen as tuples of a database ordered by time. The Mercury trace is an adaptation of the Byrd's box model [4]. The attributes of the Mercury trace are: the event number, the call number, the execution depth, the port, the determinism, the procedure (defined by a module name, a name, an arity and a mode number), the live arguments, the live non-arguments variables, the goal path and the ancestor stack. A description of those attributes is given in appendix.

3 The *collect* primitive

3.1 Specification

The collect/3 primitive is a meta-predicate that collects information about a whole execution of a Mercury program. The behavior of this primitive is

```
collect(Program, CollectModule, Result) :-
    compile(CollectModule),
    run_program_and_get_event_list(Program, EventList),
    initialize(Start),
    foldl(filter, EventList, Start, Result).
```

Figure 2: Pseudo code that specifies the collect primitive

specified in Figure 2 (the actual implementation is described later).

In collect(Program, CollectModule, Result), Program should be an invocation of a Mercury program compiled in mode *debug* and CollectModule should be the name of a Mercury module defining: (1) the type of the "collecting" variable that will contain the result of the monitoring process, (2) the initialization predicate initialize/1 and (3) the filtering predicate filter/3. This module is compiled with compile/1. run_program_and_get_event_list/2 runs a program compiled in mode *debug* and retrieves in a list all the events of its execution. initialize/1 initializes the "collecting" variable. filter/3 takes an event and a "collecting" variable and updates the variable. foldl/4 is the classical fold predicate operating left-to-right. Hence, filter is successively called with each event of the execution and an accumulator, and returns the final value of the accumulator in Result. The type of the "collecting" variable can be set thanks to the type system of Mercury. For example, in order to collect an integer, it can be defined the following way:

```
:- type collected_type == int.
```

Then initialize/1 and filter/3, which respectively initializes and updates the "collecting" variable, must be defined with the following declarations:

```
:- pred initialize(collected_type).
:- mode initialize(out) is det.

:- pred filter(event, collected_type, collected_type).
:- mode filter(in, in, out) is det.
```

Variables of type event contains all the attributes of an event. Each event attribute can be accessed with functions of the form:

```
:- func <attribute_name>(event::in) = <attribute_type>::out.
```

For example, depth(Event) returns the depth of the event Event.

3.2 Implementation

Actually, implementing collect with foldl/4 as we have just specified would be far too inefficient; it would mean to create and process a list of possibly millions of events. To efficiently implement this primitive, information needs to be collected on the fly.

The `collect` primitive is implemented on top of the Mercury trace. First, a global variable is created and initialized by the Mercury predicate `initialize/1`. Then, whenever an event is reached, the `collect` interface is called instead of the standard debugger. The `collect` interface calls the Mercury predicate `filter/3` which updates the global variable, and gives control back to the execution. It is important to note here that for performance reasons, there is no coroutining between different Operating System (OS) processes but only procedure calls that update a global variable. It was to avoid those expensive OS level context switches induced by coroutining that the `collect` primitive was initially designed (see related work section).

4 Various monitors

A *program execution monitor* is a system that oversees the dynamic runtime behavior of a program. In this section, we use the *collect* primitive to implement monitors that collect various kinds of statistics. Each of them is quite simple and available on some commercial Prolog distributions. The novelty is that they can be implemented by any user; hence users can get exactly the variants they need. The four examples given in this section are variants from each other and one could imagine a large number of other variants.

Counting predicate calls Figure 3-a shows a monitor that counts the number of predicate calls that occurs during an execution of a Mercury program. The variable we use to count calls is of type int; `initialize/1` initializes it to '0'. Then, for every event occurring during the execution, `filter/3` increments the counter whenever the event is a `call` event.

Counting the number of events at each port Figure 3-b implements a variant of the previous monitor that counts the number of events at `call`, `exit`, `redo`, `fail` and internal ports. To do this, we need counters that are coded using the 'array' module of the Mercury standard library. `init(Size, Init, Array)` creates an array *Array* with bounds from 0 to $Size - 1$, and with each element initialized to *Init*. `lookup(Array, N, V)` returns in V the Nth element of Array. `set(ArrayIn, N, V, ArrayOut)` sets the value V in the Nth element of *ArrayIn* and returns the resulting array in *ArrayOut*. `initialize/1` creates an array of size five with each element initialized to 0. `filter/3` extracts the port from the current event (`port(Event)`) and increments the corresponding counter.

Counting the number of calls at each depth Figure 3-c implements a monitor that counts the number of calls at each depth. `initialize/1` creates an array of size 32 with each elements initialized to 0. `filter/3` extracts the depth from the current event (`depth(Event)`) and increments the

```
:- import_module int.
:- type collected_type = int.

initialize(0).

filter(Event, Cpt0, Cpt) :-
  ( if
        port(Event) = call
    then
        Cpt = Cpt0 + 1
    else
        Cpt = Cpt0
  ).
```

(a) *Monitor that counts the number of calls* (count calls)

```
:- import_module int, array.
:- type collected_type == array(int).

initialize(Acc) :-
    init(32, 0, Acc).

filter(Event, Acc0, Acc) :-
  ( if port(Event) = call then
        D = depth(Event),
        ( if semidet_lookup(Acc0, D, N) then
               set(Acc0, D, N + 1, Acc)
          else
               size(Acc0, Size)
               resize(Acc0, Size*2, 0, Acc1),
               set(Acc1, D, 1, Acc)
        )
    else
        Acc = Acc0
  ).
```

(c) *Monitor that counts the number of calls at each depth* (histogram)

```
:- import_module int, array.
:- type collected_type
      == array(int).

initialize(Array) :-
    init(5, 0, Array).

filter(Event, Array0, Array) :-
    Port = port(Event),
  ( if Port = call then
        lookup(Array0, 0, N),
        set(Array0, 0, N+1, Array)
    else if Port = exit then
        lookup(Array0, 1, N),
        set(Array0, 1, N+1, Array)
    else if Port = fail then
        lookup(Array0, 2, N),
        set(Array0, 2, N+1, Array)
    else if Port = redo then
        lookup(Array0, 3, N),
        set(Array0, 3, N+1, Array)
    else
        % internal ports
        lookup(Array0, 4, N),
        set(Array0, 4, N+1, Array)
  ).
```

(b) *Monitor that counts the number of events at each port* (statistic)

```
:- import_module std_util, list.
:- type pred == string.
:- type args == list(string).
:- type solution ---> sol(pred, args).
:- type collected_type ==
      pair(pred, list(solution)).

initialize(["foo", "bar1", "bar2"] - []).

filter(Event, Acc0, Acc) :-
    Acc0 = (ListPred - ListSol0),
  ( if
        port(Event) = exit,
        member(proc_name(Event), ListPred)
    then
        Proc = procedure(Event),
        Sol = sol(Proc, arg(Event)),
        ( if member(Sol, ListSol0) then
               Acc = Acc0
          else
               ListSol = [Sol | ListSol0],
               Acc = (ListPred - ListSol)
        )
    else
        Acc = Acc0
  ).
```

(d) *Monitor that collects all the solutions* (solutions)

Figure 3: Various monitors, as specified in Mercury by users

corresponding counter. Whenever the upper bound of the array is reached, its size is doubled. `semidet_lookup/4` is a semi-deterministic version of `lookup`; the former fails if one tries to set an out of bounds element whereas the later generates an error.

Collecting solutions The monitor of Figure 3-d collects the solutions produced by a set of predicates during the execution. To do so, we define the collecting variable as being a functor with a string containing a procedure name as first argument and a list of solutions as second argument. `var initialize/1` initializes the collecting variable with a list of predicate names for which we want to collect solutions and an empty list where the solutions will be put. If the current port is `exit` and if the current predicate is a member of the list of predicates we are interested in, `filter/3` constructs the solution and adds it in the set of already collected solutions.

5 Test coverage

In this section we define two notions of test coverage for logic programs and show how to measure the corresponding coverage rate of Mercury programs execution using the *collect* primitive. However, the aim here is not to provide "the" definition of test coverage for logic programs but only to propose two possible (and rather natural) definitions and to show how the corresponding coverage rate can be measured using *collect*.

5.1 Test coverage and logic programs

The aim of test coverage is to assess the quality of a test suite in order to know whether it is necessary to generate more test cases or not. For a given coverage criterion, one can decide to stop testing when a certain percentage of coverage is reached (ideally 100 %).

The usual criteria used for imperative languages are *instructions* and *branches*[1] criteria [3]. The *branch coverage rate* achieved by a test suite is the percentage of branches that have been traversed during the execution. The *statement coverage rate* achieved by a test suite is the percentage of statements that have been executed.

One of the weaknesses of statement and branch coverage is due to boolean instructions. The problem occurs when a boolean instruction is composed by more than one atomic statement: it may be that a test suite covers each value of the whole condition without covering every values of each atomic part of the condition. For example, the condition 'A or B' may have a test suite for which it succeeds and fails without having exercised the B success. Take $A = true$, $B = false$ and $A = false$, $B = false$; in that case, every branch and every statement are exercised and nevertheless, B never succeeded. If B

---

[1] where a branch refers to an edge of the control-flow graph of the program

is erroneous, even 100% statement and branch coverage will miss it. In logic programming, this problem is crucial because every statement is a predicate.

5.2 Predicate coverage

In order to tackle the above problem, we need a coverage criterion that checks that each single predicate defined in the tested program succeeds and fails at least once. But we do not want to enforce that all predicates must fail because some, like printing predicates, are intrinsically deterministic. Therefore, we want a criterion that allows the test designer to specify if a predicate should succeed and/or fail. Hence, a possible criterion attached to a predicate could be a subset of the set {'success', 'failure'}. We call such a subset a *predicate criterion* and a *predicate coverage of a logic program* is a set of predicate criteria for every predicate in the program.

In the case of Mercury, we can take advantage of the determinism declaration to automatically determine if a predicate should succeed and/or fail. Here is an example of what could systematically be covered according to the determinism declaration of each predicate:

'det' and 'multi' predicates	{ success }
'semidet' and 'nondet' predicates	{ success, failure }
'failure' predicates	{ failure }
'erroneous' predicates	{ }

To check with the trace whether a predicate succeeded and/or failed, we simply need to look if 'exit' and/or 'fail' events have been generated. Figure 5 shows a monitor implemented with the *collect* primitive that measures predicate coverage rate of a Mercury module "foo" from which we show selected extracts in Figure 4.

```
r(X, Y) :- ...                      p(1, X) :- ...
r(X, Y) :- ...                      p(2, X) :- ...
r(X, Y) :- (h(X) -> ... ; q(Y)).    p(3, X) :- q(X).
```

Figure 4: Selected extracts of the Mercury module foo

We define the type `predicate_criterion` as being a functor with the following arguments: a procedure and a list of ports (see appendix for a description of those two attributes). `initialize/1` initializes the collecting variable to a list of predicate criteria to be covered. Note that this information can be generated automatically from the source code. If a predicate criterion is present in the collecting variable, `filter/3` removes it. `remove_if_present(Proc, Port, PathList0, PathList)` takes a procedure `Proc`, a port `Port` and a list of predicate criteria `Acc0` and returns in `Acc` the list of predicate criteria where `pc(Proc, [Port])` have been removed if needed.

```
:- import_module int, list.
:- type procedure ---> proc(module_name, pred_name, arity, mode_number).
:- type predicate_criterion ---> pc(procedure, list(port)).
:- type collected_type == list(predicate_criterion).

initialize([
    pc(proc("foo", "p", 2, 0), [exit, fail]),
    pc(proc("foo", "q", 1, 0), [fail]),
    ...
]).
filter(Event, PathList0, PathList) :-
    Port = port(Event),
  ( if (Port = exit ; Port = fail) then
        remove_if_present(procedure(Event), Port, PathList0, PathList)
    else
        PathList = PathList0
    ).
```

Figure 5: A monitor that measures predicate coverage rate of module foo

5.3 Goal coverage

The previous coverage only checks that at least one occurrence of all the predicates are covered. That coverage is weaker than statement coverage. To ensure 100 % statement coverage, we need a definition of coverage that ensures that every *predicate invocation* in the program succeeds and/or fails. Hence we need a definition attached to goals and not only to predicates: thus we define the *goal criterion* as being the *predicate criterion* of its corresponding predicate and a *goal coverage of a logic program* as a set of goal criteria of every goal invocation of the program.

A monitor that measures goal coverage rate of Mercury program executions is given in Figure 6. To be able to uniquely identify each goal invocation of the program with the information contained in the Mercury trace, we need to look at the ancestor and the goal_path attributes. Unfortunately, the goal_path attribute is only available at call, exit, fail and redo ports (see appendix for the list of Mercury tracer ports). But it is possible to "remember" it using a variable and 2 stacks: that is what perform_goal_path/6 does. Hence we enrich the type of collected_type with a variable and 2 stacks. We define the type goal_criterion as being a functor with a procedure, its ancestor, its goal path and a list of ports as arguments. initialize/1 initializes the collecting variable to a list of collecting criteria to be covered. Note that the list of collecting criteria to be covered can be generated automatically from the source code. filter/3 removes from the collecting variable the collecting criterion of the current event if needed; it also updates the variable and the stacks used to perform the goal path. remove_if_present(Proc, Anc, Port, GP,PathList0, PathList) does the same as remove_if_present/4 of Figure 5 but taking into account the richer definition of coverage. perform_goal_path/6 takes as input a

```
:- import_module int, list.
:- type procedure ---> proc(module_name, pred_name, arity, mode_number).
:- type ancestor == procedure.
:- type goal_criterion --->
    gc(procedure, ancestor, list(port), goal_path).
:- type stack == list(goal_path).
:- type collected_type --->
    acc(list(goal_criterion), goal_path, stack, stack).

initialize([
    gc(proc("foo","p",2,0), proc("foo","r",2,0), [exit, fail], "d3;e;"),
    gc(proc("foo","q",1,2), proc("foo","p",2,0), [exit], "s3"),
    ...
]).

filter(Event, Acc0, Acc) :-
    Port = port(Event),
    Acc0 = acc(PathList0, GoalPath0, Stk0, NonDetStk0),
    perform_goal_path(Event, GoalPath0, GoalPath, Stk0, Stk,
                      NonDetStk0, NonDetStk),
  ( if (Port = exit ; Port = fail) then
        remove_if_present(procedure(Event), ancestor(Event), Port,
                      GoalPath, PathList0, PathList),
    else
        Acc = acc(PathList, GoalPath, Stk, NonDetStk)
    ).
```

Figure 6: A monitor that measures goal coverage rate of module foo

goal_path, and 2 stacks and outputs a new goal_path and 2 new stacks.

A next step could be to take in account the number of solutions one would want each goal invocation to produce. For example, it would be natural to specify that multi or nondet predicates have more that one success. Performing that coverage rate would be a little bit more complex though; it would require to keep in the collecting variable the goal invocation of every goal that has not failed and has not yet been covered, and to add the goal invocation number (call attribute, cf appendix) to the goal_criterion type definition.

6 Performance issues

In order to have a rough idea of the slowdown induced by the monitoring activities of collect, we have benchmarked the previous monitors on a 1300 lines Mercury program that generates 15 millions events. The result of the measurements are on Figure 7.

The first column times the program executed alone[2]. The second measures the cost of the tracer interface: the program is executed under the

---

[2]Note that a Mercury program compiled in mode *debug* generates an executable that is bigger but not slower than the same program compiled without debugging information

without tracing	do nothing	count calls (3-a)	histogram (3-b)	statistic (3-c)	solutions (3-d)	predicate coverage (5)	goal coverage (6)
9 s	32 s	45 s	45/130 s	47 s	100-400 s	110 s	135 s

Figure 7: Timings the monitors of Figures 3, 5 and 6

control of the tracer which never calls any monitoring or debugging primitives. The next four columns time the four monitors of Figure 3. The last two ones time the monitors defined in Figures 5 and 6.

The "histogram" monitor performs the number of events at each depth. On this particular program, it happens that the depth goes down to 300000, thus most of the time here was spent in writing the result. It is the reason why we distinguished two timings; 45 seconds is the time spent collecting the results and 130 seconds is the time spent collecting the results and writing it. This particular monitor is already available on an experimental version of the Mercury compiler; for this hard-coded monitor, the timings were 11 seconds without printing the result and 95 seconds with printing it.

For the "statistic" and "histogram" monitors, using arrays lets us destructively update the accumulator; it is one of the reasons why performance for those monitors were rather good compared to the "solutions" or the "coverage" monitors. For the "solutions" monitor, the timings depend of the predicate we chose to print the solution of. Predicates that generate big solutions considerably augment the size of the accumulator and this decreases the performance. Note that for predicate and goal coverage; the result not only depends of the size of the trace but also of the size of the program (i.e. of the size of the paths to cover). On the particular program we made the timings, the size of the execution was quite large but the size of the program was rather small.

The performance of the monitored program executions range from a slowdown of 5 on casuals statistics to 50 for large collected data. As a comparison, a slowdown of 10 is common for debuggers which must be used interactively. Hence, the slowdown of 5 is very good. For the slowdown of 50, considering that monitoring is not an interactive activity (it can be done at night for example), this seems acceptable to us.

7 Related work

All the monitors presented in this article have first been implemented with Opium-M [5, 10, 11], a Mercury trace analyzer designed for *debugging* that operates in coroutining with the analyzed program. However, debugging in general does not need to collect as much data as monitoring; our experience with Opium-M is that it was a nice tool to easily prototype monitors, but performances were not sufficient on some monitors for very big executions. The reasons are that the coroutining mechanism induces too much OS level context switches and socket traffic between the two processes. It was to avoid those problems that we designed *collect*. Opium-M and *collect* approaches are quite complementary; Opium-M is more convenient when we want to interact with the program (as in a debugging session for example) whereas *collect* is more efficient to analyze a whole execution.

Jeffery and al. [12] describe Alamo, an architecture to ease the development of monitors for C programs. As in our approach, their monitoring architecture is based on events filtering and monitors can be programmed. Their system deals with trace extraction whereas we rely on an already available tracer; this saves us from a low level and tedious task, but the counterpart is that we don't have the control on the information available in an event. Note however that with our approach, lacking information can sometimes be recovered as we do in Figure 6 to get the goal path attribute at every ports. To avoid code explosion, they perform part of the event filtering at compilation time. Hence they need to recompile the program each time they want to execute another monitor whereas we only need to compile `initialize/1` and `filter/3` and then dynamically link them to the monitored program.

Eustace and Srivastava developed ATOM [7, 16], another system that aims at easing the building of monitors. The difference with Alamo is that monitors are implemented with procedures calls and global variables which is much more efficient than coroutining but less powerful.

Kishon and al. [13] automatically derive an interpreter instrumentation starting from denotational specifications of monitors and a denotational semantics. As in our approach, once the specification is written, the method is entirely automatic and guarantees that the operational semantics of the initial program is preserved. Their approach requires a continuation semantics specification of the language to monitor, which is not easy to get in Mercury because of its complex execution model. Moreover, their approach only works for interpreted languages.

Patil and Fisher [14] tackles the problems of performance of monitoring by delegating the monitoring activities to a second processor (they call it a shadow processor). Their approach is very efficient; the monitored is nearly not slowed down. However, the set of monitoring commands they propose cannot be extended as in our approach.

In [18], Voas needs to instrument source code to be able to detect hidden faults that cannot possibly be detected by simply comparing the output of the program with its expected output (coincidental correctness). Ball [1] instruments control flow graphs to implement non-regression test case selection (RTS). The information they needs is in fact available from debuggers that generally lack powerful mechanisms to filter useless information.

Ball and Larus in [2] present algorithms to place instructions of extraction (for tracing) or counting (for monitoring) in an optimal way. Indeed, using a control-flow graph, it is not necessary to put counters at every block of instructions to know how many times each instruction has been exercised.

8 Conclusion

We have designed *collect*, a high level primitive that allows users to easily specify what they want to monitor. We illustrated it on various examples that demonstrate its genericity and its simplicity of use; each example is only a few lines of Mercury. We defined two notions of test coverage for logic programs and showed how to measure coverage rates with our primitive. To our knowledge no definition of test coverage existed for logic programming so far. Measurements showed that the performance of the primitive on the above examples is acceptable for an execution of several millions of trace events. Our primitive, although simple, sets the ground to define a generic and powerful monitoring environment.

Standard testing and monitoring mechanisms are missing from many declarative systems: *collect* allows some of these mechanisms to be easily defined and implemented. Implementing the collect interface inside the Mercury system required only one week of work (by someone who already knew the implementation of the Mercury debugger system) and a few hundred lines of Mercury and C code. Of course, this was possible because of the clear distinction between the trace extraction and the debugging primitives. As advocated in [9] by Ho and Olson, analysis tools should be constructed layers by layers to allow more modularity.

Acknowledgments

The work described in this article is partially financed by the Esprit project number 25503 ARGO. We warmly thank Sarah Mallet, Olivier Ridoux, Fergus Henderson and the anonymous referees for their fruitful comments, the members of the Mercury project of the university of Melbourne for the low level tracer of Mercury, as well as the members of the ARGO project.

References

[1] T. Ball. On the limit of control flow analysis for regression test selection. In *Proceedings of the ACM SIGSOFT International Symposium on Software Testing and Analysis (ISSTA-98)*, volume 23,2 of *ACM Software Engineering Notes*, pages 134–142, New York, March2-5 1998. ACM Press.

[2] T. Ball and J. R. Larus. Optimally profiling and tracing programs. In *Principles of Programming Languages*, January 1992.

[3] B. Beizer. *Software testing techniques*, volume 2nd ed. International Thomson Computer Press, 1990.

[4] L. Byrd. Understanding the control flow of Prolog programs. In S.-A. Tärnlund, editor, *Logic Programming Workshop*, Debrecen, Hungary, 1980.

[5] M. Ducassé. Opium: An extendable trace analyser for Prolog. *The Journal of Logic programming*, 1999. Special issue on Synthesis, Transformation and Analysis of Logic Programs, A. Bossi and Y. Deville (eds).

[6] M. Ducassé and J. Noyé. Tracing Prolog programs by source instrumentation is efficient enough. In K. Sagonas, editor, *IJCSLP'98 Post-conference workshop on Implementation Technologies for Programming Languages based on Logic.*, http://www.cs.kuleuven.ac.be/ kostis/proceedings.ps.gz, June 1998.

[7] A. Eustace and A. Srivastava. ATOM: A flexible interface for building high performance program analysis tools. In *Proceedings of the Winter 1995 USENIX Conference*, January 1995.

[8] F. Henderson, T. Conway, Z. Somogyi, D. Jeffery, and P. Ross. *The Mercury Language Reference Manual.* University of Melbourne, January 1999. Available at "http://www.cs.mu.oz.au/research/mercury/".

[9] W.W. Ho and R.A. Olsson. A layered model for building debugging and monitoring tools. *Journal of Systems Software*, 34:211–222, 1996.

[10] E. Jahier and M. Ducassé. *Opium-M 0.1 User and Reference Manuals.* IRISA, Rennes, March 1999.

[11] E. Jahier and M. Ducassé. Un traceur d'exécutions de programmes ne sert pas qu'au débogage. In F. Fages, editor, *Actes des Journées francophones de Programmation Logique et programmation par Contraintes*, Lyon, juin 1999. Hermès.

[12] C. Jeffery, W. Zhou, K. Templer, and M. Brazell. A lightweight architecture for program execution monitoring. *ACM SIGPLAN Notices*, 33(7):67–74, July 1998.

[13] A. Kishon, P. Hudak, and C. Consel. Monitoring semantics: a formal framework for specifying, implementing and reasoning about execution monitors. *ACM Sigplan Notices*, 26(6):338–352, June 1991. SIGPLAN PLDI Conference.

[14] H. Patil and C. Fischer. Low-cost, concurrent checking of pointer and array accesses in C programs. *Software - Practice and Experience*, 27(1):87–110, January 1997.

[15] Z. Somogyi, F. Henderson, and T. Conway. The execution algorithm of Mercury, an efficient purely declarative logic programming language. *Journal of logic programming*, 29:17–64, October-December 1996.

[16] A. Srivastava and A. Eustace. ATOM: A system for building customized program analysis tools. In *Proceedings of the SIGPLAN '94 Conference on Programming Language Design and Implementation*, pages 196–205, June 1994.

[17] A. Tolmach and A.W. Appel. A debugger for Standard ML. *Journal of Functional Programming*, 5(2):155–200, April 1995.

[18] J. Voas, L. Morell, and K. Miller. Predicting where faults can hide from testing. *IEEE Software*, 8(2):41–48, March 1991.

Appendix - The Mercury trace

There are three kinds of attributes: attributes containing information relative to the control-flow (numbered from 1 to 6 in the following), to the data-flow (7 and 8) as well as information relative to the source code (9 and 10). The different *attributes* provided by the Mercury tracer are listed below.

1. *Event number* (chrono). It is the rank of the event in the trace.

2. *Goal invocation number* (call).

3. *Execution depth* (depth).

4. *Event type or port* (port). There are the 4 traditional ports call, exit, fail and redo introduced by Byrd [4] for Prolog. Mercury also generates *internal* events describing what occurs inside a call: an event of type disj is generated each time the execution enters a branch of a disjunction, of type switch[3] if this disjunction is a switch, of type then if it is the "then" branch of a if-then-else and of type else if it is the "else" branch.

5. *Determinism* (deter). It characterizes the number of potential solutions for each procedure. The different determinism markers are described in section 2.

6. *Procedure* (proc). It is characterized by: a flag indicating if the current procedure is a function or a predicate (proc_type), a *module name* (module), a *procedure name* (proc_name), an *arity* (arity) and a *mode number* [4] (mode_num).

7. *List of live arguments* (arg). A variable is said to be *live* at a given point of the execution if its instanciation is still available.

8. *List of local live variables* (local_var). It is the live variables that are not arguments of current procedure.

9. *Goal Path* (goal_path). It is a list indicating in which branch of the code the current event takes place. The branches *then* and *else* of a *if-then-else* are represented by t and e respectively; the *conjunctions*, *disjunctions* and the *switches* are represented by ci, di and si respectively, where i is the number of the conjunction, disjunction, or the switch. For example, an event whose path is [c3;e;d1] corresponds to an event which occurs in the first branch of a disjunction, which is itself part of an else branch of an if-then-else, which is in the third conjunction of the current procedure. For efficiency reasons, this attribute is only available at internal events.

10. *Ancestor stack* (ancestors).

A more detailed description of the contents of the Mercury trace is made in the Mercury language reference manual [8] and in the user's manual of Opium-M [10].

---

[3]A *switch* is a disjunction in which each branch unifies a ground variable with a different function symbol. In that case, at most one disjunction will provide a solution. For example, in the append predicate of Figure 1, there is a switch on the first argument.

[4]The mode number encodes the mode of a predicate or a function: when a predicate has one mode, this number is 0. If not, this number corresponds to the rank of appearance in the code of the mode declaration; 1 for the first, 2 for the second, etc.

Generating Deductive Database Explanations

Sarah Mallet[1], Mireille Ducassé[1]
IRISA/INSA

Abstract

Existing explanation systems for deductive databases show forests of proof trees. Although proof trees are often useful, they are only one possible interesting representation. We argue that an explanation system for deductive databases must be able to generate explanations at several levels of abstraction. One possible and well known technique to achieve this flexibility is to instrument meta-interpreters. It is, however, not often used because of its inefficiency. On the other hand, deductive databases often generate intermediate information stored in the physical database. This information can be considered as a low-level trace giving a faithful picture of what has happened at the relational level. The deductive reasoning is lost but can be very easily recovered by a meta-interpreter. In this article we describe a technique to generate explanations by integrating a relational trace and an instrumented meta-interpreter. The expensive aspects of meta-interpretation are reduced by the use of the trace which avoids many costly calculations. The flexibility of meta-interpretation is preserved, as illustrated by the generation of three different kinds of explanations: a box-oriented trace, a multi-SLD-AL tree and abstract AND trees. This technique enables powerful explanation systems to be implemented with very few modifications of the deductive database mechanism itself.

1 Introduction

Explaining the behaviour of a program consists of showing an abstraction of its execution. Existing explanation systems for deductive databases [20, 16, 1] show forests of proof trees. Although proof trees are often useful, they are only one possible interesting abstraction.

Deductive databases (DDB) have various kinds of users: implementors who develop the deductive part, knowledge engineers who maintain the data, and end-users who query the database. An explanation system for DDB must be useful for all of them. It must therefore be able to generate explanations at *several* levels of abstraction. A key feature of an explanation system for DDB is therefore its **flexibility**.

A well known and very flexible technique to produce explanations consists of instrumenting meta-interpreters (see for example [21]). This instrumentation can be easily adapted to users' needs, but it is in general inefficient. On the other hand, DDB often generate intermediate information stored in the physical database. This information can be considered as a low-level trace giving a faithful picture of what has happened at the relational level. In the

---

[1]Correspondance address: IRISA/INSA Campus Universitaire de Beaulieu, CS 14315, F - 35042 Rennes Cedex, France ; email : {Mireille.Ducassé}{Sarah.Mallet}@irisa.fr

DDB system that we studied, this relational trace was intended mainly for developers private usage. Indeed, the deductive reasoning was lost and only knowledgeable people could interpret the trace. We show in this article that the deduction can be easily recovered by a meta-interpreter hence making the low-level trace useful to more people.

Thus, we propose a technique for generating explanations which integrates a low-level trace with an instrumented meta-interpreter. The trace efficiently gives precise and low-level information about the extraction of data from the relational database. The meta-interpreter gives explanations about the deduction. The expensive aspects of meta-interpretation are reduced by the use of the trace which avoids many costly calculations. In particular, the accesses to the relational database are not repeated. When necessary, the meta-interpreter uses the intermediate information generated by the data extraction system, accessible via the relational trace. This feature is especially suited here as a DDB program handles *a large quantity of data*. Avoiding recalculations of these data saves a significant amount of time. In addition, the flexibility of meta-interpretation enables different traces to be easily produced, as illustrated at the end of the article.

We have implemented our technique for the Validity system based on EKS [19], in a prototype called Myrtle. Two specifics of DDB prevent usual Prolog meta-interpreters to be straightforwardly reused: *set-oriented management of data* and *termination*. These specifics are taken into account in our extension of Multi-SLD [15] : Multi-SLD-AL.

The main contribution of this work is the integration of a relational trace and a meta-interpreter. The practical impact of such a technique is important. As already mentioned, users of DDB have many different profiles. The flexibility at reasonable cost offered by our technique enables the explanations to be adapted, in particular, to end users. They will better accept the results if they can understand how they were produced. Furthermore, this technique requires very few modifications of the DDB mechanism itself.

In the following we first present the existing explanation systems for DDB and introduce our approach. We then informally describe the multi-SLD-AL resolution and the set-oriented meta-interpreter. The Validity "relational" trace and its integration with the meta-interpreter are explained in a following part. Lastly, we show three different abstractions of executions constructed by instrumenting the meta-interpreter: a box-oriented trace, a multi-SLD-AL tree and abstract AND trees.

2   Related Work

Generally, three stages can be distinguished in a debugger [6]. First, the trace is extracted from a source program or its execution, then it is filtered to be abstracted and finally the results are presented, often with a visualization tool. In the following we present several explanation tools for deductive systems and give their characteristics with respect to these three steps.

The first explanation system for DDB we are aware of was developed for Dedex [11] by Wieland [20]. The extracted trace is dedicated to the construction of proof trees, which are the only abstraction proposed for the execution. Wieland redefines an independent inference system which generates the trace. An interface allows proof trees to be visualized. This method involves a slow explanation system, disconnected from the initial system and a fixed type of abstraction.

The *Explain* system [1] was developed by Arora and al. for CORAL [13]. Like the previous system, the abstraction structure is the proof tree. The implementation of the *Explain* trace generation consists of storing derivation information during the evaluation of the query. An efficient visualization tool allows users to navigate among the proof trees. This technique of trace generation is similar to the one used in Validity as described in section 5.1 except that the information stored for *Explain* is completely dedicated to the construction of proof trees. The explanation system seems reasonably efficient but it has a fixed type of abstraction. Moreover, for optimization purposes, the user program is transformed by the Magic Set transformation [14], and unfortunately the traced program is the transformed one, not the user one.

The system designed by Specht [16] for LOLA [17] also uses proof trees as explanations. Its principle is to transform the user program to insert trace generation. In contrast to the other systems, it does not modify the deductive engine. The transformed program is queried as usual. This method, very simple to implement, makes the performance of evaluation decrease when the size of the proof trees and their number grow. With this method, to extract operational information is tricky.

Some theorem provers like Satchmo [10] are implemented in Prolog and have to manage an internal database. Their debugging problems are similar to the DDB explanation ones. SNARKS [7] is a graphical tool for debugging and explaining Satchmo's programs. The selected abstraction for explaining executions is a tree reflecting the principles of Satchmo resolution. The trace is generated by instrumenting the deductive engine. The trace is completely dedicated to the visualization tool and it is not possible to construct other abstractions.

In active database systems, rules provide automatic mechanisms to react to events. In order to understand interactions between events, rules and databases, debuggers are needed. The context is approximatively the same as in DDB: rules interact with databases; the difference is that the database can be updated during rule evaluation. Chakravarthy et al. [4] developed a tool for visualizing and explaining executions in active databases. They proposed two different causal graphs as abstractions of the interactions between the different events and rules occurring during execution. The generated trace is a general log file but it is only used for graph visualization. There are no facilities proposed to construct other abstractions. This tool is efficient, and has a general initial trace but there are no flexibility possibilities. The abstractions are subordinated to the visualization tool.

3 Explanations and flexibility

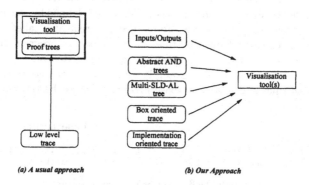

(a) A usual approach   (b) Our Approach

Figure 1: Explanation tools and abstractions

Figure 1.a reflects the approach of the systems discussed in the previous section. It consists of constructing an abstraction, namely proof trees, from a low-level trace. Users cannot get different points of view of the execution. In particular, if they want a global picture with the set by set database accesses, proof trees are totally inadapted. A query on a million tuple database can generate several million answers, each of them possibly generating several proof trees. Hence, the number of proof trees is unacceptable.

Figure 1.b illustrates our approach: users can chose among a scale of possible abstractions starting from the closest to implementation, ending with inputs/outputs of the program execution. Existing intermediate abstractions are a box-oriented trace,the Multi-SLD-AL tree which is an extension of the multi-SLD tree of Smith [15], and Abstract AND trees [2]. Alternate views could also include the abstract trees presented by Naish for declarative debugging [12] or by Comini et al. [5] for abstract debugging.

4 A Multi-SLD-AL meta-interpreter

Two specifics of DDB prevent usual Prolog meta-interpreters to be straight-forwardly reused: *set-oriented management of data* and *termination*. Tuples of the relational database are, in general, retrieved several at the same time, and not one at a time; a possibly large number of tuples can be extracted from the base during a single access. Hence, in Myrtle substitutions are managed in a set-oriented way as described in multi-SLD [15]. Lastly, the restriction to Datalog and dedicated search strategies ensure that a request on a deductive database always terminates [14]. Myrtle implements such a strategy: the SLD-AL one [19].

4.1 Principles of the Multi-SLD-AL Resolution

A DDB program defines two databases: the extentional database composed of data in the database and the intensional database defined by the deductive program. Tuples of the database are defined by predicates called database predicates. Predicates defined by rules of the deductive program are called derived predicates. The previous notions are illustrated on Fig. 2. This example is the classical ancestor example where $anc/2$ is a derived predicate, defined with rules and $p/2$ a database predicate defined by tuples stored in the database.

Rules	Database tuples		
(c1) anc(X,Y) :- p(X,Y).	p(a,b)	p(e,f)	p(f,g)
(c2) anc(X,Y) :- anc(X,Z), p(Z,Y).	p(b,c)	p(d,b)	

Figure 2: Definition of the anc program

There exist different techniques to solve the deductive part of the different DDB systems, see for example the survey of Ramakrishnan and Ullman[14]. In particular, the system we are working on, Validity, is based on SLD-AL resolution (*SLD with test of Admissibility and resolution on Lemmas*) described by Vieille in [19]. This form of resolution is an optimization of SLD resolution which cuts infinite branches from the search tree.

The aim of this resolution is to do the calculations only once. Therefore two kinds of information have to be stored: goals, solved or in the process of resolution, and solutions, produced by the solved goals. During the resolution new goals are compared with the set of stored goals. When a goal is a variant of one of the stored goals, it is called *non-admissible* and it is solved using both the solutions already produced and those that will be further produced. The solutions are called *lemmas*. Only derived predicates are concerned by the notion of non-admissibility because they are the only ones that can induce non termination. Goals using database predicates are not stored.

The SLD-AL resolution manipulates tuples one by one. On the example $anc/2$ of Fig.2, to solve $p(X,Y)$, one branch of resolution is created by tuple in the database unifying with $p(X,Y)$. However, in DDB connected to a relational database, database accesses are achieved set by set and in this case only one branch is actually created to solve $p(X,Y)$. To express this set manipulation, we introduce substitution sets in the SLD-AL resolution in the same way as in *multi-SLD* resolution presented by Smith [15].

The new resolution is called *multi-SLD-AL* and the resulting search tree of this resolution is called a multi-SLD-AL tree. A node of the tree is labeled with the resolvent and a set of substitutions. An edge is labeled with the type of the transition: the clause, if the solved goal is a derived predicate; *database*, if it is a database predicate; *lemmas*, if it is a non-admissible goal solved using lemmas and *builtin*, if it is a built-in predicate.

Figure 3 represents a multi-SLD-AL tree for the query $anc(X, Y)$ on the program of Fig. 2. The first branch of the tree corresponds to the use of the clause *c1*. At the end of this branch, some solutions (lemmas) are produced for the atom $anc(X, Y)$. Lemmas are global to the whole search space of the multi-SLD-AL resolution. The second branch, created using clause *c2*, uses the produced lemmas (1) to solve $anc(X, Z)$ which is a variant of $anc(X, Y)$. The substitution set is enriched with these lemmas. After the evaluation of $p(Z, Y)$, the result of the database access $\{\{Z/a, Y/b\}, \{Z/b, Y/c\}, \{Z/e, Y/f\}, \{Z/d, Y/b\}, \{Z/f, Y/g\}\}$ is joined with the previous substitution set $\{\{X/a, Z/b\}, \{X/b, Z/c\}, \{X/e, Z/f\}, \{X/d, Z/b\}, \{X/f, Z/g\}\}$. Some of the substitutions cannot be joined with the tuples selected during the database access, for example $\{X/b, Z/c\}$ cannot be joined as there is no solution $\{Z/c, Y/...\}$. They are suppressed from the substitution set. As soon as new lemmas are produced, new transitions are possible. The production of lemmas at the end of the second branch creates a new possible transition from the node $anc(X, Z), p(Z, Y)$ with an empty substitution set using the new lemmas (2). This third branch ends with a failure because the join between the substitution set and the database results gives an empty set.

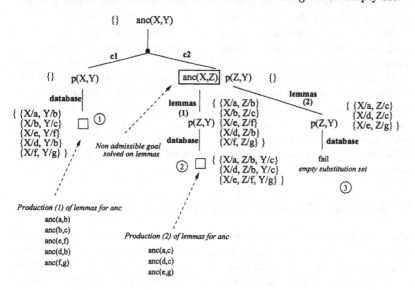

Figure 3: A multi SLD-AL tree

4.2 A set oriented meta-interpreter

The Prolog meta-interpreter, which we propose for implementing the multi-SLD-AL resolution, is an extension of SLD-AL meta-interpreters introduced in [9] which did not take substitution sets into account.

The meta-interpreter can be divided in two parts: the search tree traversal and the resolution which computes answers as sets of substitutions. We first describe the traversal and then the resolution.

Figure 4 defines the traversal of the search tree of the multi-SLD-AL resolution. This traversal starts with the predicate *solve/2*. In a first pass, *solve_goal/4* evaluates the query like a multi-SLD-AL query, leaving the non admissible goals on the side. In the second pass *solve_na/2* solves the non admissible goals using lemmas.

The first argument of *solve_goal/4* is the resolvent. Its structure may seem unusual. Indeed, the head of the unified clause is kept in the resolvent (hence the *[true ← Query]*). This allows lemmas to be generated easily, the information about the solved subgoal is still present in the resolvent.

The resolution of a subgoal is composed of two stages. Initially, the atom to be evaluated is chosen (*select/3*) then *solve_atom/7*, defined on Fig. 5, solves it according to its type following the four transitions previously described on the multi-SLD-AL tree. The evaluation of non admissible atoms is delayed. In this case, the goal and its environment are stored and the procedure fails in order to continue the traversal of the search tree.

Some functions calculate the new substitution sets of the states: when accessing the database (*access/3*), evaluating built-in predicates (*answer_builtin/3*), unifying the head of a clause with the selected atom (*unify/4*) and solving the non admissible goals using lemmas (*answer_set/3*).

The multi-SLD-AL evaluation requires storage of some information. *save_answer/2* and *answer_set/3* are respectively used to store and recover the produced lemmas. *save_subquery/3* and *variants_subquery/3* respectively store and compare subgoals to detect non admissible subgoals. Finally *save_na/4* and *na/4* respectively store and recover the non admissible states.

5 Driving the meta-interpreter with the trace

The meta-interpreter is not efficient. In particular, the construction of the answers and the storage of information take a lot of time. We show here how to drive it by a relational (low-level) trace to lighten some of the problems. Information stored in the trace do not need to be rebuilt in the meta-interpreter. The non determinism in the meta-interpreter can be reduced and substitution sets are already present in the trace.

In the following we first describe the generation of the relational trace. We, then, explain how to use information stored in the trace. Finally, we discuss the synchronization of the meta-interpreter with the trace events.

```
/* Query resolution: multi-SLD and AL part */

    /* multi-SLD part */
solve(Query, SubstSet) :-
  <initialisations>,
    solve_goal([true <- Query], emptySet, SubstSet, Query).

    /* AL part */
solve(Query, SubstSet) :-
    solve_na(Query, SubstSet).

/* Resolution of non-admissible states */

solve_na(Query, SubstSet) :-
  IF <no new answer produced>
  THEN fail
  ELSE    /* Take a non-admissible state */
  na(Atom, SubstSet0, Cont, Query),
    /* Solve it on existing lemmas */
  answer_set(Atom, SubstSet0, SubstSet1),
    /* Continue the resolution with Cont */
  solve_goal(Cont, SubstSet1, SubstSet, Query).


/* The query has been solved, a set of answers SubstSet has been produced */

solve_goal([true <- []], SubstSet, SubstSet, _).


/* A sub-goal has been solved */

solve_goal([SubGoal <- []| Rest], SubstSet0, SubstSet, Query) :-
    /* Production of lemmas for SubGoal */
  save_answer(SubGoal, SubstSet0),
    /* The resolution goes on */
  solve_goal(Rest, SubstSet0, SubstSet, Query).


/* Resolution of a SubGoal */

solve_goal([SubGoal <- ToSolve|Rest], SubstSet0, SubstSet, Query) :-
    /* Selection of Atom to solve local selection rule */
  select(ToSolve, Atom, RestToSolve),
    /* Resolution of the selected Atom */
  solve_atom(Type, Atom, [SubGoal :- NewToSolve|Rest], NewResolvent,
        SubstSet0, SubstSet, Query),
    /* Continue the resolution with NewResolvent */
  solve_goal( NewResolvent, SubstSet1, SubstSet, Query).
```

Figure 4: Multi-SLD-AL meta-interpreter: resolution of a goal

```
/* Resolution of an atom of base type */

solve_atom(base, Atom, ToSolve, ToSolve, SubstSet0, SubstSet, Query) :-
      /* Test of the atom type */
   is_basis(Atom), !,
      /* Database access*/
   access(Atom, SubstSet0, SubstSet).

/* Resolution of an atom of builtin type */

solve_atom(builtin, Atom, ToSolve, ToSolve, SubstSet0, SubstSet, Query) :-
      /* Test of the atom type */
   is_builtin(Atom), !,
      /* Resolution of the builtin */
   answer_builtin(Atom, SubstSet0, SubstSet).


/* Resolution of an atom of non-admissible type */

solve_atom(na, Atom, Resolvent, _, SubstSet0, _, Query) :-
      /* Test of the non-admissibility of the state */
   variants_subquery(Atom, SubstSet0, NonAdmSet),
      /* If the state is non-admissible on all the substitution set, */
      /* other branches of resolution are cut                        */
   IF all_non_admissible(NonAdmSet)
   THEN <cut other branches>,
      /* The non-admissible state is saved */
   save_na(Atom,  NonAdmSet, Resolvent, Query),
      /* And fail (it will backtrack to the next choice point) */
   fail.

/* Resolution of an atom of rule type */

solve_atom(rule, Atom, Resolvent, [Atom :- Body|Resolvent], SubstSet0,
            SubstSet, Query) :-
      /* Save the atom */
   save_subquery(Atom, SubstSet0, AdmSet),
      /* Selection of a rule to solve Atom */
   choose_rule(Head, Body),
      /* Unification of Atom and the Head of the clause */
   unify(Atom, Head, AdmSet, SubstSet1).
```

Figure 5: Multi-SLD-AL meta-interpreter: resolution of an atom

5.1 The Validity "Relational" Trace : Generation

An ad hoc trace has been added by implementors in order to have some low level information for debugging. It describes a succession of events which reflect the interaction with the relational database. These events are of two types: management of the control flow and operations on data.

The management of the control flow gives information about the non admissible goals. The data events give pointers to tables stored in the database. The tables contain descriptions of relations manipulated during the operations. *These tables are generated by the execution whether the trace is requested or not.* They remain accessible after the execution. Thus, at explanation time the whole information related to database accesses is available without re-executing these accesses, and this at no extra cost in terms of space.

5.2 Information in the Trace

Avoiding database accesses The sets of substitutions are no longer transmitted along the meta-interpreter to construct solutions. At each point of construction or enrichment of a set (namely in *answer_set/3*, *access/3*, *answer_builtin/3*, *unify/4*), the substitutions are replaced by an indication of how to obtain them from the intermediate relations if necessary. These sets can be accessed one by one on user request during the visualisation step or in the chosen abstraction or ignored. The arguments *SubstSet* and *SubstSet0* are no longer used in *solve_atom/5* and *solve_goal/2*. In the temporary relations, tuples are tuples of values. To reconstruct substitutions, these values have to be associated with the variables present in the corresponding query. That correspondence is present in the trace file.

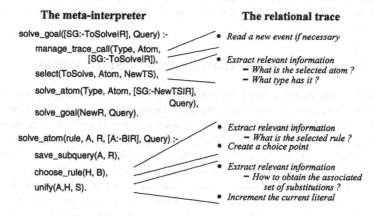

Figure 6: Using relational trace information

Reducing the non determinism The trace is an image of an execution, where choices were already made. It is not necessary to remake them in the meta-interpreter. The atom selected at a given resolution step is known from the trace. The selection function *select/3* consists then of retrieving this information. In the same way, the type of this atom is present in the table of symbols. The clause of *solve_atom/7* which is used can now be set in advance using indexing. *Type* in *solve_atom(Type, Atom, Res, NewRes, SubstSet0, SubstSet, Query)* is instantiated before invocation. Furthermore, the rule selected for the resolution of a derived predicate is also present in the trace. The choice points normally created by Prolog are no longer created. It is nevertheless necessary for the meta-interpreter to backtrack in order to follow correctly the execution. These choice points have then to be simulated: the predicate *choose_rule/2* is redefined. The principle is to repeat the choice of rules until no longer rule unifies with the current goal in the trace. In the same way, the lemmas used to solve non admissible goals can also be found in the trace. Therefore the meta-interpreter does not need to manage lemmas, now *save_answer/2* does nothing. For the non admissible states, the resolvent is not available in the trace, *save_na(Atom, Resolvent, Query)* continues to save it but does not save the associated set of substitutions anymore because they are stored in the trace.

5.3 Synchronizing the meta-interpreter with the trace events

Figure 6 sums up the connection on a small part of the meta-interpreter. In *solve_goal/2*, *manage_trace_call/3* reads a new event if necessary, then *select/3* extracts relevant information from the trace. In *solve_atom/5*, *choose_rule/2* extracts the selected rule and a choice point is created as explained before. *unify/3* gives the set of substitutions corresponding to the resolution of the atom and then increments the current literal to progress in the trace.

6 Constructing abstractions by instrumentation

Once trace information has been associated with the multi-SLD-AL resolution, the next step is to produce abstract views of executions. As already mentioned in the introduction, it is necessary to have different abstractions to adapt to different users and different debugging or understanding problems. Three possible abstractions of executions are presented. The order of presentation corresponds to a growing level of abstraction. The first one, relatively low level, is a box-oriented representation of execution. The second one reflects the operational semantics level, it is a representation of the multi-SLD-AL tree. The last one is closer to declarative semantics. The execution is abstracted by a forest of proof trees combined with substitution sets.

A box-oriented trace A box-oriented trace gives a sequence of events inspired by those proposed by Byrd in [3]. The meta-interpreter is instrumented following the tracing methods of Prolog programs described in [18, 21]. The trace format that we choose contains eight ports, including four ports for the non admissible goals. These ports are *call, fail, exit, redo, call_na, fail_na, exit_na, redo_na*. The *_na* suffix refers to non-admissible goals.

Instrumentation	Corresponding abstraction		

```
solve_na(Query) :-                     call      anc(X,Y)
  IF <no new answer produced>          unify     anc(X,Y)   rule
  THEN fail                            call      p(X,Y)
  ELSE                                 unify     p(X,Y)     base
  ( trace(call_na, Atom)               exit      p(X,Y)
  ; trace(fail_na, Atom),              exit      anc(X,Y)
      fail),                           redo      anc(X,Y)
  na(Atom, Cont, Query),               unify     anc(X,Y)   rule
  answer_set(Atom, S),                 call      anc(X,Z)
  ( trace(exit_na, Atom)               unify     anc(X,Z)   non-admissible
  ; trace(redo_na, Atom),              fail      anc(X,Z)
      fail),                           fail      anc(X,Y)
  solve_goal(Cont, Query).             call_na   anc(X,Z)
                                       exit_na   anc(X,Z)
                                       call      p(Z,Y)
                                       unify     p(Z,Y)     base
                                       exit      p(Z,Y)
                                       exit      anc(X,Y)
```

Figure 7: Instrumentation: generation of a box oriented trace

The meta-interpreter builds a trace of the resolution of the various atoms appearing during the evaluation. The predicates *solve_goal/2, solve_atom/5* and *solve_na/1* are instrumented in order to trace each resolution of an atom. The instrumentation of *solve_na/1* is presented on Fig. 7. A predicate *trace/2* is used to trace information concerning the current port and the current atom. It should be noted that the proposed instrumentation is not the only possible one. It remains adaptable. The trace obtained for the example of Fig. 2 is presented on Fig. 7. At unify time, the type of transititon is mentioned (rule, base, non-admissible, builtin). It actually corresponds to the first two branches of the multi-SLD-AL tree. This trace could be enriched with additional information such as the call depth or an action number for example.

The Multi-SLD-AL Tree This abstraction gives an operational view of execution in terms of a multi-SLD-AL tree (see Section 4.1). The management of the nodes occurs at the time of the resolution of the selected atom. The predicates *solve_atom/5* and *solve_goal/7* are instrumented to build the tree. Fig. 8 gives the instrumentation of one clause of *solve_atom/7*. The predicates *create_node/3* and *create_edge/2* are adding new nodes and new edges. An inherited argument, which is the identifier of the father node, has been added to *solve_goal* and *solve_atom*.

```
solve_atom(base, A, R, R, Q, Father,  NewCurrentNode):-
  !, access(A, S),
  value(NewCurrentNode),
  create_node(NewCurrentNode, A, S),
  create_edge(Father, NewCurrentNode).
```

Figure 8: Instrumentation: generation of a multi-SLD-AL tree

Information is associated with the nodes during their creation. It can depend on the expected use of the tree. The identifier of a node is a mandatory information, then the atom, the remainder of the goal and the associated set of substitutions can be kept. Information associated with the edges concerns transitions and can be, as in the abstraction we choose, only the type of the transition. It is necessary for non admissible goals to enrich *save_na* with the identifier of the associated node. Indeed, when the evaluation of the goal is resumed again, it should be known where to hang the subtree.

Forest of Abstract AND Trees This abstraction consists of giving one proof tree per set of solutions to a query, that is to say one proof tree per success branch of the multi-SLD-AL tree. This structure is called *abstract AND tree* by Bruynooghe [2]. This view preserves the notion of set manipulation of data without operational information. It is interesting for users querying the database who are not interested in operational information but have notions of database relations. Instrumentations of the first and third clause of *solve_goal/4* and of the fourth clause of *solve_atom/7* are presented on Fig. 9. Two new arguments are added to *solve_goal/2*, *solve_na/1* and *solve_atom/5*: the skeleton of the abstract AND tree and the current node of this tree. The skeleton of the abstract AND tree is composed of only the solved atoms, the substitution sets are not interesting during the resolution. They are only interesting when some answers are found in the first clause of *solve_goal/4*. In this clause, *traceTree/2* instantiates the skeleton of the tree with values and constructs the corresponding tree. In the third clause of *solve_goal/4*, after selecting a new atom, *modifyCurrentNode/3* puts as current node the node which corresponds to the selected atom in the skeleton. Finally, in each clauses of *solve_atom/7*, new nodes are created. In particular, in the fourth clause, one son per atom in the body of the clause is added to the current node by *createSons/4*. On the example of Fig. 2, the obtained forest contains two trees, one per success branch of the multi-SLD-AL tree. Each abstract AND tree represents several proof trees. On the example, the two trees together correspond to eight proof trees. Users can be interested in the details of proof trees. As the number of proof trees can be very important and some of them can be really big, a tool to manipulate these proof trees can be used to help the user to consult this information. In this case a tool as proposed in *Explain* is useful [1].

Instrumentation

```
solve_goal( [SG :- TS|R], Q, AbstractTree, Node) :-
  manage_trace_call(T, A, [SG :- TS|R]),
  select(TS, A, NTS),
  modifyCurrentNode(A, AbstractTree, NewNode),
  solve_atom(T, A, [SG :- NTS|R], NRes, Q, AbstractTree, NewNode),
  solve_goal(NRes, Q, AbstractTree, NewNode).

solve_goal([true :- []], _, AbstractTree, _) :-
  manage_trace_exit(S),
  traceTree(AbstractTree, S).

solve_atom(rule, A, R, [A :- B|R], Q, AbstractTree, Node) :-
  save_subquery(A),
  choose_rule(H, B),
  createSons(AbstractTree, Node, B, NewAbstractTree),
  unify(A, H, S).
```

Corresponding abstraction

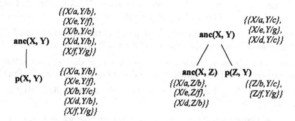

Figure 9: Instrumentation: generation of Abstract AND trees

7   Conclusion

We have presented a technique of explanation generation which consists of integrating a relational trace with an instrumented set-oriented meta-interpreter. The relational trace reduces the non determinism of meta-interpretation and avoids many costly calculations at the debugging stage that have been already performed at execution. The meta-interpreter allows different abstract views of the execution to be constructed by instrumentation. This technique has been illustrated on the Validity system. The meta-interpreter is grounded on the multi-SLD-AL semantics, which is an extension of the multi-SLD semantics to the AL technique. In order to connect the meta-interpreter to the trace produced by Validity, some calculation functions and some choice functions of the meta-interpreter have been modified.

Acknowledgments   Alexandre Lefebvre, Laurent Vieille and Bernard Wappler from Next Century Media[2] sacrificed part of their time to explain the operation of Validity. Olivier Ridoux gave fruitful comments to an earlier version of this article.

---

[2]http://www.nextcenturymedia.com

References

[1] T. Arora, R. Ramakrishnan, W.G. Roth, P. Seshadri, and D. Srivastava. Explaining program execution in deductive systems. In S. Ceri, K. Tanaka, and S. Tsur, editors, *Proceedings of the DOOD Conference, LNCS* 760, 1993.

[2] Maurice Bruynooghe. A Practical Framework for the Abstract Interpretation of Logic Programs. *JLP*, 10:91–124, 1991.

[3] L. Byrd. Understanding the control flow of Prolog programs. In S.-A. Tärnlund, editor, *Logic Programming Workshop*, 1980.

[4] S. Chakravarthy, Z. Tamizuddin, and J. Zhou. A Visualization and Explanation tool for debugging ECA rules in active databases. In Timos K. Sellis, editor, *Proc. RIDS'95, LNCS* 985, pages 197–209, 1995.

[5] M. Comini, G. Levi, and G. Vitiello. Abstract debugging of logic programs. In L. Fribourg and F. Turini, editors, *Proc. Logic Program Synthesis and Transformation and Metaprogramming in Logic, LNCS* 883, pages 440–450, 1994.

[6] M. Ducassé and J. Noyé. Logic programming environments: Dynamic program analysis and debugging. *JLP*, 19/20:351–384, May/July 1994.

[7] M. Kettner and N. Einsinger. The tableau browser SNARKS. In William McCune, editor, *Proc. CADE'97, LNCS* 1249, pages 408–411, 1997.

[8] T. Leblanc and J. Mellor-Crummey. Debugging parallel programs with Instant Replay. *IEEE Transactions on Computers*, C-36(4):471–481, April 1987.

[9] A. Lefebvre. *Evaluation de requêtes dans les bases de données déductives : aspects théoriques et pratiques.* PhD thesis, Université Descartes of Paris V, France, 1991.

[10] R. Manthey and F. Bry. SATCHMO : a theorem prover implemented in prolog. In *Proc. CADE'88*, 1988.

[11] R. Marti, C. Wieland, and B. Wüthrich. Adding inferencing to a relational database management system. In T. Härder, editor, *Datenbanksysteme in Büro, Technik und Wissenschaft*, pages 266–270. Springer Verlag, 1989.

[12] Lee Naish. A declarative debugging scheme. *JFLP*, 3, 1997.

[13] R. Ramakrishnan, D. Srivastava, and S. Sudarshan. Coral : Control, relations and logic. In Li-Yan Yuan, editor, *Proc. VLDB'92*, 1992.

[14] R. Ramakrishnan and J. D. Ullman. A survey of deductive database systems. *JLP*, 23:125–149, 1995.

[15] Donald A. Smith. MultiLog: Data Or-Parallel Logic Programming. *JLP*, 29, 1996.

[16] G. Specht. Generating explanation trees even for negations in deductive database systems. In M. Ducassé, B. Le Charlier, Y.-J. Lin, and U. Yalcinalp, editors, *Proceedings of ILPS'93 Workshop on Logic Programming Environments*, 1993.

[17] G. Specht and B. Freitag. Amos : a natural language parser implemented as a deductive database in LOLA. In R. Ramakrishnan, editor, *Applications of logic databases*, pages 197–214. Kluwer Academic Publishers, 1995.

[18] L. Sterling and E. Shapiro. *The Art of Prolog, second edition.* MIT Press, 1994.

[19] L. Vieille, P. Bayer, V. Küchenhoff, and A. Lefebvre. EKS-V1, a short overview. In *Workshop on Knowledge Base Management System*, 1990. AAAI-90.

[20] C. Wieland. Two explanation facilities for the deductive database management system DeDex. In H. Kangassalo, editor, *Proceedings of the 9th Conference on Entity-Relationship Approach*, pages 189–203, 1990.

[21] L.Ü. Yalcinalp. *Meta-programming for knowledge based systems in Prolog.* PhD thesis, Case Western Reserve University, Cleveland, Ohio 44106, August 1991. TR 91-141.

Computing large and small stable models

Mirosław Truszczyński
Department of Computer Science
University of Kentucky
Lexington, KY 40506-0046, USA
mirek@cs.uky.edu

Abstract

In this paper, we focus on the problem of existence of and computing *small* and *large* stable models. We show that for every fixed integer k, there is a linear-time algorithm to decide the problem *LSM* (large stable models problem): does a logic program P have a stable model of size at least $|P| - k$. In contrast, we show that the problem *SSM* (small stable models problem) to decide whether a logic program P has a stable model of size at most k is much harder. We present two algorithms for this problem but their running time is given by polynomials of order depending on k. We show that the problem *SSM* is *fixed-parameter intractable* by demonstrating that it is $W[2]$-hard. This result implies that it is unlikely, an algorithm exists to compute stable models of size at most k that would run in time $O(n^c)$, where c is a constant independent of k. We also provide an upper bound on the fixed-parameter complexity of the problem *SSM* by showing that it belongs to the class $W[3]$.

1 Introduction

The stable model semantics by Gelfond and Lifschitz [10] is one of the two most widely studied semantics for normal logic programs, the other one being the well-founded semantics by Van Gelder, Ross and Schlipf [17]. Among 2-valued semantics, the stable model semantics is commonly regarded as the one providing the correct meaning to the negation operator in logic programming. It coincides with the least model semantics on the class of Horn programs, and with the well-founded semantics and the perfect model semantics on the class of stratified programs [1]. In addition, the stable model semantics is closely related to the notion of a default extension by Reiter [12, 4]. Logic programming with stable model semantics has applications in knowledge representation, planning and reasoning about action. It was also recently proposed as a computational paradigm especially well suited for solving combinatorial optimization and constraint satisfaction problems [14, 15].

The problem with the stable model semantics is that, even in the propositional case, reasoning with logic programs under the stable model semantics is computationally hard. It is well-known that deciding whether a finite propositional logic program has a stable model is NP-complete [13]. Consequently, it is not at all clear that logic programming with the stable model semantics can serve as a practical computational tool.

This issue can be resolved by implementing systems computing stable models and by experimentally studying the performance of these systems. Several such projects are now under way. Niemelä and Simons [16] developed a system, *smodels*, for computing stable models of finite function symbol-free logic programs and reported very promising performance results. For some classes of programs, *smodels* decides the existence of a stable model in a matter of seconds even if an input program consists of tens of thousands of clauses. Encouraging results on using *smodels* to solve planning problems are reported in [15]. Another well-advanced system is DeReS [6], designed to compute extensions of arbitrary propositional default theories but being especially effective for default theories encoding propositional logic programs with good relaxed stratification. Finally, systems capable of reasoning with disjunctive logic programs were described in [9] and [2].

However, faster implementations will ultimately depend on better understanding of the algorithmic aspects of reasoning with logic programs under the stable model semantics. In this paper, we investigate the complexity of deciding whether a finite propositional logic program has stable models of some restricted sizes. Specifically, we study the following two problems ($|P|$ stands for the number of rules in a logic program P):

LSM (Large stable models) Given a finite propositional logic program P and an integer k, decide whether there is a stable model of P of size at least $|P| - k$.

SSM (Small stable models) Given a finite propositional logic program P and an integer k, decide whether there is a stable model of P of size no more than k.

Inputs to the problems *LSM* and *SSM* are pairs (P, k), where P is a finite propositional logic program and k is a non-negative integer. Problems of this type are referred to as *parametrized* decision problems. By fixing a parameter, a parameterized decision problem gives rise to its *fixed-parameter* version. In the case of problems *LSM* and *SSM*, by fixing k we obtain the following two fixed-parameter problems (k is now no longer a part of input):

LSM(k) Given a finite propositional logic program P, decide whether P has a stable model of size at least $|P| - k$.

SSM(k) Given a finite propositional logic program P, decide whether P has a stable model of size at most k.

The problems *LSM* and *SSM* are NP-complete. It follows directly from the NP-completeness of the problem of existence of stable models [13]. But fixing k makes a difference! Clearly, the fixed-parameter problems $SSM(k)$ and $LSM(k)$ can be solved in polynomial time. Indeed, consider a finite propositional logic program P with the set of atoms $At(P)$. Then, there are $O(|At(P)|^k)$ subsets of $At(P)$ of cardinality at most k. For each such subset M, it can be checked in time linear in the size of P (the total number of all occurrences of atoms in P; in the paper we will denote this number by $size(P)$) whether M is a stable model of P. Thus, one can decide whether P has a stable model of size at most k in time $O(size(P) \times |At(P)|^k)$.

Similarly, there are only $O(|P|^k)$ subsets of P of size at least $|P| - k$. Each such subset is a candidate for the set of generating rules of a stable model of size at least $|P| - k$ (and smaller subsets, clearly, are not). Given such a subset R, one can check in time $O(size(P))$ whether R generates a stable model for P. Thus, it follows that there is an algorithm that decides in time $O(size(P) \times |P|^k)$ whether a logic program P has a stable model of size at least $|P| - k$.

While both algorithms are polynomial in the size of the program, their asymptotic complexity is expressed by the product of the size of a program and of a polynomial of order k in the number of atoms (or rules) of the program. Even for small values of k, say for $k \geq 4$, the functions $size(P) \times |At(P)|^k$ and $size(P) \times |P|^k$ grow very fast with $size(P)$, $|At(P)|$ and $|P|$, and render the corresponding algorithms infeasible.

An important question is whether algorithms for problems $SSM(k)$ and $LSM(k)$ exist whose order is significantly lower than k, preferably, a constant independent of k. The study of this question is the main goal of our paper. A general framework for such investigations was proposed by Downey and Fellows [7, 8]. They introduced the concepts of *fixed-parameter tractability* and *fixed-parameter intractability* that are defined in terms of a certain hierarchy of complexity classes known as the *W hierarchy*.

In the paper, we show that the problem LSM is fixed-parameter tractable and demonstrate an algorithm that for every fixed k decides the problem $LSM(k)$ in linear time — a significant improvement over the straightforward algorithm presented earlier.

On the other hand, we demonstrate that the problem SSM is much harder. We outline an algorithm to decide the problems $SSM(k)$, $k \geq 1$, that is asymptotically faster than the simple algorithm described above but the improvement is rather insignificant. Our algorithm runs in time $O(size(P) \times |At(P)|^{k-1})$, an improvement only by the factor of $|At(P)|$. The difficulty in finding a substantially better algorithm is not coincidental. We provide evidence that the problem SSM is *fixed-parameter intractable* and, thus, it is unlikely that there is an algorithm to decide the problems $SSM(k)$ whose running time would be given by a polynomial of order independent of k.

The study of fixed-parameter tractability of problems occuring in the area of nonmonotonic reasoning is a relatively new research topic. Another paper that pursues this direction is [11].

2 Fixed-parameter intractability

This section recalls basic ideas of the work of Downey and Fellows on fixed-parameter intractability. The reader is referred to [7, 8] for a detailed treatment of this subject.

Informally, a *parametrized* decision problem is a decision problem whose inputs are pairs of items, one of which is referred to as a *parameter*. The graph colorability problem is an example of a parametrized problem. The inputs are pairs (G, k), where G is an undirected graph and k is a nonnegative integer. The problem is to decide whether G can be colored with at most k colors. The problems SSM and LSM are also examples of parametrized decision problems. Formally, a *parametrized* decision problem is a set $L \subseteq \Sigma^* \times \Sigma^*$, where Σ^* is a fixed alphabet.

By selecting a concrete value $y \in \Sigma^*$ of the parameter, a parametrized decision problem L gives rise to an associated *fixed-parameter* problem $L_y = \{x : (x, y) \in L\}$. For instance, by fixing the value of k to 3, we get a fixed-parameter version of the colorability problem, known as 3-colorability. Inputs to the 3-colorability problem are graphs and the question is to decide whether an input graph can be colored with 3 colors. Clearly, the problems $SSM(k)$ and $LSM(k)$ are fixed-parameter versions of the problems SSM and LSM, respectively.

The interest in the fixed-parameter problems stems from the fact that they are often computationally easier than the corresponding parametrized problems. For instance, the problems SSM and LSM are NP-complete yet, as we saw earlier, their parametrized versions $SSM(k)$ and $LSM(k)$ can be solved in polynomial time. A word of caution is in order here. It is not always the case that fixed-parameter problems are easier. For instance, the 3-colorability problem is still NP-complete.

As we already pointed out, the fact that a problem admits a polynomial-time solution does not necessarily mean that practical algorithms to solve it exist. An algorithm that runs in time $O(n^{15})$, where n is the size of the input, is hardly more practical than an algorithm with an exponential running time (and may even be a worse choice in practice). The algorithms we presented so far to argue that the problems $SSM(k)$, $LSM(k)$ are in P rely on searching through the space of n^k possible solutions (where n is the number of atoms or rules of a program). Thus, these algorithms are not practical (except for the very smallest values of k). The key question is how fast those polynomial-time solvable fixed-parameter problems can really be solved. Or, in other words, can one significantly improve over the brute-force approach?

A technique to deal with such questions is provided by the fixed-parameter intractability theory of Downey and Fellows [7]. A parametrized problem $L \subseteq \Sigma^* \times \Sigma^*$ is *fixed-parameter tractable* if there exist a constant p, an integer function f and an algorithm A such that A determines whether $(x, y) \in L$ in time $f(|y|)|x|^p$ ($|z|$ stands for the length of a string $z \in \Sigma^*$). The class of fixed-parameter tractable problems will be denoted by FPT. Clearly, if a parametrized problem L is in FPT, each of the associated fixed-parameter problems L_y is solvable in polynomial time by an algorithm whose exponent does not depend on the value of the parameter y. It is known (see [7]) that, for instance, the vertex cover problem is in FPT.

There is substantial evidence supporting a conjecture that some parametrized problems whose fixed-parameter versions belong to P are not fixed-parameter tractable. To study and compare complexity of parametrized problems Downey and Fellows proposed the following notion of reducibility[1]. A parametrized problem L can be *reduced* to a parametrized problem L' if there exist a constant p, an integer function q and an algorithm A that to each instance (x, y) of L assigns an instance (x', y') of L' such that

1. x' depends upon x and y and y' depends upon y only,

2. A runs in time $O(q(|y|)|x|^p)$,

3. $(x, y) \in L$ if and only if $(x', y') \in L'$.

Downey and Fellows also defined a hierarchy of complexity classes called the *W hierarchy*:

$$\text{FPT} \subseteq \text{W}[1] \subseteq \text{W}[2] \subseteq \text{W}[3] \ldots \tag{1}$$

The classes W[t] can be described in terms of problems that are complete for them (a problem D is *complete* for a complexity class $\mathcal{E}$ if $D \in \mathcal{E}$ and every problem in $\mathcal{E}$ can be reduced to D). Let us call a boolean formula *t-normalized* if it is of the form of products-of-sums-of-products ... of literals, with t being the number of products-of, sums-of expressions in this definition. For example, 2-normalized formulas are products of sums of literals. Thus, the class of 2-normalized formulas is precisely the class of CNF formulas. Define the *weighted t-normalized satisfiability problem* as:

WS(t) Given a t-normalized formula φ and an integer k, decide whether there is a model of φ with at most k atoms (or, alternatively, decide whether there is a satisfying valuation for φ which assigns the logical value **true** to at most k atoms).

It is believed that the problems $WS(t)$, $t \geq 2$, are *not* fixed-parameter tractable and that for different values of t they are of different difficulty. Downey and Fellows show that for $t \geq 2$, the problems $WS(t)$ are complete for the class W[t]. They also show that a restricted version of the problem $WS(2)$:

$WS_3(2)$ Given a 3CNF formula φ and an integer k (parameter), decide whether there is a model of φ with at most k atoms

---

[1] The definition given here is sufficient for the needs of this paper. To obtain structural theorems a subtler definition is needed. This topic goes beyond the scope of the present paper. The reader is referred to [7] for more details.

is complete for the class $W[1]$. Downey and Fellows conjecture that all the implications in (1) are proper[2]. In particular, they conjecture that problems complete for the classes W[t], $t \geq 1$, are not fixed-parameter tractable.

In the paper, we relate the problem SSM to the problems $WS(2)$ and $WS(3)$ to place the problem SSM in the W hierarchy, to obtain estimates of its complexity and to argue for its fixed-parameter intractability.

3 Large stable models

In this section we will show an algorithm for the parametrized problem LSM that runs in time $O(2^{k+k^2} \times size(P))$, where (P, k) is an input instance. This result implies that the problem LSM is fixed-parameter tractable and that for every fixed k there is a linear-time algorithm for the problem $LSM(k)$.

We start by introducing some basic notation. Given a logic program rule r, we define $h(r)$ to be the head of the rule r and $b(r)$ to be the set of atoms appearing in the body of r. We denote by $b^+(r)$ the set of atoms that appear positively in the body of r and by $b^-(r)$ the set of atoms that appear negated in the body of r. For a logic program P, by $H(P)$ we denote the set atoms of P that appear as heads of rules from P. Finally, given a logic program P and a set of atoms M, by P_M we denote the Gelfond-Lifschitz reduct of P with respect to M.

Given a logic program P, denote by P^* the logic program obtained from P by eliminating from the bodies of the rules in P all literals $\mathbf{not}(a)$, where a is not the head of any rule from P. The following well-known result states the key property of the program P^*.

Lemma 3.1 *A set of atoms M is a stable model of a logic program P if and only if M is a stable model of P^*.*

Since $|P| = |P^*|$, Lemma 3.1 implies that the problem LSM has a positive answer for (P, k) if and only if it has a positive answer for (P^*, k). Moreover, it is easy to see that P^* can be constructed from P in time linear in the size of P. Thus, when looking for algorithms to decide the problem LSM we may restrict our attention to programs in which every atom appearing negated in the body of a rule appears also as the head of a rule. We will denote the class of such logic programs by $\mathcal{C}$.

By P^k let us denote the program consisting of those rules r in P for which $|b^-(r)| \leq k$. We have the following lemma.

Lemma 3.2 *Let P be a logic program in $\mathcal{C}$ and let $M \subseteq H(P)$ be a set of atoms such that $|M| \geq |P| - k$.*

1. M is a stable model of P if and only if M is a stable model of P^k

---

[2]If true, this conjecture would imply that in the context of fixed-parameter tractability there is a difference between the complexity of weighted satisfiability for 3CNF and CNF formulas.

2. *If M is a stable model of P^k, then P^k has no more than $k+k^2$ different negated literals appearing in the bodies of its rules.*

The following algorithm for the problem $LSM(k)$ is implied by Lemmas 3.1 and 3.2.

1. Eliminate from the input logic program P all literals $\mathbf{not}(a)$, where a is not the head of any rule from P. Denote the resulting program by Q (that is, $Q = P^*$).

2. Compute the set of rules Q^k consisting of those rules r in Q for which $|b^-(r)| \leq k$.

3. Decide whether Q^k has a stable model M such that $|M| \geq |P| - k$.

By Lemmas 3.1 and 3.2, stable models of Q^k that have at least $|P| - k$ elements are precisely the stable models of P with at least $|P| - k$ elements. Thus, our algorithm is correct.

Notice that steps 1 and 2 can be implemented in time $O(size(P))$. To implement step 3, note that every stable model of the logic program Q^k is determined by a subset of $\bigcup\{b^-(r) : r \in Q^k\}$ [5]. By Lemma 3.2, there are no more than 2^{k+k^2} such candidate subsets to consider. Checking for each of them whether it determines a stable model of Q^k can be implemented in time $O(size(Q^k)) = O(size(P))$. Consequently, our algorithm runs in time $O(2^{k+k^2} \times size(P))$.

Theorem 3.3 *The problem LSM is fixed-parameter tractable. Moreover, for each fixed k there is a linear-time algorithm to decide whether a logic program P has a stable model of size at least $|P| - k$.*

4 Computing stable models of size at most k

As already mentioned, there is a straightforward algorithm to decide the problem $SSM(k)$ that runs in time $O(size(P) \times n^k)$, where $n = |At(P)|$. This algorithm can be somewhat improved. In this section we will outline an algorithm for the problem $SSM(k)$ that runs in time $O(size(P) \times n^{k-1})$. We will provide a detailed description in the case $k = 2$ and comment on how to extend this algorithm to the case of an arbitrary k.

We say that a logic program P is *proper* if it satisfies the following three conditions:

(P1) for every rule $r \in P$, $h(r) \notin b^+(r)$

(P2) for every rule $r \in P$, $b^+(r) \cap b^-(r) = \emptyset$

(P3) $\bigcup\{b^-(r) : r \in P\} \subseteq H(P)$ (that is, $P = P^*$).

Given a logic program P, its *proper core* is a logic program obtained from P by removing from P every clause that violates conditions (P1) or (P2) and by enforcing (P3). The following lemma is straightforward.

Lemma 4.1 *A set of atoms M is a stable model of a logic program P if and only if it is a stable model of its proper core.*

Clearly, a proper core of a program P can be constructed in time linear in the size of P. Hence, Lemma 4.1 allows us to restrict our discussion of algorithms to decide the problem $SSM(k)$ to the class of proper logic programs.

Let P be a logic program. By $P(k)$ we will denote the program obtained from P by removing from it each clause with more than k atoms appearing positively in its body. In our discussion below we will use the following result.

Lemma 4.2 *Let P be a proper logic program and let M be a set of atoms such that $|M| \leq k$. Then M is a stable model of P if and only if M is a stable model of $P(k)$.*

We will now present an algorithm to decide the problem $SSM(1)$. Define $P_0 = P(0)$ and $P_1 = P(1) \setminus P(0)$. In other words, P_i, $i = 0, 1$, consists of those rules in P that have exactly i different atoms occurring positively in the body. Next, for each atom a define:

$H_0(a) =$ the number of rules r in P_0 with $h(r) = a$ and $a \notin b^-(r)$
$H_1(a) =$ the number of rules r in P_1 with $a \in b^+(r)$ (since $r \in P_1$,
there are no other positive atoms in the body of r)
$H_2(a) =$ the number of rules r in P_0 with $h(r) \neq a$ and $a \notin b^-(r)$.

We have the following lemma.

Lemma 4.3 *Let P be a proper logic program. The set $\{a\}$ is a stable model of $P(1)$ if and only if $H_0(a) \geq 1$ and $H_1(a) = H_2(a) = 0$.*

Clearly, the tables H_0, H_1 and H_2 can be computed in time $O(size(P))$. Since it takes linear time to decide whether the empty set is a stable model of a program, Lemmas 4.2 and 4.3 imply a linear-time algorithm to decide whether a logic program P has a stable model of size at most 1.

We will next describe an algorithm to decide whether a logic program has a stable model of size at most 2. Consider a proper logic program P. As before, define $P_0 = P(0)$ and $P_1 = P(1) \setminus P(0)$. In addition, define $P_2 = P(2) \setminus P(1)$.

For every two different atoms a and b in P define:

$G_0(a, b) =$ the number of rules r in P_0 with $h(r) = a$, $a \notin b^-(r)$
and $b \notin b^-(r)$

$G_1(a, b) =$ the number of rules r in P_1 such that $h(r) = b$, $b^+(r) = \{a\}$, $a \notin b^-(r)$ and $b \notin b^-(r)$

$G_2(a, b) =$ the number of rules r in P_2 with $b^+(r) = \{a, b\}$

$G_3(a, b) =$ the number of rules r in P_1 with $b^+(r) = \{a\}$, $h(r) \neq b$ and $b \notin b^-(r)$

$G_4(a, b) =$ the number of rules r in P_0 with $h(r) \notin \{a, b\}$, $a \notin b^-(r)$ and $b \notin b^-(r)$.

We have the following lemma.

Lemma 4.4 *Let P be a proper logic program. Then, the set $\{a, b\}$ is a stable model for P if and only if $G_2(a, b) = G_3(a, b) = G_4(a, b) = 0$ and at least one of the following three conditions holds:*

1. *$G_0(a, b) \geq 1$ and $G_0(b, a) \geq 1$*

2. *$G_0(a, b) \geq 1$ and $G_1(a, b) \geq 1$*

3. *$G_0(b, a) \geq 1$ and $G_1(b, a) \geq 1$.*

Observe that each of the arrays G_i, $0 \leq i \leq 4$, can be computed in time $O(n \times size(P))$. Thus, Lemmas 4.2 and 4.4 imply the following algorithm to decide the problem $SSM(2)$:

1. Decide whether $SSM(1)$ holds. If so, output YES and stop (as shown earlier, this task takes $O(size(P))$ steps)

2. Otherwise, use the algorithm implied by Lemma 4.4 to decide whether P has stable models of size 2 (that is, compute tables G_i and check the condition of Lemma 4.4 for each set of two atoms). If so, output YES and otherwise output NO.

Let $|At(P)| = n$. Since there are $O(n^2)$ two-element subsets of $At(P)$ and since $n^2 = O(n \times size(P))$, our algorithm can be implemented to run in time $O(n \times size(P))$, where n is the number of atoms occurring in P. However, the algorithm requires that several $n \times n$ arrays be maintained.

The algorithms presented in this section can be extended to the case of an arbitrary k. We will only present a very general outline here. The details are rather complex and are omitted. First, observe that by Lemmas 4.1 and 4.2, it is enough to describe the algorithm for proper logic programs with at most k positive atoms in the body. Hence, consider such a program P. As in the case of $k = 2$, we first compute programs $P_0 = P(0)$, and $P_i = P(i) \backslash P(i-1)$, $1 \leq i \leq k$. Next, we establish a lemma, corresponding to Lemmas 4.3 and 4.4 that we used in the cases $k = 1$ and $k = 2$, characterizing stable models of size at most k in terms of the numbers of rules in the programs P_i satisfying certain properties. These numbers can be arranged in no more than $f(k)$ tables (for some function f) of dimensions no more than k. One can show that these tables can be computed in time $O(size(P) \times n^{k-1})$ and that the whole algorithm can also be implemented to run in time $O(size(P) \times n^{k-1})$.

5 Complexity of the problem SSM

The algorithm outlined in the previous section is not quite satisfactory. First, the detailed description is quite complex, Second, it poses high space requirements that are of the order $\Theta(n^k)$. A natural question to ask is: are there significantly better algorithms for the problems $SSM(k)$?

In this section we address this question by studying the complexity of the problem SSM. Our goal is to show that the problem is difficult in the sense of the W hierarchy. To this end we will show that the problem $WS(2)$ can be reduced to the problem SSM, that is, that the problem SSM is $W[2]$-hard. Given the overwhelming evidence of fixed-parameter intractability of problems that are $W[2]$-hard [7], it is unlikely that algorithms for problems $SSM(k)$ exist whose asymptotic behavior would be given by a polynomial of order independent of k. To better delineate the location of the problem SSM in the W hierarchy we also provide an upper bound on its hardness by showing that it belongs to the class $W[3]$.

We will start by showing that the problem $SSM(k)$ is reducible (in the sense of the definition from Section 2) to the problem $WS(3)$. To this end, we describe an encoding of a logic program P by means of a collection $T(P)$ of 3-normalized formulas so that P has a stable model of size at most k if and only if $T(P)$ has a model with no more than $(k+1)(k^2+2k)$ atoms. In the general setting of the class NP, an explicit encoding of the problem of existence of stable models in terms of propositional satisfiability was described in [3]. Our encoding, while different in key details, uses some ideas from that paper.

Let us consider an integer k and a logic program P. For each atom q in P let us introduce new atoms $c(q)$, $c(q,i)$, $1 \le i \le k+1$, and $c^-(q,i)$, $2 \le i \le k+1$. Intuitively, atom $c(q)$ represents the fact that in the process of computing the least model of the reduct of P with respect to some set of atoms, atom q is computed no later than during the iteration $k+1$ of the van Emden-Kowalski operator. Similarly, atom $c(q,i)$ represents the fact that in the same process atom q is computed exactly in the iteration i of the van Emden-Kowalski operator. Finally, atom $c^-(q,i)$, expresses the fact that q is computed *before* the iteration i of the van Emden-Kowalski operator. The formulas $F_1(q,i)$, $2 \le i \le k+1$, and $F_2(q)$ describe some basic relationships between atoms $c(q)$, $c(q,i)$ and $c^-(q,i)$ that we will require to hold:

$$F_1(q,i) = c^-(q,i) \Leftrightarrow c(q,1) \vee \ldots \vee c(q,i-1),$$

$$F_2(q) = c(q) \Leftrightarrow c(q,1) \vee \ldots \vee c(q,k+1).$$

Let r be a rule in P with $h(r) = q$, say

$$r = q \leftarrow a_1, \ldots, a_m, \mathbf{not}(b_1), \ldots, \mathbf{not}(b_n).$$

Define a formula $F_3(r,i)$, $2 \le i \le k+1$, by

$$F_3(r,i) = c^-(a_1,i) \wedge \ldots \wedge c^-(a_m,i) \wedge \neg c(b_1) \wedge \ldots \wedge \neg c(b_n) \wedge \neg c^-(q,i).$$

Define also $F_3(r, 1) = \mathbf{false}$ if $m \geq 1$ and

$$F_3(r, 1) = \neg c(b_1) \wedge \ldots \wedge \neg c(b_k),$$

otherwise. Speaking informally, formula $F_3(r, i)$ asserts that q is computed by means of rule r in the iteration i of the least model computation process and that it has not been computed earlier.

Let $r_1, \ldots, r_t$ be all rules in P with atom q in the head. Define a formula $F_4(q, i)$, $1 \leq i \leq k + 1$, by

$$F_4(q, i) = c(q, i) \Leftrightarrow F_3(r_1, i) \vee \ldots \vee F_3(r_t, i).$$

Intuitively, the formula $F_4(q, i)$ expresses the definition of $c(q, i)$ (recall that $c(q, i)$ stands for the following statement: when computing the least model of the reduct of P, atom q is first computed in the iteration i).

We will now define the theory $T_0(P)$ that encodes the problem of existence of small stable models. Put

$$\begin{aligned} T_0(P) \;=\; & \{F_1(q, i) : q \in At(P),\ 1 \leq i \leq k + 1\} \cup \{F_2(q) : q \in At(P)\} \cup \\ & \{F_4(q, i) : q \in At(P),\ 1 \leq i \leq k + 1\}. \end{aligned}$$

We will now establish some useful properties of the theory $T_0(P)$. First, consider a set U of atoms that is a model of $T_0(P)$. Define

$$M = \{q \in At(P) : c(q) \in U\}.$$

Lemma 5.1 *Let $q \in M$. Then there is a unique integer i, $1 \leq i \leq k + 1$, such that $c(q, i) \in U$.*

For every atom $q \in M$ define i_q to be the integer whose existence and uniqueness is guaranteed by Lemma 5.1. Define $i_U = \max\{i_q : q \in M\}$. Next, for each i, $1 \leq i \leq i_U$ define

$$M_i = \{q \in M : i_q = i\}.$$

Lemma 5.2 *For every i, $1 \leq i \leq i_U$, $M_i \neq \emptyset$.*

Lemma 5.2 implies that if $|M| \leq k$, then $i_U \leq k$.

Lemma 5.3 *Assume that $|M| \leq k$. Then M is a stable model of P.*

Consider now a stable model M of the program P and assume that $|M| \leq k$. Clearly, $M = \bigcup_{i=1}^{i} T_{P_M}^i(\emptyset)$. For each atom $q \in M$ define s_q to be the least integer s such that $q \in T_{P_M}^s(\emptyset)$. Clearly, $s_q \geq 1$. Moreover, since $|M| \leq k$, it follows that for each $q \in M$, $s_q \leq k$. Now, define

$$U_M = \{c(q), c(q, s_q) : q \in M\} \cup \{c^-(q, i) : q \in M,\ s_q < i \leq k + 1\}$$

Lemma 5.4 *The set of atoms U_M is a model of $T_0(P)$.*

Lemmas 5.1 - 5.4 add up to a proof of the following result.

Theorem 5.5 *Let k be a non-negative integer and let P be a logic program. The program P has a stable model of size at most k if and only if the theory $T_0(P)$ has a model U such that $|\{q \in At(P) : c(q) \in U\}| \leq k$.*

We will now modify the theory $T_0(P)$ to construct a theory $T(P)$ that will demonstrate that the problem $SSM(k)$ can be reduced to the problem $WS(3)$. First, for each atom $q \in At(P)$, introduce $k^2 + 2k$ new atoms $d(q, i)$, $1 \leq i \leq k^2 + 2k$, and define

$$C_0(q) = \{\neg c(q) \vee d(q, i) : 1 \leq i \leq k^2 + 2k\} \cup \{c(q) \vee \neg d(q, i) : 1 \leq i \leq k^2 + 2k\}.$$

Next, define

$$\begin{aligned} C_1(q, i) &= \{\neg c^-(q, i) \vee c(q, 1) \vee \ldots \vee c(q, i - 1)\} \cup \\ &\quad \{\neg c(q, j) \vee c^-(q, i) : 1 \leq j \leq i - 1\}, \end{aligned}$$

$$C_2(q) = \{\neg c(q) \vee c(q, 1) \vee \ldots \vee c(q, k + 1)\} \cup \{\neg c(q, j) \vee c(q) : 1 \leq j \leq k + 1\},$$

and

$$C_4(q, i) = \{\neg c(q, i) \vee F_3(r_1, i) \vee \ldots \vee F_3(r_t, i)\} \cup \{\neg F_3(r_j, i) \vee c(q, i) : 1 \leq j \leq m\},$$

where $\{r_1, \ldots, r_t\}$ is the set of all rules in P with q in the head.

Finally, define

$$\begin{aligned} T(P) &= \{C_0(q) : q \in At(P)\} \cup \{C_1(q, i) : q \in At(P), 1 \leq i \leq k + 1\} \cup \\ &\quad \{C_2(q) : q \in At(P)\} \cup \{C_4(q, i) : q \in At(P), 1 \leq i \leq k + 1\} \end{aligned}$$

It is easy to see that the set of clauses $C_1(q, i)$ is equivalent to the formula $F_1(q, i)$, the set of clauses $C_2(q)$ is equivalent to the formula $F_2(q)$, and the set $C_4(q, i)$ of disjunctions of conjunctions of literals is equivalent to the formula $F_4(q, i)$. Thus, the union of the last three sets of clauses in the definition of $T(P)$ is logically equivalent to the theory $T_0(P)$. It follows that $U \subseteq \{c(q) : q \in At\} \cup \{c(q, i) : q \in M, \ 1 \leq i \leq k + 1\} \cup \{c^-(q, i) : q \in M, \ 2 \leq i \leq k + 1\}$ is a model of $T_0(P)$ if and only if $U \cup \{d(q, i) : c(q) \in U, 1 \leq i \leq k^2 + 2k\}$ is a model of $T(P)$. Moreover, every model of $T(P)$ is of the form $U \cup \{d(q, i) : c(q) \in U, 1 \leq i \leq k^2 + 2k\}$, where $U \subseteq \{c(q) : q \in At\} \cup \{c(q, i) : q \in M, \ 1 \leq i \leq k + 1\} \cup \{c^-(q, i) : q \in M, \ 2 \leq i \leq k + 1\}$ is a model of $T_0(P)$.

The role of the clauses in the sets $C_0(q)$ is to decrease the effect of the atoms $c^-(q, i)$ and $c(q, i)$ on the size of models of $T(P)$. Consequently, given a model U of $T_0(P)$, we can derive a bound on $|\{q \in At(P) : c(q) \in U\}|$ from a bound on the size of the model of $T(P)$ corresponding to U. Specifically, one can show that $T_0(P)$ has a model U with $|\{q \in At(P) : c(q) \in U\}| \leq k$ if and only if $T(P)$ has a model of size at most $(k + 1)(k^2 + 2k)$. Thus, by

Theorem 5.5, one can show that P has a stable model of size at most k if and only if $T(P)$ has a model of size at most $(k+1)(k^2+2k)$. In other words, the problem SSM can be reduced to the problem $WS(3)$ (note that $T(P)$ consists of 3-normalized formulas).

Theorem 5.6 *The problem $SSM(k) \in W[3]$.*

Next, we will show that the problem $WS(2)$ can be reduced to the problem SSM. Let $C = \{c_1, \ldots, c_m\}$ be a collection of clauses. Let $A = \{x_1, \ldots, x_n\}$ be the set of atoms appearing in clauses in C. For each atom $x \in A$, introduce k new atoms $x(i)$, $1 \le i \le k$. By S_i, $1 \le i \le k$, we denote the logic program consisting of the following n clauses:

$$x_1(i) \leftarrow \mathbf{not}(x_2(i)), \ldots, \mathbf{not}(x_n(i))$$
$$\ldots$$
$$x_n(i) \leftarrow \mathbf{not}(x_1(i)), \ldots, \mathbf{not}(x_{n-1}(i))$$

Define $S = \bigcup_{i=1}^{k} S_i$. Clearly, each stable model of S is of the form $\{x_{j_1}(1), \ldots, x_{j_k}(k)\}$, where $1 \le j_p \le n$ for $p = 1, \ldots, k$. Sets of this form can be viewed as representations of nonempty subsets of the set A that have no more than k elements. This representation is not one-to-one, that is, some subsets have multiple representations.

Next, define P_1 to be the program consisting of the clauses

$$x_j \leftarrow x_j(i), \quad j = 1, \ldots, n, \quad i = 1, 2, \ldots, k.$$

Stable models of the program $S \cup P_1$ are of the form $\{x_{j_1}(1), \ldots, x_{j_k}(k)\} \cup M$, where M is a nonempty subset of A such that $|M| \le k$ and $x_{j_1}, \ldots, x_{j_k}$ enumerate (possibly with repetitions) all elements of M.

Finally, for each clause

$$c = a_1 \vee \ldots \vee a_s \vee \neg b_1 \vee \ldots \vee \neg b_t$$

from C define a logic program clause $p(c)$:

$$p(c) = f \leftarrow b_1, \ldots, b_t, \mathbf{not}(a_1), \ldots, \mathbf{not}(a_s), \mathbf{not}(f)$$

where f is yet another new atom. Define $P_2 = \{p(c) : c \in C\}$ and $P^C = S \cup P_1 \cup P_2$.

Theorem 5.7 *A set of clauses C has a nonempty model with no more than k elements if and only if the program P^C has a stable model with no more than $2k$ elements.*

Now the reducibility of the problem $WS(k)$ to the problem $SSM(2k)$ is evident. Given a collection of clauses C, to check whether it has a model of size at most k, we first check whether the empty set of atoms is a model of C. If so, we return the answer YES and terminate the algorithm. Otherwise, we construct the program P^C and check whether it has a stable model of size at most $2k$. Consequently, we obtain the following result.

Theorem 5.8 *The problem SSM is $W[2]$-hard.*

6 Open problems and conclusions

There is a natural variation on the problem of computing large stable models: given a logic program P and an integer k (parameter), decide whether P has a stable model of size at least $|At(P)| - k$. We conjecture that this version of the problem LSM is fixed-parameter intractable but have not been able to find a proof, yet.

Another open problem is to resolve whether there is an algorithm for the problem $SSM(k)$ that would run in time $O(n^{\alpha k})$, for some constant $\alpha < 1$.

Finally, our results show that SSM is in $W[3]$ and that it is $W[2]$-hard. Determining the exact location of the problem SSM in the W hierarchy is yet another open problems suggested by our paper.

Acknowledgments

The author thanks Victor Marek and Jennifer Seitzer for useful discussions and comments, and to an anonymous referee for pointing out inaccuracies in proofs of some of the results. This research was supported by the NSF grants IRI-9400568 and IRI-9619233.

References

[1] K. Apt, H.A. Blair, and A. Walker. Towards a theory of declarative knowledge. In J. Minker, editor, *Foundations of deductive databases and logic programming. Papers from the workshop held in Washington, D.C., August 18-22, 1986*, pages 89–142, Palo Alto, CA, 1988. Morgan Kaufmann.

[2] C. Aravindan, J. Dix, and I. Niemelä. DisLoP: Towards a disjunctive logic programming system. In *Logic programming and nonmonotonic reasoning (Dagstuhl, Germany, 1997)*, volume 1265 of *Lecture Notes in Computer Science*, pages 342–353. Springer, 1997.

[3] R. Ben-Eliyahu and R. Dechter. Propositional semantics for disjunctive logic programs. *Annals of Mathematics and Artificial Intelligence*, 12:53–87, 1994.

[4] N. Bidoit and C. Froidevaux. Negation by default and unstratifiable logic programs. *Theoretical Computer Science*, 78(1, (Part B)):85–112, 1991.

[5] A. Bondarenko, F. Toni, and R.A. Kowalski. An assumption-based framework for non-monotonic reasoning. In A. Nerode and L. Pereira, editors, *Logic programming and non-monotonic reasoning (Lisbon, 1993)*, pages 171–189, Cambridge, MA, 1993. MIT Press.

[6] P. Cholewiński, W. Marek, and M. Truszczyński. Default reasoning system deres. In *Proceedings of KR-96*, pages 518–528. Morgan Kaufmann, 1996.

[7] R. G. Downey and M. R. Fellows. Fixed-parameter tractability and completeness i: Basic results. *SIAM J. Comput*, 24:873–921, 1995.

[8] R. G. Downey and M. R. Fellows. Fixed-parameter tractability and completeness ii: On completeness for w[1]. *Theoretical Computer Science*, 141:109–131, 1995.

[9] T. Eiter, N. Leone, C. Mateis, G. Pfeifer, and F. Scarcello. A deductive system for non-monotonic reasoning. In *Logic programming and nonmonotonic reasoning (Dagstuhl, Germany, 1997)*, volume 1265 of *Lecture Notes in Computer Science*, pages 364–375. Springer, 1997.

[10] M. Gelfond and V. Lifschitz. The stable semantics for logic programs. In R. Kowalski and K. Bowen, editors, *Proceedings of the 5th International Symposium on Logic Programming*, pages 1070–1080, Cambridge, MA, 1988. MIT Press.

[11] G. Gottlob, F. Scarcello, and M. Sideri. Fixed parameter complexity in ai and nonmonotonic reasoning. In *Proceedings of LPNMR'99*, 1999. To appear.

[12] W. Marek and M. Truszczyński. Stable semantics for logic programs and default theories. In E.Lusk and R. Overbeek, editors, *Proceedings of the North American Conference on Logic Programming*, pages 243–256. MIT Press, 1989.

[13] W. Marek and M. Truszczyński. Autoepistemic logic. *Journal of the ACM*, 38(3):588–619, 1991.

[14] W. Marek and M. Truszczyński. Stable models and an alternative logic programming paradigm. In K.R. Apt, W. Marek, M. Truszczyński, and D.S. Warren, editors, *The Logic Programming Paradigm: a 25-Year Perspective*, pages 375–398. Springer Verlag, 1999.

[15] I. Niemelä. Logic programs with stable model semantics as a constraint programming paradigm. In I. Niemelä and T. Schaub, editor, *Proceedings of the Workshop on Computational Aspects of Nonmonotonic Reasoning*, pages 72–79, 1998.

[16] I. Niemelä and P. Simons. Efficient implementation of the well-founded and stable model semantics. In *Proceedings of JICSLP-96*. MIT Press, 1996.

[17] A. Van Gelder, K.A. Ross, and J.S. Schlipf. The well-founded semantics for general logic programs. *Journal of the ACM*, 38(3):620–650, 1991.

Algebra of Logic Programming

Silvija Seres, Michael Spivey, Tony Hoare

Oxford University Computing Laboratory
Wolfson Building, Parks Road, Oxford, OX1 3QD, U.K.
{Silvija.Seres,Mike.Spivey,Tony.Hoare}@comlab.ox.ac.uk

Abstract

A declarative programming language has two kinds of semantics. The more abstract helps in reasoning about specifications and correctness, while an operational semantics determines the manner of program execution. A correct program should reconcile its abstract meaning with its concrete interpretation.

To help in this, we present a kind of algebraic semantics for logic programming. It lists only those laws that are equally valid for predicate calculus and for the standard depth-first strategy of Prolog. An alternative strategy is breadth-first search, which shares many of the same laws. Both strategies are shown to be special cases of the most general strategy, that for tree searching. The three strategies are defined in the lazy functional language Haskell, so that each law can be proved by standard algebraic reasoning. The laws are an enrichment of the familiar categorical concept of a monad, and the links between such monads are explored.

1 Introduction

In an earlier paper [5] we have proposed a simple and direct embedding of the main logical constructs of Prolog in a lazy functional language. Its use of lazy lists gives rise to a natural implementation of the possibly infinite search-space and the depth-first search strategy of Prolog. We call this the *stream model* of logic programming. We have described in [5] how the embedding can be changed to implement breadth-first search by lifting the operations to streams of lists, where each list has one higher cost that the predecessor; we call this the *matrix model*. In this paper we offer a third, more flexible model based on lists of trees which accommodates *both* search strategies; we call this the *forest model* of logic programming.

We therefore have three different implementations of a logic programming language. In comparing their logical and computational properties we concentrate on those algebraic laws which are shared in all three execution models, and in this sense the three models prove to be strongly consistent with each other and with the declarative reading. We use category theory to specify how the three models are related as *semi-distributive monads*. We define three such monads – extensions of the stream, matrix and forest monads – that satisfy certain laws and that capture each of the computation models. Then we claim the existence of unique mappings between the monad corresponding to the most general model and the other two monads. The two mappings correspond exactly to the depth-first and breadth-first traversal of the search tree of a logic program.

The embedding of logic into functional programming is achieved by translating each primitive to a function or an operator. In this manner we can separately implement the logic operators and the search-control operators, so this is a realisation of Kowalski's slogan that programs are logic plus control. Our implementation is arguably the simplest possible formalisation of different operational semantics of logic programming and can be thought of as an executable operational semantics for logic programming.

We describe the concrete implementations in the functional language Haskell, for three reasons: it is rewarding to have a concrete, working prototype to experiment with; the functional languages are easy to interpret in terms of the category theory; and the proofs of the proposed algebraic laws only use the standard algebra of functions. As an alternative to Haskell any lazy language (with the Hindley-Milner type system) and λ-abstractions would do. Our implementation shows that any such functional language contains much of the expressive power of functional logic languages, but to achieve the full power of these languages further extensions (e.g. typed unification) are needed.

In section 2 we describe the ideas behind our translation of logic programs to functional ones, and in sections 3, 4 and 5 we outline the implementations of three different execution models of logic programs: one using depth-first search, one using breadth-first search and one model accommodating both search strategies. In section 6 we show how these three models can be understood in terms of monads in category theory, and in section 7 we prove the existence of shape-preserving morphisms between the forest model and the other two. Except in these two sections, we do not assume any knowledge of category theory, but some basic knowledge of functional programming is needed.

2 Functional Interpretation of Logic Programs

In our embedding of logic programs into a functional language, we aim to give rules that allow any pure Prolog program to be translated into a functional program with the same meaning. To this end, we introduce two data types *Term* and *Predicate* into our functional language, together with the following four operations:

$$
\begin{aligned}
\&, \| \;&: \quad Predicate \to Predicate \to Predicate, \\
\doteq \;&: \quad Term \to Term \to Predicate, \\
\exists \;&: \quad (Term \to Predicate) \to Predicate.
\end{aligned}
$$

The intention is that the operators & and ‖ denote conjunction and disjunction of predicates, the operator $\doteq$ forms a predicate expressing the equality of two terms, and the operation $\exists$ expresses existential quantification. In terms of logic programs, we will use & to join literals of a clause, ‖ to join clauses, $\doteq$ to express the primitive unification operation, and $\exists$ to introduce fresh local variables in a clause.

These four operations suffice to translate any pure Prolog program into a functional program. As an example, we take the well-known program for append:

```
append([], Ys, Ys) :- .
append([X|Xs], Ys, [X|Zs]) :- append(Xs, Ys, Zs).
```

As a first step, we remove any patterns and repeated variables from the head of each clause, replacing them by explicit equations written at the start of the body. The head of each clause then contains only a list of distinct variables. By renaming, we can ensure that the list of variables is the same in each clause. We complete the translation to Haskell by joining the clause bodies with the ‖ operation, the literals in each clause by the & operator, and existentially quantifying any variables that appear in the body but not in the head of a clause:

$$
\begin{aligned}
append(Ps, Qs, Rs) = \\
(Ps \doteq nil \;\&\; Qs \doteq Rs) \;\| \\
(\exists X, Xs, Ys \to Ps \doteq cons(X, Xs) \;\&\; Rs \doteq cons(X, Ys) \;\& \\
append(Xs, Qs, Ys)).
\end{aligned}
$$

Here *nil* is used for the value of type *Term* representing the empty list, and *cons* is written for the function on terms corresponding to the Prolog constructor [|]. The function *append* defined by this recursive equation has type:

$$append : (Term, Term, Term) \to Predicate.$$

This translation to a functional program obviously respects the *declarative* semantics of the original logic program; the operators &, ‖, $\doteq$ and $\exists$ have as their main role to make the declarative semantics of the logic program explicit. We will define and implement these four basic operators such that the translation *also* respects the *execution* semantics of the logic program. In fact, we show that this translation can be adapted to three different execution models.

The four operators can be divided into two groups: we call & and ‖ the *structuring* operators, and $\doteq$ and $\exists$ the *unification* operators. The choice of a concrete scheduling strategy affects mainly the basic type of predicates and the structuring operators, so the focus of this paper will be on the implementation and analysis of these. A closer semantical study of the unification operators is a task we pursue in another paper; they have interesting monotonicity properties and are important in our study of typed unification, program transformation, functional logic programming and other topics.

The implementation details of all the four operators for both the depth-first and breadth-first computation models are described in [5]. We now give an outline of the differences between these two computation models, and in section 5 we describe a model that accommodates both search strategies.

3   The Depth-First Search Strategy

The key idea of all the three implementations is that each predicate is a function taking an 'answer' (that represents the state of knowledge about the values of variables at the time the predicate is solved), and producing a *collection* of answers, where each answer corresponds to a solution of the predicate that is consistent with the input. An answer is in principle just a substitution, i.e. an associative list mapping each value to the term that is to be substituted for it.

The representation, or type, of the collections of answers is the main difference between the three models. In the depth-first model, the set of answers is represented by a lazy list, or stream:[1]

   type *Predicate = Answer → Stream Answer.*

The $\|$ operator computes the answers to the disjunction of two predicates by concatenating the streams of answers returned by its two operands. The & operator computes the answers to the conjunction of two predicates by a pairwise unification of the answers from the two streams computed by its two arguments. It combines all the answers from its two arguments by first applying the left-hand predicate to the incoming answer, followed by applying the right-hand predicate to each of the answers in the resulting stream. Finally, to preserve the types, concatenation of the resulting stream of streams into a single stream is needed. Given the standard Haskell binary concatenation operator ++ and functions *concat* and *map*, the definitions of $\|$ and & are:

$$(p \parallel q)\ x = p\ x \mathbin{+\!\!+} q\ x, \tag{1}$$

$$p\ \&\ q = concat \cdot map\ q \cdot p. \tag{2}$$

We also define constant predicates *true* and *false*, one corresponding to immediate success and the other to immediate failure:

true :: *Predicate*	*false* :: *Predicate*
true $x = [x]$,	*false* $x = [\ ]$.

---

[1]For clarity, we use the type constructor *Stream* to denote infinite streams, and *List* to denote finite lists. In a lazy functional language, these two concepts share the same implementation.

A series of interesting algebraic properties can be proved for the operators & and ‖. The proofs are based on equational reasoning using the definitions of the operators, the associativity property of functional composition (·) and the definitions of the standard functions *map*, *concat* and their following well-known properties (see [2]):

$$map\ (f \cdot g) = (map\ f) \cdot (map\ g), \tag{3}$$

$$map\ f \cdot concat = concat \cdot map\ (map\ f), \tag{4}$$

$$concat \cdot map\ concat = concat \cdot concat. \tag{5}$$

The laws are listed below. The operator & is associative (6) with unit element *true* (7). The predicate *false* is a left zero for & (8), but the & operator is strict in its left argument, so *false* is not a right zero. The ‖ operator is associative (9) and has *false* as its unit element (10). The & operator distributes through ‖ from the right (11):

$$(p\ \&\ q)\ \&\ r = p\ \&\ (q\ \&\ r), \tag{6}$$

$$p\ \&\ true = true\ \&\ p = p, \tag{7}$$

$$false\ \&\ p = false, \tag{8}$$

$$(p\ \|\ q)\ \|\ r = p\ \|\ (q\ \|\ r), \tag{9}$$

$$p\ \|\ false = false\ \|\ p = p, \tag{10}$$

$$(p\ \|\ q)\ \&\ r = (p\ \&\ r)\ \|\ (q\ \&\ r). \tag{11}$$

Other identities that are satisfied by the connectives of propositional logic are not shared by our operators because in our stream-based implementation, answers are produced in a definite order and with definite multiplicity. This behaviour mirrors the operational behaviour of Prolog. For example, neither ‖ nor & are idempotent because the number of answers to $p\ \|\ p$ and to $p\ \&\ p$ is not the same as the the number of answers to p except in the trivial cases.

Some of the missing laws could be reestablished if bags or sets were used to collect the answers. For example, if we used bags instead of streams, the order of answers would not matter. In that case both & and ‖ would become commutative, and & could distribute through ‖ also from the left. If sets were used instead, & and ‖ would in addition become idempotent. The problem with using bags or sets is that in the infinite case their equality cannot be algorithmically defined. Furthermore, some other standard laws from propositional logic, for example the distributivity of ‖ through &, or *false* being a right zero for ‖, could be established as inequalities if an ordering on predicates was used.

We can also define the predicate operators *not* and *cut*:

$$not :: Predicate \rightarrow Predicate \qquad cut :: Predicate \rightarrow Predicate$$

$$not\ p = true\ \text{if}\ p == false, \qquad cut\ p\ x = [\,]\ \text{if}\ p\ x == [\,]$$

$$\qquad\qquad\qquad\qquad\qquad\qquad\quad |\ [head\ (p\ x)]\ otherwise.$$

The *cut* operator defined here does not exactly correspond to the cut operator in Prolog, because we have made it into an operator on predicates rather than a single predicate like in Prolog. This possibly influences the way cut behaves with respect to backtracking. As compensation for our lack of faith to Prolog, we can define a set of algebraic properties, useful for optimising purposes among others:

$$cut\ (cut\ p) = cut\ p, \tag{12}$$

$$cut\ (false) = false, \tag{13}$$

$$cut\ (p\ \&\ q) = cut\ (p\ \&\ (cut\ q)), \tag{14}$$

$$cut\ (p\ \|\ q) = cut\ ((cut\ p)\ \|\ q), \tag{15}$$

$$not\ (not\ (not\ p)) = not\ p, \tag{16}$$

$$not\ (p\ \|\ q) = (not\ p)\ \&\ (not\ q). \tag{17}$$

The operator *cut* is idempotent (12), and has *false* as its zero element (13). It does not distribute through & nor $\|$, but it does satisfy the equations (14) and (15). The operator *not* is not idempotent, but does satisfy (16). Only one of the De Morgan laws holds (17).

4   The Breadth-First Search Strategy

In a model that allows breadth-first search, we need to maintain the information about the computational cost for each answer. The cost of an answer is measured by the number of resolution steps required in its computation. Therefore, the predicates in our breadth-first model return a stream of bags[2], or a *matrix*, of answers. Each bag represents the finite number of answers reached at the same depth, or level, of the search tree. All such bags are finite because there are only a finite number of branches in each node in the search tree, so the bag equality in this case is always computable. Intuitively, each successive bag of answers in the stream contains the answers with the same computational 'cost'. The type of *Predicate* is thus:

type *Predicate = Answer → Matrix Answer*,
type *Matrix a = Stream Bag a*.

The bookkeeping of the resolution costs for each of the answers to a predicate is implemented by the function *step*, with type *Predicate → Predicate*, and the definition of each predicate implementation needs to be changed to perform a call to *step* on the outermost level. In the depth-first model, *step* is the identity function on predicates, because the cost of answers is

---

[2]If lists were used instead of bags, the definite ordering of answers would imply the loss of associativity for the & operator in this model. The underlying implementation of bags and lists is same in a functional language, but we use the *Bag* type constructor to stress the semantic difference, and we use bag equality for all our algebraic laws.

irrelevant. In the breadth-first model it increases the cost of computation of the predicate by one. It does this by shifting all the bags of answers one position to the right in the main stream:

$$step\ p\ x = [\ ]:(p\ x).$$

In the breadth-first model, the implementations of the operators $\parallel$ and $\&$ need to be adapted to preserve the cost information that is embedded in the input matrices. The $\parallel$ operator simply zips the two matrices into a single one, using the function *zipwith* which concatenates all the bags of answers with the same cost and returns a single stream of these new bags. The $\&$ operator has to add the costs of its arguments; the idea is first to compute all the answers to p, then map q on each answer in the resulting matrix by the matrix-map function *mmap*, and then to use function *shuffle* to flatten the resulting matrix of matrices to a single matrix, according to the cost:

$$(p \parallel q)\ x = zipwith\ (+\!\!+)\ (p\ x)\ (q\ x), \tag{18}$$

$$p\ \&\ q = shuffle \cdot mmap\ q \cdot p. \tag{19}$$

The function *mmap* is simply a composition of *map* with itself, and the function *zipwith* is a generalisation of the standard function *zipwith* such that it does not stop when it reaches the end of the shortest of its two argument streams. The implementation of *shuffle* is too technical to be included here, please see [5] for details. From the definitions of these functions it can be proved by structural induction on the matrices that they enjoy the following algebraic properties:

$$mmap\ (f \cdot g) = (mmap\ f) \cdot (mmap\ g), \tag{20}$$

$$mmap\ f \cdot shuffle = shuffle \cdot mmap\ (mmap\ f), \tag{21}$$

$$shuffle \cdot mmap\ shuffle = shuffle \cdot shuffle, \tag{22}$$

$$zipwith\ f\ (zipwith\ f\ l_1\ l_2)\ l_3 = zipwith\ f\ l_1\ (zipwith\ f\ l_2\ l_3), \tag{23}$$

$$mmap\ f \cdot zipwith\ g\ l_1\ l_2 = zipwith\ g\ (mmap\ f\ l_1)\ (mmap\ f\ l_2), \tag{24}$$

$$shuffle \cdot zipwith\ (+\!\!+)\ l_1\ l_2 = zipwith\ (+\!\!+)(shuffle\ l_1)(shuffle\ l_2). \tag{25}$$

The law (23) requires that f is associative, and the law (24) holds if f and g commute. For these equalities to hold it is necessary to interpret the equality sign in the laws as equality of *streams of bags* rather than a stream equality.

The predicate *false* in this model has the same implementation as in the stream model: it has no answers at any cost level so it is simply the empty stream [ ]. The predicate *true* has to be lifted to matrices, where it returns its input answer as its only answer at level 0, and has no other answers. The predicate operator *not* stays the same as in the stream model, it returns true if its input predicate equals *false*, while *cut* needs to be lifted to return the matrix containing only the first element in the first non-empty bag:

$$true\ x = [[x]],$$

$$cut\ p\ x = [[head \cdot concat \cdot map\ first\ (p\ x)]],$$

where *first* returns the singleton list containing the first element of its input list if it is non-empty, or an empty list otheriwse.

All the algebraic laws for *true*, *false*, & and ‖ listed in the previous section hold in this model too, and all the laws for *not* and *cut* hold except for (14-15). The proofs of these laws are again based on equational reasoning, using the definitions of the operators, the associativity of functional composition, and the properties (20-25). For example, in the proof of the associativity of ‖, we use the associativity property of *zipwith* (23), and in the proof of the right-distributivity of & through ‖ we use the distributivity properties of *mmap* and *shuffle* through *zipwith* (24-25). As a concrete example we show the proof of the associativity of & in this model:

$$(p \ \& \ q) \ \& \ r$$

$$= shuffle \cdot mmap \ r \cdot shuffle \cdot mmap \ q \cdot p \qquad \text{by (19)}$$

$$= shuffle \cdot shuffle \cdot (mmap \ mmap \ r) \cdot mmap \ q \cdot p \qquad \text{by (21)}$$

$$= shuffle \cdot mmap \ shuffle \cdot (mmap \ mmap \ r) \cdot mmap \ q \cdot p \qquad \text{by (22)}$$

$$= shuffle \cdot mmap \ (shuffle \cdot mmap \ r \cdot q) \cdot p \qquad \text{by (20)}$$

$$= p \ \& \ (q \ \& \ r) \qquad \text{by (19)}$$

As in the previous model, the additional properties of the propositional logic operators could be established as equalities on bags or sets (rather than equalities on streams of bags), or as inequalities using the subsumption ordering on predicates. For the same constructive reasons as before, we choose not to use these.

5   The General Model

In the model that allows the use of *both* depth-first and breadth-first search the predicates can be modelled by functions returning lists of trees of answers, or *forests* of answers. The type of *Answer* is same as before. Each inner node in a tree can have an arbitrary number of children; this can be implemented by collecting all the children nodes in a new forest:

type *Predicate = Answer → Forest Answer*,

type *Forest a = List Tree a*,

data *Tree a = Leaf a | Fork (Forest a)*.

The cost of an answer corresponds to its depth in the search tree. Consequently, the function *step* pushes all the computed answers one level down the tree by adding a new parent node as a root. It forms a tree from the input forest of answers and for type correctness converts this tree to a singleton forest:

$$step \ p \ x = [\,Fork \ (p \ x)\,].$$

The implementations of ∥ and & operators in this model are similar to the implementations in the stream model. The ∥ operator actually stays the same, it simply concatenates the two forests of answers, and the costs do not change. The & in the forest model is the lifting of the original & to the forest type. The left-hand argument to & returns a list of trees. The right-hand argument is then applied to all the answers in the resulting list – which are simply all the leafs of each tree in the list – by the function *fmap*. This results in a forest of answers at each leaf, and these are grafted into the tree by the function *fgraft*:

$$(p \parallel q)\ x = p\ x \mathbin{+\!\!+} q\ x, \tag{26}$$

$$p\ \&\ q = fgraft \cdot fmap\ q \cdot p. \tag{27}$$

The motivation for choosing forests rather than just trees for the type of answers is that ∥ and & cannot be cost-preserving on trees. If simple trees were used, $p \parallel q$ would have to combine their trees of answers by inserting them under a new parent node in a new tree, but that would increase the cost of each answer to $p \parallel q$ by one. For example, the answers to $p \parallel no$ would in the tree model cost more than the answers to p, which would be wrong – the number of resolution steps performed is the same. Also, in the tree model the ∥ operation would not be associative.

The following definitions of the auxiliary functions *graft*, *graft2*, *fmap* and *tmap* are needed in the proofs in later sections:

$$fgraft = concat \cdot map\ graft2, \tag{28}$$

$$graft2\ (Leaf\ xf) = xf, \tag{29}$$

$$graft2\ (Fork\ xff) = [\,Fork\ (fgraft\ xff)\,], \tag{30}$$

$$fmap\ f = map\ (tmap\ f), \tag{31}$$

$$tmap\ f\ (Leaf\ x) = Leaf\ (f\ x), \tag{32}$$

$$tmap\ f\ (Fork\ xf) = Fork\ (fmap\ f\ xf). \tag{33}$$

From these definitions it can be proved by structural induction that *fmap* and *fgraft* both distribute through ⧺ and that they share the standard properties of the functions *map*, *concat* and functional composition:

$$fmap\ (f \cdot g) = (fmap\ f) \cdot (fmap\ g), \tag{34}$$

$$fmap\ f \cdot fgraft = fgraft \cdot fmap\ (fmap\ f), \tag{35}$$

$$fgraft \cdot fgraft = fgraft \cdot fmap\ fgraft. \tag{36}$$

As an example we give the proof of (36). The function *fgraft* is defined through indirect recursion with the function *graft2*, so a proof of (36) requires a simultaneous inductive proof of the equation (37):

$$fgraft\ \cdot graft2 = graft2 \cdot tmap\ fgraft. \tag{37}$$

Assuming that (37) holds, we prove (36):

$$
\begin{aligned}
&\textit{fgraft} \cdot \textit{fgraft} \\
&= \textit{concat} \cdot \textit{map graft2} \cdot \textit{concat} \cdot \textit{map graft2} && \text{by (28)} \\
&= \textit{concat} \cdot \textit{concat} \cdot \textit{map (map graft2)} \cdot \textit{map graft2} && \text{by (4)} \\
&= \textit{concat} \cdot \textit{map concat} \cdot \textit{map (map graft2)} \cdot \textit{map graft2} && \text{by (5)} \\
&= \textit{concat} \cdot \textit{map (concat} \cdot \textit{map graft2} \cdot \textit{graft2)} && \text{by (3)} \\
&= \textit{concat} \cdot \textit{map (fgraft} \cdot \textit{graft2)} && \text{by (28)} \\
&= \textit{concat} \cdot \textit{map (graft2} \cdot \textit{tmap fgraft)} && \text{by (37)} \\
&= \textit{concat} \cdot \textit{map graft2} \cdot \textit{map (tmap fgraft)} && \text{by (3)} \\
&= \textit{fgraft} \cdot \textit{fmap fgraft} && \text{by (28,31)}
\end{aligned}
$$

To prove (37), we need to look at both inductive cases. The proof of the base case, $\textit{fgraft (graft2 Leaf xf)} = \textit{graft2 (tmap fgraft xft)}$, follows trivialy from the definitions (29) and (32). In the induction case, if $xft = \textit{Fork xf}$ and the induction hypothesis (36) holds of xf, we find:

$$
\begin{aligned}
&\textit{fgraft} \cdot \textit{graft2 (Fork xf)} \\
&= \textit{fgraft [Fork (fgraft xf)]} && \text{by (30)} \\
&= \textit{concat (map graft2 [Fork (fgraft xf)])} && \text{by (28)} \\
&= \textit{concat [graft2 (Fork (fgraft xf))]} && \text{by (map)} \\
&= \textit{[graft2 (Fork (fgraft xf))]} && \text{by (concat)} \\
&= \textit{[Fork (fgraft (fgraft xf))]} && \text{by (30)} \\
&= \textit{[Fork (fgraft (fmap fgraft xf))]} && \text{by (36)} \\
&= \textit{graft2 (Fork (fmap fgraft xf))} && \text{by (30)} \\
&= \textit{graft2} \cdot \textit{tmap fgraft (Fork xf)} && \text{by (33)}
\end{aligned}
$$

The predicate operator *not* stays the same as in the stream model, it returns true if its input predicate equals *false*. Since the search strategy is not specified for this model, there can be several different definitions of the *cut* operator such that it is idempotent, monotonous and returns the first answer relative to some search strategy. Once again, the predicate *false* in this model has the same implementation as in the stream model; it has no sub-trees, so it always returns the empty stream [ ]. The predicate *true* has to be lifted to forests, where it returns its input answer as its only answer at level 0 in the first subtree, and has no other answers:

$$\textit{true } x = [\textit{Leaf } x].$$

The same algebraic laws for *true*, *false*, & and ‖ hold of this model as of the previous two, and the equalities in this case need to be interpreted as equalities on streams of trees. The proofs are based on equational reasoning: the laws regarding *true* and *false* follow directly from the definitions of the operators, the associativity of ‖ follows from the associativity of ++, the associativity of & has a similar proof as for matrices and uses (34-36), and the proof of the distributivity of & through ‖ from the left uses the distributivity of *fgraft* and *fmap* through ++.

6 The Three Monads

We have so far described implementations of three scheduling strategies for logic programming, and we have seen that the same set of algebraic laws holds for the structuring operators of each model. The aim of this section is to present the mathematical framework which will help us explore and express the relationships between our three models.

Phil Wadler has shown in [6, 7] that many aspects of functional programming, for example laziness or eagerness of evaluation, non-determinism and handling of input and output, can be captured by the monad construction from category theory. Here we show in a similar fashion how our models of logic programming relate to concepts from category theory.

A monad T is a triple $(map_T, unit_T, join_T)$, where T is a type constructor T with an associated function map_T, and $unit_T$ and $join_T$ are polymorphic functions, with types:

$$map_T :: (a \rightarrow b) \rightarrow T\ a \rightarrow T\ b,$$
$$unit_T :: a \rightarrow T\ a,$$
$$join_T :: T\ (T\ a) \rightarrow T\ a.$$

In addition, we use id_T for the identity function on each T. For such a triple to qualify as a monad, the following equalities must be satisfied:

$$map_T\ id_T = id_T, \tag{38}$$
$$map_T\ (f \cdot g) = map_T\ f \cdot map_T\ g, \tag{39}$$
$$map_T\ f \cdot unit_T = unit_T \cdot f, \tag{40}$$
$$map_T\ f \cdot join_T = join_T \cdot map_T\ (map_T\ f), \tag{41}$$
$$join_T \cdot unit_T = id_T, \tag{42}$$
$$join_T \cdot map_T\ unit_T = id_T, \tag{43}$$
$$join_T \cdot map_T\ join_T = join_T \cdot join_T. \tag{44}$$

Taking *Stream* for T, the standard stream function *map* for map_T, the list unit constructor [−] for $unit_T$, and *concat* for $join_T$, one can easily verify that (*map*, [−], *concat*) is a monad. The equations (39), (41) and (44) correspond to the standard laws for list operators (3-5); the rest of the equations follow from the definitions of *map* and *concat*.

The *Matrix* monad results from taking *mmap* for map_T, the matrix unit constructor [[−]] for $unit_T$ and *shuffle* for $join_T$. The equations (39), (41) and (44) for this monad correspond to the equations (20-22), and the remaining equations can be proved from the definitions of the matrix functions *mmap* and *shuffle*.

Finally, the *Forest* monad results from taking the function *fmap* for map_T, the forest unit constructor [*Leaf* −] for $unit_T$ and *fgraft* for $join_T$. Again, the equations (39), (41) and (44) for this monad are the same as the equations (34-36) described in section 5, and the remaining ones can be proved from the definitions of the forest functions *fmap* and *fgraft*.

There is an alternative definition of a monad, where the function $join_T$ is replaced by the operator $\star_T$, also called the Kleisli composition, defined as:

$$(\star) :: (a \rightarrow T\ b) \rightarrow (b \rightarrow T\ c) \rightarrow (a \rightarrow T\ c), \tag{45}$$

$$p \star_T q = join_T \cdot map_T\ q \cdot p. \tag{46}$$

The triple $(map_T, unit_T, \star_T)$ is a monad if the equations (47-49) given below are satisfied. These equations are implied by the equations (38-44):

$$(unit_T\ a) \star k = k\ a, \tag{47}$$

$$m \star unit_T = m, \tag{48}$$

$$m \star (p \star q) = (m \star p) \star q. \tag{49}$$

Conversely, the functions map_T and $join_T$ can be defined in terms of $\star_T$, and the equations (47-49) imply the original monad equations (38-44), so the two alternative definitions of a monad are equivalent.

This second definition of a monad is particularly convenient for our purposes, since the operator $\star_T$ corresponds exactly to the definition of the operator & in each of the models, and $unit_T$ corresponds to our function *true* in each model. We have already seen that in all three models & is associative with unit element *true*, so the laws (47-49) are satisfied in the *Stream*, *Matrix* and *Forest* monads. In that sense we can say that they capture the algebraic semantics of the operator & and predicate *true* in our three models of logic programming. The remaining structural parts of each model are ‖ and *false*. We now formulate the right notion of the extended monad that captures these and their properties.

In an application to our models of logic programming, we define an *extended* monad T^+ as a five-tuple, where T is one of *Stream*, *Matrix* and *Forest* monads, $true_T$ is the unit, and $\&_T$ is the Kleisli composition in each of the monads:

$$T^+ = (map_T,\ true_T,\ false_T,\ \|_T,\ \&_T),$$

such that the laws for ‖ and *false* listed in section 3 hold. The extended monads $Stream^+$, $Matrix^+$ and $Forest^+$ capture the algebraic semantics of the three different scheduling strategies for logic programming.

A *morphism* between two extended monads is a mapping which preserves the structure of the monads, i.e. which maps *true* in one monad to *true* in the other and so on with *false*, $\|_T$ and $\&_T$. We now proceed to show the existence of monad morphisms between the third, most general, extended monad and the other two.

7 Relationships between the Monads

In the most general model, each query to a logic program returns a forest corresponding to the search tree of the query. This forest can be converted to a stream of answers, by traversing the trees in either a depth-first or breadth-first manner. The functions *dfs* and *bfs* below, with type *Forest a → Stream a*, implement these two search strategies.

The *dfs* function applies the auxiliary *dfs2* function to each tree in the list and concatenates the resulting lists. The function *dfs2* returns the leaf nodes of each tree in a depth-first manner, by recursively calling *dfs*:

$$dfs = concat \cdot map\ dfs2, \tag{50}$$

$$dfs2\ (Leaf\ x) = [x], \tag{51}$$

$$dfs2\ (Fork\ xf) = dfs\ xf. \tag{52}$$

The *bfs* function needs to take account of the cost of the answers. It does this by collecting all the answers from a same level in all the search trees of the input forest in a same list, and by returning the lists in an increasing order of level. The function *bfs2* performs the sorting of input answers with respect to their cost. The function *levels* sorts the leafs of a input tree in lists by increasing cost, and the function *bfs2* lifts it to forests. The auxiliary function *combine* takes a list of lists, and reshuffles it by making the first list from all the first elements in each list, the next list from the second elements etc.

$$bfs = concat \cdot bfs2, \tag{53}$$

$$bfs2\ [\,] = [\,], \tag{54}$$

$$bfs2\ xf = combine\ (map\ levels\ xf), \tag{55}$$

$$levels\ (Leaf\ x) = [[x]], \tag{56}$$

$$levels\ (Fork\ xf) = [\,] : bfs2\ xf, \tag{57}$$

$$combine = foldr\ (zipwith\ (++))\ [\,]. \tag{58}$$

We now show that any query results in the same stream of depth-first sorted answers regardless whether one computes the answers in the stream model, or one computes the answers by the forest model and then applies *dfs* to this forest. Also, one gets the same matrix of breadth-first sorted answers, either by computing queries directly in the matrix model or by applying *bfs2* to the forest resulting from the most general model. Categorically speaking, we show that there exist *morphisms* between the three monads, and that they are exactly the functions *dfs* and *bfs2*.

The polymorphic function *dfs* is a morphism between the *Forest*[+] and *Stream*[+] extended monads if it maps the predicates $true_F$ and $false_F$ to their counterparts in the stream model and if it preserves the behaviour of the *map* functions of the two monads and of the operators & and ∥. In other words, *dfs* is a *Forest*[+] $\Longrightarrow$ *Stream*[+] morphism if it satisfies:

$$dfs \cdot true_F = true_S, \tag{59}$$

$$dfs \cdot false_F = false_S, \tag{60}$$

$$dfs \cdot fmap\ f = map\ f \cdot dfs, \tag{61}$$

$$dfs \cdot (p \mathbin{\&_F} q) = (dfs \cdot p) \mathbin{\&_S} (dfs \cdot q), \tag{62}$$

$$dfs \cdot (p \parallel_F q) = (dfs \cdot p) \parallel_S (dfs \cdot q). \tag{63}$$

The equations (59) and (60) follow directly from the definitions of *dfs* and the predicates *true* and *false*. Equation (61) can be proved by simultaneous induction for *dfs* and *dfs2*, similarly to the proof of (36). To prove (62), we need a following lemma:

$$dfs \cdot fgraft = concat \cdot (dfs * dfs). \tag{64}$$

Here *dfs* ∗ *dfs* denotes a categorical construction called the *horizontal composition* of *dfs* with itself; it is expressed as either:

$$dfs * dfs = dfs \cdot fmap\ dfs, \tag{65}$$

$$dfs * dfs = map\ dfs \cdot dfs. \tag{66}$$

These equations express the fact that it does not matter whether one first does depth-first search on the sub-forests or the main forest. The proof of (64) is done by simultaneous induction on *dfs* and *dfs2*, similarly to the proof of (36).

The proof of (62) is then:

$$
\begin{aligned}
&dfs \cdot (p \mathbin{\&_F} q) \\
&= dfs \cdot fgraft \cdot fmap\ q \cdot p && \text{by (27)} \\
&= concat \cdot map\ dfs \cdot dfs \cdot fmap\ q \cdot p && \text{by (64,66)} \\
&= concat \cdot map\ dfs \cdot map\ q \cdot dfs \cdot p && \text{by (61)} \\
&= concat \cdot map\ (dfs \cdot q) \cdot dfs \cdot p && \text{by (3)} \\
&= (dfs \cdot p) \mathbin{\&_S} (dfs \cdot q) && \text{by (2)}
\end{aligned}
$$

The proof of (63) is a simple consequence of the distributivity of *concat* and *map* through ++.

Similarly, to prove that also *bfs2* is a monad morphism, we need to show that $true_F$ and $false_F$ are correctly mapped by *bfs2* and that:

$$mmap\ f \cdot bfs2 = bfs2 \cdot fmap\ f, \tag{67}$$

$$bfs2 \cdot (p\ \&_F\ q) = (bfs2 \cdot p)\ \&_M\ (bfs2 \cdot q), \tag{68}$$

$$bfs2 \cdot (p\ \|_F\ q) = (bfs2 \cdot p)\ \|_M\ (bfs2 \cdot q). \tag{69}$$

The proofs of (67) and (69) go by structural induction on forests. The proof of (68) requires the following two lemmas which also can be proved by structural induction on forests:

$$bfs2 \cdot fgraft = shuffle \cdot (bfs2*bfs2), \tag{70}$$

$$bfs2 * bfs2 = bfs2 \cdot fmap\ bfs2 = mmap\ bfs2 \cdot bfs2, \tag{71}$$

and we get:

$$
\begin{aligned}
&bfs2 \cdot (p\ \&_F\ q) \\
&= bfs2 \cdot fgraft \cdot fmap\ q \cdot p && \text{by (27)}\\
&= shuffle \cdot mmap\ bfs2 \cdot bfs2 \cdot fmap\ q \cdot p && \text{by (70,71)}\\
&= shuffle \cdot mmap\ bfs2 \cdot mmap\ q \cdot bfs2 \cdot p && \text{by (67)}\\
&= shuffle \cdot mmap\ (bfs2 \cdot q) \cdot bfs2 \cdot p && \text{by (20)}\\
&= (bfs2 \cdot p)\ \&_M\ (bfs2 \cdot q) && \text{by (19)}
\end{aligned}
$$

Further work on this topic is to show that the monad $Forest^+$ is an *initial object* in the 'category of monads that describe logic programming'. This captures the fact that the *dfs* and *bfs2* arrows in the diagram below are unique. Another interesting monad for further algebraic survey of logic programming is the monad where the answers are returned as sets. The definitions of the operators in the set monad would necessarily have to be less operational then in the other three monads; it would be an algebraic formulation of the least Herbrand models semantics of logic programs. The existence of morphisms between the set monad and the stream and matrix monads would show that the set of answers in both stream and matrix monads is the same, i.e. it would serve as a formal proof that our implementation is correct not only with regards to the operational semantics, but also to the formal declarative semantics of logic programs. These morphisms would correspond to a forgetful functor, i.e. one that "forgets" the information about the ordering and the multiplicity of answers.

8 Conclusion and Related Work

Declarative programming, with its mathematical underpinning, was aimed to simplify mathematical reasoning about programs. Both logic and functional programming paradigms facilitate writing of mathematically clear programs and both paradigms admit variation in execution strategy (lazy or eager, breadth-first or depth-first). So far, only functional programming has allowed easy reasoning about the equality of the clear program with the corresponding efficient program. The proofs take advantage of a suite of algebraic laws for equational inductive reasoning about functions over lists. We propose a corresponding algebraic approach to reasoning about logic programs.

Such algebraic laws can be exploited at all stages of program development. They have had a significant influence on the development of the functional programs so far: designers use them to device correct algorithms, programmers use them to make efficient programs, and language implementors use them to build a language that is suited for optimisation by both programmers and compilers.

Our idea to use algebraic laws to describe and calculate logic programs is motivated by several sources: [1] uses an algebraic approach to functional programming both to derive individual programs and to study programming principles (such as algorithm design) in general, while [4] uses algebraic description to classify and study the different programming paradigms. This paper is an attempt to carry these ideas over to logic programming, emphasising the similarity between its declarative and procedural readings.

Here we have concentrated on the study of the scheduling strategies, but the algebraic approach has many other interesting applications. One interesting topic is a semantical study of functional-logic programming, with more execution details than the least complete Herbrand model in [3]. We hope that this work can stimulate other applications of algebraic reasoning to logic programs.

References

[1] R. Bird and O. de Moor. *Algebra of Programming*. Prentice Hall, 1997.

[2] R. Bird and P. Wadler. *Introduction to Functional Programming*. Prentice Hall, 1988.

[3] M. Hamana. *Semantics for Interactive Higher-order Functional-logic Programming*. PhD thesis, University of Tsukuba, 1998.

[4] C.A.R. Hoare and H. Jifeng. *Unifying Theories of Programming*. Prentice Hall, 1998.

[5] S. Seres, J.M. Spivey, and C.A.R. Hoare. Embedding Prolog in Haskell. To be presented at HASKELL99.

[6] P. Wadler. The essence of functional programming. In *19'th Annual Symposium on Principles of Programming Languages*, January 1992.

[7] P. Wadler. Monads for functional programming. In *Advanced Functional Programming*. Springer LNCS 925, 1995.

Semantic Definitions for Normal Open Programs

Fernando Orejas and Elvira Pino
Dept. Leng. Sist. Inf., Univ. Polit. Catalunya
Barcelona, SPAIN
(orejas,pino)@lsi.upc.es

Abstract

In this paper we study the semantics of normal open programs. In particular, we consider normal open logic programs in full generality, without some usual restrictions considered in previous approaches: in our case, Ω-union is defined allowing to close some, but not necessarily all, open predicates. In this context, two semantic definitions are presented: $\mathcal{Q}_{P,\Omega}$ defines the semantics of P as a certain set of formula (from a given domain) which are logic consequences of the completion of P: This semantics is shown to be compositional and fully abstract with respect to Ω-union. The second semantics, $\mathcal{FQ}_{\Omega}(P)$, easier to compute than $\mathcal{Q}_{P,\Omega}$, is defined as the least fixpoint of an immediate consequence continuous operator associated to P. This semantics is only proved to be weakly compositional and fully abstract.

1 Introduction

The full applicability of program analysis tools largely depends on the possibility of being able to decompose large programs into units that could be analized separately. But this is only possible if adequate semantic definitions are given to the kind of units considered. In the case of logic programming, different kinds of modular units have been proposed for the design of large programs that could be an adequate basis for such kind of separate analysis. One of such kind of unit, that we consider especially interesting due to its generality and its applicability in connection to deductive databases and to the incremental definition of predicates, is the notion of open logic program [4]. In this sense, the aim of this paper is the definition of a semantics for open logic programs satisfying the following requirements:

- Following ideas from [11], the semantics should be defined in terms of a syntactic domain of formulas and its definition should be constructive. The idea is that tools for program analysis could use directly the semantics or some abstraction of it.

- The semantics must be compositional. This means that it should be possible to express the semantics of the Ω-union of two programs in terms of the semantics of both programs. Compositionality is, actually, the property that guarantees that to analyze a complete program it is enough to independently analyze its components.

The semantics should be fully abstract with respect to Ω-union and a reasonable observation criteria. This means that the semantics of two open programs coincide if and only if both units behave equally in every context. If a semantics is fully abstract in this sense, this guarantees that our notion of program equivalence is the right one for dealing about implementation, i.e. a program unit could be substituted by another unit implementing the same abstraction if and only if they have the same semantics.

According to these requirements, in this paper we present two semantic definitions for open normal programs: $\mathcal{Q}_{P,\Omega}$ defines the semantics of P as a certain set of formula (from a given domain) which are logic consequences of the completion of P. This semantics is shown to be compositional and fully abstract with respect to Ω-union. The second semantics, $\mathcal{FQ}_{P,\Omega}$, easier to compute than $\mathcal{Q}_{P,\Omega}$, is defined as the least fixpoint of an immediate consequence continuous operator associated to P. This semantics is only proved to be weakly compositional and fully abstract.

There are a number of a approaches for defining the semantics of various kinds of open programs, usually paying special attention to the problem of compositionality. Unfortunately, none of these approaches provides a satisfactory solution to our requirements. The approaches presented in [9, 7] impose a restriction on the program units that we consider too severe. They require that, for putting together two program units, there cannot be clauses defining the same predicate in two programs or, similarly, that open programs should not include any clause defining an open predicate. This restriction makes impossible the incremental definition of a predicate, for instance through some form of inheritance [2]. On the other hand, none of these approaches provide full abstraction results. In [21] a slightly more general framework is considered. They study open programs where the open predicates can be axiomatized by arbitrary first-order axioms. However, compositionality is proved under certain sufficient conditions that are quite close to the restrictions imposed in [7]. In addition, that approach is based on well-founded semantics, hence not satisfying our first requirement. In [3] it is proved that Fittings immediate consequence operator can be used for defining a semantics for arbitrary program fragments which is compositional with respect to union, intersection and filtering. The main problem here is that, if only union is considered, the given semantics is too concrete to be of any use. Finally, in [16], using algebraic techniques, we proposed a semantics for program fragments which is compositional and fully abstract with respect to union. However, the semantics is very abstract, defined in terms of some categorical constructions, making the definition hardly constructive and not easy to fully understand. Actually, the original motivation of this work was to provide a concrete version of that semantics, but the results obtained have gone far beyond our original intentions. The new semantics presented in this paper is more powerful (a limitation imposing that the signature of function symbols should be unique for all programs has been removed) and simple (we do not have to deal with *ranked models* since we directly deal with three-valued models).

This paper is organized as follows. In the next section we present the basic notions and terminology for presenting our results. In section 3, we present the two semantic definitions showing their soundness and completeness. Finally, in section 4, we prove the results about compositionality and full abstraction.

2 Preliminaries

In this paper, we assume on the reader a certain knowledge of the basic literature on Normal Logic Programming (e.g. see [1]). A countable *signature* is a pair $\Sigma = (FS, \Pi)$ such that $FS = \{FS_n\}_{n \in \mathbb{N}}$ and $\Pi = \{\Pi_n\}_{n \in \mathbb{N}}$ are, respectively, families of sets of *function and predicate symbols* for each arity $n \in \mathbb{N}$. FS-terms and Σ-atoms are built, as usual, using functions and predicates from Σ and, also, variables from a prefixed countable set X of variable symbols. In particular, $H_{FS}(X)$ denotes the set of all $FS(X)$-terms. Similarly the set of all $\Sigma(X)$-atoms is denoted by $Atom_\Sigma(X)$.

Terms will be denoted by $t, s, ...$, and atoms by $a, b, ...$, maybe with subindices. Terms and atoms are called *ground* if they contain no variables. The sets of ground terms and ground atoms are, respectively, written H_{FS} and $Atom_\Sigma$ and, they are respectively called the *Herbrand universe* and the *Herbrand Base*.

Greek lowercase letters ψ , ϕ, γ,... are used to denote formulas and Greek uppercase letters Φ, Γ,... to denote sets of formulas. A *literal* is either an atom b (*positive literal*) or a negated atom $\neg b$ (*negative literal*). Literals will be denoted by $\ell_1, ..., \ell_k,..$ $\bar{x}$, $\bar{t}$, $\bar{a}$ or $\bar{\ell}$ will denote, respectively, tuples of variables, terms, atoms or literals. A variable is *free* in a formula if it is not quantified. Given any expression E, $var(E)$ will denote the free variables appearing in E. Given any set of formulas Φ, $pred(\Phi)$ will denote the set of predicate symbols appearing in Φ. Free variables of a formula will not be made explicit if they are not relevant. $\psi(\bar{x})$ indicates that $var(\psi) \subseteq \bar{x}$. Formulas $\psi^\forall, \psi^\exists$ stand for the universal and existential closures of ψ, respectively.

A *normal Σ-program* is a set of normal Σ-clauses of the form:

$$a : -\ell_1, ..., \ell_n$$

where a is a $\Sigma(X)$-atom, for each i, $0 \leq i \leq n$, ℓ_i is a $\Sigma(X)$-literal.

For simplifying some technical constructions, we consider that any normal Σ-program is written as its equivalent constraint normal program with flat head. That is, any clause:

$$p(t_1, ..., t_m) : -\ell_1, ..., \ell_n.$$

is written as the constraint clause

$$p(x_1, ..., x_m) : -\ell_1, ..., \ell_n \Box x_1 = t_1, ..., x_m = t_m$$

or just $p(\bar{x}) : -\bar{\ell}\Box\bar{x} = \bar{t}$.

Moreover, we assume that all clauses defining a predicate p in a program have exactly the same head $p(x_1, ..., x_n)$. Then, $Hd_P(p(\bar{x}))$ denotes the set $\{p(\bar{x}) : -\bar{\ell}^k\Box\bar{x} = \bar{t}^k | 1 \le k \le m\}$ of all clauses with head p appearing in P.

Constraints appearing in programs are just equality constraints, i.e. arbitrary first-order formulas over equality atoms. We denote constraints by $c, d,...$ (possibly with sub- or super-scripts). We deal with constraints in a logical way, using logical consequence of the free equality theory. The free equality theory FET_Σ for a signature Σ is the following set of formulas:

$\forall x(x = x)$
$\forall\bar{x}\forall\bar{y}(\bar{x} = \bar{y} \leftrightarrow f(\bar{x}) = f(\bar{y}))$ for each $f \in FS_\Sigma$
$\forall\bar{x}\forall\bar{y}(\bar{x} = \bar{y} \rightarrow (p(\bar{x}) \leftrightarrow p(\bar{y})))$ for each $p \in PS_\Sigma \cup \{=\}$
$\forall\bar{x}\forall\bar{y}(f(\bar{x}) \ne g(\bar{y}))$ for each pair $f, g \in FS_\Sigma$ such that $f \not\equiv g$
$\forall x(x \ne t)$ for each Σ-term t and variable x such that $x \in var(t)$ and $x \not\equiv t$.

Besides, whenever Σ is finite, FET_Σ also includes the *weak closure domain axiom*:

$$\forall x(\bigvee_{f \in FS} \exists\bar{y}(x = f(\bar{y})).$$

FET_Σ is a complete theory, that is $FET_\Sigma \models c$ or $FET_\Sigma \models \neg c$ for every constraint c. As a consequence, all models of FET_Σ are elementary equivalent.

We deal with substitutions by means of constraints. In particular, every substitution $\theta = \{x_1 = t_1, ..., x_m = t_m\}$ is identified with the equality constraint $x_1 = t_1 \wedge ... \wedge x_m = t_m$. In this context, a ground substitution $\theta = \{\bar{x} = \bar{t}\}$ ($\bar{t}$ are ground terms) is a solution for a constraint $c(\bar{x})$ iff $FET_\Sigma \models (\bar{x} = \bar{t} \rightarrow c)$.

From a logical point of view, the meaning of a normal program P is its completion [5], denoted by $Comp(P)$ and consisting of FET_Σ and, for each predicate symbol $p \in \Sigma$, a formula:

$$\forall\bar{x}(p(\bar{x}) \leftrightarrow \bigvee_{1 \le k \le m} \exists\bar{y}^k(\bar{x} = \bar{t}^k \wedge \bar{\ell}^k))$$

where $\bar{y}^k = var(\bar{t}^k, \bar{\ell}^k)\backslash\bar{x}$ and $Hd_P(p(\bar{x})) = \{p(\bar{x}) : -\bar{\ell}^k\Box\bar{x} = \bar{t}^k | 1 \le k \le m\}$ is the set of all clauses with head $p(\bar{x})$ in P.

Conjunction (resp. disjunction) of an empty set is simplified to the atomic formula *true* (resp. *false*).

As usual, this completion is interpreted in a three-valued logic [15]. In particular, in this logic the three values are true ($\underline{t}$), false ($\underline{f}$) and undefined ($\underline{u}$). The connectives $\neg$, $\vee$ and $\wedge$ and existential and universal quantification are interpreted in Kleene's partial logic [14]. The connective $\leftrightarrow$ is interpreted as the identity of truth values, so it is two-valued. With respect to implication, we have chosen Przymusinski's interpretation ([17]) defined as:

$\rightarrow$	$\underline{t}$	$\underline{f}$	$\underline{u}$
$\underline{t}$	$\underline{t}$	$\underline{f}$	$\underline{f}$
$\underline{f}$	$\underline{t}$	$\underline{t}$	$\underline{t}$
$\underline{u}$	$\underline{t}$	$\underline{f}$	$\underline{t}$

A three-valued Σ-structure A consists of a universe of values $\mathbf{A}$ and an interpretation of every function symbol f by a total function f_A from $\mathbf{A}^n$ to $\mathbf{A}$ (of adequate arity n) and of every predicate symbol p by a partial relation, which can be seen as a total function from $\mathbf{A}^n$ to the set of the three truth values: $\{\underline{t}, \underline{f}, \underline{u}\}$. The *value* of any first-order Σ-sentence ψ in a three-valued Σ-structure A will be denoted by $A(\psi)$. A three-valued structure A is a *model* of a set of sentences Φ, denoted by $A \models_3 \Phi$, iff $A(\psi) = \underline{t}$ for any formula $\psi \in \Phi$. ψ is a *three-valued logical consequence* of Φ, written $\Phi \models_3 \psi$, if for every three-valued structure A if $A \models_3 \Phi$ then $A \models_3 \psi$.

A Herbrand three-valued Σ-structure is a structure whose universe is the Herbrand universe H_{FS} and the function symbols A_{FS} are trivially interpreted. A Herbrand three-valued Σ-structure A can be represented as a pair of disjoints subsets of the Herbrand base, $A = (A^+, A^-)$, where A^+ is the set of true ground atoms and A^- is the set of false ground atoms, so that any other atom is undefined in A.

A constrained Σ-atom is a pair $p(\bar{x})\Box c(\bar{x})$ such that $p \in \Pi$ and $c(\bar{x})$ is a satisfiable Σ-constraint. A Herbrand three-valued Σ-structure of constrained atoms A, also called three-valued constrained interpretation, is a pair, $A = (A^+, A^-)$ such that:

- A^+ and A^- are sets of constrained atoms,

- A^+ and A^- are closed under variable renaming,

- (*Consistency condition*) For each $p \in \Pi$ if there exist Σ-constraints c and d such that $p(\bar{x})\Box c \in A^+$ and $p(\bar{x})\Box d \in A^-$ then $c \wedge d$ is unsatisfiable.

From now on, $\ell \Box c \in A$ stands for:

- $p \Box c \in A^+$ if $\ell = p$, and

- $p \Box c \in A^-$ if $\ell = \neg p$.

The pair $p\Box c$ (that is, $p(\bar{x})\Box c(\bar{x})$) can be logically interpreted as the formula $(c \to p)^\forall$ if $p\Box c \in A^+$, but has the logical meaning $(c \to \neg p)^\forall$ if $p\Box c \in A^-$. Consequently, we can define the following sets:

- $(A^+)^\forall = \{(c \to p)^\forall | p\Box c \in A^+\}$

- $(A^-)^\forall = \{(c \to \neg p)^\forall | p\Box c \in A^-\}$

- $A^\forall = (A^+)^\forall \cup (A^-)^\forall$.

Given a three-valued Σ-structure of constrained atoms $A = (A^+, A^-)$, $[A]$ denotes the set of all ground instances of the constrained atoms in the positive (respectively negative) part of A, that is, $p(\bar{t}) \in [A]^{\{+,-\}}$ iff there exists a constrained atom $p(\bar{x})\Box c(\bar{x}) \in A^{\{+,-\}}$ such that $FET_\Sigma \models c[\bar{t}/\bar{x}]$ or, equivalently, $FET_\Sigma \models \bar{x} = \bar{t} \to c(\bar{x})$. If c is less general than d then $[p(\bar{x})\Box c(\bar{x})] \subseteq [p(\bar{x})\Box d(\bar{x})]$.

Let us define the following closure operators with respect to disjunctions of constraints and less general constraints, respectively, over sets of constrained atoms:

$D(C) = \{p\Box c | \exists p\Box c_i \in C \text{ for } i = 1, .., n \text{ with } FET_\Sigma \models_3 (c \to \bigvee_{1 \le i \le n} c_i)^\forall\}$

$L(C) = \{p\Box c | \exists p\Box d \in C \text{ such that } FET_\Sigma \models_3 (c \to d)^\forall\}$.

If a three-valued Σ-structure of constrained atoms $A = (A^+, A^-)$ is closed with respect to less general constraints, that is $L(A) = A$, then

$$p(\bar{t}) \in [A]^{\{+,-\}} \; iff \; p(\bar{x})\Box \bar{x} = \bar{t} \in A^{\{+,-\}}$$

In [16] the truth-value of any first-order sentences in three-valued constrained structures is defined as follows. The first step is to assign truth-values to constrained (not necessarily flat) atoms:

Let $A = (A^+, A^-)$ be a three-valued constrained Σ-structure, $p(\bar{s})$ a (not necessarily ground) Σ-atom and c a satisfiable Σ-constraint:

- $A(p(\bar{s})\Box c) = \underline{t}$ if there exists $\{p(\bar{x})\Box d_k(\bar{x}) | 1 \le k \le m\} \subseteq A^+$ such that $FET_\Sigma \models (c \wedge \bar{x} = \bar{s} \to \bigvee_{1 \le k \le m} d_k)^\forall$ and $c \wedge \bar{x} = \bar{s}$ is satisfiable where $\bar{x}$ are dictint new variables.

- $A(p(\bar{x})\Box c) = \underline{f}$ if there exists $\{p(\bar{x})\Box d_k(\bar{x}) | 1 \le k \le m\} \subseteq A^-$ such that $FET_\Sigma \models (c \wedge \bar{x} = \bar{s} \to \bigvee_{1 \le k \le m} d_k)^\forall$ and $c \wedge \bar{x} = \bar{s}$ is satisfiable where $\bar{x}$ are dictint new variables.

- $A(p(\bar{s})\Box c) = \underline{u}$ Otherwise.

The above definitions can be easily extended to any arbitrary constrained formula. See, for instance [19, 16].

Now, let $A = (A^+, A^-)$ be any three-valued constrained Σ-structure. Then, the value of any first-order Σ-sentence ψ in three-valued constrained structures is defined as

$$A(\psi) = A(\psi\Box true)$$

To end the section, we define the $\mathcal{M}$-closure operator $\mathcal{M} = \langle \mathcal{M}^+, \mathcal{M}^- \rangle$ that given any set of first-order formulas Φ, returns the set of all its atomic constrained logic consequences:

$\mathcal{M}^+(\Phi) = \{p(\bar{x})\Box c(\bar{x}) | FET_\Sigma \cup \Phi \models_3 (c \to p)^\forall\}$

$\mathcal{M}^-(\Phi) = \{p(\bar{x})\Box c(\bar{x}) | FET_\Sigma \cup \Phi \models_3 (c \to \neg p)^\forall\}$.

Then, given a program P, we denote by $\mathcal{M}_P$ the set of all the atomic consequences of $Comp(P)$, i.e. $\mathcal{M}_P = \mathcal{M}(Comp(P))$

3   The semantic definition of open programs

An Ω-open program P is a logic program where some of its predicates (those included in Ω) are considered to be *open*, i.e. not completely defined. As a consequence, it is assumed that additional clauses defining these predicates will be included in other units. The operation for composing open programs, and hence *adding definition* to open predicates, is Ω-union. given two open programs $P1$ and $P2$, the Ω-union of $P1$ and $P2$ is defined only if the predicates shared by $P1$ and $P2$ are open and, in this case, the result is an Ω-open program consisting of all the clauses of $P1$ and $P2$. The set of open predicates of the result, Ω, may not include all the open predicates of $P1$ and $P2$. In this case we consider that these predicates have been closed.

Definition 3.1 *An Ω-open program is a logic program P together with a set Ω of predicate symbols. Ω is called the set of open predicates i.e. the predicates which are considered partially defined. If $P1$ is an $\Omega1$-open program and $P2$ is an $\Omega2$-open program and $pred(P1) \cap pred(P2) \subseteq \Omega1 \cap \Omega2$ and $\Omega \subseteq \Omega1 \cup \Omega2$, then the Ω-union of $P1$ and $P2$, noted $P1 \cup_\Omega P2$, is the Ω-open program $P1 \cup P2$. Otherwise $P1 \cup_\Omega P2$ is not defined.*

The usual approach (see e.g. [4, 13]) for defining a compositional semantics of logic program units consists in, first, defining as the semantic domain a class of clauses having only open or imported predicates in their tails and, second, defining the semantics of a program P as the subset of this domain obtained by certain inferences from P. For instance, in [4] the semantic domain considered is the class of all clauses having only open predicates in their tails. Then, the semantics of an open program is defined as the set of all clauses in that semantic domain that can be obtained, by successive unfolding, from the given program. We follow a similar approach, but dealing with normal programs poses some additional difficulties that should be considered carefully.

The first problem is related with the definition of the semantic domain associated to open programs. In the case of definite programs [4, 13], as said above, the semantics of an open or modular program is defined as a set of Horn clauses with only open predicates in their tales. This means that the semantics of a program is also a (special kind of) program. Unfortunately, this is not possible here. In our case, our semantics will be defined in terms of sets of implications $\ell \leftarrow \phi$, where ℓ is a (positive or negative) literal and ϕ is an arbitrary first-order formula built over open predicates. It should be obvious why we need to allow having negative literals in the heads of these formulas. With respect to the tails of these implications, the following example shows why conjunctions of literals may be insufficient. Let P be an open program consisting of the clauses:

$$p(x) \leftarrow \exists y(\neg q(x,y), r(y))$$

$$q(x,y) \leftarrow \exists z(r1(y,z), r(z))$$

where p and q are closed predicates and $r1$ and r are open predicates. Now, the formula:

$$p(x) \leftarrow \exists y(\forall z(\neg r1(y, z) \vee \neg r(z)) \wedge r(y))$$

obtained by unfolding would need to be included in the semantics of P in order to ensure completeness and compositionality.

Definition 3.2 *Given* $\Sigma = (FS, \Pi)$ *and* $\Omega \subseteq \Pi$, *the semantic domain for* Ω-*programs over* Σ *is* $Form(\Sigma, \Omega) = \langle Form^+(\Sigma, \Omega), Form^-(\Sigma, \Omega) \rangle$, *where:*

- $Form^+(\Sigma, \Omega) = \{p(\bar{x}) \leftarrow \phi(\bar{x}) | p \in \Pi$ *and* ϕ *is a* $(FS, \Omega \cup \{=\})$-*formula built over the connectives* $\{\neg, \vee, \wedge, \forall, \exists\}\}$

- $Form^-(\Sigma, \Omega) = \{\neg p(\bar{x}) \leftarrow \phi(\bar{x}) | p \in \Pi$ *and* ϕ *is a* $(FS, \Omega \cup \{=\})$-*formula built over the connectives* $\{\neg, \vee, \wedge, \forall, \exists\}\}$

Another aspect that, in our case, must be taken into account concerns the closed world assumption (CWA) considered when dealing with negation in logic programming. This means that we should define the semantics of a program P as some set of formulas which are inferred from some kind of completion of P. However, it seems reasonable to apply the completion to the closed predicates only. Actually, this is what is done in [7]. Unfortunately, this only works for open programs not including any clause defining an open predicate. The problem can be seen in the following counter-example:

Example 3.3 *Let P be the Ω-open program:*

$$p : -s, q., s : -s.$$

with $\Omega = \{p, q\}$. *If we apply the completion only to s, but not to the clauses defining p and q, we obtain the following set of formulas:*

$$p \leftarrow s \wedge q, s \leftrightarrow s$$

Now, the only implications of the form $\ell \leftarrow \phi$, which are logical consequences of P, where ℓ is a literal and ϕ includes only open predicates, are tautologies. This means that the semantics of this program whatever the kind of inferences are used to define it, as long as these inferences are sound, will at most contain tautologies. The same happens with the Ω-open program P':

$$p : -s., s : -s.$$

Hence, the semantics of P and P' are logically equivalent. Now, let $P1$ and $P1'$ be, respectively, the Ω'-union of the empty program with P and P', where Ω' is the empty set, i.e. this is equivalent to closing the predicates in Ω. However, $\neg p$ is a logic consequence of the completion of $P1$ but not of the completion of $P1'$.

Unfortunately, using the standard Clark-Kunen completion also poses problems. The first one is quite obvious. The union of the completion of two programs sharing predicates is, most often, inconsistent: if the completion of the programs $P1$ and $P2$ include, respectively, the formulas $p \leftrightarrow \phi 1$ and $p \leftrightarrow \phi 2$ then the union of $P1$ and $P2$ is inconsistent unless $\phi 1$ and $\phi 2$ are logically equivalent. On the other hand, any reasonable semantics defined in terms of the completion will inherit the problem.

However, this problem can be avoided easily. The idea consists in defining the semantics of the Ω-union of $P1$ and $P2$ in terms of the "intersection" of the negative definitions of the open predicates and in terms of the union of the rest of the definitions. In particular, this would mean, in the example above, that the semantics of the Ω-union of $P1$ and $P2$, if we assume that the predicate p is open, would include the formulas $p \leftarrow \phi 1$, $p \leftarrow \phi 2$ and $\neg p \leftarrow \neg \phi 1 \wedge \neg \phi 1$, as needed.

The second problem is a little bit more subtle: some inferences that may be used to define the semantics may cause a similar problem to the one just described above, but now with respect to the closed predicates. Let us see an example. Let $P1$ be the program consisting just of the clause $p \leftarrow \neg q$, where q is considered open and p is considered closed. Its completion consists of the formulas $p \leftrightarrow \neg q$ and $q \leftrightarrow false$. Now, if the semantics of $P1$ includes these formula and, in addition, it also includes the formula $p \leftrightarrow true$, inferred from the other two, then the semantics of the Ω-union of $P1$ and $P2$ will be inconsistent if, for instance, $P2$ just consists of the clause q. The actual problem, in this case, is that inferences over negative open literals may be unsound after Ω-union. As a consequence, the solution consists in not allowing this kind of inferences (in the example, the unfolding of $\neg q$ by $q \leftrightarrow false$ would be forbidden).

Following the above ideas, we define two different semantics for open programs. The first one, called $\mathcal{Q}_\Omega$, is defined as the set of all logic consequences (excluding the forbidden inferences), in the domain $Form(\Sigma, \Omega)$, of the completion of the given program. The second semantics, called $\mathcal{FQ}_\Omega$, is defined as the least fixpoint of a continuous immediate consequence operator.

Definition 3.4 *Let $\mathcal{Q}_\Omega() = \langle \mathcal{Q}_\Omega^+(), \mathcal{Q}_\Omega^-() \rangle : 2^{Form(\Sigma)} \to 2^{Form(\Sigma, \Omega)}$ be the logical consequence Ω-closure operator defined for every $\Phi \in 2^{Form(\Sigma)}$:*

$$\mathcal{Q}_\Omega^+(\Phi) = \{p \leftarrow \phi \in Form^+(\Sigma, \Omega) | FET_\Sigma \cup \Phi^+ \cup \Phi^-|_{\Pi \backslash \Omega} \models_3 (\phi \to p)^\forall\}$$
$$\mathcal{Q}_\Omega^-(\Phi) = \{\neg p \leftarrow \phi \in Form^-(\Sigma, \Omega) | \neg p \leftarrow \gamma \in \Phi^- \text{ and } FET_\Sigma \cup \Phi^+ \cup$$
$$\Phi^-|_{\Pi \backslash \Omega} \models_3 (\phi \to \gamma)^\forall\}$$

Then, the $\mathcal{Q}_\Omega$-semantics of a normal Σ-program P, $\mathcal{Q}_{P,\Omega}$, is defined as:

$$\mathcal{Q}_{P,\Omega} = \mathcal{Q}_\Omega(Comp(P))$$

The immediate consequence operator needed for the second semantics is defined as follows:

Definition 3.5 *Let P a normal Σ-program and $\Omega \subseteq \Pi$. Then, we define an immediate consequence operator:*

$$FQ_{P,\Omega} = \langle FQ^+_{P,\Omega}, FQ^-_{P,\Omega} \rangle : 2^{Form(\Sigma,\Omega)} \to 2^{Form(\Sigma,\Omega)}$$

such that for each set of formulas $\Phi \in 2^{Form(\Sigma,\Omega)}$:

$FQ^+_{P,\Omega}(\Phi^+, \Phi^-) = \{p(\bar{x}) \leftarrow \gamma | p(\bar{x}) : -\ell_1(\bar{s}_1),.., \ell_n(\bar{s}_n)\Box\bar{x} = \bar{t} \in P$ *and there exist formulas:* $\ell_j(\bar{x}_j) \leftarrow \phi_j(\bar{x}_j) \in \Phi^+ \cup \Phi^-|_{\Pi\backslash\Omega} \cup ID_\Omega,$ $1 \leq j \leq n,\ \gamma = \exists\bar{y}(\bigwedge_{1 \leq j \leq n} \phi_j[\bar{s}_j\backslash\bar{x}_j] \wedge \bar{x} = \bar{t})$ *and* $\bar{y} = var\{\phi_j | 1 \leq j \leq n\}\}$

$FQ^-_{P,\Omega}(\Phi^+, \Phi^-) = \{\neg p(\bar{x}) \leftarrow \gamma |$ *if* $\forall p(\bar{x}) : -\ell_1^k(\bar{s}_1^k),.., \ell_{n_k}^k(\bar{s}_{n_k}^k)\Box\bar{x} = \bar{t}^k$ *in* $Hd_P(p(\bar{x})) = \{p(\bar{x}) : -\bar{l}^k\Box\bar{x} = \bar{t}^k | 1 \leq k \leq m\}$ *there exist* $J_k \subseteq \{1,.., n_k\}$ *and (renamed apart) formulas,* $j \in J_k$: $\neg\ell_j^k(\bar{x}_j^k) \leftarrow \phi_j^k(\bar{x}_j^k) \in \Phi^+ \cup \Phi^-|_{\Pi\backslash\Omega} \cup ID_\Omega,\ \gamma = \bigwedge_{1 \leq k \leq m} \forall\bar{y}^k(\bigvee_{j \in J_k} \phi_j^k[\bar{s}_j^k\backslash\bar{x}_j^k] \vee \bar{x} \neq \bar{t}^k)$ *and* $\bar{y}^k = var\{\phi_j^k | j \in J_k, 1 \leq k \leq m\}\}$

where $ID_\Omega = \{\ell \leftarrow \ell | pred(\ell) \in \Omega\}$.

Theorem 3.6 *For each normal Σ-program P, $FQ_{P,\Omega}$ is monotonic and continuous with respect to $\subseteq$ in $2^{Form(\Sigma,\Omega)}$.*

Proof: The operator $FQ_{P,\Omega}$ is monotonic since for each $\Phi, \Gamma \in 2^{Form(\Sigma,\Omega)}$, such that $\Phi \subseteq \Gamma$, $FQ_{P,\Omega}(\Phi) \subseteq FQ_{P,\Omega}(\Gamma)$ is a direct consequence of the definition of $FQ_{P,\Omega}$.

Being $FQ_{P,\Omega}$ monotonic, to show that it is continuous, we have to prove that it is finitary: $FQ_{P,\Omega}(\cup_{i \in I}\Phi_i) \subseteq \cup_{i \in I}FQ_{P,\Omega}(\Phi_i)$ for every increasing chain $\Phi_0 \subseteq \Phi_1 \subseteq ... \subseteq \Phi_n...$ Let us suppose $\psi \in FQ_{P,\Omega}(\cup_{i \in I}\Phi_i)$.

(a) If $\psi = p(\bar{x}) \leftarrow \exists\bar{y}(\bigwedge_{1 \leq j \leq n} \phi_j \wedge c) \in FQ^+_{P,\Omega}(\cup_{i \in I}\Phi_i)$ then, we know there exists a clause $p(\bar{x}) : -\ell_1,.., \ell_n\Box\bar{x} = \bar{t} \in P$ such that, ψ is built over the following finite set of formulas:

$$\Gamma = \{\ell_j \leftarrow \phi_j | 1 \leq j \leq n\} \subseteq \cup_{i \in I}\Phi_i \cup ID_\Omega$$

Then, since $2^{Form(\Sigma,\Omega)}$ is a cpo with respect to $\subseteq$, we know that every finite set $\Gamma \subseteq \cup_{i \in I}\Phi_i$ has a least upper bound in $\Phi_{ii \in I}$. This means, $\Gamma \subseteq \Phi_n$ for some $n \in I$. Therefore, $\psi \in FQ^+_{P,\Omega}(\Phi_n) \subseteq \cup_{i \in I}FQ^+_{P,\Omega}(\Phi_i)$.

(b) If $\psi = \neg p(\bar{x}) \leftarrow \bigwedge_{1 \leq k \leq m} \forall\bar{y}^k(\bigvee_{j \in J_k} \phi_j^k \vee c^k) \in FQ^-_{P,\Omega}(\cup_{i \in I}\Phi_i)$ is similar ∎

Now we can define our second semantics:

Definition 3.7 *The $\mathcal{FQ}_\Omega$-semantics of a normal Σ-program P, $\mathcal{FQ}_\Omega(P)$, is defined as:*

$$\mathcal{FQ}_\Omega(P) = FQ_{P,\Omega} \uparrow \omega$$

The following theorem establishes the relations between the two semantics, showing that if we close $\mathcal{F}\mathcal{Q}_\Omega(P)$ under the allowed logical consequences, we obtain $\mathcal{Q}_{P,\Omega}$.

Theorem 3.8 *For each normal Σ-program P, $\mathcal{Q}_\Omega(\mathcal{F}\mathcal{Q}_\Omega(P)) = \mathcal{Q}_{P,\Omega}$.*

Proof sketch: To prove $\mathcal{Q}_\Omega(\mathcal{F}\mathcal{Q}_\Omega(P)) \subseteq \mathcal{Q}_{P,\Omega}$, it is enough to show that $FQ_{P,\Omega}(\mathcal{Q}_{P,\Omega}) \subseteq \mathcal{Q}_{P,\Omega}$, since, as a consequence of monotonicity and continuity of the operator $FQ_{P,\Omega}$, this implies:

$$FQ_{P,\Omega} \uparrow \omega \subseteq FQ_{P,\Omega}^\omega(\mathcal{Q}_{P,\Omega}) \subseteq \dots \subseteq FQ_{P,\Omega}^n(\mathcal{Q}_{P,\Omega}) \subseteq \dots \subseteq \mathcal{Q}_{P,\Omega}$$

But, since $\mathcal{Q}_\Omega$ is closed under the allowed logical consequences, we have:

$$\mathcal{Q}_\Omega(\mathcal{F}\mathcal{Q}_\Omega(P)) \subseteq \mathcal{Q}_\Omega(\mathcal{Q}_{P,\Omega}) = \mathcal{Q}_{P,\Omega}$$

Conversely, according to the def. of $\mathcal{Q}_{P,\Omega}$, to prove $\mathcal{Q}_{P,\Omega} \subseteq \mathcal{Q}_\Omega(\mathcal{F}\mathcal{Q}_\Omega(P))$, we have to show that

1) $Comp_\Omega(P) \models_3 (\phi \to p)^\forall$ implies $FET_\Sigma \cup \mathcal{F}\mathcal{Q}_\Omega(P)^+ \cup \mathcal{F}\mathcal{Q}_\Omega(P)^- |_{\Pi \backslash \Omega} \models_3 (\phi \to p)^\forall$:

Let us suppose that there exists $\ell \leftarrow \phi \in Form(\Sigma, \Omega)$ such that

$$FET_\Sigma \cup \mathcal{F}\mathcal{Q}_\Omega(P)^+ \cup \mathcal{F}\mathcal{Q}_\Omega(P)^- |_{\Pi \backslash \Omega} \not\models_3 (\phi \to \ell)^\forall$$

and prove $Comp_\Omega(P) \not\models_3 (\phi \to \ell)^\forall$, where $Comp_\Omega(P)$ denotes the completion of P, where the definitions of the open predicates are not closed.

Let A be the constrained structure satisfying $A(\phi \Box c) = \underline{t}$ but $A(\ell \Box c) \neq \underline{t}$ for some satisfiable constraint c. Therefore, we have that

$$FET_\Sigma \cup \mathcal{F}\mathcal{Q}_\Omega(P)^+ \cup \mathcal{F}\mathcal{Q}_\Omega(P)^- |_{\Pi \backslash \Omega} \cup A^\forall \models_3 (c \to \phi)^\forall$$

but $\qquad FET_\Sigma \cup \mathcal{F}\mathcal{Q}_\Omega(P)^+ \cup \mathcal{F}\mathcal{Q}_\Omega(P)^- |_{\Pi \backslash \Omega} \cup A^\forall \not\models_3 (c \to \ell)^\forall$

and this implies

$$\mathcal{M}(\mathcal{F}\mathcal{Q}_\Omega(P)^+ \cup \mathcal{F}\mathcal{Q}_\Omega(P)^- |_{\Pi \backslash \Omega} \cup A^\forall)(\phi \Box c) = \underline{t}$$

but $\qquad \mathcal{M}(\mathcal{F}\mathcal{Q}_\Omega(P)^+ \cup \mathcal{F}\mathcal{Q}_\Omega(P)^- |_{\Pi \backslash \Omega} \cup A^\forall)(\ell \Box c) \neq \underline{t}$

It is not difficult to see that $\mathcal{M}(\mathcal{F}\mathcal{Q}_\Omega(P)^+ \cup \mathcal{F}\mathcal{Q}_\Omega(P)^- |_{\Pi \backslash \Omega} \cup A^\forall)$ is a constrained model of $Comp_\Omega(P)$.

Finally, let $\tilde{A}$ be a model of $\mathcal{M}(\mathcal{F}\mathcal{Q}_\Omega(P)^+ \cup \mathcal{F}\mathcal{Q}_\Omega(P)^- |_{\Pi \backslash \Omega} \cup A^\forall)^\forall$ satisfying $\tilde{A} \models_3 (c \to \phi)^\forall$, $\tilde{A} \not\models_3 (c \to \ell)^\forall$ and $\tilde{A} \models_3 Comp_\Omega(P)$. It is not difficult to show the existence of this model. Then, we can conclude that $Comp_\Omega(P) \not\models_3 (\phi \to \ell)^\forall$.

2) If $\neg p \leftarrow \gamma \in P^-$ and $Comp_\Omega(P) \models_3 (\phi \to \gamma)^\forall$ there exists a formula $\neg p \leftarrow \delta \in \mathcal{F}\mathcal{Q}_\Omega(P)^-$ with $FET_\Sigma \cup \mathcal{F}\mathcal{Q}_\Omega(P)^+ \cup \mathcal{F}\mathcal{Q}_\Omega(P)^- |_{\Pi \backslash \Omega} \models_3 (\phi \to \delta)^\forall$: the proof for this case is similar. ∎

Finally, as a simple consequence of the previous theorem, we have that $\mathcal{Q}_{P,\Omega}$ and $\mathcal{F}\mathcal{Q}_\Omega(P)$ are sound and complete with respect to $\mathcal{M}(Comp(P))$:

Theorem 3.9 *For every normal Σ-program P:*

$$\mathcal{M}(Comp(P)) = \mathcal{M}(\mathcal{Q}_{P,\Omega}) = \mathcal{M}(\mathcal{F}\mathcal{Q}_\Omega(P)).$$

4 Compositionality and Full Abstraction

In this section we study the compositionality and full abstraction of the two semantics defined above. The first result shows that the $\mathcal{FQ}_\Omega$-semantics is weakly compositional, in the sense that, for any two open programs $P1$ and $P2$, the $\mathcal{FQ}_\Omega$-semantics of $P1 \cup_\Omega P2$ is logically equivalent (but not necessarily equal) to the result of an expression defined in terms of the $\mathcal{FQ}_\Omega$-semantics of $P1$ and $P2$. Note that, as described in the previous section, the semantical operation associated to Ω-union is defined as a kind of intersection for the negative clauses defining open predicates.

Theorem 4.1 *Let $P1$ and $P2$ be Σ-programs such that $pred(P1) \cap pred(P2) \subseteq \Omega$, $\Omega \subseteq \Pi$. Then,*

$$\mathcal{Q}_\Omega(\mathcal{FQ}_\Omega(P1 \cup_\Omega P2)) = \mathcal{Q}_\Omega(\mathcal{FQ}_\Omega(P1) \bigvee_\Omega \mathcal{FQ}_\Omega(P2))$$

where for each $\Phi 1, \Phi 2 \in 2^{Form(\Sigma)}$:

- $\Phi 1^+ \bigvee_\Omega \Phi 2^+ = \Phi 1^+ \cup \Phi 2^+$

- $\Phi 1^- \bigvee_\Omega \Phi 2^- = \{\neg p \leftarrow \phi \in Form(\Sigma, \Omega) | \neg p \leftarrow \phi \in \Phi 1^- \cup \Phi 2^-$ *if* $p \notin \Omega$, *and* $\phi = \phi 1 \wedge \phi 2$ *with* $\neg p \leftarrow \phi j \in \Phi j^-$ $j = 1, 2$ *if* $p \in \Omega\}$

Proof sketch: The right-to-left inclusion is straightforward because

$$\mathcal{FQ}_\Omega(P1) \bigvee_\Omega \mathcal{FQ}_\Omega(P2) \subseteq \mathcal{FQ}_\Omega(P1 \cup_\Omega P2)$$

For the converse inclusion, as in the proof of Theorem 3.8, it is enough to prove that

$$FQ_{P1 \cup_\Omega P2, \Omega}(\mathcal{FQ}_\Omega(P1) \bigvee_\Omega \mathcal{FQ}_\Omega(P2)) \subseteq \mathcal{Q}_\Omega(\mathcal{FQ}_\Omega(P1) \bigvee_\Omega \mathcal{FQ}_\Omega(P2)).$$

Let us assume $\ell \leftarrow \phi \in FQ_{P1 \cup_\Omega P2, \Omega}(\mathcal{FQ}_\Omega(P1) \bigvee_\Omega \mathcal{FQ}_\Omega(P2))$. Let us just see the case $\neg p(\bar{x}) \leftarrow \phi(\bar{x}) \in FQ^-_{P1 \cup_\Omega P2, \Omega}(\mathcal{FQ}_\Omega(P1) \bigvee_\Omega \mathcal{FQ}_\Omega(P2))$ with $p \in \Omega$. The other cases are similar, but simpler. Let us suppose

$$Hd_{P1}(p(\bar{x}))^\forall = \{p(\bar{x}) \leftarrow \exists \bar{y}^k (\bigwedge_{1 \leq j \leq n_k} \ell^k_j(s^{\bar{k}}_j) \wedge \bar{x} = t^k) | 1 \leq k \leq s\}$$

$$Hd_{P2}(p(\bar{x}))^\forall = \{p(\bar{x}) \leftarrow \exists \bar{y}^k (\bigwedge_{1 \leq j \leq n_k} \ell^k_j(s^{\bar{k}}_j) \wedge \bar{x} = t^k) | s < k \leq m\}$$

Then, for some $J_k \subseteq \{1, .., n_k\}$ for every $1 \leq k \leq m$, there exists a set of (renamed apart) formulas $\{\neg \ell^k_j(x^k_j) \leftarrow \phi^k_j(x^k_j) | 1 \leq k \leq m$ *and* $j \in J_k\}$ included in $\mathcal{FQ}^+_\Omega(P1) \cup \mathcal{FQ}^+_\Omega(P2) \cup \mathcal{FQ}^-_\Omega(P1)|_{\Pi \backslash \Omega} \cup \mathcal{FQ}^-_\Omega(P2)|_{\Pi \backslash \Omega} \cup ID_\Omega$, such that $\phi(\bar{x}) = \bigwedge_{1 \leq k \leq m} \forall \bar{y}^k (\bigvee_{j \in J_k} \phi_j[\bar{s}_j \backslash \bar{x}_j]) \vee \bar{x} \neq t^k)$.

Let $\delta1(\bar{x})$ and $\delta2(\bar{x})$ be the following two formulas:

$$\delta1(\bar{x}) = \bigwedge_{1\leq k\leq s} \forall\bar{y^k}((\bigvee_{j\in I1_k} \phi_j[\bar{s}_j\backslash\bar{x}_j]) \vee (\bigvee_{j\in J_k\backslash I1_k} \neg\ell_j^k(\bar{s}_j^k)) \vee \bar{x} \neq \bar{t^k}).$$

$$\delta2(\bar{x}) = \bigwedge_{s<k\leq m} \forall\bar{y^k}((\bigvee_{j\in I2_k} \phi_j[\bar{s}_j\backslash\bar{x}_j]) \vee (\bigvee_{j\in J_k\backslash I2_k} \neg\ell_j^k(\bar{s}_j^k)) \vee \bar{x} \neq \bar{t^k}).$$

where $I1_k$ (resp. $I2_k$) are the subsets of J_k such that $pred(\ell_j) \in pred(P1)\backslash\Omega$ (resp. $pred(\ell_j) \in pred(P2)\backslash\Omega$).

On the one hand, we have $\neg p(\bar{x}) \leftarrow \delta j(\bar{x}) \in \mathcal{FQ}_\Omega^-(Pj)$, for $j = 1,2$, thus,

$$\neg p(\bar{x}) \leftarrow \delta1(\bar{x}) \wedge \delta2(\bar{x}) \in \mathcal{FQ}_\Omega^-(P1) \bigvee_\Omega \mathcal{FQ}_\Omega^-(P2).$$

On the other, since $\{\neg\ell_j^k(\bar{x}_j^k) \leftarrow \phi_j^k(\bar{x}_j^k) | 1 \leq k \leq m \text{ and } j \in J_k\backslash I_k\}$ is included in $\mathcal{FQ}_\Omega^+(P1) \cup \mathcal{FQ}_\Omega^+(P2) \cup \mathcal{FQ}_\Omega^-(P1)|_{\Pi\backslash\Omega} \cup \mathcal{FQ}_\Omega^-(P2)|_{\Pi\backslash\Omega} \cup ID_\Omega$, we have:

$$FET_\Sigma \cup \mathcal{FQ}_\Omega^+(P1) \cup \mathcal{FQ}_\Omega^+(P2) \cup (\mathcal{FQ}_\Omega^-(P1) \bigvee_\Omega \mathcal{FQ}_\Omega^-(P2))|_{\Pi\backslash\Omega} \models_3 \psi(\bar{x})$$

where $\psi(\bar{x}) = (\phi(\bar{x}) \rightarrow \delta1(\bar{x}) \wedge \delta2(\bar{x}))^\forall$. ∎

Now, we have that $\mathcal{Q}_\Omega()$ is compositional with respect to $\cup_\Omega$ as a direct consequence of the above theorem and theorem 3.8.

Corollary 4.2 *Given Σ-programs $P1$ and $P2$ such that $pred(P1)\cap pred(P2) \subseteq \Omega$, for $\Omega \subseteq \Pi$, then $\mathcal{Q}_{P1\cup_\Omega P2,\Omega} = \mathcal{Q}_\Omega(\mathcal{Q}_{P1,\Omega} \bigvee_\Omega \mathcal{Q}_{P2,\Omega})$.*

$\mathcal{Q}_\Omega()$ is fully abstract with respect to $\cup_\Omega$, taking as observables the class of all constrained literals which are consequence of the completion:

Theorem 4.3 *Given two normal Σ-programs $P1$ and $P2$ and $\Omega \subseteq \Pi$. Then the following three statements are equivalent:*

1. *$\mathcal{Q}_\Omega(P1) = \mathcal{Q}_\Omega(P2)$.*

2. *For each Σ-program P such that $pred(Pi)\cap pred(P) \subseteq \Omega$, for $i = 1,2$: $\mathcal{Q}_\Omega(P1 \cup_\Omega P) = \mathcal{Q}_\Omega(P2 \cup_\Omega P)$.*

3. *For each Σ-program P such that $pred(Pi)\cap pred(P) \subseteq \Omega$, for $i = 1,2$: $\mathcal{M}(Comp(P1 \cup_\Omega P)) = \mathcal{M}(Comp(P2 \cup_\Omega P))$.*

Proof sketch: (1) implies (2) as a direct consequence of compositionality of $\mathcal{Q}_\Omega$ and, it is trivial that (2) implies (3) as a consequence of theorem 3.9.

To prove (3) implies (1), let us suppose that $\ell \leftarrow \phi \in \mathcal{Q}_\Omega(P1)\backslash\mathcal{Q}_\Omega(P2)$. Now let P be the following program:

$P = \{q : -\square d | d \text{ is satisfiable, } q(\bar{s}) \in \phi \text{ and } A(q\square d) = \underline{t}\} \cup \{q : -q\square d | d \text{ is satisfiable, } q(\bar{s}) \in \phi \text{ and } A(q\square d) = \underline{u}\}.$

It is not difficult to show that $\mathcal{M}(Comp(P1 \cup_\Omega P)) \neq \mathcal{M}(Comp(P2 \cup_\Omega P))$. ∎

Finally, as in the case of compositionality, as a consequence of Theorem 3.8, we can show that $\mathcal{F}\mathcal{Q}_\Omega()$ is weakly fully abstract with respect to $\cup_\Omega$:

Corollary 4.4 *Let $P1$ and $P2$ be two normal Σ-programs. Then, the following are equivalent*

1. $\mathcal{Q}_\Omega(\mathcal{F}\mathcal{Q}_\Omega(P1)) = \mathcal{Q}_\Omega(\mathcal{F}\mathcal{Q}_\Omega(P2))$

2. *For each Σ-program P such that $pred(Pi) \cap pred(P) \subseteq \Omega$, for $i = 1, 2$:*

$$\mathcal{Q}_\Omega(\mathcal{F}\mathcal{Q}_\Omega(P1 \cup_\Omega P)) = \mathcal{Q}_\Omega(\mathcal{F}\mathcal{Q}_\Omega(P2 \cup_\Omega P))$$

3. *for any Σ-program P such that $pred(P_i) \cap pred(P) \subseteq \Omega$, for $i = 1, 2$:*

$$\mathcal{M}(Comp(P1 \cup_\Omega P)) = \mathcal{M}(Comp(P2 \cup_\Omega P)).$$

Acknowledgments

This work has been partially supported by the Spanish CICYT project HEMOSS (ref. TIC98-0949-C02-01) and CIRIT Grup de recerca consolidat (1997SGR-00051).

References

[1] Apt, K. R., Bol, R. N. Logic Programming and Negation: A Survey *The Journal of Logic Programming* 19:9-71 (1994).

[2] Bossi, A., Bugliesi, M., Gabbrielli, M., Levi, G., Meo, M. C. Differential Logic Programming, in *Proc. POPL'93*, ACM, 1993.

[3] Brogi, A., Contiero, S., Turini, F. Programming by combining general logic programs Tech. Rep. 97/02, Dept. of Comp. Sc., Univ. of Pisa (1997).

[4] A. Bossi, M. Gabbrielli, G. Levi, M. C. Meo. A Compositional Semantics for Logic Programs. *Theoretical Computer Science* 1/2:3-47, 1994.

[5] Clark, K. L., Negation as failure, in: Gallaire, H., Minker, J. (eds), *Logic and Databases*, Plenum, 1978.

[6] Drabent, W. What is failure? An approach to constructive negation, *Acta Informática* 32:27-59 (1995).

[7] Etalle, S., Teusink, F., A compositional semantics for normal open programs, in: *Proc. ICSLP'96*, The MIT Press, 1996.

[8] Fages, F., Constructive negation by pruning, *The Journal of Logic Programming* 32:85-11 (1997).

[9] Ferrand, G., Lallouet, A., A compositional proof method of partial correctness for normal logic programs, in *Proc. ILPS*, Lloyd, J. (ed.), 1995.

[10] Fitting, M., A Kripke-Kleene Semantics for Logic Programs, *The Journal of Logic Programming*, 4:295-312 (1985).

[11] M. Falaschi, G. Levi, M. Martelli, C. Palamidessi. Declarative Modelling of the Operational Behaviour of Logic Languages. *Theoretical Computer Science*. 69, 289-318, 1989.

[12] M. Gabbrielli, G. Levi. On the semantics of Logic Programs. *Proc. ICALP'91*, J. Leach, B. Monien, M. Rodriguez-Artalejo (eds.), Springer LNCS 510 (1991) 1-19.

[13] Gaifman, H., Shapiro, E., Fully abstract compositional semantics for logic programs, in: *Proc. 16th Annual ACM POPL*, 1989.

[14] Kleene, S. C., *Introduction to Metamathematics*. North-Holland, 1952.

[15] Kunen, K., Negation in Logic Programming, *The Journal of Logic Programming* 4:289-308 (1987).

[16] P. Lucio, F. Orejas, E. Pino. An algebraic framework for the definition of compositional semantics of Normal Logic Programs. *Journal of Logic Programming*. 40(1):89-124, july 1999.

[17] Przymusinski, T. C., On the declarative semantics of deductive databases and logic programs, in: Minker, J. (ed), *Foundations of Deductive Databases and Logic Programs*, Morgan Kaufmann, 1988.

[18] Shepherdson, J. C., Negation in Logic Programming, in: Minker, J. (ed), *Foundations of Deductive Databases and Logic Programs*, Morgan Kaufmann, 1988.

[19] Stuckey, P. J., Negation and Constraint Logic Programmming, *Information and Computation* 118:12-23 (1995).

[20] van Gelder, A., Negation as failure using tight derivations for general logic programs, in: Minker, J. (ed), *Foundations of Deductive Databases and Logic Programs*, Morgan Kaufmann, Los Altos, CA, 1988.

[21] Verbaeten, S., Denecker, M., De Schreye, D., Compositionality of normal open logic programs, to appear in: *Proc. of ILPS'97*, 1997.

Declarative Priority In A Concurrent Logic Language O_N

Keiji Hirata
NTT Communication Science Laboratories
3-1, Morinosato Wakamiya, Atsugi-shi, Kanagawa, 243-0198 Japan
hirata@brl.ntt.co.jp

Kenichi Yamazaki
NTT Network Innovation Laboratories
3-9-11 Midoricho, Musashino-shi, Tokyo, 180-8585 Japan
yamazaki@t.onlab.ntt.co.jp

Abstract

It is well known that priority control is essential for real-world problems, and indeed, many real-world-oriented concurrent logic/constraint languages, such as KL1 and Oz, can deal with priority in explicit or implicit ways. However, the design policies of these languages in terms of priority were ad hoc, since priority has been considered non-logical. It turns out that its procedural meaning has been given in an informal way at most. Our aim is to construct a formal declarative semantics of a prioritized program in order to increase the applicability of concurrent logic languages to real-world problems. In this paper, we first define a model of priority and prove some properties of the model. Then, we design a concurrent logic language called O_N based on our theoretical framework and discuss some prominent characteristics that are embodied in sample programs written in O_N. The results presented in the paper provide a new insight into priority from the declarative point of view.

1 Introduction

The goals of logic programming include giving a clear-cut boundary between "what to do" and "how to do it". According to Kowalski's famous article [7], what-to-do corresponds to the logic component, and how-to-do-it to the control component. Declarative programming is the concept that a programmer concentrates on what-to-do and leaves how-to-do-it to a language processing system as much as possible. Concurrent logic programming languages (CLLs) have been developed according to this concept. Because of the what-to-do concept, CLLs have excellent programmability, and hence many of them have been successfully used for various reactive, parallel and distributed applications.

On the other hand, certain application fields still require a programmer to describe how-to-do-it. There are some cases where the how-to-do-it description contributes to speedup, and others where it is absolutely necessary in order to ensure execution control proceeds exactly as a programmer intends. In particular, for real-world concurrent processing, specifying how-to-do-it is inevitable and essential; typical and familiar examples are interrupt processing, exception handling, speculative computation, and real-time processing. The standard way to control processes according to the programmer's intention is to give a priority to each process. The concept of priority is by nature incompatible with CLLs because of their fundamental design policy, i.e. specifying what-to-do as much as possible. Therefore, it is in general considered difficult to incorporate priority into the framework of CLLs.

The authors think that in order to extend the applicability of CLLs to real-world problems, priority should be incorporated into their framework. There are three approaches to doing this:

(1) Incorporate a meta-level programming feature. In this approach, we can prioritize all object-level activities but not meta-level ones, because priority can be handled as a first-class data only from a meta-level interpreter.

(2) Provide built-in predicates and/or system libraries dedicated to priority handling. Huntback proposed a predicate for interrupt processing that checks message arrival [6]. Gregory proposed a predicate for speculative computation that checks whether a processor is idle [3]. Since such predicates are ad hoc and inconsistent from the execution-model point of view, it is difficult to understand priority in a declarative way.

(3) Reform a language so that it has a priority annotation but retains its core semantics intact. Suppose that we have two versions of a program, a prioritized one P and a non-prioritized plain one O. Let A_O be the set of all possible answers of program O and A_P that of program P. Then, we have $A_P \subseteq A_O$. Since priority just shrinks the set of answers, a priority annotation is in general regarded as logically transparent. The attempts with this approach are KL1 [11] and the work of Huntback [5]. However, in these languages, the operational semantics in terms of priority is not defined formally; priority is treated just as an implementation-dependent feature to the extent that scheduling is carried out on the best-effort basis.

These classification suggests us a new approach which we adopt in this paper; our standpoint is that (a) priority should be first-class data, (b) priority should be declaratively understood, and (c) priority should have an operational and model-theoretic semantics; a similar statement in CSP is found in [2]. From these points of view, we design a new language that amalgamates priority and the framework of CLLs so that we can give a formal semantics to priority.

This paper is organized as follows. Section 2 defines a model of priority and proves some crucial properties of the model. Section 3 designs a concurrent logic language called O_N based on our framework; priority is introduced as a first-class data to control process invocation and message passing. Then, the operational semantics of O_N is stated. Section 4 demonstrates sample programs written in O_N, including prioritized merge and prioritized event loop, and discusses some prominent characteristics that are embodied in these programs. Section 5 concludes the paper and addresses future work.

2   Formalizing Priority

This section first informally describes our design principle of a new data type and its meaning for priority, formally defines it, and proves some useful properties.

2.1   What Priority Should Be

Priority controls concurrent activities, such as process invocation and message passing, to make nondeterministic execution more or fully deterministic. The relations among priorities directly and indirectly reflect the execution order of concurrent activities. Conventional priority systems use an integer to represent priority in general. We think that this integer-based priority involves serious problems.

First, we believe a priority relation should be *binary* and *relative*. Let us consider the situation where a programmer decides the priority of each process and cannot statically predict what and how many concurrent activities are dynamically spawned. The programmer can decide that a concurrent activity should be executed prior to the other, but he/she can not make a total ordering among several or more concurrent activities. Hence, we think that the binary and relative priority relation is intuitively understandable; it allows us to read and write prioritized programs with relative ease. On the other hand, the integer-based priority relations are total and absolute.

Next, we maintain that the priority relations needed for execution control are as follows: (1) *equal*, (2) *higher* or *lower*, and (3) *unrelated*. There may be no need to explain (2). *Equal* means that the same-priority process should be scheduled fairly. *Unrelated* is further split into two cases: (3a) a programmer does not care about the order of two concurrent activities and (3b) he/she cannot make the order even if he/she is required to. Either way, it is impossible to express this intention using integer-based priority. In a sequential environment, both the "equal" relation and the "unrelated" relation may lead to (fairly) nondeterministic execution. However, in a parallel and/or distributed environment, these two relations may yield different behaviors and effects. As for (3b), let us consider a distributed environment. When a programmer wants to execute a activity A at a remote processor, he/she must know the priorities of all the activities that already exist at the remote processor in order to prioritize A. We think this is unrealistic, and therefore relations (1) and (3) should be distinguished.

Note that for instance, the equal-or-higher relation is meaningless, because there is no distinction between the behavior of this relation and that of the equal relation.

Finally, we believe a priority relation should be *stable*. To treat priority declaratively, once a priority relation is fixed, it should never change. This implies that an unrelated relation should remain unrelated. Suppose that there are two unrelated priorities A and B, and a process with A is executed earlier than one with B by chance. If a new priority relation, say, B > A is defined after the execution of the second process (one with B), the actual execution order (A then B) contradicts the defined priority relation B > A. We think that such a situation should not happen.

From our first claim, we base our priority system on a binary, relative relation, denoted as '$\succ$'. From the second, to create an equal priority, we explicitly use '='. As long as two priorities are not explicitly related to each other using $\succ$ and/or =, they are unrelated. From the third, we slightly extend the $\succ$ relation and introduce a language constructor for priority definition of the form $(H_1, H_2, \cdots) \succ P \succ (L_1, L_2, \cdots)$ to create a priority P. The form used is as follows. Here we introduce special symbols $\top$ and $\bot$, which mean the top and bottom priorities respectively. Then, if for a given priority Q we create a new priority P higher or lower than Q (satisfying $P \succ Q$ or $Q \succ P$), we write $\top \succ P \succ Q$ or $Q \succ P \succ \bot$. If for two given priorities P and Q (suppose $P \succ Q$) we create a new in-between priority R satisfying $P \succ R \wedge R \succ Q$, we just write $P \succ R \succ Q$. If we create two unrelated priorities P, Q, we write $\top \succ P \succ \bot \wedge \top \succ Q \succ \bot$. It is advantageous that the condition for stability can be simply stated with the form $(H_1, \cdots, H_n) \succ P \succ (L_1, \cdots, L_m)$. That is, this form requires that the condition $\forall i \forall j H_i \succ L_j$ holds before a new priority P is put between H_i and L_j. At the same time, this form guarantees that the condition holds after the new priority is created.

2.2   Term Model for Priority

Let us elaborate on what information a priority has to keep as a term. The form of a priority definition implies a priority P can be regarded as the function of H_i and L_j. We also have to distinguish A and B created by $\top \succ A \succ \bot \wedge \top \succ B \succ \bot$. Therefore, a priority should have the information of an identification, higher priorities H_i, and lower priorities L_i.

C is the set of all constant symbols. Var is the set of all variable names. Var(t) is the set of variables occurring in a term t and is defined as usual.

An *atomic formula* is of the form $A \star B$, where A and B are variables, $\top$ (the top symbol), or $\bot$ (the bottom symbol), and $\star$ is either $\succ$ or =. A *formula* is constructed from atomic formulas and connectives, $\wedge, \vee$, and $\neg$ as usual. A *structure* consists of a domain and an interpretation. A *valuation* into a structure is a total function from variables to the domain of the structure.

Definition   A *priority definition* is of the form $(H_1, \cdots, H_n) \succ P \succ (L_1, \cdots, L_m)$, where P is a variable, and H_i $(i = 1..n)$ and L_j $(j = 1..m)$ are variables, $\top$, or $\bot$.

Definition   Let C be the set of all constants. Then $\mathcal{T}$ is a *priority type* $C \times 2^C \times 2^C$, and an instance $t \in \mathcal{T}$ is represented as a triplet $\langle a, \{b_1, \cdots, b_n\}, \{c_1, \cdots, c_m\}\rangle$, where $a, b_1, \cdots, b_n, c_1, \cdots, c_m$ are all constants. Here a works as an identifier of a priority.

If $t \in \mathcal{T}$ is $\langle e_1, e_2, e_3 \rangle$, we introduce a dotted notation $t.i$ to access a component e_i ($i = 1, 2$ or 3). We use $\mathcal{T}$ as the set of all instances of type $\mathcal{T}$.

Definition Π is $\{\top, \bot\} \cup \mathcal{T}$. There are two kinds of binary relations on Π, denoted as $\succ$ and =, and these are subsets of $\Pi \times \Pi$, respectively. The rules prescribing these relations and special constants are as follows: for

$\alpha, \beta, \gamma, \xi \in \Pi$, (R1) $\alpha \succ \xi$ if $\alpha.1 \in \xi.2$, (R2) $\xi \succ \beta$ if $\beta.1 \in \xi.3$, (R3)
$\alpha \succ \beta \wedge \beta \succ \gamma \to \alpha \succ \gamma$, and (R4) $\alpha = \beta$ if $\alpha.i = \beta.i$ ($i = 1, 2$ and 3); $\top = \top$
and $\bot = \bot$, (R5) $\forall \alpha \in \Pi.\top \succ \alpha \vee \top = \alpha$, (R6) $\forall \alpha \in \Pi.\alpha \succ \bot \vee \bot = \alpha$.
Since we intend to build a term model for priority, we adopt Π as a semantic
domain and call it a *priority domain*. The relations and the symbols defined
by rules (R1)~(R6) are also straightforwardly mapped to the correspondings
on the priority domain Π. Although strictly speaking, we should write $\top_\Pi$,
$\bot_\Pi$ $\succ_\Pi$ and $=_\Pi$ on Π, we will use $\top$, $\bot$, $\succ$ and $=$ instead as long as there is
no confusion.

It follows from the above definition that $\top \succ \bot$ holds.

Definition $\mathcal{P}$ is a *priority structure* consisting of the priority domain Π
and the canonical interpretation.

Definition The realizability of a set of formulas is defined in the standard
way [9]. A valuation Γ *realizes* a formula ϕ in the priority structure $\mathcal{P}$ and
we write $\mathcal{P}, \Gamma \models \phi$, if for $\{V_1, \cdots, V_n\} = Var(\phi), \mathcal{P} \models \phi[\Gamma(V_1), \cdots, \Gamma(V_n)]$,
where $\phi[\alpha_1, \cdots, \alpha_n]$ means that $\alpha_1, \cdots, \alpha_n (\in \Pi)$ are respectively put as the
values of free variables $V_1, \cdots, V_n$ in ϕ.

A valuation is also represented in a set of pairs of a variable and a value:
$\Gamma = \{\langle X_1, \xi_1 \rangle, \langle X_2, \xi_2 \rangle, \cdots\}$.

Definition Let $\mathcal{D}$ be a finite set of priority definitions. We now present an
algorithm to compute a valuation of $\mathcal{D}$ into the priority structure $\mathcal{P}$, denoted
as Γ.
(S1) $\mathcal{D}_1 = \mathcal{D}$ and $\Gamma_1 = \{\}$.
(S2) Suppose that we have $\mathcal{D}_k$ and Γ_k. Choose $d \in \mathcal{D}_k$ such that $d = (H_1, \cdots, H_n) \succ P \succ (L_1, \cdots, L_m)$ and $\forall i \forall j.\mathcal{P} \models \Gamma_k(H_i) \succ \Gamma_k(L_j)$. Then,
we create a new element $\xi(\in \Pi)$, which is $\langle "P", \{\Gamma_k(H_1).1, \cdots, \Gamma_k(H_n).1\}$,
$\{\Gamma_k(L_1).1, \cdots, \Gamma_k(L_m).1\}\rangle$, where $"P"$ is a fresh constant generated from the
variable name of P. $\Gamma_{k+1} = \{\langle P, \xi \rangle\} \cup \Gamma_k$ and $\mathcal{D}_{k+1} = \mathcal{D}_k \setminus \{d\}$. Iterate Step
(S2), while $\mathcal{D}_k \neq \emptyset$.
(S3) If $\mathcal{D}_k = \emptyset$, $\Gamma = \Gamma_k \cup \{\langle X, \zeta \rangle, \cdots\}$, where X's are $Var \setminus Var(\mathcal{D})$ and ζ's
are arbitrary elements in Π.

If this computation meets the following two cases at Step (2), it terminates halfway; Γ is not generated. One is that there is no d found in $\mathcal{D}_k$
satisfying $\forall i \forall j.\mathcal{P} \models \Gamma_k(H_i) \succ \Gamma_k(L_j)$. The other is that for a variable P,
$\langle P, \xi \rangle$ is added more than once. At Step (S3), adding set $\{\langle X, \zeta \rangle, \cdots\}$ makes
Γ_k a total function. Since $\mathcal{D}$ is finite, $\mathcal{D}_k = \emptyset$ is reached eventually, and the
algorithm always terminates.

The algorithm for computing the valuation presented above is nondeterministic. This is because there are several choices for a priority definition
$d \in \mathcal{D}_k$ to create a new element ξ. Thus, the more than one valuation of
$\mathcal{D}$ may be computed with different sequences of d. However, the following
proposition states that the valuations are unique.

Definiticn A finite set of priority definitions $\mathcal{D}$ is *well-formed* if there exists
a sequence of d chosen at Step (S2) so that we successfully reach $\mathcal{D}_k = \emptyset$
and obtain an answer valuation Γ.

Proposition 2.1 *(Declarative Priority)*
Let $\mathcal{D}$ be a finite well-formed set of priority definitions. Then, the computation by the above algorithm always reaches the identical answer valuation independently from the selection sequences of $d \in \mathcal{D}$.

Outline of proof. It is obvious that all valuations, if they exist, are identical, because ξ is always uniquely determined at Step (S2). It hence suffices to show that the algorithm can always choose a priority definition at every Step (S2) and finally moves to Step (S3). Since $\mathcal{D}$ is well formed, there exists a selection sequence of priority definitions, denoted by S_1. We use proof by contradiction. Suppose that at some step (S2), the algorithm can not choose proper d, and let χ be the set of the priority definitions already selected until the step. Here we consider the sequence of priority definitions by deleting χ from the sequence S_1, denoted by S_1'. Note that the left most priority definition of S_1' can be chosen at Step (S2). Thus, if the algorithm selects the left most one of S_1' as d, it can generate a new ξ. Hence contradiction. Since $\mathcal{D}$ is finite, the algorithm always reaches $\mathcal{D}_k = \emptyset$. $\square$

Definition Let $\mathcal{D}$ be a finite well-formed set of priority definitions and Γ the valuation of $\mathcal{D}$ into the priority structure $\mathcal{P}$ computed by the above algorithm. Then, the *term model* of $\mathcal{D}$ and rules (R1)~(R6) consists of priority domain Π, the canonical interpretation, and Γ (namely $\mathcal{P}$ and Γ).

Example 2.2 *Suppose that the set of priority definitions $\mathcal{D}$ is $\{\top \succ A \succ \bot, \top \succ B \succ \bot, (A, B) \succ C \succ \bot, C \succ D \succ \bot\}$. Then, we obtain the valuation $\Gamma = \{\langle A, \langle$ "A", $\{\top\}, \{\bot\}\rangle\rangle, \langle B, \langle$ "B", $\{\top\}, \{\bot\}\rangle\rangle, \langle C, \langle$ "C", $\{$ "A", "B"$\}, \{\bot\}\rangle\rangle, \langle D, \langle$ "D", $\{$ "C"$\}, \{\bot\}\rangle\rangle \} \cup \{\langle X, \zeta\rangle, \cdots\}$, where "A", "B", "C" and "D" are distinct constants, X's are $\mathbf{Var} \setminus \mathbf{Var}(\mathcal{D})$ and ζ's are arbitrary elements in Π.*

The following graph depicts the priority relations of $\mathcal{D}$; the righthand side shows all the priority relations deduced from $\mathcal{D}$.

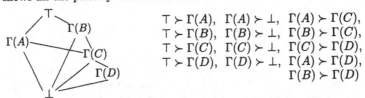

$$\top \succ \Gamma(A), \quad \Gamma(A) \succ \bot, \quad \Gamma(A) \succ \Gamma(C),$$
$$\top \succ \Gamma(B), \quad \Gamma(B) \succ \bot, \quad \Gamma(B) \succ \Gamma(C),$$
$$\top \succ \Gamma(C), \quad \Gamma(C) \succ \bot, \quad \Gamma(C) \succ \Gamma(D),$$
$$\top \succ \Gamma(D), \quad \Gamma(D) \succ \bot, \quad \Gamma(A) \succ \Gamma(D),$$
$$\Gamma(B) \succ \Gamma(D)$$

2.3 Properties

Definition Let $\mathcal{P}$ be the priority structure. For a formula ϕ, let $\phi^{\mathcal{P}}$ denote the set of all valuations $\{\Gamma \mid \mathcal{P}, \Gamma \models \phi\}$. Then, for formulas ψ and ϕ, we say that ψ *entails* ϕ and write $\psi \models \phi$ if $\psi^{\mathcal{P}} \subseteq \phi^{\mathcal{P}}$.

The new element ξ computed at Step (S2) of the above algorithm, if it exists, always satisfies the relation $\Gamma_k(H_1) \succ \xi \wedge \cdots \wedge \Gamma_k(H_n) \succ \xi \wedge \xi \succ \Gamma_k(L_1) \wedge \cdots \wedge \xi \succ \Gamma_k(L_m)$ because of rules (R1) and (R2) in Section 2.2, and this relation does not violate the existing priority relations. This implies that a priority definition $(H_1, \cdots, H_n) \succ P \succ (L_1, \cdots, L_m)$ can be logically regarded as $H_1 \succ P \wedge \cdots \wedge H_n \succ P \wedge P \succ L_1 \wedge \cdots \wedge P \succ L_m$. Therefore, we can write $P, \Gamma \models \mathcal{D}$, $\mathcal{D} \models A \succ B$ if $\mathcal{D}$ entails $A \succ B$, and $\mathcal{D} \models \neg(A \succ B)$ if it does not. Similarly, $\mathcal{D} \models A = B$ if $P, \Gamma \models A = B$. Also, $\mathcal{D} \models A \not\succ B$ is a notational convenience for $\mathcal{D} \models \neg(A \succ B \vee B \succ A \vee A = B)$.

Lemma 2.3 *Let $\mathcal{D}$ be a well-formed set of priority definitions, and let $\mathcal{V}$ be $\{\top, \bot\} \cup \text{Var}(\mathcal{D})$. Then, for $A, B \in \mathcal{V}, \mathcal{D} \models \neg(A \succ B \wedge B \succ A)$ and $\mathcal{D} \models \neg(A \succ A)$.*

Outline of proof. Induction on the construction of a valuation and proof by contradiction are used. $\square$

The lemma shows that our priority is transitive but neither antisymmetric nor reflexive. This property corresponds to that of the '$<$' predicate of the Tempo language [4].

Proposition 2.4 *(Satisfaction Completeness of Priority Relations)*
Let $\mathcal{D}$ be a well-formed set of priority definitions, and let $\mathcal{V}$ be $\{\top, \bot\} \cup \text{Var}(\mathcal{D})$. Then, for $A, B \in \mathcal{V}, \mathcal{D} \models (A \succ B \vee B \succ A \vee A = B \vee A \not\succ B)$, and these cases are mutually execution.

Outline of proof. In the case of $\Gamma(A) = \Gamma(B)$, the proof is straightforward. Otherwise, it follows from Lemma 2.3. $\square$

Thus, a well-formed set of priority definitions is consistent.

Proposition 2.5 *(Stability of Priority Relations)*
Let $\mathcal{D}$ and $\mathcal{D}'$ be finite well-formed sets of priority definitions satisfying $\mathcal{D} \subseteq \mathcal{D}'$, and let $\mathcal{V}$ be $\{\top, \bot\} \cup \text{Var}(\mathcal{D})$. Then, for $A, B \in \mathcal{V}, \mathcal{D} \models A \star B \Rightarrow \mathcal{D}' \models A \star B$, where $\star$ is either $\succ$, $=$ or $\not\succ$.

Outline of proof. Since $\mathcal{D} \subseteq \mathcal{D}'$, new priority definitions are just added to $\mathcal{D}$ and we get $\mathcal{D}'$. Consider the following cases: (i) $\mathcal{D} \models A \succ B$ is transformed to $\mathcal{D}' \models (A \succ B \wedge A \diamond B)$, (ii) $\mathcal{D} \models A = B$ to $\mathcal{D}' \models (A = B \wedge A \succ B)$, and (iii) $\mathcal{D} \models A \not\succ B$ to $\mathcal{D}' \models A \diamond B$, where $\diamond$ is either $\succ$ or $=$. It is proved by Proposition 2.4 that cases (i) and (ii) do not occur. It follows from the construction of a valuation Γ that case (iii) does not occur. $\square$

2.4 Aggregate Priority

Definition Let $\mathcal{D}$ be a well-formed set of priority definitions, and $\{\vec{A}\}$ and $\{\vec{B}\}$ nonempty sets of priority variables. The ordering between these sets is defined as follows: $\mathcal{D} \models \{\vec{A}\} = \{\vec{B}\}$ if $(\forall X \in \{\vec{A}\} \exists Y \in \{\vec{B}\}.\mathcal{D} \models X = Y) \wedge (\forall Y \in \{\vec{B}\} \exists X \in \{\vec{A}\}.\mathcal{D} \models X = Y)$, and $\mathcal{D} \models \{\vec{A}\} \succ \{\vec{B}\}$ if $\neg(\{\vec{A}\} = \{\vec{B}\}) \wedge (\forall X \in \{\vec{A}\} \exists Y \in \{\vec{B}\}.\mathcal{D} \models X \succ Y \vee X = Y) \wedge (\forall Y \in \{\vec{B}\} \exists X \in \{\vec{A}\}.\mathcal{D} \models X \succ Y \vee X = Y)$. Also, $\mathcal{D} \models \{\vec{A}\} \not\succ \{\vec{B}\}$ is a notational convenience for $\mathcal{D} \models \neg(\{\vec{A}\} \succ \{\vec{B}\} \vee \{\vec{B}\} \succ \{\vec{A}\} \vee \{\vec{A}\} = \{\vec{B}\})$.

The relations $\succ$, $=$ and $\not\succ$ between two aggregate priorities have the same properties as those between two priorities; that is, $\succ$ for $\{\vec{A}\} \succ \{\vec{B}\}$ is transitive but neither antisymmetric nor reflexive. Lemma 2.3 and Propositions 2.4 and 2.5 can be easily extended for aggregate priority.

For example, let $\mathcal{D}$ be a finite well-formed set of priority definitions, and suppose $\mathcal{D} \models A \succ B$. Then $\mathcal{D} \models \{A\} \succ \{A, B\} \wedge \{A, B\} \succ \{B\}$ holds.

The aggregate priority is used for defining an operational semantics of a new language in Section 3.3.

3 New Language

The O_N language is a concurrent logic language that is integrated with priority, the semantics of which is based on the framework given in Section 2.

3.1 Syntax

The syntax of O_N is based on FGHC [11] (Fig. 1).

Program	::=	:- Calls. Defs.				
Calls	::=	Calls, Calls $\mid$ true $\mid$ Unif $\mid$ Pred $\mid$ PDef				
Defs	::=	Defs. Defs $\mid$ Pred :- Guard $\mid$ Calls.				
Guard	::=	Guard, Guard $\mid$ true $\mid$ Unif				
Unif	::=	Var $\overset{PVar}{=}$ Term	$\cdots$ priority-annotated unification			
Pred	::=	p(Arg,$\cdots$,Arg)^{PVar}	$\cdots$ priority-annotated predicate			
PDef	::=	(Prios) $\succ$ PVar $\succ$ (Prios)	$\cdots$ priority definition			
Prios	::=	Prios, Prios $\mid$ $\top$ $\mid$ $\bot$ $\mid$ PVar				
Arg	::=	Atom $\mid$ Var $\mid$ PVar				
Term	::=	Atom $\mid$ Var $\mid$ f(Arg,$\cdots$,Arg)				

Figure 1: Syntax

Here, p in Pred represents a predicate name, and f in Term a function name. The structures of a predicate and a function are flat. Atom, Var and PVar respectively represent an atom, a logic variable, a priority variable. The domain of a logic variable is the Herbrand universe, and that of a priority variable is Π introduced in Section 2.2. As a convention in this paper, we will use P, Q, R, H, L to range over PVar. Here, we impose the following syntactical constraint: for every definition clause $p(V_1, \cdots, V_n)^P$:- $V_{i_1} \overset{Q_1}{=} t_1, \cdots, V_{i_l} \overset{Q_l}{=} t_l \mid$ Calls, variables $V_1, \cdots, V_n$, $\text{Var}(t_1), \cdots, \text{Var}(t_l), P, Q_1, \cdots, Q_l$ are distinct. This syntactical constraint enables us to explicitly add a priority annotation to every predicate call and every active/passive unification.

There are two kinds of concurrent activities in CLLs, process invocation and message passing. Prioritizing goal reduction and active unification in O_N corresponds to controlling process invocation and message passing, respectively. The intention of a priority-annotated active unification $X \overset{P}{=} t$ is to send a message with a priority P added, while that of a priority-annotated passive unification $X \overset{P}{=} t$ is to receive a message t and its associated priority P. The intention of a priority-annotated predicate call $p(V_1, \cdots, V_n)^P$ is to call a process with a priority P. If a callee is a definition clause $p(V_1, \cdots, V_n)^P$:- $V_{i_1} \overset{Q_1}{=} t_1, \cdots, V_{i_l} \overset{Q_l}{=} t_l \mid$ Calls, the priority that is associated with the call is represented as the aggregate priority $\{P, Q_1, \cdots, Q_l\}$. Note that since $P, Q_1, \cdots, Q_l$ are all elements of the set, the priority of a process invocation and that of message passing are treated equally.

3.2 Priority of Passive Unification

Definition $\Phi(G)$ is the set of priority variables occurring in Guard G; $\Phi(G) = \{Q_1, \cdots, Q_l\}$ if G is the Guard part of a definition clause, $V_1 \stackrel{Q_1}{=} t_1, \cdots, V_l \stackrel{Q_l}{=} t_l$.

We consider the priorities to which $\Phi(G)$ are instantiated. Now we have the following two types of passive unifications in O_N: $X \stackrel{P}{=} f(Y_1, \cdots)$ and $X \stackrel{P}{=} Y$. As for the former, it is usually expected that a corresponding active unification $X \stackrel{Q}{=} f(Z_1, \cdots)$ has been or will be executed elsewhere in a program. Hence, we also have to care about the implicit unifications $Y_1 = Z_1, \cdots$ that are subsequently spawned.

For simplicity, in this paper, we suppose that a program is well-moded [12]. This guarantees that there is at most one writer for every variable. Then, it suffices that the following three patterns are taken into account: (i) P for a passive unification $X \stackrel{P}{=} t$, (ii) P for a passive unification $X \stackrel{P}{=} Y$ and (iii) P_i for an implicit active unification $Y_i \stackrel{P_i}{=} Z_i$ when we have an active unification $X \stackrel{Q}{=} f(\cdots, Z_i, \cdots)$ and a passive unification $X \stackrel{P}{=} f(\cdots, Y_i, \cdots)$. Here, let t be a Term and $\mathcal{D}$ a set of priority definitions.

For (i), suppose that the chain of active unifications which instantiates a variable X is of the form $X \stackrel{P_1}{=} X_1, X_1 \stackrel{P_2}{=} X_2, \cdots, X_{n-1} \stackrel{P_n}{=} t$. Then, P for a passive unification $X \stackrel{P}{=} t$ is bound to the minimum value among the values of $P_1, P_2, \cdots, P_n$, denoted as $P_1 \downarrow \cdots \downarrow P_n$. Operator $\downarrow$ is defined as follows:
$$P_i \downarrow P_j = \begin{cases} P_j & \cdots \; \mathcal{D} \models P_i = P_j \text{ or } \mathcal{D} \models P_i \succ P_j \\ Q \text{ defined by } (P_i, P_j) \succ Q \succ \perp & \cdots \text{ otherwise.} \end{cases}$$
Operator $\downarrow$ is commutative and associative. This rule means that the lowest priority on a chain determines the whole priority.

For (ii), suppose that the priority variables of all active unifications which contribute to the bindings of X and/or Y are $P_1, \cdots, P_n$. Then, P for a passive unification $X \stackrel{P}{=} Y$ is $P_1 \downarrow \cdots \downarrow P_n$. For example, when (a) there are active unifications $X \stackrel{P_1}{=} Z, Z \stackrel{P_2}{=} Y$, (b) $X \stackrel{P_1}{=} t, Y \stackrel{P_2}{=} t$, and (c) $X \stackrel{P_1}{=} Y, Y \stackrel{P_2}{=} t$, P for a passive unification $X \stackrel{P}{=} Y$ is $P_1 \downarrow P_2$ in each case.

For (iii), suppose that an implicit active unification subsequently spawned is $Y_i \stackrel{P_i}{=} Z_i$ for every i. Then, P_i is instantiated to $\top$. This rule means that whatever priority is set to the active unification at the top level, it does not affect the priorities of the argument-level implicit unifications.

3.3 Operational Semantics

Section 2.3 defines the entailment of formulas, denoted as $\models$. On the other hand, for conventional logical formulas F and G, we also write $F \models G$ if G is a logical consequence of F [8]. So, we will properly use $\models$ in these two meanings.

Definition A *configuration* is a triplet $\langle C, S \rangle : \mathcal{V}$ in which C stands for Callsand S stands for a *constraint store*, which is a set of active unifications Unif and priority definitions PDef. $\mathcal{V}$ is the set of variables contained in S. An initial configuration is $\langle C_0, \emptyset \rangle : \emptyset$, where C_0 stands for an initial goal. Note that priority is carried into a constraint store with an active unification. This suggests that our framework for prioritizing concurrent activities is an extension of the conventional concurrent constraint (cc) framework [9].

Definition Let C be a set of goals and S a constraint store. For a goal $b \in C$, a function $\pi_S : b \rightarrow 2^{\{\top, \bot\} \cup \text{PVar}}$ calculates the aggregate priority associated with the goal reduction of b, where b is either Unif, Pred or PDef. Then, b is *executable* in S if $\pi_S(b) \neq \emptyset$. $\pi_S(b)$ is computed as follows:

(Unif) b is an active unification $X \overset{P}{=} t$: $\pi_S(b) = \{P\}$ if $S \models \top \succ P$. Otherwise, $\pi_S(b) = \emptyset$.

(Pred) b is a predicate call $p(V_1, \cdots, V_n)^P$: For every $p(W_1, \cdots, W_n)^Q$:- $G \mid B \in$ Defs, $\pi_S(b) = \{P\} \cup \Phi(G)$ if $S \models \top \succ P$ and $S \models \exists \Delta G\{V_1/W_1, \cdots, V_n/W_n\}$, where $\Delta = \text{Var}(G\{V_1/W_1, \cdots, V_n/W_n\})$. Otherwise, $\pi_S(b) = \emptyset$.

(PDef) b is a priority definition $(H_1, \cdots, H_n) \succ P \succ (L_1, \cdots, L_m)$: $\pi_S(b) = \{\top\}$ if $\forall i \forall j. S \models H_i \succ L_j$. Otherwise, $\pi_S(b) = \emptyset$.

In case (Pred), it suffices that we just check the entailment of the logical formula G and ignore all priority variables $\Phi(G)$. This is guaranteed by the Active Unification rule presented below; that is, for a passive unification $X \overset{Q}{=} t$, that Q is instantiated is equivalent to that X is instantiated.

Definition Let C be a set of goals and S a constraint store. Then, a goal $m \in C$ has the *maximum* priority in S if $m \in E = \{e \mid e \in C \text{ is executable in } S\}$ and $\forall b \in E \setminus \{m\}. S \models \pi_S(m) \succ \pi_S(b) \vee \pi_S(m) \not\succ \pi_S(b)$.

In general, there are more than one goal that have the maximum priority in S.

Program execution is represented by successive configurations $C_0, C_1, C_2, \cdots$. A transition is a binary relation on configurations, $\rightarrow \subseteq C \times C$; the transition $C_j \rightarrow C_{j+1}$ is defined by the transition rules presented in the Plotkin style in Fig. 2. A transition is made in one step and is thus atomic. In the figure, $\vec{X}$ and $\vec{Y}$ mean variable sequences of the same length.

Predicate Call
$$\langle \{p(\vec{X})^P\}, S \rangle : \mathcal{V} \rightarrow \langle B\theta, G\theta \cup S \rangle : \mathcal{V} \cup \mathcal{V}_{(G,B)}$$
if $p(\vec{X})^P$ is executable in S, the corresponding clause is $p(\vec{Y})^Q$:- $G \mid B$, $\theta = \{P/Q, \vec{X}/\vec{Y}\}$, and $\mathcal{V} \cap \mathcal{V}_{(G,B)} = \emptyset$.

Active Unification
$$\langle \{X \overset{P}{=} t\}, S \rangle : \mathcal{V} \rightarrow \langle \emptyset, \{X \overset{P}{=} t\} \cup S \rangle : \mathcal{V}$$
if $X \overset{P}{=} t$ is executable in S.

Priority Definition
$$\langle \{(H_1, \cdots, H_n) \succ P \succ (L_1, \cdots, L_m)\}, S \rangle : \mathcal{V} \rightarrow \langle \emptyset, \{(H_1, \cdots, H_n) \succ P \succ (L_1, \cdots, L_m)\} \cup S \rangle : \mathcal{V}$$
if $(H_1, \cdots, H_n) \succ P \succ (L_1, \cdots, L_m)$ is executable in S.

Goal Selection
$$\frac{\langle \{b\}, S \rangle : \mathcal{V} \rightarrow \langle C', S' \rangle : \mathcal{V}'}{\langle \{b\} \cup C, S \rangle : \mathcal{V} \rightarrow \langle C' \cup C, S' \rangle : \mathcal{V}'}$$
if b has the maximum priority in S.

Figure 2: Transition Rules

It follows from the Priority Definition rule that the priority definition is executed immediately after commitment, since its aggregate priority is always $\{\top\}$. There are illegal programs in that $C \neq \emptyset$ but no *if* condition in every rule in Fig. 2 is satisfied; thus, the execution is suspended perpetually.

4 Programming with Priority

This section demonstrates programming with priority in O_N. Basically, there are two methods in CLLs to react to an asynchronous message from an external process: event loop and merge. Thus, we take them as sample programs in the following subsections. After that, it is shown that O_N has an independency property in terms of the priority control of process invocation and message passing. We think that this property plays an important role in the process-message paradigm.

4.1 Prioritized Event Loop

Fig. 3 is a sample program that demonstrates prioritizing clause selection in O_N. The *loop*/2 predicate usually makes a recursive call while waiting for an express message from *interrupt*/1 which is executed at a higher priority. When a message from *interrupt*/1 arrives at *loop*/2, both the definition

$$:- \top \succ P \succ \perp, \top \succ Q \succ P,$$
$$interrupt(Sig)^Q,$$
$$loop(Sig, D)^P, D \stackrel{P}{=} init.$$

$$interrupt(Sig)^Q :- exception(Ex) \mid$$
$$Sig \stackrel{Q}{=} [Ex|T],$$
$$interrupt(T)^Q.$$

$$loop(Sig, D)^P :- Sig \stackrel{Q}{=} [Ex|T] \mid$$
$$handler(Ex)^Q,$$
$$loop(T, D)^P.$$
$$loop(Sig, D)^P :- true \qquad \mid$$
$$body(D, E)^P,$$
$$loop(Sig, E)^P.$$

Figure 3: Prioritized Event Loop

clauses of *loop*/2 become the candidates for commitment. Then, the aggregate priority of the first clause is $\{Q, P\}$, while that of the second is $\{P\}$. Since $Q \succ P$, we have $\{Q, P\} \succ \{P\}$. Thus, the first clause always precedes the second; as soon as a message from *interrupt*/1 arrives, it is processed.

4.2 Prioritized Merge

Suppose that process *merge*/3 receives messages from process *interrupt*/1 with higher priority than ones from process *routine*/1. O_N can implement two methods to prioritize messages from *interrupt*/1: (1) controlling the priorities set to messages and (2) controlling the priorities set to processes. In method (1), the priority of each message is made equal to that of its sender, and the process priorities are set as *interrupt* $\succ$ *routine*. Here the priority of *merge*/3 does not matter. In method (2), the priority of every message is made equal, and the process priorities are set as *interrupt* $\succ$ *merge* $\succ$ *routine*. Method (1) can be implemented only in O_N, while method (2) can also be implemented in KL1. Fig. 4 shows the prioritized merge program based on method (1).

$$:\text{-} \top \succ P \succ \bot, \top \succ Q \succ P,$$
$$\top \succ R \succ \bot,$$
$$merge(Sig, D, Z)^R,$$
$$interrupt(Sig)^Q,$$
$$routine(D)^P.$$

$interrupt(Sig)^Q$:- the same as Fig. 3
$routine(D)^P$:- $true$ |
$\quad gen\_data(X)^P,$
$\quad D \overset{P}{=} [X|Ds],$
$\quad routine(Ds)^P.$

$$merge(X, Y, Z)^R :\text{-} X \overset{Q}{=} [H|Xs] \mid Z \overset{Q}{=} [H|Zs], merge(Xs, Y, Zs)^R.$$
$$merge(X, Y, Z)^R :\text{-} Y \overset{P}{=} [H|Ys] \mid Z \overset{P}{=} [H|Zs], merge(X, Ys, Zs)^R.$$

Figure 4: Prioritized Merge

4.3 Contradictory Prioritization in KL1

To explain the concept of the independency of controlling process invocation and message passing, we show that KL1 does not have the independency property.

In KL1, process priority is controlled by @priority, and clause selection by alternatively. An integer is dynamically given to @priority as its argument. Accordingly, the priority of KL1 has the total ordering. If both the definition clauses above and below the alternatively pragma are ready for commitment (that is, their variables are sufficiently instantiated), one of the clauses on the upper side is always selected. As such, in KL1, the process control by priority is dynamic, while the clause selection is static. In other words, process priority is controlled by a message sender, while clause selection is controlled by a message receiver. Unfortunately, the KL1 priority system causes contradictory prioritization.

The following KL1 program is problematic.

```
:- (X = a)@priority(10),        p(X,Y) :- X = a | true.
   (Y = b)@priority(20),        alternatively.
   p(X,Y)@priority(Np).         p(X,Y) :- Y = b | true.
```

In this program, suppose that Np, which is given as the priority of p(X,Y), is instantiated to an integer somewhere else. Then, the commitment of p(X,Y) *depends* on not only the position of alternatively but also on the value of Np. If Np > 10, the second definition clause is selected; if Np = 10, the clause selection is nondeterministic; if Np < 10, the first is selected. This behavior is caused by the contradiction of the dynamic relation between priorities of X = a and Y = b and the static relation between the first and second clauses of p/2 posed by alternatively. It is also reported in [2] that such contradictory prioritization may appear in Ada programming.

On the other hand, O_N prevents a programmer from writing such a program with contradictory prioritization, since the aggregate priority is employed for clause selection and all the priorities for process invocation and message passing are dynamically given by message senders.

4.4 Independency of Priority Control

We show that process invocation is independent from the prioritization of message passing in O_N and vice versa. Let S be the constraint store after the completion of program execution, through this subsection.

Program Feature 4.1 *There are the following programs A and B. Which process, p/2 or q/2, precedes the other is determined only by the ordering between P and Q; it is independent from the message priority represented by R.*

$:- \top \succ P \succ \bot, \top \succ R \succ \bot, P \succ Q \succ \bot,$

$\quad p(X,Y)^P, q(X,Z)^Q, X \overset{R}{=} t.$

$p(X,Y)^P :- X \overset{R}{=} t \mid Y \overset{P}{=} a.$

$q(X,Z)^Q :- X \overset{R}{=} t \mid Z \overset{Q}{=} b.$

$:- \top \succ P \succ \bot, \top \succ R \succ \bot,$

$\quad p(X,Y)^P, q(X,Z)^P, X \overset{R}{=} t.$

The definitions of $p/2$ and $q/2$ are the same as Program A.

Program A · · · · · · · · · · · · · · · · Program B

Proof. In Program A, $S \models P \not\succ R$ and $S \models Q \not\succ R$. We consider the following three cases in terms of the invocation order of $p(X,Y)^P, q(X,Z)^Q$, and $X \overset{R}{=} t$. (A1) The order $p(X,Y)^P, q(X,Z)^Q$ and $X \overset{R}{=} t$: First the invocations of $p(X,Y)^P$ and $q(X,Z)^Q$ are suspended. When $X \overset{R}{=} t$ is executed, both $p(X,Y)^P$ and $q(X,Z)^Q$ become executable. Since their aggregate priorities are $\{P,R\}$ and $\{Q,R\}$ respectively and $\{P,R\} \succ \{Q,R\}$, $p(X,Y)^P$ precedes $q(X,Z)^Q$. (A2) The order $p(X,Y)^P, X \overset{R}{=} t$ and $q(X,Z)^Q$: First the invocation of $p(X,Y)^P$ is suspended. After $X \overset{R}{=} t$ is completed, the execution of $p(X,Y)^P$ resumes. This is followed by $q(X,Z)^Q$. (A3) The order $X \overset{R}{=} t, p(X,Y)^P$ and $q(X,Z)^Q$: Since $X \overset{R}{=} t$ has been executed, $p(X,Y)^P$ immediately becomes executable. Therefore, in every case, the commitment of $p(X,Y)^P$ always precedes that of $q(X,Z)^Q$.

Next, Program B behaves as the same FGHC program with the priority annotations ignored, since the aggregate priorities are equal. Thus, whether $p/2$ precedes $q/2$ or vice versa is nondeterministic. Consequently, the execution order of $p/2$ and $q/2$ is independent of R. $\square$

Program Feature 4.2 *There are the following programs C and D. The value of variable Z is determined only by the ordering of P and Q; it is independent from the process priority represented by R.*

$:- \top \succ P \succ \bot, \top \succ R \succ \bot, P \succ Q \succ \bot,$

$\quad X \overset{P}{=} a, Y \overset{Q}{=} b, p(X,Y,Z)^R.$

$p(X,Y,Z)^R :- X \overset{P}{=} a \mid Z \overset{P}{=} a.$

$p(X,Y,Z)^R :- Y \overset{Q}{=} b \mid Z \overset{Q}{=} b.$

$:- \top \succ P \succ \bot, \top \succ R \succ \bot,$

$\quad X \overset{P}{=} a, Y \overset{P}{=} b, p(X,Y,Z)^R.$

The definition of $p/3$ is the same as Program C.

Program C · · · · · · · · · · · · · · · · Program D

Proof. In Program C, $S \models P \not\succ R$ and $S \models Q \not\succ R$. We consider the following three cases in terms of the invocation order of $X \overset{P}{=} a, Y \overset{Q}{=} b$ and $p(X,Y,Z)^R$. (C1) The order $X \overset{P}{=} a, Y \overset{Q}{=} b$ and $p(X,Y,Z)^R$: The aggregate priorities of the two definition clauses of $p/3$ are $\{P,R\}$ and $\{Q,R\}$. Since $\{P,R\} \succ \{Q,R\}$, the first clause is always selected and $Z = a$ is obtained. (C2) The order $X \overset{P}{=} a, p(X,Y,Z)^R$ and $Y \overset{Q}{=} b$: Upon the invocation of

$p(X, Y, Z)^R$, the first clause of $p/3$ is selected and $Z = a$ is obtained. (C3)
The order $p(X, Y, Z)^R, X \overset{P}{=} a$ and $Y \overset{Q}{=} b$: The invocation of $p(X, Y, Z)^R$ first
suspends. After $X \overset{P}{=} a$ is completed, the execution of $p(X, Y, Z)^R$ resumes,
the first clause of $p/3$ is selected and $Z = a$ is obtained. Therefore, in every
case, the first clause of $p/3$ is selected and we get $Z = a$.

Next, Program D behaves as the same FGHC program with the priority
annotations ignored, since the aggregate priorities are equal. Thus, which
clause of $p/3$ is selected, the first or the second, is nondeterministic. Consequently, the clause selection of $p/3$ is independent of R. □

A counterpart of a phenomenon known as priority inversion may occur
in O_N programs. We think it is not appropriate to amalgamate into O_N
a mechanism to resolve priority inversion such as the priority-inheritance
algorithm, since the design principle of O_N is to give a means of describing
priority to a programmer. Actually, we successfully wrote a simple priority-
inheritance algorithm in O_N.

5 Concluding Remarks

From the above development and the sample programs, we think that our
framework can make priority a means for representing a programmer's intention related to execution control in declarative programming. Moreover,
thinking about priority may give us another new insight into execution control and the process-message paradigm.

According to the operational semantics of O_N, every time a goal is reduced, its language processing system must compute the aggregate priorities
of many goals and choose a goal with the maximum priority among them.
The operational semantics employs fine-grained concurrency, and it seems
quite inefficient if naively implemented. Thus, detecting specific patterns in
which the overhead of the goal selection and goal scheduling can be alleviated will be inevitable. We expect that the static analysis of priority in a
program will be able to detect some profitable characteristics for program
execution. One is the condition that makes the computation of the goal selection lightweight. Actually, we have already discovered some prioritization
patterns to be profitable. Another is the thread extraction and some other
information for goal scheduling. The analysis may suggest suspension-free
threads and as static goal-scheduling strategies as possible. This characteristic benefits the coarse-grained concurrency employed by almost all practical
implementations of CCLs [1]. In addition, if the analysis detects unrelated
threads in terms of priority, each thread may be regarded as an execution
unit in a distributed environment.

There is also another interesting approach to share our basic motivation
for treating prioritized concurrent activities, in which an agent of the form
if a else A, representing default, is introduced to detect negative information
[10]. Since we think this approach is closely related to ours, a comparison
between them will be the subject of future investigations.

We are just at the first step, where the declarative semantics for priority is
given and a concurrent logic language with the concept of priority is designed.

As stated in Section 1, priority restricts the set of answers as $A_P \subseteq A_O$; our research is motivated by the exploration of the semantics for priority. Therefore, future work will be to identify A_P and clarify how priority affects the language semantics.

Acknowledgements: We would like to thank Prof. Kazunori Ueda for his encouraging suggestions to the material of this paper. We thank the anonymous ICLP'99 referees who carefully read and gave valuable comments, although we unfortunately could not reflect all of them in this paper. We also thank Mr. Yasuyuki Tsukada of NTT for the improvement of the theoretical treatment of priority and the board members of the KLIC Association for the discussion about practical use. Thanks are due to Dr. Shunichi Uchida, the director of Research Institute For Advanced Information Technology (AITEC), for his environmental support.

References

[1] Chikayama, T., KLIC: A Portable Parallel Implementation of a Concurrent Logic Programming Language, *Proc. of Parallel Symbolic Languages and Systems (PSLS'95)*, also in *LNCS 1068*, 1995.

[2] Fidge, C. J., A Formal Definition of Priority in CSP, *ACM Trans. on Prog. Lang. and Sys.*, Vol.15, No.4, pp.681–705, Sep. 1993.

[3] Gregory, S., Experiments with Speculative Parallelism in Parlog, *Proc. of the 10th ISLP*, 1993.

[4] Gregory, S., and Ramirez, R., Tempo: a declarative concurrent programming language, *Proc. of the 12th ICLP*, 1995.

[5] Huntback, M., Speculative Computation and Priorities in Concurrent Logic Languages, *Proc. of the 3rd UK Conference on Logic Programming (ALPUK'91)*, 1991.

[6] Huntback, M. and Ringwood, G., Programming in Concurrent Logic Language, *IEEE Software*, pp.71–82, Nov. 1995.

[7] Kowalski, R., Algorithm = Logic + Control, *Comm. ACM* 22, 7, pp.424–436, 1979.

[8] Lloyd, J. W., *Foundations of Logic Programming*, Second, Extended Edition, Springer-Verlag, 1987.

[9] Saraswat, V. A., *Concurrent Constraint Programming*, The MIT Press, 1993.

[10] Saraswat, V., Jagadeesan, R. and Gupta, V., Timed Default Concurrent Constraint Programming, *J. of Symbolic Computation*, Vol.22, Nos. 5&6, pp.475-520, 1996.

[11] Ueda, K. and Chikayama, T., Design of the Kernel Language for the Parallel Inference Machine. *The Computer Journal*, Vol.33, No.6, pp.494–500, 1990.

[12] Ueda, K. and Morita, M., Moded Flat GHC and Its Message-Oriented Implementation Technique, *New Generation Computing*, Vol.13, No.1, pp.3–43, 1994.

Revising hull and box consistency

Frédéric Benhamou, Frédéric Goualard, Laurent Granvilliers
IRIN, Université de Nantes
B.P. 92208, F-44322 Nantes Cedex 3

Jean-François Puget
ILOG S.A.
B.P. 85, F-94253 Gentilly Cedex

Abstract

Most interval-based solvers in the constraint logic programming framework are based on either hull consistency or box consistency (or a variation of these ones) to narrow domains of variables involved in continuous constraint systems. This paper first presents HC4, an algorithm to enforce hull consistency without decomposing complex constraints into primitives. Next, an extended definition for box consistency is given and the resulting consistency is shown to subsume hull consistency. Finally, BC4, a new algorithm to efficiently enforce box consistency is described, that replaces BC3—the "original" solely Newton-based algorithm to achieve box consistency—by an algorithm based on HC4 and BC3 taking care of the number of occurrences of each variable in a constraint. BC4 is then shown to significantly outperform both HC3 (the original algorithm enforcing hull consistency by decomposing constraints) and BC3.

1 Introduction

Finite representation of numbers precludes computers from exactly solving continuous problems. *Interval constraint solvers* such as Prolog IV, Numerica [14], and ILOG Solver [12], tackle this problem by relying on *interval arithmetic* [10] to compute verified approximations of the solutions to constraint systems. Domains are associated to every variable occurring in the problem, and solving a particular constraint then lies in eliminating some of the values of these domains for which the constraint does not hold (inconsistency), using *local consistency techniques* and *filtering* [9].

In practice, enforced consistencies only approximate perfect local consistency since some solutions may be unrepresentable with floating-point numbers. Two worth mentioning approximate consistencies are *hull consistency* [1] and *box consistency* [2]. Most interval constraint solvers are based on either one of them. Enforcing hull consistency usually requires decomposing the user's constraints into so-called *primitive constraints* [4]. A well known drawback of this method is that the introduction of new variables induced by the decomposition hinders efficient domain tightening. On the other hand, the original algorithm enforcing box consistency processes constraints without decomposing them but is not at best with constraints involving many variables with few occurrences. In [6], some of the authors have presented DecLIC, a CLP language allowing the programmer to choose the "best fitted" consistency to use for each constraint of a system; however, deferring the choice of the consistency to the user spoils the declarativity of the language.

In this paper, HC4, an algorithm to enforce hull consistency is first presented, that traverses repeatedly from top to bottom and conversely the tree-structured representation of constraints; consequently, decomposition of complex constraints into "primitives" is no longer needed. Next, a slightly extended definition of box consistency is given, that no longer solely relies on the *natural interval extension* of constraints and captures both the original definition of box consistency [2] and the one by Collavizza *et al.* [5]. A new algorithm (BC4) permitting to efficiently enforce box consistency is then given. BC4 adapts the computation method to the number of occurrences of each variable in a constraint: domain narrowing for variables occurring only once in a constraint (which is one of the weaknesses of the "original" Newton-based method to enforce box consistency) is obtained by using HC4; variables occurring more than once are handled by searching "extreme quasi-zeros" using an interval Newton method as described in the original paper [2].

The rest of this paper is organized as follows: Section 2 presents the basics related to interval constraint solving. Section 3 presents hull consistency along with the usual scheme used to enforce it [4]; next, Algorithm HC4 to enforce hull consistency without decomposing constraints is described and its properties are pointed out. Section 4 first presents the extended definition for box consistency; Algorithm BC4 to efficiently enforce box consistency is then given. Section 5 comments results obtained on a prototype implementing BC4. Last, Section 6 summarizes the paper's contribution and points out some directions for future research.

2 Preliminary notions

In order to model the change from continuous domains to discrete domains induced by the shift from reals to machine numbers, Benhamou and Older [3] have introduced the notion of *approximate domain* over the set of reals[1] $\mathbb{R}$: an approximate domain $\mathcal{A}$ over $\mathbb{R}$ is a subset of the power set of $\mathbb{R}$, $\mathcal{P}(\mathbb{R})$, closed under intersection, containing $\mathbb{R}$, and for which the inclusion is a well-founded ordering. The *approximation w.r.t.* $\mathcal{A}$ *of a real relation* ρ, written $\mathrm{apx}_{\mathcal{A}}(\rho)$, is then defined as the intersection of all the elements of $\mathcal{A}$ containing ρ. This section focuses on two widely used approximation sets over $\mathbb{R}$, namely *intervals* and *unions of intervals*. The shift from reals to

---

[1]The original definition is more general but the one given here is sufficient for our purpose.

intervals is first described; interval constraints are then introduced; finally, the basics related to interval constraint solving are presented.

Let $\mathbb{R}$ be the set of reals compactified with the infinities $\{-\infty, +\infty\}$ in the obvious way, and $\mathbb{F} \subset \mathbb{R}$ a finite subset of reals corresponding to *binary floating-point numbers* in a given format [8]. Let $\mathbb{F}^\infty$ be $\mathbb{F} \cup \{-\infty, +\infty\}$. For every $g \in \mathbb{F}^\infty$, let g^+ be the smallest element in $\mathbb{F}^\infty$ greater than g, and g^- the greatest element in $\mathbb{F}^\infty$ smaller than g (with the conventions: $(+\infty)^+ = +\infty$, $(-\infty)^- = -\infty$, $(+\infty)^- = \max(\mathbb{F})$, $(-\infty)^+ = \min(\mathbb{F})$).

A *closed/open floating-point interval* is a connected set of reals whose lowest upper bound and greatest lower bound are floating-point numbers. The following notations are used as shorthands: $[g \mathinner{.\,.} h] \equiv \{r \in \mathbb{R} \mid g \leqslant r \leqslant h\}$, $[g \mathinner{.\,.} h) \equiv \{r \in \mathbb{R} \mid g \leqslant r < h\}$, etc. Let $\mathbb{I}_o$ be the set of closed/open floating-point intervals and $\mathbb{I}_\square$ the set of closed floating-point intervals. Let $\mathbb{U}_o$ be the set of unions of disjoint closed/open intervals, and $\mathbb{U}_\square$ the restriction of $\mathbb{U}_o$ to unions of disjoint closed intervals. Let $\mathbb{I}$ (resp. $\mathbb{U}$) denote the set of intervals (resp. unions of intervals) when the distinction between closed and closed/open bounds is useless. For the sake of clarity and otherwise explicitly stated, we will only consider hereafter (unions of) closed floating-point intervals.

A Cartesian product of n intervals $\boldsymbol{B} = I_1 \times \cdots \times I_n$ is called a *box*; a *domain* D is either an interval I or a union U of disjoint intervals. A nonempty interval $I = [g \mathinner{.\,.} h]$ is said to be *canonical* whenever $h \leqslant g^+$. An n-ary box $\boldsymbol{B}$ is canonical whenever intervals $I_1, \ldots, I_n$ are canonical.

In the sequel, a real (resp. interval) constraint is an atomic formula built from a real (resp. interval)-based structure and a set of real (resp. interval)-valued variables. Given a real constraint c, let ρ_c denote the underlying relation, $\mathsf{Var}(c)$ be the set of variables occurring in c, and $\mathsf{Multiplicity}(v, c)$ the multiplicity (i.e. the number of occurrences) of the variable v in the constraint c.

An *interval extension* of $f \colon \mathbb{R}^n \to \mathbb{R}$ is a mapping $F \colon \mathbb{I}^n \to \mathbb{I}$ such that for all $I_1, \ldots, I_n \in \mathbb{I} \colon r_1 \in I_1, \ldots, r_n \in I_n \Rightarrow f(r_1, \ldots, r_n) \in F(I_1, \ldots, I_n)$. An interval extension of a relation $\rho \subseteq \mathbb{R}^n$ is a relation $R \subseteq \mathbb{I}^n$ such that for all $I_1, \ldots, I_n \in \mathbb{I} \colon \exists r_1 \in I_1 \ldots \exists r_n \in I_n$ s.t. $(r_1, \ldots, r_n) \in \rho \Rightarrow (I_1, \ldots, I_n) \in R$.

A real relation ρ may be conservatively approximated by the smallest (w.r.t. set inclusion) union of disjoint boxes $\mathsf{Union}(\rho) = \mathrm{apx}_\mathbb{U}(\rho)$ (resp. the smallest box $\mathsf{Hull}(\rho) = \mathrm{apx}_\mathbb{I}(\rho)$) containing it. In the sequel, the following approximations are used: $\mathsf{Union}_o(\rho) = \mathrm{apx}_{\mathbb{U}_o}(\rho)$, $\mathsf{Union}_\square(\rho) = \mathrm{apx}_{\mathbb{U}_\square}(\rho)$, $\mathsf{Hull}_o(\rho) = \mathrm{apx}_{\mathbb{I}_o}(\rho)$, and $\mathsf{Hull}_\square(\rho) = \mathrm{apx}_{\mathbb{I}_\square}(\rho)$.

An n-ary interval operation $\blacklozenge$ is called the *natural* interval extension of an n-ary real operation $\Diamond$ if for all $I_1, \ldots, I_n \in \mathbb{I} \colon \blacklozenge(I_1, \ldots, I_n) = \mathsf{Hull}(\{\Diamond(x_1, \ldots, x_n) \mid x_1 \in I_1, \ldots, x_n \in I_n\})$. The *natural interval extension* of a function $f \colon \mathbb{R}^n \to \mathbb{R}$ is the interval function obtained from f by replacing each constant r by $\mathsf{Hull}(\{r\})$, each variable by an interval variable, and each operation by its natural interval extension. Given an n-ary real constraint c, let $\pi_k(\rho_c) = \{r_k \in \mathbb{R} \mid \exists r_1, \ldots, \exists r_n \in \mathbb{R}$ s.t. $(r_1, \ldots, r_n) \in \rho_c\}$ be the k-th *projection of ρ_c.*

Given a real constraint $c(x_1, \ldots, x_n)$, a constraint solver aims at reducing the domains associated to variables $x_1, \ldots, x_n$. This reduction process is abstracted by the notion of *constraint narrowing operators* [1] (shortened thereafter to CNOs) which are correct, contracting, and monotone functions taking as input a box and returning a box from which have been discarded some of the elements which do not belong to ρ_c.

Due to space requirements, we only give proof sketches for the properties stated hereinafter.

3 Hull consistency and related algorithms

Discarding all values of a box $\boldsymbol{B}$ for which a real constraint c does not hold is not achievable in general. Section 3.1 presents a coarser consistency called *hull consistency* [3] consisting in computing the smallest box that contains $\rho_c \cap \boldsymbol{B}$. Section 3.2 describes HC4, a new algorithm tackling one of the drawbacks of the original algorithm used to enforce hull consistency, that is, the decomposition of the user's constraints.

3.1 Hull consistency: the original scheme

The original definition of hull consistency is based on the approximate domain $\mathbb{I}_\square$, though it might easily be defined on $\mathbb{I}_\circ$:

Definition 3.1 (hull consistency [3]). A real constraint c is said *hull consistent w.r.t. a box* $\boldsymbol{B}$ if and only if $\boldsymbol{B} = \mathsf{Hull}_\square(\rho_c \cap \boldsymbol{B})$.

Due to round-off errors introduced by the use of floating-point numbers, computing the interval enclosure of a real set S is a difficult task in itself. Moreover, the precision of many arithmetic functions such as exp, cos ... is not guaranteed by the IEEE 754 standard [8]; consequently, their actual precision is implementation dependent.

Algorithm HC3[2] [2, 4] partly overcomes this problem by enforcing hull consistency over a decomposition c_{dec} of simple—*primitive*—constraints rather than considering the user constraint c. For example, the constraint $c: x + y * z = t$ might be decomposed into $c_{dec} = \{y * z = \alpha, x + \alpha = t\}$ with the addition of the new variable α.

Formally, given a real n-ary constraint c and a box $\boldsymbol{B}$, let $\rho_c^{(k)}(\boldsymbol{B})$ be the k-th canonical extension of ρ_c w.r.t. $\boldsymbol{B}$ defined as follows [13]:

$$\rho_c^{(k)}(\boldsymbol{B}) = \{r_k \in \mathbb{R} \mid \exists r_1 \in I_1, \ldots, \exists r_{k-1} \in I_{k-1},$$
$$\exists r_{k+1} \in I_{k+1}, \ldots, \exists r_n \in I_n \quad \text{s.t.} \quad (r_1, \ldots, r_n) \in \rho_c\}$$

---

[2]HC3 is our own denomination for Algorithm Nar given in [2] and is justified by its very close relation to AC3.

A constraint c is called a *primitive constraint* on the approximate domain $\mathcal{A}$ if and only if one can exhibit n *projection narrowing operators* $N_c^1, \ldots, N_c^n$, defined from $\mathcal{A}^n$ to $\mathcal{A}$, such that: $\forall \boldsymbol{D} = D_1 \times \cdots \times D_n, \forall k \in \{1, \ldots, n\}: N_c^k(\boldsymbol{D}) = \mathrm{apx}_{\mathcal{A}}(\rho_c^{(k)}(\boldsymbol{D}) \cap D_k)$.

The CNOs for primitive constraints are implemented using *relational interval arithmetic* [4] (see an example below). The main advantage of such an approach is that computation of hull consistency can be implemented very efficiently for the set of simple constraints supported by the constraint programming system. The drawbacks are that the introduction of new variables due to the decomposition process drastically hinders domain tightening for the variables the user is interested in. As pointed out in [2], this is particularly true when the same variables appear more than once in the constraints since each occurrence of a variable v is considered as a new variable v' with the same domain as v (*dependency problem* [10]).

Example 3.1 (A CNO for $c: x + y = z$). Enforcing hull consistency for the constraint $c: x + y = z$ and domains I_x, I_y, and I_z, is done by computing the common fixed-point included in $\boldsymbol{B} = I_x \times I_y \times I_z$ of the following projection operators: $N_c^1(\boldsymbol{B}) = I_x \cap (I_z \ominus I_y)$, $N_c^2(\boldsymbol{B}) = I_y \cap (I_z \ominus I_x)$, and $N_c^3(\boldsymbol{B}) = I_z \cap (I_x \oplus I_y)$, where $\ominus$ and $\oplus$ are interval extensions of $-$ and $+$ defined as: $[a..b] \oplus [c..d] = [a + c..b + d]$, and $[a..b] \ominus [c..d] = [a - d..b - c]$.

. As pointed out by Van Emden [13], the projection operators N_c^1, N_c^2, N_c^3, for a constraint of the form $x \lozenge y = z$ may all exist even if the function $\lozenge$ has no inverse. For example, consider the case where $\lozenge$ stands for the multiplication over $\mathbb{I}_\square$: N_c^1 computes the smallest union of intervals containing the set $\{r_x \in I_x \mid \exists r_y \in I_y, \exists r_z \in I_z : r_x \times r_y = r_z\}$. Hence, it is defined even when $0 \in I_y$.

3.2   HC4: a new algorithm for hull consistency

Algorithm 1 presents the HC4 algorithm which takes as input a set of constraints and a box, and narrows the variables' domains as much as possible. Algorithm HC4 is very similar to Algorithm HC3 [1] except that input constraints $c_1, \ldots, c_m$, are user's constraints instead of decomposed constraints, and that constraint narrowing operators associated to the constraints are implemented by Algorithm HC4revise, whose description follows.

Algorithm HC4 shares the following properties with HC3: if the computation of HC4revise terminates for any constraint and any box, HC4 terminates; the algorithm is correct: the output Cartesian product of domains is a superset of the declarative semantics of the constraint system included in the input box; the algorithm is confluent: the output is independent of the reinvocation order of constraints.

These properties are proved in the same way as for HC3 (see [11]) once HC4revise has been proved to be a constraint narrowing operator (see Prop. 1).

Algorithm 1: HC4 algorithm

HC4(in $\{c_1, \ldots, c_m\}$; inout $B = I_1 \times \cdots \times I_n$)
begin
    $S \leftarrow \{c_1, \ldots, c_m\}$
    while $(S \neq \varnothing$ and $B \neq \varnothing)$ do
        $c \leftarrow$ choose one c_i in S
        $B' \leftarrow$ HC4Revise($c,B,\mathbb{I}_\square$)
        if $(B' \neq B)$ then
            $S \leftarrow S \cup \{c_j \mid \exists x_k \in \mathsf{Var}(c_j) \wedge I'_k \neq I_k\}$
            $B \leftarrow B'$
        else % HC4revise not idempotent: next call on c may further narrow domains
            $S \leftarrow S \setminus \{c\}$
        endif
    endwhile
end

HC4 improves the compilation time (generation of primitives is useless), the solving time (no propagation needed between different primitive constraints for a given user's constraint), and the memory size.

Algorithm 2: HC4revise algorithm

HC4revise(in $c = r(t_1, \ldots, t_p)$: real constraint; inout B: box;
          in $\mathcal{A}$: approximate domain)
begin
    $D_\mathcal{A} \leftarrow B$
    foreach $i \in \{1, \ldots, p\}$ do
        ForwardEvaluation($t_i, D_\mathcal{A}$)
    endforeach
    BackwardPropagation($c, D_\mathcal{A}$)
    $B \leftarrow$ Hull$_\square(D_\mathcal{A})$
end

Algorithm 2 presents HC4revise, the new algorithm implementing the constraint narrowing operators used in HC4. Once more, note that HC4revise considers the user's constraints rather than primitives generated by decomposition: A real constraint $r(t_1, \ldots, t_p)$ is represented by an *attribute tree* where the root node contains the p-ary relation symbol r, and terms t_i are composed of nodes containing either a variable, a constant, or an operation symbol. Moreover, each node but the root contains two interval attributes $t.fwd$ (synthesized) and $t.bwd$ (inherited).

Given a real constraint and a box B, Algorithm HC4revise proceeds in two consecutive stages:

1. The *forward evaluation phase* (see Alg. 3 and Fig. 1) is a traversal of

Algorithm 3: Forward evaluation algorithm

ForwardEvaluation(**inout** t: attribute tree;
                   in $\boldsymbol{D_{\mathcal{A}}} = D_1 \times \cdots \times D_n$: Cartesian product of domains)
begin
   case (t) **of**
       $\Diamond(t_1, \ldots, t_j)$:   % a term
             foreach $i \in \{1, \ldots, j\}$ **do**
                ForwardEvaluation($t_i, \boldsymbol{D_{\mathcal{A}}}$)
             endforeach
             $t.fwd \leftarrow \blacklozenge(t_1.fwd, \ldots, t_j.fwd)$
      a: % a constant
             $t.fwd \leftarrow \mathrm{apx}_{\mathcal{A}}(\{a\})$
      x_k: % a variable
             $t.fwd \leftarrow D_k$
   endcase
end

the terms from leaves to roots in order to evaluate in $t.fwd$ the natural interval extension of every sub-term t of the constraint;

2. The *backward propagation phase* (see Alg. 4 and Fig.2) is a traversal of the tree-structured representation of the constraint from root to leaves in order to evaluate in every $t.bwd$ a projection narrowing operator associated to the father of node t. More precisely, two kinds of node are considered:

   – given the root node $r(t_1, \ldots, t_p)$, attributes $t_k.bwd$ ($k \in \{1, \ldots, p\}$) are computed by the k-th projection narrowing operator of the constraint $r(x_1, \ldots, x_p)$, where $x_1 \in t_1.fwd, \ldots, x_p \in t_p.fwd$;

   – given a term $t_{h+1} \equiv \Diamond(t_1, \ldots, t_h)$, attributes $t_k.bwd$ ($k \in \{1, \ldots, h\}$) are computed by the k-th projection narrowing operator of the constraint $x_{h+1} = \Diamond(x_1, \ldots, x_h)$, where $x_i \in t_i.fwd$ for all $i \in \{1, \ldots, h\}$, and $x_{h+1} \in t_{h+1}.bwd$; intuitively, variables x_i simulate the new ones introduced by the decomposition process.

During the backward propagation phase, the algorithm may be prematurely ended by the computation of an empty interval in some $t.bwd$. The constraint is then inconsistent w.r.t. the initial domains. If the computation is successful, the domain of each variable x_i in the constraint is intersected with the one in $x_i.bwd$.

Note: Backward propagation in a term is quite similar to automatic differentiation in reverse mode [7] for computing the partial derivatives of a real function: after the forward evaluation, the aim is either to evaluate the projection narrowing operators, or the partial derivatives for each node containing an operation symbol. At the end of the traversal in the tree, the domains are either intersected, or the derivatives summed.

Algorithm 4: Backward propagation algorithm

BackwardPropagation(**inout** t: attribute tree;
$\qquad\qquad\qquad$ **inout** $D_{\mathcal{A}} = D_1 \times \cdots \times D_n$: Cartesian product of domains)
begin
$\quad$ **case** (t) **of**
$\qquad r(t_1, \ldots, t_m)$: $\qquad\qquad\qquad$ % The root node
$\qquad\qquad c \leftarrow (r(x_1, \ldots, x_m))$
$\qquad\qquad D'_{\mathcal{A}} \leftarrow (t_1.fwd, \ldots, t_m.fwd)$
$\qquad\qquad$ **foreach** $i \in \{1, \ldots, m\}$ **do**
$\qquad\qquad\qquad t_i.bwd \leftarrow \pi_i(\mathrm{apx}_{\mathcal{A}}(\rho_c \cap D'_{\mathcal{A}}))$
$\qquad\qquad\qquad$ BackwardPropagation($t_i, D_{\mathcal{A}}$)
$\qquad\qquad$ **endforeach**
$\qquad \Diamond(t_1, \ldots, t_h)$: $\qquad\qquad\qquad$ % A term below the root
$\qquad\qquad c \leftarrow (\Diamond(x_1, \ldots, x_h) = x_{h+1})$
$\qquad\qquad D'_{\mathcal{A}} \leftarrow (t_1.fwd, \ldots, t_h.fwd, t.bwd)$
$\qquad\qquad$ **foreach** $i \in \{1, \ldots, h\}$ **do**
$\qquad\qquad\qquad t_i.bwd \leftarrow \pi_i(\mathrm{apx}_{\mathcal{A}}(\rho_c \cap D'_{\mathcal{A}}))$
$\qquad\qquad\qquad$ BackwardPropagation($t_i, D_{\mathcal{A}}$)
$\qquad\qquad$ **endforeach**
$\qquad x_j$: $\qquad\qquad\qquad\qquad\qquad$ % A variable
$\qquad\qquad D_j \leftarrow D_j \cap t.bwd$ $\quad$ % Domains intersected to take into
$\qquad\qquad\qquad\qquad\qquad\qquad$ % account multiple occurrences of x_j
$\quad$ **endcase**
end

Example 3.2. Figures 1 and 2 illustrate the computation of HC4revise over the constraint $2x = z - y^2$, with domains $I_x = [0 .. 20]$, $I_y = [-10 .. 10]$, and $I_z = [0 .. 16]$.

Backward propagation at the root node computes $[0 .. 40] \cap [-100 .. 16]$ (the intersection corresponds to the interpretation of the equality between intervals) in $(\times(2, x)).bwd$ and $(-(z, \hat{}(y, 2))).bwd$. Backward propagation at the root node of term $\times(2, x)$ computes in $x.bwd$ the interval I included in $[0 .. 20]$ (result of forward evaluation) which verifies $2 \times I_x = [0 .. 16]$. Finally, the new domains (located in the grey nodes) are $I_x = [0 .. 8]$, $I_y = [-4 .. 4]$, and $I_z = [0 .. 16]$.

Proposition 1. *Given an n-ary real constraint c, Algorithm* HC4revise *implements a constraint narrowing operator for c.*

Proof. Follows from the fact that HC4revise consists essentially in applying some primitive CNOs at each node of a finite tree, and that a composition of CNOs is also a CNO. $\qquad\qquad\qquad\qquad\qquad\qquad\qquad\qquad\qquad\qquad$ $\square$

Let HC4revise* be Algorithm HC4revise where, given a node t, the attribute $t.bwd$ is not eventually intersected with $t.fwd$.

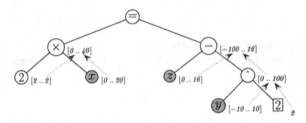

Figure 1: Annotated tree for the forward evaluation in the constraint $2x = z - y^2$

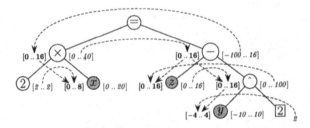

Figure 2: Annotated tree for the backward propagation in the constraint $2x = z - y^2$

As stated by the following proposition, invoking Algorithm HC4 on a set of constraints C and a box B is equivalent to the invocation of Algorithm HC3 on B and the set of constraints generated by the decomposition of the constraints in C into primitives:

Proposition 2. *Given C a set of real constraints and B a box, the output box of HC4(C,B) is equal to the one of HC3(C_{dec},B), where $C_{dec} = \bigcup_{c \in C} c_{dec}$.*

Proof. The proof is done by noticing that HC4 and HC3 use the same narrowing operators, and that the node attributes in HC4revise mimic the new variables in HC3. The proof then follows since the application order of the same constraint narrowing operators does not influence the fixed-point (confluency property of propagation algorithms [11]). □

4 Box consistency and related algorithms

Box consistency [2] has been introduced to avoid decomposing constraints, thus tackling the dependency problem for variables with many occurrences. Section 4.1 generalizes its definition and surveys the original method used to enforce it. Some connections between Algorithm HC4revise and box consistency are then stated. Finally, Section 4.2 presents a new algorithm to enforce box consistency that avoids relying on the computationally expensive Newton method when a cheaper method (straight evaluation) is available.

4.1 Box consistency

The original box consistency definition [2] is based on $\mathbb{I}_\square$ and on the natural interval extension of constraints. It is generalized below by permitting the use of other interval extensions, and by parameterizing it with two approximate domains. This last modification allows us to take into account some variations over the original definition such as the one given by Collavizza et al. [5], where quasi-zeros are approximated by open intervals while the output result is a closed one. The definition applies to (possible) different interval extensions of the original real constraint to define the projections.

Definition 4.1 (Box$_{\mathcal{A}_1,\mathcal{A}_2,\Gamma}$ consistency). Given $\mathcal{A}_1$ and $\mathcal{A}_2$ two approximate domains, let c be a real n-ary constraint, $\Gamma = \{C_1, \ldots, C_n\}$ a set of n interval extensions of c, k an integer in $\{1, \ldots, n\}$, and $D = D_1 \times \cdots \times D_n$ a Cartesian product of domains. The constraint c is said *box consistent w.r.t. D, a variable x_k of c, and C_k* if and only if:

$$D_k = \mathrm{apx}_{\mathcal{A}_1}(D_k \cap \{r_k \in \mathbb{R} \mid$$
$$C_k(D_1, \ldots, D_{k-1}, \mathrm{apx}_{\mathcal{A}_2}(\{r_k\}), D_{k+1}, \ldots, D_n)\}) \quad (1)$$

Moreover, c is said box consistent w.r.t. Γ and D iff Eq. (1) holds for all k in $\{1, \ldots, n\}$. A constraint set $\mathcal{C}$ is said box consistent w.r.t. a Cartesian product of domains D whenever every n-ary constraint $c \in \mathcal{C}$ is box consistent w.r.t. D and a set Γ of n interval extensions of c.

It is then worthwhile noting that box$_{\mathbb{I}_\square,\mathbb{I}_o,\{C,\ldots,C\}}$ consistency—where C is the natural interval extension of the considered constraint—corresponds to the definition of box consistency as given by Collavizza et al. [5], while box$_{\mathbb{I}_\square,\mathbb{I}_\square,\{C,\ldots,C\}}$ consistency is equivalent to the original definition [2].

For the sake of clarity, box$_{\mathbb{I}_\square,\mathbb{I}_\square,\{C,\ldots,C\}}$ consistency is henceforth shortened to "box$_o$ consistency."

Box$_o$ consistency is enforced by Algorithm BC3revise over a n-ary constraint c as follows: CNOs $N_1, \ldots, N_n$ (implementing typically an interval Newton method [14]) are associated to the univariate interval constraints $C_1^B, \ldots, C_n^B$ obtained from the interval extension C of c by replacing all the variables but one by their domains. Each N_k reduces the domain of one variable by computing the leftmost and rightmost *canonical intervals* such that C_k^B holds (*leftmost and rightmost quasi-zeros*).

As said in [2], box$_o$ consistency computation is far more effective than hull consistency computation when dealing with complex constraints involving the same variables many times, since the global processing of these constraints avoids losing some useful information. Nevertheless, finding the leftmost and rightmost quasi-zeros is computationally expensive. Moreover, it must be done for every variable occurring in the constraint. Therefore, box_o consistency is generally not the solution of choice when a complex constraint involves many different variables.

Given a variable x_k occurring once in a constraint c, let c' be an equivalent constraint where x_k is expressed in term of the other variables of c, and C_{x_k} the natural interval extension of c'. A property of Algorithm HC4revise can now be stated:

Proposition 3. *Let c be an n-ary constraint, C its natural interval extension, x_k a variable occurring exactly once in c, $\Gamma = \{C, \ldots, C_{x_k}, \ldots, C\}$ a set of n interval extensions, $\mathbf{B}$ a n-ary box, and $\mathbf{B'}$ the output box of HC4revise*$(c, \mathbf{B}, \mathbb{U}_\square)$. Then, c is $box_{\mathbb{I}_\square, \mathbb{I}_\square, \Gamma}$ consistent w.r.t. $\mathbf{B'}$, x_k and C_{x_k}.*

Proof. One may prove by induction on the tree-structured representation of c that, given $\mathbf{B'}$ the result of HC4revise*$(c, \mathbf{B}, \mathbb{U}_\square)$, the interval I'_k is equal to $\text{Hull}_\square(\rho_c^{(k)}(\mathbf{B}) \cap I_k)$. The results then follows from Definition 4.1. □

The exact characterization of the result provided by the execution of HC4revise is still an open problem but we have the following correctness and accuracy result w.r.t. variables with single occurrences:

Proposition 4. *Given an n-ary constraint c, a box $\mathbf{B}$, and x_k a variable occurring once, the following inclusions hold:*

$$\text{Hull}_\square(\rho_c \cap \mathbf{B}) \subseteq \text{HC4revise}(c, \mathbf{B}, \mathbb{U}_\square) \subseteq \text{HC4revise}^*(c, \mathbf{B}, \mathbb{U}_\square)$$

Proof. Inclusion $\text{Hull}_\square(\rho_c \cap \mathbf{B}) \subseteq \text{HC4revise}(c, \mathbf{B}, \mathbb{U}_\square)$ comes from HC4revise being a CNO (Prop. 1), while the other inclusion is due to HC4revise being HC4revise* where the attribute nodes are intersected with some domains. □

4.2 BC4: a new algorithm for box consistency

Let BC3 be the algorithm similar to HC3 and HC4, where the CNOs used by the *revise function* implement BC3revise.

On the one hand, Algorithm HC3 is efficient over real constraints whose variables have only one occurrence since then, the decomposition process does not amplify the dependency problem and the interval tightening methods are cheap. On the other hand, Algorithm BC3 is in general more efficient than HC3 since it is able to cancel the dependency problem over one variable with many occurrences in one constraint while the decomposition in HC3 increases it.

The previous remarks have led us to define BC4, a new propagation algorithm presented by Alg. 5. Let BC4* be Algorithm BC4 where HC4revise is replaced by HC4revise*.

Algorithm 5: Algorithm **BC4**

BC4(**in** C: set of constraints; **inout** B: box)
begin
   repeat
      $B' \leftarrow B$
      do
         NotFinished $\leftarrow$ **false**
         foreach $c \in C$ **do**
            $\mathcal{V}_c^1 \leftarrow \{x \in \mathsf{Var}(c) \mid \mathsf{Multiplicity}(x, c) = 1\}$
            $B'' \leftarrow B$
            HC4revise($c, B, \mathbb{U}_\square$)
            NotFinished $\leftarrow (B \neq \varnothing \wedge ((\exists I_k \neq I_k'' \wedge x_k \in \mathcal{V}_c^1)$
                          $\vee$ *NotFinished*))
         endforeach
      while (*NotFinished*)
      if ($B \neq \varnothing$) **then**
         BC3($\mathcal{C}_p^+, B$)
      endif
   until ($B' = B$ **or** $B = \varnothing$)
end

The set $\mathcal{C}_p^+$ is the set of projection constraints (univariate constraints obtained by replacing all occurrences of every variable but one in any constraint by the corresponding domains) generated from C, where the variable occurs more than once.

Proposition 5. *Let C be a constraint set, $\mathcal{C}_p^1 = \{C_x \mid \exists c \in C : x \in \mathsf{Var}(c) \wedge \mathsf{Multiplicity}(x, c) = 1\}$ the set of univariate interval constraints whose variable has only one occurrence, $\mathcal{C}_p^+$, the set of univariate interval constraints whose variable has more than one occurrence, B a box, and B' the output box of BC4* (C, B). Then, BC4* enjoys the same properties than HC4, namely: it is a confluent, correct and terminating algorithm. Moreover, C is $box_{\mathbb{I}_\square, \mathbb{I}_\square, \mathcal{C}_p^1 \cup \mathcal{C}_p^+}$ consistent w.r.t. B'.*

Proof. Confluency, correctness and termination are proved in the same way as for Algorithm HC4. As for box consistency, it suffices to note that HC4revise* enforces $box_{\mathbb{I}_\square, \mathbb{I}_\square, \mathcal{C}_p^1}$ consistency for variables occurring only once, while BC3 enforces $box_{\mathbb{I}_\square, \mathbb{I}_\square, \mathcal{C}_p^+}$ consistency for variables occurring more than once. Consequently, computing the common fixed point of both leads to the result. $\square$

As a consequence of Prop. 4, the result of applying Algorithm BC4 may be proved correct and included in the result of BC4*.

5 Experimental results

The propagation algorithms HC3, BC3 and BC4 have been implemented and tested on various examples from numerical analysis and CLP(Intervals) benchmarks [14, 6].

Table 5 presents the computational results obtained on a Sun Ultra-Sparc 2/166MHz for algorithms BC3 and BC4 and on an AMD K6/166MHz for HC3, then scaled to the first machine. Propagation algorithms are embedded in a more general bisection algorithm which splits the domains if the desired precision (width of domains) of 10^{-8} is not reached. Neither *improvement factor* nor weakening of box consistency (box$_\varphi$ consistency [6]) where used. Computation times exceeding one hour are replaced by a question mark.

Table 1: Experimental results

Benchmark	BC4 (s.)	BC3 (s.)	BC3/BC4	HC3 (s.)[†]	HC3/BC4
Cosnard 10	0.15	2.45	15	4.10	27
Cosnard 20	0.95	16.50	17	172.75	182
Cosnard 40	2.90	123.30	42	?	↗
Cosnard 80	13.70	916.95	67	?	↗
Broyden 10	2.40	2.35	1	?	↗
Broyden 160	86.65	86.55	1	?	↗
Kearfott 10	0.50	1.40	3	0.75	1.5
Kearfott 11	0.70	6.45	9	0.70	1
i4	32.65	160.80	5	?	↗
bifurcation	2.85	31.10	11	3.55	1.2
DC circuit	0.40	12.15	30	0.65	1.6
pentagon	1.10	12.95	12	0.70	0.6
pentagon all	44.60	2 340.00	52	124.20	2.8

[†] *Time on an AMD K6/166 scaled to a SUN Solaris 2/166.*

"Cosnard x" is the Moré-Cosnard problem obtained by discretizing a nonlinear integral equation which is composed of x equations over x variables, every variable appearing in every constraint; "Broyden x" is the Broyden-Banded problem with x variables which all have multiple occurrences in the constraints; "Kearfott 10", "Kearfott 11" and "bifurcation" are respectively some problems from chemistry, kinematics and numerical bifurcation, where the numbers of multiple and simple occurrences of variables in the constraints are approximatively equal; "i4" is a standard benchmark from the interval community; "DC circuit" models an electrical circuit with linear constraints; "pentagon all" describes the coordinates of a set of regular pentagons; "pentagon" is a restriction of "pentagon all" to one pentagon; the variables in benchmarks "i4", "DC circuit", "pentagon" and "pentagon all" have simple occurrences.

Results analysis: The well-known behaviours of HC3 and BC3 are confirmed. HC3 is not able to compute all the solutions of the Broyden-Banded problem since the decomposition of constraints amplifies the dependency problem. HC3 is slow for the Moré-Cosnard problem since the decomposition of complex constraints generates numerous primitive constraints and intermediate variables. Consequently, the domains propagation takes a long time. On the same problems, BC3 is far more efficient. HC3 outperforms BC3 on the other problems whose constraints have single occurrences of variables.

The use of HC4revise before BC3 in BC4 greatly accelerates the computations (see Column BC3/BC4). The worst case corresponds to the Broyden-Banded problem composed of multiple occurrences of variables. BC3 does not contract any domain but the overhead is insignificant due to the low cost of HC4revise. The good results for the last benchmarks are not surprising and come from the superiority of BC4 (and HC3) over BC3. The Moré-Cosnard problem is efficiently handled since HC4 is able to contract the domains of variables having multiple occurrences and then HC4 is always used instead of the interval Newton method (in BC3) which computes a sequence of intervals at a greater cost.

Last, BC4 outperforms HC3 on most of the benchmarks (see column HC3/BC4). On the one hand this comes from the superiority of BC3 over HC3 (for example on the Moré-Cosnard and Broyden-Banded problems). On the other hand, HC4 accelerates HC3 for the last benchmarks though the difference is small. A pathological case is "pentagon" which illustrates that a different propagation strategy may lead to different computation times. However the result "pentagon all" is in favour of BC4 though the benchmark is similar.

6 Conclusion

The contribution of this paper is twofold: first, an algorithm to enforce hull consistency without decomposing constraints into primitives has been presented; second, an extended definition for box consistency has been given: the original definition [2] only relies on a closed interval approximate domain and on natural interval extension, while the new one is parameterized by two approximate domains and permits defining box consistency for each variable of a constraint according to a different interval extension. As a result, the new definition captures several slightly different definitions of box consistency present in the literature and allows us to devise a new algorithm to efficiently enforce box consistency that may replace both the traditional algorithm used to enforce the original box consistency and the traditional algorithm to enforce hull consistency.

A variation of hull-consistency, *3B consistency*, has been proved to be more precise than box consistency [5], though computationally more expensive to enforce since it relies on decomposition of constraints into primitives. A promising direction for future research is to reuse Algorithm HC4 to device a new scheme for enforcing 3B consistency that might compete with BC4 in both speed and accuracy.

Acknowledgements

The research exposed here was supported in part by the INRIA LOCO project, the LTR DiSCiPl ESPRIT project #22532, and a project supported by the French/Russian A.M. Liapunov Institute.

References

[1] F. Benhamou. Interval constraint logic programming. In Andreas Podelski, editor, *Constraint programming: basics and trends.*, volume 910 of *Lecture notes in computer science*, pages 1–21. Springer-Verlag, 1995.

[2] F. Benhamou, D. McAllester, and P. Van Hentenryck. CLP(Intervals) revisited. In *Proceedings of Logic Programming Symposium*, pages 124–138, Ithaca, NY, USA, 1994. MIT Press.

[3] F. Benhamou and W. J. Older. Applying interval arithmetic to real, integer and boolean constraints. *Journal of Logic Programming*, 32(1):1–24, 1997.

[4] J. G. Cleary. Logical arithmetic. *Future Computing Systems*, 2(2):125–149, 1987.

[5] H. Collavizza, F. Delobel, and M. Rueher. Comparing partial consistencies. *Reliable Computing*, 5:1–16, 1999.

[6] F. Goualard, F. Benhamou, and L. Granvilliers. An extension of the WAM for hybrid interval solvers. *Journal of Functional and Logic Programming. The MIT Press*, 1999. To appear.

[7] A. Griewank. On automatic differentiation. In *Mathematical Programming: Recent Developments and Applications*, pages 83–108, 1989.

[8] IEEE. IEEE standard for binary floating-point arithmetic. Technical Report IEEE Std 754-1985, Institute of Electrical and Electronics Engineers, 1985. Reaffirmed 1990.

[9] A. K. Mackworth. Consistency in networks of relations. *Artificial Intelligence*, 1(8):99–118, 1977.

[10] R. E. Moore. *Interval Analysis*. Prentice-Hall, Englewood Cliffs, N.J., 1966.

[11] W. J. Older and A. Vellino. Constraint arithmetic on real intervals. In Frédéric Benhamou and Alain Colmerauer, editors, *Constraint Logic Programming: Selected Papers*. The MIT Press, 1993.

[12] J.-F. Puget. A C++ implementation of CLP. In *Proceedings of the Singapore Conference on Intelligent Systems (SPICIS'94)*, Singapore, 1994.

[13] M. H. Van Emden. Canonical extensions as common basis for interval constraints and interval arithmetic. In *Proceedings of JFPLC'97*, pages 71–83. HERMES, 1997.

[14] P. Van Hentenryck, L. Michel, and Y. Deville. *Numerica: A Modeling Language for Global Optimization*. The MIT Press, 1997.

CLAIRE: Combining Sets, Search and Rules to Better Express Algorithms

Yves Caseau, François-Xavier Josset, François Laburthe

BOUYGUES – DTN, 1 avenue Eugène Freyssinet
78061 St-Quentin en Yvelines cedex, FRANCE
{ycs,fxjosset,flaburth}@challenger.bouygues.fr

Abstract. This paper presents a programming language that includes paradigms that are usually associated with declarative languages, such as sets, rules and search, into an imperative (functional) language. Although these paradigms are separately well-known and available under various programming environments, the originality of the CLAIRE language comes from the tight integration, which yields interesting run-time performances, and from the richness of this combination, which yields new ways to express complex algorithmic patterns with few elegant lines. To achieve the opposite goals of a high abstraction level (conciseness and readability) and run-time performance (CLAIRE is used as a C++ pre-processor), we have developed two kinds of compiler technology. First, a pattern pre processor handles iterations over both concrete and abstract sets (data types and program fragments), in a completely user-extensible manner. Second, an inference compiler transforms a set of logical rules into a set of functions (demons that are used through procedural attachment).

1. Introduction

The CLAIRE language [7] is born from a research project that started 6 years ago which goal was to study the relationship between combinatorial optimization and constraints. We decided to evaluate the competitive advantages and reciprocal benefits of combinatorial optimization (CO) and constraint programming (CP) techniques, and then to combine them into hybrid algorithms. We followed a systematic approach and looked at problems such as Resource Allocation, Matching, Scheduling (job-shop, cumulative), Routing (TSP, VRP, VRPTW) or Time-Tabling. Most real industrial optimization problems are a combination of these more classical problems, thus another goal of this project was to identify a set of "building blocks" for optimization applications. For each of these problems, we have produced a library of hybrid algorithms.

The combination of hybrid algorithms can only be made at the source level, using a "white box" approach. The complexity and the inter-dependence between the various algorithms for propagation, computing lower bounds, branching, etc. is such that an approach based on components (black boxes) does not seem realistic to us (today) if one wants to take advantage of all the various techniques provided by the CO field. Thus, we have found the need for a language to express our different algorithms that would be:

- *simple and readable*, for many reasons: because reuse of algorithms requires a readable expression of the ideas, but also because CLAIRE was part of a research and teaching project and we needed an "executable pseudo-code" to demonstrate algorithms;

- *multi-paradigm* (supporting logic, imperative and functional programming styles), with few simple and well-understood concepts, such as objects, functions, rules and versioning for building search trees;

- *compiled efficiently* so that we could compare our algorithms with state-of-the-art approaches from teams in the CO community who use C or FORTRAN as their implementation language. We decided to build CLAIRE as a C++ preprocessor that would generate hand-quality C++ code (CLAIRE is now being ported to Java). The main technical contribution of the CLAIRE compiler is source-to-source optimization, which is presented in this paper.

The paper is organized as follows. The next section is a presentation of CLAIRE at a glance. CLAIRE is an object-oriented functional language with parametric polymorphism. It is also a modeling language that uses high-level abstractions such as sets or relations. Last, it includes an inference engine for object-based rules and a few tools for building tree search algorithms. The third section presents the notion of "set programming" in CLAIRE, which is derived from a set of techniques that make the use of sets as a programming paradigm both natural and efficient. The fourth section shows how logical rules are compiled into functions. This is based on previous work developed for the LAURE language [3] (one of CLAIRE's ancestors), so we focus on the application of the technique to the CLAIRE logic and the impressive performance that we now obtain (since CLAIRE functions are compiled into very efficient C++ code). The last section shows the application of CLAIRE to writing optimization algorithms. We show how we can use the built-in features to write tree search algorithms, and how the strategy of source-to-source optimization introduces new opportunities for optimization through the notion of composition polymorphism.

2. CLAIRE at a Glance

2.1 A Simple OOP Language

The object-oriented data model for CLAIRE is straightforward. Classes are defined with a simple list of typed slots (i.e., instance variables) and only single inheritance is supported. Each class is a first-class object of the system and is available at run-time (an optional list of instances is maintained for each class).

A class definition uses the < : operator (because subclasses are subtypes in CLAIRE) and consists of appending a list of new slots to the parent class. Slots support default values and unknown values, i.e., there is a special unknown object that represents the absence of value. Here are two simple examples; the second one shows a parameterized class (the usual stack class, parameterized by the type of its elements).

```
point <: object(x:integer = 0, y:integer = 0)
stack[of] <: object(of:type, contents:list = nil)
```

A rich data type complements the simplicity of the class hierarchy. A type is either a class, a constant set of objects, the union or the intersection of two types, a parameterized class, an integer interval or a typed subset of list, array or set. A parameterized class is the subset of the class such that the parameter belongs to a given type. For instance, stack[of:{integer,float}] is the set of stacks whose type parameter (of) is either integer or float.

There are three kinds of primitive collections: arrays (constant length and ordered), lists (dynamic length, ordered) and sets (dynamic length, no order and no duplicates). Both lists and sets come in two flavors: either untyped (list, *à la* LISP) or strongly typed (list<integer>, *à la* C++). Since list<X> ⊂ list, we can write generic list methods, but list subtypes are monomorphic (list<X> ⊂ list<Y> ⇒ X = Y) for type safety [4]. Besides, the tuple type is used for constant, heterogeneous, typed "arrays"; for instance, tuple(integer,integer,float) contains *tuples* with exactly three elements: two integers and a float. A *tuple* is not an *array*; its content cannot be changed. We can summarize the CLAIRE type system as follows (as usual, integer[] is the type for arrays of integers and .. is used to define integer intervals):

```
<type>  ≡ <class> | <class>[<parameter>:<type> *] |
          {<object> *} | (<integer> .. <integer>) |
          (<type> ∪ <type>) | (<type> ∧ <type>) |
          set<<type>> | list<<type>> | <type>[] |
          tuple(<type> *) | subtype[<type>]
```

Types are seen conceptually as sets of objects (more precisely, as expressions that denote a set of objects) and can be used everywhere in a program, since they are reified. Types as objects are themselves typed with the subtype[...] type; for instance, subtype[integer] contains all types that are included in integer. This set-oriented view is supported by the semantic of type subsumption. It is defined by the inclusion of the set extensions for all possible evolution in the object database. Types form an inclusion lattice with syntactical greater lower bound and subsumption (similar to LAURE [3]).

2.2 Polymorphism and Advanced Typing

Methods in CLAIRE are simply overloaded functions, where each parameter contributes to the overloading (the so-called *multi-methods* [5]) and each parameter can be typed with *any* CLAIRE type. For instance, attaching a method to a class union is useful to palliate the absence of multiple inheritance. Methods may be attached anywhere in the type lattice, not simply to the class hierarchy (more precisely, anywhere in the lattice of type Cartesian products). This makes CLAIRE closer to a language like *Haskell* than to C++. A method is called a restriction of the global function (e.g., f) which itself is called a property. For instance, the following definition (although meaningless) illustrates the resulting expressive power:

```
f(x:{0}, y:integer) : integer -> 1
f(x:integer, y:(0 .. INT+)) : integer -> f(abs(x) - 1, y + x)
f(x:integer, y:(INT- .. -1)) : integer -> f(x + y, abs(x + y))
f(x:(1 .. 10), y:((0 .. 10) U (100 .. INT+))) : integer -> 1
f(x:integer) : integer -> f(x, x)
```

Parameterized types can be used to produce parameterized signature. That means that we can use the value of a parameter (when it is a type) inside the signature. Let us consider the following example:

```
push(s:stack<X>, y:X) : void -> s.content :add y  ¹
```

The use of the type variable X states that the second argument must belong to the type contained in the slot of from the first argument (the stack). Note that there is an explicit difference in CLAIRE between `stack[of:{integer}]`[2] and `stack[of:subtype[integer]]`. The first is the set of stacks with *range parameter* integer (exactly), whereas the second can be thought of as the stacks of integers (stacks whose *range parameter* is a subtype of integer). There is no parametric subtyping with the first (i.e. `stack[of:{integer}] <= stack[of:{number}]` is false) as noticed in [8]. However, there is parametric subtyping with the second (i.e. `stack[of:subtype[integer]] <= stack[of:subtype[number]]`).

Another feature that will prove important in the next section is the fact that CLAIRE supports higher-order functions. Properties, that are function names, may be passed as arguments to a method and they can, in turn, be applied to functions. For instance, one can write:

```
exp(f:property, x:any, n:integer) : integer      // exponentiation
   -> if (n = 0)  f(x)
      else  f(exp(f, x, n - 1))
```

This example will not be type-checked by the compiler and CLAIRE will rely on dynamic typing. On the other hand, most methods are statically type-checked and the C++ code produced by the compiler is completely similar to hand-written code (on classical benchmarks for procedural languages, CLAIRE is identical to C++).

Last, second-order types can be attached to methods. A second-order type is a function, defined by a lambda abstraction, which represents the relationship between the type of the input arguments and the result. More precisely it is a function such that if it is applied to any valid type tuple for the input arguments, its result is a valid type for the result of the original function. Let us consider the two following examples:

```
Identity(x:any) : type[x] -> x
top(s:stack<x>) : type[x] -> last(s.content)
```

---

¹ for each operation op, x :op y is syntactical sugar for x := (x op y)
² `stack<integer>` is syntactical sugar for `stack[of:{integer}]`

The first classical example states that Identity is its own second-order type. The second one states that the top of a stack always belong to the type of the stack elements (of parameter). In the expression e that we introduce with the type[e] construct, we can use the types of the input variables directly through the variables themselves, we may also use the extra type variables that were introduced in a parameterized signature (as in the top example) and we use the basic CLAIRE operators on types such as ∪ or ∧ (type intersection).

In the same way that overloading becomes more powerful with a richer type system, we have introduced tables to represent binary relations. Tables extend traditional arrays by allowing the domain (and the range) to be any type. When the domain is not an integer interval (the usual case for arrays) it is implemented through hashing. The following examples illustrate CLAIRE tables:

```
square[x:(0 .. 20)] : integer := x * x
dist[x:(0 .. 10), y:(0 .. 10)] : float := 0.0
creator[c:class] : string := "who created that class"
color[s:{car, house, table}] : set<colors> := {}
married[t:tuple(person,person)] : tuple(date,place)∪{nil} := nil
```

The combination of objects, relations (with explicit and implicit inverses), heterogeneous sets and lists makes CLAIRE a good language for knowledge representation. For instance, entity-relationship modeling is straightforward.

2.3 Set and Logic Programming

Sets play an important role in CLAIRE. We saw that each type represents a set and may be used as such. A set is used through testing membership, iteration, or combining with another set and a set operation. Membership is tested using the operation ∈ (the ASCII representation is '%'). Iteration is performed with the for x in S e(x) control structure. We have also introduced two convenient expressions:

- exists(x in S | P(x)) returns true if there exists an x in S such that P(x) is true, and false otherwise
- some(x in S | P(x)) returns an x from S such that P(x) is true if one exists, and unknown else (as in ALMA [2]).

For instance (refer to [7] for further information), we may write:

```
if exists(c in (1 .. 10) | ok?(c + y))  choose(d, y)
when x := some(t in TASK | completed?(t)) in
    register(t)                           // t was found
else error("no completed task was found")
```

New sets can be formed through selection (e.g., {x in S | P(x)}) or set image (e.g., {f(x) | x in S}) [15]. When duplicates should not be removed, a list image can be formed with list{f(x) | x in S}. Using a straightforward syntax leads to straightforward examples:

```
exists(p in {x.father | x in (man ∪ woman)} | p.age < 20)

sum(list{y.salary | y in {y in person | y.dept = sales}})
```

In addition to sets, CLAIRE uses a fragment of an object-oriented logic to support inference rules (a complete description of this logic is out of scope for this paper and may be found in [3] and its associated bibliography). This logic may be seen as an object-oriented extension of binary DATALOG with object methods, set expressions and negation. The following expression is the logic part of a CLAIRE rule (e.g., the closure rule, in section 4.2):

```
edge(x,y) | exists(z, edge(x,z) & path(z,y))  => x.path :add y
```

The first extension is the introduction of interpreted functions, which are represented by object methods. These methods are either comparison methods or binary operations. For computing x.tax from x.salary, we may write:

```
exists(z, z = x.salary & z > 30000 & z < 50000 &
       y = 3000 + (z - 30000) * 0.28 )   => x.tax := y
```

The second extension is the introduction of set expressions (*à la* LDL [14]) and the creation of "invented" objects (a rule may create a new object that is completely specified by the set of its components using an implicit bijection). Here are two examples: the first one defines a relation append that associates to a pair of arguments (represented by pair) the list obtained by appending the two arguments (pair[1] and pair[2]). It shows the parameterized creation of a list u that is defined by its car and its cdr. The second example uses a set expression.

```
cdr(u) = append(make_pair(cdr(pair[1]), pair[2])) &
car(u) = car(pair[1])
    => append(pair) := u

z = 2 + size({y in person | y ∈ x.children})
    => x.family_size := z
```

The last extension is the introduction of negation (using not(P(x,y))). Although this object-oriented logic supports a top-down complete resolution strategy (with stratified negation), it is only used in CLAIRE to provide forward-chaining inference rules. A rule is defined by linking a logical condition to a conclusion, which is any CLAIRE expression. Here is a simple example:

```
compute_salary(x:person[age:(18 .. 40)]) :: rule(
    x.salary < average_salary({y in person | x.dept = y.dept})
    => x.next_salary := x.salary * 1.1)
```

To complete this brief overview of CLAIRE, we need to mention the "versioning" mechanism. A version (also called a *world*, using the AI terminology) is a virtual copy of the state of the objects. The goal is to be able to return to a previously stored state if a hypothetical branch fails during problem solving. As a consequence, worlds in CLAIRE are organized into a stack and only two operations are allowed: one for copying the current state of the database and another for returning to the previous state. The part of the objects that supports these defeasible updates is defined by the programmer and may include slots, tables, global variables or specific data structures such as lists or arrays.

Each time we ask CLAIRE to create a new world, CLAIRE saves the status of defeasible slots (and tables, variables, ...). Worlds are represented with numbers, and various operations are provided to query the current world, create and return to previous worlds, with or without "forgetting" the most recent updates. The use of worlds is also encapsulated with the branch(e) control structure which creates a world, evaluates the expression e and returns true if the result of e is true, and otherwise backtracks to the previous world and returns false. Using these programming features makes writing search algorithms, such as branch-and-bound, much simpler in CLAIRE (or another language with search primitives such as ALMA [2]). For instance, here is a simple program fragment that solves the "n queens" problem:

```
r1(x:D, y:D) :: rule(exists(z:D, column[z] = y)    // propagation rule
    => possible[x, y] := false)
r2(x:D, y:D) :: rule(exists(z:D, column[z] + z = y + x)
    => possible[x, y] := false)
r3(x:D, y:D) :: rule(exists(z:D, column[z] - z = y - x)
    => possible[x, y] := false)

queens(n:(0 .. SIZE)) : boolean
    -> (if (n = 0) true
        else exists(p in D |
            (possible[n, p] &
            branch( (column[n] := p, queens(n - 1)) ))))
```

In this program, queens(n) returns true if it is possible to place n queens. The search tree (these embedded choices) is represented by the stack of the recursive calls to the method queens. At each level of the tree, each time a decision is made (an assignment to the column table), a new world is created so that we can backtrack whether this hypothesis (this branch of the tree) leads to a failure.

3. Set-Based Programming

3.1 Sets in CLAIRE

We gave a brief overview of the use of sets in CLAIRE in the previous section. However, there is more to the concept of "Set-Based Programming". For us, it comes from the combination of two principles:

- Sets are "first-class citizens" with a choice of multiple representations (abstraction);

- Abstract sets may be used to capture "design patterns".

The first aspect in CLAIRE is illustrated by the variety of data structures that are available to represent collections of objects. These include classes, arrays, lists, sorted collections or bit-vectors. Also, we already mentioned that any type can be used as a collection, as illustrated in the following example:

```
for x in person[age:(15 .. 18)]  print(x)
```

Moreover, new collection classes can be introduced. In the following example, we introduce collections that are implemented with a hash table (hashing an object to get an index in a list is a standard method).

```
Hset<of> <: collection(of:type, content:list, index:integer)
add(s:Hset<X>, y:X) : void
        -> let i := hash(s.content, y) in ( ... )
set!(s:Hset) : set
        -> {x in s.content | known?(x)}
```

In addition to concrete sets, CLAIRE supports set expressions, which can be used freely since they are built lazily by the compiler so that any useless allocation and construction is avoided, as we shall see later. We already mentioned set construction by image or selection. New set expressions can also be introduced through the concept of pattern. A pattern is a function call that can be lazily dealt with. The first step is to define a new set operator, such as:

```
but(x:collection,y:any) : set                    // (x but y) ⟺ x \ {y}
        -> {z in x | z != y}
```

Now we can treat the pattern (s but x) lazily without building a concrete data structure that would represent it. The pattern type F[tuple(X,Y)] is the set of function calls with F as the selector (function) and two arguments (stored in the args list) of respective types X and Y. For instance, we can declare how to compute membership on the but pattern so that the compilation of the expression (x ∈ (Person but john)) will be performed by code substitution into (x ∈ Person & x != john).

CLAIRE supports true abstraction for collections since one may substitute a representation by another and not have to change a line of code in generic methods, such as the following example:

```
sum(s:subtype[integer]) : integer     // sum is an inline method (=>)
        => let d := 0 in (for x in s  d :+ x, d)
```

On the other hand, re-compiling will be necessary since the efficient implementation of abstraction relies on source-to-source transformation.

3.2 Customizable Iteration

One of the most important aspects of set programming from a practical perspective is the ability to customize set iterations. Iteration plays an important role in CLAIRE, either in an explicit form (using the for control structure) or in an implicit form (an iteration is implied in the image/selection set expressions as well as in the some/exists structures) as shown in these examples:

```
{x in (1 .. 10) | f(x) > 0}
{size(c) | c in (class but class)}
```

For each of these iterations, the compiler uses source-to-source optimization and generates the equivalent, but faster, expressions. The first one is compiled into:

```
let s := {}, x := 1 in
       (while (x <= 10)  (if (f(x) > 0)  s :add x, x :+ 1), s)
```

Since the set of collection classes is extensible, the compiler supports the extension of the iteration mechanism through the definition of the iterate method:

```
iterate(x:Hset, v:Variable, e:any) : any
       => for v in x.content  (if known?(v)  e)
```

This is also true for patterns, thus we can explain how the iteration of a pattern should be compiled lazily without building the set:

```
iterate(x:but[tuple(abstract_set,any)],v:Variable,e:any) : any
       => for v in args(x)[1]  (if (v != args(x)[2])  e)
```

This mechanism has also been used to implement the lazy iteration of image or selection sets. As a consequence, an expression such as:

```
for x in {f(x,0) | x in (myHset but 12)}  print(x)
```

will be transformed into:

```
for x in myHset.content
       (if (known?(x) & x != 12) print(f(x,0)))
```

As a consequence, it is both natural and efficient in CLAIRE to use "virtual" sets that are iterated as a programming pattern. This yields programs that are easier to read since we separate the filtering of the data from the processing.

3.3 Sets and Design Patterns

This section illustrates the previous feature through two examples of using sets as a design and programming pattern. The first example is the concept of embedded (doubly) linked lists. Linked lists are very common and useful objects, since they provide insertion and deletion in constant time. The implementation provided by most libraries is based on cells with pointers to next/previous cells in the list. This is useful but has the inconvenience of requiring dynamic memory allocation. When performance is critical, most programmer use embedded linked list, that are implemented by adding the two *next/previous* slots to the objects that must be chained. This only works if few lists (e.g., one) need to be kept, since we need a pair of slots for each kind of list, but it has the double advantage of fewer memory access (twice fewer) and no dynamic allocation as the list grows. For instance, if we have objects representing tasks and if we need a list of tasks that have to be scheduled, we may define the class Task as follows:

```
Task <: object( ..., next:Task, prev:Task, ...)
```

The obvious drawback is the loss of readability, since the concept of linked list is diluted into pointer chasing. In CLAIRE, we can use a pattern to represent the concept of a linked chain using these two slots as follows. We first define chain(x) which is the list of tasks obtained by following the next pointer:

```
chain(x:Task) : list<Task>
     -> let l := list<Task>(x) in                // x is the first member
        (while known?(next, x)  (x := x.next, l :add x), l)
```

We define the iteration of the chain pattern in a very similar way:

```
iterate(x:chain[tuple(Task)], v:Variable, e:any) : any
     => let v := args(x)[1] in
            (while true  (e, if known?(next, v)  v := v.next
                             else break()))
```

We can now use the "abstract" chains as any other collection in CLAIRE:

```
sum({weight(x) | x in chain(t0)})
count(chain(t1))
```

The interest of this approach is to keep the benefit of abstraction at no cost (we do not see the pointer slots anywhere and we can later replace embedded linked list with another representation). The code produced by the optimizer is precisely the pointer-chasing loop that we would have written in the first place.

The second example shows the power of combining patterns with the concept of iterators. Iterators are a very popular solution for iterating collection in most Java and C++ libraries. However, for most collection types they induce a needless overhead (thus, we do not use them in CLAIRE). However, there are more complex data structures for which iteration can be seen as traversing the structure, and for which the iterator embodies the traversal strategy. An iterator is simply defined by two methods, `start` and `next`, which respectively provide the entry point for the iteration and the succession relationship. The following is an example of a tree iterator. We introduce a pattern (T by I) which produces the set of nodes in T using the traversing strategy of the iterator I:

```
Tree <: object(value:any, right:Tree, left:Tree)
TreeIterator <: object(tosee:list, status:boolean)
iterate(x:by[tuple(Tree,TreeIterator)], v:Variable, e:any) : any
    => let v := start(args(x)[2], args(x)[1]) in
          while (v != unknown)
              (e, v := next(args(x)[2], args(x)[1]))
```

We can define many types of iterators corresponding to the various popular strategies for iterating a tree (Depth-First Search, Breadth-First Search, etc.):

```
TreeIteratorDFS <: TreeIterator()              // DFS strategy
DFS :: TreeIteratorDFS()
start(x:TreeIteratorDFS, y:Tree) -> ...
next(x:TreeIteratorDFS, y:Tree) -> ...
```

We may then use the pattern (T by I) as any other collection and simply write:

```
sum({y.weight | y in (myTree by DFS)})
```

which associated optimized code is the following:

```
let d := 0, y := start(DFS, myTree) in
    (while (y !=unknown) (d :+y.weight, v :=next(DFS, myTree)), d)
```

4. Rule-Based Programming

4.1 Production Rules

Here we present an example taken from our cumulative scheduling program presented in [6]: it is interesting because the propagation pattern is complex and better expressed with a rule than with a procedural description. Cumulative scheduling is defined with a set of tasks that have to be scheduled on finite capacity resources. The amount by which a task "consumes" a resource must fit between two bounds (minUse/maxUse).

The rule `throw-up` (see below) involves two classes: Task and Interval. For each Task t, we store (in slots) the required resource t.res, time bounds t.earliestStart and t.lastEnd, the associated work t.work, and its extremal resource use levels t.minUse/t.maxUse. For each Interval S, we store its bounds (S.Left/S.Right), the common resource of all tasks in the interval (S.Res), and the sum of the work amount of tasks (S.Work) in the Interval.

The rule considers a task t and an interval S. Let A be the earliest start time of the lower bound of S, B the latest end time of the upper bound of S, and a the earliest start time of t. Whenever t and S are such that:

1. they share some common resource r,
2. S is not an empty interval, but t is not included in S,
3. t cannot start before A and end before B,
4. t cannot start before A and end after B.

In such a case, the rule deduces that t necessarily starts after A, and analyses the amount of t that can be performed before B in order to update the time bounds of t. We use two update methods increaseEarliestStart and increaseLatestStart in order to maintain the Interval object.

```
throw-up(t:task, S:Interval) :: rule(
  exists(r:resource, S.Res = r & t.res = r &             // 1.
    r.capacity > 1 &
    not(empty(S)) & not(contains(S,t)) &                 // 2.
    exists(a, a = t.earliestStart &
      exists(A, A = (S.Left).earliestStart &
        exists(B, B = (S.Right).latestEnd &
          exists(slack, slack = (B - A) * r.capacity - S.Work &
            (t.work - max(0,A - a)) * t.maxUse > slack &   // 3.
            (B - A) * t.minUse > slack )))))              // 4.
  => increaseEarliestStart(t, B - (slack ceildiv t.minUse)),
     increaseLatestEnd(t, B - (slack ceildiv t.maxUse)
                       + t.minDuration) )
```

This rule is triggered whenever a time bound `earliestStart`/`latestEnd` or the `contains` relation is modified. There are multiple propagation patterns and writing the equivalent procedural code is really a tedious and error-prone task.

4.2 Compilation of Rules

CLAIRE rules are compiled into procedural demons, in three phases. First, the condition part of the rule is rewritten into an algebraic expression, which is next differentiated into many functions that are finally transformed into *if-write* demons. The process of rule compilation relies on the use of a relational algebra. This algebra $A(R)$ contains relational terms (elements of R) that represent binary relations; it is generated from a set of constants (Cartesian products of types), of variables (CLAIRE slots and tables) and a set of operators. These operators can define unions, intersections and compositions over relational terms, but also more advanced algebraic functions such as the composition of a binary operation or a comparison operation with two binary relations, etc. (see [3] for details).

We will briefly describe each step of the compilation process, and follow the transformation of two rules, from their logical expression towards the generated procedural demons.

1. The `closure` rule performs a transitive closure over a graph, described through the binary relations `edge` and `path` (& and | are usual Boolean conjunction and disjunction):

   ```
   closure(x:point, y:point) :: rule(
       edge(x,y) | exists(z, edge(x,z) & path(z,y))
     => x.path :add y )
   ```

2. The `geo` rule aims at representing a geometric line (the object L is an instance of the `line` class) both as a set of points (`Hold(L,x)` means that the point x belongs to the line L), and as a pair of points (a line L is defined by two unique points `L.p1` and `L.p2`):

   ```
   geo(L:line, x:point) :: rule(
       exists(y, y ∈ L.Hold & x ∈ line(L.p2,y).Hold)
     => L.Hold :add x )
   ```

This rule says that we can deduce that a point x belongs to a line L if there exists a point y that belongs to L, such that x belongs to the line formed by y and one (p2) of the two points that define L (see Fig1).

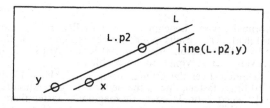

Fig1: *Representation of the process performed by the* **geo** *rule.*

- The first phase of the compilation process is the transformation of the conditional part of the rule into a relational formula that belongs to $A(R)$. Translation into the algebraic form is based on rewriting and involves a lot of knowledge about object methods. The principle is to solve the equation assertion(x,y), while considering that x is known and that y is sought. The result is the relational algorithm that explains how to get y from x, which is represented as a term in $A(R)$. The conditional part or the rule closure is transformed into the following algebraic term t1:

  t1 = edge ∪ (path o edge)

  and the conditional part of the rule geo is rewritten into the term t2:

  t2 = Hold o ψ[line](p2,Hold)

  where ∪, o and ψ[ ] are respectively the union operator, the composition operator and the composition of a binary operation (line) with two relations (p2 and Hold).

- Next, a phase of symbolic differentiation computes the effect of adding a pair of values into a table or a slot. The differentiation is a function that is applied to the algebraic term t, with respect to each relation R occurring in the condition, and that produces a term $\partial t/\partial R$ in $A(R\cup\{\mathbb{0},\mathbb{1}\})$. $\mathbb{0}$ and $\mathbb{1}$ are two constant functions that represent respectively the empty function ($\mathbb{0}$: (x,y) → ∅) and the identity function ($\mathbb{1}$: (x,y) → {(x,y)}). A set of differentiation rules (one for each operation on binary relations) is used to compute the term $\partial t/\partial R$. The term t1 computed above is differentiated with respect to the relation edge and yields the following function f1:

  f1 = ∂t1/∂edge = $\mathbb{1}$ ∪ (path o $\mathbb{1}$)

  or in other terms:

  f1 : (a,b) → {(a,b)} ∪ {(a,y) | (b,y) ∈ [path]}

  The term t2 is differentiated with respect to the relation Hold and yields the function f2:

  f2 = ∂t2/∂Hold = $\mathbb{1}$ o ψ[line](p,Hold) ∪ Hold o ψ[line](p2, $\mathbb{1}$)

- The last phase of the compilation of a rule consists of associating the set of functions (derived from each relational term occurring in the condition) and the CLAIRE expression in the conclusion, so as to build one *if-write* demon per function. For instance, the demon associated to the rule closure and the function f1 is compiled as follows (it is evaluated each time a pair (x,y) is added to the edge relation):

  ```
  if_write[edge](x, y)
     -> (x.path :add y,
            for z in y.path  x.path :add z)
  ```

  The compilation of the rule geo, with the function f2, gives the demon:

  ```
  if_write[Hold](L, y)
     -> for p in POINT
           let z := line(p, L.p1) in
              (if (L.p2 ∈ z.Hold)  z.Hold :add y),
                 for z in line(L.p2, y).Hold  L.Hold :add z)
  ```

4.3 Results

We performed several benchmarks on CLAIRE rules; some of them are reported in Table1. The results point out the efficiency of the technique of compilation by differentiation (between 600 K to 3 Mips = Million *inferences* per second), even when solving complex problems.

The improvement over the original design of LAURE [3] is one order of magnitude (10 times faster), due to the better C++ generation technique. Thus, CLAIRE is between 2 or 3 orders of magnitude faster than what we have measured with RETE-based inference engines [10] (for a comparison on a catalog of small benchmarks, see http://www.ens.fr/~caseau/rules.html). More empirically, we have noticed that CLAIRE programs written with production rules yield only about a 10 to 50 % penalty compared with hand-optimized procedural code. However, rule-written programs are about 4 to 30 times shorter than no rule-written ones, and they are easier to write.

	CPU time (P166)	Rules / s
Simple Filtering	0.33 s	3 Mips
Monkey	0.05 s	780 Kips
Triplet	0.27 s	660 Kips
Airline (rules & methods)	0.05 s	20 Kips
Zebra (heavy backtracking)	< 0.01 s	> 3 Mips

Table1: *Benchmarks on rules.*

Many industrial applications have been developed in CLAIRE, for which the choice of rules was relevant. They can be divided in two categories: applications that perform a complex task, which use all the expressive power of rules (such as cumulative scheduling), and applications that require flexibility, with an important amount of parameters. Programming with CLAIRE rules is motivated mostly by the need for flexibility (business rules change quite often) and also by the readability of the code (easier maintenance).

5. Search Algorithms

5.1 Search in an Imperative Language

The ability to write search algorithm in an imperative language is a key feature of CLAIRE, which is very similar to the ideas proposed in [2]. It is the reason why CLAIRE was used by many projects as a laboratory for exploring different search strategies, such as Limited Discrepancy Search [13], shuffling [11], or SaLSA [12].

Here is a real example of the search strategy for the jobshop problem [11]. The functional parameter `tightest` is a heuristic that returns the set of tasks (an Interval) that share the same machine and that looks for the most difficult to process.

```
solve(tightest:property) : boolean
-> when I:Interval := tightest() in
      exists(t in {x in I | canbefirst?(I, t)} |
               branch( (for t' in (I but t) t.After :add t',
                        solve(tightest) )
   else true                              // no interval was found
```

This example shows many interesting features. Some of them have already been mentioned: the iteration of a selection set (the set of tasks that can be the first in the set I), the use of the pattern (I but t) or the use of a functional parameter. We also notice the defeasible update t.After :add t', which adds t' to the list of tasks performed after t and triggers the propagation rules that represent the scheduling constraints [11].

Another interesting aspect of the `branch` control structure is contradiction handling (failure in a sub-tree). CLAIRE supports exceptions (represented as objects in a hierarchy) with a built-in `contradiction` subclass. When a contradiction is raised (for instance, by rule propagation), it is caught by the `branch(...)` instruction which backtracks and returns `false`. Thus, `branch` support a concise and readable programming style of search algorithms, an asset for defining easily new variations (other search strategies, instrumentation, ...).

We are also making good use of the extensibility of the iteration compiler. A task interval I is a set of tasks that share a same resource I.Res whose time

windows are included in a given interval [11]. Each task has a unique index and
the set of tasks that belong to I is represented by a bit-vector I.SET. Thus the
iteration of a task interval consists of iterating the set of tasks on the right
machine whose indexes belong to the bit-vector. For instance, the iteration in the
previous algorithm will be expanded into:

```
for t in (I.Res).users
    (if I.SET[t.index]
        (if canbefirst?(I, t)  branch(...) ))
```

The ability to pass function parameters at no cost from a performance point
of view is a key feature to write parametric algorithms. This is reinforced by the
fact that these parameters can be in-line methods, which means that the original
in-line method can be seen as a higher-level function generator. For instance, we
can use the following definition of max to define the method later:

```
// a generic max method
max(s:subtype[integer], greater:property, default:any) : integer
   => let x := default, empty := true in
          (for y in s
              (if empty  (x := y, empty := false)
                  else if greater(x, y)  x := y),
          x)

before(x:task, y:task) : boolean  =>  x.atleast ≤ y.atleast

later(x:Interval, t:task) : integer
        -> max(x but t, before, EndTask)
```

The code generated for the method later will be:

```
let t0 := EndTask, empty := true in
    (for t1 in (x.Res).users
        (if x.SET[t1.index]
            (if (t != t1)
                (if empty  (t0 := t1, empty := false)
                    else if (t0.atleast ≤ t1.atleast)  t0 := t1))),
    t0)
```

In that example, we have used max as a high-level code generator. This is the
first step in writing truly reusable code for complex problem solving algorithms.

5.2 Composition Polymorphism

The use of parameterization leads to the need for a new paradigm to implement
simplification (or reduction) rules. Consider the two following equations:

```
(A + B)[i,j] = A[i,j] + B[i,j]

(x ∈ (s but t)) = ((x ∈ s) & (x != t))
```

These equations may be seen as simplification rules since they respectively
allow us to extract a cell of a matrix sum without computing this sum explicitly
or evaluate membership to a "but" set without computing this set. Usually, there
is no need to represent these rules because the programmer uses them implicitly.
However, this is no longer the case when parameterization is used. For instance,
an expression M[i,j] may exist in the body of an in-line method, which gets
transformed into (A + B)[i,j] because of the form of the input parameters.
This is even more obvious with the second example if we apply a set inline
method to the set expression (s but t).

Representing these simplification rules leads to the notion of composition
polymorphism. What we need to represent is that the processing of
f(...,x,...) may be different when x is obtained as g(...). For instance, in
our first example, f is get[3] and g is +; in the second case, f is ∈ and g is but.
This type of polymorphism might be captured with a complex abstract data type

---

[3] get is used implicitly in the form ...[...] (e.g. M[i,j] = get(M,i,j))

in a statically typed language using complex pattern matching rules, but is out of reach with our concrete type approach. This is why we have introduced the notion of *patterns*, which are sets of function calls. Patterns are used to allow composition polymorphism through the definition of new inline methods whose signature are made either of any (for concrete parameters) or patterns (for expressions). The compiler uses such a restriction when it finds a function call matching its signature. We have already seen the application to the but example, here is an application with matrices:

```
get(x:+[tuple(matrix, matrix)], i:any, j:any)
    => eval(args(x)[1])[i,j] + eval(args(x)[2])[i,j]
```

Suppose that we now have this situation:

```
traceInv(m:matrix)
    => sum(list{ 1.0 / M[i,i] | i in (1 .. N) })

f(m1:matrix, m2:matrix) : boolean -> (traceInv(m1 + m2) > 0.0)
```

The macro-expansion of `traceInv(m1 + m2)` will yield an expression that involves `(m1 + m2)[i,i]`. This call matches the signature of the optimizing restriction that we defined previously (with x being the call `+(m1, m2)` and `args(x) = (m1, m2)`). Thus a further reduction is performed and the result is:

```
let x := 0.0, i := 1 in
    (while (i >= N)  (x :+ 1.0 / (m1[i,i] + m2[i,i]), i :+ 1),
     x > 0.0)
```

5.3 Writing Elegant Algorithms

We have used CLAIRE over the last 5 years to implement many graph or combinatorial algorithms, such as Edmonds' algorithm for minimum spanning arborescence [9] or the Hungarian algorithm bipartite matching problems (useful for global constraint propagation [11]). Although they do not necessarily use search mechanisms, we believe that they demonstrate the value of CLAIRE high-level features to express a complex algorithm in a more readable and elegant manner, even if not declarative.

Here is a fragment of the Hungarian algorithm in CLAIRE that illustrates some of the key ideas. The complete algorithm builds the matching by repeatedly applying growing steps and dual changes until the complete set of nodes is spanned (this is a primal-dual algorithm). The following method is the implementation of this first step, grow, which builds a Hungarian forest using a classical search for augmenting chains. This search is performed (with alternate marks even and odd?) in the reduced graph Gpi. The reduced graph is implicitly defined as the subset of all edges satisfying a given condition on the dual weights (that the corresponding constraint in the linear model is saturated). It is represented by the following pattern: Gpiset(i,a,b) is the subset of neighbors of the node i in this reduced graph where a and b are two iteration cursors.

```
// grow() returns true if the matching is improved (return value is true)
grow() : boolean
    -> let i := pop(explore) in // the stack of nodes that need to be explored
       (exists( j in {j in Gpiset(i, LastExplored[i] + 1, LastValid[i]) |
                                                          not(odd?[j])} |
           (if (sol-[j] != 0)
               //[SPEAK] grow: add (~S,~S) to forest// i,j,
               (odd?[j] := true, pushEven+(sol-[j]), tree[j] := i, false)
            else (augment(i,j), true))) |
        (if not(empty?(explore))  grow()) )
```

Although it is hard to grasp much from a short fragment of code, we may notice:

- the use of patterns such as pop(explore) or Gpiset(i,a,b) which encapsulate the complexity due to data structure handling (e.g., using the even array to implement the stack),

- the use of complex set expressions that are iterated and the use of set operators (exists),
- the use of active comments, that can be used as trace statements.

From our point of view, a description of this complex algorithm in less than 30 lines is very valuable, and is a strong advocate for using high-level languages.

The interest of the techniques presented in this paper is that they come with no penalties for run-time performance, since this CLAIRE implementation was checked to be exactly as efficient as a standard C++ implementation.

6. Conclusion

Experiments in the previous years have shown that constraint programming was best used in combination with other optimization techniques for combinatorial problem solving. The fact that hybrid algorithm engineering cannot be always performed exclusively through the use of components and may require some programming motivates the use of multi-paradigm programming languages. There have been many proposals for incorporating "advanced features" such as sets or rules into object-oriented languages, especially in the AI community. On the other hand, few have managed to incorporate as well a high degree of polymorphism and the use of higher-order functions. Among those few, the most interesting, from our point of view, are LIFE and Oz.

The major contribution of LIFE [1] (which actually may be seen as a superset of CLAIRE) is to provide with a clean integration of logic, inheritance and functions (as its name stands). LIFE played an important role when we tried to put some elegance into our "mix of features". However, there is a top-down vs. bottom-up difference in the design strategy of CLAIRE and LIFE. CLAIRE is the bottom-up integration of features that we know how to compile efficiently whereas LIFE is the top-down implementation of paradigms that are known to blend elegantly. The result is that it is easier, from our point of view, to write efficient algorithms with CLAIRE than with LIFE.

Oz is a concurrent constraint language [17] belonging to the post-CLP language generation. Its object oriented kernel offers multiple inheritance and a clean integration of higher order functions, in particular with the predefined search combinators that offer parametric search procedures [16]. In a way similar to LIFE, Oz is more ambitious than CLAIRE and has been a model for some of its features (such as the use of higher-order functions). On the other hand, Oz is still an untyped language and too high-level, from our point of view, to be a language of choice to implement propagation strategies.

To summarize, we have presented a high-level language for writing re-usable algorithms. The application of this language to various optimization problems has resulted in programs that are easier to read (and thus to maintain) and to reuse (or to combine). This is mostly due to two features:

- Declarative programming is encouraged with the use of logic rules (the programmer is freed from the concern about propagation patterns) which can be compiled into procedural demons with no run-time processing overhead.
- Set programming and set iteration raise the level of abstraction and recursively-nested expressions can be compiled with no run-time processing overhead.

We believe that our experience with CLAIRE may be of interest to the CLP community on three topics: the technology of compilation-by-differentiation for rules, the definition of a simple multi-paradigm language supported by real applications and the concern for a general purpose programming language for hybrid algorithms. On this last point, CLAIRE offers different tools for different concerns: an object oriented type system for elegant modeling, a data-driven rule compiler for declarative programming, parametric polymorphism, iteration and patterns for data structure manipulations and a version mechanism (reified in SaLSA [12]) for controlling search trees. This suggests that the scope of

CLAIRE is broader than its current use for combinatorial optimization algorithms and that it could be used for applications that have been associated with logic and rule-based programming.

CLAIRE is a public domain software and can be downloaded at www.ens.fr/~caseau/claire.html.

Acknowledgement

We would like to thank an anonymous referee who helped us in improving the paper.

References

[1]   H. Aït-Kaci. *An Introduction to LIFE—Programming with Logic, Inheritance, Functions, and Equations*, Proceedings of 10th ILPS, p. 117, 1993.

[2]   K.R. Apt, A. Schaerf. *Search and Imperative Programming*, Proceedings of the 24th ACM Symposium on Principles of Programming Languages (POPL'97), ACM Press, 1997.

[3]   Y. Caseau. *Constraint Satisfaction with an Object-Oriented Knowledge Representation Language*. Applied Intelligence, Vol. 4, no. 2, May 1994.

[4]   G. Castagna. *Covariance and Contravariance: Conflict without a Cause*. ACM Transactions on Programming Languages and Systems, Vol 17, no. 3, May 1995.

[5]   C. Chambers, G. Leavens. *Typechecking and Modules for Multi-Methods*. Proceedings of OOPSLA'94, ACM Sigplan Notices, Portland, 1994.

[6]   Y. Caseau, F. Laburthe. *Cumulative Scheduling with Tasks Intervals*. Proceedings of JICSLP'96, M. Maher ed., The MIT Press, 1996.

[7]   Y. Caseau, F. Laburthe *Introduction to the CLAIRE Programming Language*, LIENS research report 96-16, Ecole Normale Supérieure, 1996.

[8]   M. Day, R. Gruber, B. Liskov, A. Myers. *Subtypes vs. Where Clauses: Constraining Parametric Polymorphism*. Proceeding of OOPSLA'95, ACM Sigplan Notices, Austin, TX, 1995.

[9]   J. Edmonds. *Matroids and the greedy algorithm* Mathematical Programming, 1, p. 126-136, 1971.

[10]   C.L. Forgy. *Rete: A Fast Algorithm for the Many Pattern/Many Object Pattern Match Problem* Artificial Intelligence, 19, p. 17-37, 1982.

[11]   F. Laburthe. *Constraints and Algorithms in Combinatorial Optimization*, Ph. D. Thesis (in French) University of Paris VII, 1998.

[12]   F. Laburthe, Y. Caseau. *SaLSA: A Language for Search Algorithms*, Proceedings. of CP'98, M.Maher, J.-F. Puget eds., Springer, LNCS 1520, p.310-324, 1998.

[13]   C. Lepape, P. Baptiste. *Heuristic Control of a Constraint-Based Algorithm for the Preemtive Job-Shop Scheduling Problem*, Journal of Heuristics, to appear, 1999.

[14]   S. Naqvi, S. Tsur. *A Logical Language for Data and Knowledge Bases*. Computer Science Press, 1989.

[15]   J. Schwartz, R. Dewar, E. Dubinsky, E. Schonberg. *Programming with Sets: an Introduction to SETL*, Springer, New-York, 1986.

[16]   C. Schulte, G. Smolka. *Encapsulated Search for Higher-order Concurrent Constraint Programming*, Proceedings of ILPS'94, M. Bruynooghe ed., MIT Press, p. 505-520, 1994.

[17]   G. Smolka. *The Oz Programming Model*, Proceedings of Computer Science Today, J. Van Leeuwen ed., LNCS 1000, p. 324-343, Springer, 1995.

Herbrand Constraint Solving in HAL

Bart Demoen
Dept. of Computer Science, K.U.Leuven, Belgium

María García de la Banda, Warwick Harvey, Kim Marriott
School of Comp. Sci. & Soft. Eng., Monash University, Australia

Peter J. Stuckey
Dept. of Comp. Sci. & Soft. Eng., University of Melbourne, Australia

Abstract

HAL is a new constraint logic programming language specifically designed to support construction of and experimentation with constraint solvers. One of the most important constraint solvers in any logic programming language is the Herbrand (or term) constraint solver. HAL programs are compiled to Mercury but, while Mercury provides only assignment, tests for equality and construction and deconstruction of ground terms, HAL supports full unification (without the occurs check). In this paper we describe the HAL Herbrand constraint solver and show how by using PARMA bindings, rather than the standard term representation used in the WAM, we can implement a solver which is compatible with Mercury's term representation. Like Mercury, HAL supports type, mode and determinism declarations. HAL uses information from these declarations to reduce the overhead of Herbrand constraint solving wherever possible. In this paper we also systematically evaluate the effect of each kind of declaration on the efficiency of HAL programs.

1 Introduction

Mercury [6] is a recent logic programming language which is considerably faster than traditional Prolog implementations. One reason is that Mercury requires the programmer to provide type, mode and determinism declarations. Type information allows a compact representation for terms, mode information guides reordering of literals and multivariant specialization while determinism information is used to remove the overhead of unnecessary choice point creation. Another reason is that Mercury does not support full unification; only assignment, construction, deconstruction and equality testing for ground terms. This means that Mercury does not allow true logical variables, and so common logic programming idioms such as difference lists cannot be (directly) coded in Mercury.

Here we investigate whether it is possible to have Mercury-like efficiency, yet still allow true logical variables. We describe our experience with HAL, a new constraint logic programming language specifically designed to support the construction of and experimentation with constraint solvers [2]. Features of HAL include Mercury-like declarations, a well-defined solver interface, dynamic scheduling and global variables. HAL is compiled to Mercury so as to leverage from Mercury's compilation techniques. Unlike Mercury, HAL includes a built-in Herbrand constraint solver which provides full unification (without the occurs check), thus supporting logical variables. The solver uses PARMA bindings [7], rather than the standard variable representation used in the WAM [1, 8], since this allows the solver to use essentially the same term representation for ground terms as does Mercury (see Section 3.4). This is important because it allows the HAL compiler to replace calls to the Herbrand constraint solver by calls to Mercury's more efficient term manipulation routines whenever ground terms are being manipulated.[1]

The results of our empirical evaluation of HAL and its Herbrand solver are very promising. With appropriate declarations, HAL is almost as fast as Mercury, yet allows true logical variables. And without declarations, its efficiency is comparable to that of SICStus Prolog. We also systematically evaluate the effect of each kind of declaration on the efficiency of HAL programs so as to determine where most of this speedup is coming from. This is possible since HAL provides full unification and a "constrained" mode. Our results suggest that mode declarations have the most impact on execution speed while type and determinism declarations provide moderate speedup.

As far as we know, HAL is the first logic programming implementation to use the PARMA variable representation and binding scheme since this was introduced in [7]. We note that [3] discusses in detail the differences between the PARMA and WAM schemes. However, there seems to be no compelling reason to prefer one over the other. There has been some earlier work on the impact of type, mode and determinism information on the performance of Prolog, but the results are quite uneven. In [4], information about type, mode and determinism is used to (manually) generate better code. Its results show up to a factor of two speedup for mode information, and the same result for type information. [5] describes Aquarius, a Prolog system in which compile-time analysis information (including type, mode and determinism information) is used for optimizing the execution. In its results, analysis information had a relatively low impact on speed: on average about 50% for small programs without built-ins (for tak 300%) and about 12% for larger programs with built-ins (for boyer only 3%). Finally, in the context of the PARMA system, [7] also reports on speedup obtained from information provided by compile time analysis. Its results are highly benchmark dependent, with only 10% speed up for boyer but a factor of 8 for nrev. It is difficult to directly compare our results (from Section 4) with those found for Aquarius and PARMA. One problem is the differences between the underlying abstract machines and the optimizations performed by each compiler. Another problem is that their information is obtained from compile time

---

[1]Actually, as long as the term is "sufficiently" instantiated.

analysis, rather than from programmer declarations. We suspect that compile time analysis is not powerful enough to find accurate information about the larger benchmarks, while in our experiments the programmer provides this information. This would explain why our performance improvements are more uniform (and larger) across all benchmarks, regardless of size.

2   The HAL Language

In this section we provide a brief overview of the HAL language, concentrating on its support for Herbrand constraints. For more details see [2]. The basic HAL syntax follows the standard CLP syntax, with variables, rules and predicates defined as usual. The module system in HAL is similar to that of Mercury. The base language supports integer, float, string, atom and term data types. However, this support is limited to assignment, testing for equality, and construction and deconstruction of ground terms. More sophisticated manipulation is available by importing a constraint solver for the appropriate type.

As a simple example, the following is a HAL version of the Towers of Hanoi benchmark which uses difference lists to build the list of moves.

```
:- module hanoi.                                    (L1)
:- import int.                                      (L2)
:- export typedef tower    -> (a ; b ; c).          (L3)
:- export typedef move     -> mv(tower,tower).      (L4)
:- export typedef list(T)  -> ([] ; [T | list(T)]). (L5)
:-         typedef difflist -> (list(move)-list(move)). (L6)
:- herbrand list/1.                                 (L7)
:- export pred hanoi(int, list(move)).              (L8)
:-         mode hanoi(in,no) is semidet.            (L9)
hanoi(N,M) :- hanoi2(N,a,b,c,M-[]).                 (L10)
:- pred hanoi2(int,tower,tower,tower,difflist).     (L11)
:- mode hanoi2(in,in,in,in,oo) is semidet.          (L12)
hanoi2(N,A,B,C,M-Tail) :-
    ( N = 1 -> M = [mv(A,C)|Tail]
    ;          N > 1, N1 is N - 1,
               hanoi2(N1,A,C,B,M-Tail1),
               Tail1 = [mv(A,C)|Tail2],
               hanoi2(N1,B,A,C,Tail2-Tail) ).
```

The first line (L1) states that the file defines the module hanoi. Line (L2) imports the standard library module int which provides (ground) arithmetic and comparison predicates for the type int. Lines (L3), (L4), (L5) and (L6) define term types used in this module. The type tower gives the names of the towers, move defines a move as a pair of towers wrapped in a mv constructor, list defines polymorphic lists, and difflist defines a pair of lists of moves. Line (L7) states that the Herbrand constraint solver for lists will be used in the module. We will elaborate on this later. Line (L8) declares that this module exports the predicate hanoi/2 which has two arguments, an

int and a list of moves. This is the *type* declaration for `hanoi/2`. Line
(*L9*) is an example of a *mode of usage* declaration. The predicate `hanoi/2`'s
first argument has mode `in` meaning that it will be fixed (ground) when
called, the second argument has mode `no` meaning that it will be `new` on
calling (that is, never seen before) and "constrained" (`old`) on return. The
second part of the declaration "`is semidet`" is a determinism statement. It
indicates that `hanoi/2` either succeeds with exactly one answer or fails. In
general, predicates may have more than one mode of usage declaration. The
rest of the file contains the rules defining `hanoi/2` and declarations and rules
for the auxiliary predicate `hanoi2/5` (the mode `oo` means the argument is
"constrained" on both call and return).

2.1 Type, Mode and Determinism Declarations

As we can see from the above example, HAL allows programmers to an-
notate predicate definitions with type, mode and determinism declarations
(modelled on those of Mercury). Type declarations detail the representation
format of a variable or argument. Types are specified using type definition
statements such as those shown in (*L3*)–(*L6*). They are (polymorphic) regular tree type statements. Overloading of predicates and functions is allowed,
although the definitions for different type signatures must appear in different modules. For example, in the module `hanoi` the binary function "`-`" is
overloaded and may mean integer subtraction or difference list pairing.

Mode declarations associate a mode with each argument of a predicate.
A mode has the form $Inst_1 \rightarrow Inst_2$ where $Inst_1$ describes the input instantiation state of the argument and $Inst_2$ describes the output instantiation
state. The basic instantiation states for a solver variable are `new`, `old` and
`ground`. Variable X is `new` if it has not been seen by the constraint solver,
`old` if it has, and `ground` if X is constrained to take a fixed value. For terms
with more structure, such as a list of moves, more complex instantiation
states (lying between `old` and `ground`) may be used to describe the state.
Consider, for example, the instantiation state definition:

```
:- instdef old_list_of_move -> ifbound([] ; [ground|old_list_of_move]).
```

which is read as the variable may be unbound, but, if bound, it is either
bound to an empty list or to a list with a fixed head and a tail with the
same instantiation state. Another example is

```
:- instdef bound_difflist -> bound(old_list_of_move - old_list_of_move).
```

which indicates that the difference list pair is certainly constructed, but the
elements in the pair may be variables. Actually, the `bound` may be dropped
from the definition since this is HAL's default.

Determinism declarations detail how many answers a predicate may have.
We use the Mercury hierarchy: `nondet` means any number of solutions;
`multi` at least one solution; `semidet` at most one solution; `det` exactly one
solution; `failure` no solutions; and `erroneous` a runtime error.

2.2 Herbrand Constraint Solvers

HAL has been expressly designed to allow experimentation with constraint solvers. The conceptual view of a constraint solver in HAL is a module that defines a type for the constrained variable, a predicate init/1 to initialize a variable and a predicate =/2 to equate two variables. The compiler automatically adds calls to init/1 in user code where required, and may generate calls to =/2 through normalization. The constraint solver will usually provide more functionality, such as other primitive constraints and solver dependent delay conditions. This view of solvers as modules facilitates "plug and play" with different solvers.

Term manipulation is at the core of any logic programming language. As indicated previously, the HAL base language only provides limited operations for dealing with terms, corresponding to those Mercury allows. Conceptually, the HAL run-time system also provides a Herbrand constraint solver for each term type defined by the programmer. This solver supports full equality (unification) and, thus, the use of true logical variables and logic programming idioms like difference lists. If the programmer wishes to make use of this more complex constraint solving for terms of some type, then they must explicitly declare that they want to use the Herbrand constraint solver for that type.

For example, in the hanoi module, since the programmer is using difference lists, they need to use the Herbrand constraint solver for lists. Thus, the program contains the declaration :- herbrand list/1. However, elements of the other types (move, tower and difflist) are only manipulated when bound, so they don't require herbrand declarations.

Note that the herbrand declaration is local to a module. Thus, in one module terms of the list type may be handled by the Herbrand solver, while in another module they may be handled by HAL's base level term manipulation operations. Hence, the underlying term representation should support both forms of manipulation.

The main effect of the herbrand declaration occurs during mode checking. If the declaration is not present for a term type, then terms of that type can only use restricted forms of the equality predicate corresponding to assignment, constructing a new term, deconstructing a bound term or comparing two bound terms. Furthermore, a new variable of that type cannot be initialized. During mode checking, literals in the body of predicates will be reordered so as to achieve the appropriate mode. If it is not possible, then a mode error results. If the herbrand declaration is present then terms of that type can be involved in arbitrary calls to the equality predicate.

To clarify this discussion, consider the goal

```
r(X), X=[U|Z], U=1, Z=[].
```

where X and Z are lists of integers, U is an integer, the predicate r/1 has mode r(oo) and at the start of the goal all variables are new. We examine how mode checking proceeds with and without the `herbrand` declaration for lists.

Without the declaration, `r(X)` cannot be scheduled since `X` has instantiation `new` not `old`. The constraint `X=[U|Z]` cannot be scheduled since both `Z` and `U` have instantiation `new`. Obviously both `U=1` and `Z=[]` can be scheduled since they are simple assignments. These constraints fix `U` and `Z`, so then `X=[U|Z]` can be scheduled. This in turn fixes the value of `X`, so the call to `r(X)` can be scheduled. Thus the reordered goal is

> `U=1, Z=[], X=[U|Z], r(X).`

With the `herbrand` declaration, the initial call to `r(X)` can be scheduled immediately since the compiler can add a call to `init(X)`. The constraint `X=[U|Z]` can be scheduled since `X` is `old`. `U=1` and `Z=[]` can be scheduled since both variables are `old`. Thus the final code is

> `init(X), r(X), X=[U|Z], U=1, Z=[].`

As we have seen, instantiations in HAL can be quite powerful. However, defining such instantiations can be laborious, especially since they are often type specific. Typically, the HAL programmer will use the instantiation `old` for initialized variables with an associated constraint solver and `ground` if there is no associated constraint solver. For convenience, HAL allows the instantiation `old` to be used as a shorthand for the most general instantiation state of an initialized variable whose term type is "mixed", that is, some components of the term have an associated solver (e.g. are `herbrand`), while others do not. Thus, if we return to the `hanoi` program, the `old` instantiation for variables with type `difflist` actually is a shorthand for the instantiation `bound_difflist` since `list` is declared `herbrand` but `difflist` and `move` are not. Hence, terms of type `difflist` will be either `new` or `bound`.

3 Herbrand constraint solvers

In this section we describe how Herbrand constraint solvers are implemented in HAL. We briefly introduce the WAM and Mercury approaches to term representation and manipulation, as well as describe the PARMA binding scheme of Taylor. Then we show how the PARMA binding scheme is used to implement Herbrand constraint solvers in HAL.

3.1 WAM

The Warren Abstract Machine (WAM) [8, 1] forms the basis of most modern Prolog implementations. Terms are stored on a heap,[2] which is an array of data cells. A reference cell is usually broken into two parts: a tag and a reference pointer. The most important tag values are REF (a variable reference), STR (a structure) and ATM (an atomic object e.g. a constant).

---

[2]For simplicity, we ignore stack variables.

The structure $f(t_1, \ldots, t_n)$ is represented by a STR tagged pointer to a contiguous sequence of $n+1$ cells. The first cell contains the functor f and the arity n, and the next n cells hold the representations of $t_1, \ldots, t_n$. An unbound variable (on the heap) points to itself. An atom is represented by a cell with tag ATM and a pointer into the atom table. For example, the term $f(h(X), Y, a, Z)$ may be represented by:

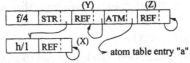

The native representation of base types such as integers and floats (usually) uses the entire width of the cell. WAM implementations either treat them as atoms, wrap them in a special functor, or assign tag values for the types and use the remaining bits to store the data.

Consider unification of two objects on the heap. First both objects are dereferenced. That is, their reference chain is followed until either a non-REF tag or a self reference is found. If at least one of the dereferenced objects is a self reference (i.e. an unbound variable) it is modified to point to the other object. Otherwise, the tags of the dereferenced objects are checked for equality. In the case of an ATM tag, they are checked to see they have the same atom table entry. In the case of a STR tag, the functor and arity are checked for equality, and, if they are, the corresponding arguments are unified.

For example, starting from the above heap state and unifying Y with the heap variable Z and then with another heap variable V results in the heap shown in Figure 1(a). If we then unify Y with U (which is bound to $h(X)$) we obtain the heap shown in Figure 1(b). Notice how references chains can exist throughout the heap.

The address of any pointer variable modified by unification is (condition-

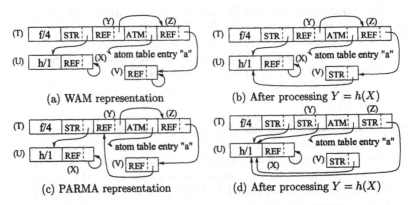

Figure 1: Different term and variable binding schemes

ally) placed in the trail. Since the modified variable is always a self reference, its previous state can be restored from this information alone.

3.2 PARMA variable representation

In the PARMA system [7], Taylor introduced a new technique for handling variables that avoided the need for dereferencing potentially long chains when checking whether an object is bound or not. A non-aliased free variable on the heap is still represented as a self-reference as in the WAM. The difference occurs when two free variables are unified. Rather than pointing one at the other, as in the WAM, a cycle of bindings is created. In general n variables which are all equal are represented by n cells forming a cycle. When one of the variables is equated to a non-variable all of the variables in the cycle are changed to direct (tagged) pointers to this structure and changes are trailed.

For example, the PARMA heap structures corresponding to Figures 1(a) and (b) are shown in Figures 1(c) and (d), respectively. Note that the chain of references is now a cycle. After processing $Y = U$ each variable in the cycle is replaced by a direct reference to the heap representation for $h(X)$.

The PARMA scheme for variable representation has the advantage that dereferencing of bound terms on the heap is never required. However, it has three potential disadvantages: (a) Checking if two unbound variables are equivalent is more involved, and is required for variable-variable binding. Essentially, each variable's cycle of aliased variables may need to be traversed. (b) When instantiating a variable cycle (conditional) trailing must occur for each cell in the cycle (rather than one as for WAM), and the trail requires two words (the variable position and its old value). (c) When creating a structure that will hold a copy of an already existing unbound variable, the cycle of variables grows, and trailing potentially occurs. The impact of each of these factors is dependent on the length of the cycles that are manipulated. As we shall see, cycles rarely grow beyond length one.

Note that only heap variables can be placed in a variable's alias cycle. An unbound initialized variable on the stack or in a register points into a cycle on the heap. If this cycle is then bound, the stack or register variable becomes a pointer to a bound object. This means that when accessing data through a stack variable or register, the PARMA scheme sometimes requires a single step dereference.

3.3 Mercury

The strong static typing of Mercury allows it to use a compact type-specific representation for terms. For more details see [6]. Assuming 32 bit words and aligned addressing, the low two bits of a pointer are zero. In Mercury these bits are used for storing the tag values, hence four different tags are available. For term types with more than four functors, the representation is modified. Since for a constant functor (such as NIL) the remaining part of the cell is unused, the remaining 30 bits can be used to store different constant functors. For term types with more non-constant functors than remaining tags, the Mercury representation uses an extra cell to store the identity of the extra functors, much like the WAM representation. In what follows, we will ignore this for simplicity.

Mercury does not allow true logical variables, so there is no analogue to the REF tagged references used in the WAM. Because there are no references and types are known at compile time, there is no need to have tags for every object. Hence, an object of a primitive type, like an integer, is free to use its entire cell to store its value.

Mercury performs program normalization, so that only two forms of equations are directly supported: $X = Y$ and $X = f(A_1, \ldots, A_n)$ for each functor f where $A_1, \ldots, A_n$ are distinct variables.

The equation $X = Y$ is only valid in two modes. The first is when X is fixed (i.e. has instantiation ground) and Y is new (i.e. has instantiation new), or vice versa. In this case the fixed variable is copied into the new. The second is when both X and Y are fixed in which case a procedure to check the two terms are identical is called. Mercury generates a specialized procedure (we'll refer to it as unify_gg) to do this for each type.

The equation $X = f(A_1, \ldots, A_n)$ is only valid in three modes. The first is when X is new and $A_1, \ldots, A_n$ are all fixed. In this case a contiguous block of n cells is allocated, the values of $A_1, \ldots, A_n$ copied into these cells, and X is set to a pointer to this block with an appropriate tag. The second is when X is fixed and each $A_1, \ldots, A_n$ is new, in which case after testing that X is of the appropriate form, the values in the contiguous block of n cells that it points to are copied into $A_1, \ldots, A_n$. The third is when all involved variables are fixed, in which case the specialized procedure is used to check that they are identical. The case where some of $A_1, \ldots, A_n$ are new and some fixed (e.g. A_4) is handled by replacing each such variable in the equation by a new variable (e.g. A_4') and a following equation (e.g. $A_4' = A_4$).

3.4 HAL

Recall that HAL allows the same term to be used with a Herbrand solver and with HAL's basic term manipulation facilities. Since HAL is compiled into Mercury, it makes considerable sense for HAL's basic term manipulation facilities to be directly implemented by those of Mercury. Therefore HAL's Herbrand solvers should use a term representation which is compatible with that of Mercury.

HAL employs the PARMA approach to variable binding with the Mercury term representation scheme. The main reason for using the PARMA approach, rather than that of the WAM, is that when a term structure becomes ground in the PARMA scheme it has no reference chains within it. Hence, it becomes a legitimate Mercury term. Even when a term is only partially bound, the HAL compiler can (mis)use the efficient Mercury operations to manipulate the bound part of the term, since they will still give the desired behavior. HAL reserves the tag 0 for all term types for use as the REF tag. This means that instead of four tags generally available for representing a type there are only three.

During compilation HAL (like Mercury) normalizes programs so that only two forms of equations arise: $X = Y$ and $X = f(A_1, \ldots, A_p)$ (where each A_i is a distinct variable). The compiler translates these equations into calls to appropriate Mercury and C code to implement the PARMA variable scheme.

Consider an equation $X = Y$. If one of X and Y is new and one is old, we simply need to assign the old variable to the new; Mercury handles this correctly. When both X and Y are new an initialization `init(Y)` is added beforehand. The initialization allocates a new cell on the heap, makes it a self-pointer and returns a reference to this cell in Y. This makes Y old and the previous case applies. If both X and Y are fixed we call Mercury's specialized procedure `unify_gg`.

The only remaining case, where both X and Y are old, corresponds to a true unification. We replace this with a call to the Herbrand unification procedure `unify_oo`, which is automatically generated by HAL for the type t of X and Y. It has the form:

```
:- pred unify_oo(t,t).
:- mode unify_oo(oo,oo).
unify_oo(X,Y) :- (var(X) -> (var(Y) -> unify_var_var(X,Y)
                  ;                     unify_var_val(X,Y))
              ;      (var(Y) -> unify_var_val(Y,X)
                  ;                     unify_val_val(X,Y))).
```

`unify_val_val` is similar to the Mercury procedure `unify_gg` except it calls `unify_oo` on the arguments of unified terms rather than `unify_gg`. The `var` procedure simply checks if its argument has tag zero (i.e. is unbound).

The procedure `unify_var_var` shown below unifies two variables. It first checks that the variables are not already the same, and then joins the cycles together, trailing the change. Note that, unlike the case for WAM, the code for unifying two variables is symmetric, treating each variable the same way. The procedure `unify_var_val` (also shown below) unifies a variable and a non-variable. It modifies all the variables in the cycle to directly refer to the non-variable, and trails the changes.

```
unify_var_var(X,Y) {                unify_var_val(X,Y) {
    QX = *X; QY = *Y;                   QX = X;
    while (QX != Y && QY != X)          repeat
       if (QX != X && QY != Y)             { Next = *QX;
          { QX = *QX; QY = *QY; }            trail(QX);
       else                                  *QX = Y;
          { trail(X); trail(Y);              QX = Next; }
            Tmp = *X; *X = *Y; *Y = Tmp;  until (QX == X) }
            break; } }
```

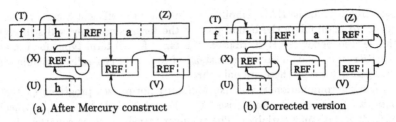

(a) After Mercury construct   (b) Corrected version

Figure 2: Adapting Mercury's term construction for Herbrand terms

Processing an equation of the form $X = f(A_1, \ldots, A_p)$ is more complicated since we may have to create objects on the heap. The first case, when X is new, will create a new structure on the heap. Each variable A_i must not be new, unless its type is **herbrand**. New variables of **herbrand** types are initialized during the building of the heap structure. Assume that variables $A_{o_1}, \ldots, A_{o_m}$ are **herbrand** and old, and $A_{n_1}, \ldots, A_{n_l}$ are **herbrand** and new. The translation to Mercury is essentially:

```
dummy_init(A_n1), ..., dummy_init(A_nl),
X = f(A1, ..., Ap),
A_n1 = init_heap(X,n1 - 1), ..., A_nl = init_heap(X,nl - 1),
fix_copy(X,o1 - 1), ..., fix_copy(X,om - 1)
```

The `dummy_init(A)` procedure is used to make Mercury's mode checker believe A is old so it can schedule the construction but contains no code; subsequent in-lining by Mercury removes it. The `init_heap(X, i)` function creates a self reference in the ith slot of heap cells pointed to by X and returns it. It is defined as:

```
init_heap(X,i) { return X[i] = &(X[i]); }
```

The `fix_copy(X, o_k - 1)` procedure handles the case when A_{o_k} is a reference, which was copied by Mercury into the new heap structure. If A_{o_k} was an unbound variable this simple copy results in a reference to the cycle in the o_k^{th} cell rather than the o_k^{th} cell being placed in the cycle. `fix_copy` adds the o_k^{th} cell into the cycle. If A_{o_k} is bound but not dereferenced (this can happen for stack and register variables) `fix_copy` replaces the contents of the o_k^{th} cell by what it refers to. It is defined as:

```
fix_copy(X,i) {
    AXi = &(X[i]); Xi = X[i];
    if (var(Xi)) if (var(*Xi)) { trail(Xi); *AXi = *Xi; *Xi = AXi }
                 else *AXi = *Xi; }
```

For example, consider the construction of $T = f(U, V, S, Z)$ where T and Z are new and U is known to be bound (to $h(X)$), S is known to be bound (to a) and V is old (and part of a cycle). After executing the Mercury $T = f(U, V, S, Z)$ the heap is as shown in Figure 2(a). Applying `init_heap(T,3)` and `fix_copy(T,1)` gives the heap shown in Figure 2(b).

The second case for handling an equation of the form $X = f(A_1, \ldots, A_p)$ occurs when X is known to be bound and $A_1, \ldots, A_p$ are new. This is simply left to Mercury. If one (or more) of $A_1, \ldots, A_p$ are not new, they are replaced by new variables and equations as in the Mercury case. The third case is when all variables involved are fixed; again this is left to Mercury. The final case is when X is old. The generated code checks if X is bound in which case it treats the equation as if it were the deconstruction $X = f(B_1, \ldots, B_p)$ followed by equations $A_i = B_i$. Otherwise X is a variable and the code constructs the term $f(A_1, \ldots, A_p)$ on the heap[3] and then equates X to this term using unify_oo.

As in the PARMA system, only heap variables can be placed in a variable's alias cycle. Thus a stack variable or register must be a pointer somewhere into the cycle and so when accessing data through a stack variable or register HAL sometimes requires a single step dereference.

One important issue we have not discussed is the treatment of variables which have a polymorphic type. HAL produces a general unification predicate unify_oo for each type, and polymorphic code is passed the appropriate version in the run-time type information. At present, the compiler does not support the use of Herbrand types for polymorphic arguments, e.g. list(T) where type T is herbrand. Handling this case is conceptually straightforward, but has not yet been implemented.

4 Evaluation

Our empirical evaluation has three aims. The first is to compare the performance of HAL and its Herbrand solver with a state-of-the-art Prolog implementation, SICStus Prolog. The second is to investigate the impact of each kind of declaration on efficiency. The third is to compare HAL with Mercury so as to determine the overhead introduced by the run-time support for Herbrand solving.

To achieve the first aim we take a number of Prolog benchmarks[4] and transform built-ins not present in HAL (such as cut) into their HAL equivalents (such as if-then-else). We then compare these with the equivalent HAL program. Although Prolog does not have type, mode and determinism declarations, the current HAL compiler requires them. We solve this problem by defining a "universal" term type for the HAL program which contains all functors occurring in the program and declaring this type to be herbrand. All predicate arguments are declared to have this type and mode oo, and all predicates are declared to have determinism nondet. All integers, floats, atoms and strings in the program must be wrapped, and each wrapping functor must appear in the "universal" term type. Most of these tasks are done automatically by a pre-processor.

For example, for the original hanoi Prolog program (the code in Section 2 minus the declarations), the preprocessor will add the declarations

---

[3]Depending on whether arguments are herbrand or not this may not be possible, causing a run-time error.

[4]See www.csse.monash.edu.au/~mbanda/hal.

272

```
:- typedef htype -> (int(int) ; float(float) ; atom(atom)
                      ; [htype|htype] ; mv(htype,htype) ; htype-htype ).
:- herbrand htype.
:- pred hanoi(htype,htype).
:- mode hanoi(oo,oo) is nondet.
:- pred hanoi2(htype,htype,htype,htype,htype).
:- mode hanoi2(oo,oo,oo,oo,oo) is nondet.
```

It will also replace the three occurrences of 1 in the program text by `int(1)`, replace `[]`, `a`, `b` and `c` by `atom([])`, `atom(a)`, `atom(b)` and `atom(c)`, and create predicates for the wrapped versions of `>`, `is` and function `-`.

To investigate the impact of each kind of declaration on efficiency we take these Prolog-equivalent HAL programs and add precise type, then mode, then determinism declarations, and compare the resulting efficiencies. In the first step type declarations are added. All types in this step must be declared as `herbrand` since the associated terms may sometimes be treated as logical variables. This also implies that we must continue to wrap integers and other primitive types since they may be placed in data structures or equated before they are fixed. In the second step mode declarations are added. Types which never have the old instantiation need not be declared as `herbrand` and, in the case of the primitive types, can have their wrapping removed. Finally, determinism declarations are added.

To compare HAL with Mercury, we run Mercury versions of the programs (with precise declarations) on a version of Mercury that does not provide trailing or reserve the extra REF tag, but is otherwise equivalent to the one used for compiling the HAL program. Since Mercury does not provide full unification, we can only do this for benchmarks with no remaining `herbrand` declarations.

Table 1 details our comparison. We have turned garbage collection off in all three systems: SICStus Prolog 3.7.1 (compact code), Mercury (May 1999 HAL development version), and HAL. All timings are in seconds on a dual Pentium II-400MHz with 384M of RAM running Linux-2.2.

We have used a subset of the standard Prolog benchmarks: `aiakl`, `boyer`, `deriv`, `fib`, `mmatrix`, `serialize`, `tak`, `warplan`, `hanoi` and `qsort`. The last two are shown in two forms, one using "normal" lists and `append/3`, the other using difference lists. The reason for choosing these benchmarks is that they did not require extensive changes to the original Prolog benchmarks (except for `boyer`, for which the starting point was a restricted Mercury version, rather than the Prolog one) and hence the comparison is fairer. The second and third columns of Table 1 detail the benchmark sizes (number of predicates and literals before normalization, excluding dead code and the query). Subsequent columns give the execution time for:

• the original program run with SICStus Prolog,
• the modified Prolog program run with SICStus Prolog,
• the Prolog-equivalent HAL program (obtained with the preprocessor),
• with precise type definitions,
• with precise type and mode declarations,

Benchmark	Size		SICStus		HAL				Merc
	Preds	Lits	Orig	Mod	None	T	+M	+D	
aiakl	7	21	0.09	0.08	0.29	0.25	0.04	0.03	0.03
boyer	14	124	0.69	0.69	2.11	1.80	0.09	0.05	0.04
deriv	1	33	2.11	3.03	2.90	2.94	0.74	0.50	0.31
fib	1	6	1.46	1.45	0.25	0.20	0.02	0.02	0.01
hanoiapp	2	7	3.42	3.43	3.57	3.23	0.61	0.22	0.23
hanoidiff	2	6	2.34	2.34	0.27	0.24	0.08	0.11	—
mmatrix	3	7	1.29	1.29	1.28	0.96	0.11	0.04	0.04
qsortapp	3	10	4.04	2.33	2.98	2.56	0.39	0.19	0.14
qsortdiff	3	10	3.94	2.26	2.87	2.58	0.37	0.21	—
serialize	5	19	1.78	1.77	1.28	1.04	0.35	0.27	—
tak	1	9	0.77	0.95	0.74	0.53	0.10	0.05	0.03
warplan	25	88	0.59	0.82	1.55	0.45	0.33	0.22	—

Table 1: Execution times in seconds

- with precise type, mode and determinism declarations,
- this last version run with Mercury (if possible).

In general, the original and modified SICStus programs have the same speed. deriv slows down because of loss of indexing, while the two versions of quick sort improve because a badly placed cut in the original program is replaced by a more efficient if-then-else. The Prolog-equivalent HAL versions have roughly similar efficiency to the modified SICStus versions. Slowdown occurs in aiakl, boyer and warplan because no indexing is currently available for possibly unbound input arguments. Surprising speed-up occurs for fib and hanoidiff; we suspect because of Mercury's handling of recursion. Generally, adding precise type information leads to a significant improvement (on average 1.4 times faster). For warplan the improvement is very large because it allows a type specialized version of univ to be used. Adding mode declarations provides the most speed-up (on average 6.8 times faster). This is because it allows calls to the Herbrand solver to be replaced by calls to Mercury's specialized term manipulation operations and also allows indexing. Determinism declarations also lead to significant speed-up (on average 1.7 times faster). The comparison between Mercury and HAL running the version with precise declarations shows that the performance is comparable although there is overhead for supporting logical variables (we believe primarily because of support for trailing). Note that the comparison is not made for hanoidiff, qsortdiff, serialize or warplan since their final HAL versions still need herbrand declarations.

We have also investigated the effect of the declarations on memory usage. Adding precise type definitions reduces the stack sizes for non-deterministic predicate calls and the heap size. Adding precise mode declarations generally reduces the heap size and greatly reduces trail size — only those benchmarks with herbrand declarations may need to use the trail.

Finally, we have investigated the size of the alias cycles constructed using

PARMA bindings. Virtually all cycles have length one immediately before being bound to a non-variable term. Only two benchmarks, `warplan` and `serialize`, have a maximum cycle length of more than two (4 and 24 respectively).

Our empirical evaluation of HAL is very pleasing. It demonstrates that it is possible to combine Mercury-like efficiency for ground data structure manipulation with Prolog-style logical variables by using PARMA bindings to ensure that the representation for terms used by HAL's Herbrand solver is consistent with that used by Mercury for ground terms. Prolog-like programs written in HAL run somewhat slower than in SICStus, in part because there is no term indexing for possibly unbound instantiations. However, once declarations are provided the programs run an order of magnitude faster. (Much of this arises from the sophisticated compilation techniques used by the underlying Mercury compiler.) Our results show that the biggest performance improvement arises from mode declarations while type and determinism declarations give moderate speed improvement. All declarations reduce the space requirements.

Acknowledgements

We would like to thank the Mercury development team, especially Fergus Henderson and Zoltan Somogyi, who have helped us with many modifications to the Mercury system to support HAL.

References

[1] H. Aït-Kaci. *Warren's Abstract Machine*. MIT Press, 1991.

[2] B. Demoen, M. García de la Banda, W. Harvey, K. Marriott, and P. Stuckey. An overview of HAL. In *Procs. of CP99*, to appear, 1999.

[3] Thomas Lindgren, Per Mildner, and Johan Bevemyr. On Taylor's scheme for unbound variables. Technical report, UPMAIL, October 1995.

[4] A. Mariën, G. Janssens, A. Mulkers, and M. Bruynooghe. The impact of abstract interpretation: an experiment in code generation. In *Proc. of the ICLP89*, pages 33–47, 1989.

[5] P. Van Roy. Can Logic Programming Execute as Fast as Imperative Programming? Report 90/600, UCB/CSD, Berkeley, California 94720, Dec 1990.

[6] Zoltan Somogyi, Fergus Henderson, and Thomas Conway. The execution algorithm of Mercury: an efficient purely declarative logic programming language. *Journal of Logic Programming*, 29:17–64, 1996.

[7] A. Taylor. PARMA–bridging the performance gap between imperative and logic programming. *Journal of Logic Programming*, 29(1–3), 1996.

[8] D. H. D. Warren. An abstract Prolog instruction set. Technical Report 309, SRI International, Menlo Park, U.S.A., Oct. 1983.

Comparing Trailing and Copying for Constraint Programming

Christian Schulte

Programming Systems Lab, Universität des Saarlandes
Postfach 15 11 50, 66041 Saarbrücken, Germany
schulte@ps.uni-sb.de

Abstract

A central service of a constraint programming system is search. In almost all constraint programming systems search is based on trailing, which is well understood and known to be efficient. This paper compares trailing to copying. Copying offers more expressiveness as required by parallel and concurrent systems. However, little is known how trailing compares to copying as it comes to implementation effort, runtime efficiency, and memory requirements. This paper discusses these issues.

Execution speed of a copying-based system is shown to be competitive with state-of-the-art trailing-based systems. For the first time, a detailed analysis and comparison with respect to memory usage is made. It is shown how recomputation decreases memory requirements which can be prohibitive for large problems with copying alone. The paper introduces an adaptive recomputation strategy that is shown to speedup search while keeping memory consumption low. It is demonstrated that copying with recomputation outperforms trailing on large problems with respect to both space and time.

1 Introduction

A central service in every constraint programming system is search. It demands that previous computation states must possibly be available at a later stage of computation. A system must take precaution by either memorizing states or by means to reconstruct them. States are memorized by *copying*. Techniques for reconstruction are *trailing* and *recomputation*. While recomputation computes everything from scratch, trailing records for each state-changing operation the information necessary to undo its effect.

Most current constraint programming systems are trailing-based. Many of them, for example CHIP [2], cc(FD) [13], Eclipse [3], and clp(FD) [5], are built on top of Prolog, which itself is trailing-based. But also systems that are not built on top of Prolog, like Screamer [12] (Lisp), and ILOG Solver [6] (C++) use trailing.

Copying offers advantages with respect to expressiveness: multiple nodes of a search tree are available simultaneously for further exploration. This is essential for concurrent, parallel, breadth-first, and user-defined search strategies. Implementation can be simpler, since copying is independent of operations and is only concerned with data structures.

On the other hand, copying needs more memory and might be slower since full copies of the computation states are created. Hence, it is not at all clear whether copying is competitive to trailing or not.

This paper shows that copying is competitive and that it offers a viable alternative to trailing for the implementation of constraint programming systems. The following points are discussed:

- The paper clarifies how much more memory copying needs. It is examined for which problems copying is competitive with respect to runtime and memory.

- For large problems with deep search trees the paper confirms that copying needs too much memory. It is shown that in these cases recomputation can decrease memory consumption considerably, even to a fraction of what is needed by trailing.

- It is shown that recomputation can also decrease runtime. The paper introduces adaptive recomputation that creates additional copies during search in order to speed up execution.

The paper uses Mozart [9], an implementation of Oz, as copying-based constraint programming system. The competitiveness of Mozart is stressed by comparing it to several trailing based constraint programming systems.

Plan of the Paper. The next section introduces some basic notions and concepts. Section 3 discusses the main implementation concepts. Section 4 introduces examples and criteria used for empirical evaluation. Section 5 gives an evaluation of copying followed by a comparison to trailing in Section 6. Recomputation is discussed in Section 7 followed by the introduction of adaptive recomputation in the next section. An empirical comparison of several constraint programming systems is given in Section 9.

2　Search for Constraint Programming

A *constraint problem* consists of a collection of *constraints* and a *distribution strategy* (also called labelling or enumeration strategy). The constraint problem defines a *search tree*. Its nodes represent computation states, whereas its arcs represent computation.

In the context of constraint programming, a computation state consists of a constraint store and propagators connected to the constraint store. The constraint store hosts basic (primitive) constraints. In the context of finite domain programming, for example, basic constraints are domain constraints like $x \in D$ where D is a finite domain. Propagators implement more complex constraints (for example, arithmetic constraints or task-serialization for scheduling). Propagators amplify the store by adding new basic constraints (*constraint propagation*) to the constraint store.

Leafs in the search tree can be either failed (constraint propagation attempted to tell a constraint incompatible with the store) or solved (no propagators are left). Inner nodes are called *choices*. For a choice N, the distribution strategy defines how to compute the descendants N_i of the node N. The N_i are also called *alternatives* (of N). For example, in the context of finite domain programming the N_i are computed by telling a basic constraint B_i to N's constraint store that starts further constraint propagation.

The computational service offered by a constraint programming system is to *explore* the search tree of a given constraint problem. In the following we always assume left-most, depth-first exploration. The system must be prepared to follow several alternatives issuing from the same node N. This paper discusses the following three approaches:

Copying. An identical copy of N is created before N is changed.

Trailing. Changes to N are recorded such that they can be undone later.

Recomputation. If needed, N is recomputed from scratch. Discussion of recomputation is postponed to Section 7.

Expressiveness. The main difference as it comes to expressiveness is the number of nodes that are simultaneously available for further exploration. With copying, all nodes that are created as copies are directly ready for further exploration. With trailing, exploration can only continue at a single node at a time.

In principle, trailing does not exclude exploration of multiple nodes. However, they can be explored in an interleaved fashion only and switching between nodes is a costly operation. For this reason all current trailing-based constraint programming systems do not support node-switching.

Having more than a single node available for exploration is essential to search strategies like concurrent, parallel, or breadth-first. The same property is also crucial for user-defined interactive exploration of search trees as implemented by the Oz Explorer [10]. By making nodes of a search tree available as first-class entities (as it is done in Oz [11]), the user can directly profit from the increased expressiveness.

Resource model. Copying essentially differs from trailing with respect to space requirements in that it is *pessimistic*: while trailing records changes exactly, copying makes the safe but pessimistic assumption that everything will change. On the other hand, trailing needs to record information on what changes as well as the original state of what is changed. In the worst case — the entire state is changed — this might require more memory than copying. This discussion makes clear that a meaningful comparison of the space requirements for trailing and copying is only possible by empirical investigations, which are carried out in Section 6.

3 Implementation Issues

This section gives a short discussion of the main implementation concepts and their properties in copying- and trailing-based systems. The most fundamental distinction is that *trailing*-based systems are concerned with *operations* on data structures while *copying*-based systems are concerned with the *data structures* themselves.

Copying. Copying needs for each data structure a routine that creates a copy and also recursively copies contained data structures. A system that features a copying garbage collector already provides almost everything needed to implement copying. For example in the Mozart implementation of Oz, copying and garbage collection share the same routines parametrized by a flag that signals whether garbage collection is performed or whether a node is being copied.

By this all operations on data structures are independent of search with respect to both design and implementation. This makes search in a system an orthogonal issue. Development of the Mozart system has proven this point: it was first conceived and implemented without search and only later search has been added.

Trailing. A trailing-based system uses a trail to store undo information. Prior to performing a state-changing operation, information to reconstruct the state is stored on the trail. In a concrete implementation, the state changing operations considered are updates of memory locations. If a memory update is performed, the location's address and its old content is stored on the trail. To this kind of trail we refer to as single-value trail. Starting exploration from a node puts a mark on the trail. Undoing the trail restores all memory locations up to the previous mark. This is essentially the technology that is used in Warren's Abstract Machine [14, 4].

In the context of trailing-based constraint programming systems two further techniques come into play:

Time-stamping. With finite domains, for example, the domain of a variable can be narrowed multiply. However it is sufficient to trail only the original value, intermediate values need no restauration: each location needs to appear at most once on the trail. Otherwise memory consumption is no longer bounded by the number of changed locations but by the number of state-changing operations performed. To ensure this property, time-stamping is used: as soon as an entity is trailed, the entity is stamped to prevent it from further trailing until the stamp changes again. Note that time-stamping concerns both the operations and the data structures that must contain the time-stamp.

Multiple-value trail. A single-value trail needs $2n$ entries for n changed locations. A multiple value trail uses the optimization that if the contents of $n > 1$ successive locations are changed, $n + 2$ entries are added to the trail: one for the first location's address, a second entry for n, and n entries for the locations' values. For a discussion of time-stamps and a multiple value trail in the context of the CHIP system, see [1, 2].

A general but brief discussion of issues related to implementation issues for trailing-based constraint programming systems can be found in [7].

Trailing requires that all operations are search-aware: search is not an orthogonal issue to the rest of the system. Complexity in design and implementation is increased: it is a matter of fact that a larger part of a system is concerned with operations rather than with basic data structure management. A good design that encapsulates update operations will avoid most of the complexity. To take advantage of multiple value trail entries, however, operations require special effort in design and implementation.

Trailing for complicated data structures can become quite complex. Consider as an example adding an element to a dictionary with subsequent reorganization of the dictionary's hash table. Here the simple model that is based on trailing locations might be unsuited, since reorganizing data structures alters a large number of locations. In general, copying offers more freedom of rearranging data structures, for a discussion in the context of finite domain constraints see [8].

The discussion in this section can be summarized as follows. A system that features a copying garbage collector already supports the essential functionality for copying. For a system that does not require a garbage collector trailing might be as easy or possibly easier depending on the number and complexity of the operations.

4 Criteria and Examples

This section introduces constraint problems that serve as examples for the empirical analysis and comparison. The problems are well known, they are chosen to be easily portable to several constraint programming systems (see Section 9).

The main characteristics of the problems are listed in Table 1. Besides of portability and simplicity they cover a broad range with respect to the following criteria.

Problem size. The problems differ in size, that is in the number of variables and constraints, and in the size of constraints (that is the number of variables each constraint is attached to). With copying, the size of

Example	Expl.	Choices	Fail.	Sol.	Depth	Var.	Constr.
Alpha	all	7435	7435	1	50	26	21
100-Queens	one	115	22	1	97	100	14850
100-S-Queens	one	115	22	1	97	100	3
10-Queens	all	6665	5942	724	29	10	135
10-S-Queens	all	6665	5942	724	29	10	3
Magic	one	13	4	1	12	500	501
18-Knights	one	266	12	1	265	7500	11205

Table 1: Characteristics of example programs.

the problem is an important parameter: it determines the time needed for copying. It also partly determines the memory requirements (which is also influenced by the search tree depth). Hence, large problem sizes can be problematic with copying.

Amount of propagation. A problem with strong propagation narrows a large number of variables. This presupposes a large number of propagation steps, which usually coincides with state changes of a large number of constraints. The amount of propagation determines how much time and memory trailing requires: the stronger the propagation, the more of the state is changed. The more of the state changes, the better it fits the pessimistic assumption "everything changes" that underlies copying.

Search tree depth. The depth of the search tree determines partly the memory requirements for both trailing and copying. Deep search trees are a bad case for trailing and even more for copying due to its higher memory requirements.

Exploration completeness. How much of the search tree is explored. A high exploration completeness means that utilization of the precaution effort undertaken by copying or trailing is high.

The criteria are not independent. Of course, the amount of propagation determines the depth of the search tree. Also search tree depth and exploration completeness are interdependent: If the search tree is deep, exploration completeness will definitely be low: Due to the exponential number of nodes, the part of the tree that can be explored is relatively small.

All example problems are familiar benchmark problems. Alpha is the well-known cryptoarithmetic puzzle: assign variables A, B, ..., Z distinct numbers between 1 and 26 such that 25 equations hold. For the popular n-Queens puzzle (place n queens on a $n \times n$ chess board such that no two queens can attack each other) two different implementations are used. The naive implementation (called n-Queens) uses $O(n^2)$ disequality constraints. This is contrasted by a smarter program (which is called n-S-Queens accordingly)

Example	Time	Copy	GC	CGC	Max
	sec	%	%	%	KB
Alpha	7.80	20.8	3.5	24.3	19
10-Queens	3.49	30.8	3.7	34.5	20
10-S-Queens	2.54	18.4	2.7	21.1	7
100-Queens	2.96	51.3	16.6	67.9	21873
100-S-Queens	0.10	31.7	0.0	31.7	592
Magic	2.61	9.9	11.5	21.5	6091
18-Knights	23.53	36.1	31.5	67.6	121557

Table 2: Runtime and memory performance of example programs.

that uses three propagators for the same constraints: this leads to much better propagation in relation to the problem size. The two different encodings of the n-Queens puzzle are chosen to analyze the difference between many small propagators and few larger propagators.

The Magic puzzle is to find a magic sequence s of 500 natural numbers, such that $0 \leq x_i \leq 500$ and i occurs in s exactly x_i times. It uses for each element of the sequence an exactly-constraint (each ranging over all variables x_i) on all elements of the sequence. The elements are enumerated in increasing order following a splitting strategy. The goal in 18-Knights is to find a sequence of knight's moves on a 18×18 chessboard such that each field is visited exactly once and that the moves return the knight to the starting field, which is fixed to the lower left field.

The paper prefers familiar benchmark programs over more realistic problems such as scheduling or resource allocation. The reason is that the programs are also intended for comparing several constraint programming systems. Choosing simple constraints ensures that the amount of constraint propagation is the same with all compared systems.

5 Copying

This section presents and analyses runtime and memory requirements for Mozart, a copying-based implementation of Oz [9]. For more information on hardware and software platforms see Appendix A.

Table 2 displays the performance of the example programs. The fields "Copy" and "GC" give the percentage of runtime that is spent on copying and garbage collection, the field "CGC" displays the sum of both fields. The field "Max" contains the maximal amount of memory used in Kilobytes, that is how much memory must at least be available in order to solve the problem.

The numbers clarify that for all but the large problems 100-Queens and 18-Knights the amount of time spent on copying and garbage collection is around one fourth of the total runtime. In addition, the memory requirements are moderate. This demonstrates that for problems with small and medium size copying does neither cause memory nor runtime problems. It

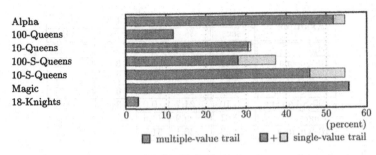

Figure 1: Memory use of trailing versus copying.

can be expected that for these problems copying is competitive.

On the other hand, the numbers confirm that *copying alone for large problems with deep search trees is unsuited*: up to two third of the runtime is spent on memory management and memory requirements are prohibitive. The considerable time spent on garbage collection is also a consequence of copying: the time used by a copying garbage collector is determined by the amount of used memory.

The two different implementations of n-Queens exemplify that copying gets considerably better for problems where a large number of small propagators is replaced by a small number of equivalent global propagators.

6 Trailing

As discussed before, one of the most essential questions in comparing trailing and copying is: how pessimistic is the assumption "everything changes" that underlies copying. An answer seems to presuppose two systems that are identical with the exception of trailing or copying. Implementing two competitive systems is not feasible.

Instead, the memory requirements of a trailing implementation are computed from the requirements of a copying implementation as follows. Before constraint propagation in a node N begins, a bitwise copy of the memory area occupied by N is created. After constraint propagation has finished, this memory area is compared to the now changed memory area occupied by N. The altered locations are those that a trailing system must have trailed.

Figure 1 shows the percentage of memory needed by a trailing implementation compared to a copying implementation. The total length of bars depicts the percentage needed by a single-value trail, whereas the dark-colored bar represents the need of a multiple-value trail implementation.

The percentage figures for the multiple-value trail are lower bounds again. Locations that are updated by separate single update operations might happen to be successive even though an implementation cannot take advantage of this fact. It is interesting to note that a multiple-value trail offers some improvement only for 10-S-Queens and 100-S-Queens (around 10%). Otherwise, its impact is quite limited (less than 2%).

The observation that for large problems with weak propagation (100-Queens and 18-Knights) trailing improves by almost up to two orders of magnitude coincides with the observation made with respect to the memory requirements in Section 5. For the other problems the memory requirements are in the same order of magnitude and trailing roughly halves them.

What is not captured at all by the comparison's method is that other design decisions for propagators would have been made to take advantage of trailing, as has already been argued in Section 3.

7 Recomputation

Recomputation trades space for time, a node N is reconstructed on demand by redoing computations. The space requirements are obviously low: only the path in the search tree leading to N must be stored (for example, as a list of integers). In particular, the space requirements for recomputation are problem independent.

Basing exploration on recomputation alone is infeasible. Suppose a complete binary search tree of height n, which has 2^n leafs. To recompute a single leaf, n exploration steps are needed. This gives a total of $n2^n$ exploration steps compared to $2^{n+1} - 2$ exploration steps without recomputation (that is, the number of arcs). Thus recomputation alone takes approximately $n/2$-times the number of exploration steps both copying and trailing need.

The basic idea of combining recomputation with copying is as follows: copy a node from time to time during exploration. Recomputation then can start from the last copy N on the path to the root. Note that this requires to start from a copy of N rather than from N itself, since N might be needed for further recomputation. The implementation of recomputation is straightforward, see [11] for example.

A simple strategy for recomputation is *fixed recomputation*: limit the number of steps needed to recompute a node by some fixed number n, to which we refer as *MRD (maximal recomputation distance)*. That is, after n exploration steps a copy of the current node is memorized.

An important optimization is as follows: after all but one alternative A of a copied node N have been explored, further recomputation from N always starts with recomputing A. The optimization now is to do the recomputation step $N \rightarrow A$ only once. This optimization corresponds to the trust_me instruction in the WAM.

Fixed recomputation with a MRD of n guarantees that the number of stored nodes decreases by a factor of n. Figure 2 displays the improvements obtained by fixed recomputation, where the numbers in parentheses give the employed MRD.

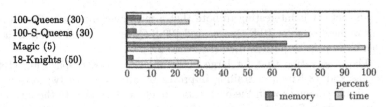

Figure 2: Runtime and memory gain with fixed recomputation.

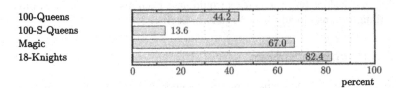

Figure 3: Memory use of fixed recomputation versus trailing.

The improvement in memory for 100-Queens and 18-Knights (the two problems for which Section 5 showed that copying entails prohibitive memory requirements) is by two orders of magnitude. 100-S-Queens enjoys the same memory-improvement as 100-Queens, since the search trees are identical. The figures for Magic exhibit that even for problems for which copying is perfectly adequate, memory consumption can be decreased without a runtime penalty.

Our motivation for recomputation was the urge to save memory. However, the numbers in Figure 2 exemplify that recomputation saves both memory and runtime. In particular, the time savings from less copying are larger than the time spent on recomputing.

Fixed recomputation uses less memory than trailing. Figure 3 shows the percentage of memory that fixed recomputation takes in comparison to the memory needed by trailing.

Trailing and copying are pessimistic in that they make the assumption that each node needs reconstruction. Recomputation, in contrast, makes the optimistic assumption that no node requires later reconstruction. For search trees that contain few failed nodes, the optimistic assumption fits well. In particular, problems with very deep search trees can profit from the optimistic assumption, since exploration completeness will definitely be low (as argued in Section 4).

Figure 4 relates the runtime to different MRDs for the 18-Knights problem. For a MRD from 1 to 10 the runtime is strictly decreasing because the time spent on copying and garbage collection decreases, while the plain runtime remains constant. With further increase of MRD the runtime increases

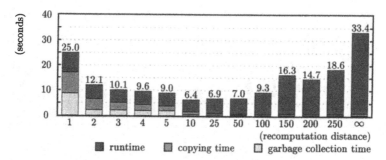

Figure 4: Runtime for 18-Knights with fixed recomputation.

due to the increasing recomputation overhead.

Figure 4 shows a small peak at a MRD of 150. The search tree for 18-Knights has five failed nodes at a depth of around 260. This means that recomputation has to perform around 110 recomputation steps for each of the nodes. This phenomenon can be observed quite often: slight changes in the MRD (like from 100 to 150 for 18-Knights) results in unexpected runtime behavior. This indicates that for some parts of the search tree the assumption of recomputation is overly optimistic.

8   Adaptive Recomputation

In the last section we made the following two observations. Firstly, the optimistic assumption underlying recomputation can save time. Secondly, the fixed choice of a MRD can inhibit this.

If exploration exhibits a failed node it is quite likely that not only a single node is failed but that an entire subtree is failed. It is unlikely that only the last decision made in exploration was wrong. This suggests that as soon as a failed node occurs during exploration, the attitude for further exploration should become more pessimistic.

The following strategy is simple and shows remarkable effect. During recomputation of a node N_2 from a node N_1 an additional copy is created at the middle of the path from N_1 to N_2. To this strategy we refer to as *adaptive recomputation*.

Figure 5 shows the runtime for adaptive recomputation applied to 18-Knights. Not only the peak for a MRD of 150 disappears, also the runtime for large MRD values remains basically constant. Even if copies are created during recomputation only (that is the MRD is ∞) the runtime remains almost unaffected.

This is the real significance of adaptive recomputation: the choice of the recomputation distance is not as important as one would think. Provided that the distance is not too small (that is, no excessive memory con-

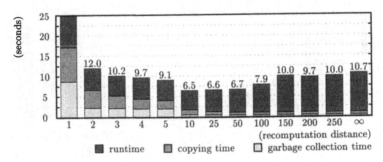

Figure 5: Runtime for 18-Knights with adaptive recomputation.

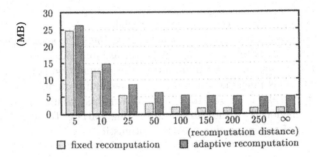

Figure 6: Memory requirements for 18-Knights.

sumption), adaptive recomputation adjusts quickly enough to achieve good performance.

While adaptive recomputation is a good strategy as it comes to runtime, it does not guarantee that memory consumption is decreased. In the worst case, adaptive recomputation does not improve over copying alone.

Figure 6 shows the active heap memory for both fixed and adaptive recomputation applied to 18-Knights. The numbers exhibit that avoidance of peaks in runtime is not paid by peaks in memory (for MRDs between 1 and 5 memory requirements for both fixed and adaptive recomputation are almost identical and thus are left out).

For deep search trees the following technique could help limit the required memory. As soon as exploration has reached a certain depth in the search tree, it is quite unlikely that nodes high above are going to be explored. Thus, copies remaining in the upper parts of the tree could be dropped. This would decrease memory consumption and would most likely not affect runtime.

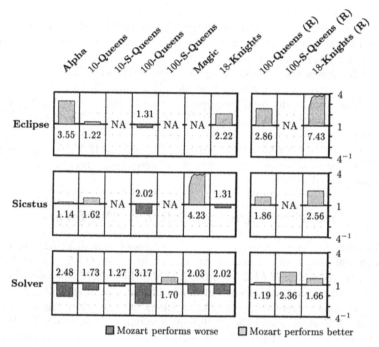

Figure 7: Empirical runtime comparison.

9 Empirical Comparison

This section compares Mozart, a copying-based system, with several trailing-based systems. For more information on the used software and hardware platforms, see Appendix A. The point to compare systems in this paper is to demonstrate that a system that is based on copying can be competitive with trailing based systems.

The runtimes of course do not depend only on the systems' search capabilities, but also on their finite domain implementation. It has been tried to keep the examples' implementations for the different systems as similar as possible. In particular, even if a system provides special propagators for a particular example, the programs do not take advantage of them.

All systems support Alpha, 10-Queens, 100-Queens, and 18-Knights. The propagators that are used for the 10-S-Queens and 100-S-Queens formulation are available in Mozart and Solver only. Eclipse does not support the exactly-constraint that is used in Magic.

Figure 7 shows a relative performance comparison of Mozart with Eclipse, SICStus, and Solver. The figures to the left are without recomputation, the figures to the right use fixed recomputation (the same MRDs as in Figure 2 are used). A number of n below the middle line together with a light gray box means that Mozart performs f-times better. Otherwise, the other system performs f-times better than Mozart.

The figures clearly indicate that a system based on the copying approach is competitive as it comes to runtime. It is worth noting that even for problems that profit from recomputation performance is still competitive without recomputation. In general, this is of course only true if the available memory is sufficient.

The numbers for Mozart with recomputation show that copying together with recomputation for large problems and deep search trees can outperform trailing-based systems.

A   Used Hardware and Software Platforms

All programs have been run on a single processor Sun ULTRASparc-1 170 with 300 Megabytes of main memory and using SunOS 5.5 as operating system. All runtimes have been taken as wall time (that is, absolute clock time), where the machine was unloaded: difference between wall and actual process time is less than 5%. All numbers presented are the arithmetic mean of 25 runs, where the coefficient of variation is less than 5% for all benchmarks and systems but 100-S-Queens for Solver, where the deviation was less than 15%.

The following systems were used: Mozart 1.1.0, Eclipse 3.7.1, SICStus Prolog 3.7.1, and ILOG Solver 4.400.

Acknowledgements. I am grateful to Thorsten Brunklaus, Katrin Erk, Leif Kornstaedt, Tobias Müller, Andreas Rossberg, and the anonymous referees for providing comments that helped to improve the paper.

References

[1] Abderrahamane Aggoun and Nicolas Beldiceanu. Time Stamps Techniques for the Trailed Data in Constraint Logic Programming Systems. In *Actes du Séminaire 1990–Programmation en Logique*, pages 487–509, Tregastel, France, May 1990. CNET.

[2] Abderrahamane Aggoun and Nicolas Beldiceanu. Overview of the CHIP Compiler System. In Frédéric Benhamou and Alain Colmerauer, editors, *Constraint Logic Programming: Selected Research*, pages 421–437. The MIT Press, Cambridge, MA, USA, 1993.

[3] Abderrahamane Aggoun, David Chan, Pierre Dufresne, Eamon Falvey, Hugh Grant, Alexander Herold, Geoffrey Macartney, Micha Meier, David Miller, Shyam Mudambi, Bruno Perez, Emmanuel Van Rossum,

Joachim Schimpf, Periklis Andreas Tsahageas, and Dominique Henry de Villeneuve. ECL^{i}PS^e 3.5. User manual, European Computer Industry Research Centre (ECRC), Munich, Germany, December 1995.

[4] Hassan Aït-Kaci. *Warren's Abstract Machine: A Tutorial Reconstruction*. Logic Programming Series. The MIT Press, Cambridge, MA, USA, 1991.

[5] Philippe Codognet and Daniel Diaz. Compiling constraints in clp(FD). *The Journal of Logic Programming*, 27(3):185–226, June 1996.

[6] ILOG. ILOG Solver: Reference manual, May 1997. Version 4.0.

[7] Joxan Jaffar and Michael M. Maher. Constraint logic programming: A survey. *The Journal of Logic Programming*, 19 & 20:503–582, May 1994. Special Issue: Ten Years of Logic Programming.

[8] Tobias Müller and Jörg Würtz. Extending a concurrent constraint language by propagators. In Jan Małuszyński, editor, *Proceedings of the International Logic Programming Symposium*, pages 149–163, Long Island, NY, USA, 1997. The MIT Press.

[9] Mozart Consortium. The Mozart programming system, 1999. Available from www.mozart-oz.org.

[10] Christian Schulte. Oz Explorer: A visual constraint programming tool. In Lee Naish, editor, *Proceedings of the Fourteenth International Conference on Logic Programming*, pages 286–300, Leuven, Belgium, July 1997. The MIT Press.

[11] Christian Schulte. Programming constraint inference engines. In Gert Smolka, editor, *Proceedings of the Third International Conference on Principles and Practice of Constraint Programming*, volume 1330 of *Lecture Notes in Computer Science*, pages 519–533, Schloß Hagenberg, Linz, Austria, October 1997. Springer-Verlag.

[12] Jeffrey Mark Siskind and David Allen McAllester. Screamer: A portable efficient implementation of nondeterministic Common Lisp. Technical Report IRCS-93-03, University of Pennsylvania, Institute for Research in Cognitive Science, 1993.

[13] Pascal Van Hentenryck, Vijay Saraswat, and Yves Deville. Design, implementation, and evaluation of the constraint language cc(FD). *The Journal of Logic Programming*, 37(1–3):139–164, October 1998.

[14] David H. D. Warren. An abstract Prolog instruction set. Technical Note 309, SRI International, Artificial Intelligence Center, Menlo Park, CA, USA, October 1983.

Stack-splitting: Or-/And-parallelism on Distributed Memory Machines[1]

Gopal Gupta and Enrico Pontelli
Department of Computer Science
New Mexico State University
http://www.cs.nmsu.edu/lldap

Abstract

We study the problem of exploiting *or-parallelism* from logic programming systems on distributed machines. We propose *stack-splitting*, a modification of the *stack-copying* technique for environment representation, that can be used for exploiting or-parallelism efficiently on distributed-memory machines. Stack-splitting coupled with *scheduling on bottom-most choice-point* leads to: (i) reduced communication during distributed execution; and, (ii) distribution of larger grain-sized work to processors. The modified technique can also be implemented on shared memory machines and performs better than standard stack-copying implementations. We also show how stack-splitting can be adapted for and-parallelism.

1 Introduction

An important characteristic of logic programming (LP) languages is that parallelism is implicitly present in the operational model of the language and can be automatically exploited. This can be done directly by the program evaluator—i.e., the runtime system—or, alternatively, it can be done by a parallelizing compiler. The task of the parallelizing compiler is essentially to unburden the evaluator from making run-time decisions regarding which parts of the program to run in parallel. Note that the program can also be parallelized by the user, through suitable source-level annotations. In all cases, the advantage offered by LP is that the process is easier because of the declarative, high level nature of the language. Two principal kinds of (implicitly exploitable) parallelism can be identified in LP. *Or-parallelism (OP)* arises when more than one clause defines some predicate and a literal unifies with more than one clause head—the corresponding bodies can then be executed in parallel with each other. *And-parallelism (AP)* arises when more than one goal is present in the query, and these goals are concurrently reduced by parallel threads. Typically two forms of AP are distinguished. *Independent AP* arises when the runtime bindings for the variables in the parallel goals make such goals *independent*, i.e., their arguments have non-intersecting sets of variables. *Dependent AP* arises when two goals in the body of a clause have a common variable and are executed in parallel.

Most research so far has focused on techniques aimed at shared-memory multiprocessors (SMMs). Relatively fewer efforts [10, 2, 7, 6, 5] have been

[1]This work has been partially supported by NSF grants CCR9625358, HRD9628450, CDA9729848, EIA9810732, CCR9875279, and from the US-Spain Fullbright program.

devoted to implementing LP systems on distributed memory multiprocessors (DMMs). Out of these efforts only a small number have been implemented as working prototypes, and even fewer have produced acceptable speedups. One can conclude that the state-of-the-art of parallel LP systems on DMMs is far behind that of parallel LP systems on SMMs.

Existing techniques developed for SMMs are inadequate for the needs of DMMs. In fact, most implementation methods require sharing of data and control stacks to work correctly. Even if the need to share data stacks is eliminated—as in *stack copying*—the need to share the control stack still exists. The control stack can be large, thus degrading the performance on DMMs. In this paper, we present a modification of the stack-copying method, called *stack-splitting*, designed to support OP on DMMs. Stack-splitting allows one to avoid sharing of the control stack, thus allowing efficient SMM techniques devised to be effectively implemented on DMMs. Stack-splitting has the potential to improve locality of computation, reduce communication between parallel threads, and improve cache behavior. Furthermore, it allows better scheduling strategies—specifically scheduling on bottom-most choice-point—even in DMM implementations of OP. The fact that our techniques for implementing LP systems on distributed architectures are based on simple modifications of efficient techniques that have proved to work on SMMs gives us confidence that they will work better than many approaches previously proposed. Our prototype implementation (on SMMs) as well as simulation studies [17] further bolster our confidence.

Stack-splitting can also be adapted for efficient implementation of AP on DMMs. In addition, it can be efficiently implemented on SMMs as well as DMMs. On SMMs we anticipate that the method's performance will be comparable to stack-copying [1]—our prototype shows that our method's performance is, in fact, better. The real benefit of the method will be apparent on DMMs, on which efficient implementation becomes possible. The ability to reuse the same technology on both SMMs and DMMs is also a key component to allow the development of LP systems on *Clusters of SMMs*, i.e., distributed architectures whose individual nodes are SMMs.

2 The Environment Representation Problem

A major problem in implementing OP is that multiple branches of the search tree are active simultaneously, each of which may produce a solution or fail. Each of these branches may bind a variable created earlier—i.e., before the choice-point. In normal sequential execution, where only one branch of the search tree is active at any time, the binding for the variable created by that branch can be stored directly in the memory location allocated for such variable. During backtracking, this binding is removed, so as to free the memory location for use by the next branch. However, in OP execution, this memory location will have to be turned into a *set of locations* shared between processors—to store the multiple bindings that may *simultaneously* exist. Also, we should be able to efficiently distinguish bindings applicable to each branch during variable access. The problem of maintaining multiple bindings is called the *multiple environments representation* problem [11, 19].

Stack-copying [1] is a successful approach for environments representation in OP. In this approach (originally developed in the Muse system), processors maintain a *separate* but *identical* address space. Whenever a processor $\mathcal{A}$ becomes idle (*idle-agent*), it will start looking for unexplored alternatives generated by another processor $\mathcal{B}$ (*active-agent*). Once a choice-point p is detected in the tree $\mathcal{T}_B$ generated by $\mathcal{B}$, $\mathcal{A}$ will create a local copy of $\mathcal{T}_B$ and restart the computation by backtracking over p. To reduce the amount of information transferred, copying is done *incrementally*, i.e., only the *difference* between $\mathcal{T}_A$ and $\mathcal{T}_B$ is actually copied.

In practice, the stack-copying operation is more involved than simply memory copying, as the choice-points have to be copied to an area accessible to all processors. This is important because the set of untried alternatives is now shared between the two processors; if this set is not accessed in mutual exclusion, then two processors may execute the same alternative. Thus, after copying, each choice-point in $\mathcal{T}_B$ will be transferred to a shared area—these will be called *shared frames*. Both active and idle agents will replace their choice-points with pointers to the corresponding shared frames. Shared frames are accessed in mutual exclusion. This whole operation of obtaining work from another processor is usually termed *sharing of or-parallel work*.

A major reason for the success of Muse [1, 4] is that it does *scheduling on bottom-most choice-point*. Each idle processor picks work from the bottom-most choice-point of an or-branch. The stack segments upwards of this choice-point are copied before the exploration of this alternative is begun. The copied stack segments may contain other choice-points with untried alternatives—which become accessible via simple backtracking. Thus, a significant amount of work becomes available to the copying processor every time a sharing is performed. The cost of having to copy potentially larger fragments of the tree is irrelevant considering that this technique drastically reduces the *number of sharing operations* performed. It is important to observe that each sharing operation requires both the processors involved to stop the regular computation and cooperate in the sharing.

3   The Split Choice-point Stack-Copying Model

Backtracking on a shared choice-point requires acquiring exclusive access to the corresponding shared frame. This solution works fine on SMMs—where mutual exclusion is easily implemented using *locks*. However, on a DMM this process is a source of overhead—access to the shared area becomes a bottleneck [3]. Sharing of information in a DMM leads to frequent exchange of messages and hence considerable overhead. Centralized data structures, such as the shared frames, are expensive to realize in a distributed setting. Nevertheless, stack copying has been recognized as the best representation methodology to support OP in a DMM setting [7, 10, 2, 6, 5]. This is because, while the choice-points are shared, at least other data-structures, such as the environment, the trail, and the heap are not. Other environment representation schemes, e.g., the Binding Arrays scheme, have been specifically designed for SMMs and share most of the computation; the communication overhead produced by these alternative schemes on DMMs is likely to be prohibitive. To avoid the problem of sharing choice-points in distributed implementations, many implementors have reverted back to the *scheduling on top-most choice-point* strategy [7, 10]. The reasoning is that untried alternatives of a choice-point created higher up in the or-tree are more likely to generate large subtrees. However, if the granularity does not turn out to be large, then another untried alternative has to be picked and a new copying operation performed. In contrast, in scheduling on bottom-most more work could be found via backtracking, since more choice-points are copied during the same sharing operation. Additionally, scheduling on bottom-most is closer to the depth-first search strategy used by sequential systems, and facilitates support of Prolog semantics. Research done on comparing scheduling strategies indicates that scheduling on bottom-most is superior to scheduling on top-most [4]. This is especially true for stack-copying because: (i) the number of copying operations is minimized; and, (ii) the alternatives in the choice-points copied are "cheap" sources of additional work, available via backtracking. However, the shared nature of choice-points is a major drawback for a DMM implementation of copying. The question we consider is: can we avoid sharing of choice-points while keeping scheduling on bottom-most? The answer is affirmative, as is discussed next.

3.1 Split Choice-point Stack Copying

In the Stack-Copying, the primary reason why a choice-point has to be shared is because we want to serialize the selection of untried alternatives, so that no two processors can pick the same alternative. The shared frame is locked while the alternative is selected to achieve this effect. However, there are other simple ways of ensuring the same property: *the untried alternatives of a choice-point can be split between the two copies of the choice-point stack*. We call this operation *Choice-point Stack-Splitting* or simply *Stack-splitting*. This will ensure that no two processors pick the same alternative.

We can envision different schemes for splitting the set of alternatives between shared choice-points—e.g., each choice-point receives half of the alternatives, or the partitioning can be guided by information regarding the unexplored computation, such as granularity and likelihood of failure. In addition, the need for a shared frame, as a critical section to protect the alternatives from multiple executions, has disappeared, as each stack copy has a choice-point with a different set of unexplored alternatives. All the choice-points can be evenly split in this way during the copying operation. The choice-point stack-splitting operation is illustrated in figure 1.

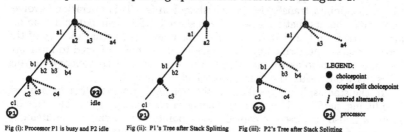

Figure 1: Stack-splitting based or-parallelism

The major advantage of stack-splitting is that scheduling on bottom-most can still be used without incurring huge communication overheads. Essentially, after splitting, the different or-parallel threads become fairly independent of each other, and hence communication is minimized during execution. This makes the stack-splitting technique highly suitable for DMMs. The possibility of parameterizing the splitting of the alternatives based on additional semantic information (granularity, non-failure, user annotations) can further reduce the likelihood of additional communications due to scheduling.

The shared frames in the stack-copying technique are used to maintain global information related to scheduling. The shared frames provide a global description of the or-tree, and each shared frame records which processor is working in which part of the tree. This last piece of information is needed to support scheduling in stack-copying systems—work is taken from the processor that is "closer" in the or-tree, thus reducing the amount of information to be copied. The shared frames ensure accessibility of this information to all processors, providing a consistent view of the computation.

However, under stack-splitting the shared frames no longer exist; scheduling and work-load information will have to be maintained in some other way. They could be kept in a global shared area similar to the case of SMMs—e.g., by building a representation of the or-tree—or distributed over multiple processors and accessed by message passing in case of DMMs. The maintenance of global scheduling information represents a problem which is orthogonal to the environment representation. This means that scheduling management in a DMM will anyway require communication between processors.

Shared frames are also employed in Muse [1] to detect the Prolog order of choice-points, needed to execute order-sensitive predicates (e.g., side-effects, extra-logical predicates) in the correct order. As in the case of scheduling, some information regarding global ordering of choice-points needs to be maintained to execute order-sensitive predicates in the correct order. Thus, stack-splitting does not completely remove the need of a shared description of the or-tree. The use of stack-splitting can mitigate the impact of accessing shared resources—e.g., stack-splitting allows scheduling on bottom-most which, in general, leads to a reduction of the number of calls to the scheduler.

3.2   The Cost of Stack-Splitting

The stack-copying operation in Stack-Splitting is slightly more involved than in regular stack-copying. In Muse, the choice-point stack is traversed and the choice-points transferred to the shared area. This operation involves only choice-points that have never been shared before—shared choice-points already reside in the shared area. For this reason the actual *sharing* of the choice-points is performed by the *active-agent*—which is forced to interrupt its computation to assist the sharing process. The actual memory copying takes place only after the sharing of the choice-points.

In the stack-splitting technique, the sharing is replaced first by a phase of splitting, performed by the active agent; after the copying is done, the idle agent will also traverse the copied choice-points, completing the splitting of the untried alternatives. In the case of SMM implementations, this operation is expected to be considerably cheaper than transferring the choice-points to the shared area. The actual splitting can be represented by a simple pair of indices that refer to the list of alternatives. In the case of DMM implementations, the situation is similar: since each processor maintains a local copy of the code, the splitting can be performed by communicating to the copying processor which alternatives it can execute for each choice-point (e.g., a pair of pointers to the list of alternatives). It is simple to encode such information within the choice-point itself during copying.

In both cases we expect the sharing operation to have comparable complexity; a slight delay may occur in stack-splitting, due to the traversal of the choice-point stack performed by each processor. On the other hand, in stack-splitting the two traversals—one in the *idle-agent* and one in the *active-agent*—can be overlapped, while in the Muse scheme the *idle-agent* is suspended until the *active-agent* has completed the sharing operation. However, if the stack being copied, S_o, is itself a copy of some other stack, then unlike regular stack-copying, we may still need to traverse both the source and target stacks and split the choice-points. The presence of this additional step depends on the policy adopted for the partitioning of the alternatives between processors. For example, it is required if we adopt a policy which assigns half of the alternatives to each of the processors. In such cases, the cost of sharing will be slightly more than the cost of regular stack-copying.

Once a processor selects new work, it will look for work again only after it finishes the exploration of all alternatives acquired via stack-splitting. Incremental copying and other optimizations developed for Muse may still apply to stack-splitting. E.g., processors should not immediately deallocate shared areas on backtracking, to allow for incremental copying.

3.3 Supporting Prolog's Sequential Semantics

In order to support Prolog semantics, we should execute the side-effects in the order in which they would be executed in a sequential implementation of Prolog. Also, it is desirable to explore the branches in the search tree in the left to right order. Performing the side-effects in the sequential order requires considerable synchronization between the different or-branches. In a distributed implementation, this synchronization may generate considerable message traffic; however, this traffic is really independent of the environment representation technique used. As far as exploring the search space with a bias towards exploring the branches to the left is concerned, it will depend on the choice-point splitting strategy used. Consider the choice-point with alternatives **a1** through **a5** shown in Fig. 2(i). Two possible splittings are shown in Fig. 2(ii) and 2(iii). In the first one (Fig. 2(ii)), the list of alternatives is split in the middle: processor P1 will be working on the left half of the tree rooted at this choice-point **a**, processor P2 on the right half. In contrast, in Fig. 2(iii), the untried alternatives are distributed alternately between the two choice-points. This splitting strategy is more likely to produce a search that is biased to the left.

If we are interested in all solutions to a goal, then the order in which the alternatives are explored is immaterial. This is frequently the case in CLP(FD) systems, where we wish to narrow the domains to the fullest extent. However, if we are interested in producing the first solution as quickly as possible, then the splitting strategy acquires considerable importance.

3.4 Optimizing Stack-splitting Cost

The cost incurred in splitting the untried alternatives between the copied stack and the stack from which the copy is made, can be eliminated by

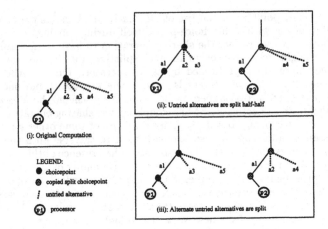

Figure 2: Distribution of Unexplored Alternatives

amortizing it over the operation of picking untried alternatives. Let us assume that the untried alternatives will be split evenly (Fig. 2(ii)).

In the modified approach, no traversal and modification of the choice-points is done during copying. The untried alternatives are organized as a binary tree. The binary alternatives can be efficiently maintained in an array, using standard techniques found in any data-structures textbook. In addition, each choice-point maintains the "copying distance" from the very first original choice-point as a bit string. This number is initially 0 when the computation begins. When stack-splitting takes place and a choice-point whose bit string is n is copied from, then the new choice-point's bit string is $n1$ (1 tagged to bit string n), while the old choice-point's bit string is changed to $n0$ (0 tagged to bit string n). When a processor backtracks to a choice-point, it will use its bit string to navigate in the tree of untried alternatives, and find the alternatives that it is responsible for. For example, if the bit-string of a processor is 10, then all the alternatives in the left subtree of the right subtree of the or-tree are to be executed by that processor.

However, it is not very clear which of the two strategies—incurring cost of splitting at copying time vs amortizing the cost over the selection of untried alternatives—would be more efficient. In case of amortization, the cost of picking an alternative from a choice-point is now slightly higher, as the binary tree of choice-points needs to be traversed to find the right alternative.

3.5 Applicability and Effectiveness

Stack-splitting essentially performs static work distribution, as the untried alternatives are split at the time of picking work. If the choice-points that are split are balanced, then we can expect good performance. Thus, we should expect to see good performance when the choice-points generated by the computation that are parallelized contain a large number of alternatives. This is the case for applications which fetch data from databases and for most generate & test type of applications.

For choice-points with a small number of alternatives, stack-splitting is more susceptible to problems created by the static work distribution strategy that implicitly results from it: for example, in cases where OP is extracted from choice-points with only two alternatives. Such choice-points arise quite frequently, from the use of predicates like member and select:

member(X,[X|_]).   select(X,[X|Y],Y).
member(X,[_|Y]) :- member(X,Y).   select(X,[Y|Z],[Y|R]) :- select(X,Z,R).

Both these predicates generates choice-points with only two alternatives—thus, at the time of sharing, a single alternative is available in each choice-point. The different alternatives are spread across different choice-points. Stack-splitting would assign all the alternatives to the copying processor, thus leaving the original processor without local work. However, the problems raised by such situations can be solved using a number of techniques:

- Use knowledge about the inputs and partial evaluation, or automatic optimizations (e.g., *Last Alternative Optimization (LAO)* [12]) to collapse the different choice-points into a single one.

- Perform a *vertical* splitting of the choice-points, i.e., each processor is given all the alternatives of alternate choice-points (See Figure 3). In this case, the list of choice-points is split between the two processors. In fact, vertical splitting is even more efficient than the *horizontal* splitting introduced in Section 3.1 and described thus far. Horizontal splitting can be resorted to when very few choice-points are present in the stack. Different mixes of vertical and horizontal splitting of can be tried to achieve a good balance of load. Eventually, the user can also be given control regarding how the splitting is done.

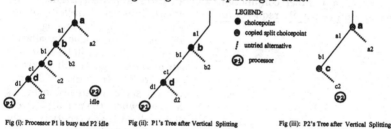

Fig (i): Processor P1 is busy and P2 idle   Fig (ii): P1's Tree after Vertical Splitting   Fig (iii): P2's Tree after Vertical Splitting

Figure 3: Vertical Splitting of Choice-points

4 Distributed Implementation of And-parallelism

In traditional logic programming independent and-parallel (IAP) computations are commonly managed using the *marker based scheme* devised in the RAPWAM model [14] and refined by various researchers [16, 20]. The marker model works by creating a *parcall* frame on the stack when a parallel conjunction of goals is encountered. The parcall frame keeps track of information related to execution of each of the goal in the parallel conjunction: a *goal-slot* is created in the parcall frame for every goal in the parallel conjunction; the slot keeps track of control information related to that goal. An input-marker is inserted in the stack before execution of one of the goals is begun by a processor, and an end-marker is inserted after the execution is over. Backtracking becomes complicated in presence of AP, since it has to be done in the correct order to ensure the integrity of the execution [14, 16].

4.1 Stack-splitting for Independent And-parallelism

The stack-splitting technique can also be applied to obtain a distributed implementation of AP. This observation is based on the *duality* [18] between OP and AP: a technique that benefits OP also benefits AP and vice versa. OP and AP are fundamentally the same, in that in both cases multiple threads concurrently work in the creation of a computation tree. The only difference is that while in the case of OP the threads are independent, in the case of AP these threads have to be *joined* as the effect of the computation in different threads is needed in the computation that corresponds to the continuation (the goal that comes after the parcall frame). A choice-point (source of OP) and a parcall frame (source of AP) are similar structures since both are used to manage the multiple threads that give rise to OP and AP respectively. Thus, just as choice-points can be split in our improved technique at the time a processor picks OP work from another processor, parcall frames can likewise be split when AP work is sought by another processor. Of course, we will have to consider how the split-computations on different processors working in AP can be "joined" so that the continuation goal can be correctly executed, an issue that is absent in the case of OP.

4.2 Stack-splitting Implementation of And-parallelism

Consider a processor P_1 executing a goal g. Suppose after some time P_1 reaches a parallel conjunction and allocates a parcall frame. Suppose idle processor P_2 requests an AP subgoal from the parallel conjunction. Following the analogy with OP, the parcall frame (analogous to a choice-point) will be split, and half of the AP goals will be transferred to P_2. In addition, P_2 will copy the stacks up to and including the point where the parcall frame is allocated, so that execution of the AP goals picked up by P_2 can be done independently of P_1 (See Figure 4). Copying of stack frames is done because goals picked up by P_2 may access/bind variables that arise in the goals occurring before the parallel conjunction. The goal-slots in the parcall frame need to be maintained as a list on the heap, so that they can be easily split—a feature needed anyway to support optimizations such as the *Last Parallel Call Optimization (LPCO)* [13]. Most of the techniques discussed for OP (e.g., incremental stack copying, amortization of overhead of splitting, etc.) apply to the case of AP, if we think of the parcall frame as analogous to a choice-point and the various AP goals in the corresponding parallel conjunction as analogous to the alternatives of that choice-point. However, the main issue that we need to tackle is the joining of various AP computations so that the continuation goal after the parallel conjunction can be correctly executed.

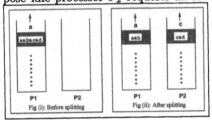

Fig (i): Before splitting   Fig (ii): After splitting

Figure 4: And-parallel stack-splitting

Consider the goal `g`, `(p & q)`, `r`, which indicates that the goals `p` and `q` are executed in IAP. During the execution, the goals `p` and `q` may access and bind variables created by `g`. Likewise, the goal `r`, which is the continuation of the parallel conjunction, may access and bind variables created by `p`, `q` as well as **g**. The only guarantee that independence gives is that **p** will never access variables created in **q** and vice versa. The continuation goal, **r**, only needs to know the bindings created for unbound variables that are reachable from the arguments of **p** and **q**. If the unbound variables appearing in the arguments of **p** and **q** are *globalized* [14], then these bindings will be found either in the stacks of the goals preceding the parallel conjunction or the heap (but not in the stacks of **p** and **q**). Bindings created by **p** and **q** for variables allocated space in the stacks corresponding to **g** can be easily recorded by setting up a *value-trail* in each processor. Essentially, any bindings made to a variable allocated space above the parcall frame is recorded in a separate trail (called *and-trail*). Both the address of the variable and its binding are recorded in this trail. Now the bindings created by **p** and **q** for variables that have been allocated space in **g**'s stack can be obtained by the processor executing **r** by simply copying the corresponding segment of the and-trails of processor executing **p** and **q**, and installing the bindings therein. This installation process will also require copying terms from the heaps of **p** and **q** to the heap of **r**, since **p** or **q** may bind a variable created in **g** to a term. Variables occuring in such a term may not be present in the and-trail. However, these terms are easily accessible as they are referred by values in the and-trails of **p** and **q**. Thus, during installation, while traversing the and-trails of **p** and **q**, if a term is found, then it has to be copied onto **r**'s heap. This process can be optimized using various techniques, such as copy-on-demand (as in the DAOS system [7]) and backtracking independence [16].

4.3 Discussion

The advantages of stack-splitting for realizing AP are similar to those for OP. When a processor steals work, it gets a large grain of work. Coupled with LPCO which increases the size of the parcall frame, larger grain-sized work can be obtained. Also, if additional processors are not available, optimizations [13] can keep the AP computation as close to sequential execution as possible—just as in OP, where choice-point can be explored via backtracking.

The stack-splitting technique is expected to be reasonably effective for distributed implementations of AP. Copying of stacks may seem to be an inordinate amount of effort for AP implementations, but given that implementations such as Muse are quite efficient, a stack-copying based and-parallel system should also be efficient. Also, the overhead in setting up the bindings while *joining* the multiple and-parallel threads, so that the parcall's continuation goal can be correctly executed, may be quite high; however, we hope that the use of and-trails will keep it to a minimum. Furthermore, the issue of joining will arise in any distributed implementation of AP, where bindings of commonly accessible variables have to be exchanged between processors to allow for a coherent execution. The use of and-trail is similar—but more efficient—than existing techniques such as *environment closing* [9].

5 Performance Results

A prototype SMM implementation of the stack-splitting technique has been realized by modifying the Muse OP system. This prototype was easier to build, compared to a true distributed implementation of stack-splitting, and enabled us to (i) perform a preliminary feasibility study of our ideas, (ii) compare performance to the original stack-copying method, and, (iii) quickly obtain a system that can used for a low-level study of locality-of-reference, communication overhead, etc., using simulators: this gives us a good indication of how our technique will perform in a distributed setting.

Benchmark	# Processors							
	1		3		5		7	
	Muse	SS	Muse	SS	Muse	SS	Muse	SS
Tina	21.4	22.5	25.1	10.1	25.1	8.3	25.0 (0.85)	7.6 (2.97)
Large	131.7	144.9	118.0	54.3	120.1	38.8	118.4 (1.11)	32.3 (4.49)
Queens1	56.8	63.6	49.8	39.5	42.9	36.1	42.1 (1.35)	34.4(1.85)
FQueens	51.3	59.0	18.8	24.5	10.8	13.1	7.5 (6.88)	9.9 (5.95)
Salt	98.8	104.7	38.7	36.2	25.1	23.3	18.6 (5.32)	18.2 (5.76)
Solitaire	22.9	24.4	8.4	8.7	5.3	5.6	4.6 (4.95)	4.1 (5.91)
Houses	37.1	41.2	13.7	14.5	8.9	9.3	6.7 (5.53)	6.9 (5.92)
constraint	67.0	69.7	25.0	25.7	15.2	15.5	10.6 (6.35)	10.8 (6.44)

Table 1: Execution Times on Sequent: Muse vs. Stack-Splitting (SS)

The timing results (in seconds) along with speedups obtained are shown in Table 1 and Table 2. All the benchmarks for which results are reported involve search—we have requested all solutions in each of them. The benchmarks used are classical benchmarks used for evaluating the parallel behavior of or-parallel systems. The results reported have been obtained using a Pentium-Pro 4-node SMM and an 8-node Sequent SMM. The Sequent is relatively old with respect to current industry standards, but it gives a good feeling for the parallel behavior of the system. The figures reported are average execution times over a sequence of 10 runs. The table presents the results obtained using Muse and using Stack-splitting. Table 2 presents the results (in milliseconds) obtained on the Pentium hardware. It can be observed that the speedups on the two systems are very similar. All benchmarks have been executed by requiring the system to exploit parallelism only from selected promising predicates. We believe this situation better reflects the kind of behavior needed to guarantee good performance in a distributed execution.

As from Table 1, stack-splitting leads in general to better speed-ups. The execution time of stack-splitting is occasionally slightly worse than Muse—on average the sequential stack-splitting system is 5% to 12% slower than sequential Muse. This is due to the temporary removal of some sequential optimizations from stack-splitting (to facilitate the development of the prototype) and the presence of one additional comparison during the backtracking phase—needed to distinguish between split and unsplit choice-points.

The first problem will be solved in the next version of our prototype. The second problem is inherent in the representation of choice-point alternatives in Muse. All choice-points associated to the same predicate share the same list of alternatives. This complicates the implementation of stack-splitting, as the list of alternatives cannot be directly manipulated. The simple alternative of duplicating the alternatives is too inefficient.

Benchmark	# Processors		
	1	2	3
Tina	1215	719 (1.69)	535 (2.27)
Large	8093	4422 (1.83)	3065 (2.64)
Queens1	3520	2466 (1.43)	2207 (1.59)
Salt	6117	3274 (1.87)	2155 (2.84)
Solitaire	1364	704 (1.94)	488 (2.79)
Houses	2425	1263 (1.92)	859 (2.82)
constraint	3030	1569 (1.93)	1102 (2.75)

Table 2: Execution on Solaris X86

At present we have introduced two pointers in the choice-point to identify the alternatives of interest—this leads to the need of discriminating between split and non-split choice-points during back-tracking. The use of alternative representations could solve this problem—but requires tedious changes to the compiler.

In the case of *Tina*, Muse suffers a slowdown irrespective of the number of processors employed. This behavior is at odds with the speed-ups reported in the literature. We conjecture it originates from having explicitly identified all choice-points as parallel/sequential. Stack-splitting is capable of extracting parallelism from this benchmark, with a maximum speedup of about 3. The *Large* benchmark generates a small and balanced number of deep branches—an ideal situation for the splitting approach. Muse obtains marginal speed-up, while stack-splitting produces better speedups. Better parallel behavior is obtained for almost all benchmarks, except *FQueens*. This benchmark generates a single choice-point with a large number of alternatives—each alternative is small and leads quickly to success/failure. In this case stack-splitting pays the price of a more expensive sharing phase—this is not the situation in which a distributed execution is desired. In the current proto-type we have also explored the use of different strategies for splitting the work available in one branch of the tree. The graphs in Fig. 5 compares *horizontal* stack-splitting with *vertical* splitting for some benchmarks.

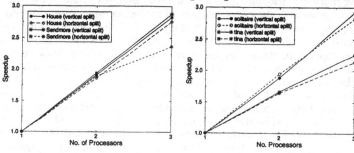

Figure 5: Basic Stack-splitting vs. Vertical Stack-splitting

We are currently carrying out a low-level performance study of our SMM implementation of stack-splitting, using the SimICS Sparc simulator [15] and other performance analysis tools. The goal of this study is to determine caching behavior, locality of access, etc., in order to assess the performance one can expect from a DMM implementation of stack-splitting. The pre-liminary results from this study are very encouraging. For SimICS, we have executed simulations with data cache size of 8MB, and cache lines of both 4 bytes (i.e., single word) and 4K (memory page size). Fig. 6 compares the largest difference in cache miss rate observed while executing different bench-marks. This shows that the worst case cache miss rate using stack-splitting is considerably lower than the one observed for Muse. Similar results have been observed by taking the best case miss rate.

The number of misses generated by vertical stack-splitting is usually lower than the corresponding numbers obtained from Muse. Note that hori-zontal splitting does not perform as well, and this is primarily because most parallel choice-points have only two alternatives (see Section 3.5). In fact, a major factor that leads to increased cache misses in our prototype im-

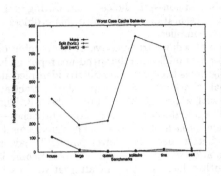

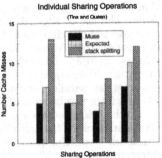

Figure 6: Worst Case Miss Rate   Figure 7: Single sharing

plementation of stack-splitting is the less-than-optimal implementation of incremental copying. This is borne out by data shown in Figure 7, in which the cache-misses observed in some *individual sharing operations* are plotted: during sharing, stack-splitting suffers more cache-misses than Muse—the bar labeled "expected" shows the number of misses we were approximately expecting in stack-splitting based on the status of the caches. Our ongoing performance study shows that if the number of cache-misses during incremental copying in stack-splitting were identical to that in Muse, then the overall cache-misses in stack-splitting would be lower than that of Muse.

The goal of our low-level performance study is to assess how well a distributed implementation of stack-splitting will perform. Our performance study indeed convinces us that a distributed implementation will perform quite well (provided incremental copying is fully incorporated in the implementation). At this point it should also be mentioned that the cache-miss rate is not an accurate estimate of the number of messages exchanged. The number of cache-misses is an overestimate of the network traffic, since a cache miss is caused either by the "local" behavior of the execution (such as a missing data-item because of an insufficiently large cache) or by the "global" behavior of the execution (data being marked as invalid in the cache of one processor by another). Cache misses due to the latter reason are more reflective of the message traffic in a DMM, as cache misses due to the former can be eliminated by having a very large memory in each node of the DMM. This estimate of the purely global behavior can be obtained by measuring the number of cache invalidates performed during the execution. Fig. 8 compares the average number of net invalidates observed in the different benchmarks. Here, once again, vertical splitting seems to perform quite well. These figures should also improve once sophisticated incremental copying techniques found in Muse are incorporated in our prototype.

6   Conclusion and Related Work

In this paper, we presented a technique called stack-splitting for implementing OP and discussed its advantages and disadvantages. Stack-splitting is a slight modification of stack-copying. Its main advantage, compared to other techniques for implementing OP, is that it allows large grain-sized work to

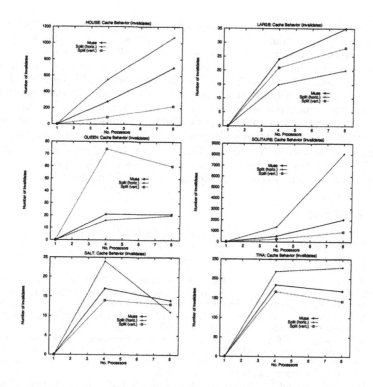

Figure 8: Average Number of Net Invalidates

be picked up by idle processors and be executed efficiently without incurring excessive communication overhead. The technique bears some similarity to the Delphi model [8] (the Delphi model was not the inspiration for our stack-splitting technique), where computation leading to a goal with multiple alternatives is replicated in multiple processors, and each processor chooses a different alternative when that goal is reached. Instead of recomputing we use stack-copying, which, we believe, is more efficient. We also showed how stack-splitting can be used for implementing independent AP.

Distributed implementations of Prolog have been proposed by several researchers [10, 2, 7]. However, none of these systems are very effective in producing speedups over a wide range of benchmarks. Foong's system [10] and Castro et al's system [7] are based directly on stack-copying and generate communication overhead due to the shared choice-points (no real implementation exist for the two of them). Araujo's system uses recomputation [8] rather than stack-copying. Using recomputation for maintaining multiple environments is inherently inferior to stack-copying. The stack frames that are copied in the stack-copying technique capture the effect of a computation. In the recomputation technique these stack-frames are reproduced by re-running the computation. A computation may run for hours and yet produce only a single stack frame (e.g., a tail-recursive computation). Distributed implementations of Prolog have been developed on Transputer systems (The Opera System [6] and the system of Benjumea and Troya [5]).

Of these, Benjumea's system has produced quite good results. However, both the Opera system and the Benjumea's system have been developed on now-obsolete Transputer hardware, and, additionally, both rely on a stack-copying mechanism which will produce poor performance in programs where the task-granularity is small. A DMM implementation of Prolog based on stack-splitting is currently in progress. Finally, the idea of stack-splitting bears some similarities with some of the loop transformation techniques which are commonly adopted for parallelization of imperative programming languages, such as loop fission, loop tiling, and index set splitting [21].

Acknowledgements: Thanks to Claudio Geyer, Luis Castro, and Inês Dutra for discussions that lead to some of the ideas in this paper, and to P. Magnusson and Virtutech for providing the SimICS simulator.

References

[1] K.A.M. Ali and R. Karlsson. Full Prolog and Scheduling Or-parallelism in Muse. *International Journal of Parallel Programming*, 1991. 19(6):445–475.

[2] L. Araujo and J. Ruz. A Parallel Prolog System for Distributed Memory. *J. Logic Programming*, 1998.

[3] H. Babu. Porting muse on ipsc860. Master's thesis, New Mexico State Univ., 1996.

[4] T. Beaumont and D.H.D. Warren. Scheduling Speculative Work in Or-Parallel Prolog Systems. In *Int'l Conf. on Logic Programming*, MIT Press, 1993.

[5] V. Benjumea and J.M. Troya. An OR Parallel Prolog Model for Distributed Memory Systems. *Procs. PLILP*, Springer Verlag, 1993.

[6] J. Briat et al. OPERA: Or-Parallel Prolog System on Supernode. In *Implementations of Distributed Prolog*, J. Wiley & Sons, 1992.

[7] L.F. Castro et al. DAOS: Distributed And-Or in Scalable Systems. Technical report, Federal University of Rio Grande del Sul, 1998.

[8] W.F. Clocksin and H. Alshawi. A Method for Efficiently Executing Horn Clause Programs Using Multiple Processors. *New Generation Computing*, 5:361–376, 1988.

[9] J. S. Conery. Binding Environments for Parallel Logic Programs in Nonshared Memory Multiprocessors. In *Int. Symp. on Logic Programming*, IEEE, 1987.

[10] W-K. Foong. *Combining and- and or-parallelism in Logic Programs: a distributed approach*. PhD thesis, University of Melbourne, 1995.

[11] G. Gupta and B. Jayaraman. Analysis of or-parallel execution models. *ACM TOPLAS*, 15(4), 1993.

[12] G. Gupta and E. Pontelli. Last Alternative Optimization for Or-parallel Logic Programming Systems. *Symp. on Parallel and Distrib. Proc.* IEEE, 1996.

[13] G. Gupta and E. Pontelli. Optimization Schemas for Parallel Implementation of Nondeterministic Languages. *Int. Parallel Proc. Symposium.* IEEE, 1997.

[14] M. Hermenegildo and K. Greene. &-Prolog and its Performance: Exploiting Independent And-Parallelism. *Int'l Conf. on Logic Prog.*, MIT Press, June 1990.

[15] P.S. Magnusson et al. SimICS/sun4m: a Virtual Workstation. In *Usenix Annual Techn. Conf.*, 1998.

[16] E. Pontelli. *High-Performance Parallel Logic Programming*. PhD thesis, New Mexico State Univ., 1997.

[17] E. Pontelli and G. Gupta. *A Simulation Study of Distributed Execution of (Constraint) Logic Programs*. Internal Paper, 1999.

[18] E. Pontelli and G. Gupta. On the Duality Between And-parallelism and Or-parallelism. In *Proc. of Euro-Par'95*. Springer Verlag, 1995.

[19] E. Pontelli, D. Ranjan, and G. Gupta. On the Complexity of Or-Parallelism. In *New Generation Computing*, 17(3), 1999.

[20] K. Shen. Exploiting Dependent And-parallelism in Prolog. *Proc. Joint Int'l Conf. and Symp. on Logic Prog.*, MIT Press, 1992.

[21] M. Wolfe. *High Performance Compiler for Parallel Computing*. Addison Wesley, 1996.

Mutable Terms in a Tabled Logic Programming System

Baoqiu Cui   **David S. Warren**
Department of Computer Science
SUNY at Stony Brook
Stony Brook, NY 11794-4400, U.S.A.
{cbaoqiu, warren}@cs.sunysb.edu

Abstract

Mutable terms in Prolog form an abstract data type that supports back-trackable destructive assignment. They are intensively used in Constraint Logic Programming and the implementation of constraint solvers. When implemented in XSB, a tabled logic programming system, the underlying mechanism to support mutable terms provides in addition an important way to save table space.

In this paper we describe our implementation of mutable terms in XSB. The implementation of mutable terms is considerably more complex than in a normal Prolog system. First, since mutable terms can appear in a subgoal call and may be updated in an answer, the substitution factoring mechanism in XSB's variant engine must be extended to handle them. Second, to ensure that direct invocation and retrieval from the table give equivalent results, multiple occurrences of the same mutable term in a subgoal and/or an answer must be maintained as shared whenever we copy terms into and out of a table. The XSB tabling engine has to be extended, and special modifications are required for the structure of subgoal table and answer table. The mechanism to preserve the sharing of mutable terms is also proved to be an efficient way of reducing table sizes, as an unchanged mutable term is only saved once in the subgoal table or answer table no matter how many times it appears in the subgoal and the corresponding answer (the new value of a changed mutable term is saved once in the answer table). Used in tabled programs, this mechanism can significantly improve time and space performance.

1   Introduction

In pure Prolog, a term is an immutable object of the Herbrand universe, which can be modified only by instantiating its non-ground parts. However, in many practical applications, destructive assignment is needed for performance. The *mutable term* is an abstract data type that supports backtrackable destructive assignment.

Mutable terms are first implemented in SICStus version 3. Used with attributed variables, mutable terms play an important role in the implementation of the CLP(FD) solver [2] and Constraint Handling Rules (CHRs) [4] that come with SICStus. One of our original motivations to implement mutable terms in XSB [6] is to introduce constraints to XSB and apply tabling techniques to them. To combine tabling with constraints and implement a tabled CLP system in XSB, supporting mutable terms in the tabling engine becomes necessary.

Compared to a non-tabled logic programming system (e.g. SICStus), implementing mutable terms in XSB is considerably more complex. Some special issues related to tabling have to be considered. First, since mutable terms can appear in a subgoal call and may be updated in an answer, the answer is not necessarily an instance of the subgoal. Thus, for a mutable term appearing in the subgoal, we may need to keep in the table both the old value (on entry to a subgoal) and the new value (on exit from a subgoal, in case this mutable term is updated). So the substitution factoring mechanism [10] in XSB's variant engine does not work for mutable terms and has to be extended. Second, to ensure that direct invocation and retrieval from the table give equivalent results, multiple occurrences of the same mutable term in a subgoal and/or an answer must be maintained as shared whenever we copy a term into and out of a table. All later updates to one of the occurrences of a mutable term must be seen by others. However, in the current XSB engine, when we copy a term into and out of a table, all the occurrences of embedded (mutable) terms become new instances and the sharing of mutable terms would be lost. This can lead to inconsistent results. To overcome these problems, the XSB tabling engine has to be extended, and special modifications are required in the structure of subgoal and answer tables.

In XSB, subgoal tables and answer tables are represented in a data structure called the *tabling trie* [10], a tree-structured automaton with the root as the start state and each leaf state associated with a term. It is used for both looking up and inserting an input term into the table. The major advantage of trie-based tabling is that only a single traversal of the term is necessary for the subgoal and answer lookup/insertion. Another advantage is that tabling tries can save table space because of the prefix sharing of terms in subgoals and answers. Answer tries can also be dynamically compiled into WAM-like instructions called *trie instructions*, and the trie instructions can be executed in the same manner as compiled program clauses. When an answer table for a subgoal has been completed, the trie instructions (also called *trie code*) in the answer trie can be executed directly to return all the answers to this subgoal call.

To support mutable terms in tabling tries and to maintain their sharing properties, three new types of trie nodes have been added to tries, and nine new trie instructions have been added to the trie instruction set. The basic idea is that, during the table lookup and insertion of a term, when we first encounter a mutable term, we mark and number it, and then copy it into the table as a normal term. Each later occurrence of this mutable term is represented by a newly added trie node. This new trie node type contains an index number by which we know which mutable term this node refers to. Therefore, every mutable term that appears in a pair of subgoal and answer is stored only once in the subgoal trie and answer trie.

While the original tries can save table space only when two different terms share a prefix, mutable terms provide another way to save more table space. If we know that a large term appears in the subgoal call and/or answer multiple times, we can wrap it up in a mutable term, so that the XSB engine knows only one copy is needed in the table for this term. Therefore, just as substitution factoring can reduce the overheads in table lookup and insertion operations, mutable terms can reduce the overheads even further because the overheads of table lookup/insertion operations are in proportion to the table size. Experimental results show that the use of mutable terms can significantly improve space and time performance in many applications.

The rest of the paper is organized as follows. The next section briefly describes tabling tries, the data structure of tables in XSB, and the substitution factoring mechanism. In Section 3 we explain the problems with mutable terms and tabling. How to modify the trie structure, and how to extend the XSB tabling engine and extend the substitution factoring mechanism to correctly support mutable terms are described in Section 4. Two examples of using mutable terms in XSB programs are given in Section 5: The first one is about parsing strings written in DCG's, which shows how mutable terms can be used in a tabling environment. The second one shows how to use mutable terms to save table space, and experimental results and analysis are given.

2   Tabling Tries and Substitution Factoring

The tabling engine of XSB is based on *tabling tries* [10]. Each predicate has a *subgoal table* associated with it, and each subgoal call at run time has an *answer table* associated with it. Both the subgoal table and answer table are represented using tabling tries, called *subgoal tries* and *answer tries* respectively.

The basic idea of tabling tries is to partition a set of terms based on their structure. Tabling tries are used for both looking up a term in a table and inserting a term into the table. A trie is a tree-structured automaton where the root is the start state and each leaf is associated with a term, which can be constructed by following the branch from the root to this leaf. Each state specifies the position to be inspected in the input term on reaching that state, and the outgoing transitions of the state specify the symbols expected at that position. If the current symbol in the input term matches the symbol on a transition, that transition is taken. On reaching a leaf state we say that the input term matches the term associated with the leaf state. The root-to-leaf path taken to reach the leaf state corresponds to a pre-order traversal of the matching term. When no outgoing transition can be taken,

308

we say the look up operation fails (if we are looking up the input term in the table), or we create a new transition with the current symbol in the input term and a new destination state for this transition (if we are inserting the input term into the table).

Looking up a term in a trie and inserting a term into a trie is illustrated by Figure 1, where (b) is the trie representation for the three terms in (a), and (c) is the trie obtained from (b) after adding a new term $p(a,g(b,c),c)$ to it. To look up the term $p(a,f(a,b),a)$ in (b), we begin at state s_1. Since the pre-order symbol sequence of the input term is $[a,f/2,a,b,a]$, we can make the corresponding transitions and follow the path $s_1 \rightarrow s_2 \rightarrow s_3 \rightarrow s_4 \rightarrow s_5 \rightarrow s_6$ till we reach state s_6, which is a leaf state and declares a match. Thus the term $p(a,f(a,b),a)$ is found in the trie of (b). Now, to insert a new term, $p(a,g(b,c),c)$, into (b), we again start at state s_1 and make a transition to state s_2. At s_2, since there is no outgoing transition labeled $g/2$, we create a new transition for $g/2$ and a new destination state for this transition, s_{12} (see Figure 1(c)). At state s_{12}, we will inspect the symbol in the input term (which is b). Continuing in this fashion we will create three new states and finally get the trie shown in (c).

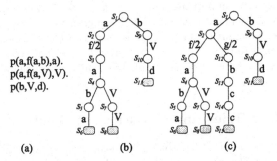

p(a,f(a,b),a).
p(a,f(a,V),V).
p(b,V,d).

(a)   (b)   (c)

Figure 1: Term looking up/inserting

Though the representation of terms using tries, and term looking up and inserting procedures are the same, the subgoal table and answer table are different in XSB. The difference comes from *substitution factoring*. As mentioned before, an answer table is associated with every subgoal in the subgoal table. Unlike the subgoal trie, which stores the whole term of the subgoal call (actually all the arguments of the call), the answer trie stores only the answer substitutions. This means that the constant symbols in the subgoal need not be examined again during either answer check/insert or answer backtracking, and that answer check/insert and answer backtracking can be performed in time proportional to the size of the answer substitution.

Figure 2 shows the idea of substitution factoring. The left side of the figure is the subgoal trie which contains two subgoal calls: $p(X,Y,Z)$ and $p(X,f(Y,a),X)$. On the other side is the answer trie for the subgoal $p(X,f(Y, a),X)$, and there are two answers for this subgoal: $p(a,f(b,a),a)$ and

309

p(c,f(d,a),c), each containing 5 symbols (excluding the symbol p/2). Instead of storing all 5 symbols in the answer trie, for each answer only its *answer tuple* is stored. For these two answers, the answer substitutions are {X = a, Y = b} and {X = c, Y = d} respectively, and their corresponding answer tuples are <a,b> and <c,d>, each containing only 2 symbols.

The concept of substitution factoring is generalized to support mutable terms (in Section 4), but the general idea will be the same. More information about the implementation of tabling tries and substitution factoring can be found in [10] and [9].

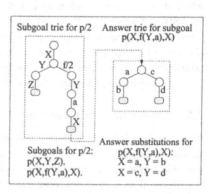

Figure 2: Substitution Factoring

3 Mutable Terms and their Problems with Tabling

3.1 Representation and Related Predicates

In XSB, a *mutable term* is represented as a compound term, '_$mutable' (*Value*, *Timestamp*), where *Value* is the current value of this mutable term and *Timestamp* is reserved for internal use to avoid unnecessary trailing [1] (it has another use when mutable terms are used to save table space, see Section 4). '_$mutable'/2 is a reserved functor in XSB.

Following SICStus [7], the system in which mutable terms were first implemented, we provide the following four predicates for operations on mutable terms:

- create_mutable(+*Value*, -*Mutable*)
  To create a new mutable term *Mutable*, whose initial value is *Value*. *Value* cannot be an unbound variable.

- get_mutable(?*Value*, +*Mutable*)
  To get/check the value of a mutable term *Mutable*, *Value* is unified with the current value of *Mutable*.

- update_mutable(+*Value*, +*Mutable*)
  To update the current value of mutable term *Mutable*, setting it to *Value*. *Value* must not be an unbound variable. This update will be undone upon backtracking.

- is_mutable(?*Mutable*)
  To check if *Mutable* is currently instantiated to a mutable term.

Backtrackable destructive assignment is realized by maintaining a pre-image trail, which saves the old value of a mutable term in the trail stack when it is updated, and resets it to its previous value on backtracking. In XSB, a forward trail is used for tabled-based evaluation [14, 11]. Each forward trail frame contains three fields: the pointer to previous trail frame, the value to which the variable is to be bound (the post-image), and the address of the trailed variable. Besides these fields, a pre-image trail frame contains another one to save the old value to which the variable was bound.

3.2 Problems with Tabling

When tabling is not considered, the implementation of the above operations of mutable terms is straight-forward for Prolog evaluation. However, when mutable terms are involved with tabled predicates, the old trie-based tabling engine requires a more complex extension to handle them correctly.

Problem 1: *A mutable term in the subgoal call may be updated in the answer, so the answer pattern of a subgoal may not be an instance of the call pattern. Thus, the old substitution factoring mechanism no longer works.*

Consider the small program and a query in Figure 3 (a):

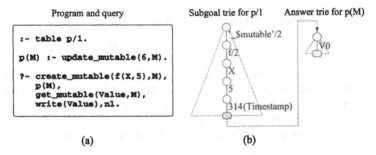

(a) (b)

Figure 3: Problem 1 (Answer is not an instance of the call)

When the query is executed for the first time, it will print out **6** and nothing seems to be wrong. But if we look at the subgoal trie for **p/1** and the answer trie for the subgoal call **p(M)** that were built during the execution (Figure 3 (b)), we see that neither of them saves any information about the update of mutable term **M**. Actually, since **X** is the only variable in the subgoal call, the answer trie contains only the answer substitution of **X**, which, in this example, is still a variable and stored as **V0** (the first variable in a trie). Thus, when the subgoal of **p(M)** has been completed and is called again (the value of **M** is **f(X,5)**), it uses the table and immediately succeeds. Nothing is changed in the call and the value of the mutable term **M** in the answer remains **f(X,5)**, which is not the answer **6** we want.

Problem 2: *If a mutable term appears in a subgoal call and/or an answer more than once, all its occurrences become new instances of this mutable* *term when they are copied into and out of a table. Sharing of the mutable term is not preserved and this can produce inconsistent results.*

This problem can be shown by the program and query in Figure 4 (a). Here, p/2 is a tabled predicate, and we assume that the same call of p(M,T) in this query has been called and completed. Now, in this query, the call of p(M,T) succeeds immediately and an answer will be returned from the completed answer table. After T is unified with f(M1,M2), M1 and M2 should have the same value (6). This is done correctly by the current XSB engine. But there is a problem with the second part of this query: when M1 is updated to value 7, both M and M2 should also be updated to the same value (because they are actually the same mutable term), i.e. both Value and Value2 should be 7. However the current XSB engine prints out 5 (for Value) and 6 (for Value2)

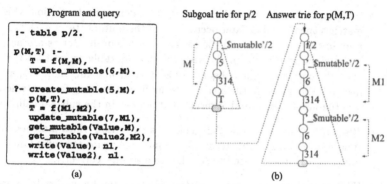

(a)   (b)

Figure 4: Problem 2 (The same mutable term are not shared)

The reason why Value is still 5 is already shown in Figure 3: it is because the update of mutable term M in the call is not saved in the answer trie. The reason why Value2 is 6 can be shown by Figure 4 (b). In the answer trie for subgoal p(M,T), only the substitution of variable T in the subgoal call, <f(M,M)>, is saved, and the two occurrences of M in T are saved as two difference instances of M. Therefore M1 and M2 are two totally different mutable terms on the heap when the answer is copied out of the answer trie. So in the answer, M, M1 and M2 are three *separate* terms. Updating any one of them will not affect others. The sharing of one mutable term among M, M1 and M2 is lost.

4 Modifications of Tabling Engine for Mutable Terms

To reflect the updates of mutable terms in the answer tries, and to preserve the sharing of mutable terms when we copy terms into and out of a table, special modifications have to be done in the XSB tabling engine, mostly in the trie structure and the substitution factoring mechanism.

Since an answer may not be an instance of the subgoal call when the subgoal contains mutable terms, it is easy to think that the current substitution factoring mechanism cannot work for mutable terms and we have to store the full subgoal in the answer trie. But, with careful design, we can use the current substitution factoring mechanism and extend it to support mutable terms. Basically, mutable terms are treated as special variables, or "pseudo-variables", and they are included as part of the substitution factor. We will add new trie nodes to the trie structure to represent mutable terms, just as the current variable trie nodes represent variables.

In our implementation, three kinds of trie nodes (i.e. transitions) are added to tabling tries to handle mutable terms: UM, TS, and UPM. (UM and UPM nodes contain a number that is the index of the mutable term involved):

- $UM(num)$ (Unify Mutable): a node that denotes a transition which matches the second or later occurrence of the mutable term with index num in the input term. In the subgoal tries, mutable terms are numbered starting from 0; in the answer tries, mutable terms that come from the corresponding subgoal call keep their indexing numbers, and new mutable terms in the answer are numbered starting from n, where n is the number of mutable terms that appear in the subgoal call.

- TS (Time Stamp): a node that denotes a transition which matches the time stamp in a mutable term. When mutable terms are copied out of tables, TS nodes are used to set the time stamps correctly.

- $UPM(num)$ (Update Mutable): a node that can be used only in answer tries to update the value of a mutable term that appears in the associated subgoal call. It denotes a transition that leads to a state where the new value of the mutable term with index num is stored.

Just as we number distinct variables in terms in tries [10], we number all the mutable terms in the subgoal call and answer. This is done by using a *mutable term array* (mt_array) and a counter (mt_count) to keep track of all the mutable terms we encounter when we copy terms into and out of tries (and when trie code is executed).

On copying a subgoal into the subgoal trie, when we encounter a mutable term for the first time, we point mt_array[mt_count] (initially mt_count is 0) to this mutable term, point the time stamp field of the mutable term to mt_array[mt_count], and then increase mt_count by 1. Then we copy the mutable term into the subgoal trie just as a normal term (except that the time stamp is copied as a TS node). Later if we encounter a mutable term whose time stamp is already pointing to an element of mt_array, say mt_array[num], we know this mutable term has been encountered before and already saved in the trie. To keep the sharing of this mutable term, we simply insert a UM(num) node into the subgoal trie instead of copying the whole term again. We call num the index of this mutable term in mt_array.

On copying an answer into the answer trie, we do the similar things, except

1. mt_array is initialized as the array of mutable terms appearing in the subgoal call (how to get these mutable terms will be explained below), and mt_count is initialized as n (the number of mutable terms in the subgoal call). New mutable terms that appear only in the answer are numbered from n. (By doing this, we make sure mutable terms are shared between subgoal tries and answer tries.)

2. After putting the substitutions of the variables in the subgoal call into the answer trie, we continue putting the new values of the mutable terms that appear in the call and are updated (by update_mutable/2) in the answer into the answer trie, using UPM nodes.

To initialize mt_array in copying an answer into the answer trie, we need to obtain all the mutable terms in the subgoal call. This can be done by changing the substitution factor record SF [10] as follows: instead of saving only the variables of the subgoal in the (generator or consumer) choice points, we also save the mutable terms obtained during the traversal of the subgoal. The new SF record is divided into two parts: variables in the subgoal, and mutable terms in the subgoal.

Corresponding to this, the answer trie is also divided into two parts (see Figure 5). Figure 5 (a) shows the new subgoal trie of p/2 and the new answer trie of p(M,T) in Figure 4. We can see that the answer trie contains two parts: the upper part stores the normal answer substitutions for the variables in the subgoal, and the lower part stores the new values of all the mutable terms that appear in the subgoal call and are updated in the answer. Now suppose we add another clause in the program shown in Figure 4:

```
p(M,T) :- create_mutable(10,A),
          T = f(M,g(A,A)),
          update_mutable(20,M).
```

Then there is another answer for the call p(M,T): p(M,f(M,g(A,A))) (the values for M and A in the answer are 20 and 10 respectively). When this subgoal has been completed, its answer trie will contain two answers, which are shown in Figure 5 (b). In the branch for the second answer, the first occurrence of mutable term A in the answer is saved as a normal term (except for the time stamp field), and its second occurrence is just saved as a node UM(1) (A is the mutable term with index 1 in the answer).

Comparing Figures 4 and 5, we find that the same mutable term in the subgoal and the corresponding answer is saved only once in the modified subgoal trie and answer trie (other occurrences are represented by a single node UM). So this implementation of mutable terms not only keeps the

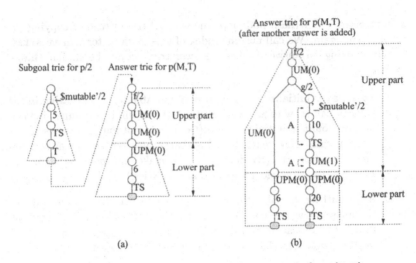

Figure 5: Modified subgoal trie and answer trie for p(M,T)

updating information of mutable terms in the answer table, but also provides a special way to reduce the table space. If a large term appears in the subgoal call and/or answer multiple times, we can wrap it up in a mutable term, so that only one copy of this term is needed in the table space.

One critical problem in the implementation is how to check whether a mutable term in the call is updated in the answer, since only the new values of changed mutable terms are stored in the answer trie. This problem is solved with the help of the time stamp field in mutable terms.

To avoid unnecessary pre-image trailing, the time stamp of a mutable term is initialized as the current **Breg** (the last choice point) when this mutable term is created, and is updated to the new value of **Breg** every time this mutable term is updated. In XSB, whenever a subgoal of a tabled predicate is called, a tabled choice point is laid down on the choice point stack, and the old **Breg** is saved in this tabled choice point frame [11]. If there is a mutable term in the call, its time stamp will be less than or equal to the old **Breg** at the call time. If this mutable term is updated during the evaluation, its time stamp will be set to the new **Breg** which should be greater than the old **Breg** at the call time. When an answer is returned for this subgoal (in the **new_answer** instruction [13, 12]), by comparing the time stamp of the mutable term in the answer with the old **Breg** saved in the tabled choice point frame, we can detect whether this mutable term has been updated: it has been updated if the timestamp is greater than the old **Breg**.

5 Applications

5.1 Grammars

Although the backtrackable destructive assignment afforded by mutable terms does not in general fit well with the declarative semantics of logic programming, when used in structured ways mutable terms can be declarative in many practical applications.

As a first example, we consider grammars and their representation as DCG's. DCG's are a notation for specifying certain kinds of state transition systems. Given a DCG rule, two arguments are added to each nonterminal to thread a state, allowing each predicate to take an input state and produce a new output state. We can replace the two added variables in each subgoal with one variable whose value is a mutable term. Then each predicate can update the mutable term to indicate its effective change of state.

So for example, consider the grammar:

```
S --> Sa
S --> Sb
S --> c
```

We can write an XSB program using mutable terms to parse strings in this grammar as follows:

```
:- table s/2.
s(r1(P,a), M) :- s(P, M), match_word(M, a).
s(r2(P,b), M) :- s(P, M), match_word(M, b).
s(r3(c), M)   :- match_word(M, c).
```

where the single variable M will hold a mutable term that contains the parser's current location in the input string; M is updated during the processing of the input string.

We assume that the input string to be parsed is stored as a series of facts word(Loc, Sym), where Sym is the symbol in the input string at location Loc. With this representation, we match input symbols with the following predicate (which replaces the 'C'/3 of regular DCG's):

```
match_word(M,Word) :- get_mutable(Loc,M),
                      word(Loc,Word),
                      Loc1 is Loc+1,
                      update_mutable(Loc1,M).
```

All that remains is to create and initialize the mutable term, call the parser, and on return check that the entire string has indeed been parsed.

With the table declaration, this XSB program will correctly process the left-recursive grammar, using the mechanisms described above to store and retrieve mutable terms from tables.

This example shows how mutable terms provide another way to think about and program state update problems in XSB. However in this particular case, it is not more efficient than the original DCG program. Indeed it is somewhat less efficient in that now a mutable term and its updated value must be stored in the tries instead of just two simple atoms. However, there are other examples in which the state has more complex structure and where the sharing does provide for significant performance improvement. We turn next to such an example.

5.2 Model Checking

Using the sharable properties of mutable terms, XSB programmers have more power to control the internal representation of tables, and are able to reduce the table space in their applications. This can help improve the performance of their programs in terms of both space and time.

Our implementation of mutable terms has been tested on several benchmarks in the LMC project [5], in which a system called XMC based on XSB is used for model checking [8, 3]. System or protocol specifications are coded in a language called XL and compiled into XSB code, and then XSB is used as a fixed-point engine to verify properties of the system or protocol.

As one of the benchmarks, a protocol called *leader election protocol* is modeled in a state transition system which contains a number of parallel processes. The processes can communicate with each other, and the system can perform different transitions from one state to another. Each state is represented as a compound term, $s(P_1, P_2, \ldots, P_n)$, where n is the number of processes in the system, and each P_i is a term representing the current value of process i. The transitions are coded as a number of rules for predicate `trans/3`, and `trans(S0,Act,S1)` means the system can make an `Act` transition from state `S0` to state `S1`.

To model check properties (e.g., dead-lock freedom) of this protocol, an exploration of the entire state-space of the system is required. A tabled predicate `reachable/1` is called to find all the reachable states starting from an initial state:

```
:- table reachable/1.
reachable(S) :- startstate(S).
reachable(S) :- reachable(S0), trans(S0,_,S).
```

Note that since `trans/3` may contain recursive structure, it has to be tabled. As the number of processes in the system increases, the numbers of possible transitions and the reachable states increase rapidly. The total table space allocated for the subgoal tables and answer tables for `reachable/1` and `trans/3` increases from about 138KB (for 6 processes) to 420MB (for 16 processes).

One reason for the huge space cost is that, since the call pattern of `trans/3` in the execution of `reachable/1` is always (+,-,-), all the processes in the input state are saved again in the answer table for a subgoal of `trans/3` even they are not changed in the transition. Analysis of the transition rules shows that, in each transition, only one or two processes are

Number of processes		6	8	10	12	14	16
Table space (MB)	Old program	0.138	0.740	3.816	18.89	90.35	420.56
	With mutable terms	0.128	0.608	2.819	12.76	56.49	245.76
Time (Sec)	Old program	0.02	0.11	0.53	2.34	11.47	51.28
	With mutable terms	0.02	0.08	0.42	1.92	9.07	40.78

Table 1: Space and time performance (process size = 4)

changed. Thus, the subgoal table and answer table of predicate trans/3 contain much redundant information.

If we represent each process as a mutable term, every process is only saved once in the subgoal trie and corresponding answer trie, and only the new values of the changed processes have to be stored in the answer trie (by the *UM* nodes). Thus, by using mutable terms, we can save about 50% of the table space (if the prefix sharing of the tries and the overhead caused by mutable terms are not considered). To use mutable terms, some modifications need to be done to the original program. A trans/3 clause in the original program of the form:

```
trans(s(P₁,P₂,...,Pᵢ,...,Pₙ), Act, S1) :-
    do-some-check-and-preprocess,
    get-process-new-value(Pᵢ, NewPᵢ),
    S1 = s(P₁,P₂,...,NewPᵢ,...,Pₙ).
```

is changed to

```
trans(s(MP₁,MP₂,...,MPᵢ,...,MPₙ), Act, S1) :-
    do-some-check-and-preprocess,
    get_mutable(Pᵢ,MPᵢ),
    get-process-new-value(Pᵢ, NewPᵢ),
    update_mutable(NewPᵢ, MPᵢ),
    S1 = s(MP₁,MP₂,...,MPᵢ,...,MPₙ).
```

where MP_k $(1 \leq k \leq n)$ is the mutable term representation of process P_k. Only one process (P_i) is changed in this transition. For the transition rules where two processes are changed, similar transformations can be done. Notice that, in the above new clause, the new state S1 is the same as the old input state, so S1 can be omitted from the head and trans/3 can actually be simplified to trans/2.

Experimental results show that mutable terms indeed help save table space and speed up the program. As shown in Table 1, compared to the old program, using mutable terms we can save up to 42% of the table space and speed up the program by about 20%. The more processes, the more notable the space-saving and speedup.

It is worthwhile noting that, in Table 1, each process consists of about 4 symbols in the old program. But, to transform a process into a mutable term, two more symbols ('_$mutable'/2 and the time stamp) are added. So the overhead is about 50% for each process. When the process size is set to 16 (so the overhead is about 12.5%), we can save up to almost 60% of the

Number of processes		6	8	10	12	14	16
Table space	Old program	0.450	2.399	12.34	61.04	292.07	1359.98
(MB)	With mutable terms	0.326	1.498	6.77	29.95	129.92	554.63
Time	Old program	0.04	0.14	0.74	3.83	17.96	85.29
(Sec)	With mutable terms	0.02	0.12	0.59	2.83	13.42	61.13

Table 2: Space and time performance (process size = 16)

table space and speed up the program by about 25% (see Table 2).

6 Conclusion

We introduced the implementation of mutable terms in XSB, and showed how the XSB engine and tabling tries can be extended to support mutable terms. To keep the correct semantics, mutable terms must be shared when they are copied into and out of tables. A significant amount of work has been done to extend the tries and XSB's tabling engine.

Most importantly, we found an efficient way to save table space: by sharing terms in the subgoal tables and answer tables. Instead of supporting only prefix sharing, the extended tries can support the sharing of arbitrary terms in a single branch of a subgoal trie and the corresponding answer trie. The XSB programmers can specify which terms can be shared in the table by putting these terms into mutable terms, then the XSB engine knows which terms can be saved only once in the tables. Therefore, besides the backtrackable destructive assignment, mutable terms have more functionality in the tabled logic programming system. They provide a tool for the programmers to control the operations of the XSB engine and to improve the performance of the programs in terms of both space and time.

Acknowledgments

This work is partially supported by NSF Grants CCR-9702681, CCR-9705998, and CCR-9711386. We thank C. R. Ramakrishnan for valuable discussions and suggestions, and thank Yifei Dong for providing the benchmarks in the LMC project and translating them into code using mutable terms. Thanks are also due to the anonymous referees for their comments.

References

[1] A. Aggoun and N. Beldiceanu. Time stamps techniques for the trailed data in constraint logic programmin systems. In *Actes du séminaires Programmation en Logique*, Trégastel, France, May 1990.

[2] M. Carlsson, G. Ottosson, and B. Carlson. An open-ended finite domain constraint solver. In H. Glaser, P. Hartel, and H. Kuchen, editors, *Pro-*

gramming Languages: Implementations, Logics, and Programs, volume 1292 of *Lecture Notes in Computer Science*, pages 191–206. Springer-Verlag, 1997.

[3] B. Cui, Y. Dong, X. Du, K. N. Kumar, C. R. Ramkarishnan, I. V. Ramakrishnan, A. Roychoudhury, S. A. Smolka, and D. S. Warren. Logic programming and model checking. In *Proceedings of the 5th International Static Analysis Symposium (SAS 98)*, Pisa, Italy, Sept. 1998.

[4] T. Frühwirth. Theory and practice of constraint handling rules. *Special Issue on Constraint Logic Programming, Journal of Logic Programming*, 37(1-3):95–138, Oct. 1998.

[5] The LMC Group. The Logic-Based Model Checking Project, 1998. Available from http://www.cs.sunysb.edu/~lmc.

[6] The XSB Group. The XSB logic programming system, version 2.0, 1999. Available from http://www.cs.sunysb.edu/~sbprolog.

[7] The Intelligent Systems Laboratory. *SICStus Prolog User's Manual Version 3.7.1*. Swedish Institute of Computer Science, Oct. 1998.

[8] Y. S. Ramakrishna, C. R. Ramakrishnan, I. V. Ramakrishnan, S. Smolka, T. Swift, , and D. S. Warren. Efficient model checking using tabled resolution. In *Proceedings of the Ninth International Conference on Computer Aided Verification (CAV '97)*, volume 1243, Haifa, Israel, July 1997. Lecture Notes in Computer Science, Springer-Verlag.

[9] P. Rao. *Efficient data structures for tabled resolution*. PhD thesis, SUNY at Stony Brook, 1997.

[10] P. Rao, I. V. Ramakrishnan, K. Sagonas, T. Swift, and D. S. Warren. Efficient table access mechanisms for logic programs. In L. Sterling, editor, *ICLP*, pages 697–711, 1995.

[11] K. Sagonas. *The SLG-WAM: A Search-Efficient Engine for Well-Founded Evaluation of Normal Logic Programs*. PhD thesis, SUNY at Stony Brook, 1996.

[12] K. Sagonas and T. Swift. An abstract machine for tabled execution of fixed-order stratified logic programs. *ACM Transactions on Programming Languages and Systems*, 20(3):586–634, May 1998.

[13] K. Sagonas, T. Swift, and D. S. Warren. An abstract machine for fixed-order stratified programs. In *Proc. of 13th Conference on Automated Deduction.*, pages 328–342, 1996.

[14] D. S. Warren. Efficient Prolog memory management for flexible control. In *ILPS*, pages 198–202, 1984.

Concurrency in Prolog Using Threads and a Shared Database*

Manuel Carro
mcarro@fi.upm.es

Manuel Hermenegildo
herme@fi.upm.es

School of Computer Science, T.U. Madrid (UPM)

Abstract

Concurrency in Logic Programming has received much attention in the past. One problem with many proposals, when applied to Prolog, is that they involve large modifications to the standard implementations, and/or the communication and synchronization facilities provided do not fit as naturally within the language model as we feel is possible. In this paper we propose a new mechanism for implementing synchronization and communication for concurrency, based on atomic accesses to designated facts in the (shared) database. We argue that this model is comparatively easy to implement and harmonizes better than previous proposals within the Prolog control model and standard set of built-ins. We show how in the proposed model it is easy to express classical concurrency algorithms and to subsume other mechanisms such as Linda, variable-based communication, or classical parallelism-oriented primitives. We also report on an implementation of the model and provide performance and resource consumption data.

1   Introduction

Concurrency has been studied in the context of a wide range of programming paradigms, and many different mechanisms have been devised for expressing concurrent computations in procedural programming languages [4]. In this paper we are interested in developing a model of concurrency for Prolog. In fact, concurrency has also received much attention in the context of logic languages. However, most previous proposals have the drawback that they either involve large modifications to standard Prolog implementations, and/or the communication and synchronization facilities provided do not fit as naturally within the Prolog language model as we feel is possible.

One approach to concurrency is represented by the family of *concurrent logic languages*, which includes PARLOG, Concurrent Prolog, Guarded Horn Clauses, Janus, and others (see [25, 30] and their references). These languages share a number of characteristics. First, concurrency is implicit, i.e., every literal in a clause body represents a concurrent process. While this can be attractive in principle, it can cause an unnecessarily high number of processes to be generated, and can also make it difficult to write sequential code. Consequently, we feel that the spawning of a concurrent computation should preferably be done via an explicit language primitive (or, conversely, that the language should have an explicit operator for sequential composition of processes) [17, 8]. While there is certainly still much debate on this issue, it is noteworthy that designs which started out as implicitly concurrent languages, such as Oz [13], have opted for the explicit concurrency approach in more recent versions.

---

*This work has been partially supported by the CICYT Project ELLA, TIC 96-1012-C02-01, and Fulbright UPM-NMSU Technology Exchange Program project ECCOSIC. We also want to thank the anonymous referees for their very valuable comments.

Another common characteristic of the family of concurrent logic languages is that communication and synchronization between processes is performed by means of shared variables. This initially extremely attractive model has turned out to suffer from a number drawbacks in practice. The most important one is that backtracking has been found very difficult to implement. As a result, most of these languages have simply eliminated backtracking altogether. However, we feel that backtracking is an integral part of the Prolog control model, and that eliminating it is therefore not an option in our context.

A more recent family of languages, including Andorra-I [24] and AKL [18] directly addresses the backtracking problem. In Andorra-I, choices are suspended until a deterministic path can be taken. AKL allows *encapsulated search* while, at the same time, communicating deterministic bindings outside such encapsulated operations. While these very interesting proposals solve to some extent the backtracking problem, they still have what we perceive as drawbacks in our context: apart from supporting the implicit concurrency approach, they require quite specialized implementation technology, particularly with regard to the representation of variables (which sometimes also results in a slowdown of sequential execution). As a result, they require what would be major changes to standard Prolog abstract machines, which are almost invariably based on the WAM [1, 31]. Also, the operational semantics of these models (specially in the case of AKL) are far removed from that of Prolog and it does not appear straightforward to adapt the related ideas to Prolog without affecting the language in a significant way.

Another interesting approach to concurrency is to use the capabilities of parallel Prolog implementations such as &-Prolog [16], Aurora [22], MUSE [2], ACE [12], etc. These systems proved early on that it is possible to construct very efficient multi-worker (i.e., multi-thread) Prolog engines. While these systems were designed with parallelism in mind, they contain many useful basic building blocks for a concurrent system. In fact, some of these engines have been used for some time now to implement concurrent applications (e.g., Aurora in [28]) or even fully concurrent and distributed Prolog systems (e.g., &-Prolog in [8, 15], which uses explicit creation of threads and a combination of a blackboard and marked shared variables for communication). Our approach builds on these experiences, but tries to improve on them in several areas. First, from the engine point of view, although these systems were all designed as extensions of the WAM, we feel that for practical purposes a model that requires smaller modifications to the WAM is useful. Furthermore, we are interested in finding better solutions to the communication and synchronization among threads.

The difficulties associated with shared variable-based communication have led to the development of other communication and synchronization primitives. One of them is *ports* [18], used for example by MT-SICStus [10]. MT-SICStus implements a relatively simple design, some aspects of which are derived from Erlang [3]. Threads can be spawned (with an initial goal) and killed. They can also send and receive fresh copies of terms, using a single port per thread. This allows creating a simple *goal server* which executes whichever goal it receives. This is certainly a quite useful model, but we feel that it can be improved upon: ports (similarly to streams) do not have a clean interaction with backtracking (what is sent down a port is not put back on backtracking), the overall model is somewhat restrictive, and the explicit codification of the above mentioned server seems to be needed for most applications. In Oz 2.0 [13] threads are started using an explicit construction which returns a value as if it were an expression. Message passing and synchronization use (in a similar way to AKL) shared variables and also an abstract data type Port, which can be shared among threads and passed to other functions/procedures, perhaps as parts of other data structures. A shared stack allows fast communication among threads. Exceptions can be *injected* into other threads. A very interesting characteristic of Oz is the caching and coherence mechanism used in concurrent, distributed execution.

An alternative to ports is to use Linda blackboards [9]. Linda is a simple but powerful concurrency paradigm which focuses on (and unifies) the mechanisms for communication and synchronization. The Linda model assumes a shared memory area (the blackboard) where tuples are written and read (using pattern matching) by concurrent processes. Writing and reading are performed through a number of primitives and are atomic actions. Reading may suspend if the requested tuple is not present in the blackboard, this being the main synchronization mechanism. This approach has been made available either natively or as libraries in several logic programming systems (e.g., [6, 27, 8, 15, 29, 5]). A practical example of this approach is the BinProlog-based Jinni system [29]. Jinni has a relatively rich set of primitives for creating threads (called *engines*), also providing them with a starting goal and means for recovering the answers returned. Obtaining multiple answers from an engine is possible by asking the engine, until this call finally fails. Coordination among engines is achieved using a Linda-style set of primitives, which access and modify a shared blackboard. These operations allow writing and reading (with pattern matching) from the blackboard, and gathering in a list and at once all the tuples which match a pattern. A form of constraint-based synchronization is also available, as well as the possibility of migrating computations to remote places. Jinni is quite attractive, but still the main means for communication, the blackboard, is an external object to the Prolog model.

Although the approaches proposed to date are undoubtedly interesting and useful, we feel that they either do not provide all the features we perceive as most interesting in a practical concurrent Prolog system or they require complex implementations. The main novelty of the model we present in this paper is that both communication and synchronization are based on concurrent, atomic accesses to the shared Prolog database, which we argue can be used in the same way as a blackboard. We will show that, apart from the conceptual simplification, this choice creates very useful synergies in the overall language design, while remaining reasonably easy to implement. In our approach, an extension of the assert/retract family of Prolog calls allows suspension on calls and redos. We show that these primitives, when combined with the Prolog module system, have the same or richer functionality than blackboard-based systems, while fitting well within the Prolog model: they offer full unification instead of pattern matching on tuples and provide a clean interaction with Prolog control, naturally supporting backtracking. The model, as described in this paper, is available in the current distribution of CIAO (a next-generation, public domain Prolog system – see http://www.clip.dia.fi.upm.es/Software).

2   A First Level Interface

As mentioned before, the significant effort realized by the logic programming community in building parallel Prolog systems has proven that it is possible to construct sophisticated and very efficient multi-worker Prolog engines. However, it is also true that the inherent complication of these systems has prevented their availability as part of mainstream Prolog systems (with the possible exception of SICStus/MUSE, and, to a more limited extent, &-Prolog, Aurora, Andorra-I, and ACE). One of our main objectives in the design of the proposed concurrency model has been to simplify the low-level implementation, i.e., the modifications to the Prolog *engine* required, in order to make it as easy as possible to incorporate into an existing WAM-based Prolog system. Such simplicity should also result in added robustness.

With this in mind, we start by defining a set of basic building blocks for concurrency which we argue can be efficiently implemented with small effort. We will then stack higher-level functionality as abstractions over these basic building blocks.

2.1 Primitives for Creating Threads

A thread corresponds conceptually to an independent Prolog evaluator, capable of executing a Prolog goal to completion in a local environment, i.e., unaffected by other threads. It is related to the notion of *agent* [16] or *worker* [22, 2] used in parallel logic programming systems.

Basic Thread Creation and Management: Thread creation is performed by calling launch_goal/2, which is similar in spirit to the &/1 operators of &-Prolog, the spawn of MT-SICStus, or the new_engine of BinProlog. A call to launch_goal(Goal, GoalHandle) first copies Goal and its arguments to the address space of a new thread and returns a *handle* in GoalHandle which allows the creating thread to have (restricted) control of and access to the state of the created thread. Execution of Goal then proceeds in the new thread within an independent environment. An exception may be raised if the spawning itself is not successful, but otherwise no further communication or synchronization with the caller occurs until a call to join_goal(GoalHandle) is made, unless explicitly programmed using the synchronization and communication primitives (Section 2.2).

A call to join_goal(GoalHandle) waits for the success or failure of the goal corresponding to GoalHandle. If a solution is found by the concurrent goal, this goal can at a later time be forced to backtrack and produce another solution (or fail) using backtrack_goal(GoalHandle). When no more solutions are needed from a given goal, the builtin release_goal(GoalHandle) must be called to release the corresponding thread. This also frees the memory areas used during the execution of the goal, and makes them available for other goals.

A number of specializations of launch_goal/2 are useful in practice. A simplified version launch_goal(Goal) causes Goal to be executed to completion (first solution or failure) in a new thread, which (conceptually) then dies silently. This behavior is useful when the created thread is to run completely detached from its parent, or when all the communication is performed using the communication / synchronization primitives (Section 2.2). There are also other primitives, such as kill_goal(GoalHandle), which kills the thread executing that goal and releases the memory areas taken up by it, which are useful in practice to handle exceptions and recover from errors.

Implementation Issues and Performance: The implementation requires the Prolog engine to be *reentrant*, i.e., several invocations of the engine code must be able to proceed concurrently with separate states. The modifications required are well understood from the parallel Prolog implementation work (we follow [16]).

A concurrent goal is launched by copying it with fresh, new variables, to the storage areas of a separate *engine*, which has its own working storage (*stack set*[1]) and attaching a thread (*agent*) to this stack set. The code area is shared and visible by all engines. Goal copying ensures that execution is completely local to the receiving WAM. This avoids many complications related to the concurrent binding and unbinding (on backtracking) of shared variables, since bindings/trailing, backtracking, and garbage collection are always local to a WAM, and thus need no changes with respect to the original, single-threaded implementation.

An important issue is how to handle goals which are suspended (e.g., are waiting at a *join*, or have executed other primitives which may cause suspension, to be described later) and goals which have returned a solution but are waiting to be joined. This issue was studied in [14, 26]. There are two basic solutions: one is to *freeze* the corresponding stack set, which then cannot be used until the goal is resumed. The same occurs with a stack set containing the execution of a goal which has produced a solution but has pending alternatives. When this stack set

---

[1]The memory areas used by a WAM, which are usually managed using a stack policy.

324

Thread creation	Engine coupling	Engine creation
2.03 ms / 702 LI	3.16 ms / 1091 LI	10.3 ms / 3579 LI

Table 1: Profile of engine and thread creation (average for 800 threads).

is asked for another alternative a thread attaches to it and forces backtracking. This approach has the advantage of great simplicity at the cost of some memory consumption: it causes memory areas of the WAM (the upper parts of frozen stack sets) to be unused, since a new WAM is created for every new goal if the other WAMs are frozen and cannot be reused. WAMs are reused when a goal detaches after completion or when they are explicitly freed via a call to release_goal/1, in which case they are left empty and ready to execute another goal. The alternative is to reuse frozen stacks using *markers* to separate executions corresponding to different concurrent goals [14, 26]. This can be more efficient in memory consumption, but is also more complicated to implement. We have implemented an intermediate approach which is possible if the stacks in the engine can be resized dynamically. We start with very small stacks which are expanded automatically as needed. This has allowed us to run quite large benchmarks with a considerable number of threads without running into memory exhaustion problems. It is also possible to shrink the stacks upon goal success, so that no memory is wasted in exchange for a small overhead. This is planned for future versions.

For our experiments we implemented the proposed primitives in the CIAO Prolog engine (essentially a simplified version of the &-Prolog engine, itself an independent evolution from SICStus 0.5-0.7, and whose performance is comparable to current SICStus versions running emulated code). We have used a minimal set of the POSIX thread primitives, in the hope of abstracting away the quite different management of threads provided in different operating systems, and to favor porting among UNIX flavors. All the experiments reported in this paper have been run on a SparcCenter 2000, with 10 55MHz processors, Solaris 2.5, CIAO-Prolog 0.9p75. All the measurements have been made using *walltime* clock.

Table 1 provides figures for several operations involving threads. Since the overhead per thread seems to remain fairly constant with the number of threads used, we show the average behavior for 800 (simultaneous) threads. Measurements correspond to the Prolog view of the execution: they reflect the time from a launch_goal(Goal) is issued, to the time Goal is started. Times are given in ms. and, to abstract away from the processor speed, in "number of naive-reverse Logical Inferences" (at the ratio of 345 logical inferences per millisecond, the result given by nrev in the machine used). Although these numbers depend heavily on the implementation of O.S. primitives, we feel that providing them is interesting, since they are real indications of the cost of thread management.

The column labeled "Thread creation" reflects the time needed to start a thread, including the time used in copying the goal. The column labelled "Engine coupling" adds the time needed to locate an already created, free WAM, and to attach to it, and includes the initialization of the WAM registers. The column "Engine creation" takes into account the time used in actually creating a new engine (i.e., memory areas) and attaching to it. The last one is, as expected, larger, and this supports the idea of not disposing of the engines which are not being used. These figures are also useful in order to determine the threshold which should be used to decide whether execution should be sequential or parallel, based on granularity considerations [11]. Regarding memory consumption, the addition of thread support increased only very marginally the memory space needed per WAM.

A Note on Avoiding the Copy of the Calling Goal: Copying goals on launch, despite its advantages, may be very expensive. We support an additional set of

Operation	Linda	concurrent/1 Facts	
Put tuple	`out`	`asserta/1, assertz/1`	
Wait, read tuple	`read`	`call/1`, simple call	
Wait, read, delete tuple	`in`	`retract/1`	
Read tuple or fail	`read_noblock`	`call_nb/1`	(+)
Read and delete or fail	`in_noblock`	`retract_nb/1`	(+)
No more tuples	—	`close_predicate/1`	
(More tuples may appear)	—	`(open_predicate/1)`	

Table 2: Comparing Linda primitives and database-related Prolog primitives

primitives which perform sharing of arguments instead of copying.[2] To simplify the implementation and avoid a performance impact on sequential execution, concurrent accesses to the shared variables are not protected. The programmer has to ensure correct, locked accesses to them, including the effects of backtracking in other agents.

More complex management of variables can be built on top of these primitives by using, for example, attributed variables for automatic locking and publication of deterministic bindings, with techniques similar to those in [15], and incremental, on demand copying of goal arguments, as shown in [8, 20].

2.2 Synchronization and Communication Primitives

For the reasons argued previously, in this design we would like to use communication and synchronization primitives simpler to implement than those based on shared-variable instantiation. The use of the dynamic database that we propose as a concurrent shared repository of terms for communication and synchronization requires some (local) modifications to the semantics of the accesses to the dynamic database, but also results in some very interesting synergies.

Making the Database Concurrent: We start by assuming that we can mark certain dynamic predicates as concurrent by using a `concurrent/1` declaration. The implication is that these predicates can be updated concurrently and atomically by different threads. We also assume for simplicity that these predicates will only contain facts, i.e., they are `data/1` predicates in the sense of [7] and Ciao (this makes them faster and helps global analysis). Finally, we assume that if a concurrent predicate is called and no matching fact exists at that time in the database, then the calling thread *suspends* and is resumed only when such a matching fact appears (i.e., is asserted by a different thread, instead of failing). With these assumptions, there is a relationship between the Linda primitives (Table 2, middle column) and the Prolog *assert/retract/call* family of builtins in the context of concurrent predicates (right column). The first three Linda operations, out/read/in, have now clear counterparts in terms both of information sharing and synchronization. In the following example:

```
:- concurrent state/1.
p:- launch_goal(q),              q:- <...produce Result...>, !,
    state(X), !,                     asserta(state(correct(Result))).
    (X = failed -> ... ; ...).   q:- asserta(state(failed)).
```

p launches predicate q and waits for notification of its final state, which may be a Result or a *failed* state (the use of the Prolog cuts will be clarified further later). Making the dynamic predicate `state/1` be concurrent ensures atomic updates and the suspension of the call to `state(X)` in p.

---

[2]That is, as long as the goals are being executed in the same machine (Section 3).

One interesting difference with Linda primitives appears at this point: it is clear that we may want to be able to backtrack into a call to a concurrent predicate (such as the one to state(X) above). The behavior on backtracking of calls to concurrent predicates is as follows: if an alternative unifying fact exists in the database, then the call matches with it and proceeds forward again. If no such fact exists, then execution suspends until one is asserted. This is the natural extension of the behavior when the predicate is called the first time, and makes sense in our concurrent environment where facts of this predicate can be generated by another thread and may appear at any time. It allows, for example, implementing producer-consumer relations using simple failure-driven loops. In the following temperature example a thread accesses a device for making temperature readings, and asserts these, while a concurrent reader accesses them in a failure driven loop as they become available.

```
:- concurrent temp/1.
temperature:- launch_goal(read_temp), produce_temp.
produce_temp:-                      read_temp:- temp(Temp),
    ( read_temp_device(Temp) ->       ( Temp = end ->
        assertz(temp(Temp)),              true
        produce_temp                  ; <...work with Temp...>,
    ; assertz(temp(end)) ).               fail ).
```

When no more temperature readings are possible, read_temp_device/1 fails and the end token, instead of a a temperature, is stored, which causes the reader to exit. Conceptually, when backtracking is performed, the *next clause pointer* moves downwards in the clauses of the temp/1 predicate until the last fact is reached. Then, the calling thread waits for more facts to appear. Note that assertion is done using assertz/1, which adds new clauses at the end of the predicate, so that they can be seen by the reader waiting for them. If asserta/1 were used, newly added facts would not be visible, and thus the reader would not wake up and read the new data available. Also, note that the data produced remains, so that other readers could process it as well by backtracking over it. For example, assume the temperature asserted has the time of the reading associated with it. Different readers can then to consult the temperature at a given time concurrently, suspending if the temperature for the desired time has not been posted yet. Alternatively, if the call to temp(Temp) above is replaced with a call to retract(temp(Temp)), then each consumer will eliminate a piece of data which will then not be seen by the other consumers. This is useful for example for implementing a task scheduler, where consumers "steal" a task which will then not be performed by others.

The concurrent database thus allows representing a changing outside world in a way that is similar to other recent proposals in computational logic, such as condition-action rules [19]. A sequence of external states can be represented by a predicate to which a series of suitably timestamped facts are added monotonically, as in the temperature sensor example above. Processes can sense this state and react to it or suspend waiting for a given outside event to happen.

One nice characteristic of the approach, apart from naturally supporting back-tracking, is that many concurrent programs using shared facts are very similar to the non-concurrent ones. There is, however, a subtle difference which must be taken into account: when calling standard, non-concurrent facts with alternatives, the choicepoint disappears when the last fact is accessed. In the reader the "last fact" was assumed to be that with the "end" token, but this did not make the choicepoint pushed in by the access to the database go away. A failure at a later point of the reader would cause it to backtrack to this choicepoint, and probably suspend — which may or may not be desired. Getting around this behavior is possible by simply putting an explicit cut at the point in which we decide that no more facts are needed (i.e., the communication channel has been conceptually closed), so that the dynamic concurrent choicepoint is removed. This is the reason for the cut in the first example of synchronization: we just wanted to wait for a fact to be present, and then we did not want to leave the choicepoint lying around.

Closing Concurrent Predicates: There are cases in which we prefer failure instead of suspension, if no matching is possible. This can be achieved in two ways. The first one is using non-blocking (_nb) versions of the retract and call primitives (marked + in Table 2), which fail instead of suspending, while still ensuring atomic accesses and updates. The second, and more interesting one, is explicitly *closing* the predicate using close_predicate/1. This states that all alternatives for the predicate have been produced, and any reader backtracking over the *last* asserted fact will then fail rather than suspending. The example can now be coded as:

```
:- concurrent temp/1.
temperature:- launch_goal(read_temp), produce_temp.
produce_temp:-                            read_temp:-
    ( read_temp_device(Temp) ->             temp(Temp),
        assertz(temp(Temp)),                <...work with Temp...>,
        produce_temp                        fail.
    ; close_predicate(temp/1) ).          read_temp.
```

where the call to temp(Temp) eventually fails after the predicate is closed. This is useful for example for marking that a stream modeled by a concurrent predicate is closed: all the threads reading/consuming facts from this predicate will fail upon the end of the data. For completeness, a symmetrical open_predicate/1 call is available in order to make a closed predicate behave concurrently again (although it is arguably best practice not to re-open closed predicates).

Local Concurrent Predicates: New, concurrent predicates can be created dynamically by calling the builtin concurrent/1. The argument to concurrent/1 can be a new predicate. Also, if the argument of the call to concurrent/1 contains a variable in the predicate name, the system will create dynamically a new, local predicate name. This allows *encapsulating* the communication, which is now private to those threads having access to the variable:

```
temp:- concurrent(T/1), launch_goal(read_temp(T)), produce_temp(T).
produce_temp(T):-                         read_temp(T):-
    ( read_temp_device(Temp) ->             T(Temp),
        assertz(T(Temp)),                   <...work with Temp...>,
        produce_temp                        fail.
    ; close_predicate(T/1) ).             read_temp(_).
```

where we could replace the higher-order syntax T(X) supported by CIAO Prolog with calls to =.. and call/n (e.g., call(T,Data)). Note that the functionality at this point is not unlike that of a *port*, but with a richer backtracking behavior.

Another way of encapsulating communication stems from an interesting synergy between the concurrent database and the module system. Concurrent predicates are, as usual, in principle local to the module in which they appear. If they are not exported, they constitute is a channel which is local to the module and can only be used by the predicates in it. The module-local database thus acts as a local blackboard. By exporting and reexporting concurrent predicates between modules, separate, *private blackboards*, can be easily created whose accessibility is restricted to those importing the corresponding module. This is particularly useful when several instantiations (objects) are created from a given module (class) – see [23].

Logical View vs. Immediate Update: A final difference between concurrent predicates and standard dynamic predicates is that the logical view of database updates [21], while convenient for many reasons, is not really appropriate for them. In fact, if this view were implemented then consumers would not see the facts produced by sibling producers. Thus, an immediate update view is implemented for concurrent predicates so that changes are immediately visible to all threads.

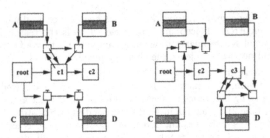

Figure 1: Choicepoints and suspended calls before and after updating clauses

Locks on Atoms/Predicate Names: A method for associating semaphores [4] to atoms / predicate names is available. Mimicking those in procedural languages, a counter is associated with each atom which can be tested or set atomically using `atom_lock_state(+Atom, ?Value)`. It can be atomically tested and decremented if its value is non-zero, or waited on if it is zero, using `lock_atom(+Atom)`, and incremented atomically using `unlock_atom(+Atom)`. The implementation is very cheap, avoiding the overkill of simulating semaphores with concurrent predicates, when only a simple means of synchronization is needed.

Implementation Issues and Performance: Concurrent accesses are made atomic by using internal, user-transparent locks, one per predicate. Every call to a concurrent predicate creates a dynamic choicepoint with special fields. In particular, its *next alternative* field points to the next clause to try on backtracking through an indirect pointer. All the indirect pointers from different choicepoints leading to a given clause are linked together into a chain reachable from that clause, so that any goal updating the predicate can access and relocate all of them atomically if needed (for example, if the clause is removed). Calls which suspend do not have their associated choicepoint removed, and the corresponding indirect pointers are linked in a separate suspension chain (Figure 1, left). When a thread tries to access its next alternative and no alternative matching clause exists, the thread waits on changes to that indirect pointer instead of failing. This behavior ultimately depends on whether the call was blocking or not, and on whether the predicate was closed or not at the time. We discuss the interesting case of blocking calls on open predicates.

When a clause is removed, the chain of indirect pointers leading to it is checked: some of the pointers might be moved forwards in the clause list to the next possibly matching instance (as dictated by indexing), and in some cases it can be determined that no matching clause exists. In the latter case, they are linked to the chain of suspended calls. On the other hand, every time a new clause is appended, the list of suspended calls is checked, and those which may match the new clause (again, according to indexing), are made to point to that new clause. This is performed even if the affected goal is not actively waiting on an update of the clause, but executing some other code.

Figure 1 depicts a possible state of the database before and after some clause updates take place. On the left, choicepoints **A** and **B** point (indirectly) to clause c1 as next clause to try. Choicepoints **C** and **D** point to *null* clauses, and they are either suspended, or they would suspend should they backtrack now. Let us remove c1 and add c3. The thread which adds / removes clauses is in charge of updating the affected pointers, based on indexing considerations. The call from **A**, which was pointing to c1, does not match neither c2 nor c3, so it points to the *null* clause now, and is enqueued in the list of calls to suspend. The call from **B** may match c3 but does not match c2, and its indirect pointer is set accordingly. The call from **C** does not match c3 and so its state does not change. And, finally, the

Primes	Conc	Data
5000	1511	1915
10000	2475	5204
15000	4775	9100
20000	6386	12560
25000	9061	17804
30000	11900	24298
35000	13252	29450

Table 3: Sieve of Erathostenes

Fact spec	Memory	bytes/fact	bytes/arg
p/0	1264	21.57	—
p/1	1753	29.91	8.34
p/2	1871	31.93	5.18
p/4	2105	35.92	3.58
p/8	2571	43.87	2.78
p/16	3507	59.85	2.39
p(g/1)	1615	27.56	5.99
p(g/2)	1753	29.91	4.17
p(g/4)	1967	33.57	3.00
p(g/8)	2435	41.86	2.53
p(g/16)	3373	57.56	2.24

Table 4: Memory usage, 60000 facts

call from **D** might match c3, and it is updated to point to this clause.

The cut needs some additional machinery to retain its semantics. Not only the (dynamic) choicepoints in the scope of a cut should be swept away (which boils down to updating a pointer), but also the possibly suspended goals corresponding to the concurrent choicepoints must be removed. This is currently done by traversing part of the choicepoint stack, following the links to suspended calls, and removing them.

The implementation of concurrent predicates is not trivial, but we argue that it is much simpler than implementing variable-based communication that behaves well on backtracking. Also, it affects only one part of the abstract machine, database access, which is typically well isolated from the rest. In our experience, the changes to be performed are fairly local. The resulting communication among threads based on access to the database may be slower than communication using shared variables, although, depending on the implementation, reading can be faster. However, note that in this design we are not primarily interested in speed, but rather in flexibility and robustness, for which we believe the proposed solution is quite appealing. Also, in the proposed implementation the execution speed of sequential code which makes no use of concurrency is not affected in any way, which is not as easy with a shared-variable approach. Furthermore, the fact that concurrent predicates should not meet the logical view of database updates [21], eliminates the need to check whether a fact is alive or not within the time window of a call, which makes, in some cases, the access and modification of concurrent predicates up to more than twice as fast as that of standard dynamic predicates.

As an example of the impact on speed of the immediate database updates, Table 3 shows timings (in milliseconds) for a database implementation of the well-known Sieve of Erathostenes, using a failure loop to both traverse the table of live elements and to remove multiples. The "Data" column corresponds to the version which uses the CIAO data/1 declaration (which is faster than dynamic, and specialized for facts). The "Conc" row uses the concurrent/1 declaration. Clause liveness (i.e., whether a given clause should or not be seen by a given call) must be tested quite often in this case, which accounts for the performance jump. On the other hand, other patterns of accesses to database perform this liveness test quite sparingly (if at all), and benefit less from the immediate update, suffering instead from the mandatory lock of the predicates being accessed. However, the factors seem to compensate even in the worst cases since we have not been able to find noticeable slowdowns.

With respect to memory consumption, Table 4 lists average memory usage per fact and per argument for the CIAO Prolog implementation in a benchmark which asserts 60000 facts to the database. A fact p with different arguments (integers)

330

1	2	4	6	12
4327	2823	1687	1400	1625

Table 5: Adding and removing facts from a database, 10 processors available

```
:- concurrent fork/1.

philosophers:-
    atom_lock_state(room, 0),
    launch_goal(philosopher(1)),
    launch_goal(philosopher(2)),
    launch_goal(philosopher(3)),
    launch_goal(philosopher(4)),
    launch_goal(philosopher(5)),
    atom_lock_state(room, 4).

eat:- ...      fork(1). fork(2).
think:- ...    fork(3). fork(4). fork(5).


philosopher(ForkLeft):-
    ForkRight is (ForkLeft mod 5) + 1,
    think,
    lock_atom(room),
    retract(fork(ForkLeft)),
    retract(fork(ForkRight)), !,
    eat,
    assertz(fork(ForkLeft)),
    assertz(fork(ForkRight)),
    unlock_atom(room),
    philosopher(ForkLeft).
```

Figure 2: Code for the Five Dining Philosophers

was asserted, as well as a fact with a single argument, containing a functor with different numbers of arguments (integers again). It is encouraging that these figures are well behaved, as we may expect large numbers of facts asserted in the database.

Another interesting issue is the impact of contention in concurrent predicate accesses. Our implementation ensures that concurrent accesses to different predicates will not interfere with each other: Table 5 shows speeds for the access and removal of a total of 10000 facts using different numbers of threads. Each thread accesses a different predicate name, which results in speedups until the number of threads is greater than the number of available processors, when other contention factors appear. However, there is obviously some interference in the concurrent accesses to the same predicate.

3 Some Applications and Examples

We now illustrate the use of the proposed concurrency scheme with some examples.

The Five Dining Philosophers: Figure 2 presents the code for the problem of the Five Dining Philosophers, with the aim of showing how a standard solution can be adapted to the concurrent database approach. The code mimics the solution presented in [4]. Each philosopher is modeled as a concurrent goal which receives its number as an argument. Fork-related actions are modeled by accesses to a concurrent predicate fork/1. A global semaphore, associated with the atom room, controls the maximum number of philosophers in the dining room, and also makes sure that all philosophers start at once.[3] No attempt is made to record when a philosopher is thinking or eating, but this can be done by asserting a concurrent predicate recording what every philosopher is doing at each time.

A Skeleton for a Server: A *server* is a perpetual process which receives requests from other programs (clients) and attends them. Typically, the server should accept more queries while previous ones are being serviced, since otherwise the service would stop temporarily. Therefore, servers usually are multithreaded, and children

---

[3] Actually, this is not strictly needed: letting philosophers think and eat as they become alive does not change the behavior of the algorithm, but this decision illustrates the use of atom-based locks for global synchronization.

	Start thread	Gather bindings
No handle, local	`..., G &, ...`	—
Handle, local	`..., G &> H, ...`	`H <&`
Remotely concurrent	`(G &) @ S`	—
Locally concurrent, remote execution	`(G @ S) &`	—
Remote handle, remotely concurrent	`(G &> H) @ S`	`(H <&) @ S`
Local handle, remote execution	`(G @ S) &> H`	`H <&`

Table 6: Starting concurrent / distributed goals and waiting for bindings.

fork from the parent in order to handle individual requests. A simple skeleton for a server is shown in Figure 3. The main thread waits for a request and, when one arrives, launches a child thread to process it. The server itself is started within the context of a catch/throw construction which will exit the execution should the server receive any external signal.[4]

Possible internal errors of the server can be dealt with by the service/1 predicate itself, since each one of its invocations is detached from the main thread. The shared database provides a communication means in case the children have to report any data to the dispatcher.

```
main:- catch(server, _AnyError, halt).
server:-
      wait_for_request(Query),
      launch_goal(service(Query)),
      server.
```

Figure 3: A skeleton for a server

Implementing Higher-Level Concurrency Primitives: The interface offered by the primitives related to threads, locks, and database is sufficient for building many different concurrent programs, but it is somewhat low-level. For example, the number of simultaneous threads has to be controlled explicitly as part of the application code. Similarly, waiting for completion of the computation of a thread and accessing the bindings created by it need the execution of a (fixed) sequence of steps. Also, implementing backtracking over concurrent goals requires some often repeated coding sequences. Such sequences are clear candidates to be abstracted as higher-level constructs.

Using the basic primitives, we have implemented the set of concurrency and distributed execution constructs proposed in [15, 8], some examples of which are shown in table 6. Remote goals are executed in a server S, specified with the placement operator @/2 (so that, for example, G @ S means "execute G at S, wait for its completion, and import the bindings performed"). Handles (H) allow waiting for the (remote) completion of the goal, and gathering the bindings. Lack of space prevents us from including the actual implementation code, but it is easy to port the implementations given in [15, 8]. Using concurrent predicates instead of the external blackboard used there results in a simplification of the code. Significant simplifications also stem from the fact that with the proposed primitives goals which have produced a solution can be left frozen and then asked for additional solutions. Thus, concurrent and distributed goals now need not be called in the context of findall.

As a simple example, we discuss the implementation of a version of the traditional &-Prolog &/2 operator, which, placed instead of a comma, specifies that the two adjacent goals are to be executed in parallel and independently: GoalA & GoalB. This operator was implemented at a very low-level (i.e., modifying the underlying abstract machine) in the &-Prolog system [16] and in other systems [12], which resulted in very good performance, but at the cost of a non-trivial amount of implementation work. Figure 4 shows the code for our source-level implementation

---

[4]Exceptions in CIAO Prolog are installed on a per-thread basis, so every concurrent goal can have its own exception handlers without altering the behavior of the other threads.

```
:- concurrent goal_to_execute/2.
:- concurrent solution/3.

GoalA & GoalB :- new_id(IdA), assertz(goal_to_execute(IdA, GoalA)),
                 call_with_result(GoalB, ResultB),
                 (   retract_nb(goal_to_execute(IdA, GoalA)) ->
                     call_with_result(GoalA, ResultA)
                 ;   repeat, perform_some_other_work(IdA, GoalA, ResultA), !),
                 ResultA = success, ResultB = success.

perform_some_other_work(Id, Sol, Res):- retract_nb(solution(Id, Sol, Res)).
perform_some_other_work(_Id, _Sols, _Result):-
        retract_nb(goal_to_execute(Id, Goal)), !,
        call_with_result(Goal, Result),
        assertz(solution(Id, Goal, Result)),
        fail.

scheduler:- retract(goal_to_execute(Id, Goal)),
            call_with_result(Goal, Result),
            assertz(solution(Id, Goal, Result)),
            fail.

call_with_result( Goal, success) :- call(Goal), !.
call_with_result(_Goal, failure).
```

Figure 4: Code for an and-parallel scheduler for deterministic goals

which assumes that the goals to be executed are deterministic. Extending it for non-deterministic goals is easy, but makes the code too long for our space limitations. However, we will compare performance results for both the simple implementation and the one which fully supports backtracking.

In this implementation, the parallel operator &/2 assigns a unique identifier to every parallel conjunction. One of the parallel goals is executed locally, while the other is stored in the database, together with its identifier, waiting for a scheduler to pick it up. Such a scheduler is implemented by the predicate scheduler/0. To use N processors of a parallel machine, $N - 1$ threads should be created, all running initially scheduler/0. As soon as one goal is posted to the database, one of the threads running the scheduler grabs and executes it, leaves the solution in the database, and fails in order to wait for another goal. If no free schedulers are available, the main thread may find, upon completion of the local goal, that the goal stored in the database is still there. Then, this local thread picks it up and executes it locally. On the other hand, if the solution waited for is not in the database, and the goal left there from the conjunction has been taken, the main thread switches personality and tries to execute any other goals present in the database while also checking whether the solution it requires for the original goal has been posted or not.

This very naive implementation cannot, of course, achieve the same performance as &-Prolog (and this is obviously not the objective of the exercise). However, it is interesting that a correct selection of the granularity level [11] does produce speedups due to parallel execution on at least some benchmarks. Table 7 shows times (in milliseconds) for the parallel execution of the doubly recursive Fibonacci benchmark (computing the 24th Fibonacci number) using the scheduler for deterministic goals. Each column is labelled with a different granularity level, i.e., the column labeled "17" corresponds to a call which stops spawning goals from the call to compute the 17th Fibonacci number downwards. Table 8 shows results for the same benchmark using a scheduler which supports non-deterministic goals. The

333

	17	18	19	20	21	22	23	24	25
1	1289	1253	1253	1287	1266	1264	1285	1305	1309
3	463	455	480	491	524	623	533	820	1309
5	287	290	312	312	376	319	510	818	1309
7	219	220	210	244	309	318	504	823	1309
9	178	178	197	220	213	330	519	836	1309

Table 7: Deterministic and-parallel scheduler: granularity against no. of agents

	17	18	19	20	21	22	23	24	25
1	1621	1555	1530	1549	1541	1582	1584	1613	1325
3	571	570	570	588	611	746	635	1062	1332
5	367	363	380	392	453	411	617	1029	1332
7	286	290	266	299	378	393	628	1081	1332
9	246	229	247	256	262	403	633	1040	1332

Table 8: Non deterministic and-parallel scheduler: granularity against no. of agents

lower the granularity level, the more goals are executed in parallel, and the smaller they are. The speedups shown approach linearity when execution is performed at a large enough granularity level. As expected, execution also speeds up as more parallel goals are available, until a turning point is reached (at the level of granularity of 17). At this level of granularity the cost of accessing the database for copying goals and recovering the solutions exceeds the speedup obtained from parallel execution. The nondeterministic scheduler, additionally, adds an overhead to the execution, which for this benchmark case ranges from 16% to 30%, with an isolated peak of 39%—and therefore, has a higher granularity, with the "turning point" in 18.

References

[1] Hassan Ait-Kaci. *Warren's Abstract Machine, A Tutorial Reconstruction.* MIT Press, 1991.

[2] K. A. M. Ali and R. Karlsson. The Muse Or-Parallel Prolog Model and its Performance. In *1990 North American Conference on Logic Programming*, pages 757–776. MIT Press, October 1990.

[3] J. Armstrong, R. Virding, C. Wistrom, and M. Williams. *Concurrent Programming in Erlang.* Prentice Hall, 1996.

[4] M. Ben-Ari. *Principles of Concurrent Programming.* Prentice Hall International, 1982.

[5] K. De Bosschere. Multi–Prolog, Another Approach for Parallelizing Prolog. In *Proceedings of Parallel Computing*, pages 443–448. Elsevier, North Holland, 1989.

[6] A. Brogi and P. Ciancarini. The Concurrent Language, Shared Prolog. *ACM Transactions on Programming Languages and Systems*, 13(1):99–123, 1991.

[7] F. Bueno, D. Cabeza, M. Hermenegildo, and G. Puebla. Global Analysis of Standard Prolog Programs. In *European Symposium on Programming*, number 1058 in LNCS, pages 108–124, Sweden, April 1996. Springer-Verlag.

[8] D. Cabeza and M. Hermenegildo. Implementing Distributed Concurrent Constraint Execution in the CIAO System. In *Proc. of the AGP'96 Joint Conference on Declarative Programming*, pages 67–78, July 1996.

[9] N. Carreiro and D. Gelernter. Linda in Context. *Comm. of the ACM*, 32(4), 1989.

[10] J. Eskilson and M. Carlsson. SICStus MT—A Multithreaded Execution Environment for SICStus Prolog. In *PLILP'98*, volume 1490 of *LNCS*. Springer, September 1998.

[11] P. López García, M. Hermenegildo, and S. K. Debray. A Methodology for Granularity Based Control of Parallelism in Logic Programs. *Journal of Symbolic Computation, Special Issue on Parallel Symbolic Computation,* 22:715–734, 1996.

[12] G. Gupta, M. Hermenegildo, E. Pontelli, and V. Santos-Costa. ACE: And/Or-parallel Copying-based Execution of Logic Programs. In *International Conference on Logic Programming,* pages 93–110. MIT Press, June 1994.

[13] S. Haridi. A Tutorial of Oz 2.0. Technical report, SICS, 1996.

[14] M. Hermenegildo. Relating Goal Scheduling, Precedence, and Memory Management in AND-Parallel Execution of Logic Programs. In *Fourth International Conference on Logic Programming,* pages 556–575. University of Melbourne, MIT Press, May 1987.

[15] M. Hermenegildo, D. Cabeza, and M. Carro. Using Attributed Variables in the Implementation of Concurrent and Parallel Logic Programming Systems. In *ICLP'95.* MIT Press, June 1995.

[16] M. Hermenegildo and K. Greene. The &-Prolog System: Exploiting Independent And-Parallelism. *New Generation Computing,* 9(3,4):233–257, 1991.

[17] M. Hermenegildo and The CLIP Group. Some Methodological Issues in the Design of CIAO - A Generic, Parallel Concurrent Constraint System. In Evan Tick, editor, *Proc. of the 1994 ICOT/NSF Workshop on Parallel and Concurrent Programming.* U. of Oregon, March 1994.

[18] S. Janson and S. Haridi. Programming Paradigms of the Andorra Kernel Language. In *ILPS'91,* pages 167–183. MIT Press, 1991.

[19] R. A. Kowalski. Logic Programming with Integrity Constraints. In *Proceedings of JELIA,* pages 301–302, 1996.

[20] E. Lamma, P. Mello, C. Stefanelli, and P. Van Hentenryck. Improving Distributed Unification through Type Analysis. In *Proceedings of Euro-Par 1997,* volume 1300 of *LNCS,* pages 1181–1190. Springer-Verlag, 1997.

[21] T. G. Lindholm and R. A. O'Keefe. Efficient Implementation of a Defensible Semantics for Dynamic Prolog Code. In Jean-Louis Lassez, editor, *JICSLP'87.* The MIT Press, 1987.

[22] E. Lusk et al. The Aurora Or-Parallel Prolog System. *New Generation Computing,* 7(2,3), 1990.

[23] A. Pineda and M. Hermenegildo. O'ciao: An Object Oriented Programming Model for (Ciao) Prolog. Technical Report CLIP 5/99.0, Facultad de Informática, UPM, July 1999.

[24] V. Santos-Costa, D.H.D. Warren, and R. Yang. Andorra-I: A Parallel Prolog System that Transparently Exploits both And- and Or-parallelism. In *Proc. 3rd. ACM SIGPLAN PPoPP Symposium.* ACM, April 1990.

[25] E.Y. Shapiro. The Family of Concurrent Logic Programming Languages. *ACM Computing Surveys,* 21(3):412–510, September 1989.

[26] K. Shen and M. Hermenegildo. Flexible Scheduling for Non-Deterministic, And-parallel Execution of Logic Programs. In *Proceedings of EuroPar'96,* number 1124 in LNCS, pages 635–640. Springer-Verlag, August 1996.

[27] Swedish Institute of Computer Science, P.O. Box 1263, S-16313 Spanga, Sweden. *Sicstus Prolog V3.0 User's Manual,* 1995.

[28] P. Szeredi, K. Molnár, and R. Scott. Serving Multiple HTML Clients from a Prolog Application. In *Proc- of the 1st Workshop on Logic Programming Tools for INTER-NET Applications,* JICSLP"96, Bonn, September 1996.

[29] Paul Tarau. Jinni: Intelligent Mobile Agent Programming at the Intersection of Java and Prolog. In *PAAM'9.* The Practical Applications Company, 1999.

[30] E. Tick. The Deevolution of Concurrent Logic Programming Languages. *The Journal of Logic Programming,* 23(1–3):89–125, 1995.

[31] D.H.D. Warren. An Abstract Prolog Instruction Set. Technical Report 309, SRI International, 1983.

Proving Termination of Input-Consuming Logic Programs

Jan–Georg Smaus[*]

INRIA-Rocquencourt

BP 105, 78153 Le Chesnay Cedex, France

Abstract

A class of predicates is identified for which termination does not depend on left-to-right execution. The only assumption about the selection rule is that derivations are *input-consuming*, that is, in each derivation step, the input arguments of the selected atom do not become instantiated. This assumption is a natural abstraction of previous work on programs with delay declarations. The method for showing that a predicate is in that class is based on level mappings, closely following the traditional approach for LD-derivations. Programs are assumed to be well and nicely moded, which are two widely used concepts for verification. Many predicates terminate under such weak assumptions. Knowing these predicates is useful even for programs where not *all* predicates have this property.

1   Introduction

Termination of logic programs has been widely studied for LD-derivations, that is derivations where the leftmost atom in a query is always selected [1, 3, 7, 8, 9, 10, 12]. These works are based on the following idea: when an atom a in a query is selected, it is possible to *pin down the size*[1] of a. This size cannot change via further instantiation. It is then shown that for the atoms introduced in this derivation step, it is again possible to pin down their size when eventually they are selected, and these atoms are smaller than a.

This idea has also been applied to arbitrary derivations [6]. Since no restriction is imposed on when an atom can be selected, it is required that in each query in a derivation, the size of each atom is always bounded. Programs that fulfill this requirement are called *strongly terminating*. The class of strongly terminating programs is very limited.

For most logic programs, it is necessary for termination to require a certain degree of instantiation of an atom before it can be selected. This can be achieved using delay declarations [2, 16, 17, 18, 19, 22, 23]. The problem is that, depending on what kind of delay declarations and selection rule are used, it is often not possible to pin down the size of the selected atom, since this size may depend on the resolution of other atoms in the query that are

---

[*]Formerly: University of Kent at Canterbury, United Kingdom.

[1]The technical meaning of "pinning down the size" differs among different methods. This will be discussed in Sect. 7.

not yet resolved. Nevertheless, the approaches by Marchiori and Teusink [17] and Martin and King [18], and to a limited extent Lüttringhaus-Kappel [16] are based on the idea described above.

Our approach falls between the two extremes of making no assumptions about the selection rule on the one hand and making very specific assumptions on the other. We believe that a reasonable minimal requirement for termination can be formulated in terms of *modes*:

> In each derivation step, the input arguments of the selected atom cannot become instantiated.

In other words, an atom in a query can only be selected when it is sufficiently instantiated so that the most general unifier (MGU) with the clause head does not bind the input arguments of the atom. We call derivations which meet this requirement *input-consuming*.

This paper is about identifying predicates for which all input-consuming derivations are finite. Other works in this area have usually made specific assumptions about the selection rule and the delay declarations, for example *local* selection rules [17], delay declarations that test arguments for groundness or rigidness [16, 18], or the default left-to-right selection rule of most Prolog implementations [19, 22, 23]. In contrast, we show how previous results about LD-derivations can be generalised, the only assumption about the selection rule being that derivations are input-consuming.

We exploit that under certain conditions, it is enough to rely on a *relative* decrease in the size of the selected atom.

Example 1.1 Consider the usual append program, where the first two argument positions are input positions. The following is an input-consuming derivation. The selected atom is always underlined. On the right hand side, we indicate some of the variable bindings made in this derivation.

$$\underline{\text{append}([1], [], \text{As})}, \text{append}(\text{As}, [], \text{Bs}) \rightsquigarrow \qquad (\text{As} = [1|\text{As}'])$$
$$\text{append}([], [], \text{As}'), \underline{\text{append}([1|\text{As}'], [], \text{Bs})} \rightsquigarrow \qquad (\text{Bs} = [1|\text{Bs}'])$$
$$\text{append}([], [], \text{As}'), \underline{\text{append}(\text{As}', [], \text{Bs}')} \rightsquigarrow \qquad (\text{As}' = [])$$
$$\underline{\text{append}([], [], \text{Bs}')} \rightsquigarrow \square \qquad (\text{Bs}' = [])$$

When append([1|As'], [], Bs) is selected, it is not possible to pin down its size in any meaningful way. In fact, nothing can be said about the length of the (input-consuming) derivation associated with append([1|As'], [], Bs) without knowing about other atoms which might instantiate As'. However, the derivation could be infinite only if some derivation associated with append([], [], As') was infinite. Our method is based on such a dependency between the atoms of a query.

As discussed in Sect. 7, previous approaches [6, 16, 17, 18] cannot formally show termination of derivations with coroutining such as the one above.

Even though the class of programs for which all input-consuming derivations are finite is obviously larger than the class of strongly terminating programs, it is still quite limited. The following example illustrates this.

Example 1.2 Consider the following program, where for both predicates, the first position is the only input position.

```
permute([], []).                    delete([X|Z], X, Z).
permute(Y, [U | X]) :-              delete([U|Y], X, [U|Z]) :-
  delete(Y, U, Z),                    delete(Y, X, Z).
  permute(Z, X).
```

Then we have the following infinite input-consuming derivation:

$$\underline{\texttt{permute}([1], W)} \rightsquigarrow \qquad\qquad\qquad (W = [U'|X'])$$
$$\underline{\texttt{delete}([1], U', Z')}, \texttt{permute}(Z', X') \rightsquigarrow \qquad (Z' = [1|Z''])$$
$$\texttt{delete}([], U', Z''), \underline{\texttt{permute}([1|Z''], X')} \rightsquigarrow \qquad (X' = [U''|X''])$$
$$\texttt{delete}([], U', Z''), \underline{\texttt{delete}([1|Z''], U'', Z''')}, \texttt{permute}(Z''', X'') \rightsquigarrow$$
$$\texttt{delete}([], U', Z''), \texttt{delete}(Z'', U'', Z''''), \underline{\texttt{permute}([1|Z''''], X'')} \rightsquigarrow \dots$$

To ensure termination even for programs like the one above, most authors have made stronger assumptions about the selection rule, thereby neglecting the important class for which assuming input-consuming derivations is sufficient. We have attempted to formulate our results as generally as possible to make them widely applicable.

The rest of this paper is organised as follows. The next section fixes the notation. Section 3 introduces well and nicely moded programs and Section 4 shows that for these, it is sufficient to prove termination for one-atom queries. Section 5 then deals with how one-atom queries can be proven to terminate. In Sect. 6 we sketch how the method presented here could be applied. Section 7 discusses the results and the related work.

2 Preliminaries

Our notation follows Apt [1] and Etalle et al. [12]. For the examples we use Prolog syntax. We recall some important notions. The set of variables in a syntactic object o is denoted as $vars(o)$. A syntactic object is **linear** if every variable occurs in it at most once. The **domain** of a substitution σ is $dom(\sigma) = \{x \mid x\sigma \neq x\}$.

For a predicate p/n, a **mode** is an atom $p(m_1, \ldots, m_n)$, where $m_i \in \{I, O\}$ for $i \in \{1, \ldots, n\}$. Positions with I are called **input positions**, and positions with O are called **output positions** of p. We assume that a fixed mode is associated with each predicate in a program. To simplify the notation, an atom written as $p(\mathbf{s}, \mathbf{t})$ means: $\mathbf{s}$ is the vector of terms filling the input positions, and $\mathbf{t}$ is the vector of terms filling the output positions. An atom $p(\mathbf{s}, \mathbf{t})$ is **input-linear** if $\mathbf{s}$ is linear, **output-linear** if $\mathbf{t}$ is linear.

A **query** is a finite sequence of atoms. Atoms are denoted by a, b, h, queries by B, F, H, Q, R. We write $a \in B$ if a is an atom in B. A **derivation step** for a program P is a pair $\langle Q, \theta \rangle; \langle R, \theta\sigma \rangle$, where $Q = Q_1, p(\mathbf{s}, \mathbf{t}), Q_2$ and $R = Q_1, B, Q_2$ are queries; θ is a substitution; $p(\mathbf{v}, \mathbf{u}) \leftarrow B$ a renamed variant of a clause in P and σ an MGU of $p(\mathbf{s}, \mathbf{t})\theta$ and $p(\mathbf{v}, \mathbf{u})$. We call $p(\mathbf{s}, \mathbf{t})\theta$ the **selected atom** and $R\theta\sigma$ the **resolvent** of $Q\theta$ and $h \leftarrow B$. A derivation step is **input-consuming** if $dom(\sigma) \cap vars(\mathbf{s}\theta) = \emptyset$.[2]

A **derivation** ξ for a program P is a sequence $\langle Q_0, \theta_0 \rangle; \langle Q_1, \theta_1 \rangle; \ldots$ where each pair $\langle Q_i, \theta_i \rangle; \langle Q_{i+1}, \theta_{i+1} \rangle$ in ξ is a derivation step. Alternatively, we also say that ξ is a **derivation of** $P \cup \{Q_0\theta_0\}$. We sometimes denote a derivation as $Q_0\theta_0; Q_1\theta_1; \ldots$. An **LD**-derivation is a derivation where the selected atom is always the leftmost atom in a query. An **input-consuming** derivation is a derivation consisting of input-consuming derivation steps.

If $(F, a, H); (F, B, H)\theta$ is a step in a derivation, then each atom in $B\theta$ is a **direct descendant** of a, and $b\theta$ is a **direct descendant** of b for all $b \in F, H$. We say b is a **descendant of** a if (b, a) is in the reflexive, transitive closure of the relation *is a direct descendant*. The descendants of a *set* of atoms are defined in the obvious way. Consider a derivation $Q_0; \ldots; Q_i; \ldots; Q_j; Q_{j+1}; \ldots$. We call $Q_j; Q_{j+1}$ an a-**step** if a is an atom in Q_i and the selected atom in $Q_j; Q_{j+1}$ is a descendant of a.

3 Modes

In this section we introduce well moded and nicely moded programs, which are standard concepts used for verification of logic programs [2, 5, 11, 12, 13].

Well-modedness has been introduced by Dembinski and Małuszyński [11] and widely used since. In Mercury it is even mandatory that programs are well moded (possibly after reordering of atoms by the compiler), which is one of the reasons for its remarkable performance [24].

Definition 3.1 [well moded] A query $Q = p_1(\mathbf{s}_1, \mathbf{t}_1), \ldots, p_n(\mathbf{s}_n, \mathbf{t}_n)$ is **well moded** if for all $i \in \{1, \ldots, n\}$ and $L = 1$

$$vars(\mathbf{s}_i) \subseteq \bigcup_{j=L}^{i-1} vars(\mathbf{t}_j) \qquad (1)$$

The clause $p(\mathbf{t}_0, \mathbf{s}_{n+1}) \leftarrow Q$ is **well moded** if (1) holds for all $i \in \{1, \ldots, n+1\}$ and $L = 0$. A program is **well moded** if all of its clauses are well moded.

Note that a one-atom query $p(\mathbf{s}, \mathbf{t})$ is well moded if and only if $\mathbf{s}$ is ground.

Another widely used concept is the following.

Definition 3.2 [nicely moded] A query $Q = p_1(\mathbf{s}_1, \mathbf{t}_1), \ldots, p_n(\mathbf{s}_n, \mathbf{t}_n)$ is **nicely moded** if $\mathbf{t}_1, \ldots, \mathbf{t}_n$ is a linear vector of terms and for all $i \in \{1, \ldots, n\}$

$$vars(\mathbf{s}_i) \cap \bigcup_{j=i}^{n} vars(\mathbf{t}_j) = \emptyset. \qquad (2)$$

---

[2]Since the MGU is unique up to variable renaming, we may assume that whenever possible, an MGU σ is used such that $dom(\sigma) \cap vars(\mathbf{s}\theta) = \emptyset$.

The clause $C = p(\mathbf{t}_0, \mathbf{s}_{n+1}) \leftarrow Q$ is **nicely moded** if Q is nicely moded and

$$vars(\mathbf{t}_0) \cap \bigcup_{j=1}^{n} vars(\mathbf{t}_j) = \emptyset. \tag{3}$$

A program is **nicely moded** if all of its clauses are nicely moded.

Note that a one-atom query $p(\mathbf{s}, \mathbf{t})$ is nicely moded if and only if $vars(\mathbf{s}) \cap vars(\mathbf{t}) = \emptyset$ and $\mathbf{t}$ is linear. We can thus state the following proposition which follows from the definitions.

Proposition 3.1 A one-atom query $p(\mathbf{s}, \mathbf{t})$ is well and nicely moded if and only if $\mathbf{s}$ is ground and $\mathbf{t}$ is linear.

Example 3.1 The program in Ex. 1.2 is well and nicely moded in mode $\{\text{permute}(I, O), \text{delete}(I, O, O)\}$. It is neither well moded nor nicely moded in mode $\{\text{permute}(O, I), \text{delete}(O, I, I)\}$, however it can easily be made well and nicely moded by interchanging the two body atoms in the second clause.

The example shows that multiple modes of a predicate can be obtained by maintaining multiple (renamed) versions of a predicate, which differ in the order of atoms in the clause bodies. This is why some authors assume that each predicate has a fixed mode [12, 19, 24]. However, in those works, assuming a fixed mode is, from a formal point of view, a real restriction.

In this paper, assuming a fixed mode for each predicate is *not at all* a restriction. It is merely for notational convenience that we assume, in all formal statements, a "left-to-right" data flow in the above definitions. Our results generalise to multiple modes *without* having multiple versions of each predicate, since we consider derivations where the textual position of an atom within a query is irrelevant for its selection. For reasons of space, we cannot explain this in more detail, and refer to [20, Subsect. 5.3].

The following lemmas state persistence properties of well-modedness and nicely-modedness.

Lemma 3.2 Every resolvent of a well moded query Q and a well moded clause C, where $vars(C) \cap vars(Q) = \emptyset$, is well moded [2, Lemma 16].

Lemma 3.3 Every resolvent of a nicely moded query Q and a nicely moded clause C, where $vars(C) \cap vars(Q) = \emptyset$ and the head of C is input-linear, is nicely moded [2, Lemma 11].

For input-consuming derivations, the requirement that the clause head is input-linear can be dropped. It is assumed that the selected atom is sufficiently instantiated, so that a multiple occurrence of the same variable in the input arguments of the clause head cannot cause any bindings to the query. Note that requiring input-linear clause heads is a severe restriction since it rules out input arguments of the selected atom being tested for equality.

Lemma 3.4 Every resolvent of a nicely moded query Q and a nicely moded clause C, where the derivation step is input-consuming and $vars(C) \cap vars(Q) = \emptyset$, is nicely moded. *(Proof see [21].)*

For a nicely moded program and query, it is guaranteed that every input-consuming derivation step only instantiates other atoms in the query that occur to the right of the selected atom.

Lemma 3.5 Let P be a nicely moded program, $Q = Q_1, p(\mathbf{s}, \mathbf{t}), Q_2$ a nicely moded query, and $\langle Q, \emptyset \rangle; \langle Q_1, B, Q_2, \sigma \rangle$ an input-consuming derivation step. Then $dom(\sigma) \cap vars(Q_1) = \emptyset$.

PROOF. Since the derivation step is input-consuming, $dom(\sigma) \cap vars(Q) \subseteq vars(\mathbf{t})$. Thus since Q is nicely moded, $dom(\sigma) \cap vars(Q_1) = \emptyset$. $\square$

This section mainly served the purpose of recalling some well-known mode concepts. However, Lemma 3.4 is an original result.

4 Controlled Coroutining

In this section we define *atom-terminating* predicates. A predicate p is atom-terminating if (under certain conditions) all input-consuming derivations of a query $p(\mathbf{s}, \mathbf{t})$ are finite. Like Etalle et al. [12], we then show that termination for one-atom queries implies termination for arbitrary queries.

For LD-derivations, it is almost obvious that it is sufficient to show termination for one-atom queries, and it only requires that programs and queries are well moded [12, Lemma 4.2]. Given an LD-derivation ξ for a query $a_1, \ldots, a_n$, the sub-derivations for each a_i do not interleave, and therefore ξ can be regarded as a derivation for a_1 followed by a derivation for a_2 and so forth. The following example illustrates that in the context of interleaving sub-derivations (coroutining), this is by no means obvious.

Example 4.1 Consider the usual append program

```
append([],Y,Y).
append([X|Xs],Ys,[X|Zs]) :-
  append(Xs,Ys,Zs).
```

in mode $\mathtt{append}(I, I, O)$ and the query

$$\mathtt{append}([], [], \mathtt{As}), \mathtt{append}([1|\mathtt{As}], [], \mathtt{Bs}), \mathtt{append}(\mathtt{Bs}, [], \mathtt{As}).$$

This query is well moded but not nicely moded. Then we have the following infinite input-consuming derivation:

$$\mathtt{append}([], [], \mathtt{As}), \underline{\mathtt{append}([1|\mathtt{As}], [], \mathtt{Bs})}, \mathtt{append}(\mathtt{Bs}, [], \mathtt{As}) \rightsquigarrow$$
$$\mathtt{append}([], [], \mathtt{As}), \underline{\mathtt{append}(\mathtt{As}, [], \mathtt{Bs}')}, \mathtt{append}([1|\mathtt{Bs}'], [], \mathtt{As}) \rightsquigarrow$$
$$\mathtt{append}([], [], [1|\mathtt{As}']), \underline{\mathtt{append}([1|\mathtt{As}'], [], \mathtt{Bs}')}, \mathtt{append}(\mathtt{Bs}', [], \mathtt{As}') \rightsquigarrow \ldots$$

This well-known termination problem of programs with coroutining has been identified as *circular modes* [19].

To avoid the problem, we require programs and queries to be nicely moded. Recall that by Prop. 3.1, a one-atom query $p(\mathbf{s}, \mathbf{t})$ is well and nicely moded if and only if $\mathbf{s}$ is ground and $\mathbf{t}$ is linear.

Definition 4.1 [atom-terminating predicate/atom] Let P be a well and nicely moded program. A predicate p in P is **atom-terminating** if for each well and nicely moded query $p(\mathbf{s}, \mathbf{t})$, all input-consuming derivations of $P \cup \{p(\mathbf{s}, \mathbf{t})\}$ are finite. An atom is **atom-terminating** if its predicate is atom-terminating.

The following lemma says that an atom-terminating atom cannot proceed indefinitely unless it is repeatedly fed by some other atom. It is similar to [22, Lemma 4.2]. For space reasons, we cannot state the precise differences, but note that here, we do not require that clause heads are input-linear. There is a lemma [20, Lemma 6.2] which subsumes [22, Lemma 4.2] and Lemma 4.1, but using this lemma would complicate this paper considerably.

Lemma 4.1 Let P be a well and nicely moded program and F, b, H a well and nicely moded query where b is an atom-terminating atom. An input-consuming derivation of $P \cup \{F, b, H\}$ can have infinitely many b-steps only if it has infinitely many a-steps, for some $a \in F$. *(Proof see [21].)*

The following theorem is a consequence of Lemma 4.1 and states that atom-terminating atoms on their own cannot produce an infinite derivation.

Theorem 4.2 Let P be a well and nicely moded program and Q a well and nicely moded query. An input-consuming derivation of $P \cup \{Q\}$ can be infinite only if it contains infinitely many steps where an atom is resolved that is not atom-terminating. *(Proof see [21].)*

Theorem 4.2 provides us with the formal justification for restricting our attention to one-atom queries. Thus the question is how it can be shown that a predicate is atom-terminating.

5 Showing that a Predicate is Atom-Terminating

Termination proofs usually rely, more or less explicitly, on measuring the size of the *input* in a query [1, 3, 7, 8, 9, 10, 12]. We agree with Etalle et al. [12] that it is reasonable to make this dependency explicit. This gives rise to the concept of *moded level mapping* [12], which is an instance of *level mapping* [6]. $\mathbf{B}_P$ denotes the set of ground atoms using predicates occurring in P.

Definition 5.1 [moded level mapping] Let P be a program. $|.|$ is a **moded level mapping** if

1. it is a level mapping, that is a function $|.| : \mathbf{B}_P \rightsquigarrow \mathbb{N}$,

2. for any $\mathbf{t}$ and $\mathbf{u}$, $|p(\mathbf{s}, \mathbf{t})| = |p(\mathbf{s}, \mathbf{u})|$.

For $a \in \mathbf{B}_P$, $|a|$ is the **level** of a.

Thus the level of an atom only depends on the terms in the input positions.

The following concept is useful for proving termination for a whole program incrementally, by proving it for one predicate at a time [1].

Definition 5.2 [depends on] Let p, q be predicates in a program P. We say p **refers to** q if there is a clause in P with p in its head and q in its body, and p **depends on** q (written $p \sqsupseteq q$) if (p, q) is in the reflexive, transitive closure of *refers to*. We write $p \sqsupset q$ if $p \sqsupseteq q$ and $q \not\sqsupseteq p$, and $p \approx q$ if $p \sqsupseteq q$ and $q \sqsupseteq p$.

Abusing notation, we shall also use the above symbols for *atoms*, where $p(\mathbf{s}, \mathbf{t}) \sqsupseteq q(\mathbf{u}, \mathbf{v})$ stands for $p \sqsupseteq q$, and likewise for $\sqsupset$ and $\approx$. Furthermore, we denote the equivalence class of a predicate p with respect to $\approx$ as $[p]_\approx$.

The following definition provides us with a criterion to prove that a predicate is atom-terminating.

Definition 5.3 [ICD-acceptable] Let P be a program and $|.|$ a moded level mapping. A clause $C = h \leftarrow B$ is **acceptable for input-consuming derivations (with respect to $|.|$)** if for every substitution θ such that $C\theta$ is ground, and for every $a \in B$ such that $a \approx h$, we have $|h\theta| > |a\theta|$. We abbreviate *acceptable for input-consuming derivations* by **ICD-acceptable**.

A set of clauses is **ICD-acceptable with respect to $|.|$** if each clause is ICD-acceptable with respect to $|.|$.

Let us compare this concept with some similar concepts in the literature: *recurrent* [6], *well-acceptable* [12] and *acceptable* [4, 10] programs.

Like Decorte and De Schreye [10] and Etalle et al. [12] but unlike Apt and Pedreschi [4] and Bezem [6], we require $|h\theta| > |a\theta|$ only for atoms a where $a \approx h$. This is consistent with the idea that termination should be proven incrementally: to show termination for a predicate p, it is assumed that all predicates q with $p \sqsupset q$ have already been shown to terminate. Therefore we can restrict our attention to the predicates q where $q \approx p$.

Like Bezem but unlike Apt and Pedreschi, Decorte and De Schreye and Etalle et al., our definition does not involve models or computed answer substitutions. Traditionally, the definition of acceptable programs is based on a model M of the program, and for a clause $h \leftarrow a_1, \ldots, a_n$, $|h\theta| > |a_i\theta|$ is only required if $M \models (a_1, \ldots, a_{i-1})\theta$. The reason is that for LD-derivations, $a_1, \ldots, a_{i-1}$ must be completely resolved before a_i is selected. By the correctness of LD-resolution [15] and well-modedness [5], the accumulated answer substitution θ, just before a_i is selected, is such that $(a_1, \ldots, a_{i-1})\theta$ is ground and $M \models (a_1, \ldots, a_{i-1})\theta$.

Such considerations count for little when derivations are merely required to be input-consuming. This is illustrated in Ex. 1.2. In the third line of the derivation, permute($[1|Z'']$, X$'$) is selected, although there is no instance of delete($[]$, U$'$, Z$''$) in the model of the program. This problem has been described by saying that delete makes a *speculative output binding* [19, 23].

Theorem 5.1 Let P be a well and nicely moded program and p be a predicate in P. Suppose all predicates q with $p \sqsupset q$ are atom-terminating, and all clauses defining predicates $q \in [p]_\approx$ are ICD-acceptable. Then p, and hence every predicate in $[p]_\approx$, is atom-terminating. *(Proof see [21].)*

Obviously the above theorem applies in particular if there exists no q such that $p \sqsupset q$, in which case trivially all predicates q with $p \sqsupset q$ are atom-terminating.

Example 5.1 We now give a few examples. We denote the *term size* of a term t, that is the number of function and constant symbols that occur in t, as $TSize(t)$.

The clauses defining append(I, I, O) (Ex. 4.1) are ICD-acceptable, where $|\text{append}(s_1, s_2, t)| = TSize(s_1)$. Thus append($I, I, O$) is atom-terminating. The same holds for append(O, O, I), defining $|\text{append}(t_1, t_2, s)| = TSize(s)$.

The clauses defining delete(I, O, O) (Ex. 1.2) are ICD-acceptable, where $|\text{delete}(s, t_1, t_2)| = TSize(s)$. Thus delete($I, O, O$) is atom-terminating. The same holds for delete(O, I, I), defining $|\text{delete}(t, s_1, s_2)| = TSize(s_2)$.

In a similar way, we can show that permute(O, I) is atom-terminating.[3] However, permute(I, O) is not atom-terminating.

The book on the Gödel language [14, page 81] shows a program that contains a clause, which in Prolog would be written as

```
slowsort(X,Y) :-
  permute(X,Y),
  sorted(Y).
```

The meaning and the modes of the predicates should be obvious from their names, and there are delay declarations to ensure that derivations are input-consuming. The predicate slowsort is *not* atom-terminating, but it could be made atom-terminating by replacing permute(X,Y) with permute(Y,X), so that permute is used in the mode in which it is atom-terminating.

Note that according to the Gödel specification, no guarantees are given about the selection rule that go beyond ensuring that derivations for the above program are input-consuming. Hence the program is not guaranteed to terminate even for a "well-behaved" query such as slowsort($[1,2]$,Y). Even though Hill and Lloyd do not claim that the program terminates, one would still expect it to do so. However, we can modify the program as stated, and guarantee that the modified program terminates using the method of this paper.

---

[3]Here we assume that the program is made well and nicely moded by interchanging the body atoms of the second clause.

```
nqueens(N,Sol) :-              safe_aux([],_,_).
  sequence(N,Seq),             safe_aux([M|Ms],Dist,N) :-
  permute(Seq,Sol),              no_diag(N,M,Dist),
  safe(Sol).                     Dist2 is Dist+1,
                                 safe_aux(Ms,Dist2,N).
safe([]).
safe([N|Ns]) :-                no_diag(N,M,Dist) :-
  safe_aux(Ns,1,N),              Dist =\= N-M,
  safe(Ns).                      Dist =\= M-N.
```

Figure 1: A program for n-queens

Figure 1 shows a fragment from a program for the n-queens problem. The mode is $\{nqueens(I,O), sequence(I,O), permute(I,O), safe(I), is(O,I), safe\_aux(I,I,I), no\_diag(I,I,I), =\setminus=(I,I)\}$. Again using as level mapping the term size of one of the arguments, one can see that the clauses defining $\{no\_diag, safe\_aux, safe\}$ are ICD-acceptable and thus these predicates are atom-terminating. Note that for efficiency reasons, this program relies on input-consuming derivations where atoms using safe are selected as early as possible [22].

As a more complex example, consider the following program, whose mode is $\{plus\_one(I), minus\_two(I), minus\_one(I)\}$.

```
plus_one(X) :- minus_two(succ(X)).

minus_two(succ(X)) :- minus_one(X).
minus_two(0).

minus_one(succ(X)) :- plus_one(X).
minus_one(0).
```

We define

$$|plus\_one(s)| = 3 * TSize(s) + 4$$
$$|minus\_two(s)| = 3 * TSize(s)$$
$$|minus\_one(s)| = 3 * TSize(s) + 2$$

Then the program is ICD-acceptable and therefore all predicates are atom-terminating.

We see that whenever in some argument position of a clause head, there is a compound term of some recursive data structure, such as [X|Xs], and all recursive calls in the body of the clause have a strict subterm of that term, such as Xs, in the same position — then the clause is ICD-acceptable using as level mapping the term size of that argument position. Since this situation occurs very often, it can be expected that an average program contains many atom-terminating predicates. However, it is unlikely that in any real program, *all* predicates are atom-terminating.

The last example shows that more complex scenarios than the one described above are possible, but we doubt that they would often occur in practice. Therefore level mappings such as the one used in the example will rarely be needed.

Consider again Def. 5.3. Given a clause $h \leftarrow a_1, \ldots, a_n$ and an atom $a_i \approx h$, we require $|h\theta| > |a_i\theta|$ for all grounding substitutions θ, rather than only for θ such that $(a_1, \ldots, a_{i-1})\theta$ is in a certain model of the program. This is of course a serious restriction. In Ex. 1.2, assuming mode permute(I, O), there cannot exist a moded level mapping such that $|\text{permute}(\text{Y}, [\text{U}|\text{X}])\theta| > |\text{permute}(\text{Z}, \text{X})\theta|$ for all θ. That however is not surprising since permute(I, O) is not atom-terminating.

Similarly, there cannot be a moded level mapping such that the usual recursive clause for quicksort, in the usual mode, is ICD-acceptable, although we conjecture that quicksort is atom-terminating. This shows a limitation of our method. The author is currently working on ways of overcoming this limitation, but the fact remains that many predicates are not atom-terminating.

6 Applying the Method

The requirement of input-consuming derivations merely reflects the very meaning of *input*: an atom must only consume its own input, not produce it. Thus if one accepts that (appropriately chosen) modes are useful for verification and reflect the programmer's intentions, then one should also accept this requirement and regard any violation of it as pathological. This does not exclude multiple modes, that is, the same program being used in a different mode at each run.

The requirement of input-consuming derivations is trivially met for LD-derivations of a well moded query and program,[4] since the leftmost atom in a well moded query is ground in its input positions. It can also be ensured by using delay declarations as in Gödel [14] that require the input arguments of an atom to be ground before this atom can be selected. Moreover, it might be ensured using *guards* as in GHC [25]. Finally, it can be ensured using delay declarations that check for partial instantiation of the input arguments, such as the block declarations of SICStus. Note that under certain conditions, delay declarations can ensure input-consuming derivations with respect to several, alternative modes [20, Chapter 7] [22].

Consequently, this paper is mainly aimed at logic programs with delay declarations, but unlike previous work [2, 16, 17, 18, 19, 22, 23], abstracts from the details of particular delay constructs. We only assume what we see as the basic purpose of delay declarations: ensuring that derivations are input-consuming.

As we have said in the introduction, the class of predicates for which all input-consuming derivations terminate is quite limited. In an average program, some predicates are atom-terminating but some are not. In general,

---

[4]In particular, this means that it is met in Mercury [24].

one has to make stronger assumptions about the selection rule. We sketch three ways in which the method presented here might be incorporated into a more comprehensive method for proving termination. This boils down to the question: how do we deal with predicates that are not atom-terminating?

The first way has actually been developed already [22]. We have previously considered atom-terminating predicates in a more concrete setting than here and called them *robust* predicates. The default left-to-right selection rule of most Prolog implementations is assumed. It is exploited that the textual position of atoms using robust predicates in clause bodies is irrelevant for termination. The other atoms must be placed such that the atoms producing their input occur earlier.

Secondly, we could build on a technique by Martin and King [18]. They consider coroutining derivations, but impose a bound on the depth of each sub-derivation by introducing auxiliary predicates with an additional argument that serves as depth counter. Applying the results of this paper, we only have to impose this depth bound for the predicates that are not atom-terminating. For the atom-terminating predicates, we can save the overheads involved in this technique.

Thirdly, we could use delay declarations as they are provided for example in Gödel [14]. For the atom-terminating predicates, it is sufficient to check for partial instantiation of the input positions using a DELAY...UNTIL NONVAR... declaration. For the other predicates, it must be ensured that the input positions are ground using a DELAY...UNTIL GROUND... declaration. Note that according to its specification, Gödel does not guarantee a (default) left-to-right selection rule, and therefore delay declarations are crucial for termination. Note also that a groundness test is usually more expensive than a test for partial instantiation. To the best of our knowledge, there has never been a systematic treatment of the question when GROUND declarations are needed, and when NONVAR declarations are sufficient.

7   Discussion

We have identified the class of predicates for which all input-consuming derivations are finite. An input-consuming derivation is a derivation where in each step, the input arguments of the selected atom are not instantiated. Predicates can be shown to be in that class using the notions of *level mapping* and *acceptable clause* [7, 10, 12].

Most previous approaches, including approaches for programs with delay declarations, can only show termination making stronger assumptions about the selection rule [16, 17, 18]. We have argued in the previous section that knowing the predicates that terminate under our weaker assumptions is useful even for programs where not *all* predicates have this property.

This paper builds on our own previous work [22], but attempts to formulate the results more abstractly, without getting involved in the details of particular delay constructs. For example, we previously imposed a restriction that all clause heads in a program must be input-linear, which is necessary so that block declarations can ensure input-consuming derivations. In this paper, we do not impose this restriction. Hence if input-consuming derivations can be ensured without imposing this restriction, say by using guards as in GHC [25], then the results of this paper could be applied to show termination.

We have claimed that most other approaches to termination rely on the idea that the size of an atom can be pinned down when the atom is selected. Technically, this usually means that the atom is *bounded* with respect to some level mapping [4, 6, 12, 18]. There are exceptions though [8, 10], where termination can be shown for the query, say, append([X], [], Zs) using as level mapping the term size of the first argument, even though the term size of [X] is not bounded. However, the method only works for LD-derivations and relies on the fact that any future instantiation of X cannot affect the derivation for append([X], [], Zs). Therefore it is effectively possible to pin down the size of append([X], [], Zs).

In contrast, we show that under certain conditions, it is enough to rely on a *relative* decrease in the size of the selected atom, even though this size cannot be pinned down. This is crucial to show termination of derivations with coroutining. More precisely, we exploit that an atom in a query cannot proceed indefinitely unless it is repeatedly fed by some other atom occurring earlier in the query. This implies that every derivation for the query is finite.

Bezem [6] has identified the class of strongly terminating programs, which are programs that terminate under *any* selection rule. While it is shown that every total recursive function can be computed by a strongly terminating program, this does not change the fact that few existing programs are strongly terminating. Transformations are proposed for three example programs to make them strongly terminating, but the transformations are complicated and ad-hoc.

On the whole, there seems to be a strong reluctance to give up the idea that the size of an atom must be pinned down when the atom is selected. This is true even for Bezem [6]. It is also true for Marchiori and Teusink [17], who assume a *local selection rule*, that is a rule under which only most recently introduced atoms can be resolved in each step. Martin and King [18] achieve a similar effect by bounding the depth of the computation introducing auxiliary predicates. It is more difficult to assess Lüttringhaus-Kappel [16] since his contribution is mainly to *generate* delay declarations automatically rather than *prove* termination.[5] However in some cases, the delay declarations that are generated require an argument of an atom to be a rigid list before that atom can be selected, which is similar to [17, 18]. Such uses of delay declarations go well beyond ensuring that derivations are input-consuming.

None of the above approaches [6, 16, 17, 18] can formally show termination under the weak assumptions we make here, even for derivations as trivial as the one in Ex. 1.1. Apt and Luitjes [2] give conditions for the termination

---

[5] For the reader familiar with that work, it is not said how programs are shown to be *safe*.

of **append**, but those are ad-hoc and do not address the general problem. Naish [19] gives heuristics to ensure termination, but no formal results.

We have assumed that queries are well and nicely moded, which means that the atoms in the query are ordered[6] so that there is a left-to-right data-flow. As a topic for future work, we envisage to prove termination of programs where these conditions are relaxed, such as programs using *layered modes* [13]. We believe that the crucial idea will be the same as in this paper, namely that one must rely on a *relative* decrease in size of the selected atom in each derivation step, rather than an absolute one. Therefore this paper should provide a good basis for this extension.

Acknowledgements

The author would like to thank Florence Benoy for proofreading this paper, and Sandro Etalle and Pat Hill for some helpful comments. This work was funded by EPSRC Grant No. GR/K79635.

References

[1] K. R. Apt. *From Logic Programming to Prolog*. Prentice Hall, 1997.

[2] K. R. Apt and I. Luitjes. Verification of logic programs with delay declarations. In V. S. Alagar and M. Nivat, editors, *Proceedings of AMAST'95*, LNCS, Berlin, 1995. Springer-Verlag. Invited Lecture.

[3] K. R. Apt and D. Pedreschi. Studies in pure Prolog: Termination. In J. W. Lloyd, editor, *Proceedings of the Symposium in Computational Logic*, LNCS, pages 150–176. Springer-Verlag, 1990.

[4] K. R. Apt and D. Pedreschi. Modular termination proofs for logic and pure Prolog programs. In G. Levi, editor, *Advances in Logic Programming Theory*, pages 183–229. Oxford University Press, 1994.

[5] K. R. Apt and A. Pellegrini. On the occur-check free Prolog programs. *ACM Transactions on Programming Languages and Systems*, 16(3):687–726, 1994.

[6] M. Bezem. Strong termination of logic programs. *Journal of Logic Programming*, 15(1 & 2):79–97, 1993.

[7] D. De Schreye and S. Decorte. Termination of logic programs: The never-ending story. *Journal of Logic Programming*, 19/20:199–260, 1994.

[8] D. De Schreye, K. Verschaetse, and M. Bruynooghe. A framework for analysing the termination of definite logic programs with respect to call patterns. In *Proceedings of FGCS*, pages 481–488. ICOT Tokyo, 1992.

[9] S. Decorte and D. De Schreye. Automatic inference of norms: A missing link in automatic termination analysis. In *Proceedings of the 10th International Logic Programming Symposium*, pages 420–436. MIT Press, 1993.

---

[6] Or more generally: *can be* ordered (see [20, Subsect. 5.3] or the discussion after Example 3.1).

[10] S. Decorte and D. De Schreye. Termination analysis: Some practical properties of the norm and level mapping space. In J. Jaffar, editor, *Proceedings of the 15th JICSLP*, pages 235–249. MIT Press, 1998.

[11] P. Dembinski and J. Małuszyński. AND-parallelism with intelligent backtracking for annotated logic programs. In *Proceedings of the 2nd International Logic Programming Symposium*, pages 29–38. MIT Press, 1985.

[12] S. Etalle, A. Bossi, and N. Cocco. Termination of well-moded programs. *Journal of Logic Programming*, 38(2):243–257, 1999.

[13] S. Etalle and M. Gabbrielli. Layered modes. *Journal of Logic Programming*, 39:225–244, 1999.

[14] P. M. Hill and J. W. Lloyd. *The Gödel Programming Language*. MIT Press, 1994.

[15] J. W. Lloyd. *Foundations of Logic Programming*. Springer-Verlag, 1987.

[16] S. Lüttringhaus-Kappel. Control generation for logic programs. In D. S. Warren, editor, *Proceedings of the 10th International Conference on Logic Programming*, pages 478–495. MIT Press, 1993.

[17] E. Marchiori and F. Teusink. Proving termination of logic programs with delay declarations. In J. W. Lloyd, editor, *Proceedings of the 12th International Logic Programming Symposium*, pages 447–461. MIT Press, 1995.

[18] J. C. Martin and A. M. King. Generating efficient, terminating logic programs. In M. Bidoit and M. Dauchet, editors, *Proceedings of TAPSOFT'97*, LNCS, pages 273–284. Springer-Verlag, 1997.

[19] L. Naish. Coroutining and the construction of terminating logic programs. Technical Report 92/5, University of Melbourne, 1992.

[20] J.-G. Smaus. *Modes and Types in Logic Programming*. PhD thesis, University of Kent at Canterbury, September 1999. Draft available from www.cs.ukc.ac.uk/people/staff/jgs5/thesis.ps.

[21] J.-G. Smaus. Proving termination of input-consuming logic programs. Technical Report 10-99, Computing Laboratory, University of Kent at Canterbury, United Kingdom, 1999.

[22] J.-G. Smaus, P. M. Hill, and A. M. King. Termination of logic programs with block declarations running in several modes. In C. Palamidessi, editor, *Proceedings of PLILP/ALP*, LNCS. Springer-Verlag, 1998.

[23] J.-G. Smaus, P. M. Hill, and A. M. King. Preventing instantiation errors and loops for logic programs with multiple modes using block declarations. In P. Flener, editor, *Proceedings of LOPSTR'98*, LNCS. Springer-Verlag, 1999.

[24] Z. Somogyi, F. Henderson, and T. Conway. The execution algorithm of Mercury, an efficient purely declarative logic programming language. *Journal of Logic Programming*, 29(1–3), 1996.

[25] K. Ueda. Guarded Horn clauses. In E. Wada, editor, *Proceedings of the 4th Japanese Conference on Logic Programming*, LNCS, pages 168–179. Springer-Verlag, 1986.

Bounded Nondeterminism of Logic Programs

Dino Pedreschi and **Salvatore Ruggieri**
Dipartimento di Informatica, Università di Pisa
Corso Italia 40, 56125 Pisa, Italy
{pedre, ruggieri}@di.unipi.it

Abstract

The notion of bounded nondeterminism for logic programs and queries is introduced. A program and a query have bounded nondeterminism iff there are finitely many refutations for them via any selection rule. We offer a declarative characterization of the class of programs and queries that have bounded nondeterminism by introducing *bounded* programs and queries. A direct application of the theoretical framework is concerned with the automatic generation of a terminating control for a given program and query. We provide a simple transformational approach that, under the assumption of boundedness, ensures strong termination of the transformed programs and queries, while preserving refutations. Also, we outline an adaptation of an automatic termination method to the purpose of inferring boundedness.

Keywords: Bounded Nondeterminism, Bounded Programs, Universal Termination, Recurrent Programs, Acceptable Programs.

1 From Universal Termination to Bounded Nondeterminism

Logic programming is a declarative paradigm, where nondeterministic specifications can be directly executed as programs and the generation of a complete control is demanded to the underlying system. By *a complete control,* it is usually meant a selection rule s such that every logical consequence of a program and a query has a refutation via s. By Strong Completeness of SLD-resolution, any selection rule is complete in this sense. However, a stronger form of completeness is usually intended, which takes into account termination as well. By *a complete control* for a program P and a query Q, we mean any selection rule s such that every SLD-derivation of P and Q via s is finite. With this definition, the problem of proving universal termination of P and Q via a selection rule s coincides with showing that s is a complete control for P and Q. Among the classes of programs and queries that have a complete control, we recall:

- recurrent programs and queries, introduced by Bezem [4], for which every selection rule is a complete control (*strong termination*);

- acceptable programs and queries, introduced by Apt and Pedreschi [3], for which the leftmost selection rule is a complete control (*left termination*);

- fair-bounded programs and queries, introduced by Ruggieri [12, 13], for which fair-selection rules are a complete control ($\exists$-*termination*).

In particular, Ruggieri shows that fair-bounded programs and queries precisely characterize the class of programs and queries for which a complete control exists, i.e. if a complete control exists then any fair-selection rule is a complete control. In general, however, a complete control in the sense above may not exist.

Example 1.1 The ODDEVEN program:

```
even(s(X)) ← odd(X).
even(0).

odd(s(X)) ← even(X).
```

defines the even and odd predicates, with the usual intuitive meaning. The query even(X),odd(X) is intended to check whether the program defines a number that is both even and odd.

Even though the program is recurrent in the sense of Bezem [4] (which implies that every ground query strong terminates), ODDEVEN and the (non ground) query above do not have a complete control, i.e. they have an infinite derivation via any selection rule. Notice, however, that they have no refutation. □

In addition, very few systems adopt fair selection rules, due to implementation reasons.

Example 1.2 The well-known program PERMUTATION checks whether two lists are permutations of each other.

```
(p1)   perm([], []).
(p2)   perm([X|Xs], Ys) ←
           delete(X, Ys, Zs),
           perm(Xs, Zs).

(d1)   delete(X, [X|Y], Y).
(d2)   delete(X, [H|Y], [H|Z]) ←
           delete(X, Y, Z).
```

PERMUTATION and the query perm([a, b], Ys) have a complete control, e.g., the rightmost or any fair selection rule. However, it may be the case that the underlying system does not support those selection rules. Thus, we are still left with the termination problem. Notice, however, that the program and the query above have finitely many SLD-refutations via any selection rule. □

In this paper, we introduce the notion of *bounded nondeterminism* of (definite) logic programs and queries, which is adapted from a similar notion in the context of imperative (parallel) programming (see e.g., [2]).

Definition 1.3 Let P be a program and Q a query. We say that P and Q have bounded nondeterminism iff for every selection rule s there are finitely many SLD-refutations of P and Q via s. □

The relation between this definition and the notion of universal termination is tight. In fact, if P and Q have a complete control, then P and Q have bounded nondeterminism. Conversely, if P and Q have bounded nondeterminism then there exists an upper bound to the length of the SLD-refutations of P and Q. If the upper bound is known, then we can transform P and Q into an equivalent program and query that strong terminate, i.e. such that any selection rule will be a complete control for them. As an example, the programs and queries of the examples above have bounded nondeterminism.

In the rest of this paper, we offer a declarative characterization of programs and queries that have bounded nondeterminism, by introducing the class of *bounded* programs and queries. The definition is given in terms of level mappings and Herbrand interpretations, in the style of the already mentioned classes of terminating programs [3, 4, 12, 13]. Notably, the definition is *purely declarative* in the sense that neither any procedural notion is needed in order to prove a program bounded, nor the definition reflects some fixed ordering of the atoms. A direct application to termination of the proposed theoretical framework is a source-to-source transformation that yields programs and queries that strong terminate, while retaining the set of refutations. The transformation adds a counter that allows for cutting derivations at an appropriate length, which is an upper bound for the length of refutations. In practice, however, such a counter can be easily implemented at compiler-level, with the advantage that the added run-time overhead is negligible. Also, we discuss by means of an example the problem of inferring boundedness. In particular, we show how the method of Decorte, De Schreye and Vandecasteele [9], originally devised for inferring left termination, can be directly adapted to bounded programs.

Preliminaries. We adhere to the notation of Apt [1], when not otherwise specified. In particular, we assume that L is the language underlying programs. Thus, B_L is the Herbrand base on L. N is the set of natural numbers. The size $size(t)$ of a ground term t is the number of function symbols occurring in it, excluding constants. The list-length function, from ground terms to natural numbers, is defined as follows: $|f(\ldots)| = 0$ if $f \neq [.|.]$, $|[x|t]| = 1 + |t|$ otherwise. In particular, for a ground list $[t_1, \ldots, t_n]$ the list-length is n. $ground_L(P)$ denotes the set of ground instances of clauses from the program P. Analogously, $ground_L(Q)$ denotes the set of ground instances of the query Q.

2 Bounded Programs

We use a generalization of level mappings, and of the ordering relation over naturals.

Definition 2.1 An *extended level mapping* is a function $|\ | : B_L \to N^\infty$ of ground atoms to N^∞, where $N^\infty = N \cup \{\infty\}$. For $A \in B_L$, $|A|$ is called the level of A. □

Level mappings play the role of terminating functions. However, in contrast to the more standard definition (see e.g. [4]), we included ∞ in the codomain of extended level mappings. The rationale is to use ∞ as a means to model uninteresting instances of program clauses and queries. First, we need to extend the $>$ order on naturals to a relation $\triangleright$ on N^∞.

Definition 2.2 We define the relation $n \triangleright m$ for $n, m \in N^\infty$ as follows:

$$n \triangleright m \quad \text{iff} \quad n = \infty \text{ or } n > m.$$

We write $n \trianglerighteq m$ iff $n \triangleright m$ or $n = m$. □

With this definition, $\infty \triangleright \infty$ and $\infty \triangleright n$ for any $n \in N$ hold. Thus ∞ models the level of uninteresting ground atoms. The need for reasoning on a subset of B_L is motivated by the fact that logic programs are untyped, and then queries may have instances that in the intended interpretation of the programmer are unintended, or ill-typed. Another reason for introducing ∞ is the fact that a program may have bounded nondeterminism for a proper subset of (ground) queries only. Therefore, ∞ allows for modeling the absence of bounded nondeterminism.

Let us introduce a class of programs and queries that will be shown to be a declarative characterization of those that have bounded nondeterminism.

Definition 2.3 Let $|\ |$ be an extended level mapping, and I a Herbrand interpretation. A logic program P is *bounded by* $|\ |$ *and* I iff I is a model of P such that for every $A \leftarrow B_1, \ldots, B_n$ in $ground_L(P)$:

$$I \models B_1, \ldots, B_n \quad implies \quad \text{for } i \in [1, n] \quad |A| \triangleright |B_i|.$$
□

Intuitively, the definition of boundedness only requires the decreasing of the extended level mapping when the body atoms are true in some model of the program, i.e. they might have a refutation. Also, notice that proof obligations are *modular*, in the sense that program clauses are taken into consideration separately, and the notion of boundedness is *purely declarative*, in the sense that neither any procedural notion is needed in order to prove a program bounded, nor the definition reflects some fixed ordering of the atoms. Also, observe that the well-studied classes of recurrent [4], acceptable [3] and fair-bounded [12, 13] logic programs are subclasses of bounded programs (this is a declarative counterpart of the fact that if a program and a query have a complete control then they have bounded nondeterminism). The next definition extends boundedness to queries.

Definition 2.4 Let $|\ |$ be an extended level mapping, and I a Herbrand interpretation. A query Q is *bounded by* $|\ |$ *and I* iff there exists $k \in N$ such that for every $A_1, \ldots, A_n \in ground_L(Q)$:

$$I \models A_1, \ldots, A_n \quad implies \quad \text{for } i \in [1, n] \quad k \vartriangleright |A_i|.$$

$\square$

Example 2.5 Consider again the ODDEVEN program. We write $s^n(0)$ as a shorthand for $s(\ s(\ \ldots s(0)\ \ldots)\ \ )$, where s is repeated $n \in N$ times. It is readily checked that ODDEVEN is bounded by defining:

$$|even(x)| = |odd(x)| = \begin{cases} size(x) & \text{if } x = s^n(0) \text{ for some } n \in N \\ \infty & \text{otherwise} \end{cases}$$

$$I = \{\ even(s^{2 \cdot i}(0)), odd(s^{2 \cdot i + 1}(0)) \mid i \geq 0\ \}.$$

Intuitively, ∞ is the level of those ground atoms that have not a natural number as argument, i.e. ∞ models unintended atoms. The query $even(X)$, $odd(X)$ is bounded by $|\ |$ and I. In fact, since no ground instance of its is true in I, Definition 2.4 imposes no requirement. $\square$

Example 2.6 Consider the PERMUTATION program and the query $perm([a, b], Ys)$. Let us show they are bounded by $|\ |$ and I, where:

$$|perm(xs,\ ys)| = |xs|$$
$$|delete(x,\ xs,\ ys)| = |ys|,$$

$$I = \{\ perm(xs,\ ys) \mid |xs| = |ys|\ \}$$
$$\{\ delete(x,\ xs,\ ys) \mid |xs| = |ys| + 1\ \}.$$

We recall that $|t|$ is the list-length of the ground term t. The only non-trivial proof obligations are those regarding clause *(p2)*. Let

$$perm([x|xs],\ ys) \leftarrow delete(x,\ ys,\ zs),\ perm(xs,\ zs).$$

be a ground instance of that clause. If the body is true in I, then $|xs| = |zs|$ and $|ys| = |zs| + 1$. This implies:

$$
\begin{aligned}
(a) \qquad |perm([x|xs],\ ys)| \ &= \ |xs| + 1 \\
&= \quad \{\ |xs| = |zs|\ \} \\
&\quad\ |zs| + 1 \\
&\vartriangleright \ |zs| \\
&= \ |delete(x,\ ys,\ zs)|,
\end{aligned}
$$

(b)
$$|\texttt{perm([}x\texttt{|}xs\texttt{], }ys\texttt{)}| \;=\; |xs|+1$$
$$\rhd\; |xs|$$
$$=\; |\texttt{perm(}xs\texttt{, }zs\texttt{)}|.$$

(c)
$$\texttt{perm([}x\texttt{|}xs\texttt{], }ys\texttt{)} \in I \quad \textit{iff} \quad |xs|+1 = |ys|$$
$$\textit{iff} \quad \{\, |ys| = |zs|+1 \,\}$$
$$|xs| = |zs|$$
$$\textit{iff} \quad \{\, |xs| = |zs| \,\}$$
$$\textit{true}.$$

(a,b) show the decreasing of the extended level mapping as required in Definition 2.3, while *(c)* shows that I is a model of the clause.

Finally, by fixing $k = |\,\texttt{perm([a, b], Ys)}\,|+1 = |\,\texttt{[a,b]}\,|+1 = 3$, the proof obligations of Definition 2.4 are satisfied. □

3 Soundness and Completeness

3.1 Soundness

The notion of boundedness is persistent along SLD-derivations. For full proofs of the results in this paper we refer the reader to [13, Chapter 2].

Lemma 3.1 (Persistency) *Let P be a program and Q a query both bounded by $|\;|$ and I. Every SLD-resolvent Q' of P and Q is bounded by $|\;|$ and I.* □

To show that bounded programs and queries have bounded nondeterminism, we follow an approach that relies on properties of multisets over well-founded orderings (see e.g., [1]). In particular, we associates a multiset over natural numbers to every bounded query.

Definition 3.2 Let $Q = A_1, \dots, A_n$ be a query bounded by $|\;|$ and I. We define the sets $^b|Q|_i^I$ for $i \in [1, n]$ as follows:

$$^b|Q|_i^I = \{|A_i'| \mid A_1', \dots, A_n' \in ground_L(Q) \;\wedge\; I \models A_1', \dots, A_n' \}.$$

We define $^b|Q|^I$ as the finite multiset

$$^b|Q|^I = bag(max^{\,b}|Q|_1^I, \dots, max^{\,b}|Q|_n^I),$$

if $I \models \exists\,(A_1, \dots, A_n)$, and $^b|Q|^I = bag()$ if $I \not\models \exists\,(A_1, \dots, A_n)$. □

The next Lemma states that the multiset associated to queries decreases along refutations. This derives from the fact that every query in a refutation is satisfiable in any model of the program. $\succ_m$ and $\succeq_m$ denote the multiset ordering and its reflexive closure.

Lemma 3.3 *Let P be a program and Q a query both bounded by $|\;|$ and I. For every SLD-resolvent Q' of P and Q, we have that:*

(i) $^b|Q|^I \succeq_m {}^b|Q'|^I$, *and*

(ii) *if $I \models \exists\, Q'$ then $^b|Q|^I \succ_m {}^b|Q'|^I$.* $\qquad\qquad\square$

Based on this property, we can state the soundness result.

Theorem 3.4 (Soundness) *Let P be a program and Q a query both bounded by $|\;|$ and I. Then P and Q have bounded nondeterminism.* $\qquad\square$

3.2   Completeness

First, we introduce a function targeted to measure refutation length.

Definition 3.5 We define $rlength_s^P(Q)$ as ∞ if there exist infinitely many SLD-refutations of P and Q via the selection rule s, and as the maximum length of a SLD-refutation of P and Q via s otherwise. $\qquad\square$

The next lemma states that every program is bounded by an extended level mapping defined in terms of the length of SLD-refutations.

Lemma 3.6 *Let P be a program and s a selection rule. Then there exist an extended level mapping $|\;|$ and a Herbrand interpretation I such that:*

(i) *P is bounded by $|\;|$ and I, and*

(ii) *for every $A \in B_L$, $|A| \in N$ iff there are finitely many SLD-refutations of P and A via s.*

Proof. Take I as the least Herbrand model of P and $|A| = rlength_s^P(A)$. $\square$

Theorem 3.7 (Completeness) *Let P be a program and Q a query that have bounded nondeterminism. Then there exist $|\;|$ and I such that P and Q are both bounded by $|\;|$ and I.*

Proof. Consider the program $P' = P \cup \{\, \mathbf{new} \leftarrow Q \,\}$, where **new** is a fresh predicate symbol. By Lemma 3.6 *(i)*, P' is bounded by some $|\;|$ and I. Moreover, the assumption of the Theorem implies that there are finitely many SLD-refutations of P and **new** via some selection rule s. By Lemma 3.6 *(ii)*, $|\mathbf{new}| \in N$. Consider now the restrictions of $|\;|$ and I to B_L, i.e. not including **new**. Since proof obligations of Definition 2.3 are modular, it is readily checked that P is bounded by the restrictions of $|\;|$ and I. Turning the attention on Q, since $\mathbf{new} \leftarrow Q$ is bounded by $|\;|$ and I, we have that for every ground instance $A_1, \ldots, A_n$ of Q, if $I \models A_1, \ldots, A_n$ then for $i \in [1, n], |\mathbf{new}| \rhd |A_i|$. In conclusion Q is bounded by the restrictions of $|\;|$ and I on B_L, by fixing $k = |\mathbf{new}|$ in Definition 2.4. $\qquad\square$

4 From Bounded Nondeterminism to Strong Termination

So far, we have developed a theoretical framework for the analysis of bounded nondeterminism of logic programs. Next, we propose a syntactic transformational approach that prunes SLD-derivations in such a way that the SLD-tree is cut at a level that includes all refutations. This will provide us with a terminating control procedure for bounded programs and queries. For notational convenience, we denote by $\mathbf{T}$ a sequence $T_1, \ldots, T_n$ of terms, with $n \geq 0$.

Definition 4.1 Let P be a program and Q a query both bounded by $|\ |$ and I, and let $k \in N$. We define $Ter(P)$ as the program such that:

- for every clause in P

$$\mathtt{p_0(T_0)} \leftarrow \mathtt{p_1(T_1)}, \ldots, \mathtt{p_n(T_n)}.$$

  with $n > 0$, the clause

$$\mathtt{p_0(T_0, s(D))} \leftarrow \mathtt{p_1(T_1, D)}, \ldots, \mathtt{p_n(T_n, D)}.$$

  is in $Ter(P)$, where $\mathtt{D}$ is a fresh variable,

- and, for every clause in P

$$\mathtt{p_0(T_0)}.$$

  the clause

$$\mathtt{p_0(T_0, D)}.$$

  is in $Ter(P)$, where $\mathtt{D}$ is a fresh variable.

Finally, if Q is $\mathtt{p_1(T_1)}, \ldots, \mathtt{p_n(T_n)}$ then we define $Ter(Q, k)$ as the query:

$$\mathtt{p_1(T_1, s^k(0))}, \ldots, \mathtt{p_n(T_n, s^k(0))}.$$

$\square$

Theorem 4.2 *Let P be a program and Q a query both bounded by $|\ |$ and I, and let k be a given natural number satisfying Definition 2.4.*

Then, for every $n \in N$, $Ter(P)$ and $Ter(Q, n)$ universally terminate via every selection rule.

Moreover, there is a bijection between SLD-refutations of P and Q via a selection rule s and SLD-refutations of $Ter(P)$ and $Ter(Q, k-1)$ via s. $\square$

The intuitive reading of this result is that the transformed program and query maintain the same *success semantics* of the original program and query, in the sense that no computed answer is lost. It is worth noting that no assumption is made on the selection rule s, i.e. any selection rule is a complete control for the transformed program and query.

Example 4.3 Reconsider the program `PERMUTATION` and the query `perm([a,`
`b], Ys)` of Example 1.2. The transformed program $Ter(\text{PERMUTATION})$ is:

```
perm([], [], D).
perm([X|Xs], Ys, s(D)) ←
    delete(X, Ys, Zs, D),
    perm(Xs, Zs, D).
delete(X, [X|Y], Y, D).
delete(X, [H|Y], [H|Z], s(D)) ←
    delete(X, Y, Z, D).
```

and the transformed query for $k = 3$ is `perm([a,b], Ys, s`^{2}`(0))`. By Theorem 4.2, the transformed program and query provide us with a terminating
control for the original program and query independently of the selection
rule adopted, modulo the extra argument added to each predicate. □

The transformations $Ter(P)$ and $Ter(Q,k)$ are of *pure theoretical interest*.
The run-time overhead due to the arguments added to predicates can be
completely avoided in practice. A realistic implementation of the transformation can be outlined as follows.

First an extended level mapping and a model are inferred such that P
and Q are bounded, and a natural k is computed satisfying Definition 2.4
(see the next Section 5).

Then the logic programming system (usually, a compiler) associates to
every atom in a derivation a counter (that plays the role of the parameter introduced by the transformation) and adds to the pure SLD-resolution
mechanism a very simple check that restricts the search space to atoms with
associated non-negative counters. With this approach, the run-time overhead turns out to be negligible.

5 Inferring Boundedness

On a theoretical level, the problem of deciding whether a program is bounded
is undecidable (see [13] for a proof). On a practical level, however, many
(sufficient) approaches are currently available to automatically infer (usually,
left) termination. We argue that most approaches can be directly adapted
for proving the proof obligations of boundedness. In the following, we outline
the adaptation of the constraint-based method of Decorte et al. [9] to the
case of an example program.

Let us consider again `PERMUTATION`, and the query `perm([a, b], Ys)`. Consider now the problem to infer that `PERMUTATION` and the query above are
bounded by a same extended level mapping | | and Herbrand interpretation
I. Here, we make the following assumptions:

(**Assumption A1**). Every n-ary predicate symbol p is annotated with a *mode*, namely a function d_p from $\{1, \ldots, n\}$ in $\{+, -\}$. If $d_p(i) = {}'+'$ we call i an *input* position. If $d_p(i) = {}'-'$ then i is called an *output* position. We write d_p in the form $p(d_p(1), \ldots, d_p(n))$. Intuitively, a mode specifies the use of predicate arguments of p, with the intended meaning that terms occurring in output positions are determined from the computation of the terms occurring in input positions. As an example, the following are intuitive modes for the predicates of PERMUTATION and of the query above:

$$\texttt{perm(+, -)} \qquad \texttt{delete(+, -, +)}$$

(**Assumption A2**). $|\ |$ is defined as a linear combination of the list-length of the predicate arguments which occur in input positions, i.e.:

$$|\texttt{perm}(xs,\ ys)| = p_0 + p_1|xs|$$
$$|\texttt{delete}(x,\ xs,\ ys)| = d_0 + d_1|x| + d_2|ys|,$$

where p_0, p_1, d_0, d_1, d_2 denote natural numbers that need to be determined.

(**Assumption A3**) I is characterized as the set of atoms whose predicate arguments satisfy a linear inequation, such as:

$$I = \{\ \texttt{perm}(xs,\ ys) \mid p_0' + p_1'|xs| \geq p_2'|ys|\ \} \cup$$
$$\{\ \texttt{delete}(x,\ xs,\ ys) \mid d_0' + d_1'|x| + d_3'|ys| \geq d_2'|xs|\ \}$$

where $p_0', p_1', p_2', d_0', d_1', d_2', d_3'$ denote natural numbers that need to be determined. Observe that the linear inequations are syntactically derived by fixing the arguments occurring in input positions to the left of the inequation, and those occurring in output positions to the right.

Let us write the proof obligations of Definition 2.3 for clauses of PERMUTATION.

(p1) For clause *(p1)*, we have only to show that I is a model of it, i.e. $\texttt{perm([], [])}$ is in I. This leads us to the symbolic constraint:

c1. $p_0' \geq 0$.

(p2) Consider a ground instance of *(p2)*:

$$\texttt{perm([x|xs], ys)} \leftarrow \texttt{delete(x, ys, zs), perm(xs, zs)}.$$

The body is true in I iff ϕ holds, where:

$$\phi \equiv d_0' + d_1'|x| + d_3'|zs| - d_2'|ys| \geq 0 \ \wedge\ p_0' + p_1'|xs| - p_2'|zs| \geq 0.$$

Therefore, the decreasing of the level mapping from the head to the leftmost atom in the body imposes the constraint:

$$\forall\ x, xs, ys, zs \quad \phi \Rightarrow p_0 + p_1|xs| + p_1 > d_0 + d_1|x| + d_2|zs|$$

which after some rearrangement, can be written as:

c2. $\forall\, x, xs, ys, zs \quad \phi \Rightarrow p_1|xs| - d_1|x| - d_2|zs| + (p_0 + p_1 - d_0) > 0.$

The decreasing from the head to the second body atom, and the requirement that I must be a model of the clause lead to:

c3. $\forall\, x, xs, ys, zs \quad \phi \Rightarrow p_1 > 0.$

c4. $\forall\, x, xs, ys, zs \quad \phi \Rightarrow p_1'|xs| - p_2'|ys| + (p_1' + p_0') \geq 0.$

(d1) We have only to show that I is a model of it, i.e.

c5. $\forall\, x, y, \;\; (d_3' - d_2')|y| + d_1'|x| + (d_0' - d_2') \geq 0.$

(d2) The decreasing from the head to the body atom, and the requirement that I must be a model of the clause yield:

c6. $\forall\, x, y, z \;\; d_1'|x| + d_3'|z| - d_2'|y| + d_0' \geq 0 \Rightarrow d_2 > 0.$

c7. $\forall\, x, y, z \;\; d_1'|x| + d_3'|z| - d_2'|y| + d_0' \geq 0 \Rightarrow d_1'|x| + d_3'|z| - d_2'|y| + (d_3' + d_0' - d_2') \geq 0.$

A general method to solve conditional constraints $c1 - c7$ of the form above is not known. However, Decorte et al. [9] propose a method that reduces those constraints to a set of linear constraints over the variables $p_0, p_1, p_2, p_0', p_1', \ldots$. The basic idea consists of observing that $c1 - c7$ are solvable by imposing that all the coefficients appearing in the inequations at the right of the implications are non-negative (and at least one is positive in the case that the inequation is strict). However, since this *sufficient* condition is in many cases too strong, they propose to apply first a weakening of the original constraint by *nondeterministically* rewriting a constraint of the form $\forall \ldots e \geq 0 \wedge \ldots \Rightarrow e' \geq 0$ into

$$\forall \ldots e \geq 0 \wedge \ldots \Rightarrow e' - e \geq 0$$

For instance, when applied to constraint $c2$ and the second conjunct in ϕ, this rule produces:

c2'. $\forall\, x, xs, ys, zs \quad \phi \Rightarrow$
$\quad -d_1|x| + (p_1 - p_1')|xs| + (-d_2 + p_2')|zs| + (p_0 + p_1 - d_0 - p_0') > 0.$

A sufficient condition to satisfy this constraint is then to require:

$$-d_1 \geq 0, \qquad p_1 - p_1' \geq 0$$
$$-d_2 + p_2' \geq 0, \quad p_0 + p_1 - d_0 - p_0' > 0.$$

With the same approach, we derive the following constraints from $c1, c3 - c7$:

$$p_1 > 0, \qquad -d_1' \geq 0,$$
$$p_2' - d_3' \geq 0, \quad d_2' - p_2' \geq 0,$$
$$p_1' - d_0' \geq 0, \quad d_3' - d_2' \geq 0,$$
$$d_0' - d_2' \geq 0, \quad d_2 > 0,$$

where variables range over naturals. Such constraints are directly solvable by a constraint solver over finite domains – and often over boolean suffices. A solution of those constraints is the following:

$$p_1 = d_2 = p_1' = p_2' = d_0' = d_2' = d_3' = 1$$
$$p_0 = d_0 = d_1 = d_1' = p_0' = d_0' = 0,$$

which lead to the level mapping and the interpretation:

$$|\mathbf{perm}(xs,\ ys)| = |xs|$$
$$|\mathbf{delete}(x,\ xs,\ ys)| = |ys|,$$

$$I \; = \; \{\ \mathbf{perm}(xs,\ ys) \mid |xs| \geq |ys|\ \} \cup$$
$$\cup \; \{\ \mathbf{delete}(x,\ xs,\ ys) \mid 1 + |ys| \geq |xs|\ \}.$$

Notice how $|\ |$ and I closely resemble the level mapping and the interpretation of Example 2.6. Let us see now the proof obligations of Definition 2.4. Consider a ground instance $\mathbf{perm}(xs,\ ys)$ of an atomic query. We have to find out a natural k such that:

$$I \models \mathbf{perm}(xs,\ ys) \; \Rightarrow \; k > |\mathbf{perm}(xs,\ ys)|,$$

which by definition of $|\ |$ and I, can be rewritten as: $|xs| \geq |ys| \Rightarrow k > |xs|$. In the case of the query $\mathbf{perm}(\mathtt{[a,b]},\ \mathtt{Ys})$, we have then the constraint:

$$\forall\, ys \;\; 2 \geq |ys| \; \Rightarrow \; k > 2.$$

It is worth noting that it is of the same form as the constraints derived from program clauses: so, it can be solved by the same approach. In conclusion, we have that $k = 3$ is a solution, and it turns out to coincide with the k of Example 2.6.

It should be observed that, even though the assumptions **(A2)** and **(A3)** use a predefined function on terms, namely the list-length, the approach can be defined in general terms, i.e. with also the construction of those functions involved in the termination analysis. This is actually the approach of Decorte et al. [9]. We conclude by mentioning that we are currently addressing the construction of an automated tool that uses the principles outlined in this section.

6 Related Work

A comprehensive survey on termination of logic programs can be found in the paper by De Schreye and Decorte [7]. They classify three types of approaches: techniques that express necessary and sufficient conditions for termination, techniques that provide decidable *sufficient* conditions, and techniques that prove decidability or undecidability for subclasses of programs and queries. Under this classification, this paper mainly falls in the first type, with a discussion on a possible automation of the method.

The class of bounded logic programs is an extension of the class originally introduced by Ruggieri [11] in the context of semantics decidability. There, the interest on bounded programs was restricted only to properties of ground queries. In particular, a meta-programming version of the transformation *Ter* was presented, and showed correct for ground queries.

The idea of pruning SLD-derivations is common to the research area of loop checking (see e.g., [5]). While a run-time analysis is potentially able to cut more unsuccessful branches, the evaluation of a pruning condition at run-time, such as for loop checks, involves a considerably high computational overhead. On the contrary, our approach combines both the advantages of a static analysis (termination) method, i.e. the analysis is conducted once and no run-time overhead is added, with those of pruning mechanisms, i.e. not being restricted to terminating derivations. In particular, observe that, by the Completeness Theorem 3.7, bounded programs and queries are the largest class such that a pruning mechanism can find out all refutations in a finite time.

Martin and King [10] showed a transformation for Gödel programs, that shares with the transformation *Ter*, the idea of not following derivations longer than a certain length. However, compared with our approach, they rely on sufficient conditions for evaluating an upper bound on the length of refutations, namely termination via a class of selection rules called *semilocal*. Also, their transformation adds run-time overhead, since the maximum length is computed at run time.

Sufficient (semi-)automatic methods to approximate the number of computed instances by means of lower and upper bounds have been studied in the context of cost analysis of logic programs [8] and of cardinality analysis of Prolog programs [6]. Of course, if ∞ is a lower bound to the number of computed instances of P and Q then they have not bounded nondeterminism. Dually, if $n \in N$ is an upper bound then P and Q have bounded nondeterminism. In this case, however, we are still left with the problem of determining a level of the SLD-tree that includes all the refutations.

Finally, let us briefly discuss on the adaptation of the approach of Decorte and De Schreye [9] to infer acceptability. On the one hand, we have replaced the generation of proof obligations for acceptability with those for boundedness. This results in fewer proof obligations, hence fewer constraints to be satisfied. On the other hand, their notion of acceptability reasons at non-ground level (i.e., considers not-necessarily-ground instances of clauses and queries). This implies a further proof obligation, known as *rigidity* of level mappings, that is tackled separately. In our approach, the equivalent of rigidity is represented by the requirements on queries, which are tackled in the same constraint satisfaction framework of the other requirements.

7 Conclusions

We have introduced the notion of bounded nondeterminism for logic programs and queries. On the one hand, bounded nondeterminism is an extension of the various notions of universal termination extensively studied in the literature. On the other hand, programs and queries that have bounded nondeterminism can be transformed, under determinate conditions, into programs and queries that universally terminate.

We have offered a declarative characterization of bounded nondeterminism in terms of bounded programs and queries. The characterization is simple, modular, easy to apply in *paper & pencil* proofs and also suitable for automation. In particular, we have outlined an adaptation of a termination method to infer level mappings and models. Starting from them, an upper bound to the length of refutations can be computed.

By adding a derivation length counter to compiled code, we then obtain a finite search space via any selection rule. In particular, the approach is sound also for dynamic selection rules, such as Gödel's, or for static reorderings, such as Mercury's.

Acknowledgements

We are grateful to the anonymous referees for many helpful comments.

References

[1] K.R. Apt. *From Logic Programming to Prolog*. CAR Hoare Series Editor. Prentice Hall, 1996.

[2] K.R. Apt and E.R. Olderog. *Verification of sequential and concurrent programs*. Texts and monographs in computer science. Springer-Verlag, Berlin, 1997. Second edition.

[3] K.R. Apt and D. Pedreschi. Reasoning about termination of pure prolog programs. *Information and computation*, 106(1):109–157, 1993.

[4] M.A. Bezem. Strong Termination of Logic Programs. *Journal of Logic Programming*, 15(1 & 2):79–98, 1993.

[5] R.N. Bol, K.R. Apt, and J.W. Klop. An analysis of loop checking mechanism for logic programs. *Theoretical Computer Science*, 86(1):35–79, 1991.

[6] C. Braema, B. Le Charlier, S. Modart, and P. Van Hentenryck. Cardinality analysis of prolog. In M. Bruynooghe, editor, *Proceedings of the 1994 International Logic Programming Symposium*, pages 457—471, 1994.

[7] D. De Schreye and S. Decorte. Termination of logic programs: the never-ending story. *Journal of Logic Programming*, 19-20:199–260, 1994.

[8] S. K. Debray and N. W. Lin. Cost analysis of logic programs. *ACM Toplas*, 15(5):826–875, 1993.

[9] S. Decorte, D. De Schreye, and H. Vandecasteele. Constraint-based Automatic Termination Analysis for Logic Programs. *ACM Toplas*, To appear. Preliminary version in ICLP 1997.

[10] J. Martin and A. King. Generating Efficient, Terminating Logic Programs. In *Proceedings of TAPSOFT'97*, number 1214 in Lecture Notes in Computer Science, pages 273–284, 1997.

[11] S. Ruggieri. Decidability of Logic Program Semantics and Applications to Testing. In *Proc. of PLILP'96*, number 1140 in Lecture Notes in Computer Science, pages 347–362. Springer-Verlag, Berlin, 1996.

[12] S. Ruggieri. ∃-Universal Termination of Logic Programs. Technical Report 98-02, Dipartimento di Informatica, Università di Pisa, 1998. To appear in *Theoretical Computer Science*.

[13] S. Ruggieri. *Verification and Validation of Logic Programs*. PhD thesis TD 6/99, Dipartimento di Informatica, Università di Pisa, March 1999.

Termination Analysis for Abductive General Logic Programs

Sofie Verbaeten
Department of Computer Science, K.U.Leuven
Celestijnenlaan 200A, B-3001 Heverlee, Belgium.
sofie.verbaeten@cs.kuleuven.ac.be

Abstract

We present an extension of the methods of Apt and Bezem for proving termination of general logic programs, to the case of abductive general logic programs. We consider programs executed under SLDNFA resolution, an abductive extension of SLDNF proposed by Denecker and De Schreye, w.r.t. an arbitrary safe selection rule. We show that the termination conditions for SLDNF of Apt and Bezem, namely acyclicity of the program and boundedness of the query, are not sufficient for ensuring termination of SLDNFA. A third syntactical condition, namely abductive nonrecursivity of the program and query, is proposed which prevents the abduction of an infinite number of abducible atoms. Acyclicity of the program, boundedness of the query and abductive nonrecursivity of the program and query form our sufficient termination condition for SLDNFA. By the best of our knowledge, this is the first work on termination of an abductive procedure for general logic programs.

1 Introduction

The role of abduction as a reasoning paradigm in AI is widely accepted. Abduction is a form of reasoning which, given a knowledge base and an observation Q, finds possible explanations of Q in terms of a particular set of predicates, called the abducible predicates. In the context of logic programming, abductive procedures have been used for planning, knowledge assimilation and belief revision, database updating, reasoning in the context of temporal domains with uncertainty, ... (we refer to [5] for references to such works). In [5], Denecker and De Schreye present an abductive extension of SLDNF [1], called SLDNFA. We investigate the termination behaviour of abductive general logic programs executed under SLDNFA w.r.t. an arbitrary safe selection rule. We show that the termination conditions for SLDNF of Apt and Bezem [2], namely acyclicity of the program and boundedness of the query w.r.t. a level mapping, are not sufficient for ensuring termination of SLDNFA. In particular, these conditions do not prevent that, in an SLDNFA-derivation, an infinite number of abducible atoms are abduced. We propose a third, syntactical condition, namely abductive nonrecursivity of the program and query. This condition together with the acyclicity of the program and boundedness of the query are sufficient for proving termination of an SLDNFA-derivation using a safe selection rule. For definite programs and queries as well as for programs and queries without abducible predicates, the condition of abductive nonrecursivity is trivially satisfied. So, in these cases, termination of SLDNFA is implied by the acyclicity of the program and boundedness of the query. By the best of our knowledge, this is the first work on termination of an abductive procedure for general logic programs.

Besides SLDNFA, a number of other abductive extensions of SLDNF resolution have been proposed. However, as discussed in [5], either these procedures have not been formalized and proved correct, or they can be proved correct only for a restricted class of abductive logic programs, or they do not provide a way of checking the consistency of the abductive answers, or they do not provide a treatment for floundering abduction (which is an analog problem of the negation floundering problem and arises when a nonground abductive atom is selected). An exception is the iff procedure of [6]. SLDNFA and iff are in many respects complementary. However, while SLDNFA is formalized in a logic programming style, iff is formalized as a rewrite procedure using completion. We refer to [5] for a formal discussion on these works and a detailed comparison with SLDNFA.

After a section of preliminaries, we recall in Section 3 the SLDNFA proof procedure as defined in [5]. In Section 4, we present a sufficient termination condition, extending the condition of [2], for SLDNFA executed under an arbitrary safe selection rule. We conclude in Section 5. We refer to the full version of the paper, [8], for all the proofs, more details and more examples.

2 Preliminaries

We assume familiarity with the basic concepts of logic programming [7]. Throughout the paper, P will denote a general logic program based on an alphabet Σ. With $ground_\Sigma(P)$ we denote the set of Σ-ground instances of clauses of P. Let $\Sigma^p \subset \Sigma$ denote the set of predicate symbols of Σ. With U_P, resp. B_P, we denote the *Herbrand Universe*, resp. *Herbrand Base*, associated with (Σ underlying) P. With $\neg B_P$ we denote the set of negative ground literals $\{\neg A \mid A \in B_P\}$.

Let $p, q \in \Sigma^p$. We say that p *refers to* q in P iff there is a clause in P with p in the head and q occurring in the body. When necessary, we distinguish between two kinds of "refers to"-arcs: there is a *positive*, resp. *negative*, *arc* from p to q iff there is a clause in P with p in the head and q occurring positively, resp. negatively, in the body. We say that p *depends on* q in P, and write $p \sqsupseteq q$, iff (p, q) is in the reflexive, transitive closure of the relation refers to. We write $p \simeq q$ iff $p \sqsupseteq q$ and $q \sqsupseteq p$ (p and q are mutually recursive or $p = q$), and $p \sqsupset q$ iff $p \sqsupseteq q$ and $q \not\sqsupseteq p$. If L is a literal $p(t_1, \ldots, t_n)$ or $\neg p(t_1, \ldots, t_n)$, then we define $Rel(L) = p$. With a *signed predicate* of a set P of predicate symbols, we mean p or $\neg p$, where $p \in P$. An atom of the form

$p(\bar{t})$ will be called a *p-atom*.

3   The SLDNFA Proof Procedure

An abductive logic program P^A based on Σ is a general program P based on Σ together with a subset $A \subset \Sigma^p$ of undefined predicates, called *abducible*. The other predicates in $\Sigma^p \setminus A$ are called *nonabducible*. Without loss of generality, we assume that for any nonpropositional abductive logic program P^A, equality $=$ is defined by one unit clause, $X = X \leftarrow$, in P (without explicitly stating this in the examples).

In [5], the *3-valued completion semantics* for abductive logic programs and the notion of *abductive solution* for a query w.r.t. a program are defined. By the lack of space, we will not go into detail here and we will only give the proof procedure, called SLDNFA. This section is based on [5] and we refer to [5] for the soundness and completeness results and for more details.

An SLDNFA computation can be understood as a process of deriving formulas $\forall(Q_0 \leftarrow \Phi)$, with $\leftarrow Q_0$ the initial query and the conjunction Φ composed of two types of unsolved queries:

- For any query $\leftarrow Q$ for which a derivation still needs to be computed (in the sequel, a *positive query*), Φ contains the open formula Q (denoting the open conjunction of literals in Q).

- For any query $\leftarrow Q$ for which a failure tree still needs to be constructed (in the sequel, a *negative query*), Φ contains the open formula $\forall \overline{X}. \leftarrow Q$ with $\overline{X}$ a subset of the variables of Q.

SLDNFA selects *unsolved* positive or negative queries $\leftarrow Q$ and literals in $\leftarrow Q$ and rewrites these queries depending on the sort of selection. These rewrite operations can be interpreted as theorem proving steps on Φ. Resolution is applied on nonabducible atoms selected in positive and negative queries, as in SLDNF. Negative literals are deleted from positive queries and added as negative queries and vice versa, just as in SLDNF. Abducible atoms in positive queries are never selected: they are treated as residual atoms. They are called *abduced atoms*. The process of computing an increasing set of residual abducible atoms can be understood as the incremental construction of a definition for the abducible predicates. Abducible atoms selected in negative queries are resolved with the residual atoms in the positive queries.

Note that Φ contains two types of variables: free variables (universally quantified in front of $\forall(Q_0 \leftarrow \Phi)$) and variables universally quantified in a conjunct of Φ. This distinction plays a crucial role in SLDNFA. The variables that appear free in Φ will be called *positive* and the variables that appear universally quantified in Φ will be called *negative*. Whether variables in queries in a derivation are positive or negative depends on the way they are introduced in the derivation. The positive variables are either variables of the initial query Q_0 or are the variables of input program clauses used for resolution with positive queries. The negative variables are the variables of program clauses used for resolution with negative queries. What follows is a precise description of how the basic operations of unification and resolution are modified to take the difference between positive and negative variables into account.

Definition 3.1 (marking) *A marking α is a partial function of the set of variables of an alphabet Σ to the set $\{+, -\}$. Given a marking α, a variable X is marked iff $\alpha(X)$ is defined. A marked atom, equality set, query, program clause is one in which all variables are marked.*

Given a marking α, we denote with X^+, resp. Y^-, that $\alpha(X) = +$, resp. $\alpha(Y) = -$. A marking can be seen as a memo to inform unification and resolution in SLDNFA about the logical nature of the variables.

Definition 3.2 (positive solved form; solvable equality set)
An equality set is in solved form iff it is a set of equality atoms of the form $X = t$ such that X is a variable different from the term t and X occurs only once at the left and not at the right.
Given a marking α, a marked equality set is in positive solved form iff it is in solved form and it contains no atoms of the form $X^+ = Y^-$.
An equality set E_s is a (positive) solved form of an equality set E iff E_s is in (positive) solved form and E_s is a mgu of E. An equality set with a solved form is called solvable; an equality set without solved form is called unsolvable.
Two atoms $p(\bar{t})$, $p(\bar{s})$ are said to be unifiable iff $\{\bar{t} = \bar{s}\}$ is solvable.

It is straightforward that (given some marking α) a marked equality set has a solved form iff it has a positive solved form.

Definition 3.3 (positive resolution) *Given is a marking α, a marked query $\leftarrow Q = \leftarrow B_1, p(\bar{t}), B_2$ and $C \equiv p(\bar{s}) \leftarrow B'$ a marked clause.*
$\leftarrow Q'$ is derived from $\leftarrow Q$ and C by positive resolution on $p(\bar{t})$ using θ if the following holds: (1) θ is a solved form of $\bar{t} = \bar{s}$ and (2) $\leftarrow Q'$ is the query $\theta(\leftarrow B_1, B', B_2)$. We call $\leftarrow Q'$ the positive resolvent.

In SLDNFA, positive resolution is applied to positive queries. If E is a marked equality set in positive solved form, define E_+, resp. E_-, as the subset of E having a positive variable, resp. negative variable, at the left.

Definition 3.4 (negative resolution) *Given is a marking α, a marked query $\leftarrow Q = \leftarrow B_1, p(\bar{t}), B_2$ and $C \equiv p(\bar{s}) \leftarrow B'$ a marked program clause or a marked abducible atom $(B' = \{\ \})$.*
$\leftarrow Q'$ is derived from $\leftarrow Q$ and C by negative resolution on $p(\bar{t})$ if the following holds: (1) $\bar{t} = \bar{s}$ has a positive solved form E and (2) $\leftarrow Q'$ is the query $E_-(\leftarrow B_1, E_+, B', B_2)$. We call $\leftarrow Q'$ the negative resolvent.

Definition 3.5 (irreducible equality atom) *We call* $s = t$ *irreducible when s is a positive variable and t is either a nonvariable term or another positive variable.*

Negative resolution is applied to negative queries. In such a negative query, an irreducible atom formulates a disequality constraint on a positive variable. Negative resolution will never bind positive variables; instead it generates disequality constraints on them.

Note that, for queries and program clauses that contain only positive (resp. negative) variables, positive (resp. negative) resolution and classical resolution coincide.

The following notion of prederivation serves as a kind of skeleton for the notion of an SLDNFA-derivation.

Definition 3.6 (prederivation) *Given is an abductive logic program* P^A *based on an alphabet* Σ*. A prederivation* K *is a tuple* $((\theta_1, \ldots, \theta_n), T, \alpha)$ *with* $(\theta_1, \ldots, \theta_n)$ *a sequence of substitutions,* T *a tree of labeled queries* $\leftarrow Q$ *and labeled arcs, and* α *a marking of the variables of* Σ*. Each query is labeled positive or negative. A query* $\leftarrow Q$ *in the tree may or may not be labeled by a literal in* $\leftarrow Q$*, called the selected literal.*
An arc from a negative query $\leftarrow Q_1, L, Q_2$ *with a selected atom* L *arrives in a negative query* $\leftarrow Q'$ *and is labeled with a program clause* $H \leftarrow B$ *(or an abducible atom* H*), called the* applied resolvendus*.* $\leftarrow Q'$ *is derived from* $\leftarrow Q_1, L, Q_2$ *and* $H \leftarrow B$ *(resp.* H*) by negative resolution on* L*.*

The sequence of substitutions in a prederivation will be the sequence of substitutions computed at *positive* resolution steps.

Given an abductive logic program P^A and a prederivation K, a *resolvendus* of a node N in K with a nonabducible selected atom L is any program clause $H \leftarrow B$ of P^A such that L and a variant of H are unifiable. If the selected atom L of N is abducible, then a resolvendus of N is any abducible atom L' in a positive query of K such that L and L' are unifiable. For a negative query $\leftarrow Q$ in K, we distinguish between *applied resolvendi* (those appearing as applied resolvendi of arcs leaving $\leftarrow Q$ in K) and the other, *nonapplied resolvendi*.

Definition 3.7 (selection) *Given is a prederivation* K*.*
A first SLDNFA-selection in K *is a tuple* (N, L)*, where* N *is a positive or negative query in* K *without selected literal, and* L *is a literal in* N*. If* N *is a positive query, then* L *is not an abducible atom.*
An SLDNFA-reselection in K *is a tuple* (N, C)*, where* N *is a negative query in* K *labeled with a selected atom* L *and* C *is a nonapplied resolvendus of* N *(w.r.t.* K *and* P^A*).*
An SLDNFA-selection in K *is a first selection or reselection in* K*.*

Note that an abducible atom in a positive query cannot be selected. The only queries that can be selected more than once are negative queries with a selected atom for which different branches of the failure tree are to be explored.

In [5] it is shown that the safety condition on the selection rule in SLDNF (namely that only *ground* negative literals can be selected) can be weakened in the SLDNFA procedure: positive variables may appear in selected negative literals. However, SLDNFA does not offer a solution for the treatment of negative variables in positive queries. Therefore, the following (weak) safety condition is imposed on the selection rule in SLDNFA.

Definition 3.8 (safe selection) *Given is a prederivation K. A selection is safe iff it is a reselection or if it is a first selection (N, L) such that L is not a negative literal containing negative variables.*

A program clause C' is called a *standardized apart* variant of a program clause C w.r.t. a prederivation $K = ((\theta_1, \ldots, \theta_n), T, \alpha)$ iff C' is a variant of C and the variables in C' appear neither in C, nor in $\theta_1, \ldots, \theta_n$ nor in T.

Definition 3.9 (SLDNFA-derivation) *Let P^A be an abductive logic program and $\leftarrow Q_0$ be a query. An SLDNFA-derivation is defined by induction:*

- *The tuple $(( ), T_0, \alpha_0)$, with T_0 a tree consisting of a single positive query $\leftarrow Q_0$ and α_0 the marking that marks the variables of Q_0 positive, is an SLDNFA-derivation.*

- *Given an SLDNFA-derivation K, an SLDNFA-extension of K using some safe selection in K is an SLDNFA-derivation.*

An SLDNFA-extension of a prederivation $K = ((\theta_1, \ldots, \theta_n), T, \alpha)$ is defined as follows.
Let (N, L) be a first selection in K with $N \equiv \leftarrow Q$.
An SLDNFA-extension of K using first selection (N, L) is a prederivation $K' = ((\theta_1, \ldots, \theta_n, \theta), T', \alpha')$ such that T' is obtained from T by adding a set S with zero, one, or two descendants to N, marking N with selected literal L, and applying θ on all queries and labels of T. α', θ and the set of descendants S satisfy one of the following conditions:

- *Let N be a positive query and L be an atom $p(\bar{t})$ with p nonabducible.*

  α' extends α by marking all variables of a standardized apart variant C' of a program clause $C \in P$ positive. S is a singleton containing a positive query $\leftarrow Q'$, which is derived by positive resolution from $\leftarrow Q$ and C' on $p(\bar{t})$ using θ.

  In all other cases $\theta = \epsilon$ (the empty substitution) and $\alpha' = \alpha$. Depending on the type of selection, S satisfies the following conditions:

- *Let N be a positive query and $L = \neg A$.*

  S is a pair consisting of a negative query $\leftarrow A$ and a positive query $\leftarrow Q'$ obtained by deleting $\neg A$ in $\leftarrow Q$.

- *Let N be a negative query and $L = \neg A$.*

  Either S is the singleton containing one positive query $\leftarrow A$, or S is the singleton consisting of a negative query $\leftarrow Q'$ obtained by deleting $\neg A$ in $\leftarrow Q$.

- *Let N be a negative query and $L = p(\bar{t})$.*

  S is empty[1].

Let (N, C) be a reselection in K where $N \equiv \leftarrow Q$.
An SLDNFA-extension *of K using reselection (N, C) is the prederivation $K' = ((\theta_1, \ldots, \theta_n, \epsilon), T', \alpha')$, such that T' is obtained from T by adding one new descendant N' to N and labeling the arc from N to N' with C as applied resolvendus. N' is a negative query $\leftarrow Q'$, which is derived as follows. Recall that by definition of reselection, N has a selected atom A appearing in $\leftarrow Q$.*

- *If A is nonabducible, then α' extends α by marking the variables of a standardized apart variant C' of C negative. $\leftarrow Q'$ is derived from $\leftarrow Q$ and C' by negative resolution on A.*

- *If A is abducible, then $\alpha' = \alpha$ and $\leftarrow Q'$ is derived from $\leftarrow Q$ and C by negative resolution on A.*

In [5], the following is proven: two different queries of an SLDNFA-derivation K that do not occur in the same branch may share positive but no negative variables; positive queries contain only positive variables; the substitutions $\theta_1, \ldots, \theta_n$ of K contain only positive variables.

Definition 3.10 (finitely failed derivation) *An SLDNFA-derivation K is* finitely failed *if K contains a positive query that contains a nonabducible atom without resolvendi w.r.t. P^A or if K contains the empty negative query.*

A negative query N in an SLDNFA-derivation K is called *completed* iff N has a selected literal L and either L is a negative literal or L is an atom such that each resolvendus of L w.r.t. P^A and K is an applied resolvendus of N.

Definition 3.11 (SLDNFA-refutation) *An SLDNFA-refutation K for a query $\leftarrow Q$ is an SLDNFA-derivation K for $\leftarrow Q$ such that all positive leaves contain only abducible atoms and all negative queries are completed or they have no selected literal and contain an irreducible equality atom.*

---

[1] K and K' differ by the fact that N in K has no selected literal, whereas N in K' has the selected literal L. .Branches of the failure tree below N are added in later stages, when N is reselected.

In [5], it is shown in detail how to extract abductive solutions from an SLDNFA-refutation. Roughly, an abductive solution is extracted from an SLDNFA-refutation by completing the abduced atoms and adding the irreducible equality atoms as constraints (without going into detail, we mention that more general answers can be derived, as shown in [5]).

In the following section, we study termination under SLDNFA-execution w.r.t. an arbitrary selection rule. However, we put three natural conditions on the selection in SLDNFA, namely: (1) no abducible atom is selected in a positive query (by Definition 3.7 of selection); (2) no negative literal containing negative variables is selected in a negative query (by Definition 3.9 of SLDNFA-derivation: the selection is *safe*); (3) no irreducible equality atom is selected in a negative query (this is a reasonable condition, since the descendant in that case would be identical to the negative query). For the rest of this paper, we consider SLDNFA-derivations using a selection rule satisfying the above conditions. We illustrate the above concepts with a small fault diagnosis problem of [5].

Example 3.1 A faulty lamp problem is caused by a broken lamp or by a power failure of a circuit without backup, that is, a loaded battery. The only circuit with battery is $c1$; its battery is $b1$. A battery is unloaded iff one of its energy cells is dry. This is formalized in $P^{\{broken/1, power\_failure/1, dry\_cell/1\}}$:

$$
\begin{aligned}
lamp(l1) &\leftarrow \\
battery(c1, b1) &\leftarrow \\
faulty\_lamp &\leftarrow lamp(X), broken(X) \\
faulty\_lamp &\leftarrow power\_failure(X), \neg backup(X) \\
backup(X) &\leftarrow battery(X, Y), \neg unloaded(Y) \\
unloaded(X) &\leftarrow dry\_cell(X)
\end{aligned}
$$

An SLDNFA-refutation for the query $\leftarrow faulty\_lamp$ is shown in Fig. 1. As a notational convenience, we prefix positive, resp. negative, queries with +, resp. -. The selected literal in a query is underlined and the arcs are numbered to indicate the sequence of computation steps. The answer that can be extracted from this refutation is that there is a power failure on a circuit X^+ that is not $c1$.

In Example 4.5, we'll prove that all SLDNFA-derivations for $\leftarrow faulty\_lamp$ are finite. In Example 4.7, we will even show that for every query, all SLDNFA-derivations in $P^{\{broken/1, power\_failure/1, dry\_cell/1\}}$ are finite.

4 SLDNFA-Termination

Let P^A be an abductive logic program and $\leftarrow Q$ be a query, both based on the alphabet Σ.

Definition 4.1 (SLDNFA-terminating program w.r.t. a query)
P^A *is SLDNFA-terminating w.r.t.* $\leftarrow Q$ *iff all SLDNFA-derivations of* $\leftarrow Q$ *in* P^A *are finite.*

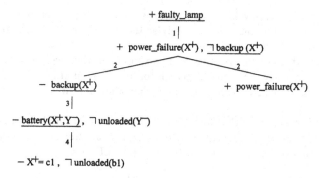

Figure 1: SLDNFA-refutation for $\leftarrow faulty\_lamp$.

As in most termination analyses for logic programs (see [4] for a survey), our termination condition relies on the concepts of level mapping and boundedness.

Definition 4.2 (level mapping, boundedness) *A level mapping for P^A is a function $|.| : B_P \cup \neg B_P \rightarrow \mathbb{N}$, with $|\neg B| = |B|$ for all $B \in B_P$.*
A literal L is called bounded *w.r.t. $|.|$ iff $|.|$ is bounded on the set $[L]$ of Σ-ground instances of L. If L is bounded w.r.t. $|.|$, then we define $|L|$ as the maximum $|.|$ takes on $[L]$. If $|L| \leq k$, with $k \in \mathbb{N}$, then we say that L is* bounded by k.
A query $\leftarrow Q$ is called bounded *w.r.t. $|.|$ iff all its literals are. If $|L_i| \leq k$ for all $i \in \{1, \ldots, n\}$, with $k \in \mathbb{N}$, then we say that $\leftarrow Q$ is bounded by k.*

We introduce the notion of semi-acyclic program.

Definition 4.3 (semi-acyclic program) *Let $|.|$ be a level mapping for the program P^A. Then, P^A is semi-acyclic w.r.t. $|.|$ iff $\forall H \leftarrow L_1, \ldots, L_n \in Ground_\Sigma(P)$ and $\forall i \in \{1, \ldots, n\}$:*

$$|H| > |L_i| \quad \text{if } Rel(H) \simeq Rel(L_i),$$
$$|H| \geq |L_i| \quad \text{if } Rel(H) \sqsupset Rel(L_i).$$

P^A is semi-acyclic iff there exists a level mapping $|.|$ such that P^A is semi-acyclic w.r.t. $|.|$.

The notion of semi-acyclic program is equivalent to the notion of acyclic program [2]. Recall from [2] that a program is *acyclic w.r.t.* a level mapping $|.|$ iff for every ground instance of each program clause, the level of the head is *strictly* greater than the level of *all* body literals. A proof of this equivalence in the case of definite programs (in which case (semi-)acyclicity is called (semi-)recurrency) is given in [3]. The proof in the general case is similar. Although the notions of acyclicity and semi-acyclicity are equivalent, the notion of semi-acyclic program allows more natural level mappings and provides means for constructing modular termination proofs (as noted in [3] in the case of definite programs).

Note that abducible predicates do not occur in the head of a clause and cannot be recursive. So, in the search for a level mapping such that P^A is semi-acyclic, it can be safely assumed that abducible literals are assigned the value 0.

In [2] it was proven that for an acyclic general program P and a bounded query $\leftarrow Q$, all SLDNF-derivations of $\leftarrow Q$ in P are finite. In the following example we show that this is not the case for SLDNFA.

Example 4.1 Consider the program $P^{\{p/1\}}$ with query $\leftarrow \neg r, p(X)$.

$$P^{\{p/1\}} : \begin{cases} r & \leftarrow p(X), \neg q(X) & (C_1) \\ q(X) & \leftarrow p(f(X)) & (C_2) \end{cases}$$

Consider the following level mapping $|.|$ for $P^{\{p/1\}}$: $|r| = 2$, $|q(t)| = 1$ and $|p(t)| = 0$ for all $t \in U_P$. Then, $P^{\{p/1\}}$ is (semi-)acyclic w.r.t. $|.|$ and the query $\leftarrow \neg r, p(X)$ is bounded by 2 w.r.t. $|.|$. An SLDNFA-derivation for $\leftarrow \neg r, p(X)$ in $P^{\{p/1\}}$ is shown in Fig. 2. Note that the derivation is not

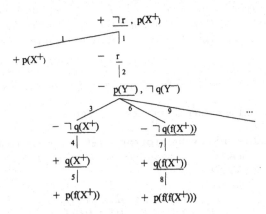

Figure 2: SLDNFA-derivation for $\leftarrow \neg r, p(X)$ in $P^{\{p/1\}}$.

finite, since there is an infinitely branching (negative) node[2].

As the above example suggests, an additional condition (besides (semi-)acyclicity of the program and boundedness of the query) is needed in order that the program is SLDNFA-terminating w.r.t. the query. That is,

---

[2]Resolution of the selected abducible atom $p(Y^-)$ in the negative query $-p(Y^-), \neg q(Y^-)$, with the abduced atom $p(X^+)$ (step 3) leads to the abduction of $p(f(X^+))$ (step 5), which in turn has to be resolved with $p(Y^-)$ (step 6), leading to the abduction of $p(f(f(X^+)))$ (step 8), which in turn ...

we have to impose a condition which prevents an SLDNFA-derivation from being infinitely branching in a node. Note that a derivation can only be infinitely branching in a node which contains a negative query with a selected abducible p-atom and there are an infinite number of abduced p-atoms in positive queries. Hence, the additional condition should ensure that, for every derivation of $\leftarrow Q$ in P^A, the set of abduced atoms in the derivation is finite. Note that for propositional programs and queries, this condition is satisfied. So, in the propositional case, SLDNFA-termination is implied by the (semi-)acyclicity of the program and boundedness of the query. Concerning the predicate case, we introduce a syntactical condition on a program and query, called abductive nonrecursivity (Definition 4.5), which, together with the (semi-)acyclicity of the program and boundedness of the query, implies termination of SLDNFA (Theorem 4.2). We introduce the necessary concepts.

Definition 4.4 (reductions and paths) *Let P^A be a program and $\leftarrow Q$ be a query. Let start be a new (i.e. not occurring in Σ^p) predicate symbol of arity 0. We define reductions between elements of the form $*sp$, where $* \in \{+,-\}$ and sp is a signed predicate symbol of $\Sigma^p \cup \{start\}$. The reductions will be denoted with an arrow "$\rightarrow$", indexed with the query Q, a clause of P^A, or the symbol s.*

- *Suppose $\leftarrow Q = \ldots, p(\bar{t}), \ldots, \neg q(\bar{s}), \ldots$. Then we have the following $\rightarrow_Q$-reductions:*

$$+start \rightarrow_Q +p \qquad + start \rightarrow_Q +\neg q$$

- *Let $C = h(\bar{u}) \leftarrow \ldots, p(\bar{t}), \ldots, \neg q(\bar{s}), \ldots$ be a clause of P^A. Then we have the following $\rightarrow_C$-reductions:*

$$+h \rightarrow_C +p \qquad +h \rightarrow_C +\neg q \qquad -h \rightarrow_C -p \qquad -h \rightarrow_C -\neg q$$

- *For all predicate symbols $p \in \Sigma^p$, we have the following $\rightarrow_s$-reductions:*

$$+\neg p \rightarrow_s -p \qquad -\neg p \rightarrow_s +p$$

A reduction sequence of the form

$$+start \rightarrow_Q .(\rightarrow_s). \rightarrow_C .(\rightarrow_s). \rightarrow_{C'} \ldots .(\rightarrow_s). \rightarrow_{C''} \ldots$$

where C, C', C'' are clauses of P^A, is called a path from $\leftarrow Q$ in P^A. If there is a subpath (possibly of length 0) in a path from $\leftarrow Q$ in P^A starting in $*sp$ and ending in $*'sq$, where $*, *' \in \{+,-\}$ and sp, sq are signed predicates of $\Sigma^p \cup \{start\}$, then we denote this with $*sp \rightarrow^{Q,P,s} *'sq$. If in this subpath from $*sp$ to $*'sq$, no reduction of the sort $\rightarrow_s$ occurs, then we denote this with $*sp \rightarrow^{Q,P} *'sq$ (note that in this case $* = *'$).

An element of the form $*sp$, with $* \in \{+, -\}$ and sp a signed predicate (as it appears in the above definition) can be seen as an abstraction of a positive or negative (depending on $*$) query which contains a positive or negative (depending on the sign of sp) literal with as predicate symbol the predicate of sp. Branches in an SLDNFA-derivation of $\leftarrow Q$ in P^A can then be abstracted by paths from $\leftarrow Q$ in P^A. We give an example.

Example 4.2 Recall the program $P^{\{p/1\}}$ and query $\leftarrow Q = \leftarrow \neg r, p(X)$ of Example 4.1. We have e.g. the following paths from $\leftarrow \neg r, p(X)$ in $P^{\{p/1\}}$: $+start \rightarrow_Q +\neg r \rightarrow_s -r \rightarrow_{C_1} -p$ and $+start \rightarrow_Q +\neg r \rightarrow_s -r \rightarrow_{C_1} -\neg q \rightarrow_s +q \rightarrow_{C_2} +p$. Notice that these paths can be found as the branches 1-2 and 1-2-3-4-5 (or 1-2-6-7-8) resp. in the SLDNFA-derivation of Fig. 2. It follows e.g. that $-r \rightarrow^{Q,P} -p$ and $-r \rightarrow^{Q,P,s} +p$.

The next definition introduces the syntactical notion of abductive recursive program and query. The concept of abductive *nonrecursive* program and query will be the additional requirement in our termination condition (Theorem 4.2).

Definition 4.5 (abductive recursive program and query) *Let P^A be a program and $\leftarrow Q$ be a query. We call $P^A \cup \{\leftarrow Q\}$ abductive recursive iff there are abducible predicates $p_1, \ldots, p_n \in A$ and predicates $q_1, \ldots, q_n \in \Sigma^p \setminus (A \cup \{=\})$, $n \geq 1$, such that*

$$
\begin{array}{cccccc}
-q_1 & \rightarrow^{Q,P} & -p_1 & -q_2 & \rightarrow^{Q,P} & -p_2 & & -q_n & \rightarrow^{Q,P} & -p_n \\
-q_1 & \rightarrow^{Q,P,s} & +p_2 & -q_2 & \rightarrow^{Q,P,s} & +p_3 & \cdots & -q_n & \rightarrow^{Q,P,s} & +p_1
\end{array}
$$

We call $P^A \cup \{\leftarrow Q\}$ abductive nonrecursive iff $P^A \cup \{\leftarrow Q\}$ is not abductive recursive.

Example 4.3 Recall the program and query of Example 4.1. We have that $P^{\{p/1\}} \cup \{\leftarrow \neg r, p(X)\}$ is abductive recursive, since $-r \rightarrow^{Q,P} -p$ and $-r \rightarrow^{Q,P,s} +p$ (see Example 4.2).

In the next Proposition 4.1, we give the meaning of the notion of abductive recursive program and query in terms of SLDNFA-derivations. We first introduce some notation. Let $K = ((\theta_1, \ldots, \theta_l), T, \alpha)$ be an SLDNFA-derivation. A positive, resp. negative, query N in T will be prefixed with $+$, resp. $-$; e.g. $+N$, resp. $-N$. If a query N (positive or negative) in T contains an atom $p(\bar{t})$, then this will be denoted as $N(p)$. If a node N is an ancestor of a node M in T, then this will be denoted with $N \rightsquigarrow M$.

Proposition 4.1 *Let P^A be a program and $\leftarrow Q$ be a query. Suppose there is an SLDNFA-derivation $K = ((\theta_1, \ldots, \theta_l), T, \alpha)$ of $\leftarrow Q$ in P^A with nodes $-N_1(p_1), +M_1(p_2), -N_2(p_2), +M_2(p_3), \ldots, -N_n(p_n), +M_n(p_1)$ in T with $n \geq 1$ and $p_1, p_2, \ldots, p_n \in A$, such that*

$$-N_1(p_1) \rightsquigarrow +M_1(p_2) \quad -N_2(p_2) \rightsquigarrow +M_2(p_3) \quad \cdots \quad -N_n(p_n) \rightsquigarrow +M_n(p_1)$$

Then, $P \cup \{\leftarrow Q\}$ is abductive recursive.

Example 4.4 Recall the program $P^{\{p/1\}}$ and query $\leftarrow Q = \leftarrow \neg r, p(X)$ of Example 4.1. We have, for the SLDNFA-derivation of Fig. 2 of $\leftarrow \neg r, p(X)$ in $P^{\{p/1\}}$, that $-N_1(p) \rightsquigarrow +M_1(p)$ with $-N_1 = -p(Y^-), \neg q(Y^-)$ and $+M_1 = +p(f(X^+))$. Hence, by Proposition 4.1 (with $n = 1$), $P^{\{p/1\}} \cup \{\leftarrow \neg r, p(X)\}$ is abductive recursive. Indeed, this was already noted in Example 4.3, by using Definition 4.5 of abductive recursive program and query.

We are now able to formulate the main theorem of this paper.

Theorem 4.2 *Let P^A be a semi-acyclic program w.r.t. a level mapping $|.|$, and let $\leftarrow Q$ be a bounded query w.r.t. $|.|$. Suppose that $P^A \cup \{\leftarrow Q\}$ is abductive nonrecursive. Then, P^A is SLDNFA-terminating w.r.t. $\leftarrow Q$.*

Example 4.5 Recall the program and query of Example 3.1. Let $|.|$ be the following level mapping: $|broken(t)| = |power\_failure(t)| = |dry\_cell(t)| = 0$, $|lamp(t)| = |battery(t, s)| = |unloaded(t)| = 1$, $|backup(t)| = 2$ and $|faulty\_lamp| = 3$, with $t, s \in U_P$. P is (semi-)acyclic w.r.t. $|.|$ and the query $\leftarrow faulty\_lamp$ is bounded by 3 w.r.t. $|.|$. One can easily verify that $P \cup \{\leftarrow faulty\_lamp\}$ is abductive nonrecursive, so, P SLDNFA-terminates w.r.t. $\leftarrow faulty\_lamp$. In Example 4.7, we prove that P SLDNFA-terminates w.r.t. all queries.

Example 4.6 Recall the program $P^{\{p/1\}}$ of Example 4.1. As we already noted in Examples 4.3 and 4.4, $P^{\{p/1\}} \cup \{\leftarrow \neg r, p(X)\}$ is abductive recursive. Consider next the query $\leftarrow r$. Note that $P^{\{p/1\}} \cup \{\leftarrow r\}$ is abductive nonrecursive. By the fact that $P^{\{p/1\}}$ is (semi-)acyclic and $\leftarrow r$ is bounded by 2 w.r.t. the level mapping proposed in Example 4.1, we have that $P^{\{p/1\}}$ SLDNFA-terminates w.r.t. $\leftarrow r$.

Note that, in case $A = \emptyset$, a program $P^{\{\ \}}$ and query $\leftarrow Q$ are trivially abductive nonrecursive. So, the termination condition of Theorem 4.2 boils down to the termination condition of Apt and Bezem [2] for SLDNF in that case. Note also that a definite program and query are trivially abductive nonrecursive. So, also in that case, termination is ensured by the (semi-) acyclicity of the program[3] and boundedness of the query.

The notion of abductive recursivity of Definition 4.5 depends on the program *and* the query in question. We refer to Example 4.6 where a program and two queries are given such that the program and first query are abductive recursive (and do not SLDNFA-terminate) whereas the program and second query are abductive recursive (and do SLDNFA-terminate). Next, in Definition 4.6, we state a condition on the program only, which we will also call abductive nonrecursivity (but now with no reference to a particular query), such that the program P^A is abductive nonrecursive (Definition 4.6) iff for all queries $\leftarrow Q$, $P^A \cup \{\leftarrow Q\}$ is abductive nonrecursive (Definition

---

[3]For definite programs, the notion of (semi-)acyclicity is called (semi-)recurrency [3].

4.5). We introduce some notation. For predicates p and q, define "$q \rightarrow^P p$" as "q depends on p in P and there is a dependency of q on p which consists of positive arcs only", and define "$q \rightarrow^{P,s} p$" as "q depends on p in P and there is a dependency of q on p which consists of an odd number of negative arcs".

Definition 4.6 (abductive recursive program) *The program P^A is abductive recursive iff there are abducible predicates $p_1, \ldots, p_n \in A$ and predicates $q_1, \ldots, q_n \in \Sigma^p \setminus (A \cup \{=\})$, $n \geq 1$, such that*

$$
\begin{array}{llll}
q_1 & \rightarrow^P & p_1 & \qquad q_2 & \rightarrow^P & p_2 & \qquad \cdots & \qquad q_n & \rightarrow^P & p_n \\
q_1 & \rightarrow^{P,s} & p_2 & \qquad q_2 & \rightarrow^{P,s} & p_3 & & \qquad q_n & \rightarrow^{P,s} & p_1
\end{array}
$$

We call P^A abductive nonrecursive iff P^A is not abductive recursive.

The above definition can also be formulated in terms of the reductions introduced in Definition 4.4. We refer to [8].

Proposition 4.3 *The program P^A is abductive nonrecursive iff for all queries $\leftarrow Q$, $P^A \cup \{\leftarrow Q\}$ is abductive nonrecursive. Or, P^A is abductive recursive iff there is a query $\leftarrow Q$ such that $P^A \cup \{\leftarrow Q\}$ is abductive recursive.*

Hence, as a corollary to the main theorem (Theorem 4.2) and Proposition 4.3, we can state the following termination condition.

Theorem 4.4 *Let P^A be a semi-acyclic program w.r.t. a level mapping $|.|$. Suppose that P^A is abductive nonrecursive. Then, for all bounded queries $\leftarrow Q$ w.r.t. $|.|$, P^A is SLDNFA-terminating w.r.t. $\leftarrow Q$.*

Example 4.7 Recall the program of Example 3.1. Note that the program is abductive nonrecursive. As we showed in Example 4.5, the program is (semi-)acyclic w.r.t. the level mapping $|.|$ proposed in Example 4.5. Note also that all queries are bounded (by 3) w.r.t. $|.|$. So, by Theorem 4.4, the program is SLDNFA-terminating w.r.t. all queries.

5 Conclusions and Future Work

We presented an extension of the methods of Apt and Bezem [2] for proving termination of general logic programs executed under SLDNF, to the case of abductive general logic programs executed under SLDNFA [5]. Whereas the conditions of Apt and Bezem (i.e. acyclicity of the program and boundedness of the query) are also sufficient for proving termination of SLDNFA in the case of definite programs and queries, in the propositional case, as well as in the case of the empty set of abducible predicates, these conditions are not sufficient in general for proving SLDNFA-termination. We proposed a third, syntactical condition, namely abductive nonrecursivity of the program and query, which together with the acyclicity of the program and boundedness of the query implies termination of SLDNFA. By the best of our knowledge, this is the first work on termination of an abductive procedure for general logic programs.

Our termination condition (Theorem 4.2) is sufficient but not necessary. In particular, there are (semi-)acyclic programs and bounded queries which SLDNFA-terminate, but which are abductive recursive. It remains a topic for future work to refine the notion of abductive recursivity and to find a characterisation of SLDNFA-termination. Another topic for future research is to study termination of SLDNFA w.r.t. a particular selection rule.

Acknowledgements

Sofie Verbaeten is research assistant of the Fund for Scientific Research - Flanders (Belgium) (F.W.O.).

References

[1] K.R. Apt and K. Doets. A new definition of SLDNF-resolution. *Journal of Logic Programming*, 18:177–190, 1994.

[2] K.R. Apt and M. Bezem. Acyclic programs. *New Generation Computing*, 9:335–363, 1991.

[3] K.R. Apt and D. Pedreschi. Modular termination proofs for logic and pure Prolog programs. In *Advances in Logic Programming Theory*, pages 183–229. Oxford University Press, 1994.

[4] D. De Schreye and S. Decorte. Termination of logic programs: the never-ending story. *Journal of Logic Programming*, 19 & 20:199–260, 1994.

[5] M. Denecker and D. De Schreye. SLDNFA: an abductive procedure for abductive logic programs. *Journal of Logic Programming*, 34(2):111–167, 1998.

[6] T.H. Fung and R. Kowalski. The iff proof procedure for abductive logic programming. *Journal of Logic Programming*, 33(2):151–165, 1997.

[7] J.W. Lloyd. *Foundations of logic programming*. Springer-Verlag, 1987.

[8] S. Verbaeten. Termination analysis for abductive general logic programs. Technical report, Department of Computer Science, K.U.Leuven, 1999. Available at http://www.cs.kuleuven.ac.be/~sofie.

The Relative Complement Problem for Higher-Order Patterns

Alberto Momigliano
Department of Philosophy

Frank Pfenning
Department of Computer Science
Carnegie Mellon University
Pittsburgh, PA 15213, U.S.A.
{mobile|fp}@cs.cmu.edu

Abstract

We address the problem of complementing higher-order patterns without repetitions of free variables. Differently from the first-order case, the complement of a pattern cannot, in general, be described by a pattern, or even by a finite set of patterns. We therefore generalize the simply-typed λ-calculus to include an internal notion of *strict function* so that we can directly express that a term must depend on a given variable. We show that, in this more expressive calculus, finite sets of patterns without repeated variables are closed under complement and unification. Our principal application is the transformational approach to negation in higher-order logic programs.

1 Introduction

In most functional and logic programming languages the notion of a pattern, together with the requisite algorithms for matching or unification, play an important role in the operational semantics. Besides unification other problems such as generalization or complement also arise frequently. In this paper we are concerned with the problem of pattern complement in a setting where patterns may contain binding operators, so-called *higher-order patterns* [10, 12]. Higher-order patterns have found applications in logic programming [10, 13], logical frameworks [13], rewriting [12], and functional logic programming [5]. Higher-order patterns inherit many pleasant properties from the first-order case. In particular, most general unifiers [10] and least general generalizations [14] exist, even for complex type theories.

Unfortunately, the complement operation does not generalize as easily. Lugiez [8] has studied the more general problem of higher-order disunification and had to go outside the language of patterns and terms to describe complex constraints on sets of solutions. We can isolate one basic difficulty: a pattern such as $\lambda x.\, E\, x$ for an existential variable E matches any term of appropriate type, while $\lambda x.\, E$ matches precisely those terms $\lambda x.\, M$ where M does not depend on x. The complement then consists of all terms $\lambda x.\, M$ such that M *does* depend on x. However, this set cannot be described by a pattern, or even a finite set of patterns.

This formulation of the problem suggests that we should consider a λ-calculus with an internal notion of *strictness* so that we can directly express that a term must depend on a given variable. For reasons of symmetry and elegance we also add the dual concept of *invariance* expressing that a given term does not depend on a given variable. As in the first-order case, it is useful to single out the case of *linear patterns*, namely those where no existential variable occurs more than once.[1] We show that patterns in our calculus have the following properties:

1. The complement of a linear pattern is a finite set of linear patterns.

2. Unification of two patterns is decidable and leads to a finite set of most general unifiers.

Consequently, finite sets of linear patterns in the strict λ-calculus are closed under complement and unification. If we think of finite sets of linear patterns as representing the set of all their ground instances, then they form a boolean algebra under simple union, intersection (implemented via unification) and the complement operation.

The paper is organized as follows: Section 2 briefly reviews related work, while Section 3 introduces some preliminary definitions. In Section 4 we introduce a strict λ-calculus and note some basic properties such as the existence of canonical forms. Section 5 introduces a restriction of the language for which complementation is possible. The algorithm for negation is presented in Section 6. In Section 7 we give a unification algorithm for our fragment. We conclude in Section 8 with some applications and speculation on future research. For reasons of space, a number of lemmas and proofs are omitted here and can be found in [11].

2   Related Work

Complement problems have a number of applications in theoretical computer science (see [4] for a list of references). For example, they are used in functional programming to produce non-ambiguous function definitions by patterns and to improve their compilation, and in rewriting systems to check whether an algebraic specification is sufficiently complete. They can also be employed to analyze communicating processes expressed by infinite transition systems. Other applications lie in the areas of machine learning and inductive theorem proving. In logic programming, Kunen [6] used term complement to represent infinite sets of answers to negative queries. Our main motivation has been the explicit synthesis of the negation of higher-order logic programs, as discussed in Section 8.

---

[1] This notion of linearity should not be confused with the eponymous concept in linear logic and λ-calculus.

Lassez and Marriot [7] proposed the seminal *uncover* algorithm for computing relative complements and introduced the now familiar restriction to linear terms. We quote the definition of the "Not" algorithm for the (singleton) complement problem given in [1] which we generalize in Definition 9. Given a finite signature Σ and a linear term t we define:

$$\begin{aligned}
\mathrm{Not}_\Sigma(x) &= \emptyset \\
\mathrm{Not}_\Sigma(f(\overline{t_n})) &= \{g(\vec{x}) \mid \text{for all } g \in \Sigma \text{ distinct from } f\} \\
&\cup \{f(z_1, \ldots, z_{i-1}, s, z_{i+1}, \ldots, z_n) \mid s \in \mathrm{Not}_\Sigma(t_i), i \in [1, n]\}
\end{aligned}$$

An alternative solution to the relative complement problem is *disunification* (see [4] for a survey and [8] for an extension to the simply-typed λ-calculus): here operations on sets of terms are translated into conjunctions or disjunctions of equations and disequation under explicit quantifiers. Non-deterministic application of a few dozen rules eventually turns a given problem into a solved form. Though a reduction to a significant subset of the disunification rules is likely to be attainable for complement problems, control is a major problem. We argue that using disunification for this purpose is unnecessarily general. Moreover the higher-order case results in additional complications, such as restrictions on the occurrences of bound variables, which fall outside an otherwise clean framework. As we show in this paper, this must not necessarily be the case. We believe that our techniques can also be applied to analyze disunification, although we have not investigated this possibility at present.

3 Preliminaries

In this section we introduce some preliminary definitions and examples which guide our development. We write P for atomic types, c for term-level constants, and x for term-level variables.

$$\begin{aligned}
\textit{Simple Types} \quad A &::= P \mid A_1 \rightarrow A_2 \\
\textit{Terms} \quad M &::= c \mid x \mid \lambda x{:}A.\, M \mid M_1\, M_2 \\
\textit{Signatures} \quad \Sigma &::= \cdot \mid \Sigma, P{:}\mathrm{type} \mid \Sigma, c{:}A \\
\textit{Contexts} \quad \Gamma &::= \cdot \mid \Gamma, x{:}A
\end{aligned}$$

We require that signatures and contexts declare each constant or variable at most once. Furthermore, we identify contexts which differ only in their order and promote "," to denote disjoint set union. As usual we identify terms which differ only in the names of their bound variables. We restrict attention to well-typed terms, omitting the standard typing rules. We generally fix a signature Σ so it does not have to be repeatedly mentioned in the typing rules and statements of theorems.

In applications such as logic programming or logical frameworks, λ-abstraction is used to represent binding operators in some object language. In such a situation the most useful notion of normal form are long $\beta\eta$-normal forms (which we call *canonical forms*), since the canonical forms are almost always the terms in bijective correspondence with the objects we are trying to represent. Every well-typed term in the simply-typed λ-calculus has a unique canonical form—a property which persists in the strict λ-calculus introduced in Section 4.

We denote existential variables of type A (also called logical variables, meta-variables, or pattern variables) by E_A, although we mostly omit the type A when it is clear from the context. We think of existential variables as syntactically distinct from bound variables or free variables declared in a context. A term possibly containing some existential variables is called a *pattern* if each occurrence of an existential variable appears in a subterm of the form $E\, x_1 \ldots x_n$, where the arguments x_i are distinct occurrences of free or bound variables (but not existential variables).

Semantically, a variable E_A stands for all canonical terms M of type A in the empty context with respect to a given signature. We extend this to arbitrary well-typed terms in the usual way, and write $\Gamma \vdash M \in \|N\| : A$ when a term M is a ground instance of a pattern N at type A. In this setting, unification of two patterns without shared existential variables corresponds to an intersection of the set of terms they denote [10, 14]. This set is always either empty, or can be expressed again as the set of instances of a single pattern. That is, patterns admit most general unifiers.

The class of higher-order patterns inherits many properties from first-order terms. However, as we will see, it is *not* closed under complement, but a special subclass is. We call a canonical pattern $\Gamma \vdash M : A$ *fully applied* if each occurrence of an existential variable E under binders $y_1, \ldots, y_m$ is applied to some permutation of the variables in Γ and $y_1, \ldots, y_m$. Fully applied patterns play an important role in functional logic programming and rewriting [5] because any fully applied existential variable $\Gamma \vdash E\, x_1 \ldots x_n$ denotes all canonical terms with free variables from Γ. It is this property which makes complementation particularly simple.

Example 1 *Consider the untyped λ-calculus.*

$$e \quad ::= \quad x \mid \lambda x.e \mid e_1\, e_2$$

We encode these expressions using the usual techniques of higher-order abstract syntax (see, for example, [9]) as canonical forms over the following signature.

$$\Sigma \quad = \quad exp : type, lam : (exp \to exp) \to exp, app : exp \to exp \to exp$$

The representation function is given by.

$$
\begin{aligned}
\ulcorner x \urcorner &= x \\
\ulcorner \lambda x.e \urcorner &= lam\ (\lambda x{:}exp.\ulcorner e \urcorner) \\
\ulcorner e_1\, e_2 \urcorner &= app\ \ulcorner e_1 \urcorner\ \ulcorner e_2 \urcorner
\end{aligned}
$$

The representation of an object-language β-redex then has the form

$$\ulcorner(\lambda x\,.\,e)\,f\urcorner \;=\; app\,(lam\,(\lambda x\!:\!exp.\,\ulcorner e\urcorner))\,\ulcorner f\urcorner$$

where $\ulcorner e\urcorner$ my have free occurrences of x. When written as a pattern with variables $E_{exp\to exp}$ and F_{exp} ranging over closed *terms, this is expressed as $app\,(lam\,(\lambda x:exp.\,E\,x))\,F$. The complement of the right-hand side considered as a pattern with respect to the empty context contains every top-level λ-abstraction plus every application where the first argument is not an abstraction:*

$$\mathrm{Not}(app\,(lam\,(\lambda x\!:\!exp.\,E\,x))\,F) =$$
$$\{lam\,(\lambda x\!:\!exp.\,H\;x), app\,(app\,H_1\,H_2)\,H_3\}$$

For patterns which are not fully applied, the complement cannot be expressed as a finite set of patterns, as the following example illustrates.

Example 2 *The encoding of an η-redex takes the form*

$$\ulcorner\lambda x\,.\,e\;x\urcorner \;=\; lam(\lambda x\!:\!exp.\,app\,\ulcorner e\urcorner\,x)$$

where $\ulcorner e\urcorner$ may contain no free occurrence of x. The side condition is expressed in a pattern by introducing an existential variable E_{exp} which does not *depend on x. Hence, its complement with respect to the empty context should contain, among others, also all terms $lam\,(\lambda x : exp.\,app\,(Ex)\,x)$ where E does depend on x.*

Note that there is no finite set of patterns which has as its ground instances exactly those terms M which depend on a given variable x. Following standard terminology, we call such terms *strict in x* and the corresponding function $\lambda x{:}A.\,M$ a *strict function*. As the example above shows, the complement of patterns which are not fully applied can therefore not be represented as a finite set of patterns. This failure of closure under complementation cannot be avoided similarly to the way in which left-linearization bypasses the limitation to linear patterns and it needs to be addressed directly.

One approach is taken by Lugiez [8]: he modifies the language of terms to permit occurrence constraints. For example $\lambda xyz.\,M\{1,3\}$ would denote a function which depends on its first and third argument. The technical handling of those objects then becomes awkward as they require specialized rules which are foreign to the issues of complementation.

Since our underlying λ-calculus is typed, we use typing to express that a function *must* or *must not* depend on its argument. In the next section we develop such a λ-calculus and generalize the complement algorithm to work on such terms.

4   A Strict λ-Calculus

As we have seen in the preceding section, the complement of some patterns in the simply-typed λ-calculus cannot be expressed in a finitary manner within the same calculus. We thus generalize our language to include *strict functions* of type $A \xrightarrow{1} B$ (which are guaranteed to depend on their argument) and *invariant functions* of type $A \xrightarrow{0} B$ (which are guaranteed **not** to depend on their argument). Of course, any concretely given function either will or will not depend on its argument, but in the presence of existential variables we still need the ability to remain uncommitted. Therefore our calculus also contains the full function space $A \xrightarrow{u} B$. A similar calculus have been independently investigated in [16] where the Curry-Howard connection with relevant logic is explained.

$$
\begin{array}{rclcl}
Labels & k & ::= & 1 \mid 0 \mid u \\
Types & A & ::= & P \mid A_1 \xrightarrow{k} A_2 \\
Terms & M & ::= & c \mid x \mid \lambda x^k{:}A.\ M \mid M_1\ M_2{}^k \\
Contexts & \Gamma & ::= & \cdot \mid \Gamma, x{:}A
\end{array}
$$

Note that there are three different forms of abstractions and applications, where the latter are distinguished by different labels on the argument. It is not really necessary to distinguish three forms of application syntactically, since the type of function determines the status of the application, but it is convenient for our purposes. A label u it is called *undetermined*.

We use a formulation of the typing judgment with three zones, containing the undetermined, irrelevant and strict hypotheses, denoted by Γ, Ω, and Δ, respectively. We implicitly assume a fixed signature Σ which would otherwise clutter the presentation.

Our system is biased towards a bottom-up reading of the rules in that variables never disappear, i.e., they are always propagated from the conclusion to the premises, although their status might be changed.

Let us go through the typing rules in detail. The requirement for the strict context Δ to be empty in the Id^u and Id^1 rules expresses that strict variables must be used, while undetermined variables in Γ or irrelevant variables in Ω can be ignored. Note that there is no rule for irrelevant variables, which expresses that they cannot be used.

The introduction rules for undetermined, invariant, and strict functions simply add a variable to the appropriate context and check the body of the function.

The difficult rules are the three elimination rules. First, the undetermined context Γ is always propagated to both premises. This reflects that we place no restriction on the use of these variables.

Next we consider the strict context Δ. Recall that this contains the variables which should occur strictly in a term. An undetermined function $M : A \xrightarrow{u} B$ may or may not use its argument. An occurrence of a variable in the argument to such a function can therefore not be guaranteed to be

$$\frac{c{:}A \in \Sigma}{\Gamma; \Omega; \cdot \vdash c : A} \; Con$$

$$\frac{}{(\Gamma, x{:}A); \Omega; \cdot \vdash x : A} \; Id^u \qquad no \; Id^0 \; rule \qquad \frac{}{\Gamma; \Omega; x{:}A \vdash x : A} \; Id^1$$

$$\frac{(\Gamma, x{:}A); \Omega; \Delta \vdash M : B}{\Gamma; \Omega; \Delta \vdash \lambda x^u{:}A.\; M : A \overset{u}{\to} B} \; \overset{u}{\to} I \qquad \frac{\Gamma; (\Omega, x{:}A); \Delta \vdash M : B}{\Gamma; \Omega; \Delta \vdash \lambda x^0{:}A.\; M : A \overset{0}{\to} B} \; \overset{0}{\to} I$$

$$\frac{\Gamma; \Omega; (\Delta, x{:}A) \vdash M : B}{\Gamma; \Omega; \Delta \vdash \lambda x^1{:}A.\; M : A \overset{1}{\to} B} \; \overset{1}{\to} I$$

$$\frac{\Gamma; \Omega; \Delta \vdash M : A \overset{u}{\to} B \qquad (\Gamma, \Delta); \Omega; \cdot \vdash N : A}{\Gamma; \Omega; \Delta \vdash M \; N^u : B} \; \overset{u}{\to} E$$

$$\frac{\Gamma; \Omega; \Delta \vdash M : A \overset{0}{\to} B \qquad (\Gamma, \Omega, \Delta); \cdot; \cdot \vdash N : A}{\Gamma; \Omega; \Delta \vdash M \; N^0 : B} \; \overset{0}{\to} E$$

$$\frac{(\Gamma, \Delta_N); \Omega; \Delta_M \vdash M : A \overset{1}{\to} B \qquad (\Gamma, \Delta_M); \Omega; \Delta_N \vdash N : A}{\Gamma; \Omega; (\Delta_M, \Delta_N) \vdash M \; N^1 : B} \; \overset{1}{\to} E$$

Figure 1: Typing rules for $\lambda^{\overset{l}{\to}}$

used. Hence we must require in the rule $\overset{u}{\to} E$ for an application $M \; N^u$ that all variables in Δ occur strictly in M. No further restrictions on occurrences of strict variables in the argument are necessary, which is reflected in the rule by adding Δ to the undetermined context while checking the argument N. The treatment of the strict variables in the vacuous application $M \; N^0$ is similar.

In the case of a strict application $M \; N^1$ each strict variable should occur strictly in either M or N. We therefore split the context into Δ_M and Δ_N guaranteeing that each variable has at least one strict occurrence in M or N, respectively. However, strict variables can occur more than once, so variables from Δ_N can be used freely in M, and variables from Δ_M can occur freely in N. As before, we reflect this by adding these variables to the undetermined context.

Finally we consider the irrelevant context Ω. Variables declared in Ω cannot be used *except* in the argument to an irrelevant function (which is guaranteed to ignore its argument). We therefore add the irrelevant context Ω to the undetermined context when checking the argument of a vacuous application $M \; N^0$.

Our strict λ-calculus satisfies the expected properties, including uniqueness of typing and the existence of canonical forms, which is critical for the intended applications. A full account can be found in [11].

Let us examine the structural properties of contexts. Exchange is directly built into the formulation. Weakening is allowed in the undetermined and in the irrelevant contexts. Contraction holds anywhere.

The notions of reduction and expansion derive directly from the ordinary β and η rules.

$$(\lambda x^k{:}A.\ M)\ N^k \xrightarrow{\beta} [N/x]M$$

$$M : A \xrightarrow{k} B \xrightarrow{\eta} \lambda x^k{:}A.\ M\ x^k$$

The subject reduction and expansion theorems are an immediate consequence of the structural and substitution properties generalized to this three-zoned calculus. The substitution properties again follow by straightforward structural inductions.

The above results culminate in the canonical form theorem: for every term M such that $\Gamma; \Omega; \Delta \vdash M : A$, there exists a unique N in canonical ($=$ β-normal η-long) form, denoted $\Gamma; \Omega; \Delta \vdash N \Uparrow A$, such that M is convertible to N. The proof employs the standard method of logical relations, adapted to the specific λ-calculus we consider.

The following lemma establishes a consistency property of the type system relevant to complementation.

Lemma 3 (Exclusivity) *It is not the case that both* $\Gamma; \Omega; (\Delta, x{:}A) \vdash M : C$ *and* $\Gamma; (\Omega, x{:}A); \Delta \vdash M : C$.

5   Embedding the Simply-Typed λ-Calculus

Now that we have developed a calculus which is potentially strong enough to represent the negation of linear patterns, we need to answer two questions: how do we embed the original λ-calculus, and is the calculus now closed under complement?

In this paper, we do not answer the second question conclusively. However, our algorithm is sound and complete for the fragment which results from the natural embedding of the original simply-typed λ-calculus which is sufficient for all applications we have presently considered (see Section 8).

Recall that we introduced strictness to capture occurrence conditions on variables in canonical forms. This means that constants (and by extension bound variables) should be considered *strict* functions of their argument, since these arguments will indeed occur in the canonical form. On the other hand, if we have a second order constant, we cannot restrict the argument function to be either strict or vacuous, since this would render our representations inadequate.

Example 4 *Continuing Example 1, we see*

$$\ulcorner \lambda x.\, \lambda y.\, x \urcorner = lam\ (\lambda x{:}exp.\, lam\ (\lambda y{:}exp.\, x))$$

so the argument to the first occurrence of 'lam' is a strict function, while the argument to the second occurrence is an invariant function. If we can give only one type to 'lam' it must therefore be $(exp \xrightarrow{u} exp) \xrightarrow{1} exp$.

Generalizing this observation means that positive occurrences of function types are translated to strict functions, while negative occurrences become undetermined functions. We can formalize this as an embedding of simply-typed λ-terms into a fragment of strict terms via two mutually recursive translations $()^-$ and $()^+$. First, the definition on types.

$$(A \rightarrow B)^- = A^+ \xrightarrow{u} B^-$$
$$(A \rightarrow B)^+ = A^- \xrightarrow{1} B^+$$
$$P^- = P^+ = P$$

We extend it to canonical terms (including existential variables), signatures, and contexts as follows:

$$
\begin{aligned}
M^- &= M^+ \quad \text{for } M : P & (\lambda x{:}A.\, M)^- &= \lambda x^u{:}A^+.\, M^- \\
x^+ &= x & (\Sigma, P{:}type)^+ &= \Sigma^+, P{:}type \\
c^+ &= c & (\Sigma, c{:}A)^+ &= \Sigma^+, c{:}A^+ \\
(E_A\ x_1 \ldots x_n)^+ &= F_{A^-}\ x_1^u \ldots x_n^u & (\cdot)^+ &= \cdot \\
(M\ N)^+ &= M^+\ (N^-)^1 & (\Gamma, x{:}A)^+ &= \Gamma^+, x{:}A^+
\end{aligned}
$$

The image of the embedding of the canonical forms of the simply-typed λ-calculus gives rise to the following fragment, which we call *simple terms*.

$$\text{Simple Terms}\quad M \ ::= \ \lambda x^u{:}A^+.\, M \mid h\ M_1{}^1 \ldots M_n{}^1 \mid E_A\ x_1^{l_1} \ldots x_n^{l_n}$$

We sometimes abbreviate $h\ M_1{}^1 \ldots M_n{}^1$ as $h\ \overline{M_n^1}$. Note that by the restriction to long normal forms such terms and applications of pattern variables must be of base type. For every judgment J on simple terms, we will shorten $\Gamma; \cdot; \cdot \vdash J$ into $\Gamma \vdash J$.

The correctness of the embedding is easily established by induction over the structure of canonical forms.

Theorem 5 *If* $\Gamma \vdash M \Uparrow A$ *then* $\Gamma^+ \vdash M^- \Uparrow A^-$.

From now on we drop the $\pm$ embedding annotations from terms, types and contexts. We may also hide the $()^1$ decoration from strict application of constants in examples.

Simple terms enjoy the tightening property which is related to exclusivity (Theorem 3) and is crucial for the correctness proof of our complement algorithm. It expresses that every closed *simple* term is either strict or vacuous in a given undetermined variable. After appropriate generalization, the result follows by induction on the given derivation.

Theorem 6 (Tightening) *Let M be a simple term without existential variables such that $(\Gamma, x{:}C); \Omega; \Delta \vdash M \Uparrow A$. Then $\Gamma; \Omega; (\Delta, x{:}C) \vdash M \Uparrow A$ or $\Gamma; (\Omega, x{:}C); \Delta \vdash M \Uparrow A$.*

It simplifies the presentation of the algorithms for complement and later unification if we extend every existentially quantified variable to be applied to all bound variables in their declaration order. This is possible for simple linear patterns without changing the set of its ground instances. We just insert vacuous applications, which guarantees that the extra variables are not used. We furthermore permute the argument to the standard order, which also does not affect the set of ground instances of linear patterns. In slight abuse of notation we call the resulting terms *fully applied*.

Example 7 *The term from Example 2, lam $(\lambda x^u{:}exp.\, app\, E\, x)$, has fully applied form lam $(\lambda x^u{:}exp.\, app\, (Z\, x^0)\, x)$ for a fresh existential variable Z of type $exp \overset{0}{\to} exp$.*

Theorem 8 *Let N be a simple term and Q its fully applied translation. Then $\Gamma \vdash M \in \|N\| : A$ iff $\Gamma \vdash M \in \|Q\| : A$.*

From now on we tacitly assume that all simple terms are fully applied. We call a term $E\, x_1^{l_1} \ldots x_n^{l_n}$ (of base type) a *generalized variable*.

6 The Complement Algorithm

The idea of complementation for applications and abstractions is quite simple and similar to the first-order case. For generalized variables we consider each argument in turn. If an argument variable is undetermined it does not contribute to the negation. If an argument variable is strict then any term where this variable does not occur contributes to the negation. We therefore complement the corresponding label from 0 to 1 while all other arguments are undetermined. For vacuous argument variables we proceed dually. In preparation for the rules we define $\text{Not}(1) = 0$ and $\text{Not}(0) = 1$. If $\Gamma = x_1{:}A_1, \ldots, x_n{:}A_n$, we write $E\, \Gamma^u$ for the application of $E\, x_1^u \ldots x_n^u$. Such an application represents the set of all terms without existential variables and free variables from Γ.

Definition 9 (Higher-Order Pattern Complement) *For a linear simple term M such that $\Gamma \vdash M : A$, define $\Gamma \vdash \text{Not}(M) \Rightarrow N : A$ with the meaning that N is in the complement of M of type A in context Γ by the following rules.*

$$\frac{1 \le i \le n \quad k \in \{1,0\}}{\Gamma \vdash \mathrm{Not}(E \; x_1^{l_1} \ldots x_{i-1}^{l_{i-1}} \; x_i^{k} \; x_{i+1}^{l_{i+1}} \ldots x_n^{l_n}) \Rightarrow H \; x_1^{u} \ldots x_{i-1}^{u} \; x_i^{\mathrm{Not}(k)} \; x_{i+1}^{u} \ldots x_n^{u} : P}$$

$$\frac{\Gamma, x{:}A \vdash \mathrm{Not}(M) \Rightarrow N : B}{\Gamma \vdash \mathrm{Not}(\lambda x^u{:}A.\, M) \Rightarrow \lambda x^u{:}A.\, N : A \xrightarrow{u} B}$$

$$\frac{g \in \Sigma \cup \Gamma, g : A_1 \xrightarrow{1} \ldots \xrightarrow{1} A_m \xrightarrow{1} P, m \ge 0, h \ne g}{\Gamma \vdash \mathrm{Not}(h \; \overline{M_n}^1) \Rightarrow g \; (H_1 \Gamma^u)^1 \ldots (H_m \Gamma^u)^1 : P}$$

$$\frac{\Gamma \vdash \mathrm{Not}(M_i) \Rightarrow N : A_i \qquad 1 \le i \le n}{\Gamma \vdash \mathrm{Not}(h \; \overline{M_n}^1) \Rightarrow h \; (H_1 \Gamma^u)^1 \ldots (H_{i-1} \Gamma^u)^1 \; N^1 \; (H_{i+1} \Gamma^u)^1 \ldots (H_n \Gamma^u)^1 : P}$$

where the H's are new variables, $h \in \Sigma \cup \Gamma$, and $\Gamma \vdash h : A_1 \xrightarrow{1} \ldots \xrightarrow{1} A_n \xrightarrow{1} P$.
Finally we define $\Gamma \vdash \mathrm{Not}(M) = \mathcal{N} : A$ if $\mathcal{N} = \{N \mid \Gamma \vdash \mathrm{Not}(M) \Rightarrow N : A\}$.

Note that if E_A is a generalized variable considered in the empty context, it has the canonical form $\lambda \overline{x_n^u}.\, E \; \overline{x_n^u}$. Hence $\cdot \vdash \mathrm{Not}(E_A) = \emptyset : A$ as expected.

We remark that the members of a complement set are not mutually disjoint, due to the indeterminacy of u. We can achieve a representation by exclusive patterns if we resolve this indeterminacy, that is, by considering for every argument x^u the two possibilities x^1 and x^0. It is clear that in the worst case scenario the number of terms in a complement set is bound by 2^n; hence the usefulness of this further step needs to be pragmatically determined.

We can now revisit Example 2:

$$\mathrm{Not}(lam(\lambda x^u{:}exp.\, app \; (E \; x^0) \; x)) =$$
$$\{lam(\lambda x^u{:}exp.\, app \; (H \; x^1) \; (H' \; x^u)),$$
$$lam(\lambda x^u{:}exp.\, app \; (H \; x^u) \; (app \; (H' \; x^u) \; (H'' x^u))),$$
$$lam(\lambda x^u{:}exp.\, app \; (H \; x^u) \; (lam(\lambda y^u{:}exp.\, H' \; x^u \; y^u))),$$
$$lam(\lambda x^u{:}exp.\, lam(\lambda y^u{:}exp.\, H \; x^u \; y^u)),$$
$$lam(\lambda x^u{:}exp.\, x),$$
$$app \; H \; H'\}$$

We can show that simple terms are closed under complementation by induction over the construction of the complement.

Theorem 10 *If M is simple, so are all N such that $\Gamma \vdash \mathrm{Not}(M) \Rightarrow N : A$.*

We address the soundness and completeness of the complement algorithm in the following theorem. Termination is obvious as the algorithm is syntax-directed and only finitely branching. We write $\Gamma \vdash M \in \|\mathrm{Not}(N)\| : A$ if $\Gamma \vdash \mathrm{Not}(N) \Rightarrow Q : A$ and $\Gamma \vdash M \in \|Q\| : A$.

Theorem 11 (Partition) *Let* $\Gamma \vdash N : A$ *be a simple linear term.*

1. *(Exclusivity) It is not the case that both*
   $\Gamma \vdash M \in \|N\| : A$ *and* $\Gamma \vdash M \in \|\mathrm{Not}(N)\| : A$.

2. *(Exhaustivity) If* $\Gamma \vdash M : A$ *then*
   either $\Gamma \vdash M \in \|N\| : A$ *or* $\Gamma \vdash M \in \|\mathrm{Not}(N)\| : A$.

Note that exclusivity is based on Theorem 3, which holds for *any* strict term. In contrast, exhaustivity requires tightening (Theorem 6) which holds only for simple terms.

7 Unification of Simple Terms

We now address the issue of unification, i.e., intersection of simple linear higher-order patterns. We start by determining when two labels are compatible and define their intersection as the idempotent and symmetric extension of $u \cap 1 = 1$ and $u \cap 0 = 0$. The remaining cases $1 \cap 0$ and $0 \cap 1$ are undefined since no variable can be both strict and vacuous in a given term.

We use Φ for sequences of labeled bound variables and write $\Phi(x) = k$ if $x^k \in \Phi$. We also extend the intersection operations to these such sequences in the obvious way. Following standard terminology we call atomic terms whose head is a free or bound variable *rigid*, while terms whose head is an existential variable are called *flexible*.

Definition 12 (Higher-Order Pattern Intersection) *For simple linear terms* M *and* N *without shared variables such that* $\Gamma \vdash M : A$ *and* $\Gamma \vdash N : A$, *we define* $\Gamma \vdash M \cap N \Rightarrow Q : A$ *by the following rules.*

$$\frac{}{\Gamma \vdash E\ \Phi_1 \cap F\ \Phi_2 \Rightarrow H\ (\Phi_1 \cap \Phi_2) : P}\ \cap\_FF$$

$$\frac{c \in \Sigma \quad \Gamma \vdash H_1\ \Phi_1 \cap M_1 \Rightarrow N_1 : A_1 \cdots \Gamma \vdash H_n\ \Phi_n \cap M_n \Rightarrow N_n : A_n}{\Gamma \vdash E\ \Phi \cap c\ \overline{M_n^1} \Rightarrow c\ \overline{N_n^1} : P}\ \cap\_FR^c$$

$$\frac{y \in \Gamma \quad \Gamma \vdash H_1\ \Phi_1 \cap M_1 \Rightarrow N_1 : A_1 \cdots \Gamma \vdash H_n\ \Phi_n \cap M_n \Rightarrow N_n : A_n}{\Gamma \vdash E\ \Phi \cap y\ \overline{M_n^1} \Rightarrow y\ \overline{N_n^1} : P}\ \cap\_FR^y$$

$$\frac{h \in \Gamma \cup \Sigma \quad \Gamma \vdash M_1 \cap N_1 \Rightarrow Q_1 : A_1 \cdots \Gamma \vdash M_n \cap N_n \Rightarrow Q_n : A_n}{\Gamma \vdash h\ \overline{M_n^1} \cap h\ \overline{N_n^1} \Rightarrow h\ \overline{Q_n^1} : P}\ \cap\_App$$

$$\frac{\Gamma, x{:}A \vdash M \cap N \Rightarrow Q : B}{\Gamma \vdash \lambda x^u{:}A.\,M \cap \lambda x^u{:}A.\,N \Rightarrow \lambda x^u{:}A.\,Q : A \to B}\ \cap\_Lam$$

where the H's *are fresh variables of correct typing and* $n \geq 0$.

We have omitted two rules $\cap\_RF^c$ *and* $\cap\_RF^y$ *which are symmetric to* $\cap\_FR^c$ *and* $\cap\_FR^y$. *The rules* $\cap\_FR^c$ *and* $\cap\_RF^c$ *have the following proviso:*

for all $x \in \Phi$ *and* $1 \le i \le n$:

$$\forall x.\Phi(x) = 0 \to \forall i \,.\, \Phi_i(x) = 0$$
$$\forall x.\Phi(x) = u \to \forall i \,.\, \Phi_i(x) = u$$
$$\forall x.\Phi(x) = 1 \to \exists i \,.\, \Phi_i(x) = 1 \land \forall j, j \ne i.\Phi_j(x) = u$$

The rules $\cap\_FR^y$ *and* $\cap\_RF^y$ *are subject to the proviso*

$$\forall x.\Phi(x) = 0 \to \forall i \,.\, \Phi_i(x) = 0$$
$$\forall x.\Phi(x) = u \to \forall i \,.\, \Phi_i(x) = u$$
$$\forall x.x \ne y \land \Phi(x) = 1 \to \exists i \,.\, \Phi_i(x) = 1 \land \forall j, j \ne i.\Phi_j(x) = u$$
$$\Phi(y) = u \lor (\Phi(y) = 1 \land \forall i.\Phi_i(y) = u)$$

Finally we define $\Gamma \vdash M \cap N : A = Q$ *if* $Q = \{Q \mid \Gamma \vdash M \cap N \Rightarrow Q : A\}$.

In rule $\cap\_FF$ we can assume that the same list of variables, though possibly with different labeling, is the argument of E, F and H, since simple terms are fully applied and due to linearity we can always reorder the context to the same list. Since patterns are linear and M and N share no pattern variables, the flex-flex case arises only with distinct variables. This also means we do not have to apply substitutions or perform the customary occurs-check. In the flex/rigid and rigid/flex rules, the proviso enforces the typing discipline since each strict variable x must be strict in some premise. The modified condition on y takes into account that the head of an application constitutes a strict occurrence.

The following example illustrates how the Flex-Rigid rules, in this case $\cap\_FR^c$, make unification on simple terms finitary:

$$x{:}A \vdash E \; x^1 \cap \; c \; (F \; x^u)^1 \; (F' \; x^u)^1 =$$
$$\{c \; (H \; x^1)^1 \; (H' \; x^u)^1, c \; (H \; x^u)^1 \; (H' \; x^1)^1\}$$

Note that, similarly to complementation, intersection returns a solution with possible overlaps between the patterns. Again it is possible, in a post-processing phase, to transform the results into disjoint form.

As for complement, the termination of the algorithm is straightforward since the judgment is term-directed with finite branching. The adequacy proof for the unification algorithm on linear simple terms requires two implications which follow inductively, at the heart relying on properties of strict typing derivations.

Theorem 13 (Correctness of Pattern Intersection) *For simple linear terms* N_1 *and* N_2 *without shared existential variables such that* $\Gamma \vdash N_1 : A$ *and* $\Gamma \vdash N_2 : A$, *we have* $\Gamma \vdash M \in \|N_1\| : A$ *and* $\Gamma \vdash M \in \|N_2\| : A$ *iff* $\Gamma \vdash M \in \|N_1 \cap N_2\| : A$.

8   Conclusion

We have shown that the complement of linear higher-order patterns cannot be expressed as a finite union of such patterns. To close the language under complement we generalized to a λ-calculus in which strict and vacuous functions can be expressed in the type system. The original language can be embedded compositionally into *simple patterns*. On this language, both complement and intersection (that is, unification) can be expressed as a finite union of simple linear patterns. From this it is easy to see that finite sets of simple linear patterns form a boolean algebra. Indeed, we can trivially define the *relative complement* of two terms via complement and intersection; namely, extending as expected the latter operation to operate on sets of terms, we have $\mathcal{M} - \mathcal{N} = \mathcal{M} \cap \mathcal{N}^c$.

Our main application lies in higher-order logic programming, where pattern complement is a necessary component in any algorithm to synthesize the negation of a given program. This synthesis includes two basic operations: negation to compute the complements of heads of clauses in the definition of a predicate, and intersection to combine results of negating individual clause heads. In this paper we have provided algorithms to compute both.

While this approach has been investigated for first-order Horn clauses [1] and CLP programs [2], the field has been little explored with respect to higher-order logics and logical frameworks. This is the most important future work we are considering; the algorithms presented here provide the central foundation.

We also plan to extend the results to dependent types to endow intentionally weak frameworks such as Twelf [15] with a logically meaningful notion of negation along the lines of [1]. Finally, we hope to address the general case of complementation and unification in the strict λ-calculus which is likely to be useful in linear logical frameworks as *LLF* [3].

Acknowledgments

We are grateful to Iliano Cervesato, Carsten Schürmann and Roberto Virga for useful comments on previous versions of this paper. This work has been partially supported by NSF Grant CCR-9619584.

References

[1] R. Barbuti, P. Mancarella, D. Pedreschi, and F. Turini. A transformational approach to negation in logic programming. *Journal of Logic Programming*, 8:201–228, 1990.

[2] P. Bruscoli, F. Levi, G. Levi, and M. C. Meo. Compilative constructive negation in constraint logic programs. In S. Tiso, editor, *Proceedings of the 19th International Colloquium on Trees in Algebra and Programming (CAAP'94)*, pages 52–76. Springer-Verlag LNCS 787, 1994.

[3] I. Cervesato and F. Pfenning. A linear logical framework. In E. Clarke, editor, *Proceedings of the Eleventh Annual Symposium on Logic in Computer Science*, pages 264–275, New Brunswick, New Jersey, July 1996. IEEE Computer Society Press.

[4] H. Comon. Disunification: A survey. In J.-L. Lassez and G.Plotkin, editors, *Computational Logic*. MIT Press, Cambridge,MA, 1991.

[5] M. Hanus and C. Prehofer. Higher-order narrowing with definitional trees. In *Proc. Seventh International Conference on Rewriting Techniques and Applications (RTA'96)*, pages 138–152. Springer LNCS 1103, 1996.

[6] K. Kunen. Answer sets and negation-as-failure. In J.-L. Lassez, editor, *Proceedings of the Fourth International Conference on Logic Programming (ICLP '87)*, pages 219–228, Melbourne, Australia, May 1987. MIT Press.

[7] J.-L. Lassez and K. Marriot. Explicit representation of terms defined by counter examples. *Journal of Automated Reasoning*, 3(3):301–318, Sept. 1987.

[8] D. Lugiez. Positive and negative results for higher-order disunification. *Journal of Symbolic Computation*, 20(4):431–470, Oct. 1995.

[9] S. Michaylov and F. Pfenning. Natural semantics and some of its meta-theory in Elf. In L.-H. Eriksson, L. Hallnäs, and P. Schroeder-Heister, editors, *Proceedings of the Second International Workshop on Extensions of Logic Programming*, pages 299–344, Stockholm, Sweden, Jan. 1991. Springer-Verlag LNAI 596.

[10] D. Miller. A logic programming language with lambda-abstraction, function variables, and simple unification. *Journal of Logic and Computation*, 1(4):497–536, 1991.

[11] A. Momigliano. *Elimination of negation in a logical framework*. PhD thesis, Carnegie Mellon University, Forthcoming.

[12] T. Nipkow. Higher-order critical pairs. In G. Kahn, editor, *Sixth Annual IEEE Symposium on Logic in Computer Science*, pages 342–349, Amsterdam, The Netherlands, July 1991.

[13] F. Pfenning. Logic programming in the LF logical framework. In G. Huet and G. Plotkin, editors, *Logical Frameworks*, pages 149–181. Cambridge University Press, 1991.

[14] F. Pfenning. Unification and anti-unification in the Calculus of Constructions. In *Sixth Annual IEEE Symposium on Logic in Computer Science*, pages 74–85, Amsterdam, The Netherlands, July 1991.

[15] C. Schürmann and F. Pfenning. Automated theorem proving in a simple meta-logic for LF. In C. Kirchner and H. Kirchner, editors, *Proceedings of the 15th International Conference on Automated Deduction (CADE-15)*, pages 286–300, Lindau, Germany, July 1998. Springer-Verlag LNCS 1421.

[16] D. A. Wright. *Reduction types and intensionality in the lambda-calculus*. PhD thesis, University of Tasmania, Sept. 1992.

Extensionality of Simply Typed Logic Programs

Marc Bezem
Utrecht University, Department of Philosophy
P.O. Box 80126, NL-3508 TC, Utrecht, The Netherlands

Abstract

We set up a framework for the study of extensionality in the context of higher-order logic programming. For simply typed logic programs we propose a novel declarative semantics, consisting of a model class with a semi-computable initial model, and a notion of extensionality. We show that the initial model of a simply typed logic program, in case the program is extensional, collapses into a simple, set-theoretic representation. Given the undecidability of extensionality in general, we develop a decidable, syntactic criterion which is sufficient for extensionality. Some typical examples of higher-order logic programs are shown to be extensional.

1 Introduction

Higher-order logic programming is an extension of logic programming where variables for predicates (and predicates of predicates, and so on) are allowed and predicates can be used in terms.

Some restricted forms of higher-order logic programming are already supported by Prolog, but in the more recent logic languages, following functional languages, the higher order has been incorporated in the design from the very beginning: Lambda Prolog [8], Hilog [2], Gödel [5], and Mercury [11]. Good references are [10] and [9].

In this paper we address the problem of assigning meaning to higher-order logic programs, and study in particular the phenomenon of extensionality. The basis of the proposed semantics is the theory of simple types, founded by Church [3]. In order to get a clear picture of the notion of extensionality itself, we keep the terms and the types as simple as possible. For this reason we do not yet consider lambda abstraction, higher-order unification, polymorphism, subtyping and so on, but we are well aware of the importance of these features for the languages cited above.

Let us start with an instructive example. Consider a higher-order logic program P, which includes the following clauses, besides the definition of a number of first-order predicates.

```
stepwise(R,[]).
stepwise(R,[_]).
stepwise(R,[X,Y|Z]):- R(X,Y),stepwise(R,[Y|Z]).
```

These three clauses show one of the key features of higher-order logic programming: the variable R stands for an arbitrary binary predicate and is used in a term position of stepwise, which is a predicate of (binary) predicates and lists of individuals. The meaning of stepwise is clear: if r is a binary predicate and l is a list, then stepwise(r,l) holds iff r holds between every two successive elements of the list l. Note that stepwise(r,l) only depends on the *extension* of r, that is, on its set of pairs, and not on the *intension*, its name r. We call the program P *extensional*, as its meaning can be explained in terms of extensions. See also Example 4.3.

Next, assume we want to use the predicate stepwise to define when a list is ordered with respect to an ordering relation. It is easy to add the following clause to the program.

```
ordered(R,L):- ordering(R),stepwise(R,L).
```

But then we have to face the problem of defining the predicate (of binary predicates) ordering. As the extensions of binary predicates can be recursively enumerable (Σ_1), cf. [1], deciding whether such an extension is irreflexive is co-enumerable (Π_1) and transitivity has already the complexity of the universal halting problem (Π_2). In fact we can do no better than, for a number of known orderings involved, state explicitly so:

```
ordering(r1).
ordering(r2).
...
```

Now the meaning of the predicate ordered has become: if r is a binary predicate and l is a list, then ordered(r,l) holds iff ordering(r) and the list l is ordered with respect to the extension of r. The subtle point here is that ordering(r) does not depend on the extension of r, but on its intension, the name r itself. If some other binary predicate s has the same extension as r (verifying this has the complexity of the universal halting problem), then it is not warranted that ordering(s) iff ordering(r) holds, and hence we can have mismatches between ordered(r,l) and ordered(s,l), although r and s have the same extension. As a consequence, the meaning of the extended program cannot be explained in terms of extensions only, whence we call such programs *intensional*, as opposed to the *extensional* program above.

Many properties of extensions are highly undecidable. Due to the unification process, logic programming seems to be inherently intensional. Completeness of the operational behaviour seems incompatible with an extensional semantics. Is this hopeless?

On the positive side, extensions of predicates are important to describe their semantics, and extensionality, if it holds, is an important structural property of a predicate, which simplifies its semantics and thus contributes to a better understanding of the program. Let us see how far we can come.

2   Terms and types

Under the restrictions we adopted, the terms of higher-order logic programming are in fact extremely simple: they are built up from constants and variables by application. To arrive at this simplicity, however, we must adopt a fully curried version of the syntax (named after Curry). This means that a function of more than one argument is viewed as a function of one argument to functions of one argument, and so on. In other words, not the tuple is the argument, but its components are successive arguments of the function (values). Then we do not need cartesian products like in $(D \times D) \rightarrow D$, but we can do with the type constructor $\rightarrow$ only, such as in $D \rightarrow (D \rightarrow D)$.

For compliance with the usual syntax we practise a liberal way of currying. For example, the following denotations are all identified:

$$pxa \equiv (px)a \equiv p(x, a) \equiv p(x)a \equiv p(x)(a)$$

This means that brackets and argument lists can be used freely, but serve only as alternative denotations of curried terms.

The (untyped) terms of logic programming are given by the following abstract syntax:

$$\mathcal{T} ::= \mathcal{C} \mid \mathcal{V} \mid (\mathcal{T}\mathcal{T})$$

Here $\mathcal{C}$ and $\mathcal{V}$ are sets of constants and variables, respectively, and $\mathcal{T}\mathcal{T}$ are terms obtained by application. In principle $\mathcal{C}$ and $\mathcal{V}$ contain all correct Prolog constants and variables, respectively, but in most examples we will tacitly assume that $\mathcal{C}$ contains only those constants that are explicitly mentioned in the example. We use x, y, z, u, v, w to denote variables, a, b, c, d, p, q, r as constants, and s, t to denote arbitrary terms. Application is taken to be left associative, so $p(xa)$ is notably different from the denotations above. The *head symbol* of a term is its leftmost symbol, either a variable or a constant.

Example 2.1 Examples of (untyped) terms are $c(x, a), c(c), xxy, x(xy)$. The first and the last will turn out to be typable, the others are not.   □

A *clause* is an expression of the form $t_0 \leftarrow t_1, \ldots, t_n$, where all t_i are terms $(0 \le i \le n)$. A program is a finite set of clauses. We use C for clauses and P for programs. In the examples we use Prolog notation for clauses and programs.

Example 2.2 Consider the following clauses.

```
call/2(X,Y1,Y2):- X(Y1,Y2).
foo(Z):- Z(Z).
X(Y1,Y1).       % every binary relation is reflexive
```

The first and the last clause will turn out to be typable, the second is not. Note that we allow a variable as head symbol of the head of a clause.   □

In order to single out the well-typed higher-order logic programs we use types. The fragment consisting of first-order terms can be typed with types given by the following abstract syntax:

$$\boldsymbol{D} ::= D \mid (D{\rightarrow}\boldsymbol{D})$$

Here D is the base type of a (fixed) domain of individuals and $(D{\rightarrow}D)$, $(D{\rightarrow}(D{\rightarrow}D))$, ... are the types of unary functions, binary functions, and so on. Here and below we let $\rightarrow$ associate to the right and we drop outermost brackets.

The types for the higher-order objects are given by the following abstract syntax:

$$\boldsymbol{T} ::= A \mid (\boldsymbol{T}{\rightarrow}\boldsymbol{T}) \mid (D{\rightarrow}\boldsymbol{T})$$

Here A is the base type of atoms. The types $D{\rightarrow}A$, $D{\rightarrow}D{\rightarrow}A$, ... are the types of unary predicates, of binary predicates, and so on. The types $A{\rightarrow}A$, $(D{\rightarrow}A){\rightarrow}A$, ... are the types of predicates on atoms, on unary predicates, and so on. More complicated types can easily be constructed, for example, $((A{\rightarrow}A){\rightarrow}A){\rightarrow}(D{\rightarrow}D{\rightarrow}A){\rightarrow}A$.

The set of types for higher-order logic programming is the union of $\boldsymbol{D}$ and $\boldsymbol{T}$. The former will only play a minor role in this paper, and we will focus attention on the latter. We use σ, τ to denote arbitrary types.

Lemma 2.3 *Every type σ in $\boldsymbol{T}$ is of the form*

$$\sigma \equiv \sigma_1 {\rightarrow} \cdots {\rightarrow} \sigma_k {\rightarrow} A$$

for some $k \geq 0$, with σ_i either D or in $\boldsymbol{T}$, for every $1 \leq i \leq k$.

Proof: By induction on σ. In the base case we have $\sigma \equiv A$ and we take $k = 0$. There are two induction steps, namely $D{\rightarrow}\tau$ with $\tau \in \boldsymbol{T}$ and $\tau'{\rightarrow}\tau$ with $\tau, \tau' \in \boldsymbol{T}$. Both are settled by applying the induction hypothesis to τ. Assume $\tau \equiv \tau_1 {\rightarrow} \cdots {\rightarrow} \tau_k {\rightarrow} A$ as in the lemma. Now the lemma is proved for σ by incrementing k, putting $\sigma_{i+1} \equiv \tau_i$ and $\sigma_1 \equiv D$ or $\sigma_1 \equiv \tau'$. □

Due to the absence of abstraction, the typing system for terms is very simple and consists of one single typing rule:

$$\frac{t : \sigma{\rightarrow}\tau \quad s : \sigma}{ts : \tau} \; (\rightarrow)$$

We will now formally define when a higher-order logic program is typable.

Definition 2.4 A *declaration* is an expression either of the form $x : \sigma$ with x a variable, or of the form $c : \sigma$ with c a constant, stating that x (respectively c) has type σ. The variable (constant) on the left hand side is called the *declarandum* of the declaration.

A *context* is a finite list of declarations with different declaranda. Contexts are denoted by Γ.

The *typing relation* $\Gamma \vdash t : \sigma$ is defined inductively as the smallest relation which holds whenever $t : \sigma$ is a declaration in Γ and which is closed under the typing rule ($\rightarrow$) above.

A term t is *typable* by Γ if there exists σ such that $\Gamma \vdash t : \sigma$.

A clause $t_0 \leftarrow t_1, \ldots, t_n$ is *typable* by Γ if $\Gamma \vdash t_i : A$ for all $0 \leq i \leq n$. In that case we write $\Gamma \vdash t_0 \leftarrow t_1, \ldots, t_n : A$.

A program P consisting of clauses $C_1, \ldots, C_n$ is *typable* by Γ if $\Gamma \vdash C_i : A$ for all $1 \leq i \leq n$. In that case we write $\Gamma \vdash P : A$.

We call a term (clause, program) *typable* if it is typable by Γ for suitable Γ. If we speak of a clause (term) in relation to a typable program, then we implicitly assume the clause (term) to be typable by the same context. □

Intuitively, $\Gamma \vdash P : A$ means that the declarations in Γ ensure that each atom in P is of the base type A. Note that one and the same variable may occur in different clauses of P, but always with the same type as declared in Γ. In cases in which different types are required, the program clauses should be standardized apart.

An alternative characterization of the typing relation is the following: $\Gamma \vdash t : \sigma$ holds if and only if there exists a derivation tree according to ($\rightarrow$) with root $t : \sigma$ and leaves in Γ.

Due to the absence of abstraction, the typing system is in fact a subsystem of that for simply typed combinatory logic. We rely on the well-established techniques on principal type schemes for type checking and type synthesis. Space limitations prevent us from entering this important subject, instead we refer to the original source [6], or [7] for a modern exposition, and to the ML literature.

To give the reader at least some idea, the principal type scheme of the term xy is $x : \alpha \rightarrow \beta$, $y : \alpha$, with α, β arbitrary types. The principal type scheme of the atom xy is $x : \alpha \rightarrow A$, $y : \alpha$, and of the clause $xy \leftarrow y$ it is the context $x : A \rightarrow A$, $y : A$.

Example 2.5 Recall the program from Example 2.2. The first and the last clause are typable by the context:

```
call/2: (D->D->A)->D->D->A
X: D->D->A
Y1,Y2: D
```

This means that `call/2` takes three arguments of types D->D->A, D and D, respectively. The second clause of Example 2.2 is not typable, since Z cannot have both type σ and type $\sigma \rightarrow A$. □

3   Operational semantics

The operational semantics is in fact an extension of the usual one for first-order logic programming. Space limitations prevent us from entering soundness and completeness issues. We treat only some key points needed for a proper understanding of the sequel, namely unification, well-typed substitution and the immediate consequence operator. The latter will play a role in inductive proofs.

We extend the Martelli-Montanari algorithm such as described in [1]. Unification of two terms can only succeed if they have the same type, say τ, in a context Γ. In unifying them, we first write the terms in the form $t_0 t_1 \ldots t_k$ and $s_0 s_1 \ldots s_l$, where t_0 and s_0 are the respective head symbols. If the head symbols have the same type, then $k = l$ and the algorithm proceeds in the usual way. If $t_0 : \tau_1 \to \cdots \to \tau_k \to \tau$ and $s_0 : \sigma_1 \to \cdots \to \sigma_l \to \tau$ have different types, then the unification fails in all but the following two symmetric cases.

- $l < k$, $\sigma_i \equiv \tau_{i+k-l}$ for $1 \leq i \leq l$ and s_0 is a variable. Now the algorithm proceeds by binding s_0 to $t_0 t_1 \ldots t_{k-l}$ and by unifying s_i with t_{i+k-l} for all $1 \leq i \leq l$.

- $k < l$, etcetera, symmetric to the previous case.

Type persistence under well-typed substitution (and hence under resolution) is ensured by the following lemma.

Lemma 3.1 *If* $\Gamma, x : \sigma \vdash t : \tau$ *and* $\Gamma, \Gamma' \vdash s : \sigma$, *then* $\Gamma, \Gamma' \vdash t[x/s] : \tau$.

Proof: By induction on the derivation of $\Gamma, x : \sigma \vdash t : \tau$. $\qquad \square$

We recall the familiar notions of Herbrand Base, Herbrand Universe, immediate consequence operator and its least fixed point. These notions are now slightly more general as the terms involved stem from the higher-order syntax. By convention all terms are assumed to be typable in the context of the program.

Definition 3.2 Let P be a typable higher-order logic program. We define the *Herbrand Base* B_P (resp. the *Herbrand Universe* U_P) to be the set of all closed terms of type A (resp. D). For every $S \subseteq B_P$ we define $T_P(S) \subseteq B_P$ by $t \in T_P(S)$ iff there exists a closed instance of a program clause in P with head t and all body atoms in S. The operator T_P is called the *immediate consequence operator* of P. As usual, $T_P{\uparrow}0 = \emptyset$, $T_P{\uparrow}(n+1) = T_P(T_P{\uparrow}n)$ and $M_P = T_P{\uparrow}\omega = \bigcup_{n \geq 0} T_P{\uparrow}n$. $\qquad \square$

4 Declarative semantics

Some introductory remarks may help to grasp the intuition behind the proposed declarative semantics. Objects of type $\sigma \in \mathcal{D}$ are never defined in a logic program. The reason is that such objects only occur in argument positions in atoms. Hence we simply put the interpretation $[\sigma]_P$ of types $\sigma \in \mathcal{D}$ to be the set of closed terms of type σ. This includes $[D]_P = U_P$.

For types from $\mathcal{T}$, in particular for the base type A, the situation is entirely different. At first thought one may expect $[\![A]\!]_P$ to be the set of truth values $\{\mathbf{T}, \mathbf{F}\}$, indeed the domain of interpretation of atoms in classical, extensional logic. However, intensionality makes the applicative behaviour of the higher-order objects non-truth-functional. The right interpretation of $[\![A]\!]_P$ turns out to be the graph of the characteristic function of the least fixed point M_P (see also [9]). This graph contains all information about the names as well as about the truth values of the atoms. In other words, the interpretation of atoms consists of pairs of intensions and extension. This will also be the case for objects of the other types in $\mathcal{T}$, i.e. for predicates, predicates of predicates, and so on.

For every typable program P we shall define, successively,

- $|\sigma|_P$ the set of all intensions of type σ,

- $|t|_P$ the intension of closed term t of type σ,

- $[\sigma]_P$ the set of (possible) extensions of type σ,

- $[t]_P$ the extension of closed term t of type σ.

- $[\![\sigma]\!]_P$ the interpretation of type σ,

- $[\![t]\!]_P$ the interpretation of closed term t of type σ.

For every type σ, $[\![\sigma]\!]_P$ will be the set consisting of all $[\![t]\!]_P$ with t a closed term of type σ. For t of type σ in $\mathcal{D}$, $[\![t]\!]_P$ will be the intension $|t|_P$. For t of type σ in $\mathcal{T}$, $[\![t]\!]_P$ will be the pair $(|t|_P, [t]_P)$ consisting of the intension t and the extension of t.

The *intension* of a closed term is simply the closed term itself. The *extension* of a closed term depends on its type and is either

- the term itself (this is the case for terms of type in $\mathcal{D}$), or

- a truth value (extension of type A), or

- a function mapping intensions of type σ to extensions of type τ (extension of type $\sigma \to \tau$ in $\mathcal{T}$).

For every type σ, $[\sigma]_P$ will be a set containing at least all $[t]_P$ with t a closed term of type σ.

We are now in a position to give a formal definition of the interpretations of types and terms.

Definition 4.1 Let P be a typable higher-order logic program. We shall define the six items listed above, distinguishing between types $\sigma \in \mathcal{D}$ and $\sigma \in \mathcal{T}$.

$\mathcal{D}$: We put $[\![t]\!]_P = [t]_P = |t|_P = t$ for all closed terms of type $\sigma \in \mathcal{D}$, and $[\![\sigma]\!]_P = [\sigma]_P = |\sigma|_P$ consist of all such terms.

$\mathcal{T}$: We put $|t|_P = t$ for all closed terms of type $\sigma \in \mathcal{T}$, and $|\sigma|_P$ consists of all such terms. For $[\sigma]_P$ we proceed by induction on σ, hence we distinguish the base case A and two induction steps. In all these cases $[\cdot]_P$ is defined in terms of $|\cdot|_P$ and $[\cdot]_P$.

For the base type A we put $[A]_P = \{\mathbf{T}, \mathbf{F}\}$ and $[\![A]\!]_P = \{[\![t]\!]_P \mid t : A \text{ closed}\}$ with $[\![t]\!]_P = (t, \mathbf{T})$ if $t \in M_P$ and $[\![t]\!]_P = (t, \mathbf{F})$ otherwise.

For the induction steps, let σ be $\sigma' \to \tau$ with either $\sigma' \equiv \tau'$ or $\sigma' \equiv D$ and assume $[\cdot]_P$ has already been defined for τ such that $[t]_P \in [\tau]_P$ for every closed term of type $t : \tau$. Define $[\sigma' \to \tau]_P$ to be the set of all functions from $|\sigma'|_P$ to $[\tau]_P$. Note that the domain of these functions consists of intensions, whereas the co-domain contains extensions. Next define

$$[\![\sigma' \to \tau]\!]_P = \{[\![t]\!]_P \mid t : \sigma' \to \tau \text{ closed}\}$$

where (and this is the crucial pairing of intension and extension)

$$[\![t]\!]_P = (t, [t]_P)$$

with $[t]_P \in [\sigma' \to \tau]_P$ defined by

$$[t]_P t' = [tt']_P$$

for every closed term t' of type σ'. Observe that $[t]_P$ is well-defined since tt' is a closed term of type τ, so that indeed $[tt']_P \in [\tau]_P$. □

We shall omit the subscript P in $[\![\cdot]\!]_P$, $[\cdot]_P$, $|\cdot|_P$ when no confusion can arise.

Lemma 4.2 *Let P be a typable higher-order logic program. For all types σ and all $\sigma_i \in \mathcal{T}$ we have:*

1. *$[t] \in [\sigma]$ for all closed $t : \sigma$;*

2. *$[\sigma_1 \to \ldots \to \sigma_n \to A]$ is isomorphic to the powerset of $|\sigma_1| \times \ldots \times |\sigma_n|$.*

Proof: By a simple induction on σ and n, respectively. □

It follows from Definition 4.1 that the interpretation of a higher-order logic program is completely determined by the extensions of all closed terms. In our examples we often give only these extensions, leaving it to the reader to pair the extensions with the intensions into interpretations. We shall also refer frequently and implicitly to Lemma 4.2, clause 2, by presenting extensions as subsets rather than as characteristic functions of these subsets.

Example 4.3 Consider the following typable higher-order logic program P.

```
p(a).             % a: D, p: D->A
holds(X,Y):- X(Y). % Y: D, X: D->A, holds: (D->A)->D->A
```

We have the following extensions (and one intension) relative to P.

```
[D]={a}
[D->A]={{},{a}}
|D->A|={p,holds(p),holds(holds(p)),...}
[p]=[holds(p)]=[holds(holds(p))]=...={a}
[holds]={(p,a),(holds(p),a),(holds(holds(p)),a),...}
```

The extension of holds is already quite complicated. The notion of model proposed in [9] labours similar complications.

Anticipating the introduction of extensionality, we state that P is extensional and that by virtue of this property it is possible to collapse the extension [holds] into {({a},a)}, that is, a subset of the product of the *extensions* [D->A] and [D], instead of the (generally more complicated) *intensions*. See also Lemma 4.2 and Corollary 6.5.   □

Definition 4.4 Let P be a typable higher-order logic program. We define the declarative semantics $\mathcal{M}_P$ of P to be the structure consisting of sets $[\![\sigma]\!]_P$ for all types σ, with application mappings

$$ap_{\sigma,\tau} : [\![\sigma \to \tau]\!]_P \times [\![\sigma]\!]_P \to [\![\tau]\!]_P$$

defined by

$$ap_{\sigma,\tau}([\![t]\!]_P, [\![t']\!]_P) = [\![tt']\!]_P.$$

We denote application by juxtaposition and associate to the left. Another way of phrasing $[\![t]\!]_P[\![t']\!]_P = [\![tt']\!]_P$ is that $[\![\cdot]\!]_P$ is a homomorphism with respect to syntactic and semantic application. Note that, for $t : \sigma \to \tau \in \mathcal{T}$ and $t' : \sigma$, we have

$$[\![t]\!]_P[\![t']\!]_P = (t, [\![t]\!]_P)(t', [\![t']\!]_P) = (tt', [\![tt']\!]_P) = (tt', [\![t]\!]_P t').$$

5 Models for higher-order logic programs

The interpretation $\mathcal{M}_P$ from Section 4 raises the more general question about the nature of models for higher-order logic programs. In this section we propose a large model class for higher-order logic programs. The idea is to separate the applicative behaviour of higher-order objects from the logical behaviour. Although this semantical framework may seem overly general at first sight, there are strong reasons in favour of this generality:

- The extensional collapse, see Example 4.3, to be introduced in the next section, can be carried out within the model class. This does not seem to·be the case in the set-up of [9, Section 3.4]. [1]

---

[1] [9, page 521] states that all models are extensional, but extensionality is used there in a weaker sense of non-truth-functional behaviour: $D_o = [\![A]\!]$ and not $[A]$.

- A greater flexibility with respect to future extensions of the typing system is achieved.

- The larger the model class is, the more applications there are.

Definition 5.1 A *type structure* $\mathcal{D}$ consists of sets D_σ for every type σ and application mappings

$$ap_{\sigma,\tau} : D_{\sigma \to \tau} \times D_\sigma \to D_\tau$$

for all types σ, τ. We denote application by juxtaposition and associate to the left.

A type structure is extended to an interpretation for higher-order logic programs in the following way. First we add an interpretation function I which assigns an element of D_σ to every constant of type σ. Next we add a valuation function V assigning a truth value (**T** or **F**) to every element of D_A. What follows now is a standard development of the interpretation of terms, but with application according to the given type structure. An *assignment* is a function mapping variables to domain elements of the corresponding types. Given an assignment α, the interpretation function I can be extended to an *interpretation* $[\![t]\!]_\alpha$ for all terms t in the following way:

- $[\![c]\!]_\alpha = I(c)$ for every constant c,

- $[\![x]\!]_\alpha = \alpha(x)$ for every variable x, and

- $[\![tt']\!]_\alpha = [\![t]\!]_\alpha [\![t']\!]_\alpha$.

Thus defined the interpretation function is a homomorphism with respect to syntactic and semantic application.

A term t of type A (that is, an atom) is *true* (*false*) under an assignment α if $V([\![t]\!]_\alpha) = \mathbf{T}$ (**F**). The valuation V is extended to formulas according to the usual meaning of the logical connectives and quantifiers.

A type structure $\mathcal{D}$ with interpretation functions I and V is called a *model* of higher-order logic program P if it makes true every clause of P under any assigment α. □

As an example, we proceed by a simple lemma stating that the construct $\mathcal{M}_P$ from the previous section indeed yields an initial model of P.

Lemma 5.2 *Let P be a typable higher-order logic program. Consider the type structure $\mathcal{M}_P$ from Definition 4.4, with interpretation function $I_P(c) = [\![c]\!]_P$ for every constant c, and with valuation function $V_P([\![t]\!]_P) = [t]_P$ for every closed term t of type A. Then $\mathcal{M}_P$ is a model of P. Moreover, $\mathcal{M}_P$ is initial in the following sense: for every closed term t of type A, if t is true in $\mathcal{M}_P$, then t is true in every model of P.*

Proof: Use that $[\![\cdot]\!]_P$ is a homomorphism and that $[\![A]\!]_P$ is the characteristic function of $\mathcal{M}_P$. Initiality is proved for $t \in T_P{\uparrow}n$ by induction on n. □

6 The extensional collapse

In this section we define a notion of extensionality for higher-order logic programs and show that for extensional programs the semantics can be considerably simplified. This so-called extensional collapse originates from the model theory of finite type arithmetic and is described and attributed to Zucker in [12].

Definition 6.1 Let P be a typable higher-order logic program, with $|\cdot|_P$ and $[\cdot]_P$ as in Definition 4.1. We define relations $\approx_P^\sigma$ on $|\sigma|_P$, expressing extensional equality of type σ.

$\mathbf{D}$: We put $\approx_P^\sigma$ to be $=$, equality on $|\sigma|_P$, for every $\sigma \in \mathbf{D}$.

$\mathbf{T}$: By induction on $\sigma \in \mathbf{T}$.

For the base type A we put $t \approx_P^A s$ if and only if $[t]_P = [s]_P$.

For the induction steps $\tau' \to \tau$ with $\tau' \equiv D$ or $\tau \in \mathbf{T}$ we define $t \approx_P^{\tau' \to \tau} s$ if and only if $tt' \approx_P^\tau ss'$ for all t', s' such that $t' \approx_P^{\tau'} s'$.

We will often omit type superscripts and the subscript P. A closed term t is called *extensional* if $t \approx t$. We call P *extensional* if all closed terms are extensional. □

We give some examples and counterexamples of extensional programs. Proofs are postponed till after Theorem 6.7.

Example 6.2 The following clauses form an extensional program:

```
R(a,b).   % (a,b) in every binary relation D->D->A
call(X):- X.
or(X,Y):- X.
or(X,Y):- Y.
tc(R,XD,YD) :- R(XD,YD).            % tc = transitive closure
tc(R,XD,ZD) :- R(XD,YD),tc(R,YD,ZD). % XD,YD,ZD: D
```

Counterexamples, i.e., examples of non-extensionality, are:

```
eq(Y,Y).  % Y: A
apply(F,Z,F(Z)).  % F: (D->D->A)->D->D->A
```

For example, we have $p \approx^A or(p,p)$, but not $eq(p,p) \approx^A eq(p,or(p,p))$, and hence not $eq \approx^{A \to A \to A} eq$. The non-extensionality of the second clause arises when, for example, one considers a transitive relation r, so that r has the same extension as $tc(r)$, and $apply(tc,r,tc(r))$ holds, whereas $apply(tc,r,r)$ does not hold. □

Lemma 6.3 *Let P be a typable higher-order logic program. Then $\approx_P^\sigma$ is a partial equivalence relation for every type σ. More precisely, for every type σ, the relation $\approx_P^\sigma$ is symmetric and transitive (whence reflexive only where defined: $t \approx_P^\sigma s \Rightarrow t \approx_P^\sigma t$ for all closed terms $t, s : \sigma$). If $\approx_P^\sigma$ is reflexive for every σ, then the usual form of extensionality holds: if $tr \approx sr$ for all r, then $t \approx s$.*

Proof: Symmetry and transitivity are proved simultaneously by induction on σ. If reflexivity also holds, then $tr \approx sr$ and $r \approx r'$ imply $tr \approx sr'$. □

Theorem 6.4 *Let P be a typable, extensional, higher-order logic program, with $[\cdot]_P$ as in Definition 4.1. Then we have $t \approx_P^\sigma s$ if and only if $[t]_P = [s]_P$, for every type σ and all closed terms $t, s : \sigma$.*

Proof: Let conditions be as above, in particular P is extensional. Thus we have $t \approx_P^\sigma t$ for all types σ and closed terms t of type σ. For types $\sigma \in \mathcal{D}$ there is nothing to prove, and for $\sigma \in \mathcal{T}$ we proceed by induction. For the base type A the result holds by definition. For the induction step $\tau' \to \tau$ with $\tau' \equiv D$ or $\tau' \in \mathcal{T}$, assume the result has been proved for type $\tau \in \mathcal{T}$. Let $t \approx_P^{\tau' \to \tau} s$, then $tt' \approx_P^\tau st'$ for all closed terms t' of type τ', as all terms are extensional. By the induction hypothesis for type τ we have $[tt']_P = [st']_P$, so $[t]_P t' = [s]_P t'$ for all closed terms t' of type τ'. It follows that $[t]_P = [s]_P$. For the converse, assume $[t]_P = [s]_P$, so $[tt']_P = [t]_P t' = [s]_P t' = [st']_P$ for all closed terms t' of type τ'. By the induction hypothesis for type τ we have $tt' \approx_P^\tau st'$ for all closed terms t' of type τ'. In order to prove $t \approx_P^{\tau' \to \tau} s$, assume $t' \approx_P^{\tau'} s'$ and calculate $tt' \approx_P^\tau st' \approx_P^\tau ss'$, using $s \approx_P^{\tau' \to \tau} s$. □

Corollary 6.5 *Generalize the relations $\approx_P^\sigma$ from $|\sigma|_P$ to $[\sigma]_P$ by putting $[t]_P \approx_P^\sigma [s]_P$ if and only if $t \approx_P^\sigma s$. Under the conditions of the theorem, with $\mathcal{M}_P$ as in Definition 4.4, we then have the following:*

1. *The relations $\approx_P^\sigma$ on $[\sigma]_P$ are congruences with respect to application.*

2. *The quotient structure $[\sigma]_P/\approx_P^\sigma$ is a model of P that is elementarily equivalent to $\mathcal{M}_P$ with respect to the clausal language of P. [2]*

3. *$[\sigma_1 \to \ldots \to \sigma_n \to A]_P/\approx_P$ is isomorphic to a subset of the powerset of $[\sigma_1]_P/\approx_P \times \ldots \times [\sigma_n]_P/\approx_P$.*

Proof: By the assumption that P is extensional we have that $\approx_P^\sigma$ is an equivalence relation on closed terms of type σ, and hence on $[\sigma]_P$, for all σ. Congruence with respect to application holds by definition. This proves 1.

Since equivalent terms have the same extension, we can identify $[\sigma]_P/\approx_P^\sigma$ with $\{[t]_P \mid t : \sigma \text{ closed}\}$. (The latter set should not be confused with its

---

[2] The quotient structure is in fact an extensional general model in the sense of Henkin [4], cf. the previous footnote.

superset $[\sigma]_P$.) In this quotient structure, application, interpretation and valuation can be defined in terms of the extensions: $[t]_P[t']_P = [tt']_P$, $I(t) = [t]_P$, $V(t) = [t]_P$. The elementary equivalence of the quotient structure with the original structure follows easily, since both structures make true the same closed atoms. This proves 2.

For every closed term $t : \sigma_1 \to \ldots \to \sigma_n \to A$ we can view $[t]_P$ as a mapping from $[\sigma_1]_P/\approx_P \times \ldots \times [\sigma_n]_P/\approx_P$ to $\{\mathbf{T}, \mathbf{F}\}$, so as the characteristic function of a subset of $[\sigma_1]_P/\approx_P \times \ldots \times [\sigma_n]_P/\approx_P$. This proves 3. □

The quotient structure from Corollary 6.5 is called the *extensional collapse* of $\mathcal{M}_P$, anticipated in Example 4.3. The dramatic simplification of the semantics can be explained by comparing Lemma 4.2 to Corollary 6.5, clause 3.

In the remaining part of this section we develop a syntactic criterion which is sufficient for extensionality. The criterion is not necessary. It is important to stress that detemining extensionality is highly undecidable. There will certainly be room for improvement of the criterion presented below. We conjecture in particular that the conditions imposed on the body atoms of a program clause can be alleviated.

In order to acquire some familiarity with proving extensionality, we start with proving that the clauses defining the transitive closure in Example 6.2 are extensional. This boils down to proving $\mathbf{tc} \approx^{(D \to D \to A) \to D \to D \to A} \mathbf{tc}$, so $[\mathbf{tc}(r, s, t)] = [\mathbf{tc}(r', s', t')]$ for all closed terms r, r', s, s', t, t' satisfying $r \approx^{D \to D \to A} r'$, $s \approx^D s'$, $t \approx^D s'$. We shall prove by induction on n the following proposition (omitting type superscripts):

$$\mathbf{tc}(r, s, t) \in T_P\uparrow n \Rightarrow \forall r', s', t' \ (r \approx r' \wedge s \approx s' \wedge t \approx t' \Rightarrow \mathbf{tc}(r', s', t') \in T_P\uparrow\omega)$$

which entails $\mathbf{tc} \approx \mathbf{tc}$. For $n = 0$ there is nothing to prove. Assume the result has been proved for n and let $\mathbf{tc}(r, s, t) \in T_P\uparrow(n+1)$ for some closed terms r, s, t of appropriate types and assume $r \approx r' \wedge s \approx s' \wedge t \approx t'$. Since there are two defining clauses for $\mathbf{tc}$, there are two cases to distinguish.

First we consider the case in which $\mathbf{tc}(r, s, t) \in T_P\uparrow(n+1)$ since $r(s, t) \in T_P\uparrow n$. By $r \approx r' \wedge s \approx s' \wedge t \approx t'$ we have $[r(s, t)] = [r'(s', t')]$, so $r'(s', t') \in T_P\uparrow\omega$. It follows that $\mathbf{tc}(r', s', t') \in T_P\uparrow\omega$.

In the second case we have $\mathbf{tc}(r, s, t) \in T_P\uparrow(n+1)$ since for some closed term t_s we have $r(s, t_s) \in T_P\uparrow n$ and $\mathbf{tc}(r, t_s, t) \in T_P\uparrow n$. By $r \approx r' \wedge s \approx s' \wedge t \approx t'$, as well as $t_s \approx t_s$ since t_s is of type D, we have $[r(s, t_s)] = [r'(s', t_s)]$, so $r'(s', t_s) \in T_P\uparrow\omega$. Moreover, by the induction hypothesis, we have $\mathbf{tc}(r', t_s, t') \in T_P\uparrow\omega$. Again it follows that $\mathbf{tc}(r', s', t') \in T_P\uparrow\omega$. This completes the induction step, and hence the proof of $\mathbf{tc} \approx \mathbf{tc}$.

The following definition and theorem generalize the above result.

Definition 6.6 Let P be a typable higher-order logic program. We define a syntactic criterion for atoms, clauses and programs.

- an *atom* $t_0 t_1 \ldots t_n : A$ is *good* if t_0 is either a variable or a constant, and for $0 < i \leq n$, if t_i has a type in $\mathcal{T}$, then t_i is a variable.

- a *clause* is *good* if it consists of good atoms, all variables of type in $\mathcal{T}$ in the head are distinct, every variable that occurs in the body but not in the head has type D or the type of a first-order predicate, and if the head atom is of the form $x t_1 \ldots t_n$, then the variable x occurs in the body atoms only as head symbol.

- a *program* is *good* if it consists of good clauses. □

Examples of good atoms (clauses, programs) can be found in Example 6.2. The counterexamples there provide reasons for some aspects of the definition of the notions of good atom (clause, program).

Theorem 6.7 *Let P be a typable higher-order logic program. If P is good, then P is extensional.*

Proof: Let P be a typable, good program. We will prove $c \approx c$ for every constant c. Then the extensionality of P follows immediately, since $\approx$ is closed under application.

First we remark that $t \approx t$ holds by definition for all closed terms $t : D$. Furthermore, as $\approx$ for type D coincides with identity, $t \approx t$ also holds for closed terms having the type of a first-order predicate, that is, type $D{\to}A$, $D{\to}D{\to}A$, and so on.

We shall prove by induction on n the following proposition:

$$c t_1 \ldots t_k \in T_P{\uparrow}n \Rightarrow \forall t'_1, \ldots, t'_k \ (t_1 \approx t'_1 \wedge \cdots \wedge t_k \approx t'_k \Rightarrow c t'_1 \ldots t'_k \in T_P{\uparrow}\omega),$$

for all constants c simultaneously. For convenience, we will simply ignore arguments of type D in the proof. For $n = 0$ there is nothing to prove. Assume the result has been proved for n and let $c t_1 \ldots t_k \in T_P{\uparrow}(n+1)$ for some closed terms t_i of appropriate types. Assume $t'_1, \ldots, t'_k$ such that $t_1 \approx t'_1 \wedge \cdots \wedge t_k \approx t'_k$. For $c t_1 \ldots t_k \in T_P{\uparrow}(n+1)$, there are basically two possibilities.

The first is a good program clause

$$c x_1 \ldots x_k \leftarrow x_i(\vec{x}, \vec{y}), \ldots, d(\vec{x}, \vec{y})$$

where $\vec{x}, \vec{y}$ are sequences of variables x_i and y_j that may occur as (multiple) arguments in the good atoms of the body, and d is a constant, possibly $d \equiv c$. The variables y_j occur in the body but not in the head. Atoms with head symbol y_j are unproblematic. The two body atoms shown correspond exactly to the two forms of a good atom. Let $t_i(\vec{t}, \vec{s}), \ldots, d(\vec{t}, \vec{s}) \in T_P{\uparrow}n$ for suitable closed terms $\vec{s}$. By the assumption on the types of the variables y_j it follows that $\vec{s} \approx \vec{s}$ (componentwise). Since we also have $\vec{t} \approx \vec{t}'$, it follows that $t_i(\vec{t}, \vec{s}) \approx t_i'(\vec{t}', \vec{s})$, so $t_i'(\vec{t}', \vec{s}) \in T_P{\uparrow}\omega$. Moreover, by the induction hypothesis, it follows that $d(\vec{t}', \vec{s}) \in T_P{\uparrow}\omega$, and hence $ct_1' \ldots t_k' \in T_P{\uparrow}\omega$.

The second possibility is a good program clause

$$x_p \ldots x_k \leftarrow x_i(\vec{x}, \vec{y}), \ldots, d(\vec{x}, \vec{y})$$

with $\vec{x} \equiv x_{p+1} \ldots x_k$ and $\vec{y}$ as above, and $0 \le p \le i \le k$. Now the argument for $ct_1' \ldots t_k' \in T_P{\uparrow}\omega$ is very similar as above, with x_p bound to $ct_1 \ldots t_p$ and $ct_1' \ldots t_p'$, respectively. $\square$

Acknowledgements

I am grateful to Krzysztof Apt for providing the opportunity to work on the subject of higher-order logic programming at CWI (Amsterdam), and for many discussions on earlier versions of this paper.

Thanks to an anonymous referee the paper [13] by Wadge came to my notice. Its result may be rendered as follows: every *definitional* higher-order logic program has a minimal *standard* model. In a standard model, see also [4], $[A]$ is $\{\mathbf{T}, \mathbf{F}\}$ and $[\sigma{\to}\tau]$ is the full function space $[\sigma] \to [\tau]$ (hence standard models are extensional, but uncountable if $[D]$ is infinite). The notions 'definitional' and 'good' are very similar in spirit, but mathematically different. For example, the body of a good clause may contain local higher-order variables, provided their types do not surpass the type of a first-order predicate. Hence the transitive closure of a binary predicate of unary predicates is good but not definitional. All Wadge's examples of definitional programs are good programs in our sense, but his definition appears to include programs beyond this. Furthermore, Wadge's argument is model theoretic, whereas ours is proof theoretic. We are happy to take over his plea for extensionality and its relevance for software engineering. For future research we conjecture that the result of [13] can be extended from definitional programs to extensional programs as defined here.

References

[1] K. R. Apt. Logic programming. In J. van Leeuwen (ed.) *Handbook of Theoretical Computer Science*, Vol. B, pp. 493–574. Elsevier, Amsterdam, 1990.

[2] W. Chen, M. Kifer and D.S. Warren. Hilog: a foundation for higher-order logic programming. *Journal of Logic Programming*, 15(3):187–230, 1993.

[3] A. Church. A formulation of the simple theory of types. *Journal of Symbolic Logic*, 5:56–68, 1940.

[4] L. Henkin. Completeness in the theory of types. *Journal of Symbolic Logic*, 15:81–91, 1950.

[5] P. M. Hill and J. W. Lloyd. *The Gödel Programming Language*. MIT Press, Cambridge, Massachusetts, 1994.

[6] J.R. Hindley. The principal type-scheme of an object in combinatory logic. *Transactions of the AMS*, 146:29–60, 1969.

[7] J.R. Hindley. *Basic simple type theory*. Cambridge tracts in TCS 42, CUP, 1997.

[8] G. Nadathur and D.A. Miller. An overview of λProlog. In K. Bowen and R. Kowalski (eds.) *Proceedings of the Fifth International Conference on Logic Programming*, pp. 810–827, Seattle. MIT Press, Cambridge, Massachusetts, 1988.

[9] G. Nadathur and D.A. Miller. Higher-order logic programming. In D. Gabbay e.a. (eds.) *Handbook of logic in artificial intelligence*, Vol. 5, pp. 499–590. Clarendon Press, Oxford, 1998.

[10] F. Pfenning (ed.). *Types in Logic Programming*. MIT Press, Cambridge, Massachusetts, 1992.

[11] Z. Somogyi, F.J. Henderson and T. Conway. The execution algorithm of Mercury, an efficient purely declarative logic programming language. *Journal of Logic Programming*, 29(1–3):17–64, 1996.

[12] A.S. Troelstra. *Metamathematical Investigation of Intuitionistic Arithmetic and Analysis*. Number 344 in Lecture Notes in Mathematics. Springer-Verlag, Berlin, 1973.

[13] W.W. Wadge. Higher-order Horn logic programming. In V. Saraswat and K. Ueda (eds.) *Proceedings of the 1991 International Symposium on Logic Programming*, pp. 289–303. MIT Press, Cambridge, Massachusetts, 1991.

Lightweight Lemmas in λProlog

Andrew W. Appel
Bell Labs and Princeton University
appel@princeton.edu

Amy P. Felty
Bell Labs, 600 Mountain Avenue, Murray Hill, NJ 07974, USA
felty@research.bell-labs.com

Abstract

λProlog is known to be well-suited for expressing and implementing logics and inference systems. We show that lemmas and definitions in such logics can be implemented with a great economy of expression. We encode a polymorphic higher-order logic using the ML-style polymorphism of λProlog. The terms of the metalanguage (λProlog) can be used to express the statement of a lemma, and metalanguage type-checking can directly type-check the lemma. But to allow polymorphic lemmas requires either more general polymorphism at the meta-level or a less concise encoding of the object logic. We discuss both the Terzo and Teyjus implementations of λProlog as well as related systems such as Elf.

1 Introduction

It has long been the goal of mathematicians to minimize the set of assumptions and axioms in their systems. Implementers of theorem provers use this principle: they use a logic with as few inference rules as possible, and prove lemmas outside the core logic in preference to adding new inference rules. In applications of logic to computer security – such as *proof-carrying code* [12] and distributed authentication frameworks [1] – the implementation of the core logic is inside the trusted code base (TCB), while proofs need not be in the TCB because they can be checked.

Two aspects of the core logic are in the TCB: a set of logical connectives and inference rules, and a program in some underlying programming language that implements proof checking – that is, interpreting the inference rules and matching them against a theorem and its proof.

Definitions and lemmas are essential in constructing proofs of reasonable size and clarity. A proof system should have machinery for checking lemmas, and applying lemmas and definitions, in the checking of proofs. This machinery also is within the TCB. Many theorem-provers support definitions and lemmas and provide a variety of advanced features designed to help with tasks such as organizing definitions and lemmas into libraries, keeping track of dependencies, and providing modularization; in our work we are particularly concerned with separating that part of the machinery necessary for proof checking (i.e., in the TCB) from the programming-environment support that is used in proof development. In this paper we will demonstrate a definition/lemma implementation that is about two dozen lines of code.

The λProlog language [8] has several features that allow concise and clean implementation of logics, proof checkers, and theorem provers [4]. We use λProlog, but many of our ideas should also be applicable in logical frameworks such as Elf/Twelf [14, 17]. An important purpose of this paper is to show which language features allow a small TCB and efficient representation of proofs. We will discuss *higher-order abstract syntax, dynamically constructed clauses, dynamically constructed goals, meta-level formulas as terms*, and *prenex* and *non-prenex polymorphism*.

2 A core logic

The clauses we present use the syntax of the Terzo implementation of λProlog [20]. λProlog is a higher-order logic programming language which extends Prolog in essentially two ways. First, it replaces first-order terms with the more expressive simply-typed λ-terms; λProlog implementations generally extend simple types to include ML-style prenex polymorphism [3, 9], which we use in our implementation. Second, it permits implication and universal quantification (over objects of any type) in goal formulas.

We introduce types and constants using `kind` and `type` declarations, respectively. Capital letters in type declarations denote type variables and are used in polymorphic types. In program goals and clauses, λ-abstraction is written using backslash \ as an infix operator. Capitalized tokens not bound by λ-abstraction denote free variables. All other unbound tokens denote constants. Universal quantification is written using the constant `pi` in conjunction with a λ-abstraction (e.g., `pi X\` represents universal quantification over variable X). The symbols *comma* and `=>` represent conjunction and implication. The symbol `:-` denotes the converse of `=>` and is used to write the top-level implication in clauses. The type `o` is the type of clauses and goals of λProlog. We usually omit universal quantifiers at the top level in definite clauses, and assume implicit quantification over all free variables.

We will use a running example based on a sequent calculus for a higher-order logic. We call this the *object logic* to distinguish it from the *metalogic* implemented by λProlog. We implement a proof checker for this logic that is similar to the one desribed by Felty [4]. We introduce two primitive types: `form` for object-level formulas and `pf` for proofs in the object logic. We introduce constants for the object-level connectives, such as `and` and `imp` of type `form → form → form`, and `forall` of type `(A → form) → form`. We also have `eq` of type `A → A → form` to represent equality at any type. We use infix notation for the binary connectives. The constant `forall` takes a functional argument, and thus object-level binding of variables by quantifiers is defined in terms of meta-level λ-abstraction. This use of higher-order data structures is called *higher-order abstract syntax* [16]; with it, we don't need to describe the mechanics of substitution explicitly in the object logic [4]. Program 1

```
initial proves A :- assume A.
(imp_r Q) proves (A imp B) :- (assume A) => (Q proves B).
(and_l A B Q) proves C :-
    assume (A and B), (assume A) => (assume B) => (Q proves C).
(forall_r Q) proves (forall A) :- pi y\ ((Q y) proves (A y)).
(cut Q1 Q2 A) proves C :-
    Q1 proves A, (assume A) => (Q2 proves C).
(congr X Z H Q P) proves (H X) :-
    Q proves (eq X Z), P proves (H Z).
refl proves (eq X X).
```

Program 1: Some type declarations and inference rules of the object logic.

shows λProlog clauses for some of the inference rules. The following two declarations illustrate the types of proof constructors.

```
type  forall_r  (A → pf) → pf.
type  congr     A → A → (A → form) → pf → pf → pf.
```

To implement assumptions (that is, formulas to the left of the sequent arrow) we use implication. The goal A => B adds clause A to the λProlog clause database, evaluates B, and then (upon either the success or failure of B) removes A from the clause database. It is a dynamically scoped version of Prolog's `assert` and `retract`. For example, suppose we use (imp_r initial) to prove ((eq x y) imp (eq x y)); then λProlog will execute the (instantiated) body of the imp_r clause:

```
(assume (eq x y))  =>  (initial proves (eq x y))
```

This adds (assume (eq x y)) to the database; then the subgoal

```
initial proves (eq x y)
```

generates a subgoal (assume (eq x y)) which matches our dynamically added clause.

We have used λProlog's ML-style prenex polymorphism to reduce the number of inference rules in the TCB. Instead of a different `forall` constructor at each type – and a corresponding pair of inference rules – we have a single polymorphic `forall` constructor. Our full core logic (not shown in this paper) uses a base type `exp` of machine integers, and a type `exp → exp` of functions, so if we desire quantification both at expressions and at predicates (let alone functions at several types) we have already saved one constructor and two inference rules.

We have also used polymorphism to define a general congruence rule on the `eq` operator, from which many other desirable facts (transitivity and symmetry of equality, congruence at specific functions) may be proved as lemmas.

Theorem 1 shows the use of our core logic to check a simple proof.

It is important to show that our encoding of higher-order logic in λProlog is *adequate*. To do so, we must show that a formula has a sequent proof if and only if its representation as a term of type `form` has a proof term that can be checked using the inference rules of Program 1. Proving such a theorem should be straightforward. In particular, since we have encoded our logic

```
(forall_r I\ forall_r J\ forall_r K\
 (imp_r (and_l (eq J I) (eq J K)
         (congr I J (X\ (eq X K))
              (congr J I (eq I) initial refl) initial))))
proves
 (forall I\ forall J\ forall K\ (eq J I and eq J K) imp eq I K).
```

Theorem 1. $\forall I \, \forall J \, \forall K \, (J = I \wedge J = K) \rightarrow I = K$.

```
type   lemma   (A→o) → A → (A→pf) → pf.

(lemma Inference Proof Rest) proves C :-
 pi Name\ (valid_clause (Inference Name),
          Inference Proof,
          (Inference Name) => ((Rest Name) proves C)).
```

Program 2: The lemma proof constructor.

using prenex polymorphism, we can expand out instantiated copies of all of the polymorphic expressions in terms of type pf; the expanded proof terms will then map directly to sequent proof trees. Although we do not discuss it, it should be easy to extend such an adequacy proof to account for the extensions to this core logic that we discuss in the rest of the paper.

3 Lemmas

In mathematics the use of lemmas can make a proof more readable by structuring the proof, especially when the lemma corresponds to some intuitive property. For automated proof checking (in contrast to automated or traditional theorem proving) this use of lemmas is not essential, because the computer doesn't need to understand the proof in order to check it. But lemmas can also reduce the *size* of a proof (and therefore the time required for proof checking): when a lemma is used multiple times it acts as a kind of "subroutine." This is particularly important in applications like proof-carrying code where proofs are transmitted over networks to clients who check them.

The heart of our lemma mechanism is the clause shown in Program 2. The proof constructor lemma takes three arguments: (1) a derived inference rule Inference (of type A → o) parameterized by a proof constructor (of type A), (2) a term of type A representing a proof of the lemma built from core-logic proof constructors (or using other lemmas), and (3) a proof of the main theorem C that is parameterized by a proof constructor (of type A).

For example, we can prove a lemma about the symmetry of equality; the proof uses congruence and reflexivity of equality:

```
pi A\ pi B\ pi P\ (P proves (eq B A) =>
                    ((congr B A (eq A) P refl) proves (eq A B))).
```

This theorem can be checked as a successful λProlog query to our proof checker: for an arbitrary P, add (P proves (eq B A)) to the logic, then check the proof of congruence using this fact. The syntax F => G means

```
(lemma
  (Symmx\ pi A\ pi B\ pi P\
    (Symmx A B P) proves (eq A B) :- P proves (eq B A))
  (A\B\P\(congr B A (eq A) P refl))
  (symmx\ (forall_r I\ forall_r J\ imp_r (symmx J I initial))))
proves (forall I\ forall J\ eq I J imp eq J I).
```

Theorem 2. $\forall I \, \forall J \, (I = J \rightarrow J = I)$.

exactly the same as G :- F, so we could just as well write this query as:

```
pi A\ pi B\ pi P\ ((congr B A (eq A) P refl) proves (eq A B) :-
                   P proves (eq B A)).
```

Now, suppose we abstract the proof (roughly, `congr B A (eq A) P refl`) from this query:

```
(Inference = (PCon\ pi A\ pi B\ pi P\
               (PCon A B P) proves (eq A B) :- P proves (eq B A)),
 Proof = (A\B\P\ congr B A (eq A) P refl),
 Query = (Inference Proof),
 Query)
```

The solution of this query proceeds in four steps: the variable `Inference` is unified with a λ-term; `Proof` is unified with a λ-term; `Query` is unified with the application of `Inference` to `Proof` (which is a term β-equivalent to the query of the previous paragraph), and finally `Query` is solved as a goal (checking the proof of the lemma).

Once we know that the lemma is valid, we make a new λProlog atom **symmx** to stand for its proof, and we prove some other theorem in a context where the clause (`Inference symmx`) is in the clause database; remember that (`Inference symmx`) is β-equivalent to

```
pi A\ pi B\ pi P\ (symmx A B P proves eq A B :- P proves eq B A).
```

This looks remarkably like an inference rule! With this clause in the database, we can use the new proof constructor **symmx** just as if it were primitive.

To "make a new atom" we simply pi-bind it. This leads to the recipe for lemmas shown in Program 2 above: first execute (`Inference Proof`) as a query, to check the proof of the lemma itself; then pi-bind `Name`, and run `Rest` (which is parameterized on the lemma proof constructor) applied to `Name`. Theorem 2 illustrates the use of the **symmx** lemma. The **symmx** proof constructor is a bit unwieldy, since it requires A and B as arguments. We can imagine writing a primitive inference rule

```
(symm P) proves (eq A B) :- P proves (eq B A).
```

using the principle that the proof checker doesn't need to be told A and B, since they can be found in the formula to be proved.

Therefore we add three new proof constructors – **elam**, **extract**, and **extractGoal** – as shown in Program 3. These can be used in the following stereotyped way to extract components of the formula to be proved. First bind variables with **elam**, then match the target formula with **extract**. Theorem 3 is a modification of Theorem 2 that makes use of these constructors. The **extractGoal** asks the checker to run λProlog code to help construct

```
type elam          (A → pf) → pf.
type extract       form → pf → pf.
type extractGoal   o → pf → pf.
```

```
(elam Q) proves B :- (Q A) proves B.
(extract B P) proves B :-  P proves B.
(extractGoal G P) proves B :- valid_clause G, G, P proves B.
```

Program 3: Proof constructors for implicit arguments of lemmas.

```
(lemma
  (Symm\ pi A\ pi B\ pi P\
    (Symm P) proves (eq A B) :- P proves (eq B A))
  (P\ elam A\ elam B\ extract (eq A B) (congr B A (eq A) P refl))
  (symm\ (forall_r I\ forall_r J\ imp_r (symm initial))))
proves (forall I\ forall J\ eq I J imp eq J I).
```

Theorem 3. $\forall I \, \forall J \, (I = J \to J = I)$.

the proof. Of course, if we want proof checking to be finite we must restrict what kinds of λProlog code can be run, and this is accomplished by
valid_clause (see below). The proof of lemma def_1 in Section 4 is an
example of extractGoal.

Of course, we can use one lemma in the proof of another.

Since the type of (Inference Proof) is o, the lemma Inference might
conceivably contain any λProlog clause at all, including those that do in-
put/output. Such λProlog code cannot lead to unsoundness – if the resulting
proof checks, it is still valid. But there are some contexts where we wish to
restrict the kind of program that can be run inside a proof. For example, in
a proof-carrying-code system, the code consumer might not want the proof
to execute λProlog code that accesses private local resources.

To limit the kind and amount of execution possible in the executable part
of a lemma, we introduce the valid_clause predicate of type o → o (Program 4). A clause is valid if contains pi, comma, :-, =>, proves, assume,
and nothing else. Of course, a proves clause contains subexpressions of
type pf and form, and an assume clause has a subexpression of type form,
so all the connectives in proofs and formulas are also permitted. Absent
from this list are λProlog input/output (such as print) and the semicolon
(backtracking search).

```
valid_clause (pi C) :-   pi X\ valid_clause (C X).
valid_clause (A,B) :-    valid_clause A, valid_clause B.
valid_clause (A :- B) :- valid_clause A, valid_clause B.
valid_clause (A => B) :- valid_clause A, valid_clause B.
valid_clause (P proves A).
valid_clause (assume A).
```

Program 4: Valid clauses.

```
(lemma (Define\ pi F\ pi P\ pi B\
          ((Define F P) proves B :-
            pi D\ (assume (eq d F) => (P D) proves B)))
        (F\P\ (cut refl (P F) (eq F F)))
    define\

(lemma (Def_r\ pi Name\ pi B\ pi F\ pi P\
          ((Def_r Name B P) proves (B Name) :-
            assume (eq Name F), P proves (B F)))
        (Name\B\P\ elam F\ (extract (B Name)
         (extractGoal (assume (eq Name F))
          (congr Name F B initial P))))
    def_r\

(lemma (Def_l\ pi Name\ pi B\ pi D\ pi F\ pi Q\
          ((Def_l Name B Q) proves D :- assume (B Name),
            assume (eq Name F), (assume (B F) => Q proves D)))
        (Name\B\Q\ elam F\ (extractGoal (assume (eq Name F))
         (cut (congr F Name B (symm initial) initial) Q (B F))))
    def_l\ ...
```

Program 5: Machinery for definitions.

In principle, we do not need lemmas at all. Instead of the symmetry lemma, we can prove (forall A\ forall B\ (eq B A imp eq A B)) and then cut it into the proof of a theorem using the ordinary cut of sequent calculus. To make use of the fact requires two forall_l's and an imp_l. This approach adds undesirable complexity to proofs.

4 Definitions

Definitions are another important mechanism for structuring proofs to increase clarity and reduce size. If some property (of a base-type object, or of a higher-order object such as a predicate) can be expressed as a logical formula, then we can make an abbreviation to stand for that formula.

For example, we can express the fact that f is an associative function by the formula $\forall X \, \forall Y \, \forall Z \, f \, X \, (f \, Y \, Z) = f \, (f \, X \, Y) \, Z$. Putting this formula in λProlog notation and abstracting over f, we get the predicate:

    F\ forall X\ forall Y\ forall Z\ eq (F X (F Y Z)) (F (F X Y) Z)

A definition is just an association of some name with this predicate:

    eq associative
    (F\ forall X\ forall Y\ forall Z\ eq (F X (F Y Z)) (F (F X Y) Z))

To use definitions in proofs we introduce three new proof rules: (1) define to bind a λ-term to a name, (2) def_r to replace a formula on the right of a sequent arrow with the definition that stands for it (or viewed in terms of backward sequent proof, to replace a defined name with the term it stands for), and (3) def_l to expand a definition on the left of a sequent arrow during backward proof. All three of these proof constructors are just lemmas provable in our system using congruence of equality, as Program 5 shows.

To check a proof (define Formula (Name\ (RestProof Name))) the system interprets the pi D within the define lemma to create a new atom D to stand for the Name. It then adds (assume(eq D Formula)) to the clause database. Finally it substitutes D for Name within RestProof and checks the resulting proof. If there are occurrences of (def_r D) or (def_l D) within (RestProof D) then they will match the newly added clause.

To check that (def_r associative (A\ A f) P) is a proof of the formula (associative f) the prover checks that (A\ A f)(associative) matches (associative f) and that (assume (eq associative Body)) is in the assumptions for some formula, predicate, or function Body. Then it applies (A\ A f) to Body, obtaining the subgoal (Body f), of which P is required to be a proof.

To check that (def_l associative (A\ A f) P) proves some formula D, the checker first reduces (A\ A f)(associative) to associative f, and checks that (assume (associative f)) is among the assumptions in the λProlog database. Then it verifies that (assume (eq associative Body)) is in the assumption database for some Body. Finally the checker introduces (assume (Body f)) into the assumptions and verifies that, under that assumption, Q proves D.

5   Dynamically constructed clauses and goals

Our technique allows lemmas and definitions to be contained *within* the proof. We do not need to install new "global" lemmas and definitions into the proof checker. The dynamic scoping also means that the lemmas of one proof cannot interfere with the lemmas of another, even if they have the same names. This machinery uses several interesting features of λProlog:

Metalevel formulas as terms.   As we have seen, the symm lemma
   (Symm\pi A\pi B\pi P\(Symm P) proves eq A B :- P proves eq B A)
occurs inside the proofs as an argument to the lemma constructor and so is just a data structure (parameterized by Symm); it does not "execute" anything, in spite of the fact that it contains the λProlog connectives :- and pi. This gives us the freedom to write lemmas using the same syntax as we use for writing primitive inference rules.

Dynamically constructed goals.   When the clause from Program 2 for the lemma proof constructor checks the validity of a lemma by executing the goal (Inference Proof), we are executing a goal that is built from a run-time-constructed data structure. Inference will be instantiated with terms such as the one above representing the symm lemma. It is only when such a term is applied to its proof and thus appears in "goal position" that it becomes the current subgoal on the execution stack.

Dynamically constructed clauses.   When, having successfully checked the proof of a lemma, the lemma clause executes

```
(lemma Inference Proof Rest) proves C :-
  pi Name\ (valid_clause (Inference Name),
            Inference Proof,
            cl (Inference Name) => ((Rest Name) proves C)).

P proves A :- cl Cl, backchain (P proves A) Cl.

backchain G G.
backchain G (pi D) :- backchain G (D X).
backchain G (A,B) :-  backchain G A; backchain G B.
backchain G (H <<== G1) :-  backchain G H, G1.
backchain G (G1 ==>> H) :-  backchain G H, G1.

(D ==>> G) :- (cl D) => G.
(G <<== D) :- (cl D) => G.
```

Program 6: An interpreter for dynamic clauses.

```
(Inference Name) => ((Rest Name) proves C))
```
it is adding a dynamically constructed clause to the λProlog database.

The Teyjus system does not allow => or :- to appear in arguments of predicates. It also does not allow variables to appear at the head of the left of an implication. These restrictions come from the theory underlying λProlog [7]; without this restriction, a runtime check is needed to insure that every dynamically created goal is an acceptable one. We now show that it is possible to relax the requirements on dynamically constructed clauses and goals to accommodate Teyjus's restrictions.

We can avoid putting :- inside arguments of predicates by writing the lemma as
```
(Symm\ pi A\ pi B\ pi P\
  (Symm P) proves (eq A B) <<== P proves (eq B A))
```
where <<== is a new infix operator of type $o \rightarrow o$ But this, in turn, means that the clause for checking lemmas cannot add (Inference Name) as a new clause, since <<== has no operational meaning. Instead, Program 6 contains a modifed lemma clause that adds the clause (cl (Inference Name)) where cl is a new atomic predicate of type $o \rightarrow o$. The rest of Program 6 implements an interpreter to handle clauses of the form (cl A) and goals of the form (A <== B) and (A ==>> B). The use of cl is the only modification to the lemma clause. The new clause for the proves predicate is used for checking nodes in a proof representing lemma applications and illustrates the use of the new atomic clauses. The (cl Cl) subgoal looks up the lemmas that have been added one at a time and tries them out via the backchain predicate. This predicate processes the clauses in a manner similar to the λProlog language itself. The remaining two clauses are needed in both checking lemmas and in checking the rest of the proof for interpreting the new implication operators when they occur at the top level of a goal.

Handling new constants for :- and => is easy enough operationally. However, it is an inconvenience for the user, who must use different syntax in

```
(lemma (Symm\ pi A\ pi B\ pi P\
        (Symm P) proves (eq A B) :- P proves (eq B A))
       (P\ elam A\ elam B\
        (extract (eq A B) (congr B A (eq A) P refl)))
       (symm\ (forall_r f\ forall_r g\ forall_r x\
        (imp_r (imp_r (and_r (symm initial) (symm initial)))))))))
 proves (forall f\ forall g\ forall x\
        (eq f g) imp (eq (f x) x) imp ((eq g f) and (eq x (f x))))).
```

Theorem 6. $\forall f, g, x. f = g \rightarrow f(x) = x \rightarrow (g = f \wedge x = f(x))$.

lemmas than in inference rules.

6   Meta-level types

In the encoding we have presented, ML-style prenex polymorphism is used in the `forall_r` and `congr` rules of Program 1 and in implementing lemmas as shown in Program 2. We now discuss the limitations of prenex polymorphism for implementing lemmas which are themselves polymorphic; and we discuss ways to overcome these limitations both at the meta-level and at the object level. The `symm` lemma is naturally polymorphic: it should express the idea that $a = 3 \rightarrow 3 = a$ (at type int) just as well as $f = \lambda x.3 \rightarrow (\lambda x.3) = f$ (at type int $\rightarrow$ int). But Theorem 6, which uses `symm` at two different types, fails to type-check in our implementation. When the λProlog type-checker first encounters `symm` as a λ-bound variable, it creates an uninstantiated type metavariable to hold its type. The first use of `symm` unifies this metavariable type variable with the type T of x, and then the use of `symm` at type T $\rightarrow$ T fails to match. Prohibiting λ-bound variables from being polymorphic is the essence of prenex polymorphism. On the other hand, the proof of Theorem 3 type-checks because `symm` is used at only one type.

We can generalize the prenex polymorphism of the metalanguage by removing the restriction that all type variables are bound at the outermost level and allow such binding to occur anywhere in a type, to obtain the second-order λ-calculus. We start by making the bindings clear in our current version by annotating terms with fully explicit bindings and quantification. The result will not be λProlog code, as type quantification and type binding are not supported in that language. So we will use the standard λProlog **pi** and \ to quantify and abstract term variables; but we'll use Π and Λ to quantify and abstract type variables, and use *italics* for type arguments and other nonstandard constructs.

```
type congr     ΠT. T → T → (T → form) → pf → pf → pf.
type forall_r  ΠT. (T → pf) → pf.
```

```
ΠT. pi X: T\ pi Z: T\ pi H: T → form\ pi Q: pf\ pi P: pf\
  (congr T X Z H Q P) proves (H X) :-
    Q proves (eq T X Z), P proves (H Z).
```

```
type   lemma ΠT. (T → o) → T → (T → pf) → pf.

(lemma T Inference Proof Rest) proves C :-
 pi Name:T\ (valid_clause (Inference Name),
             Inference Proof,
             (Inference Name) => ((Rest Name) proves C)).
 (lemma  T
         (Symm: ΠT. pf → pf \        ← here!
          ΠT. pi A:T\ pi B:T\ pi P:pf\
              (Symm T P) proves (eq T A B) :- P proves (eq T B A))
         (ΛT. P:pf\ elam A:T\ elam B:T\
              (extract (eq T A B) (congr T B A (eq T A) P refl)))
         (symm\ (forall_r I:int\ forall_r J:int\
          (imp_r (symm int initial)))))
     proves (forall I\ forall J\ (eq int I J) imp (eq int J I)).
```

Figure 7: Explicitly typed version of Theorem 3.

```
ΠT. pi A: T → form\ pi Q: T → pf\
    (forall_r T Q) proves (forall T A) :- pi Y:T\ (Q Y proves A Y).
```
Every type quantifier is at the outermost level of its clause; the ML-style prenex polymorphism of λProlog can typecheck this program. However, we run into trouble when we try to write a polymorphic lemma. The lemma itself is prenex polymorphic, but the lemma definer is not.

Figure 7 is pseudo-λProlog in which type quantifiers and type bindings are shown explicitly. The line marked *here* contains a λ-term, λSymm.body, in which the type of Symm is ΠT.pf → pf. Requiring a function argument to be polymorphic is an example of non-prenex polymorphism, which is permitted in second-order λ-calculus but not in an ML-style type system.

Polymorphic definitions (using **define**) run into the same problems and also require non-prenex polymorphism. Thus prenex polymorphism is sufficient for polymorphic inference rules; non-prenex polymorphism is necessary to directly extend the encoding of our logic to allow polymorphic lemmas, although one can scrape by with monomorphic lemmas by always duplicating each lemma at several different types within the same proof.

There are also several ways to encode our polymorphic logic and allow for polymorphic lemmas without changing the metalanguage. One possibility is to encode object-level types as meta-level terms. The following encoding of the **congr** rule illustrates this approach.

```
kind tp      type.
kind tm      type.
type arrow   tp → tp → tp.
type form    tp.
type eq      tp → tm → tm → tm.
type congr   tp → pf → pf → (A → tm) → A → A → pf.

congr T Q P H X Z proves H X :-
  typecheck X T, typecheck Z T, Q proves (eq T X Z), P proves H Z.
```

This encoding also requires the addition of explicit **app** and **abs** constructors, primitive rules for β- and η-reduction, and typechecking clauses for terms of types **exp** and **form**, but not **pf**. To illustrate, the new constructors and corresponding type checking clauses are given below.

```
type app  tp → tm → tm → tm.
type lam  (tm → tm) → tm.
typecheck (app T1 F X) T2 :-
   typecheck F (arrow T1 T2),  typecheck X T1.
typecheck (lam F) (arrow T1 T2) :-
   pi X\ (typecheck X T1 => typecheck (F X) T2).
```

This encoding loses some economy of expression because of the extra constructors needed for the encoding, and requires a limited amount of typechecking, though not as much as would be required in an untyped framework. For instance, in addition to typechecking subgoals such as the ones in the **congr** rule, it must also be verified that all the terms in a particular sequent to be proved have type **form**. In this encoding, polymorphism at the meta-level is no longer used to encode formulas, although it is still used for the **lemma** constructor. Lemma polymorphism can also be removed by using an application constructor at the level of proofs, though this would require adding typechecking for proofs also.

Another alternative is to use an encoding similar to one by Harper et al. [5] (for a non-polymorphic higher-order logic) in a metalanguage such as Elf/Twelf [14, 17]. The extra expressiveness of dependent types allows object-level types to be expressed more directly as meta-level types, eliminating the need for any typechecking clauses. This encoding still requires explicit constructors for **app** and **abs** as well as primitive rules for $\beta\eta$-reduction. The following Twelf clauses, corresponding to λProlog clauses above, illustrate the use of dependent types for this kind of encoding.

```
tp : type.
tm : tp → type.
form : tp.
pf : tm form → type.
arrow : tp → tp → tp.
eq : {T:tp}tm T → tm T → tm form.
congr : {T:tp}{X:tm T}{Z:tm T}{H:tm T → tm form}
        pf (eq T X Z) → pf (H Z) → pf (H X).
```

Elf [14] and Twelf [17] are both implementations of LF [5], the Edinburgh logical framework. Elf 1.5 has full (nonprenex) statically checked polymorphism with explicit type quantification and explicit type binding, which we have used to implement polymorphic lemmas approximately as shown in Figure 7. But polymorphism in Elf 1.5 is undocumented and discouraged [15], so we recommend the above encoding instead. Twelf is the successor to Elf. Like Elf, it has higher-order data structures with a static type system, but Twelf is monomorphic. Thus, the above encoding is the only possibility.

Both of the above λProlog and Twelf encodings look promising as a basis for a proof system with polymorphic lemmas [2].

7 Other issues

Although we are focusing on the interaction of the meta-level type system with the object-logic lemma system, are other aspects of metalanguage implementation are also relevant to our needs for proof generation and checking.

Type abbreviations In the domain of proof-carrying code, we encode types as predicates which themselves take predicates as arguments. For example, our program has declarations like this one:

```
type hastype (exp → form) →  (exp → exp) →  exp →
              ((exp → form) → (exp → exp) → exp → form)  → form.
```

Neither Terzo nor Teyjus allow such abbreviations and this is rather an inconvenience. ML-style (nongenerative) type abbreviations would be very helpful. In the object-types-as-meta-terms encoding (Section 6), Twelf definitions can act as type abbreviations, which is a great convenience.

Arithmetic. For our application, proof-carrying code, we wish to prove theorems about machine instructions that add, subtract, and multiply; and about load/store instructions that add offsets to registers. Therefore we require some rudimentary integer arithmetic in our logic.

Some logical frameworks have powerful arithmetic primitives, such as the ability to solve linear programs [13] or to handle general arithmetic constraints [6]. For example, Twelf will soon provide a complete theory of the rationals, implemented using linear programming [18]. Some such as Elf 1.5 have no arithmetic at all, forcing us to define integers as sequences of booleans. On the one hand, linear programming is a powerful and general proof technique, but we fear that it might increase the complexity of the trusted computing base. On the other hand, synthesizing arithmetic from scratch is no picnic. The standard Prolog is operator seems a good compromise and has been adequate for our needs.

Representing proof terms. Parameterizable data structures with higher-order unification modulo β-equivalence provide an expressive way of representing formulas, predicates, and proofs. We make heavy use of higher-order data structures with both direct sharing and sharing modulo β-reduction. The implementation of the metalanguage must preserve this sharing; otherwise our proof terms will blow up in size.

Any logic programming system is likely to implement sharing of terms obtained by copying multiple pointers to the same subterm. In Terzo, this can be seen as the implementation of a reduction algorithm described by Wadsworth [19]. But we require even more sharing. The similar terms obtained by applying a λ-term to different arguments should retain as much sharing as possible. Therefore some intelligent implementation of higher-order terms within the metalanguage—such as Teyjus's use of explicit substitutions [10, 11]—seems essential.

Programming the prover. In this paper, we have concentrated on an encoding of the logic used for proof checking. But of course, we will also need to construct proofs. For the proof-carrying code application, we need an automatic theorem prover to prove the safety of programs. For implementing this prover, we have found that the Prolog-style control primitives (such as the cut (!) operator and the is predicate), which are also available in λProlog, are quite important. λProlog also provides an environment for implementing tactic-style interactive provers [4]. This kind of prover is useful for proving the lemmas that are used by the automatic prover. Neither Elf nor Twelf have any control primitives. However, there are plans to add an operator to Twelf similar to Prolog cut [15], which would allow us to implement the automatic prover in the same way as in λProlog. It is not possible to build interactive provers in Elf or Twelf, so proofs of lemmas used by the automatic prover must be constructed by hand.

8 Conclusion

The logical frameworks discussed in this paper are promising vehicles for proof-carrying code, or in general where it is desired to keep the proof checker as small and simple as possible. We have proposed a representation for lemmas and definitions that should help keep proofs small and well-structured, and it appears that each of these frameworks has features that are useful in implementing, or implementing efficiently, our machinery.

Although the lemma system shown in this paper is particularly lightweight and simple to use, its lack of polymorphic definitions and lemmas has led us to further investigate the encodings (sketched in Section 6) that use object-level polymorphic types [2].

Acknowledgements

We thank Robert Harper, Frank Pfenning, Carsten Schürmann for advice about encoding polymorphic logics in a monomorphic dependent-type metalanguage; Robert Harper and Daniel Wang for discussions about untyped systems; Ed Felten, Neophytos Michael, Kedar Swadi, and Daniel Wang for providing user feedback; Gopalan Nadathur and Dale Miller for discussions about λProlog.

References

[1] Andrew W. Appel and Edward W. Felten. Proof-carrying authentication. In *6th ACM Conf. on Computer and Communications Security*, Nov. 1999.

[2] Andrew W. Appel and Amy P. Felty. Polymorphic lemmas in LF and λProlog. In preparation, 1999.

[3] Luis Damas and Robin Milner. Principal type-schemes for functional programs. In *Ninth ACM Symposium on Principles of Programming Languages*, pages 207–12, New York, 1982. ACM Press.

[4] Amy Felty. Implementing tactics and tacticals in a higher-order logic programming language. *J. Automated Reasoning*, 11(1):43–81, August 1993.

[5] Robert Harper, Furio Honsell, and Gordon Plotkin. A framework for defining logics. *Journal of the ACM*, January 1993.

[6] Joxan Jaffar and Jean-Louis Lassez. Constraint logic programming. In *Proceedings of the SIGACT-SIGPLAN Symposium on Principles of Programming Languages*, pages 111–119. ACM, January 1987.

[7] Dale Miller, Gopalan Nadathur, Frank Pfenning, and Andre Scedrov. Uniform proofs as a foundation for logic programming. *Annals of Pure and Applied Logic*, 51:125–157, 1991.

[8] Gopalan Nadathur and Dale Miller. An overview of λProlog. In K. Bowen and R. Kowalski, editors, *Fifth International Conference and Symposium on Logic Programming*. MIT Press, 1988.

[9] Gopalan Nadathur and Frank Pfenning. *The Type System of a Higher-Order Logic Programming Language*, pages 243–283. MIT Press, 1992.

[10] Gopalan Nadathur and Debra Sue Wilson. A representation of lambda terms suitable for operations on their intensions. In *Proc. 1990 ACM Conf. on Lisp and Functional Programming*, pages 341–348. ACM Press, 1990.

[11] Gopalan Nadathur and Debra Sue Wilson. A notation for lambda terms: A generalization of environments. *Theoretical Computer Science*, 198(1-2):49–98, 1998.

[12] George Necula. Proof-carrying code. In *24th ACM SIGPLAN-SIGACT Symposium on Principles of Programming Languages*, pages 106–119, New York, January 1997. ACM Press.

[13] George Ciprian Necula. *Compiling with Proofs*. PhD thesis, School of Computer Science, Carnegie Mellon University, Pittsburgh, PA, September 1998.

[14] Frank Pfenning. Logic programming in the LF logical framework. In Gérard Huet and Gordon Plotkin, editors, *Logical Frameworks*, pages 149–181. Cambridge University Press, 1991.

[15] Frank Pfenning. personal communication, June 1999.

[16] Frank Pfenning and Conal Elliot. Higher-order abstract syntax. In *Proceedings of the ACM-SIGPLAN Conference on Programming Language Design and Implementation*, pages 199–208, 1988.

[17] Frank Pfenning and Carsten Schürmann. System description: Twelf — a metalogical framework for deductive systems. In *The 16th International Conference on Automated Deduction*. Springer-Verlag, July 1999.

[18] Roberto Virga. Twelf(X): Extending Twelf to rationals and beyond. In preparation, 1999.

[19] C. P. Wadsworth. *Semantics and Pragmatics of the Lambda Calculus*. PhD thesis, Oxford University, 1971.

[20] Philip Wickline. The Terzo implementation of λProlog. http://www.cse.psu.edu/~dale/lProlog/terzo/index.html, 1999.

Well-founded Abduction via Tabled Dual Programs

José Júlio Alferes[1]
Luís Moniz Pereira[2]
Terrance Swift[3]

Abstract

Abductive Logic Programming offers a formalism to declaratively express and solve problems in areas such as diagnosis, planning, belief revision and hypothetical reasoning. Tabled Logic Programming offers a computational mechanism that provides a level of declarativity above that of Prolog, and which has supported successful applications in fields such as parsing, program analysis, and model checking. In this paper we show how to use tabled logic programming to evaluate queries to abductive frameworks with integrity constraints when these frameworks contain both default and explicit negation. Our approach consists of a transformation and an evaluation method. The transformation adjoins to each rule R of a finite ground program a new rule that is true if and only if R is false. We call the resulting program a *dual* program. The evaluation method, ABDUAL, then operates on the dual program. ABDUAL is sound and complete for evaluating queries to abductive frameworks whose entailment method is based on either the well-founded semantics with explicit negation, or answer sets. Further, ABDUAL is asymptotically as efficient as any known method for either class of problems. In addition, when abduction is not desired, ABDUAL operating on a dual program provides a novel tabling method for evaluating queries to ground extended programs whose complexity and termination properties are similar to those of the best tabling methods for the well-founded semantics. A publically available meta-interpreter has been developed for ABDUAL using the XSB system.

1 Introduction

Abductive Logic Programming [11] is a general non-monotonic formalism whose potential for applications is striking. As is well known, problems in domains such as diagnosis, planning, and temporal reasoning can be naturally modeled through abduction. In this paper we lay the basis for efficiently computing queries over ground three-valued abductive frameworks based on extended logic programs and whose notion of entailment rests on the well-founded semantics. Our query processing technique, termed ABDUAL, relies on a mixture of program transformation and tabled evaluation. In our abductive frameworks, a transformation removes negative literals from both the program over which abduction is to be performed and from the integrity rules. Specifically a *dual transformation* is used, that defines for each rule R a dual rule, that is true if and only if R is false. Tabled evaluation of the resulting program turns out to be much simpler than for untransformed normal programs, when abduction is needed, while at the same time maintaining the termination and complexity properties of tabled evaluation of extended programs when abduction is not needed.

The contributions of this paper are

- We describe ABDUAL fully and first consider its use over abductive frameworks whose entailment method is based on the well-founded semantics with explicit negation. ABDUAL is sound, complete, and terminating for queries to such frameworks over finite ground programs and integrity rules.

- We show that over abductive frameworks whose entailment method is based on the well-founded semantics

---

[1] Dep. Matematica, Univ. Évora and A.I. Centre, Univ. Nova de Lisboa, 2825-114 Caparica, Portugal. jja@dmat.uevora.pt
[2] A.I. Centre, Faculdade de Ciências e Tecnologia, Univ. Nova de Lisboa, 2825-114 Caparica, Portugal. lmp@di.fct.unl.pt
[3] Department of Computer Science, University of Maryland, College Park, MD, USA. tswift@cs.umd.edu

with explicit negation, the complexity of ABDUAL is in line with the best known methods. In addition, for normal and extended programs — viewed as abductive frameworks containing no abducibles or integrity constraints — query evaluation has polynomial data complexity.

- We provide a transformation whereby generalized stable models [12] can be computed using ABDUAL and show that ABDUAL provides a sound and complete evaluation method for computing such models. Furthermore, the efficiency of ABDUAL in computing generalized stable models is in line with the best known methods.

- Finally, we provide access to an ABDUAL meta-interpreter, written using the XSB system, illustrating how to evaluate ABDUAL in practice and describe how ABDUAL can be applied to medical diagnosis.

2 Preliminaries

2.1 Terminology and assumptions

Throughout this paper, we use the terminology of Logic Programming as defined in [13] with the following modifications. An *objective literal* is either an atom A, or the *explicit negation* of A, denoted $-A$. If an objective literal O is an atom A, the explicit conjugate of O ($conj_E(O)$) is the atom $-A$; otherwise if O has the form $-A$, the explicit conjugate of O is A. A *literal* either has the form O, where O is an objective literal, or $not(O)$ the *default negation* of O. Default conjugates are defined similiarly to explicit conjugates: the default conjugate ($conj_D(O)$) of an objective literal O is $not(O)$, and the default conjugate of $not(O)$ is O. Thus, every atom is an objective literal and every objective literal is a literal. An extended program P, formed over some countable language of function and predicate symbols $\mathcal{L}_P$, is the set of rules of the form H :- $Body$ in which H is an objective literal, and $Body$ is a possibly empty sequence of literals. If no objective literals in a program P contain the explicit negation symbol, P is called *normal*. The set of literals occurring in P is termed *literals*(P).

The extended Herbrand base of a program P, denoted $\mathcal{H}_P$, is the set of all ground objective literals in $\mathcal{L}_P$. By a *3-valued interpretation* I of a program P we mean a set of literals over $\mathcal{H}_P$. We denote as I_T the set of objective literals in I, and I_F the set of literals of the form $not(O)$ in I. For a ground objective literal, O, if neither O nor $not(O)$ is in I, the truth value of O is undefined. An interpretation I is *consistent* if there is no objective literal O such that $O \in I_T$ and $not(O) \in I_F$; I is *coherent* if $O \in I_T$ implies $not(conj_E(O)) \in I_F$[4]. The *information ordering* of interpretations is defined as follows. Given two interpretations, I^1 and I^2, $I^1 \subseteq_{Info} I^2$ if I_F^1 is a subset of I_F^2, and I_T^1 is a subset of I_T^2. Given a program P, we denote by $WFS(P)$ the three-valued well-founded model of P [17], and by $WFSX(P)$ the three-valued well-founded model with explicit negation [1] of P, which generalizes WFS. Any consistent 3-valued interpretation can be viewed as a function from $\mathcal{H}_P$ to the set $\{\mathbf{f}, \mathbf{u}, \mathbf{t}\}$. Accordingly, for convenience we assume that the symbols $\mathbf{t}$ and $not(\mathbf{f})$ belong to every model, while neither $\mathbf{u}$ nor $not(\mathbf{u})$ belong to any model. For simplicity of presentation, we assume a left-to-right literal selection strategy throughout this paper, although any of the results presented here will hold for any fixed literal selection strategy. Finally, because dual programs (introduced below) allow any literal as the head of a rule, the terms *goal*, *query* and *literal* are used interchangibly.

2.2 The Well-Founded Semantics with Explicit Negation

We first recall definitions of the well-founded and stable models for extended programs. Both of these definitions make use of the operator θ_J^X [4].

Definition 2.1   [The θ_J^X Operator] Let P be an extended program and J an interpretation. The operator θ_J^X maps interpretations of P to interpretations of P and is defined as follows. If I and J are 3-valued

---

[4]In a coherent interpretation if some atom is explicitly false (resp. true) then it must be false (resp. true) by default.

interpretations of P and A an objective literal, then $\theta_J^X(I)$ is defined as

1. $A \in \theta_J^X(I)$ iff there is a rule $A :\text{-} L_1, ..., L_n$ in P such that for $1 \leq i \leq n$, L_i is an objective literal and $L_i \in I$, or L_i is of the form $not(O)$, and $not(O) \in J$.

2. $not(A) \in \theta_J^X(I)$ iff

   (a) for every rule $A :\text{-} L_1, ..., L_n$ in P, there is a literal L_i for $1 \leq i \leq n$, such that either L_i is of the form $not(G)$ and $G \in J$, or L_i is an objective literal and $not(L_i) \in I$; or

   (b) $conj_E(A) \in J$

$\square$

The θ_J^X operator is an extension of a similar operator for normal programs (e.g. [15]). Indeed, the only addition required for explicit negation is clause 2b, which ensures coherency. It can be shown [4] that θ_J^X is monotonic on the truth ordering for 3-valued interpretations, so that it has a unique least fixed point for a given J, denoted by $\omega^X(J) = lfp(\theta_J^X(Neg\_Olits))$, where $Neg\_Olits = \{not(O)|O \in \mathcal{H}_P\}$. Furthermore, it can be shown [4] that the operator ω^X is also monotonic on the information ordering of interpretations leading to the following definition of the well-founded semantics with explicit negation.

Definition 2.2 [Paraconsistent Well-founded Semantics with Explicit Negation] Let P be an extended program. Then $WFSX_P(P)$ is defined as the least fixed point of $\omega^X(\emptyset)$. $\square$

Example 2.1 Let P be the program containing the rules $\{c :\text{-} not(b); \quad b :\text{-} a; \quad -b; \quad a :\text{-} not(a)\}$. Then $WFSX_P(P) = \{-b, c, not(-a), not(b), not(-c)\}$. Note that to compute c, coherency (condition 2b of Definition 2.1) must be used to infer $not(b)$ from $-b$.

Using the operator ω^X it is possible to define a stability operator for extended programs that allows partial, and possibly paraconsistent models.

Definition 2.3 [Partial Stable Interpretation of an Extended Program] Let P be an extended program. We call an interpretation J a *partial stable interpretation* of P if $J = \omega^X(J)$ $\square$

If an interpretation I contains both O and $-O$, then through coherency, $\omega^X(I)$ will contain both O and $not(O)$ and so will be inconsistent. Thus, by definition an interpretion I can be a partial stable interpretation even if it is inconsistent. However as we will see, within abductive frameworks consistency can be ensured by means of integrity constraints — for instance, prohibiting O and $-O$ to be true for any objective literals O.

2.3 Three-Valued Abductive Frameworks

The definitions of three-valued abductive frameworks modify those of [5].

Definition 2.4 [Integrity Rule] An *integrity rule* for a program P has the form

$$\perp :\text{-} L_1, ..., L_n$$

where each L_i, $1 \leq i \leq n$ is a literal formed over an element of $\mathcal{L}_P$. $\square$

Definition 2.5 [Abductive Framework] An abductive framework is a triple $\langle P, \mathcal{A}, I \rangle$ where $\mathcal{A}$ is a set of ground objective literals of $\mathcal{L}_P$ called *abducibles*, such that for any objective literal O, $O \in \mathcal{A}$ iff $conj_E(O) \in A$, I is a set of ground integrity rules, and P is a ground program such that (1) there is no rule in P whose head is in $\mathcal{A}$; and (2) $\perp /0$ is a predicate symbol not occurring in $\mathcal{L}_P$.

An *abductive subgoal* $S = \langle A, Set \rangle$ is a literal A together with a set of abducibles, *Set*, called the *context* of A. If the context contains both an objective literal and its (explicit or default) conjugate, it is termed *inconsistent* and is *consistent* otherwise. $\square$

The requirement that there can be no rule in P whose head is an abducible leads to no loss of generality, since any program with abducibles can be rewritten to obey it [5].

---

[5]For instance, if it is desired to abduce A, one may introduce a new abducible predicate A', along with a rule $A :\text{-} A'$ [11].

Definition 2.6 [Abductive Scenario] A scenario of an abductive framework $\langle P, \mathcal{A}, I \rangle$ is a tuple $\langle P, \mathcal{A}, \mathcal{B}, I \rangle$, where $\mathcal{B}$ is a consistent 3-valued interpretation of each $A \in \mathcal{A}$. $P_{\mathcal{B}}$ contains, for each $A \in \mathcal{A}$, the rule $A :\!\!- \mathbf{t}$ iff $A \in \mathcal{B}$; $A :\!\!- \mathbf{f}$ iff $not(A) \in \mathcal{B}$; and $A :\!\!- \mathbf{u}$ if neither A nor $not(A)$ is in $\mathcal{B}$. □

Definition 2.7 [Abductive Solution] An abductive solution is a scenario $\sigma = \langle P, \mathcal{A}, \mathcal{B}, I \rangle$ of an abductive framework, such that $\perp$ is false in $M(\sigma) = WFSX_P(P \cup P_{\mathcal{B}} \cup I)$. □

We say that $\sigma = \langle P, \mathcal{A}, \mathcal{B}, I \rangle$ is an abductive solution for a query Q if $M(\sigma) \models Q$. σ is minimal, if there is no other abductive solution $\sigma = \langle P, \mathcal{A}, \mathcal{B}', I \rangle$ for Q such that $WFM(\mathcal{B}') \subseteq_{info} WFM(\mathcal{B})$.

3 Evaluation of the Abductive Solutions for a Query over the Well-Founded Semantics With Explicit Negation

We informally introduce ABDUAL through a series of examples.

Example 3.1 We first illustrate how ABDUAL can be used to compute queries to ground programs according to the well-founded semantics when neither abduction nor integrity constraints are needed. Accordingly, consider the abductive framework $\langle P_1, \emptyset, \emptyset \rangle$, in which the set of abducibles and the set of integrity rules are both empty, and $P_1 =$

```
s  :- not(p), not(q), not(r).
p  :- not(s), not(r), q.
q  :- not(p), r.
r  :- not(q), p.
```

Note that, taken as a normal program, $WFM(P_1) = \{s, not(p), not(q), not(r)\}$. In order to evaluate the query ?-s through ABDUAL, we first create the dual form of P_1 taken together with a *query rule*

```
query :- s, not(⊥).
```

where query is assumed not to be in $\mathcal{L}_{P_1}$. This rule ensures that integrity constraints are checked for any abductive solutions that are derived. This dual program, $dual(P_1 \cup query :\!\!- s, not(\perp))$ is shown in Figure 1.

```
s  :- not(p), not(q), not(r).              not(s)      :- p.
                                           not(s)      :- q.
                                           not(s)      :- r.
p  :- not(s), not(r), q.                   not(p)      :- s.
                                           not(p)      :- r.
                                           not(p)      :- not(q).
q  :- not(p), r.                           not(q)      :- p.
                                           not(q)      :- not(r).
r  :- not(q), p.                           not(r)      :- q.
                                           not(r)      :- not(p).
query :- s,not(⊥).                         not(query)  :- not(s).
                                           not(query)  :- ⊥.
                                           not(⊥).
```

```
            not(p)  :- -p.    not(-p)  :- p.
            not(q)  :- -q.    not(-q)  :- q.
            not(r)  :- -r.    not(-r)  :- r.
            not(s)  :- -s.    not(-s)  :- s.
```

Figure 1: *Dual Program for* $(P_1 \cup query :\!\!- s, not(\perp))$

Note that in the dual form of a program, rules can have default literals of the form $not(A)$ in their heads, and a rule for $not(A)$ is designed to be true if and only if A is false. The last four lines of Figure 1 are *coherency axioms* so-named because they ensure coherency of the model computed by ABDUAL. As is usual with tabled evaluations (e.g. [2]), the ABDUAL evaluation of a query to $dual(P_1)$ is represented as a sequence $\mathcal{F}_0, ..., \mathcal{F}_i$, of forests of ABDUAL trees. $\mathcal{F}_0$ is the forest consisting of the single tree $< query, \emptyset > :- |query$, which calls the query rule. Given a successor ordinal $i + 1$, a forest $\mathcal{F}_{i+1}$ is created when an ABDUAL operation either adds a new tree to $\mathcal{F}_i$ or expands a node in an existing tree in $\mathcal{F}_i$. A forest of trees at the end of one possible ABDUAL evaluation of the above query is shown in Figure 2 [6]. Nodes in Figure 2 are all *regular* having the form *Abductive_subgoal :- GoalList|DelayList*, where *Abductive_subgoal* is an abductuve subgoal (Definition 2.5), and *GoalList* and *DelayList* are sequences of literals. In ABDUAL terminology, when an evaluation encounters

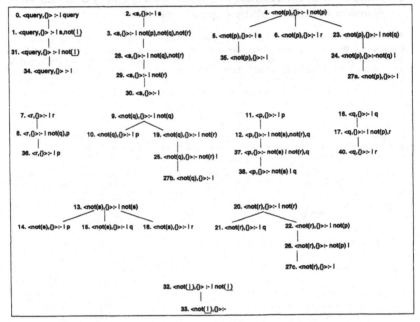

Figure 2: Simplified ABDUAL Evaluation of a Normal Program

a new literal, S, a tree with root $S :- |S$ is added to the forest via the NEW SUBGOAL operation. Thus, in Figure 2, when the literal s is selected in node 1, a NEW SUBGOAL operation creates node 2 as a single tree. Children of the roots of trees are created via PROGRAM CLAUSE RESOLUTION operations. The left-to-right literal selection strategy can be broken by a DELAYING operation of a non-root node, which moves a selected literal from the *GoalList* to the *DelayList* of the node — nodes 24, 25, and 26 are created in this way. An

---

[6]For simplicity of presentation, Figure 2 does not include computation paths that include the coherency axioms.

answer is a leaf node with an empty *GoalList*. In the subforest of Figure 2 consisting of nodes whose index is 26 or less, nodes 24, 25, and 26 are all answers. Because each of their delay lists is non-empty they are termed *conditional answers*. However, in the well-founded model of P_1 each of these answers should be unconditionally true, and in order to derive this a CO-UNFOUNDED SET REMOVAL operation is needed. Note that nodes 24, 25, and 26 together form an analogue in the dual program to an unfounded set [17] consisting of p, q, and r in P_1. Such an analogue is called a *co-unfounded set*. Whereas positive literals of an unfounded set are all false, negative literals for a co-unfounded set are all true. When a set of conditional answers is determined to form a co-unfounded set, the answers are all made unconditionally true. Answers are returned to other nodes via the ANSWER CLAUSE RESOLUTION operation which also combines the abductive contexts of the answer and the node. For instance, the answer `<not(p),{}>  :- |` is returned to the node 3 through ANSWER CLAUSE RESOLUTION.

We now formalize the definitions of some concepts introduced in Example 3.1.

Definition 3.1 [Dual Program] Let P be an extended program. The *dual transformation* creates a *dual program dual(P)*, defined as the union of P with smallest program containing a set of rules R_1 and R_2 as follows:

1. If O is an objective literal for which there are no facts in P, and all of its rules are:

$$O :- \quad L_{1,1}, ..., L_{1,n_1}$$
$$\vdots$$
$$O :- \quad L_{m,1}, ..., L_{m,n_m}$$

    (a) then R_1 contains the rule

$$not(O) :- \quad fold\_O_1, ..., fold\_O_m.$$

    (b) and for $1 \leq i \leq m$, R_1 contains the rules $fold\_O_i, 1 \leq i \leq m$

$$fold\_O_i :- \quad conj_D(L_{i,1}).$$
$$\vdots$$
$$fold\_O_i :- \quad conj_D(L_{i,n_i}).$$

    where $fold\_O_i$ is assumed not to occur in $\mathcal{L}_P$ for $1 \leq i \leq m$ (such rules are termed *folding rules*, and literals formed from atoms whose predicate symbol is $fold\_O_i$ are called *folding literals*).

    (c) Otherwise, if $not(O)$ is in *literals(P)*, but there is no rule with head O in P, then R contains the rule $not(O) :-$

    (d) R_2 consists of *axioms of coherence* that relate explicit and default negation, defined as:

$$not(O) :- conj_E(O)$$

    For each objective literal $not(O)$ in either *literals(P ∪ R_1)* or A.

                                                                 □

In the *dual(P)* form, $not(O)$ is true iff O is false in P. For instance, if there is a fact in P for some objective literal O then the dual has no rule for $not(O)$.

Definition 3.2 [ABDUAL Trees and Forest] An ABDUAL forest consists of a forest of ABDUAL trees. Nodes of ABDUAL trees are either *failure nodes* of the form *fail*, or *regular nodes* of the form

$$Abductive\_Subgoal :- DelayList|GoalList$$

where *Abductive_subgoal* is an abductive subgoal. Both *DelayList* and *GoalList* are sequences of literals (also called delay literals and goal literals, respectively).

We call a (non-failure) leaf node N an *answer* when *GoalList* is empty. If *DelayList* is also empty, N is *unconditional*; otherwise it is *conditional*. □

Definition 3.7 ensures that the root node of a given ABDUAL tree, T, has the form $\langle S, \emptyset \rangle :- |S$, where S is a literal. In this case, we say that S is the *root goal* for T or that T is the *tree for S*. Similarly by Definitiondef:ops, a forest contains a root goal S if the forest contains a tree for S. Literal selection rules apply to the *GoalList* of a node; as mentioned in Section 2, we use a fixed left-to-right order for simplicity of presentation.

The next example illustrates how ABDUAL can evaluate queries to general abductive frameworks.

Example 3.2 Consider the abductive framework $\langle P_2, A, I \rangle$, in which P_2 is the program

$$\text{p :- not(q*).}$$
$$\text{q :- not(p*).}$$

$A = \{p*, q*, -p*, -q*\}$, and I is the program

```
⊥ :- p_constr
⊥ :- q_constr
p_constr :- p, -p*.
q_constr :- q, -q*.
```

So that the (ground) integrity constraints represent an abductive interpretation of default negation. Let the query rule be

$$\text{query :- q,not($\perp$).}$$

The dual program is shown in Figure 3.

```
p :- not(q*).              not(p) :- q*.
q :- not(p*).              not(q) :- p*.
⊥ :- p_constr              not(⊥) :- not(p_constr),not(q_constr)
⊥ :- q_constr
p_constr :- p, -p*.        not(p_constr) :- not(p)
                           not(p_constr) :- not(-p*).
q_constr :- q, -q*.        not(q_constr) :- not(q)
                           not(q_constr) :- not(-q*).
query :- q,not(⊥).         not(query) :- not(q).
                           not(query) :- not(⊥).


not(-p)  :- p.             not(p)  :- -p.
not(-q)  :- q              not(q)  :- -q
not(-p*) :- p*             not(p*) :- -p*
not(-q*) :- q*             not(q*) :- -q*
not(-p_constr) :- p_constr not(p_constr) :- -p_constr
not(-q_constr) :- q_constr not(q_constr) :- -q_constr
```

Figure 3: *Dual program for $(P_2 \cup$ query :- q,not($\perp$)).*

Figure 4 illustrates a forest of trees created by an ABDUAL evaluation of this initial query. As with Figure 2, derivations stemming from coherency axioms are not presented. When abducibles are encountered in an evaluation, provision must be made for when the selected literal of a given node is an abducible, as well as for propagation of abducibles among abductive goals. In the first case, if the selected atom of a node N is an abducible, and the addition of the selected atom to the context of the abductive subgoal of N does not make the context inconsistent (Definition 2.5), an ABDUCTION operation is applicable to N. As an example, ABDUCTION is used to create a child for node 3, $\langle q, \{\} \rangle :- \text{not(p*)}$. Abducibles are propagated through the ANSWER CLAUSE RESOLUTION operation, which has the restriction that the context of the answer must be consistent with the context of the node to which the answer is returned. For instance, of the two unique abductive solutions to not($\perp$) only one can be returned to the node $\langle \text{query}, \{p*\} \rangle :- \text{not}(\perp)$, namely

433

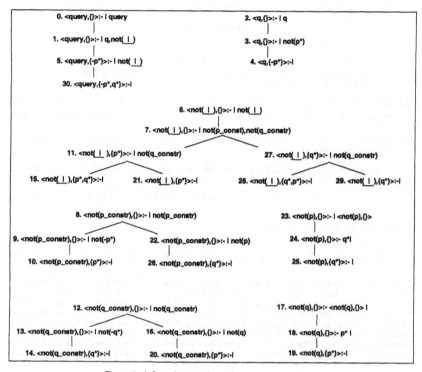

Figure 4: *A finite* ABDUAL *forest the query* ?- q *to* P_2.

434

$<\texttt{not}(\perp),\{\texttt{q*}\}>$.

The final definitions for ABDUAL are now provided. First, a notion is needed to determine when a set of trees has produced all abductive answers that it will ever produce. This is captured by the notion of a set of trees being completely evaluated.

Definition 3.3 [Completely Evaluated] Given a forest $\mathcal{F}$, a set $\mathcal{T}$ of ABDUAL trees is *completely evaluated* iff at least one of the following conditions is satisfied for each tree $T \in \mathcal{T}$:

1. T contains an unconditional answer whose context is empty; or

2. For each node N in $\mathcal{T}$ with selected literal SL

   - The tree for SL belongs to a set S' of completely evaluated trees; and
   - No NEW SUBGOAL, PROGRAM CLAUSE RESOLUTION, or ANSWER CLAUSE RESOLUTION operations (Definition 3.7) are applicable to N.

A literal L is completely evaluated in $\mathcal{F}$ if the tree for L belongs to a completely evaluated set in $\mathcal{F}$. □

Evaluation of the program in Example 3.1 required detection of a co-unfounded set, whose formal definition is as follows.

Definition 3.4 [Co-Unfounded Set of Answers] Let $\mathcal{F}$ be an ABDUAL forest, and S a set of answers in $\mathcal{F}$. Then S is a co-unfounded set in $\mathcal{F}$ iff

1. Each literal S_i, such that $< S_i, C_i >$ is the abductive subgoal of an answer in S, is completely evaluated.

2. The set
$$Context = \{C_i| < S_i, C_i > \text{ is the abductive subgoal of an answer in } S\}$$
   is consistent; and

3. For each answer $< S_i, C_i > \ :- DL_i| \in S$

   (a) DL_i is non-empty; and
   (b) for each $S_j \in DL_i$, there exists an answer $< S_j, Context_j > \ :- DL_j| \in S$. □

An ABDUAL evaluation consists of a (possibly transfinite) sequence of ABDUAL forests. Our definition here follows that of [16] for generalized SLG trees. In order to define the behavior of an ABDUAL evaluation at a limit ordinal, we define a notion of a least upper bound for a set of ABDUAL trees. If a global ordering on literals is assumed, then the elements in the *Context* of a node can be uniformly ordered, and using this ordering an equivalence relation can be defined for nodes of ABDUAL trees. Furthermore, any rooted tree can be viewed as a partially ordered set in which each node N is represented as $\{N, P\}$ in which P is a tuple representing the path from N to the root of the tree. When represented in this manner, it is easily seen that when T_1 and T_2 are rooted trees, $T_1 \subseteq T_2$ iff T_1 is a subtree of T_2, and furthermore, that if T_1 and T_2 have the same root, their union can be defined as their set union, for T_1 and T_2 taken as sets.

Definition 3.5 [ABDUAL Evaluation] Let $\mathcal{A} = \langle P, A, I \rangle$ be an abductive framework and Q a query. An ABDUAL evaluation $\mathcal{E}$ of Q to $\mathcal{A}$ is a sequence of ABDUAL forests $\mathcal{F}_0, \mathcal{F}_1, ..., \mathcal{F}_n$ operating on the ground instantiation of $dual(P \cup I \cup \{query :- not(\perp), Q\})$ such that:

- $\mathcal{F}_0$ is the forest containing the single tree, $< query, \{\} > \ :- |query$,

- For each successor ordinal $n + 1 \leq \beta$, $\mathcal{F}_{n+1}$ is obtained from $\mathcal{F}_n$ by applying an ABDUAL operation from Definition 3.7.

- For each limit ordinal $\alpha \leq \beta$, $\mathcal{F}_\alpha$ is defined such that $T \in \mathcal{F}_\alpha$ iff

– The root node of T, $< S, \{\} >$:- $|S$ is the root node of some a tree in a forest F_i, $i < \alpha$;

– $T = \cup(\{T_i | T_i \in \mathcal{F}_i, i < \alpha$ and T_i has root S :- $|S)$

If no operation is applicable in $\mathcal{F}_n$, then it is called a *final forest* of $\mathcal{E}$. $\qquad\square$

Similarly to SLG, ABDUAL does not propagate delay lists of delayed answers — that is if an answer p :- $q, r|$ is returned to a node a :- $|p, s$ the resulting node will be a :- $p|s$ rather than a :- $q, r|s$. This action is necessary for ABDUAL to have polynomial complexity for normal programs in the absence of abduction (c.f. Theorem 3.3). However, in certain special cases it is possible to propagate conditional answers that cannot be simplified away. In this case the answers become unsupported (see [2] for an example of this).

Definition 3.6 [Supported Answers] Let $\mathcal{F}$ be a forest, and S the root goal for a tree T in $\mathcal{F}$. Then S is supported in $\mathcal{F}$ iff

1. T is not completely evaluated; or

2. there exists an answer $< S, Context >$:- $DL|$ of S such that, for every (positive) delayed literal L_1 in DL, L_1 is supported in $\mathcal{F}$.

$\qquad\square$

Definition 3.7 [ABDUAL Operations] Let $\mathcal{F}_n$ be an ABDUAL forest for an evaluation of a query Q to an abductive framework $\mathcal{A} = \langle P, A, I \rangle$, and suppose n is a successor ordinal. Then $\mathcal{F}_{n+1}$ may be produced by one of the following operations

1. NEW SUBGOAL: Let $\mathcal{F}_n$ contain a non-root node

$$N = AbductiveSubgoal \text{ :- } DL|S, GoalList.$$

Assume $\mathcal{F}_n$ contains no tree with root goal S. Then add the tree: $< S, \{\} >$:- $|S$.

2. PROGRAM CLAUSE RESOLUTION: Let $\mathcal{F}_n$ contain a root node

$$N = < S, \{\} > \text{ :- } |S$$

and C be a program clause S :- $Body$. Assume that in $\mathcal{F}_n$, N does not have a child:

$$N_{child} = < S, \{\} > \text{ :- } |Body$$

Then add N_{child} as a child of N.

3. ANSWER CLAUSE RESOLUTION: Let $\mathcal{F}_n$ contain a non-root node $N = < S, C_1 >$:- $DL_0|G, Body$ and suppose that $\mathcal{F}_n$ contains an answer node $< G, C_2 >$:- $DL_1|$ for G, such that $C_1 \cup C_2$ is consistent. Let $DL_2 = DL_0, G$ if DL_1 is not empty, and $DL_2 = DL_0$ otherwise. Finally, assume that in $\mathcal{F}_n$, N does not have a child

$$N_{child} = < S, C_1 \cup C_2 > \text{ :- } DL_2|Body$$

Then add N_{child} as a child of N.

4. DELAYING: Let $\mathcal{F}_n$ contain a non-root leaf node

$$N = < S, Context > \text{ :- } DelayList|not(G), Body$$

where G is not an abducible, and where $\mathcal{F}_n$ contains a tree for $not(G)$, but no answer of the form $< not(G), \{\} >$:- $|$. Then add: $< S, Context >$:- $DelayList, not(G)|Body$ as a child of N.

5. SIMPLIFICATION: Let $N = < S, C_1 >$:- $DL|$ be a node for a tree with root goal S, and let D be a delayed literal in DL. Then

- if $\mathcal{F}_n$ contains an unconditional answer node $< D, C_2 > \ :\text{-} |$, and if $C_1 \cup C_2$ is consistent, let $DL_1 = DL - D$. If

$$N_{child} = < S, C_1 \cup C_2 > \ :\text{-} DL_1|$$

is not a descendent of N in $\mathcal{F}$, add N_{child} as a child of N.

- if the tree for D is completely evaluated and contains no answers; or if D is non-supported, then create a child *fail* of N.

6. CO-UNFOUNDED SET REMOVAL: Let S be a co-unfounded set and let C_{union} be the consistent union of all contexts of answers in S. Then for each

$$N = < S, C_1 > \ :\text{-} DL| \in S$$

create a child of N: $N_{child} = < S, C_{union} > \ :\text{-} |$

7. ABDUCTION: Let

$$N = < S, Context > \ :\text{-} DL|G, Body$$

where G is an abducible, and suppose that $G \cup Context$ is consistent. Finally, assume that in $\mathcal{F}_n$, N does not have a child

$$N_{child} = < S, Context \cup G > \ :\text{-} DL|Body$$

Then add N_{child} as a child of N.

$\square$

The definitions of ABDUAL bear some similarity to those of SLG (see Section 4).

Theorem 3.1 [7] *Let $\mathcal{A} = \langle P, A, I \rangle$ be an abductive framework such that P is an extended program, and I a set of extended integrity rules. Let $\mathcal{E}$ be an ABDUAL evaluation of Q against $\mathcal{A}$. Then*

- $\mathcal{E}$ *will have a final forest $\mathcal{E}_\beta$;*
- *if $< query, Set > \ :\text{-} |$ is an answer in $\mathcal{E}_\beta$ $\sigma = \langle P, A, Set, I \rangle$ is an abductive solution for $\mathcal{A}$;*
- *if $\langle P, A, Set, I \rangle$ is a minimal abductive solution for Q, then $< query, Set > \ :\text{-} |$ is an answer in $\mathcal{E}_\beta$.*

3.1 Finite Termination and Complexity of ABDUAL for Extended Programs

Termination of ABDUAL evaluations is characterized by the following theorem.

Theorem 3.2 *Let $\mathcal{A} = \langle P, A, I \rangle$ be an abductive framework such that P and I are finite ground extended programs, and A is a finite set of abducibles. Let $\mathcal{E}$ be an ABDUAL evaluation of a query Q against $\mathcal{A}$. Then $\mathcal{E}$ will reach a final forest after a finite number of ABDUAL operations.*

It is known that the problem of query evaluation to abductive frameworks is NP-complete, even for those frameworks in which entailment is based on the well-founded semantics. However, in the special case in which an abductive framework reduces to an extended (or normal) program ABDUAL can evaluate queries with polynomial data complexity, the definition of which we now recall.

Definition 3.8 [17] *The intension of a program P, P_I, consists of all rules in P with non-empty bodies; the extension of P, P_E, consists of all rules in P whose body is empty. The data complexity of P is the computational complexity of deciding an answer to a ground atomic query as a function of the size of P_E.*
$\square$

Theorem 3.3 *Let P be an extended program, and $\mathcal{A} = \langle P, \emptyset, \emptyset \rangle$ be an abductive framework of P, such that the ground instantiation of P is finite. Let $\mathcal{E}$ be an ABDUAL evaluation of a non-abductive query Q against $\mathcal{A}$, whose final forest is $\mathcal{E}_\beta$. Then $\mathcal{E}_\beta$ can be constructed in time polynomial in $|P_E|$.*

---

[7]Proofs of theorems are provided in the full version of this paper, available at http://www.cs.sunysb.edu/~tswift.

3.2 Construction of Generalized Stable Models through ABDUAL

The three-valued abductive frameworks of Section 2 are not the only semantics used for abduction: Generalized Stable Models [12] provide an important alternative. In [5] it was shown that the abductive framework of Section 2 has the same expressive power as generalized stable models [11]. In this section, we reformulate these results to show that ABDUAL can be used to evaluate abductive queries over generalized stable models. By allowing all positive literals to be inferred through abduction, ABDUAL can be used to construct partial stable interpretations (Definition 2.3). By choosing appropriate integrity constraints, these interpretations can be constrained to be consistent and total. We begin by adapting the concept of a generalized stable model to the terminology of Section 2.

Definition 3.9 [Generalized Partial Stable Interpretation and Model] Let σ be scenario $\sigma = \langle P, A, \mathcal{B}, I \rangle$ of an abductive framework. Then $M(\mathcal{B})$ is a generalized partial stable interpretation of $\langle P, A, I \rangle$ if

- $M(\mathcal{B})$ is a partial stable interpretation of $(P \cup P_{\mathcal{B}} \cup I)$; and

- $\perp$ is false in $M(\mathcal{B})$.

If in addition $M(\mathcal{B})$ is an answer set of $(P \cup P_{\mathcal{B}} \cup I)$, σ is a generalized stable model of $\langle P, A, I \rangle$. $\square$

Generalized stable models can be computed by adding additional program rules, abducibles, and integrity constraints to abductive frameworks and computing the solution to these frameworks as per Definition 2.7.

Definition 3.10 Let $\mathcal{A} = \langle P, A, I \rangle$ be an abductive framework. Then for each objective literal O, let abd_O be a new objective literal, not in $\mathcal{H}_P$. Let

$$R = O \text{ :- } Body$$

be a rule in P. Then a *shadow rule* for R is a rule

$$R_{shadow} = O \text{ :- } Body_{abd}$$

in which each literal of the form $not(O')$ in $Body$ ($O' \in \mathcal{H}_P$) is replaced by $not(abd\_O')$. Corresponding to the shadow rules are *shadow constraints* (I_{shadow}) of the form

$$\perp \text{ :- } O, not(abd\_O).$$
$$\perp \text{ :- } not(O), abd\_O.$$

for each abd_O such that $not(abd\_O) \in S(P)$.

The *consistency constraints* ($I_{consist}$) for $\mathcal{A}$ consist of integrity rules of the form

$$\perp \text{ :- } O, not(O).$$
$$\perp \text{ :- } O, not(abd\_O).$$
$$\perp \text{ :- } not(O), abd\_O.$$

The *totality rules* (I_{total}) for $\mathcal{A}$ have the form

$$\perp \text{ :- } not(defined_O)$$
$$defined_O \text{ :- } O$$
$$defined_O \text{ :- } not(O)$$

for each $O \in \mathcal{H}_P$. $\square$

Applying the transformations in Definition 3.10 allows ABDUAL to compute GSMs.

Theorem 3.4 Let $\langle P, A, \mathcal{B}, I \rangle$ be an abductive scenario, let $S(P)$ be the set of shadow rules for P, and $A_{shadow} = \{abd\_O | not(abd\_O) \in S(P)\}$. Then

438

1. $M(\mathcal{B})$ is a generalized partial stable interpretation of $\langle P, A, I\rangle$ iff there exists an abductive solution

$$\langle (P \cup S(P)), (A \cup A_{shadow}), \mathcal{B}, (I \cup I_{shadow}) \rangle$$

such that $M(\sigma) = M(\mathcal{B})$.

2. $M(\mathcal{B})$ is a generalized stable model of $\langle P, A, I\rangle$ iff there exists an abductive solution

$$\langle (P \cup S(P)), (A \cup A_{shadow}), \mathcal{B}, (I \cup I_{shadow} \cup I_{consist} \cup I_{total}) \rangle$$

such that $M(\sigma) = M(\mathcal{B})$.

Theorem 3.4 has several implications. First, since the paraconsistent well-founded model of a program is a partial stable interpretation, use of the shadow program and constraints includes computation of the paraconsistent well-founded model as a special case. In addition, because Theorem 3.1 states that ABDUAL can be used for query evaluation to abductive frameworks based on $WFSX_P$, ABDUAL can be used to compute generalized partial stable interpretations and generalized stable models. The cost of these computation, of course, includes the cost of potentially evaluating shadow rules and the various additional integrity constraints. It is known that the problem of deciding the answer to a ground query to an abductive framework is NP-complete when the entailment method is based on the well-founded semantics [8], as is the problem of deciding whether an abductive framework has a generalized stable model. The lack of polynomial data complexity of ABDUAL for arbitrary abductive frameworks is therefore understandable, given the power of these frameworks.

4 Discussion

A Meta-interpreter for ABDUAL **and its Application to Diagnosis** A preliminary meta-interpreter for ABDUAL, written using the XSB system, is available from http://www.cs.sunysb.edu/~tswift. This meta-interpreter has the termination property of Theorem 3.2, but does not have the complexity property of Theorem 3.3. Work is underway on the XSB system so that the CO-UNFOUNDED SET REMOVAL operation can be implemented at the engine level and the complexity results of Theorem 3.3 attained.

ABDUAL was originally motivated by a desire to implement psychiatric diagnosis. Knowledge about psychiatric illnesses is codified by *DSM-IV* [7] sponsored by the American Psychiatric Association. Knowledge in DSM-IV can be represented as a directed graph with positive links to represent relations from diagnoses to sub-diagnoses or to symptoms. These graphs also have negative links, called *exclusion* links that represent symptoms or diagnoses that must shown false in order to derive the diagnosis. The DSM-IV graph requires both abduction and non-stratified negation, as can be seen by considering the diagnosis of Adjustment Disorder ([7], pg. 626). One criterion for this diagnosis is

Once the stressor (or its consequences) has terminated, the symptoms do not persist for more than an additional 6 months.

Thus, to diagnose a patient as presently undergoing adjustment disorder, a physician must hypothesize about events in the future — a step naturally modeled with abduction. Adjustment disorder requires an exclusion criterion

The stress-related disturbance does not meet the criteria for another specific Axis I disorder and is not merely an exacerbation of a preexisting Axis I or Axis II disorder.

that admits the possibility of a loop through negation between adjustment disorder and another diagnosis. This can in fact occur, for instance with Alzheimer's Dementia ([7], pg. 142-143). If, as far as a physician can tell, a patient fulfills all criteria for adjustment disorder besides the above criterion, as well as all criteria for Alzheimer's (besides the criterion that the disturbance is not better accounted for by another disorder), the physician will essentially be faced with the situation:

The patient has an Adjustment Disorder if he does not have Alzheimer's Dementia, and has Alzheimer's Dementia of the patient does not have an Adjustment Disorder.

It is unclear whether such a situation was envisioned by the DSM-IV committees, or how to model what a physician should do in such a situation. A physician to make a provisional diagnosis of the Adjustment Disorder based on a revision of his beliefs about Alzheimer's Dementia; alternatively a physician might choose Adjustment Disorder using a mechanism based on argumentation semantics [11]. Work has begun to use ABDUAL to implement psychiatric diagnosis for a commercial system, Diagnostica 2.0, which is being developed using the ABDUAL interpreter mentioned above.

Comparisons with Other Methods The use of dual programs to compute the well-founded semantics of normal programs was introduced in [14], but this method has several limitations compared with ABDUAL: it does not handle abduction or explicit negation; and it can have exponential complexity for some queries. Many of the definitions of ABDUAL are derived from SLG [2] (as reformulated in [16]) which computes queries to normal programs according to the well-founded semantics. For normal programs, ABDUAL shares the same finite termination and complexity properties as SLG. ABDUAL adds the capability to handle abduction, the use of the dual transformation for extended programs and the CO-UNFOUNDED SET REMOVAL operation, but ABDUAL does not allow evaluation of a non-ground program as does SLG. Unfortunately, performance tradeoffs of ABDUAL and SLG are not yet available, due to the lack of an engine-level implementation of the CO-UNFOUNDED SET REMOVAL operation of ABDUAL.

The main contribution of ABDUAL is its incorporation of abduction. We are not aware of any other efforts that have added abduction to a tabling method. Indeed, it is the use of tabling that is responsible for the termination and complexity results of Sections 3.1 and 3.2. Furthermore, ABDUAL evaluations are confluent in the sense that Theorem 3.1 holds for *any* ordering of applicable ABDUAL operations. The complexity and termination for WFS distinguishes ABDUAL from approaches such as the IFF proof procedure [9] and SLDNFA [6]. These approaches do allow variables in rules which ABDUAL does not. The methods of [3] and [10] compute abductive explanation based on some form of two-valued rule completion for non-abducible predicates (the former based on Clark's completion, and the latter based on the so-called transaction programs). This is similar to our use of the dual program[8]. In both methods, abductive explanations are computed by using the only-if part of the completion in a bottom-up fashion. However, both methods have a severe restriction on the class of programs: they apply generally only to acyclic programs. This restriction is due to their being based on completion. In contrast, ABDUAL is based on the well-founded semantics, and does not impose any restriction on cycles in programs.

Generalizing ABDUAL to Programs with Variables Generalizing ABDUAL for non-ground covered programs[9] with ground queries is not a difficult task: as in Clark's completion, consider rule heads with free variables, and explicitly represent unifications in the body; the dual is then obtained from these rules as usual, where the negation of = is \=. Allowing non-ground queries in covered programs can be obtained by considering as abducibles all terms of the form X \= T, and by adding an appropriate method for verifying consistency of sets of such inequalities. The most difficult step in order to fully generalize ABDUAL to deal with non-ground programs is to abandon the restriction of covered programs. This is so because free variables in the body of program rules introduce universally quantified variables in the body of rules in the dual program — a problem similar to that of floundering in normal programs. Work is underway to generalize ABDUAL to deal with non-ground noncovered programs using constructive negation methods.

A practical advantage of ABDUAL is that it allows the easy propagation of abducibles through both positive and negative literals. As an abductive answer is returned to an abductive subgoal, contexts can be immediately checked for consistency, regardless of whether the subgoal is positive or negative, and regardless of how many levels of negation were needed to produce the answer.

---

[8]Note that the dual for non-abducible predicates in acyclic programs is the same as the completion.

[9]A program is covered iff all variables appearing in the body of rules also appear in the corresponding head.

Acknowledgements This work was partially supported by NSF grants CCR-9702581, EIA-97-5998, and INT-96-00598. The authors also thank PRAXIS XXI projects MENTAL and ACROPOLE and FLAD-NSF project REAP for their support.

References

[1] J. Alferes, C. Damásio, and L. M. Pereira. A logic programming system for non-monotonic reasoning. *Journal of Automated Reasoning*, 14(1):93–147, 1995.

[2] W. Chen and D. S. Warren. Tabled Evaluation with Delaying for General Logic Programs. *JACM*, 43(1):20–74, January 1996.

[3] L. Console, D. Dupré, and P. Torasso. On the relationship between abduction and deduction. *Journal of Logic and Computation*, 1(5):661–690, 1991.

[4] C. Damásio. *Paraconsistent Extended Logic Programming with Constraints*. PhD thesis, Univ. Nova de Lisboa, 1996.

[5] C. Damásio and L. M. Pereira. Abduction over 3-valued extended logic programs. In *LPNMR*, pages 29–42. Springer-Verlag, 1995.

[6] M. Denecker and D. De Schreye. SLDNFA: An abductive procedure for normal abductive programs. In *JICSLP*, pages 868–700. MIT Press, 1992.

[7] *Diagnostic and Statistical Manual of Mental Disorders*. American Psychiatric Association, Washington,DC, 4th edition, 1994. Prepared by the Task Force on DSM-IV and other committees and work groups of the American Psychiatric Association.

[8] Thomas Eiter, Georg Gottlob, and Nicola Leone. Abduction From Logic Programs: Semantics and Complexity. *Theoretical Computer Science*, 189(1-2):129–177, December 1997.

[9] T. Fung and R. Kowalski. The IFF proof procedure for abductive logic programming. *Journal of Logic Programming*, 33(2):151–165, 1997.

[10] K. Inoue and C. Sakama. Computing extended abduction through transaction programs. *Annals of Mathematics and Artificial Intelligence*, 1999. To appear.

[11] A. Kakas, R. Kowalski, and F. Toni. Abductive logic programming. *Journal of Logic and Computation*, 2(6):719–770, 1993.

[12] A. Kakas and P. Mancarella. Generalized stable models: A semantics for abduction. In *ECAI*, pages 385–391. Morgan-Kaufmann, 1990.

[13] J. W. Lloyd. *Foundations of Logic Programming*. Springer-Verlag, Berlin Germany, 1984.

[14] L. M. Pereira, J. Aparício, and J. Alferes. Derivation procedures for extended stable models. In *International Joint Conference on Artificial Intelligence*, 1991.

[15] T.C. Przymusinski. Every logic program has a natural stratification and an iterated least fixed point model. In *ACM PODS*, pages 11–21. ACM Press, 1989.

[16] T. Swift. A new formulation of tabled resolution with delay. In *EPIA 99*, 1999. Available at http://www.cs.sunysb.edu/~tswift.

[17] A. van Gelder, K.A. Ross, and J.S. Schlipf. Unfounded sets and well-founded semantics for general logic programs. *JACM*, 38(3):620–650, 1991.

Optimization of Disjunctive Queries[1]

Sergio Greco
DEIS
Università della Calabria
87030 Rende, Italy
greco@si.deis.unical.it

Abstract

This paper presents a technique for the optimization of bound queries on disjunctive deductive databases. The optimization is based on the rewriting of the source program into an equivalent program which can be evaluated more efficiently. The proposed optimization reduces the size of the data relevant for the query and, consequently, greatly reduces the number of models to be considered to answer the query. Several experiments have confirmed the value of our technique.

1 Introduction

Disjunctive databases are a natural extension of deductive databases which permit to express, by allowing clauses to have disjunctions in their heads, incomplete knowledge of the world [15]. The presence of disjunctions in the head of rules increases the expressive power of the language but it makes the computation of queries very difficult. This is because no efficient techniques, such as the ones defined for standard Datalog (e.g. magic-set), have been defined, and due to the presence of multiple models (generally the number of models can be exponential with respect to the size of the input [1]).

Computation algorithms for disjunctive queries are based on the evaluation of the ground instantiation of programs and the only significant technique so far presented, known as intelligent grounding, is mainly based on the elimination of ground rules whose head cannot be derived from the program [7]. However, in many cases it is not necessary to compute all the models of the program. Take for instance a query asking if, given a graph G, a Hamiltonian path from the node a to the node b there exists. In this case it is not necessary to check all models but just the ones containing paths with source node a and end node b. Although intelligent grounding reduces the number of ground rules, by eliminating useless rules (or heads of rules), it does not reduce the number of models to be checked.

Therefore, techniques which reduce the number of models, by eliminating the ones which are not useful for answering the query, should be exploited. The following example, presents a program where only a strict subset of the minimal models needs to be considered to answer the query.

Example 1.1 Consider the disjunctive program P consisting of the following rule

$$p(X) \vee q(X) \leftarrow a(X)$$

and a database D consisting of the set of facts $\{a(1), a(2), ..., a(n)\}$. Then consider a query asking

---

[1] Work partially supported by ISI-CNR and by a MURST grant under the project "Interdata".

if there is some model for $P \cup D$ containing the atom $p(m)$. A 'brute force' approach, based on an exhaustive search of the minimal models of $P \cup D$, would consider 2^n minimal models.

However, to answer the query we could consider only the ground rule

$$p(m) \vee q(m) \leftarrow a(m)$$

and, therefore consider at most two minimal models: if $a(m)$ is in the database the rewritten program has two minimal models $M_1 = \{p(m)\} \cup D$ and $M_2 = \{q(m)\} \cup D$, otherwise it has only one minimal model $M_3 = D$. □

The main result of this paper is the introduction of a technique which permits us to exploit binding propagation into disjunctive Datalog programs. The proposed technique permits the application of binding propagation methods, previously defined for Datalog queries, to disjunctive Datalog queries. Although, for the sake of presentation, we consider only the extension of the magic-set method [2, 20], other methods such as supplementary magic-set, factorization techniques and special techniques for linear and chain queries [3, 13, 17, 19, 20], can be applied as well.

We point out that a technique for the propagation of bindings into disjunctive queries was proposed in [12]. However, this technique, based on the rewriting of queries into disjunctive queries with nested rules, i.e. rules where heads may also be rules, cannot be used by current systems since the rewritten program is not a standard disjunctive program. Our technique is based on the rewriting of queries into standard disjunctive queries.

The rest of the paper is organized as follows. In Section 2 we present the syntax and semantics of Disjunctive Datalog. In Section 3 we present our technique for the optimization of Disjunctive Datalog queries. In Section 4 we present some experimental results to show the relevance of our technique. Finally, in Section 5 we present our conclusions. Appendix A contains an informal presentation of the magic-set rewriting technique for standard Datalog queries.

2 Disjunctive Deductive Databases

For background and concepts unexplained here, see [15]. A *disjunctive Datalog rule* r is a clause of the form

$$a_1 \vee \cdots \vee a_n \leftarrow b_1, \cdots, b_k, \neg b_{k+1}, \cdots, \neg b_{k+m}$$

where $n \geq 1$, $k, m \geq 0$ and $a_1, \cdots, a_n, b_1, \cdots, b_{k+m}$ are function-free atoms.

We denote by $Head(r)$ (resp. $Body(r)$) the set of head atoms (resp. body literals) of r. If $n = 1$, then r is *normal* (i.e. $\vee$-free); if $m = 0$, then r is *positive* (or $\neg$-free). A *disjunctive Datalog program* $\mathcal{P}$, also called *disjunctive deductive database*, is a finite set of rules; it is *normal* (resp. *positive*) if all its rules are normal (resp. positive). The definition of stratified program defined for standard programs (i.e. programs with only one atom in the head) also applies to disjunctive programs. In the following we shall first consider positive disjunctive deductive databases and then disjunctive programs with stratified negation.

Minker proposed in [16] a model-theoretic semantics for positive $\mathcal{P}$, which assigns to $\mathcal{P}$ the set $MM(\mathcal{P})$ of its *minimal models*, where a model M for $\mathcal{P}$ is minimal, if no proper subset of M is a model for $\mathcal{P}$. Accordingly, the program $\mathcal{P} = \{a \vee b \leftarrow\}$ has the two minimal models $\{a\}$ and $\{b\}$, i.e. $\mathrm{MM}(\mathcal{P}) = \{ \{a\}, \{b\} \}$.

The more general stable model semantics also applies to programs with (unstratified) negation. An interpretation M is a (disjunctive) stable model of $\mathcal{P}$ if and only if $M \in MM(\mathcal{P}^M)$ where $\mathcal{P}^M$ is the ground positive program derived from $ground(\mathcal{P})$ (1) by removing all rules that contain a negative literal $\neg a$ in the body and $a \in M$, and (2) by removing all negative literals from the remaining rules. For general $\mathcal{P}$, the stable model semantics assigns to $\mathcal{P}$ the set $\mathrm{SM}(\mathcal{P})$ of its *stable models*. For positive $\mathcal{P}$, stable model and minimal model semantics coincide, i.e. $\mathrm{SM}(\mathcal{P}) = \mathrm{MM}(\mathcal{P})$.

The result of a query $\mathcal{Q} = \langle G, \mathcal{P} \rangle$ on an input database D is defined in terms of the minimal models of $\mathcal{P} \cup D$, by taking either the union of all models (*possible inference*) or the intersection (*certain inference*). Thus, given a program $\mathcal{P}$ and a database D, a ground atom G is true, under possible (brave) semantics, if there exists a minimal model M for $\mathcal{P} \cup D$ such that $G \in M$. Analogously, G is true, under certain (cautious) semantics, if G is true in every minimal model for $\mathcal{P} \cup D$.

3 Binding Propagation in Disjunctive Databases

In this section we present a technique for propagating bindings into disjunctive programs. Before presenting how disjunctive queries are rewritten to propagate bindings into the bodies of rules, let us first define the equivalence of queries for disjunctive programs. A disjunctive Datalog *query* over a database defines a mapping from the database to a finite (possibly empty) set of finite (possibly empty) relations for the goal.

Given an atom G and an interpretation M, $A(G, M)$ denotes the set of substitution for the variables in G such that G is true in M. The answer to a query $\mathcal{Q} = \langle G, \mathcal{P} \rangle$ over a database D under *possible* (resp. *certain*) semantics, denoted $Ans_p(\mathcal{Q}, D)$ (resp., $Ans_c(\mathcal{Q}, D)$) is the relation $\cup_M A(G, M)$ such that $M \in SM(\mathcal{P}, D)$ (resp., $\cap_M A(G, M)$ such that $M \in SM(\mathcal{P}, D)$). Two queries $\mathcal{Q}_1 = \langle G_1, \mathcal{P}_1 \rangle$ and $\mathcal{Q}_2 = \langle G_2, \mathcal{P}_2 \rangle$ are said to be *equivalent* under semantics s ($\mathcal{Q}_1 \equiv_s \mathcal{Q}_2$) if for every database D on a fixed schema DS is $Ans_s(\mathcal{Q}_1, D) = Ans_s(\mathcal{Q}_2, D)$. Moreover, if $\mathcal{Q}_1 \equiv_p \mathcal{Q}_2$ and $\mathcal{Q}_1 \equiv_c \mathcal{Q}_2$ (the two queries are equivalent under both brave and cautious semantics) we simply write $\mathcal{Q}_1 \equiv \mathcal{Q}_2$.

The main problem in propagating bindings in disjunctive rules is that, generally, we cannot apply standard techniques since by propagating bindings from some atom in the head into the body, we restrict the body of the rule and, consequently, all head atoms. In standard Datalog we propagate binding from the head of rules into the body since the truth value of the head atom depends on the truth value of the body atoms. Moreover, in disjunctive Datalog the truth value of an atom appearing in the head of a given rule depends on the truth value of the atoms appearing in both head and body. Thus, we have to propagate binding from a head atom into the body and also into the other atoms appearing in the head.

We next present how bindings are propagated in disjunctive rules. First we consider the case of positive programs and then we extend the method to programs with stratified negation.

3.1 Positive Programs

In this section we present an algorithm for the optimization of disjunctive Datalog queries. We will use the following running example, known as strategic companies [4], to explain our rewriting method.

Example 3.1 A holding owns companies, each of which produces some goods. Moreover, several companies may have joint control over another company. Then, some companies can be sold, on condition that all goods can be still produced, and that no company which would still be controlled by the holding after the transaction is sold. A company is *strategic*, if it belongs to a *strategic set*, which is a minimal set of companies satisfying these constraints. The query consist in checking if a given company a is strategic. This query can be expressed as $\langle st(a), SC \rangle$ where SC is defined as follows:

$$st(C_1) \vee st(C_2) \leftarrow pb(P, C_1, C_2).$$
$$st(C) \leftarrow cb(C, C_1, C_2, C_3),\ st(C_1),\ st(C_2),\ st(C_3).$$

Here $st(C)$ means that C is strategic, $pb(P, C_1, C_2)$ that product P is produced by companies C_1 and C_2, and $cb(C, C_1, C_2, C_3)$ that C is jointly controlled by C_1, C_2 and C_3; as in [4] each product is produced by at most two companies and each company is jointly controlled by at most three other companies. The problem consists in checking if company a is strategic, i.e. if there is a minimal model containing $st(a)$. □

The strategic companies problem is Σ_2^P-complete and, therefore, it cannot be expressed by Datalog with negation.

Definition 3.2 Let $\mathcal{P}$ be a disjunctive Datalog program. The *standard* version of $\mathcal{P}$, denoted $sv(\mathcal{P})$, is the Datalog program derived from $\mathcal{P}$ by replacing each disjunctive rule $A_1 \vee ... \vee A_m \leftarrow B$ with the m rules of the form $A_i \leftarrow B$ for $1 \leq i \leq m$. Moreover, given a query $\mathcal{Q} = \langle G, \mathcal{P} \rangle$, we denote with $sv(\mathcal{Q})$ the query $\langle G, sv(\mathcal{P}) \rangle$. □

Example 3.3 The standard version of the program SC of Example 3.1, denoted $sv(SC)$, is as follows

$$st(C_1) \leftarrow pb(P, C_1, C_2).$$
$$st(C_2) \leftarrow pb(P, C_1, C_2).$$
$$st(C) \leftarrow cb(C, C_1, C_2, C_3),\ st(C_1),\ st(C_2),\ st(C_3).$$ □

Observe that we are considering negation free programs and, therefore, the standard version of a disjunctive program has a unique minimal model.

Fact 3.4 *Let $\mathcal{P}$ be a positive disjunctive Datalog program and let N be the minimal model of $sv(P)$. Then, every minimal model for $\mathcal{P}$ is contained in N.* □

In order to consider all data which are relevant to answer a query we also need to propagate bindings among atoms in the head of disjunctive rules.

Definition 3.5 Let $\mathcal{P}$ be a disjunctive Datalog program. The *extended standard* version of $\mathcal{P}$, denoted $esv(\mathcal{P})$, is the Datalog program derived from $\mathcal{P}$ by replacing each disjunctive rule $A_1 \vee \ldots \vee A_m \leftarrow B$ with

1. m rules of the form $A_i \leftarrow B$ for $1 \leq i \leq m$, and
2. $m \times (m-1)$ rules of the form $A_i \leftarrow A_j, B$ for $1 \leq i, j \leq m$ and $i \neq j$.

Moreover, given a query $\mathcal{Q} = \langle G, \mathcal{P} \rangle$, we denote with $esv(\mathcal{Q})$ the query $\langle G, esv(\mathcal{P}) \rangle$.   ☐

For instance, the extended standard version of the program of Example 3.1 consists of the rules reported in Example 3.3 plus the following rules

$$\begin{aligned}
\mathrm{st}(C_1) &\leftarrow \mathrm{st}(C_2), \ \mathrm{pb}(P, C_1, C_2). \\
\mathrm{st}(C_2) &\leftarrow \mathrm{st}(C_1), \ \mathrm{pb}(P, C_1, C_2).
\end{aligned}$$

Given a disjunctive Datalog program $\mathcal{P}$, we denote with $SV(\mathcal{P})$ (resp., $ESV(\mathcal{P})$) the standard program derived from $sv(\mathcal{P})$ (resp., $esv(\mathcal{P})$) by replacing each derived predicate symbol q with a new predicate symbol Q. Moreover, given a query $\mathcal{Q} = \langle g(t), \mathcal{P} \rangle$, we denote with $SV(\mathcal{Q})$ (resp. $ESV(\mathcal{Q})$) the query $\langle G(t), SV(\mathcal{P}) \rangle$ (resp. $\langle G(t), SV(\mathcal{P}) \rangle$) where G is the new symbol used to replace g.

Example 3.6 The standard version $ESV(\mathrm{SC})$ of the program SC of Example 3.1 is derived from the program $esv(\mathrm{SC})$ of Example 3.3 by replacing the predicate symbol **st** with the new predicate symbol ST.

$$\begin{aligned}
\mathrm{ST}(C_1) &\leftarrow \mathrm{pb}(P, C_1, C_2). \\
\mathrm{ST}(C_2) &\leftarrow \mathrm{pb}(P, C_1, C_2). \\
\mathrm{ST}(C) &\leftarrow \mathrm{cb}(C, C_1, C_2, C_3), \ \mathrm{ST}(C_1), \ \mathrm{ST}(C_2), \ \mathrm{ST}(C_3).
\end{aligned}$$

$$\begin{aligned}
\mathrm{ST}(C_1) &\leftarrow \mathrm{ST}(C_2), \ \mathrm{pb}(P, C_1, C_2). \\
\mathrm{ST}(C_2) &\leftarrow \mathrm{ST}(C_1), \ \mathrm{pb}(P, C_1, C_2).
\end{aligned}$$
☐

The application of the magic-set method to $ESV(\mathcal{Q})$ gives an equivalent query which can be evaluated more efficiently [3, 20]. An informal description of the technique is reported in Appendix A.

Example 3.7 Consider the program of Example 3.6 and the query goal ST(a). The first step consists in the generation of adornments for derived predicates. The query goal has only one bound argument. From the propagation of bindings we derive only one binding for the predicate ST. Thus, the query obtained by applying the magic-set method is $\langle \mathrm{ST}^b(\mathrm{a}), \ Magic(ESV(\mathrm{SC})) \rangle$ where the rewritten program $Magic(ESV(\mathrm{SC}))$ is as follows:

$$\begin{aligned}
\mathrm{magic\_ST}^b(\mathrm{a}). & \\
\mathrm{magic\_ST}^b(C_1) &\leftarrow \mathrm{magic\_ST}^b(C), \ \mathrm{cb}(C, C_1, C_2, C_3). \\
\mathrm{magic\_ST}^b(C_2) &\leftarrow \mathrm{magic\_ST}^b(C), \ \mathrm{cb}(C, C_1, C_2, C_3). \\
\mathrm{magic\_ST}^b(C_3) &\leftarrow \mathrm{magic\_ST}^b(C), \ \mathrm{cb}(C, C_1, C_2, C_3). \\
\mathrm{magic\_ST}^b(C_2) &\leftarrow \mathrm{magic\_ST}^b(C_1), \ \mathrm{pb}(P, C_1, C_2). \\
\mathrm{magic\_ST}^b(C_1) &\leftarrow \mathrm{magic\_ST}^b(C_2), \ \mathrm{pb}(P, C_1, C_2).
\end{aligned}$$

$$ST^b(C_1) \leftarrow \quad \texttt{magic\_}ST^b(C_1), \quad pb(P, C_1, C_2).$$
$$ST^b(C_2) \leftarrow \quad \texttt{magic\_}ST^b(C_2), \quad pb(P, C_1, C_2).$$
$$ST^b(C) \leftarrow \quad \texttt{magic\_}ST^b(C), \quad cb(C, C_1, C_2, C_3), \quad ST^b(C_1), \quad ST^b(C_2), \quad ST^b(C_3).$$

$$ST^b(C_1) \leftarrow \quad \texttt{magic\_}ST^b(C_1), \quad ST^b(C_2), \quad pb(P, C_1, C_2).$$
$$ST^b(C_2) \leftarrow \quad \texttt{magic\_}ST^b(C_2), \quad ST^b(C_1), \quad pb(P, C_1, C_2).$$

Here the predicate $\texttt{magic\_}ST^b$ computes all companies which are relevant to establishing if the company a is strategic.

Fact 3.8 *Let Q be a positive disjunctive Datalog query. Then, $Magic(ESV(Q)) \equiv ESV(Q)$.* □

Observe that rules generated in Step 2 of Definition 3.5 have been used to transfer bindings among head atoms. It is worth nothing that the application of the magic-set rewriting could generate useless rules which can be deleted from the final program. For instance, in our running example (see Example 3.7), the magic set rewriting produces the rules

$$ST^b(C_1) \leftarrow \quad \texttt{magic\_}ST^b(C_1), \quad ST^b(C_2), \quad pb(P, C_1, C_2).$$
$$ST^b(C_2) \leftarrow \quad \texttt{magic\_}ST^b(C_2), \quad ST^b(C_1), \quad pb(P, C_1, C_2).$$

which are useless since the rewritten program also contains the rules

$$ST^b(C_1) \leftarrow \quad \texttt{magic\_}ST^b(C_1), \quad pb(P, C_1, C_2).$$
$$ST^b(C_2) \leftarrow \quad \texttt{magic\_}ST^b(C_2), \quad pb(P, C_1, C_2).$$

Redundant rules, which are derived from rules used to propagate bindings among head atoms (introduced by Step 2 of Definition 3.5), can be deleted since they do not give any contribution. We are now in the position to present our rewriting algorithm.

Notation. Given a program $\mathcal{P}$ and an atom $r(t_1, ..., t_k)$ in $\mathcal{P}$, $R(t_1, ..., t_k)$ denotes the atom which replaces $r(t_1, ..., t_k)$ in $SV(\mathcal{P})$. Moreover, given an adornment α for R, $R^\alpha(t_1, ..., t_k)$ denotes the adorned version of $R(t_1, ..., t_k)$ w.r.t. α.

The algorithm implementing the rewriting of disjunctive queries is reported in Fig. 1. It receives in input a positive disjunctive query, say $Q = \langle g, \mathcal{P} \rangle$, and returns a positive disjunctive query, say $Q' = \langle g, \mathcal{P}' \rangle$. Initially the algorithm generates the set of standard rules $ESV(\mathcal{P})$. In the next step it applies the standard magic-set rewriting technique to the query $ESV(Q) = \langle G, ESV(\mathcal{P}) \rangle$ where G is the atom derived from g by rewriting the predicate symbol. In Step 3 the rules to collect tuples of relations with different adornment and the same predicate symbol are generated. In the last step the *extended* rules are generated.

The rules generated in the second and third steps are called *new rules*, whereas the rules generated in Step 4 are called *extended rules*. The rules produced in the last two steps are not adorned. We now present an example showing the output generated by Algorithm 1.

Example 3.9 The complete program obtained from the application of Algorithm 1 to the program of Example 3.1 with the query goal $st(a)$, consists of the rule in $Magic(ST(a), ESV(SC))$ (reported in Example 3.7) plus the following 'extended' rules

$$ST(C) \leftarrow \quad ST^b(C).$$

Algorithm 1 *Rewriting disjunctive queries*
Input: *Positive safe disjunctive query* $Q = \langle g, \mathcal{P} \rangle$
Output: $Q' = \langle g, \mathcal{P}' \rangle$
begin
(1) $\mathcal{P}_1 = ESV(\mathcal{P})$;
(2) $\mathcal{P}_2 = Magic(\langle G, \mathcal{P}_1 \rangle)$;
(3) **for each** *predicate* R^α *generated in Step (2) add to* $\mathcal{P}'$ *the following rule with* $k = arity(R)$
$\qquad R(X_1, ..., X_k) \leftarrow R^\alpha(X_1, ..., X_k)$;
(4) *Replace every rule* $a_1(X_1) \vee ... \vee a_m(X_m) \leftarrow B(W)$ *(m $\geq$ 1) with*
$\qquad a_1(X_1) \vee ... \vee a_m(X_m) \leftarrow A_1(X_1), ..., A_m(X_m), B(W)$
end.

Figure 1: Optimization of disjunctive queries

$$st(C_1) \vee st(C_2) \quad \leftarrow \quad ST(C_1),\ ST(C_2),\ pb(P, C_1, C_2).$$
$$st(C) \quad \leftarrow \quad ST(C),\ cb(C, C_1, C_2, C_3),\ st(C_1),\ st(C_2),\ st(C_3).$$

where the first rule defining the predicate ST is added in Step 3 and the last two rules defining the predicate st are added in Step 4. $\qquad\qquad\qquad\qquad\qquad\qquad\qquad\qquad\qquad\qquad\qquad\square$

Notation Given a disjunctive Datalog query $Q = \langle g, \mathcal{P} \rangle$ and let $Q' = \langle g, \mathcal{P}' \rangle$ be the query generated by Algorithm 1. The program $\mathcal{P}'$ consists of the two distinct sets of rules $New(g, \mathcal{P})$ and $Extended(\mathcal{P})$ containing the rules generated, respectively, in the first three steps and in Step 4 of Algorithm 1. Clearly $Magic(G, \mathcal{P}) \subseteq New(g, \mathcal{P})$. Given an interpretation M and an atom g we denote with $M(g)$ the set of atoms in M which match with g.

Theorem 3.10 *Let* $Q = \langle g, \mathcal{P} \rangle$ *be a disjunctive Datalog query and let* $Q' = \langle g, \mathcal{P}' \rangle$ *be the query derived by applying Algorithm 1 to* Q. *Then,* $Q \equiv Q'$. $\qquad\qquad\qquad\qquad\qquad\qquad\square$

Note that when a predicate symbol R has associated a unique adornment α it is possible to replace the predicate R^α with R and to cancel the rule $R(X_1, ..., X_k) \leftarrow R^\alpha(X_1, ..., X_k)$ introduced in Step 4 of Algorithm 1.

The magic-set technique is general and can be applied to all queries. However, there are several programs such as *left-linear*, *right-linear*, *counting linear*, *factorized* and *chain* programs for which specialized methods, which are much more efficient than the magic-set method, exist [17, 19, 13]. For instance, the query of the following example presents a disjunctive program which can be optimized by using the classical right-linear optimization technique [17, 20].

Example 3.11 Consider the query $\langle anc(john, Y), ANC \rangle$ where the program ANC consists of the following rules:

$$father(X, Y) \vee mother(X, Y) \leftarrow parent(X, Y).$$

$$anc(X, Y) \leftarrow father(X, Y).$$
$$anc(X, Y) \leftarrow father(X, Z),\ anc(Z, Y).$$

Since the program $esv(\text{ANC})$ is linear it is possible to apply optimization techniques specialized for linear programs. □

The rewriting of disjunctive queries is orthogonal with respect to the specific rewriting technique used to optimize the standard version of the query (step (2) in Algorithm 1). Thus, for special classes of queries, it is possible to apply specialized optimization techniques.

3.2 Stratified Programs

The minimal model semantics is not able to capture the intuitive meaning of programs with negation. Stable models and perfect models have been proposed to capture the semantics of general disjunctive programs. Although both semantics have been defined for general disjunctive programs, the perfect model semantics is particularly suited for stratified disjunctive programs. Given a program $\mathcal{P}$, $SM(\mathcal{P})$ and $PF(\mathcal{P})$ denote, respectively, the sets of stable and perfect models of $\mathcal{P}$. Moreover, for stratified programs we have that $PM(\mathcal{P}) = SM(\mathcal{P})$ whereas for positive programs $MM(\mathcal{P}) = PM(\mathcal{P}) = SM(\mathcal{P})$ [18].

Now, letting $\mathcal{P}$ be a stratified disjunctive program, we denote with $psv(\mathcal{P})$ (resp. $PSV(\mathcal{P})$) the positive standard program derived from $esv(\mathcal{P})$ (resp. $ESV(\mathcal{P})$) by deleting negative literals. The algorithm for the rewriting of Q can be derived from Algorithm 1 by simply generating in Step 1 the query $PSV(Q)$ instead of the query $ESV(Q)$. We will denote the modified algorithm as *Algorithm 2*.

Theorem 3.12 *Let $Q = \langle g, \mathcal{P} \rangle$ be a stratified disjunctive linear Datalog query and let Q' be the query derived by applying Algorithm 2 to Q. Then, $Q \equiv Q'$.* □

Example 3.13 Consider the following query $\langle s(m), P \rangle$ where the program P consists of the following rules:

```
p(X) ∨ q(X) ←   a(X).
s(X) ←          p(X), ¬q(X).
```

and the database D consists of the unary relation a. The optimized program generated by Algorithm 2 is as follows:

```
p(X) ∨ q(X) ←   P(X), Q(X), a(X).
s(X) ←          S(X), p(X), ¬q(X).

magic_S(m).
magic_P(X) ← magic_S(X).               P(X) ← magic_P(X), a(X).
magic_Q(X) ← magic_P(X).               Q(X) ← magic_Q(X), a(X).
magic_P(X) ← magic_Q(X).               S(X) ← magic_S(X), P(X).
```

where adornments and rules collecting tuples (generated at Step 4) have been deleted since there is only one adornment for each predicate. The evaluation of the rules in $New(P)$ (the last seven rules) gives, if the tuple $a(m)$ is in the database D, a set of tuples $M = \{\text{magic\_S}(m), \text{magic\_P}(m), \text{magic\_Q}(m), P(m), Q(m), S(m)\}$ otherwise a set $M = \emptyset$. To answer the query it is sufficient to compute the first two rules using as database facts $D \cup M$, i.e., it is sufficient to evaluate at most two ground rules. □

4   Experimental Results

In this section we report some experimental results to give some idea of the improvement which can be obtained by means of the technique proposed here. The experiments have been carried out by means of the system prototype presented in the previous section and obtained on a SUN Sparc 10 workstation under Solaris 2.5.1.

Example 1.1

The results for the query of Example 1.1 are reported in Figure 2, where the x-axis shows the number of tuples in the database. The y-axis shows the time to evaluate the query (in seconds). The improvement on this program is extremely high (observe that the scale of the y-axis is logarithmic).

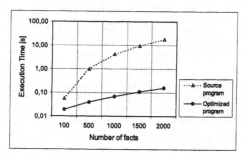

Figure 2.   Results for the query of Example 1.1

Example 3.11

For the query of Example 3.11 we have used instances for the relation *parent* as depicted in Figure 3 with *base* = *height* and output *grade* = 2. Each node in the graph represent a person and an arc (i, j) represents a tuple *parent*(j, i). The number of nodes in the graph is *base* × *height* whereas the number of arcs is $base \times (height - 1) \times grade$.

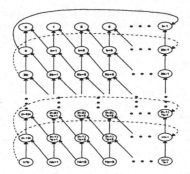

Figure 3.   Parent relation

The results of the query are reported in Figure 4 where the x-axis shows the size of the graph, i.e. the number of nodes for base and height (we have assumed in this experiment that $height = base$ and $grade = 2$). Also in this case the improvement is extremely high. For graphs with a number of nodes varying between 100 and 400 the improvement is between 2 and 3 orders of magnitude.

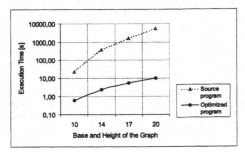

Figure 4.   Results for the query of Example 3.11

Strategic companies (Example 3.1)

For the query of Example 3.1 we have used a database where companies and products are partitioned into distinct groups. Each group has the structure like the one reported in Figure 5 where squared nodes represent products, circled nodes represent companies, an arc from product p_{ki} to company c_{kj} means that p_{ki} is produced by c_{kj} whereas an arc from c_{ki} to c_{kj} means that company c_{ki} is controlled by company c_{kj} (k denotes the group).

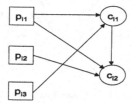

Figure 5.   Database Structure

Figure 6 reports some experimental results. Here we have assumed that the structure of each group is fixed and consists of 10 companies and 30 products and that the number of groups is variable. The improvement is very high since the evaluation of the optimized program considers only the group containing the company specified in the query goal whereas the evaluation of the source program considers all groups.

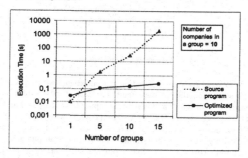

Figure 6.   Results for the query of Example 3.1

Full adder

Logic based diagnostic problems can be formulated by means of disjunctive programs. We consider a circuit consisting of a n-bits numbers adder as depicted in Figure 7. The system computes the sum of two n-bits numbers $A_0 A_1 ... A_{n-1}$ and $B_0 B_1 ... B_{n-1}$ and gives as a result the sequence

$S_0 S_1 ... S_{n-1}$. C_i is the report of stage $i-1$ which is an input of stage i. Clearly C_{-1} is equal to 0.

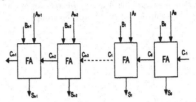

Figure 7.   Structure of the n-bits adder

Each stage in the adder is as depicted in Figure 8. The description of a single gate and the connection among gates and stages are described by means of logic rules and constraints.

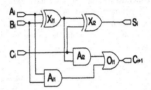

Figure 8.   Full Adder

The problem is as follows: given an observation at some stage i which differs from the expected one, to discover possible anomalies in the circuit, i.e. sets of gates which could be abnormal. Consider, for instance, a 1-bit adder and assume as input $A_0 = 1$, $B_0 = 0$ and $C_0 = 1$ stored by means of the facts $\text{in1}(1, \text{x1}, 1)$, $\text{in2}(1, \text{x1}, 0)$ and $\text{in1}(1, \text{a2}, 1)$ whereas the observation is $S_0 = 1$ and $C_1 = 0$ stored by means of a rule of the form $g \leftarrow \text{out}(1, \text{x2}, 1), \text{out}(1, \text{o1}, 0)\}$ where g is a predicate symbol used a goal in the query. Since the expected output is $S_0 = 0$ and $C_1 = 1$, the circuit does not work correctly. Possible anomalies are inferred by using disjunction (the rule $ab(I, X) \lor noab(I, X) \leftarrow gate(I, X)$ states that gate X in stage I can be either normal or abnormal). The semantics of the program gives three alternative models containing the sets of tuples $\Delta_1 = \{\text{ab}(1, \text{x1})\}$, $\Delta_2 = \{\text{ab}(1, \text{x2}), \text{ab}(1, \text{o1})\}$ and $\Delta_3 = \{\text{ab}(1, \text{x2}), \text{ab}(1, \text{a2})\}$ which correspond to alternative diagnostics (sets of abnormal gates). For space limitation the code implementin an n-bits adder is not reported here and it can be found in the extended version of the paper.

Figure 9 reports some experimental results on a 4-bits adder. The x-axis reports the observation stage whereas the y-axis shows the time to evaluate the query (in seconds). The improvement is very high. Assuming that the anomaly has been observed at stage 2, the gain is of more than three orders of magnitude. The complexity of the optimized program is comparable with the complexity of the source program only when the anomaly is noticed at the last stage of the adder.

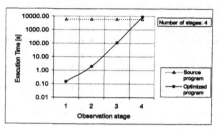

Figure 9.   Results for the 4-bits adder

The above experiments show that the improvement of our technique is extremely high since the number of models to be considered is strongly reduced. We conclude by mentioning that a prototype of an optimizer has been developed at the the University of Calabria. Such a prototype is written in Prolog and implements a module which can be easily included in any system evaluating disjunctive Datalog queries.

References

[1] Abiteboul, S., Hull, R., Vianu, V., *Foundations of Databases*. Addison-Wesley. 1995.

[2] Bancilhon F., D. Mayer, Y. Sagiv, and J.F. Ullman. Magic sets and other strange ways to implement logic programs. *Proc. PODS Conf.*, 1986, pages 1-16.

[3] Beeri, C. and R. Ramakrisnhan, On the power of magic. *Journal of Logic Programming*, 1991, pages 255-299 .

[4] Cadoli M, T. Eiter and G. Gottlob, Default Logic as a Query Language, TKDE, 9(3), 1997, pages 448-463.

[5] Dix J., U. Furbach and A. Nerode (eds.) *Proc. Int. Conf. Logic Progr. and Nonmon. Reasoning* (System Descriptions). 1997.

[6] Eiter, T., Gottlob, G. and Mannila, Disjunctive Datalog, in *ACM Trans. on Database Systems*, 22(3), 1997, pages 364-418, (Prel. vers. in PODS-94).

[7] Eiter T., N. Leone, C. Mateis, G. Pfeifer and F. Scarcello. A Deductive System for Non-monotonic Reasoning. *Proc. LPNMR Conf.*, 1997. 363-374.

[8] Eiter T., W. Faber, N. Leone and G. Pfeifer. The diagnostic frontend of the dlv systems *Research Report*, DBAI-TR-98-20, 1998.

[9] Fernández, J.A. and Minker, J., Semantics of Disjunctive Deductive Databases, in *Proc. 4th ICDT Conf.* 1992, pages 21-50.

[10] Gelfond, M., Lifschitz, V., The Stable Model Semantics for Logic Programming, in *Proc. Fifth Conf. on Logic Progr.*, 1988, pages 1070-1080.

[11] Gelfond, M. and Lifschitz, V., Classical Negation in Logic Programs and Disjunctive Databases, *New Generation Computing*, **9**, 1991, 365–385.

[12] Greco, S., Binding Propagation into Disjunctive Databases, *Proc. Int. Conf. Very Large Databases*, 1998, pages 287–298.

[13] S. Greco, D. Sacca and C. Zaniolo, The PushDown Method to Optimize Chain Logic Programs. *Proc. International Colloquium on Automata, Logic and Programming*, 1995, pages 523–534.

[14] R. Hasegawa, K. Inoue, Y. Ohta, M. Koshimura, Non-Horn Magic Sets to Incorporate Top-down Inference into Bottom-up Theorem Proving. *Proc. International Conference on Automated Deduction*, 1997, pages 176–190

[15] Lobo, J., Minker, J. and Rajasekar, A., *Foundations of Disjunctive Logic Programming* MIT Press, Cambridge, MA, 1992.

[16] Minker, J., On Indefinite Data Bases and the Closed World Assumption, *in "Proc. 6th CADE Conference*, 1982, pages 292–308.

[17] J. Naughton, R. Ramakrisnhan, Y. Sagiv, and J.F. Ullman. Efficient evaluation of right-, left-, and multi-linear rules. *Proc. SIGMOD Conf.*, 1989, pages 235–242.

[18] Przymusinski, T., Stable Semantics for Disjunctive Programs, *New Generation Computing*, **9**, 1991, pages 401–424.

[19] R. Ramakrisnhan, Y. Sagiv, J.F. Ullman, and M.Y. Vardi. Logical Query Optimization by Proof-Tree Transformation. *JCSS*, 47, 1993, pp. 222-248.

[20] J.D. Ullman, *Principles of Database and Knowledge-Base Systems*, Computer Science Press, 1989.

APPENDIX A: Magic-set rewriting

We recall now the magic-set rewriting techniques for Datalog queries. The technique presented here applies only to negation free linear programs where bindings are propagated only through predicates which are not mutually recursive with the head predicate.

The magic-set method consists of three separate steps

1. An *Adornment step* in which the relationship between a bound argument in the rule head and the bindings in the rule body is made explicit.
2. A *Generation step* in which the adorned program is used to generate the *magic rules* which simulate the top-down evaluation scheme.
3. A *Modification step* in which the adorned rules are modified by the magic rules generated in step (2); these rules will be called *modified rules*.

We now informally recall the above steps for the case of linear programs, i.e. programs containing at most one predicate mutually recursive with the head predicate in the body of rules.

An *adorned program* is a program whose predicate symbols have associated a string α, defined on the alphabet $\{b, f\}$, of length equal to the arity of the predicate. A character b (resp. f) in the i-th position of the adornment associated with a predicate p means that the i-th argument of p is bound (resp. free).

The adornment step consists in generating a new program whose predicates are adorned. Given a rule r and an adornment α of the rule head, the adorned version of r is derived as follows:

1. Identify the distinctive arguments of the rules as follows: an argument is distinctive if it is bound in the adornment α, is a constant or appears in a base predicate of the rule-body which includes an adornment argument;

2. Assume that the distinctive arguments are bound and use this information in the adornment of the derived predicates in the rule body.

Adornments containing only f symbols can be omitted.

Given a query $Q = \langle q(T), P \rangle$ and letting α be the adornment associated with $q(T)$, the set of adorned rules for Q is generated by 1) first computing the adorned version of the rules defining q and 2) next generating, for each new adorned predicate p^β introduced in the previous step, the adorned version of the rules defining p w.r.t. β; Step 2 is repeated until no new adorned predicate is generated.

The second step in the process is to use the adorned program for the generation of the magic rules. For each of the adorned predicates in the body of the adorned rule:

1. Replace the derived predicates symbol p^α with $magic\_p^\alpha$ and eliminate the variables which are free w.r.t. α;
2. Replace the head predicates symbol q^β with $magic\_q^\beta$ and eliminate the variables which are free w.r.t. β;
3. Interchange the transformed head and derived predicate in the body.

Finally, the modification step of an adorned rule is performed as follows. For each adorned rule whose head is $p^\alpha(X)$, where X is a list of variables, extend the rule body with $magic\_p^\alpha(X')$ where X' is the list of variables in X which are bound w.r.t. α.

The final program will contain only the rules which are needed to answer the query.

Example 4.1 Consider the query $Q = \langle p(1,C), P \rangle$ where P is defined as follows:

$$p(X,C) \leftarrow \quad q(X,2,C).$$
$$q(X,Y,C) \leftarrow \quad a(X,Y,C).$$
$$q(X,Y,C) \leftarrow \quad b(X,Y,Z,W), \ q(Z,W,D), \ c(D,C).$$

The adorned program P' is

$$p^{bf}(X,C) \leftarrow \quad q^{bbf}(X,2,C).$$
$$q^{bbf}(X,Y,C) \leftarrow \quad a(X,Y,C).$$
$$q^{bbf}(X,Y,C) \leftarrow \quad b(X,Y,Z,W), \ q^{bbf}(Z,W,D), \ c(D,C).$$

The rewritten query is $Q' = \langle p^{bf}(1,C), P' \rangle$ where P' is as follows:

$$\text{magic\_}p^{bf}(1).$$
$$\text{magic\_}q^{bbf}(X,2) \leftarrow \quad \text{magic\_}p^{bf}(X).$$
$$\text{magic\_}q^{bbf}(Z,W) \leftarrow \quad \text{magic\_}q^{bf}(X,Y), \ b(X,Y,Z,W).$$

$$p^{bf}(X,C) \leftarrow \quad \text{magic\_}p^{bf}(X), \ q^{bbf}(X,2,C).$$
$$q^{bbf}(X,Y,C) \leftarrow \quad \text{magic\_}q^{bbf}(X,Y), \ a(X,Y,C).$$
$$q^{bbf}(X,Y,C) \leftarrow \quad \text{magic\_}q^{bbf}(X,Y), \ b(X,Y,Z,W), \ q^{bbf}(Z,W,D), \ c(D,C).$$

$\square$

Observe that, although the technique presented here applies only to negation free linear programs, it is general and can also be applied to non-linear programs with some form of negation (e.g. stratified negation) where bindings are also propagated through derived predicates.

Let $Q = \langle G, \mathcal{P} \rangle$ be a query, then $Magic(Q)$ denotes the query derived from Q by applying the magic-set method. The query $Magic(Q)$ will be also denoted as $\langle G\alpha, magic(G, \mathcal{P}) \rangle$ where G^α denotes the adorned version of G whereas $magic(G, \mathcal{P})$ denotes the rewriting of $\mathcal{P}$ w.r.t. the goal G. The rewritten program consists of two distinct sets of rules: a set of new rules (generated in Step (2)), called *magic rules*, and the set of *modified rules*, (generated in Step (3)) which is derived from the set of rules in the source program.

Well-Founded Semantics by Transformation: The Non-Ground Case

Ulrich Zukowski and Burkhard Freitag
Fakultät für Mathematik und Informatik
Universität Passau
D-94030 Passau, Germany
{zukowski,freitag}@fmi.uni-passau.de
http://daisy.fmi.uni-passau.de/

Abstract

We present a transformation system that supports the goal-directed computation of the well-founded semantics of normal logic programs using any strategy from set-oriented bottom-up to single-answer top-down or any combination in this range by just rearranging the order of elementary transformations. The well-known problems of the magic set transformation in the context of the well-founded semantics are avoided while still not being tied to a top-down tuple-at-a-time strategy. Most bottom-up methods based on the alternating fixpoint approach and also the well-founded model computation used in smodels are subsumed. However, the extended version of the transformation approach presented in this paper is not restricted to range-restricted or ground programs. It even extends the search strategies possible within the *SLG* approach by allowing the activation of more than one body literal at a time. This leads to more efficient computations for some programs and enables even the parallel evaluation of several body literals in applications where it is appropriate.

Our rewriting system gives the formal background to analyze and combine different evaluation strategies in a common framework, or to design new algorithms and prove the correctness of its implementations at a high level just by changing the order of program transformations.

1   Introduction

In recent years there has been a considerable amount of work on the formal investigation of declarative logic programming. For normal logic programs, i.e. non-disjunctive logic programs with negation, the leading declarative approaches are the well-founded semantics [18] and the stable model semantics [10]. In the meantime, several different evaluation algorithms and implementations have been developed, each of it having its own advantages.

The basic *bottom-up* algorithm for computing the complete well-founded model of a range-restricted program is the *alternating fixpoint procedure* [17]. Although it can be implemented efficiently using differential fixpoint iteration and relational techniques for processing large amounts of data, it is well-known that it often performs many unnecessary recomputations. The smodels approach [13, 14] includes an algorithm computing the well-founded model of a range-restricted function-free program, that avoids the recomputations of the alternating fixpoint procedure and is much more efficient for many programs. However, the main algorithm operates on ground programs only, which implies that always a grounding phase has to be prepended.

To answer queries w.r.t. to the well-founded semantics, bottom-up algorithms usually are extended by techniques like the *magic set* [2] or the *magic templates transformation* [15]. It is well-known that problems arise when magic-facts get undefined truth values in the well-founded model of the transformed program. In [11, 12] different solutions are proposed, but none of them guarantees that only relevant magic facts are used. In the *well-founded ordered search* method [16] magic facts are treated in a particular way to avoid undefined truth values. However, complex data structures are needed for this, and whenever a negative cyclic dependency is detected, the evaluation falls back to the alternating fixpoint procedure with its redundant recomputations.

Top-down methods avoid all these problems since they are inherently goal-directed. The most prominent top-down algorithm is the *SLG resolution* [6, 7] implemented in the XSB system. However, as usual for resolution based systems, SLG defaults to a tuple-at-a-time depth-first strategy that is unsuitable for set-oriented data access that is provided e.g. by external database systems. Therefore SLG has been extended by alternative scheduling strategies [9] including breadth first search.

As it has been stated by many authors, the *combination of several methods* and its advantages would be ideal for practical applications. For instance, to compute the complete well-founded model the relational bottom-up techniques of the alternating fixpoint procedure for non-ground programs could be combined with the efficient reduction algorithm for ground programs used in smodels. Most other bottom-up algorithms based on the alternating fixpoint method can be made more efficient by such a combination. For query answering a goal-directed method like SLG is appropriate. However, to process large sets of intermediate results, it should be combined with set-oriented breadth-first search strategies or relational techniques known from bottom-up methods.

In this paper we present a transformation system that supports the computation of the well-founded semantics of normal logic programs using any strategy from set-oriented bottom-up to single-answer top-down or any combination in this range by just rearranging the order of elementary transformations. The rewriting system builds on and extends those presented in [3, 4, 5, 19]. However, as opposed to these it is not restricted to range-restricted or ground programs. Further it allows goal-directed search strategies directly and thus avoids the well-known problems of the magic set transformation in the context of the well-founded semantics.

The rest of the paper is organized as follows. Section 2 contains some notation and preliminaries. Sections 3 and 4 introduce the concept of transformation states and the well-founded transformation. Section 5 shows how different search strategies can be applied. After discussing the selection of strategies in Section 6 we conclude the paper with Section 7.

2 Preliminaries

A rule is of the form $A \leftarrow L_1 \wedge \cdots \wedge L_n$, where the head A is an atom and each body literal L_i is an atom B or a negated atom $\mathbf{not}\,B$. We treat the rule body as a set of literals and write also $A \leftarrow \mathcal{B}$ with $\mathcal{B} = \{L_1, \ldots, L_n\}$. Consequently, a fact A is represented by the rule $A \leftarrow \emptyset$. A program is a set of rules as introduced above. $BASE(P)$ denotes the Herbrand base of a program P, i.e. the set of all ground atoms over the language of P. We write $ground(P)$ for the Herbrand instantiation of P.

The complement of a literal L is denoted by $\sim L$, i.e., $\sim(B) = \mathbf{not}\,B$ and, conversely, $\sim(\mathbf{not}\,B) = B$. For a set S of literals, $\sim S$ denotes the set of the complements of the literals in S. S is *consistent* if and only if $S \cap \sim S = \emptyset$. Let P be a logic program. A *partial interpretation* for P is a consistent set I of ground literals such that the set of its atoms is a subset of the Herbrand base of P. A *total interpretation* for P is a partial interpretation I such that for each atom A of the Herbrand base of P either A or its complement is contained in I. Two partial interpretations are said to agree on an atom Q if they contain the same ground instances of Q and $\mathbf{not}\,Q$.

Definition 2.1 (Greatest Unfounded Set [18])
Let P be a normal program. Let I be a partial interpretation. Let $\mathcal{A} \subseteq BASE(P)$ be a set of ground atoms. $\mathcal{A}$ is an unfounded set of P w.r.t. I, if for every atom $A \in \mathcal{A}$ and every ground rule instance $A \leftarrow \mathcal{B} \in ground(P)$ at least one of the following conditions holds: 1. at least one body literal $L \in \mathcal{B}$ is false in I, or 2. at least one positive body literal $B \in \mathcal{B}$ is contained in $\mathcal{A}$. The greatest unfounded set of P w.r.t. I is the union of all unfounded sets of P w.r.t. I.

Definition 2.2 (Positive and Negative Immediate Consequences)
Let P be a normal program. Let I be a partial interpretation. The three monotonic operators T_P, U_P, and W_P are defined as follows:

$$T_P(I) \;:=\; \{A \in BASE(P) \mid \text{ there is a rule instance}$$
$$(A \leftarrow \mathcal{B}) \in ground(P)$$
$$\text{such that } \mathcal{B} \subseteq I\}$$
$$U_P(I) \;:=\; \text{the greatest unfounded set of } P \text{ w.r.t. } I$$
$$W_P(I) \;:=\; T_P(I) \cup \sim U_P(I)$$

Definition 2.3 (Partial and Total Well-Founded Model [18])
Let P be a program. The well-founded partial model of P, W_P^*, is the least fixpoint of W_P. If W_P^* is a total interpretation, it is called the well-founded model *of P.*

3   Transformation States

The transformation system presented in this paper operates on transformation states that are defined as follows.

Definition 3.1 (Transformation State)
Let G be a set of atoms. Let R and U be sets of rule instances. Then

$$S := (G, R, U)$$

is called a transformation state. *G is called the set of* activated goals. *R is called the set of* active rule instances. *U is called the set of* used rule instances.

The set G is the set of queries to be answered. To keep the presentation simple, we will assume that an initial query atom Q is given. More queries are added later during the transformation. However, it is also possible to start with a larger set G of queries. For example, to compute the complete model of P all rules of P can be activated by adding a query atom for each predicate defined in P. If an (not necessarily ground) atom B is contained in G, all instances of B are considered as activated as well.

Definition 3.2 (Active Goals)
Let $S = (G, R, U)$ be a transformation state. An atom A is activated in S, iff there is an atom $B \in G$ such that A is an instance of B.

The set R is what is actually transformed: the set of relevant rule instances to compute the intended result. It is initialized with instances of the rules of P the head of which is unifiable with Q.

Definition 3.3 (Relevant Rule Instances)
Let P be a normal program. Let A be an atom. The set of relevant rule instances of P w.r.t. A is defined by

$$instances(P, A) := \{(H \leftarrow B)\sigma \mid \begin{array}{l} (H \leftarrow B) \in P \text{ and} \\ H \text{ and } A \text{ are unifiable and} \\ \sigma = mgu(H, A)\}. \end{array}$$

The set R changes during transformation. To keep track of the transformation process and enable us to determine its progress the set U stores the rule instances that have added new information to R. To this end, we need to identify variants of rule instances.

Definition 3.4 (Used and New Rule Instances)
Let $S = (G, R, U)$ be a transformation state. A rule instance $A \leftarrow B$ is used in S if U contains a variant of $A \leftarrow B$. Otherwise $A \leftarrow B$ is new in S.

For a normal program P and a query atom Q, the initial transformation state contains Q as the only activated atom and the corresponding set of relevant rule instances as the initial rule set.

Definition 3.5 (Initial Transformation State)

Let P be a normal program. Let Q be an atom. Then

$$S_0 := (\{Q\}, instances(P, Q), instances(P, Q))$$

is called the initial transformation state *of P w.r.t. Q.*

With each transformation state S we associate a partial interpretation $I(S)$, where facts contained in the rule set R are considered to be true and activated atoms that are not unifiable with any rule head from R are considered to be false.

Definition 3.6 (Interpretation of a State)

Let $S = (G, R, U)$ be a transformation state. An atom A is called true in S, if A is activated in S and there is a fact B in R such that A is an instance of B. An atom is called false in S if A is activated in S and there is no rule in R with a head that is unifiable with A. A negative literal $L = $ not A is called true (false) in S, if A is false (true) in S.

The set $true(S)$ of true ground atoms and the set $false(S)$ of false ground atoms in S are defined as follows:

$$
\begin{aligned}
true(S) &:= \{A \in BASE(P) \mid A \text{ is true in } S\}, \\
false(S) &:= \{A \in BASE(P) \mid A \text{ is false in } S\}.
\end{aligned}
$$

The interpretation of S, *that contains all ground literals that are true in S is defined as follows:*

$$I(S) := true(S) \cup {\sim}false(S).$$

Remark 3.7 (Non-Ground Facts)

If a non-ground atom B is true or false in a transformation state S, all ground instances of B are contained in $true(S)$ or $false(S)$, respectively. Thus, non-ground true or false facts can be considered to represent all of their ground instances to be true or false, respectively.

Example 3.8 (Initial Transformation State)

Consider the following program P that is also used as an example in [6].

$$
\begin{array}{ll}
q(X) \leftarrow p(X). & p(X) \leftarrow q(X). \\
q(a). & p(X) \leftarrow \text{not } r. \\
r \quad\;\; \leftarrow \text{not } s. & s \quad\;\; \leftarrow \text{not } r.
\end{array}
$$

Let the initial query be $Q = q(X)$. In the initial transformation state $S_0 = (G_0, R_0, U_0)$ of P w.r.t. Q we have $G_0 = \{q(X)\}$ and

$$R_0 = U_0 = \{q(X) \leftarrow p(X). \; q(a).\}.$$

The interpretation $I(S_0) = \{q(a)\}$ contains the first answer.

4 Well-Founded Transformation

In this section we will define a set of transformations that are to be applied to the initial transformation state until the answer of the initial query is derived. The first transformation activates new atoms.

Definition 4.1 (Activation)
Let P be a normal program. Let $S_1 = (G_1, R_1, U_1)$ and $S_2 = (G_2, R_2, U_2)$ be transformation states of P. S_2 results from S_1 by activation, $S_1 \leadsto_A S_2$, iff there is a rule instance $A \leftarrow B$ in $\mathcal{R}_1$ and a positive or negative literal $(\textbf{not})B \in \mathcal{B}$ such that B is not activated in S_1 and

$$
\begin{aligned}
G_2 &= G_1 \ \cup \ \{B\} \\
R_2 &= R_1 \ \cup \ instances(P, B) \\
U_2 &= U_1 \ \cup \ instances(P, B)
\end{aligned}
$$

holds.

This transformation corresponds to selecting a literal and resolving it with all possible rules of P in a top-down resolution method.

Example 4.2 (Activation)
The only body literal that can be activated in the initial transformation state S_0 of Example 3.8 is $p(X)$. Thus in a new transformation state we add $p(X)$ to G and the two rule instances $p(X) \leftarrow \textbf{not}\, r$ and $p(X) \leftarrow q(X)$ to R and U. Then we can activate r and add the rule $r \leftarrow \textbf{not}\, s$ and finally activate s and add the rule $s \leftarrow \textbf{not}\, r$. The rule set R of the new transformation state S contains all rules from P. But until now there are no new answers in $I(S)$.

Note, that Definition 4.1 allows to activate more than one body literal of a rule instance at a time. In Example 5.3 we illustrate that this can lead to more efficient search strategies.

The following four transformations remove obviously true body literals from rule instances or delete rule instances containing body literals that are false in the current transformation state.

Definition 4.3 (Success)
Let P be a normal program. Let $S_1 = (G_1, R_1, U_1)$ and $S_2 = (G_2, R_2, U_2)$ be transformation states of P. S_2 results from S_1 by success, $S_1 \leadsto_S S_2$, iff $G_1 = G_2$ and $U_1 = U_2$ and there is a rule instance $A \leftarrow \mathcal{B}$ in $\mathcal{R}_1$ and a positive literal $B \in \mathcal{B}$ such that B is true in S_1 and

$$R_2 = R_1 \setminus \{A \leftarrow \mathcal{B}\} \ \cup \ \{A \leftarrow (\mathcal{B} \setminus \{B\})\}.$$

Definition 4.4 (Failure)
Let P be a normal program. Let $S_1 = (G_1, R_1, U_1)$ and $S_2 = (G_2, R_2, U_2)$ be transformation states of P. S_2 results from S_1 by failure, $S_1 \leadsto_F S_2$, iff $G_1 = G_2$ and $U_1 = U_2$ and there is a rule instance $A \leftarrow \mathcal{B}$ in $\mathcal{R}_1$ and a positive literal $B \in \mathcal{B}$ such that B is false in S_1 and

$$R_2 = R_1 \setminus \{A \leftarrow \mathcal{B}\}.$$

Definition 4.5 (Positive Reduction)
Let P be a normal program. Let $S_1 = (G_1, R_1, U_1)$ and $S_2 = (G_2, R_2, U_2)$ be transformation states of P. S_2 results from S_1 by positive reduction, $S_1 \leadsto_P S_2$, iff $G_1 = G_2$ and $U_1 = U_2$ and there is a rule instance $A \leftarrow \mathcal{B}$ in R_1 and a negative literal **not** $B \in \mathcal{B}$ *such that B is false in S_1 and*

$$R_2 = R_1 \setminus \{A \leftarrow \mathcal{B}\} \cup \{A \leftarrow (\mathcal{B} \setminus \{\textbf{not } B\})\}.$$

Definition 4.6 (Negative Reduction)
Let P be a normal program. Let $S_1 = (G_1, R_1, U_1)$ and $S_2 = (G_2, R_2, U_2)$ be transformation states of P. S_2 results from S_1 by negative reduction, $S_1 \leadsto_N S_2$, iff $G_1 = G_2$ and $U_1 = U_2$ and there is a rule instance $A \leftarrow \mathcal{B}$ in R_1 and a negative literal **not** $B \in \mathcal{B}$ *such that B is true in S_1 and*

$$R_2 = R_1 \setminus \{A \leftarrow \mathcal{B}\}.$$

In Definitions 4.3 to 4.6 of the basic transformations, an activated body literal of a rule instance is considered to be true or false if *all* its ground instances are true or false in S (cf. Remark 3.7). The *instantiation* transformation to be defined next allows to focus on single instances of positive body literals rather than having to consider the entire set of ground instances.

Definition 4.7 (Instantiation)
Let P be a normal program. Let $S_1 = (G_1, R_1, U_1)$ and $S_2 = (G_2, R_2, U_2)$ be transformation states of P. S_2 results from S_1 by instantiation, $S_1 \leadsto_I S_2$, iff $G_1 = G_2$ and there is a rule instance $A \leftarrow \mathcal{B}$ in R_1 and an atom $B \in \mathcal{B}$ such that B is activated and there is a rule instance $B' \leftarrow C'$ in R_1 such that B and B' are unifiable and $\sigma = mgu(B, B')$ and $(A \leftarrow \mathcal{B})\sigma$ is new in S_1 and

$$
\begin{aligned}
R_2 &= R_1 \cup \{(A \leftarrow \mathcal{B})\sigma\} \\
U_2 &= U_1 \cup \{(A \leftarrow \mathcal{B})\sigma\}
\end{aligned}
$$

holds.

Example 4.8 (Instantiation and Success)
In the transformation states of Example 4.2, we can apply instantiation and add the instance $p(a) \leftarrow q(a)$ of $p(X) \leftarrow q(X)$ and then the instance $q(a) \leftarrow p(a)$ of $q(X) \leftarrow p(X)$ to R and U. A subsequent application of success removes the body atoms $q(a)$ and then $p(a)$ from the new instances in R. In the resulting transformation state S we have

$$
\begin{aligned}
G = \{ &\ q(X),\ p(X),\ r,\ s\ \} \\
R = \{ &\ q(a).\ p(a).\ q(X) \leftarrow p(X).\ p(X) \leftarrow q(X). \\
&\ p(X) \leftarrow \textbf{not } r.\ r \leftarrow \textbf{not } s.\ s \leftarrow \textbf{not } r. \qquad \} \\
U = \{ &\ q(a) \leftarrow p(a).\ p(a) \leftarrow q(a).\ q(X) \leftarrow p(X).\ p(X) \leftarrow q(X). \\
&\ q(a).\ p(X) \leftarrow \textbf{not } r.\ r \leftarrow \textbf{not } s.\ s \leftarrow \textbf{not } r. \qquad \}
\end{aligned}
$$

The corresponding interpretation $I(S)$ contains the atoms $q(a)$ and $p(a)$.

If a rule has been continuously instantiated successively using all rule heads that are unifiable with an activated body literal, the rule itself has become useless and can be removed.

Definition 4.9 (Complete Instantiation)
Let $S = (G, R, U)$ be a transformation state. Let $A \leftarrow \mathcal{B}$ be a rule instance in R, and let $B \in \mathcal{B}$ be an atom that is activated in S. $A \leftarrow \mathcal{B}$ is completely instantiated through B w.r.t. R in S, iff for every rule $B' \leftarrow C'$ in R holds: if B and B' are unifiable with $\sigma = mgu(B, B')$ then $(A \leftarrow \mathcal{B})\sigma$ is used in S and $(A \leftarrow \mathcal{B})\sigma$ is no variant of $A \leftarrow \mathcal{B}$.

Definition 4.10 (Completion)
Let P be a normal program. Let $S_1 = (G_1, R_1, U_1)$ and $S_2 = (G_2, R_2, U_2)$ be transformation states of P. S_2 results from S_1 by completion, $S_1 \leadsto_C S_2$, iff $G_1 = G_2$ and there is a rule instance $A \leftarrow \mathcal{B}$ in R_1 and an atom $B \in \mathcal{B}$ such that $A \leftarrow \mathcal{B}$ is completely instantiated through B w.r.t. R_1 in S_1 and

$$R_2 = R_1 \setminus \{A \leftarrow \mathcal{B}\}.$$

Remark 4.11 (Completion subsumes Failure)
If a rule instance $A \leftarrow \mathcal{B}$ can be deleted by failure, i.e., an atom $B \in \mathcal{B}$ is false in S, then $A \leftarrow \mathcal{B}$ is completely instantiated through B and can be deleted by completion.

By definition, $\leadsto_C$ is not applicable to rule instances whose activated body depends (directly or indirectly) on the rule head. The last transformation deletes simultaneously a set of mutually recursive rule instances that cannot produce new answers.

Definition 4.12 (Loop Detection)
Let P be a normal program. Let $S_1 = (G_1, R_1, U_1)$ and $S_2 = (G_2, R_2, U_2)$ be transformation states of P. S_2 results from S_1 by loop detection, $S_1 \leadsto_L S_2$, iff $G_1 = G_2$ and $U_1 = U_2$ and there is a set $R' \subseteq R_1$ such that for each rule instance $A \leftarrow \mathcal{B}$ in R' there is an activated atom $B \in \mathcal{B}$ such that B is unifiable with some rule head in R' and $A \leftarrow \mathcal{B}$ is completely instantiated through B w.r.t. $R_1 \setminus R'$ in S_1, and $R_2 = R_1 \setminus R'$.

Definition 4.13 (Well-Founded Transformation)
Let $\leadsto_X$ denote our final rewriting system:

$$\leadsto_X := \leadsto_A \cup \leadsto_S \cup \leadsto_F \cup \leadsto_P \cup \leadsto_N \cup \leadsto_I \cup \leadsto_C \cup \leadsto_L.$$

Theorem 4.14 (Termination)
Let P be a function-free normal program. Let Q be an atom. Let S_0 be the initial transformation state of P w.r.t. Q. Then every sequence of transformation states generated by applying $\leadsto_X$ starting from S_0 reaches a transformation state that is irreducible w.r.t. $\leadsto_X$ after a finite number of transformation steps.

Proof: The proof of this theorem is based on the fact that all transformations either 1) strictly reduce the size of the set of active rule instances by removing body literals or deleting rules or 2) add new elements to the set of used rule instances. □

Note, that we have allowed to activate non-ground negative literals. *Instantiation* is not allowed w.r.t. a negative literal, because as usual negative literals are not allowed to produce bindings. If its atom becomes false or true in one of the following transformation states, the literal can be reduced by *positive* or *negative reduction*, respectively. If the negative literal can not be reduced in a later step the transformation is floundered.

Definition 4.15 (Floundering)
Let $S = (G, R, U)$ be a transformation state. Let S be irreducible w.r.t. $\rightsquigarrow_X$ and let R contain a rule $A \leftarrow B$ that contains a non-ground negative body literal. Then S is called floundered.

The central result of this paper is expressed by the following theorem.

Theorem 4.16 (Partial Correctness and Completeness)
Let P be a normal program. Let Q be an atom. Let S_n be a transformation state of P that is the result of n transformations starting from the initial transformation state S_0 of P w.r.t. Q. If S_n is irreducible w.r.t. $\rightsquigarrow_X$ and S_n is not floundered, then $I(S_n)$ and W_P^* agree on Q, i.e. contain exactly the same ground instances of Q and **not** Q.

Proof: To prove this theorem, we show that each transformation applied to a transformation state S adds only ground literals to the corresponding interpretation I(S) that are also contained in $W_P(I)$ (cf. Definition 2.2). □

Example 4.17 (Well-Founded Model)
The final transformation state S of Example 4.8 is irreducible w.r.t. $\rightsquigarrow_X$ and is not floundered. The answer to the initial query $q(X)$ is that $q(X)$ is true for $X = a$ in the well-founded model of P and undefined for all other possible bindings of X. In this example, we have actually computed the complete well-founded model of P since during the computation all rule heads in P have been activated. Thus we have $W_P^* = I(S) = \{q(a), p(a)\}$.

Of course, in general the transformation method does not compute the entire well-founded model to answer a given query. Consider the program

$$P' := P \cup \{ m(X) \leftarrow p(X). \}$$

extending the program P of Example 3.8. To answer the query $Q = q(x)$ the new rule is not activated by the transformation method.

Remark 4.18 (Non-Ground Answers)
Note, that the well-founded transformation approach is not restricted to range-restricted programs. Thus, as illustrated in Example 4.17, the rules of the final transformation state do not have to be ground and may contain non-ground facts.

5 Flexible Scheduling Strategies

Due to Theorem 4.16, we can apply the transformations in any order starting from the initial transformation state S_0 of P w.r.t. an atom Q. Whenever an irreducible transformation state S is reached its interpretation $I(S)$ contains the correct answer to the query Q. However, the rewriting system $\leadsto_X$ is not confluent. Thus the order of transformations applied significantly influences the number of transformations needed to reach an irreducible transformation state S and also the number of activated atoms and used rule instances in S.

Actually, by rearranging the order of transformations we can choose any evaluation strategy in the range from tuple-at-a-time top-down to set-oriented bottom-up or any combination. In this section we will show that many existing computation methods can be subsumed by appropriate transformation strategies and how new combinations can be built easily.

Remark 5.1 (Correctness of New Strategies)
A main contribution of the well-founded transformation approach is, that new strategies can be designed without having to provide correctness proofs. Every strategy is correct w.r.t. to the well-founded semantics, if the following conditions are satisfied:

1. *The transformation starts with the initial transformation state of the given program w.r.t. the given query (cf. Definition 3.5).*

2. *Only the eight transformations defined in Section 4 are applied.*

3. *The search strategy is fair, i.e., every applicable transformation is eventually applied.*

4. *The transformation system is applied until an irreducible transformation state is reached.*

5.1 Top-Down Strategies

The Examples 3.8, 4.2, 4.8, and 4.17 already illustrated that the transformation approach allows a top-down strategy similar to that of the SLG resolution. The following theorem states that the computation of SLG can be fully subsumed by the well-founded transformation.

Theorem 5.2 (Relation to SLG)
Let P be a normal program. Let Q be an atom. Then there exists a sequence of transformation states that corresponds exactly to the computation performed by the SLG resolution when answering the query Q w.r.t. P.

Proof: To prove this theorem we show that the data structures used by the SLG resolution carry the same information as the transformation states defined in this paper and that for every operation of the SLG resolution there are transformations that have the same effect on the transformation state. $\square$

As a consequence of Theorem 5.2, the SLG resolution can be seen as the implementation of one possible transformation strategy. However, SLG is restricted to select only one body literal of a rule instance at a time. Only negative body literals or literals depending on the latter can be delayed to enable the selection of another body literal. Our transformation approach does not use explicit delaying but treats all remaining body literals equally. While the delaying of negative body literals is necessary to compute the well-founded semantics, the parallel activation of more than one positive body literal can lead to more efficient search strategies. This is illustrated by the following example.

Example 5.3 (Parallel Activation)
Consider the following program fragment

$$p(X) \leftarrow r(X), s(X).$$
$$r(a) \leftarrow \ldots$$
$$s(b) \leftarrow \ldots$$

and the query $Q = p(X)$ where we assume that the goals $r(a)$ and $s(b)$ need a considerable amount of evaluation effort. By the SLG resolution the body literal first selected in the first clause has to be evaluated completely before an answer is returned. Then the other body literal can be selected and will fail.

By our transformation the first clause can be instantiated w.r.t. any body literal using $\leadsto_I$. Then the original rule instance can be deleted by $\leadsto_C$ and the instantiated rule can be deleted by $\leadsto_F$ after having activated the other body literal. Thus the query fails directly without having to evaluate $r(a)$ or $s(b)$.

The implementation of the SLG resolution in the XSB system defaults to a tuple-at-a-time depth-first search strategy. When base relations are provided by external databases this tuple-at-a-time strategy leads to many expensive database operations. Therefore the SLG implementation has been extended by alternative scheduling strategies [9] including a breadth-first search strategy for a set-oriented processing of database queries and their results.

Due to the arbitrary order of transformations our approach supports this strategy, too. The following example shows a top-down evaluation with a set-oriented breadth-first search strategy.

Example 5.4 (Hybrid Set-Oriented Top-Down Strategy)
Consider the following program fragment

$$q(X, Y) \leftarrow r(X, Z), s(Z, Y).$$

and the query $Q = q(a, Y)$. This time we assume that the predicates r and s are defined by relations stored in an external database system. In the initial transformation state $S_0 = (G, R, U)$ we have $G = \{q(a, Y)\}$ and

$$R = U = \{q(a, Y) \leftarrow r(a, Z), s(Z, Y).\}.$$

The activation of r(a, Z) leads to a database query that returns the set of all facts matching r(a, Z). For each such fact r(a, b) we apply $\leadsto_I$ and $\leadsto_S$ to get a new rule instance q(a, Y) ← s(b, Y). Then we activate all atoms s(b, Y) leading to another database query returning all atoms matching s(b, Y). For each such atom s(b, c) we apply $\leadsto_I$ and $\leadsto_S$ and get all answer atoms of the form q(a, c).

A pure tuple-at-a-time top-down strategy usually causes frequent page faults. Assuming that s is clustered on its first attribute the hybrid approach illustrated above applies a set-oriented strategy that increases the locality of the data access and thus reduces the number of page faults.

Remark 5.5 (Relation to Magic Set Transformation)
The hybrid search strategy illustrated in Example 5.4 combines a goal-directed top-down strategy with a set-oriented bottom-up processing of intermediate results. Note, that this strategy fully subsumes the magic set transformation and thus avoids its well-known problems in the context of the well-founded semantics.

5.2   Bottom-Up Strategies

For *range-restricted* programs efficient bottom-up algorithms have been developed using differential fixpoint iterations and techniques known from relational databases. In this section we will show that also these methods can be subsumed by the well-founded transformation, and thus can be integrated into combined evaluation strategies.

Lemma 5.6 (Relation to Bottom-Up Fixpoint Iteration)
Let P be a range-restricted program. Then there is a sequence of transformation states that corresponds to the bottom-up fixpoint iteration of P as performed by the alternating fixpoint procedure or the grounding algorithm in [13, 14] or [19].

Remark 5.7 (Relation to Differential Fixpoint Iteration)
Note, that the bottom-up fixpoint iteration performed by the well-founded transformation in Lemma 5.6 corresponds to a differential fixpoint iteration [1], since every derived rule instance is generated only once.

The characterization of the bottom-up fixpoint iteration for range-restricted programs has two advantages. First, since only ground facts or ground rule instances are derived, and thus only matching is required instead of unification, efficient evaluation techniques have been developed. Whenever a combined transformation strategy chooses to completely evaluate a range-restricted part of a program, one of these optimized implementations can be used. Second, since the result of such a fixpoint iteration is always ground, efficient evaluation techniques optimized for ground programs can be used to further process the result.

5.3 Strategies for Ground Programs

Since for ground programs, that can be transformed easily into equivalent propositional programs, neither unification nor matching is needed, several efficient algorithms have been developed. A linear-time algorithm to compute the least model of propositional definite programs has been described in [8]. This algorithm has been extended in [13] to a linear-time implementation of the fitting-operator for ground normal programs which is used in smodels for an efficient computation of well-founded and stable models for range-restricted programs. In [19] a confluent transformation system $\mapsto_X$ for the well-founded model computation of ground programs has been defined. The following lemma states that our non-ground rewriting system $\leadsto_X$ subsumes the ground rewriting system $\mapsto_X$.

Theorem 5.8 (Relation to Ground Transformation)
Let P_1 and P_2 be two ground programs such that $P_1 \mapsto_X^* P_2$, i.e., P_1 is reducible to P_2 by a number of applications of $\mapsto_X$ as defined in [19]. Then there exist transformation states $S_1 = (G_1, P_1, U_1)$ and $S_2 = (G_2, P_2, U_2)$ such that $S_1 \leadsto_X^* S_2$ holds.

In [19] it has been proven that the ground rewriting system $\mapsto_X$, in combination with a suitable grounding algorithm for range-restricted programs like that of Lemma 5.6, subsumes the alternating fixpoint procedure, and is even much more efficient for many programs. This leads to the following result.

Corollary 5.9 (Relation to Alternating Fixpoint)
Let P be a range-restricted normal program. Then there exists a sequence of transformation states of the non-ground transformation $\leadsto_X$ that corresponds exactly to the computation performed by the alternating fixpoint procedure to compute the well-founded model of P. If unnecessary applications of loop detection are avoided, the transformation is much more efficient than the alternating fixpoint procedure for many programs.

Note, that the transformation approach computes the entire well-founded model of a program P if for each predicate defined in P a query atom containing mutually different variables is added to the initial set G.

Remark 5.10 (Relation to smodels)
The well-founded model computation used in the smodels approach corresponds exactly to the computation described in Corollary 5.9 if loop detection is applied only if no other transformation is applicable. If loop detection is not needed, the well-founded model can be computed in linear time w.r.t. the size of the ground program.

We have shown that the well-founded transformation can subsume many prominent bottom-up evaluation methods. Thus, in combined strategies these methods can be integrated smoothly and their implementations can be used for the corresponding sub-computations.

Remark 5.11 (Relation to other Bottom-Up Methods)
Note, that due to Corollary 5.9 most bottom-up algorithms based on the alternating fixpoint algorithm (cf. [11, 12, 16]) could be subsumed by the well-founded transformation, too. However, since the well-founded transformation is able to perform a goal-directed computation directly without the magic set transformation (cf. Remark 5.5) we omit the details here.

6 Strategy Selection

We have implemented a prototypical transformation system in Java. An important part of this implementation is a strategy component, that selects an appropriate search strategy depending on the given program and the query. We propose the following strategy selection guidelines.

The default strategy for query answering should be a *top-down* strategy like that of Theorem 5.2. If it is important to find the first answer quickly in a main memory application the default *depth-first search* strategy is used. If the set of all answers to a query is needed or base relations are provided by an external database a *breadth-first search* like that in Example 5.4 is preferred. Note, that in any case no magic set transformation is needed (cf. Remark 5.5) since our transformation is able to apply goal-directed strategies directly.

Here a remark on depth-first search and the fairness condition of Remark 5.1 seems in order: for function-free programs fairness is guaranteed by Theorem 4.14. In general, an appropriate fair strategy is crucial for termination.

If the complete well-founded model of a program is to be computed the selected strategy depends on whether the program is range-restricted or not. If it is *not* range-restricted still a top-down strategy has to be applied that is able to produce non-ground answers (cf. Remark 4.18). If the program *is* range-restricted a combined strategy consisting of a differential fixpoint computation (cf. Lemma 5.6) and an efficient reduction of the ground result (cf. Remark 5.10) can be used.

Further combinations are possible. For instance, if during top-down evaluation a query occurs that needs the complete answer relation for some predicates, a bottom-up fixpoint iteration of the corresponding sub-program can be integrated as one part of a mixed search strategy. Due to Theorem 4.16 the correctness of all combined strategies is guaranteed, as long as the conditions of Remark 5.1 are satisfied.

7 Conclusion

We have presented a transformation approach to the goal-directed computation of the well-founded semantics for non-ground normal logic programs. We have shown that just by rearranging the order of transformations any strategy in the range from set-oriented bottom-up fixpoint-iteration to tuple-at-a-time goal-directed top-down resolution can be performed.

References

[1] I. Balbin and K. Ramamohanarao. A differential approach to query optimisation in recursive databases. TR 86/7, University of Melbourne, Dep. of Computer Science, Parkville, Australia, 1986.

[2] C. Beeri and R. Ramakrishnan. On the power of magic. *JLP*, 10:255–299, 1991.

[3] S. Brass and J. Dix. Characterizations of the Disjunctive Stable Semantics by Partial Evaluation. *JLP*, 32(3):207–228, 1997.

[4] S. Brass and J. Dix. Characterizations of the Disjunctive Well-founded Semantics: Confluent Calculi and Iterated GCWA. *Journal of Automated Reasoning*, 20(1):143–165, 1998.

[5] S. Brass and J. Dix. Semantics of (Disjunctive) Logic Programs Based on Partial Evaluation. *JLP*, accepted for publication, 1998. (Extended abstract in: *Proc. ICLP'95, Tokyo*, pages 199–213, 1995. MIT Press.).

[6] W. Chen, T. Swift, and D. S. Warren. Efficient Top-Down Computation of Queries under the Well-Founded Semantics. *JLP*, 24(3):219–245, 1995.

[7] W. Chen and D. S. Warren. Tabled evaluation with delaying for general logic programs. *JACM*, 43(1):20–74, 1996.

[8] W. F. Dowling and J. H. Gallier. Linear-time algorithms for testing the satisfiability of propositional horn formulae. *JLP*, 1(3):267–284, 1984.

[9] J. Freire, T. Swift, and D. S. Warren. Beyond depth-first strategies: Improving tabled logic programs through alternative scheduling. *Journal of Functional and Logic Programming*, 1998(3), 1998.

[10] M. Gelfond and V. Lifschitz. The Stable Model Semantics for Logic Programming. In *Proc. ICLP/SLP'88*, pages 1070–1080. MIT Press, 1988.

[11] D. B. Kemp, D. Srivastava, and P. J. Stuckey. Bottom-up evaluation and query optimization of well-founded models. *TCS*, 146:145–184, 1995.

[12] S. Morishita. An extension of Van Gelder's alternating fixpoint to magic programs. *Journal of Computer and System Sciences*, 52:506–521, 1996.

[13] I. Niemelä and P. Simons. Efficient implementation of the well-founded and stable model semantics. TR 7/96, Universität Koblenz-Landau, 1996.

[14] I. Niemelä and P. Simons. Efficient Implementation of the Well-founded and Stable Model Semantics. In *Proc. JICLP'96*, pages 289–303, Bonn, Germany, September 1996. The MIT Press.

[15] R. Ramakrishnan. Magic templates: A spellbinding approach to logic programs. In *Proc. ICLP/SLP'88*, pages 140–159, 1988. MIT.

[16] P. J. Stuckey and S. Sudarshan. Well-founded ordered search: Goal-directed bottom-up evaluation of well-founded models. *JLP*, 32(3):171–205, 1997.

[17] A. Van Gelder. The alternating fixpoint of logic programs with negation. *Journal of Computer and System Sciences*, 47(1):185–221, 1993.

[18] A. Van Gelder, K. A. Ross, and J. S. Schlipf. The well-founded semantics for general logic programs. *JACM*, 38:620–650, 1991.

[19] U. Zukowski, S. Brass, and B. Freitag. Improving the alternating fixpoint: The transformation approach. In *Proc. LPNMR'97*, LNAI 1265, pages 40–59, 1997.

Monotonicity in Rule Based Update

Yan Zhang
School of Computing and Information Technology
University of Western Sydney, Nepean
Kingswood, NSW 2747, Australia
E-mail: yan@cit.nepean.uws.edu.au

Abstract

An important characteristic for many formulations of knowledge representation and reasoning is that they are nonmonotonic. It has been, however, illustrated that under certain conditions, a formulation may satisfy some restricted monotonicity in its reasoning [2]. In this paper, we investigate this issue under the context of rule based update. We first present a general framework of rule based update in which a knowledge base is viewed as a set of literals and can be updated with a set of update rules which is represented by an extended logic program (also called update program). We then show that given a knowledge base $\mathcal{B}$ and an update program Π, (1) there exist some facts that can be always added into $\mathcal{B}$ such that updating the expansion of $\mathcal{B}$ with Π will not destroy any fact obtained from the update of $\mathcal{B}$ with Π, and (2) on the other hand, there also exist some update rules that can be always added into Π such that updating $\mathcal{B}$ with the expansion of Π will not destroy any fact obtained from the update of $\mathcal{B}$ with Π. We illustrate how these results can be used to simplify an update evaluation. Our proofs of restricted monotonicity theorems are based on a generalization of Lifschitz-Turner's Splitting Set Theorem on extended logic programs [4].

1 Introduction

An important characteristic for many formulations of knowledge representation and reasoning is that they are nonmonotonic. It has been, however, illustrated that under certain conditions, a formulation may satisfy some restricted monotonicity in its reasoning [2]. The purpose of this paper is to investigate this issue under the context of rule based update.

Generally, the rule based update addresses the following problem: given a knowledge base and a set of update rules, what is the resulting knowledge base after updating this knowledge base with the set of update rules? For example, consider a domain of specifying user access rights to a computer system. Given an access policy base including facts that *Peter* can access file F and he is in group G, if the computer system officer wants to update the policy base in terms of a rule saying that if a user belongs to group G, then the user is no longer allowed to access file F, then after updating this policy base with the rule, we would expect that *Peter* cannot access file F

any more.

Although some syntactic and semantic aspects of rule based update has been studied by some researchers [5, 1, 6], the monotonicity property related to rule based update still remains unclear. In this paper, we first present a general framework of rule based update in which a knowledge base is viewed as a set of literals and can be updated with a set of update rules where an update rule may include both classical negation and negation as failure. To handle the possible conflict between inertia rules and update rules, a prioritized logic program is employed to formalize the update specification in our framework. We then show that given a knowledge base $\mathcal{B}$ and an update program Π, (1) there exist some facts that can be always added into $\mathcal{B}$ such that updating the expansion of $\mathcal{B}$ with Π will not destroy any fact obtained from the update of $\mathcal{B}$ with Π, and (2) on the other hand, there also exist some update rules that can be always added into Π such that updating $\mathcal{B}$ with the expansion of Π will not destroy any fact obtained from the update of $\mathcal{B}$ with Π. We illustrate how these results can be used to simplify an update evaluation. Our proofs of restricted monotonicity theorems are based on a generalization of Lifschitz-Turner's Splitting Set Theorem on extended logic programs [4], which presents another contribution of this paper.

The paper is organized as follows. Next section presents a general framework of rule based update. Section 3 investigates restricted monotonicity properties of our rule based update. Section 4 presents a generalization of Lifschitz-Turner's splitting theorem on extended logic programs, which provides a basis of proving our major restricted monotonicity results discussed in section 3. Section 5 then gives the proofs of two restricted monotonicity theorems for rule based update. Finally, section 6 concludes the paper with some remarks.

2   A Framework of Rule Based Update

In this section, we develop a general framework of rule based update. As we allow an update rule to include both classical negation and negation as failure, possible conflict between inertia rules and update rules may occur in the evaluation of an update. To solve this kind of conflict, a prioritized logic program is then used in our framework.

2.1   PLPs - An Overview

To begin with, we need to briefly review prioritized logic programs (PLPs) proposed by Zhang and Foo recently [8]. We first introduce the extended logic program and its answer set semantics defined by Gelfond and Lifschitz [3]. A language $\mathcal{L}$ of extended logic programs is determined by its object constants, function constants and predicates constants. *Terms* are built as in the corresponding first order language; *atoms* have the form $P(t_1, \cdots, t_n)$, where t_i $(1 \leq i \leq n)$ is a term and P is a predicate symbol of arity n; a *literal* is either an atom $P(t_1, \cdots, t_n)$ or a negative atom $\neg P(t_1, \cdots, t_n)$. A *rule* is an expression of the form:

$$L_0 \leftarrow L_1, \cdots, L_m, not L_{m+1}, \cdots, not L_n, \qquad (1)$$

where each L_i ($0 \le i \le n$) is a literal. L_0 is called the *head* of the rule, while $L_1, \cdots, L_m, not\ L_{m+1}, \cdots, not\ L_n$ is called the *body* of the rule. Obviously, the body of a rule could be empty. A term, atom, literal, or rule is *ground* if no variable occurs in it. An *extended logic program* Π is a collection of rules.

To evaluate a extended logic program, Gelfond and Lifschitz proposed the answer set semantics for extended logic programs. For simplicity, we treat a rule r in Π with variables as the set of all ground instances of r formed from the set of ground literals of the language of Π. In the rest of paper, we will not explicitly declare this assumption whenever there is no ambiguity in our discussion. Let Π be an extended logic program not containing *not* and *Lit* the set of all ground literals in the language of Π. The *answer set* of Π, denoted as $Ans(\Pi)$, is the smallest subset S of *Lit* such that (i) for any rule $L_0 \leftarrow L_1, \cdots, L_m$ from Π, if $L_1, \cdots, L_m \in S$, then $L_0 \in S$; and (ii) if S contains a pair of complementary literals, then $S = Lit$. Now let Π be an extended logic program. For any subset S of *Lit*, let Π^S be the logic program obtained from Π by deleting (i) each rule that has a formula *not* L in its body with $L \in S$, and (ii) all formulas of the form *not* L in the bodies of the remaining rules[1]. We define that S is an *answer set* of Π, denoted $Ans(\Pi)$, iff S is an answer set of Π^S, i.e. $S = Ans(\Pi^S)$.

It is easy to see that an extended logic program may have one, more than one, or no answer set at all. A rule with the form (1) is *satisfied* in a set of ground literals S if and only if the fact that $L_1, \cdots, L_m$ are in S and $L_{m+1}, \cdots,$ and L_n are not in S implies the fact that L_0 is in S. Clearly, each rule of an extended logic program Π is satisfied in every answer set of Π.

The language $\mathcal{L}^P$ of PLPs is a language $\mathcal{L}$ of extended logic programs [3] with the following augments:
- *Names:* $N, N_1, N_2, \cdots$.
- A strict partial ordering $<$ on names.
- A naming function $\mathcal{N}$, which maps a rule to a name.

A *prioritized logic program* (PLP) $\mathcal{P}$ is a triple $(\Pi, \mathcal{N}, <)$, where Π is an extended logic program, $\mathcal{N}$ is a naming function mapping each rule in Π to a name, and $<$ is a strict partial ordering on names. The partial ordering $<$ in $\mathcal{P}$ plays an essential role in the evaluation of $\mathcal{P}$. Intuitively $<$ represents a preference of applying rules during the evaluation of the program. In particular, if $\mathcal{N}(r) < \mathcal{N}(r')$ holds in $\mathcal{P}$, rule r would be preferred to apply over rule r' during the evaluation of $\mathcal{P}$ (i.e. rule r is more preferred than rule r'). Consider the following classical example represented in our formalism:

$\mathcal{P}_1$:
$\quad N_1 : Fly(x) \leftarrow Bird(x), not\ \neg Fly(x),$

---

[1] We also call Π^S is the Gelfond-Lifschitz transformation of Π in terms of S.

$N_2 : \neg Fly(x) \leftarrow Penguin(x), not\ Fly(x),$
$N_3 : Bird(Tweety) \leftarrow,$
$N_4 : Penguin(Tweety) \leftarrow,$
$N_2 < N_1.$

Obviously, rules N_1 and N_2 conflict with each other as their heads are complementary literals, and applying N_1 will defeat N_2 and *vice versa*. However, as $N_2 < N_1$, we would expect that rule N_2 is preferred to apply first and then defeat rule N_1 after applying N_2 so that the desired solution $\neg Fly(Tweety)$ can be derived. This idea is formalized by following definitions.

Definition 1 *Let* Π *be an extended logic program and* r *a rule with the form* $L_0 \leftarrow L_1, \cdots, L_m, not\ L_{m+1}, \cdots, not\ L_n$ *(r does not necessarily belong to* Π*). Rule* r *is defeated by* Π *iff* Π *has answer set(s) and for every answer set* $Ans(\Pi)$ *of* Π*, there exists some* $L_i \in Ans(\Pi)$*, where* $m + 1 \leq i \leq n$.

Definition 2 *Let* $\mathcal{P} = (\Pi, \mathcal{N}, <)$ *be a PLP and* $\mathcal{P}(<^+)$ *denote the* $<$*-closure of* $\mathcal{P}$ *(i.e.* $\mathcal{P}(<^+)$ *is the smallest set containing all preference relations of* $\mathcal{P}$ *and closed under transitivity).* $\mathcal{P}^<$ *is a reduct of* $\mathcal{P}$ *with respect to* $<$ *iff there exists a sequence of sets* Π_i *($i = 0, 1, \cdots$) such that:*

1. *$\Pi_0 = \Pi$;*

2. *$\Pi_i = \Pi_{i-1} - \{r_1, \cdots, r_k \mid$ (a) there exists $r \in \Pi_{i-1}$ such that $\mathcal{N}(r) < \mathcal{N}(r_i) \in \mathcal{P}(<^+)$ ($i = 1, \cdots, k$) and $r_1, \cdots, r_k$ are defeated by $\Pi_{i-1} - \{r_1, \cdots, r_k\}$, and (b) there does not exist a rule $r' \in \Pi_{i-1}$ such that $\mathcal{N}(r_j) < \mathcal{N}(r')$ for some j ($j = 1, \cdots, k$) and r' is defeated by $\Pi_{i-1} - \{r'\}\}$;*

3. *$\mathcal{P}^< = \bigcap_{i=0}^{\infty} \Pi_i$.*

Clearly $\mathcal{P}^<$ is an extended logic program obtained from Π by eliminating some rules from Π. In particular, if $\mathcal{N}(r) < \mathcal{N}(r')$ and $\Pi - \{r'\}$ defeats r', rule r' is eliminated from Π if no *less preferred rule* can be eliminated (i.e. conditions (a) and (b) in (ii)). This procedure is continued until a fixed point is reached. Note that due to the transitivity of $<$, we need to consider each $\mathcal{N}(r) < \mathcal{N}(r')$ in the $<$-closure of $\mathcal{P}$. It should be also noted that the reduct of a PLP may not be unique generally [8]. Now it is quite straightforward to define the answer set for a prioritized logic program.

Definition 3 *Let* $\mathcal{P} = (\Pi, \mathcal{N}, <)$ *be a PLP and Lit the set of all ground literals in the language of* $\mathcal{P}$*. For any subset* S *of Lit,* S *is an answer set of* $\mathcal{P}$*, denoted as* $Ans^P(\mathcal{P})$*, iff* $S = Ans(\mathcal{P}^<)$*, where* $Ans(\mathcal{P}^<)$ *is an answer set of extended logic program* $\mathcal{P}^<$*. A ground literal* L *is derivable from a PLP* $\mathcal{P}$*, denoted as* $\mathcal{P} \vdash L$*, iff* $\mathcal{P}$ *has answer set(s) and* L *belongs to every answer set of* $\mathcal{P}$.

Example 1 Using Definition 1 and 2, it is not difficult to conclude that $\mathcal{P}_1$ has a unique reduct: $\mathcal{P}_1^{<} = \{\neg Fly(x) \leftarrow Penguin(x), \; not \; Fly(x), \; Bird(Tweety) \leftarrow, \; Penguin(Tweety) \leftarrow\}$, and then from Definition 3, it has a unique answer set $Ans^P(\mathcal{P}_1) = \{Bird(Tweety), \; Penguin(Tweety), \; \neg Fly(Tweety)\}$. ∎

2.2 Generalized Rule Based Update

Consider a language $\mathcal{L}$ of extended logic programs as described in section 2. We specify that a *knowledge base* $\mathcal{B}$ is a *consistent* set of ground literals of $\mathcal{L}$ and an *update program* Π is a set of rules of $\mathcal{L}$ with form (1) that are called *update rules*. Note that we allow a knowledge base to be *incomplete*. That is, a literal not in a knowledge base is treated as *unknown*.

We will use a prioritized logic program to specify an update of $\mathcal{B}$ by Π, where Π is an extended logic program. For this purpose, we first need to extend language $\mathcal{L}^P$ by the following way. We specify $\mathcal{L}^P_{new}$ to be a language of PLPs based on $\mathcal{L}^P$ with one more augment: For each predicate symbol P in $\mathcal{L}^P$, there is a corresponding predicate symbol $New\text{-}P$ in $\mathcal{L}^P_{new}$ with the same arity of P.

To simplifying our presentation, in $\mathcal{L}^P_{new}$ we use notation $New\text{-}L$ to denote the corresponding literal L in $\mathcal{L}$. For instance, if a literal L in $\mathcal{L}$ is $\neg P(x)$, then notation $New\text{-}L$ simply means $\neg New\text{-}P(x)$. We use Lit_{new} to denote the set of all ground literals of $\mathcal{L}^P_{new}$. Clearly, $Lit_{new} = Lit \cup \{New\text{-}L \mid L \in Lit\}$. Now we are ready to formalize our generalized rule-based update.

Definition 4 *Let* $\mathcal{B}$, Π, $\mathcal{L}$, $\mathcal{L}^P$ *and* $\mathcal{L}^P_{new}$ *be defined as above. The specification of updating* $\mathcal{B}$ *with* Π *is defined as a PLP of* $\mathcal{L}^P_{new}$, *denoted as* $Update(\mathcal{B}, \Pi) = (\Pi^*, \mathcal{N}, <)$, *as follows:*

1. Π^* *consists of following rules:*
   Initial knowledge rules: *for each* L *in* $\mathcal{B}$, *there is a*
      rule $L \leftarrow$;
   Inertia rules: *for each predicate symbol* P *in* $\mathcal{L}$,
      there are two rules:
      $New\text{-}P(x) \leftarrow P(x), \; not \; \neg New\text{-}P(x)^2$, *and*
      $\neg New\text{-}P(x) \leftarrow \neg P(x), \; not \; New\text{-}P(x)$,
   Update rules: *for each rule*
      $L_0 \leftarrow L_1, \cdots, L_m, \; not \; L_{m+1}, \cdots, \; not \; L_n \; in \; \Pi$,
      there is a rule
      $New\text{-}L_0 \leftarrow New\text{-}L_1, \cdots, New\text{-}L_m,$
         $not \; New\text{-}L_{m+1}, \cdots, \; not \; New\text{-}L_n$;

2. *Naming function* $\mathcal{N}$ *assigns a unique name* N *for each rule in* Π^*;

3. *For any inertia rule with name* N *and update rule with name* N', *we specify* $N < N'$.

---

[2] x might be a tuple of variables.

An update specification $Update(\mathcal{B}, \Pi)$ is well defined *if it has answer set(s) and all its answer sets are consistent.*

It should be noted that in the above definition, we specify inertia rules to be more preferred than update rules in $Update(\mathcal{B}, \Pi)$. The intuitive idea behind this is that a preference ordering between an inertia rule and an update rule in $Update(\mathcal{B}, \Pi)$ will affect the evaluation of $Update(\mathcal{B}, \Pi)$ *only if* these two rules conflict with each other, eg. applying one rule causes the other inapplicable. On the other hand, a fact in the initial knowledge base $\mathcal{B}$ is always preferred to persist during an update whenever there is no violation of update rules[3]. Therefore, when conflicts occur between inertia and update rules, inertia rules should defeat the corresponding update rules. without conflicts between inertia and update rules, the preference ordering does not play any role in the evaluation of $Update(\mathcal{B}, \Pi)$. Also note that there will be at most $2k \cdot l$ <-relations in $Update(\mathcal{B}, \Pi)$, where k is the number of predicate symbols of $\mathcal{L}_P$ and l is the number of update rules in Π.

Finally, on the basis of Definition 4, we can formally define a knowledge base $\mathcal{B}'$ resulting from updating $\mathcal{B}$ with Π in a straightforward way.

Definition 5 *Let $\mathcal{B}, \mathcal{P}, \mathcal{L}, \mathcal{L}^P$ and $\mathcal{L}_{new}^P$ be specified as before, and $Update(\mathcal{B}, \Pi)$ the specification of updating $\mathcal{B}$ with Π as defined in Definition 4. A set of ground literals of $\mathcal{L}$, $\mathcal{B}'$, is called a* possible resulting knowledge base *with respect to the update specification $Update(\mathcal{B}, \Pi)$, iff $\mathcal{B}'$ satisfies the following conditions:*

1. *if $Update(\mathcal{B}, \Pi)$ has a consistent answer set, say $Ans^P(Update(\mathcal{B}, \Pi))$, then $\mathcal{B}' = \{L \mid New\text{-}L \in Ans^P(Update(\mathcal{B}, \Pi))\}$.*

2. *if $Update(\mathcal{B}, \Pi)$ is not well defined, then $\mathcal{B}' = \mathcal{B}$.*

Example 2 Let $\mathcal{B} = \{\neg A, B, C\}$ and $\Pi = \{\neg B \leftarrow not\ B,\ A \leftarrow C\}$. From Definition 4, the specification of updating $\mathcal{B}$ by Π, $Update(\mathcal{B}, \Pi)$, is as follows:

Initial knowledge rules:
$N_1 : \neg A \leftarrow,$
$N_2 : B \leftarrow,$
$N_3 : C \leftarrow,$
Inertia rules:
$N_4 : New\text{-}A \leftarrow A, not\ \neg New\text{-}A,$
$N_5 : New\text{-}B \leftarrow B, not\ \neg New\text{-}B,$
$N_6 : New\text{-}C \leftarrow C, not\ \neg New\text{-}C,$
$N_7 : \neg New\text{-}A \leftarrow \neg A, not\ New\text{-}A,$
$N_8 : \neg New\text{-}B \leftarrow \neg B, not\ New\text{-}B,$
$N_9 : \neg New\text{-}C \leftarrow \neg C, not\ New\text{-}C,$

---

[3]Note that an update rule in $Update(\mathcal{B}, \Pi)$ is defeasible if it contains a weak negation *not* in the body.

Update rules:

$N_{10} : \neg New\text{-}B \leftarrow not\ New\text{-}B,$

$N_{11} : New\text{-}A \leftarrow New\text{-}C,$

$<:$

$N_4 < N_{10}, N_5 < N_{10}, N_6 < N_{10},$

$N_7 < N_{10}, N_8 < N_{10}, N_9 < N_{10},$

$N_4 < N_{11}, N_5 < N_{11}, N_6 < N_{11},$

$N_7 < N_{11}, N_8 < N_{11}, N_9 < N_{11}.$

Now from Definitions 2 and 3, it is not difficult to see that $Update(\mathcal{B}, \Pi)$ has a unique answer set: $\{\neg A, B, C, New\text{-}A, New\text{-}B, New\text{-}C\}$. Note that in $Update(\mathcal{B}, \Pi)$, only $N_5 < N_{10}$ is used in $Update(\mathcal{B}, \Pi)$'s evaluation, while other $<$-relations are useless (see Definition 2). Hence, from Definition 5, the only resulting knowledge base $\mathcal{B}'$ after updating $\mathcal{B}$ with Π is: $\{A, B, C\}$ ∎

It is worth to mention that the major difference between our approach and other formulations of rule based update is that our approach can deal with a more general case by allowing the set of update rules to have both classical negation and negation as failure, while in previous methods, an update rule can only have classical negation, e.g. [1]. It is also observed that by allowing an update rule to have two types of negations, previous methods may result in some unintuitive solution. For instance, in the case of Example 2 described above, Przymusinski and Turner's method will imply a solution that literal B may or may not be changed after updating $\{\neg A, B, C\}$ with $\{\neg B \leftarrow not\ B,\ A \leftarrow C\}$.

3 Restricted Monotonicity Properties

In this section, we examine basic properties, specifically, monotonicity properties related to the generalized rule based update described above. Firstly we show that the update specification $Update(\mathcal{B}, \Pi)$ in language $\mathcal{L}_{new}^P$ defined in Definition 4 can be simplified to a PLP in language $\mathcal{L}^P$.

Lemma 1 *Let $Update(\mathcal{B}, \Pi)$ be a well defined update specification as defined in Definition 4. $\mathcal{B}'$ is a resulting knowledge base after updating $\mathcal{B}$ with Π if and only if $\mathcal{B}'$ is an answer set of prioritized logic program $\mathcal{P} = (\Pi \cup \{L \leftarrow not\overline{L} \mid L \in \mathcal{B}\}, \mathcal{N}, <)$, where for each rule $r : L \leftarrow not\overline{L}$ with $L \in \mathcal{B}$, and each rule r' in Π, $\mathcal{N}(r) < \mathcal{N}(r')$[4].*

Consider a knowledge base $\mathcal{B}$ and a rule r with the form (1). Recall that $\mathcal{B}$ *satisfies* r iff if facts $L_1, \cdots, L_m$ are in $\mathcal{B}$ and facts $L_{m+1}, \cdots,$ and L_n are not in $\mathcal{B}$, then fact L_0 is in $\mathcal{B}$. Let Π be a set of rules with the form (1). $\mathcal{B}$ satisfies Π if $\mathcal{B}$ satisfies each rule in Π. We show that after

---

[4]$\overline{L}$ stands for the complement of literal L.

updating knowledge base $\mathcal{B}$ with Π, every possible resulting knowledge base $\mathcal{B}'$ satisfies Π as stated in the following proposition.

Proposition 1 *Given a knowledge base $\mathcal{B}$ and an update program Π. Suppose the update specification $Update(\mathcal{B}, \Pi)$ is well defined. Let $\mathcal{B}'$ be a resulting knowledge base with respect to $Update(\mathcal{B}, \Pi)$. Then $\mathcal{B}'$ satisfies Π.*

Let $\mathcal{B}$ and $\mathcal{B}'$ be two knowledge bases. We use $Diff(\mathcal{B}, \mathcal{B}')$ to denote the symmetric set difference on ground atoms between $\mathcal{B}$ and $\mathcal{B}'$, i.e.

$$Diff(\mathcal{B}, \mathcal{B}') = \{|L| \mid L \in (\mathcal{B} - \mathcal{B}') \cup (\mathcal{B}' - \mathcal{B})\},$$

where notation $|L|$ indicates the corresponding ground atom of ground literal L, and $Min(\mathcal{B}, \Pi)$ to denote the set of all consistent knowledge bases satisfying Π but with minimal differences from $\mathcal{B}$, i.e.

$$Min(\mathcal{B}, \Pi) = \{\mathcal{B}' \mid \mathcal{B}' \text{ satisfies } \Pi \text{ and } Diff(\mathcal{B}, \mathcal{B}') \text{ is minimal}$$
$$\text{with respect to set inclusion}\}.$$

Then we have the following minimal change theorem for update, which guarantees that our generalized rule based update satisfies the principle of minimal change.

Theorem 1 (Minimal Change) *Let $\mathcal{B}$ be a knowledge base, Π an update program, and $Update(\mathcal{B}, \Pi)$ the well defined update specification as defined in Definition 4. If $\mathcal{B}'$ is a resulting knowledge base with respect to $Update(\mathcal{B}, \Pi)$, then $\mathcal{B}' \in Min(\mathcal{B}, \Pi)$.*

The above theorem guarantees that our generalized rule based update satisfies the principle of minimal change. However, it should be noted that not every element of $Min(\mathcal{B}, \Pi)$ could be a resulting knowledge base of updating $\mathcal{B}$ by $\mathcal{P}$.

It is not surprising that in general our rule based update is nonmonotonic in the sense that adding more facts into a knowledge base $\mathcal{B}$ or more update rules into an update program Π may destroy some facts obtained from the update of $\mathcal{B}$ with Π. Therefore, instead of obtaining a general monotonicity result, our goal here is to investigate some kinds of restricted monotonicity properties related to our rule based update. In particular, we are interested in two forms of restricted monotonicity properties: (1) under what conditions will the result of updating a knowledge base $\mathcal{B}$ with Π be preserved in the result of updating an expanded knowledge base $\mathcal{B} \cup \mathcal{B}'$ with Π? (2) under what conditions will the result of updating a knowledge base $\mathcal{B}$ with Π be preserved in the result of updating $\mathcal{B}$ with an expanded update program $\Pi \cup \Pi'$?

Before we present our restricted monotonicity theorems, we first introduce some useful notations. Let r be a rule in Π:

$$L_0 \leftarrow L_1, \cdots, L_m, \text{ not } L_{m+1}, \cdots, \text{ not } L_n.$$

We use $pos(r)$ to denote the set of literals in the body of r without negation as failure $\{L_1, \cdots,$
$L_m\}$ in r, and $neg(r)$ the set of literals in the body of r with negation as failure $\{L_{m+1}, \cdots, L_n\}$ in r. We specify $body(r)$ to be $pos(r) \cup neg(r)$. We also use $head(r)$ to denote the head of r: $\{L_0\}$. Then we use $lit(r)$ to denote $head(r) \cup body(r)$. By extending these notations, we use $pos(\Pi)$, $neg(\Pi)$, $body(\Pi)$, $head(\Pi)$, and $lit(\Pi)$ to denote the unions of corresponding components of all rules in Π, e.g. $body(\Pi) = \bigcup_{r \in \Pi} body(r)$. Given a set of literals $\mathcal{B}$, we also use $\overline{\mathcal{B}}$ to denote the set of complement literals of $\mathcal{B}$ with respect to classical negation sign $\neg$.

Theorem 2 *(Restricted Monotonicity Theorem 1) Given two knowledge bases $\mathcal{B}_1$ and $\mathcal{B}_2$ where $\mathcal{B}_1 \subseteq \mathcal{B}_2$ and an update program Π. Suppose both update specifications $Update(\mathcal{B}, \Pi_1)$ and $Update(\mathcal{B}, \Pi_2)$ are well defined. Let $\mathcal{B}'_1$ be a resulting knowledge base with respect to $Update(\mathcal{B}_1, \Pi)$. Then there exists a resulting knowledge base $\mathcal{B}'_2$ with respect to $Update(\mathcal{B}_2, \Pi)$ such that $\mathcal{B}'_1 \subseteq \mathcal{B}'_2$ if $body(\Pi) \cap (\mathcal{B}_2 - \mathcal{B}_1) = \emptyset$. In this case, $\mathcal{B}'_2 = \mathcal{B}'_1 \cup \{L \mid L \in (\mathcal{B}_2 - \mathcal{B}_1)$ and $\overline{L} \notin \mathcal{B}'_1\}$.*

Theorem 3 *(Restricted Monotonicity Theorem 2) Given a knowledge base $\mathcal{B}$ and two update programs Π_1 and Π_2 where $\Pi_1 \subseteq \Pi_2$. Suppose both update specifications $Update(\mathcal{B}_1, \Pi)$ and $Update(\mathcal{B}_2, \Pi)$ are well defined. Let $\mathcal{B}'$ be a resulting knowledge base with respect to $Update(\mathcal{B}, \Pi_1)$. Then there exists a resulting knowledge base $\mathcal{B}''$ with respect to $Update(\mathcal{B}, \Pi_2)$ such that $\mathcal{B}' \subseteq \mathcal{B}''$ if $head(\Pi_2 - \Pi_1) \cap (\overline{\mathcal{B}} \cup body(\Pi_1)) = \emptyset$. In this case, $\mathcal{B}''$ is an answer set of program $\{L \leftarrow \mid L \in \mathcal{B}'\} \cup (\Pi_2 - \Pi_1)$.*

The intuitive idea behind Theorem 2 is described as follows. If a knowledge base $\mathcal{B}_1$ is expanded to $\mathcal{B}_2$ by adding some facts and all these added facts do not occur in the body of any rule in Π, then the result of updating $\mathcal{B}_1$ with Π is preserved in the result of updating $\mathcal{B}_2$ with Π. Furthermore, the latter can be simply computed from the result of updating $\mathcal{B}_1$ with Π. On the other hand, Theorem 3 says that if an update program Π_1 is expanded to Π_2 by adding some rules and the head of each added rule does not occur in the bodies of rules in update specification $Update(\mathcal{B}, \Pi_1)$, then the result of updating $\mathcal{B}$ with Π_1 is preserved in the result of updating $\mathcal{B}$ with Π_2, and the latter is reduced to an answer set of a corresponding extended logic program.

Given a knowledge base $\mathcal{B}$ and an update program Π, we can apply the restricted monotonicity theorems above to simplify the computation of $Update(\mathcal{B}, \Pi)$ when $\mathcal{B}$ or Π can be split into parts. The following example illustrates such application.

Example 3 Let $\mathcal{B} = \{A, B, C, D\}$, and $\Pi = \{\neg A \leftarrow B, \neg C \leftarrow B, \neg B \leftarrow not \; B\}$. We consider the update of $\mathcal{B}$ with Π. Since $body(\Pi) \cap \{A, C, D\} = \emptyset$, from Theorem 2, we can actually reduce the update of $\mathcal{B}$ with Π into the update of $\{B\}$ with Π. It is clear that the unique result of $Update(\{B\}, \Pi)$ is $\{\neg A, B, \neg C\}$. So according to Theorem 2, the unique resulting knowledge base with respect to $Update(\mathcal{B}, \Pi)$ is $\{\neg A, B, \neg C, D\}$.

Let us consider another situation. Let $\mathcal{B} = \{A, B\}$, and $\Pi = \{\neg B \leftarrow not\ C, \neg C \leftarrow A\}$. Consider a rule $r : \neg C \leftarrow A$ in Π. Since $head(r) \cap (\overline{\mathcal{B}} \cup body(\neg B \leftarrow not\ C)) = \{\neg C\} \cap \{\neg A, \neg B, C\} = \emptyset$, according to Theorem 3, the update of $\mathcal{B}$ with Π can be reduced to the update of $\mathcal{B}$ with $\{\neg B \leftarrow not\ C\}$, which has the unique result $\{A, \neg B\}$. So the result of $Update(\mathcal{B}, \Pi)$ is an answer set of program $\{A \leftarrow, \neg B \leftarrow, \neg C \leftarrow A\}$, which has the unique answer set $\{A, \neg B, \neg C\}$. ∎

4 A Generalization of Splitting Theorem

Our proofs of Theorems 2 and 3 described previously are based on a nontrivial generalization of Lifschitz-Turner's Splitting Set Theorem on extended logic programs [4]. To describe Lifschitz-Turner's Splitting Theorem , we first define the following transformation. Let X be a set of literals and Π an extended logic program. The *e-reduct* of Π with respect to set X is an extended logic program, denoted as $e(\Pi, X)$, obtained from Π by deleting

1. each rule in Π that has a formula *not L* in its body with $L \in X$; and

2. all formulas of form L in the bodies of the remaining rules with $L \in X$.

Consider an example with $X = \{C\}$ and Π is a set of the following rules:

$A \leftarrow B, not\ C,$
$B \leftarrow C, not\ A.$

Then it is clear that $e(\Pi, \{C\}) = \{B \leftarrow not\ A\}$. Intuitively, *e*-reduct of Π with respect to X can be viewed as a simpled program of Π given the fact that every literal in X is true. Now Lifschitz-Turner's Splitting Set Theorem on extended logic program can be presented as follows[5].

Lifschitz and Turner's Splitting Set Theorem [4]
Let $\Pi = \Pi_1 \cup \Pi_2$ be an extended logic program and $lit(\Pi_1) \cap head(\Pi_2) = \emptyset$. Then a set of literals $\mathcal{B}$ is a consistent answer set of Π if and only if $\mathcal{B} = \mathcal{B}_1 \cup \mathcal{B}'$, where $\mathcal{B}_1$ is an answer set of Π_1, $\mathcal{B}'$ is an answer set of $e(\Pi_2, \mathcal{B}_1)$, and $\mathcal{B}_1 \cup \mathcal{B}'$ is consistent.

As illustrated by Lifschitz and Turner, with the splitting theorem, computing the answer set of an extended logic program can be simplified when the program is split into parts. In the above example, if we expand Π as $\Pi \cup \{C \leftarrow\}$, we can rewrite Π as $\Pi_1 \cup \Pi_2$, where $\Pi_1 = \{C \leftarrow\}$ and $\Pi_2 = \{A \leftarrow B, not\ C, B \leftarrow C, not\ A\}$. Clearly, $lit(\Pi_1) \cap head(\Pi_2) = \emptyset$. So

---

[5]For our purpose, we slightly reformulate this theorem according to Lifschitz and Turner's original form.

it is easy to see that $\{C, B\}$ is an answer set of $\Pi \cup \{C \leftarrow\}$. This splitting theorem, however, can be further generalized. Let us consider the following example.

Example 4 Let Π be a program consisting of following rules:

$$A \leftarrow not\ C,$$
$$A \leftarrow not\ B,$$
$$B \leftarrow not\ A.$$

It is not difficult to see that Π can not be split into two parts Π_1 and Π_2 such that $lit(\Pi_1) \cap head(\Pi_2) = \emptyset$ if we do not consider the trivial case by setting $\Pi_1 = \emptyset$ or $\Pi_2 = \emptyset$. Therefore, the above splitting theorem cannot be used to compute the answer set of Π. However, Π can be split into Π_1 and Π_2 as follows:

Π_1: Π_2:
$A \leftarrow not\ C,$ $A \leftarrow not\ B,$
                    $B \leftarrow not\ A,$

such that $body(\Pi_1) \cap head(\Pi_2) = \emptyset$. It is observed that $\{A\}$ is the unique answer set of Π_1, and the unique answer set of Π is then obtained from Π_1's answer set $\{A\}$ and the answer set of $e(\Pi_2, \{A\})$, which is also $\{A\}$. So we get the unique answer set of Π $\{A\}$. ∎

From the above observation, we can see that since the head of each rule in Π_2 does not occur in the body of each rule in Π_1, Π_2 actually does not play any role in affecting rules in Π_1 when we compute the answer set of Π. Therefore, Π can be still split into two parts to evaluate its answer set. In general, we have the following generalized splitting theorem.

Theorem 4 (Generalized Splitting Theorem) *Let $\Pi = \Pi_1 \cup \Pi_2$ be an extended logic program and $body(\Pi_1) \cap head(\Pi_2) = \emptyset$. Then a set of literals $\mathcal{B}$ is a consistent answer set of Π if and only if $\mathcal{B} = \mathcal{B}_1 \cup \mathcal{B}'$, where $\mathcal{B}_1$ is an answer set of Π_1, $\mathcal{B}'$ is an answer set of $e(\Pi_2, \mathcal{B}_1)$, and $\mathcal{B}_1 \cup \mathcal{B}'$ is consistent.*

Proof: ($\Leftarrow$) Let $\mathcal{B} = \mathcal{B}_1 \cup \mathcal{B}'$ and $\Pi = \Pi_1 \cup \Pi_2$, where $\mathcal{B}_1$ is an answer set of Π_1 and $\mathcal{B}'$ is an answer set of $e(\Pi_2, \mathcal{B}_1)$ and $\mathcal{B}_1 \cup \mathcal{B}'$ is consistent. Consider the Gelfond-Lifschitz transformation of Π in terms of $\mathcal{B}$, $\Pi^{\mathcal{B}}$. $\Pi^{\mathcal{B}}$ is obtained from Π by deleting (i) each rule in $\Pi_1 \cup \Pi_2$ that has a formula $not\ L$ in its body with $L \in \mathcal{B}$; and (ii) all formulas of the form $not\ L$ in the bodies of the remaining rules. Since $body(\Pi_1) \cap head(\Pi_2) = \emptyset$, during the step (i) in the above transformation, for each literal $L \in \mathcal{B}_1$, only rules with the form $L' \leftarrow \cdots, not\ L$ in Π_1 or Π_2 will be deleted. On the other hand, for each literal $L \in \mathcal{B}'$, only rules with the form $L' \leftarrow \cdots, not\ L$ in Π_2 will be deleted and no rules in Π_1 can be deleted. Therefore, we can denote $\Pi^{\mathcal{B}}$ as $\Pi_1' \cup \Pi_2'$, where Π_1' is obtained from Π_1 in terms of literals in

$\mathcal{B}_1$, and Π'_2 is obtained from Π_2 in terms of literals in $\mathcal{B}_1 \cup \mathcal{B}'$ during the above transformation procedure. Then it is easy to see that $\Pi'_1 = \Pi_1^{\mathcal{B}_1}$. So $\mathcal{B}_1$ is an answer set of Π'_1.

On the other hand, from the construction of $e(\Pi_2, \mathcal{B}_1)$, it is observed that there exists the following correspondence between Π'_2 and $e(\Pi_2, \mathcal{B}_1)$: for each rule $L_0 \leftarrow L_1, \cdots, L_k, L_{k+1}, \cdots, L_m$ in Π'_2, there is a rule with the form $L_0 \leftarrow L_1, \cdots, L_k, not\ L_{m+1}, \cdots, not\ L_n$ in $e(\Pi_2, \mathcal{B}_1)$ such that $L_{k+1}, \cdots, L_m \in \mathcal{B}_1$ and $L_{m+1}, \cdots,$ or $L_n \notin \mathcal{B}_1$; on the other hand, for each rule $L_0 \leftarrow L_1, \cdots, L_k,$ $not\ L_{m+1}, \cdots, not\ L_n$ in $e(\Pi_2, \mathcal{B}_1)$, if none of $L_{m+1}, \cdots, L_n$ is in $\mathcal{B}'$, then there exists a rule $L_0 \leftarrow L_1, \cdots, L_k, L_{k+1}, \cdots, L_m$ in Π'_2 such that $L_{k+1}, \cdots, L_m \in \mathcal{B}_1$. From this observation, it can be seen that there exists a subset Δ of $\mathcal{B}_1$ such that $\Delta \cup \mathcal{B}'$ is an answer set of Π'_2. This follows that $\mathcal{B}_1 \cup \mathcal{B}'$ is the smallest set such that for each rule $L_0 \leftarrow L_1, \cdots, L_m \in \Pi^{\mathcal{B}}, L_1, \cdots, L_m \in \mathcal{B}$ implies $L_0 \in \mathcal{B}$. That is, $\mathcal{B}$ is an answer set of $\Pi^{\mathcal{B}}$ and also an answer set of Π.

($\Rightarrow$) Let $\Pi = \Pi_1 \cup \Pi_2$ and $\mathcal{B}$ be a consistent answer set of Π. It is clear that for each literal $L \in \mathcal{B}$, there must be some rule with the form $L \leftarrow \cdots$ in Π. So we can write $\mathcal{B}$ as a form of $\mathcal{B}'_1 \cup \mathcal{B}'_2$ such that $\mathcal{B}'_1 \subseteq head(\Pi_1)$ and $\mathcal{B}'_2 \subseteq head(\Pi_2)$. Note that $\mathcal{B}'_1 \cap \mathcal{B}'_2$ may not be empty. Now we transfer set $\mathcal{B}'_1$ into $\mathcal{B}_1$ by the following step: if $\mathcal{B}'_1 \cap \mathcal{B}'_2 = \emptyset$, then $\mathcal{B}_1 = \mathcal{B}'_1$; otherwise, let $\mathcal{B}_1 = \mathcal{B}'_1 - \{L \mid L \in \mathcal{B}'_1 \cap \mathcal{B}'_2,$ and for each rule $L \leftarrow L_1, \cdots, L_m,$ $notL_{m+1}, \cdots, notL_n$ in Π_1, there exists some $L_j\ (1 \leq j \leq m) \notin \mathcal{B}'_1$ or L_j $(m+1 \leq j \leq n) \in \mathcal{B}'_1\}$. In above translation, since every L deleted from $\mathcal{B}_1$ is also in $\mathcal{B}'_2$, the answer set $\mathcal{B}$ of Π can then be expressed as $\mathcal{B} = \mathcal{B}_1 \cup \mathcal{B}'_2$. An important fact is observed from the construction of $\mathcal{B}_1$:

Fact 1. $L \in \mathcal{B}_1$ iff there exists some rule in Π_1 with the form $L \leftarrow L_1, \cdots, L_m, notL_{m+1}, \cdots, notL_n$, such that $L_1, \cdots, L_m \in \mathcal{B}_1$ and $L_{m+1}, \cdots,$ or $L_n \notin \mathcal{B}_1$.

Now we prove $\mathcal{B}_1$ is an answer set of Π_1. We do Gelfond-Lifschitz transformation on Π in terms of set $\mathcal{B} = \mathcal{B}_1 \cup \mathcal{B}'_2$. After such transformation, we can write $\Pi^{\mathcal{B}}$ as form $\Pi'_1 \cup \Pi'_2$, where $\Pi'_1 \subseteq \Pi_1$ and $\Pi'_2 \subseteq \Pi_2$. As $body(\Pi_1) \cap head(\Pi_2) = \emptyset$, any literal in $\mathcal{B}'_2$ will not cause a deletion of a rule from Π_1 in the Gelfond-Lifschitz transformation. Then it is easy to see that $\Pi'_1 = \Pi_1^{\mathcal{B}_1}$. From **Fact 1**, it concludes that literal $L \in \mathcal{B}_1$ iff there is a rule $L \leftarrow L_1, \cdots L_m$ in $\Pi_1^{\mathcal{B}_1}$ and $L_1, \cdots, L_m \in \mathcal{B}_1$. This follows that $\mathcal{B}_1$ is an answer set of $\Pi_1^{\mathcal{B}_1}$, and then an answer set of Π_1.

Now we transfer $\mathcal{B}'_2$ into $\mathcal{B}_2$ by the following step: if $\mathcal{B}_1 \cap \mathcal{B}'_2 = \emptyset$, then $\mathcal{B}_2 = \mathcal{B}'_2$; otherwise, let $\mathcal{B}_2 = \mathcal{B}'_2 - \{L \mid L \in \mathcal{B}_1 \cap \mathcal{B}'_2,$ and for each rule $L \leftarrow L_1, \cdots, L_m, not\ L_{m+1}, \cdots, not\ L_n$ in Π_2, there exists some $L_j(1 \leq j \leq m) \notin \mathcal{B}_1 \cup \mathcal{B}'_2$, or $L_j(m + 1 \leq j \leq n) \in \mathcal{B}_1 \cup \mathcal{B}'_2\}$. After this translation, $\mathcal{B}$ can be expressed as $\mathcal{B} = \mathcal{B}_1 \cup \mathcal{B}_2$. An important fact is also observed from the translation of $\mathcal{B}_2$:

Fact 2. $L \in \mathcal{B}_2$ iff there exists some rule in Π'_2 with the form $L \leftarrow L_1, \cdots, L_k, L_{k+1}, \cdots, L_m$ such that $L_1, \cdots, L_k \in \mathcal{B}_1$ and $L_{k+1}, \cdots, L_m \in \mathcal{B}_2$.

Now we prove $\mathcal{B}_2$ is an answer set of $e(\Pi_1, \mathcal{B}_1)$. Recall that $\Pi^\mathcal{B} = \Pi'_1 \cup \Pi'_2 = \Pi_1^{\mathcal{B}_1} \cup \Pi'_2$. From **Fact 2**, it is clear that there exists a subset Δ of $\mathcal{B}_1$ such that $\mathcal{B}_2$ is an answer set of $e(\Pi'_2, \Delta)$ and $e(\Pi'_2, \Delta)^{\mathcal{B}_2} = e(\Pi'_2, \Delta)$. On the other hand, from the construction of $e(\Pi_2, \mathcal{B}_1)$, it is easy to see that $e(\Pi_2, \mathcal{B}_1)^{\mathcal{B}_2} = e(\Pi'_2, \Delta) = e(\Pi'_2, \Delta)^{\mathcal{B}_2}$. So $\mathcal{B}_2$ is also an answer set of $e(\Pi_2, \mathcal{B}_1)$. ∎

5 Proofs of Restricted Monotonicity Theorems

From the Generalized Splitting Theorem (Theorem 4), we can prove the following Lemma 2 which will be needed in the proof of Restricted Monotonicity Theorem 1 (Theorem 2), and from Lemma 3 we can prove Restricted Monotonicity Theorem 2 (Theorem 3). Due to a space limit, details of the proofs for these lemmas are referred to our full paper [9]. Here we only give proofs of Theorems 2 and 3.

Lemma 2 *Let Π_1 and Π_2 be two extended logic programs, where each rule in Π_2 has form $L \leftarrow not\overline{L}$, $head(\Pi_2) \cap body(\Pi_2) = \emptyset$ and $body(\Pi_1) \cap head(\Pi_2) = \emptyset$. Suppose both Π_1 and $\Pi_1 \cup \Pi_2$ have consistent answer sets. Then $\mathcal{B}$ is a consistent answer set of $\Pi_1 \cup \Pi_2$ if and only if $\mathcal{B} = \mathcal{B}' \cup \{L \mid L \leftarrow not\overline{L} \in \Pi_2 \text{ and } \overline{L} \notin \mathcal{B}'\}$, where $\mathcal{B}'$ is a consistent answer set of Π_1.*

Lemma 3 *Let $\mathcal{P} = (\Pi, \mathcal{N}, <)$ be a PLP which has consistent answer set(s). Then each answer set of $\mathcal{P}$ is also an answer set of Π.*

Proof of Restricted Monotonicity Theorem 1
From Lemma 1, $Update(\mathcal{B}_1, \Pi)$ and $Update(\mathcal{B}_2, \Pi)$ are equivalent to following two PLPs respectively: $\mathcal{P}_1 = (\Pi \cup \{L \leftarrow not\overline{L} \mid L \in \mathcal{B}_1\}, \mathcal{N}, <)$ and $\mathcal{P}_2 = (\Pi \cup \{L \leftarrow not\overline{L} \mid L \in \mathcal{B}_2\}, \mathcal{N}, <)$, where $<$ relations in $\mathcal{P}_1$ are specified as stated in Lemma 1 respectively. Let $\mathcal{B}'_1$ be a consistent answer set of $\mathcal{P}_1$. We assume $\mathcal{B}_1 = \{L_1, \cdots, L_k\}$, and $\mathcal{B}_2 = \mathcal{B}_1 \cup \{L_{k+1}, \cdots, L_m\}$. Observing the construction of $\mathcal{P}_2$, besides rules in $\mathcal{P}_1$, $\mathcal{P}_2$ also contains following rules: $r_{k+1} : L_{k+1} \leftarrow not\overline{L_{k+1}}, \cdots, r_m : L_m \leftarrow not\overline{L_m}$. Let $\Pi' \cup \Pi''$ be a reduct of $\mathcal{P}_2$, where each rule in Π' is also in $\mathcal{P}_1$, and $\Pi'' = \{r_{k+1}, \cdots, r_m\}$. Note that since for each rule $r \in \Pi''$, there is no other rule r^* such that $\mathcal{N}(r^*) < \mathcal{N}(r)$, all rules $r_{k+1}, \cdots, r_m$ will be included in each reduct of $\mathcal{P}_2$. Now we show $\mathcal{B}'_2$ is an answer set of $\Pi' \cup \Pi''$. If Π' is a reduct of $\mathcal{P}_1$, then $\mathcal{B}'_1$ is an answer set of Π' and the result is true from Lemma 2.

Now suppose Π' is a proper subset of some reduct Π^* of $\mathcal{P}_1$, where $\Pi' = \Pi^* - \{r_p, \cdots, r_q\}$. Clearly, all rules $r_p, \cdots, r_q$ are eliminated from Π^* due to additional rules $r_{k+1}, \cdots, r_m$ are added into $\mathcal{P}_1$ to form $\mathcal{P}_2$. Therefore, we can assume that in the evaluation of reduct $\Pi' \cup \Pi''$ of $\mathcal{P}_2$, there exists some integer h such that

$$\Pi_0 = \Pi \cup \{L \leftarrow not\overline{L} \mid L \in \mathcal{B}_2\},$$

$\Pi_h = \Pi^* \cup \Pi''$,

$\Pi_{h+1} = \Pi_h - \{r_i, \cdots, r_j \mid$ there exists some $r \in \Pi''$ such that $\mathcal{N}(r) < \mathcal{N}(r_i), \cdots, \mathcal{N}(r) < \mathcal{N}(r_j)$ and $r_i, \cdots, r_j$ are defeated by $\Pi_h - \{r_i, \cdots, r_j\}\}$,

$\cdots$,

where $r_i, \cdots, r_j$ are the first set of rules eliminated from the reduct Π^* of $\mathcal{P}_1$ due to preferences $\mathcal{N}(r) < \mathcal{N}(r_i), \cdots, \mathcal{N}(r) < \mathcal{N}(r_j)$ for some $r \in \Pi''$. Note that since Π^* is a reduct of $\mathcal{P}_1$, no any other rules in Π^* can be further eliminated from preferences between rules in $\{L \leftarrow not\neg L \mid L \in \mathcal{B}_1\}$ and rules in Π. On the other hand, since for any rule $r' \in \{L \leftarrow not\overline{L} \mid L \in \mathcal{B}_1\}$, $\mathcal{N}(r') < \mathcal{N}(r_i), \cdots, \mathcal{N}(r') < \mathcal{N}(r_j)$, Π_{h+1} can be also specified as

$\Pi_{h+1} = \Pi_h - \{r_i, \cdots, r_j \mid$ there exists some $r' \in \{L \leftarrow not\overline{L} \mid$ $L \in \mathcal{B}_1\}$ such that $\mathcal{N}(r') < \mathcal{N}(r_i), \cdots,$ $\mathcal{N}(r') < \mathcal{N}(r_j)$ and $r_i, \cdots, r_j$ are defeated by $\Pi_h - \{r_i, \cdots, r_j\}\}$.

But this contradicts the fact that Π^* is a reduct of $\mathcal{P}_1$ where no any other rules can be further eliminated from preferences between rule r' and rules $r_i, \cdots, r_j$. So Π' must be a reduct of $\mathcal{P}_1$. ∎

Proof of Restricted Monotonicity Theorem 2
From Lemma 1, we know that $Update(\mathcal{B}, \Pi_2)$ is equivalent to a PLP $\mathcal{P} = (\{L \leftarrow not\overline{L} \mid L \in \mathcal{B}\} \cup \Pi_2, \mathcal{N}, <)$, where for each rule $r \in \{L \leftarrow not\overline{L} \mid L \in \mathcal{B}\}$ and each rule and each rule r' in Π_2, $N(r) < N(r')$. Then from Lemma 3, we know that each answer set of $\mathcal{P}$ is also an answer set of extended logic program $\{L \leftarrow not\overline{L} \mid L \in \mathcal{B}\} \cup \Pi_2$. Again from Lemmas 1 and 3, a resulting knowledge base with respect to $Update(\mathcal{B}, \Pi_1)$ can be viewed as an answer set of program $\{L \leftarrow not\overline{L} \mid L \in \mathcal{B}\} \cup \Pi_1$. Therefore, it is sufficient to prove that each consistent answer set $\mathcal{B}''$ of Π', where $\Pi' = \{L \leftarrow not\overline{L} \mid L \in \mathcal{B}\} \cup \Pi_2$, is also an answer set of $\{L \leftarrow \mid L \in \mathcal{B}'\} \cup (\Pi_2 - \Pi_1)$, where $\mathcal{B}'$ is an answer set of $\{L \leftarrow not\overline{L} \mid L \in \mathcal{B}\} \cup \Pi_1$. From condition $head(\Pi_2 - \Pi_1) \cap (\overline{\mathcal{B}} \cup body(\Pi_1)) = \emptyset$, this is simply followed from the Generalized Splitting Theorem (Theorem 4). ∎

6 Conclusion

In this paper we analyzed restricted monotonicity properties for rule based update. In particular, we provided two forms of restricted monotonicity theorems. Example 3 presented in section 3 illustrated an application of how these results are used to simplify update evaluations. In general, given an update specification $Update(\mathcal{B}, \Pi)$, two restricted monotonicity theorems can be applied alternatively and sequentially to split both $\mathcal{B}$ and Π into smaller and smaller parts such that the evaluation of $Update(\mathcal{B}, \Pi)$ can be significantly simplified (details have been shown in [9]).

Another contribution of this paper is that we proved a generalization of Lifschitz-Turner's Splitting Set Theorem. As Lifschitz-Turner's Splitting Set Theorem has illustrated its broad applications in exploring declarative semantics of logic programs, logic program based knowledge representation, and reasoning about action, e.g. [7], it is clear that our generalized splitting theorem will enhance these applications under an even weaker condition.

Acknowledgement

The author thanks Vladimir Lifschitz for examining the author's early version of the proof of the generalized splitting theorem. Thanks are also due to four anonymous referees for their criticisms and useful comments.

References

[1] C. Baral, Rule based updates on simple knowledge bases. In *Proceedings of the Eleventh National Conference on Artificial Intelligence (AAAI-94)*, pp 136-141. AAAI Press, 1994.

[2] J. Engelfriet, Monotonicity and persistence in preferential logics. *Journal of Artificial Intelligence Research*, 8: 1-12, 1998.

[3] M. Gelfond and V. Lifschitz, Classical negation in logic programs and disjunctive databases. *New Generation Computing*, **9** (1991) 365-386.

[4] V. Lifschitz and H. Turner, Splitting a logic program. In *Proceedings of Eleventh International Conference on Logic Programming*, pp 23-37. MIT Press, 1994.

[5] V.W. Marek and M. Truszczyński, Update by means of inference rules. In *Proceedings of JELIA'94, Lecture Notes in Artificial Intelligence*, 1994.

[6] T.C. Przymusinski and H. Turner, Update by means of inference rules. In *Proceedings of LPNMR'95, Lecture Notes in Artificial Intelligence*, pp 156-174. Springer-Verlag, 1995.

[7] H. Turner, Representing actions in logic programs and default theories: A situation calculus approach. *Journal of Logic Programming*, **31**, 1997.

[8] Y. Zhang and N.Y. Foo, Answer sets for prioritized logic programs. In *Proceedings of the 1997 International Logic Programming Symposium (ILPS'97)*, pp 69-83. MIT Press, 1997

[9] Y. Zhang, A framework of rule based update. Manuscript, April, 1999.

Transforming Inductive Definitions

Maurizio Proietti
IASI-CNR
Viale Manzoni 30, I-00185 Roma, Italy
proietti@iasi.rm.cnr.it

Alberto Pettorossi
DISP, University of Roma Tor Vergata,
Via di Tor Vergata, I-00133 Roma, Italy
adp@iasi.rm.cnr.it

Abstract

The main goal of this paper is to provide a common foundation to the theories
of correctness of program transformations for a large variety of programming languages.

We consider the notion of *rule set* and the notion of *inductive set* which is defined
by a rule set. We also consider a class of transformations of rule sets, called *rule
replacements*, which replace an old rule set by a new rule set. These replacements
can be viewed as generalizations of the most commonly used transformations, such
as folding and unfolding.

We study two methods for proving the correctness of rule replacements, that is,
for showing that the old rule set and the new rule set define the same inductive set.
These methods are: (i) the Unique Fixpoint Method, based on the well-foundedness
property of the new rule set, and (ii) the Improvement Method, based on the fact
that the premises of the old rule set are replaced by premises which have 'smaller'
proofs w.r.t. a suitable well-founded relation. Our Unique Fixpoint and Improvement Methods generalize many methods described in the literature which deal with
transformation rules for functional and logic programming languages. Our methods
have also the advantages of: (i) being parametric w.r.t. the well-founded relation
which is actually used, and (ii) being applicable to rules with finite or infinite sets
of premises.

1 Introduction

A large number of program transformation rules, which we will also call *transformations*, for brevity, have been proposed in the literature (see, for instance, [4, 13]
and [9] for a survey). These transformations may vary according to the programming language considered and the semantics to be preserved. For instance, program
transformations have been proposed for functional languages with eager or lazy semantics, for logic languages with least Herbrand model or computed answer semantics, for constraint and concurrent languages. For each language, the correctness of
these transformations is usually proved from scratch. The main goal of this paper
is to provide a common foundation to many different transformations proposed for
the different programming languages.

A methodology which is often used for defining the semantics of programming languages, is based on the concept of *inductive definitions* presented by means of *rule sets* (see, for instance, [1] for a survey of some theoretical results on inductive definitions, and [16] for their application to the definition of the operational semantics of some imperative, functional, and concurrent programming languages). A rule is pair of the form (X/y), also written as $\frac{X}{y}$, where X is a set of *premises* and y is a *conclusion*.

For instance, in the case of a simple recursive equation language with (i) integer constants n, (ii) variables x, (iii) binary operators **op** (such as $+$ and $\times$), (iv) the **if-then-else** construct, (iv) function applications, and (v) function declarations, we may define the operational semantics of call-by-value by the infinite set R of rules which are derived, as we will indicate below, from the following five schematic rules (here and in what follows we feel free to omit the curly brackets when writing a *set* of premises) [16]:

$$(r1) \quad \frac{}{n \rightarrow n} \qquad\qquad (r2) \quad \frac{t_1 \rightarrow n_1 \qquad t_2 \rightarrow n_2}{t_1 \text{ op } t_2 \ \rightarrow \ n} \ \text{ if } n = (n_1 \ op \ n_2)$$

$$(r3) \quad \frac{t_0 \rightarrow 0 \qquad t_1 \rightarrow n_1}{\text{if } t_0 \text{ then } t_1 \text{ else } t_2 \ \rightarrow \ n_1} \qquad (r4) \quad \frac{t_0 \rightarrow n_0 \qquad t_2 \rightarrow n_2}{\text{if } t_0 \text{ then } t_1 \text{ else } t_2 \ \rightarrow \ n_2} \ \text{ if } n_0 \neq 0$$

$$(r5) \quad \frac{t_1 \rightarrow n_1 \quad \dots \quad t_k \rightarrow n_k \quad d[n_1/x_1, \dots, n_k/x_k] \rightarrow n}{f(t_1, \dots, t_k) \ \rightarrow \ n}$$

where: (i) f is assumed to be defined by the declaration $f(x_1, \dots, x_k) = d$, (ii) $d[n/x]$ denotes the substitution of x by n in the expression d, and (iii) op is the semantic operator corresponding to the syntactic operator **op**.

Every rule in R is obtained as an instance of a schematic rule by replacing the metavariables $n, n_0, \dots, t_0, t_1, \dots$, by suitable elements of the set $\mathbf{N}$ of integers and the set **CTerms** of closed terms so that the given constraints (such as $n_0 \neq 0$ in rule $r4$) are satisfied.

Thus, the rule $\dfrac{3+1 \ \rightarrow \ 4 \qquad 2 \ \rightarrow \ 2}{(3+1)+2 \ \rightarrow \ 6}$ is in R because it is an instance of the schematic rule $r2$.

The set R of rules defines the binary relation $\rightarrow$ as a subset of **CTerms** $\times \mathbf{N}$ which is said to be the *inductive set* defined by R. The relation $\rightarrow$ is constructed as follows:
(i) take the following operator T_R from the powerset of **CTerms** $\times \mathbf{N}$ to the powerset of **CTerms** $\times \mathbf{N}$:

$$T_R(A) = \{(t \rightarrow n) \in \mathbf{CTerms} \times \mathbf{N} \mid \text{ there exists } \frac{X}{(t \rightarrow n)} \in R \text{ and } X \subseteq A\}$$

and then
(ii) take the relation $\rightarrow$ to be the least fixpoint of T_R (recall that T_R is a monotonic operator on the complete lattice given by the powerset of **CTerms** $\times \mathbf{N}$ ordered by $\subseteq$).

The methodology for specifying the semantics of programs based on inductive definitions, generalizes the technique for specifying the semantics of a definite logic program P which consists in taking the least fixpoint of the immediate consequence operator T_P [15]. Indeed, in the case a definite logic program P the set of rule instances is the set $Ground(P)$ of all ground instances of the clauses of P, and the operator $T_{Ground(P)}$ is equal to T_P.

Similarly, by means of rule sets one may define other semantics for logic programs such as the *computed answer* and the *finite failure* semantics (see, for instance, [7]).

In order to study the correctness of program transformations in a way that is independent of the specific programming language, in this paper we assume that the semantics of the language in use is defined by means of a set of rules whose premises and conclusions belong to a suitable domain.

Our approach relies on the fact that the transformation of a program P into a program Q induces a transformation on the rule set, say $R(P)$, that defines the semantics of P into the rule set, say $R(Q)$, that defines the semantics of Q. Thus, the preservation of the semantics of P which expresses the *correctness* of the transformation as we will specify below, can be established by proving that the two sets of rules $R(P)$ and $R(Q)$ define the same inductive set.

In this paper we consider transformations of sets of rules, called *rule replacements*, which are very general. Indeed, we have that the most commonly used program transformations, such as folding and unfolding [4], induce rule replacements.

Usually, a program transformation is a *conditional* transformation, that is, a transformation which is applied to a program P only if a given property holds w.r.t. the semantics of P. Typical properties which are required to hold, are often expressed as *implications* or *equivalences*. Thus, we are lead to consider the problem of showing the correctness of a rule replacement when a suitable implication or equivalence formula holds in the inductive set defined by the given rule set. For instance, consider the rule set:

$$R: \quad \frac{}{a} \quad \frac{a}{b} \quad \frac{a \; b}{c}$$

We have that the inductive set $I(R)$ defined by R is $\{a,b,c\}$. We may say that the sets $\{a,b\}$ and $\{a\}$ of premises are equivalent w.r.t. the inductive set $I(R)$ in the sense that $\{a,b\}$ is a subset of $I(R)$ iff so is $\{a\}$. Now, if we replace the rule $\frac{a \; b}{c}$ with the set $\{a,b\}$ of premises, by the rule $\frac{a}{c}$ with the equivalent set $\{a\}$ of premises (and this replacement can be viewed as an unfolding transformation whereby b is replaced by a according to the second rule $\frac{a}{b}$), then we get:

$$S_1: \quad \frac{}{a} \quad \frac{a}{b} \quad \frac{a}{c}$$

and we have that the inductive set $I(S_1)$ defined by the new set S_1 of rules, is equal to $I(R)$.

Also $\{a\}$ and $\{b\}$ are equivalent w.r.t. $I(R)$. Unfortunately, in spite of this equivalence, if we replace a with b in the premise of the second rule of R (and this replacement can be viewed as a folding transformation), we get the following new set of rules:

$$S_2: \quad \frac{}{a} \quad \frac{b}{b} \quad \frac{a \; b}{c}$$

and now we have that the inductive set defined by S_2, which is $\{a\}$, is *not* equal to $I(R)$.

This example shows that when transforming an old rule set R into a new rule set by replacing some rules in R with other rules which have equivalent sets of premises w.r.t. $I(R)$, one may change the corresponding inductive set. Below we will present some sufficient conditions which ensure the preservation of the inductive sets, both in a weak form (*partial correctness*) and in a strong form (*total correctness*), and we will also present two methods which guarantee total correctness.

The plan of the paper is as follows. In Section 2 we give some preliminary definitions concerning rule sets and the corresponding inductive sets, and we present some basic results. In Section 3 we introduce our rule replacement transformation and we prove its partial correctness and completeness. Then in Sections 4 and 5, we consider two methods, namely the Unique Fixpoint Method and the Improvement Method, to prove the total correctness of a rule replacement. In Section 6 we provide a generalization of the Improvement Method where the notion of improvement is parametric w.r.t. the measure of the proof trees constructed via rule sets.

2 Inductive Definitions by Rule Sets

In this section we summarize some well-known basic concepts and results in the theory of inductive definitions (see, for instance, [1, 16]).

Definition 1 (Rule Set) Let D be a set.
(i) A *rule* over D is a pair (X/y) where $X \subseteq D$ and $y \in D$. X is said to be the set of *premises* of the rule and y is said to be the *conclusion* of the rule. A rule (X/y) will also be written as

$$\frac{}{y} \quad \text{if } X = \emptyset, \text{ and as} \quad \frac{x_1 \ \cdots \ x_n \ \cdots}{y} \quad \text{if } X = \{x_1, \ldots, x_n, \ldots\}.$$

(ii) A *rule set* over D is a (finite or infinite) set of rules over D.
(iii) Given a rule set R over D, a set $A \subseteq D$ is *R-closed* iff for every rule (X/y) in R, if $X \subseteq A$ then $y \in A$.

Given a rule set R over D we can introduce, as indicated in the following definitions, a set $I(R) \subseteq D$, called the *inductive set* defined by R. Let $\wp(D)$ denote the powerset of D.

Definition 2 (Immediate Consequence Operator) Let R be a rule set over D. (i) The *immediate consequence operator associated with R* is the function $T_R : \wp(D) \to \wp(D)$, defined as follows:

$$T_R(A) = \{y \in D \mid \text{there exists } (X/y) \in R \text{ and } X \subseteq A\}$$

(ii) A set $A \subseteq D$ is a *fixpoint* of T_R iff $T_R(A) = A$. A is a *prefixpoint* of T_R iff $T_R(A) \subseteq A$. A is a *postfixpoint* of T_R iff $T_R(A) \supseteq A$.

T_R is a monotonic operator on the complete lattice $\wp(D)$ ordered by $\subseteq$. We have the following properties.

Theorem 1 (i) T_R has a least fixpoint, denoted by $lfp(T_R)$, which is equal to its least prefixpoint.
(ii) T_R has a greatest fixpoint, denoted by $gfp(T_R)$, which is equal to its greatest postfixpoint.

Definition 3 (Inductive Set) *The* inductive set *defined by a rule set R over D, denoted by $I(R)$, is the least fixpoint of the operator T_R.*

It follows directly from the definitions and Theorem 1 that $I(R)$ is the *smallest R-closed subset of D*.

3   Transformations of Rule Sets

In this section we consider the *rule replacement* transformation which given a rule set R, generates a new rule set S by replacing some rules of R by new rules, if suitable implications or equivalences hold w.r.t. the inductive set $I(R)$. We present a sufficient condition for the partial correctness of rule replacement, that is, a condition which ensures that $I(R) \supseteq I(S)$. We also show that the rule replacement transformation is *complete*, in the sense that given any two rule sets which define the same inductive set, we can derive one from the other by suitable rule replacements.

Every set of rules can be partitioned into subsets of rules which have the same conclusion. Thus, every rule replacement which derives the rule set S from the rule set R, can be viewed as replacing, for each conclusion d, the set R_d of the sets of premises relative to d, by a new set S_d of sets of premises. In what follows we will study the correctness of rule replacements when suitable implications or equivalences hold between the sets of sets of premises which correspond to the same conclusion.

We start off by defining the following concept of implication between sets of sets of premises.

Definition 4 Let R be a rule set over D and $\mathbf{X}$, $\mathbf{Z}$ be sets of subsets of D. We write:
(i) $I(R) \models \mathbf{X} \rightarrow \mathbf{Z}$ iff   for all $X \in \mathbf{X}$, if $X \subseteq I(R)$ then there exists $Z \in \mathbf{Z}$ such that $Z \subseteq I(R)$,
(ii) $I(R) \models \mathbf{X} \leftarrow \mathbf{Z}$ iff $I(R) \models \mathbf{Z} \rightarrow \mathbf{X}$,
(iii) $I(R) \models \mathbf{X} \leftrightarrow \mathbf{Z}$ iff $I(R) \models \mathbf{X} \rightarrow \mathbf{Z}$ and $I(R) \models \mathbf{X} \leftarrow \mathbf{Z}$.

The following properties follow directly from the definition. Let us consider a rule set R over D. Let A be a subset of D and $\mathbf{W}$, $\mathbf{X}$, and $\mathbf{Z}$ be sets of subsets of D. We have that:

(i) if $\forall X \in \mathbf{X}.\ \exists Z \in \mathbf{Z}.\ Z \subseteq X$ then $I(R) \models \mathbf{X} \rightarrow \mathbf{Z}$

(ii) for any $\mathbf{X} \subseteq \mathbf{Z}$, $I(R) \models \mathbf{X} \rightarrow \mathbf{Z}$, and in particular,
for any $\mathbf{X}$, $I(R) \models \{\} \rightarrow \mathbf{X}$, $I(R) \models \mathbf{X} \rightarrow \wp(D)$, and $I(R) \models \mathbf{X} \rightarrow \mathbf{X}$ (*reflexivity*)

(iii) for any $\mathbf{X}$, $\mathbf{W}$, and $\mathbf{Z}$, if $I(R) \models \mathbf{X} \rightarrow \mathbf{W}$ and $I(R) \models \mathbf{W} \rightarrow \mathbf{Z}$ then $I(R) \models \mathbf{X} \rightarrow \mathbf{Z}$ (*transitivity*)

(iv) for any A, $\mathbf{X}$, $\mathbf{W}$, and $\mathbf{Z}$, if $I(R) \models \mathbf{X} \rightarrow \mathbf{Z}$ then
$\quad I(R) \models \mathbf{W} \cup \mathbf{X} \rightarrow \mathbf{W} \cup \mathbf{Z}$ (*monotonicity* w.r.t. $\cup$) and
$\quad I(R) \models \{A \cup X \mid X \in \mathbf{X}\} \rightarrow \{A \cup Z \mid Z \in \mathbf{Z}\}$ (*distributivity*).

Definition 5 (Rule Replacement) (i) A *rule replacement* ρ is a pair (R, S) of rule sets over D, denoted by $\rho : R \mapsto S$. Given $\rho : R \mapsto S$, we say that the rule set S *is derived from* the rule set R *via* ρ.

(ii) Given a rule set R over D, for each $d \in D$ we define $R_d = \{X \subseteq D \mid (X/d) \in R\}$.

(iii) The rule replacement $\rho : R \mapsto S$ is *implication-based*, written $I(R) \models R \Rightarrow S$, iff for all $d \in D$, $I(R) \models R_d \rightarrow S_d$.
ρ is *reverse-implication-based*, written $I(R) \models R \Leftarrow S$, iff for all $d \in D$, $I(R) \models R_d \leftarrow S_d$.
ρ is *equivalence-based*, written $I(R) \models R \Leftrightarrow S$, iff for all $d \in D$, $I(R) \models R_d \leftrightarrow S_d$.

(iv) The rule replacement $\rho : R \mapsto S$ is *partially correct* iff $I(R) \supseteq I(S)$; it is *increasing* iff $I(R) \subseteq I(S)$; it is *totally correct* iff it is partially correct and increasing, that is, $I(R) = I(S)$.

The rules for unfolding, folding, and goal replacement usually considered in logic program transformation are examples of rule replacements. For instance, let us consider the following logic program:

$$P = \{p \leftarrow q, r \quad q \leftarrow t \quad q \leftarrow \quad r \leftarrow\}.$$

Every clause $h \leftarrow body$ of P can be viewed as the rule $\dfrac{body}{h}$ over the domain $D = \{p, q, r, t\}$. By unfolding the atom q in the first clause of P, we get the new program:

$$Q = \{p \leftarrow t, r \quad p \leftarrow r \quad q \leftarrow t \quad q \leftarrow \quad r \leftarrow\}.$$

We have that $I(P) = \{p, q, r\}$. We also have that for each element $d \in D$, $I(P) \models P_d \leftrightarrow Q_d$. Indeed,
for p, $I(P) \models \{\{q, r\}\} \leftrightarrow \{\{t, r\}, \{r\}\}$,
for q, $I(P) \models \{\{t\}, \emptyset\} \leftrightarrow \{\{t\}, \emptyset\}$,
for r, $I(P) \models \{\emptyset\} \leftrightarrow \{\emptyset\}$, and
for t, $I(P) \models \{\} \leftrightarrow \{\}$. Thus, $I(P) \models P \Leftrightarrow Q$.

We show below that reverse-implication-based rule replacement is partially correct. However, in general, equivalence-based rule replacement is not increasing, and thus, it is not totally correct, that is, $I(R) \models R \Leftrightarrow S$ does not imply $I(R) = I(S)$.

To see this, let us consider the following rule replacement $\rho : R \mapsto S$, where R and S are the following rule sets over $D = \{a, b\}$:

$$R : \frac{}{a} \quad \frac{a}{b} \qquad S : \frac{}{a} \quad \frac{b}{b}$$

We have that $I(R) = \{a, b\}$. $I(R) \models R \Leftrightarrow S$ holds because: (i) for a we have that $I(R) \models \{\emptyset\} \leftrightarrow \{\emptyset\}$, and (ii) for b we have that $I(R) \models \{\{a\}\} \leftrightarrow \{\{b\}\}$. However, $I(S) = \{a\} \neq I(R)$.

The following theorem shows that equivalence-based rule replacement is *complete* for the derivation of equivalent rule sets, in the sense that for any two rule sets, say R and S, which define the same inductive set, we can derive S from R via an equivalence-based rule replacement.

Theorem 2 (Completeness of Equivalence-Based Rule Replacement)
If $I(R) = I(S)$ then $I(R) \models R \Leftrightarrow S$.

Proof. Since $I(S)$ is a fixpoint of T_S and $I(R) = I(S)$, we have that $I(R) = T_S(I(R))$.

We have to prove that for any $d \in D$, $I(R) \models R_d \rightarrow S_d$ and $I(R) \models S_d \rightarrow R_d$. Let us now consider an element $d \in D$.

If $X \in R_d$ and $X \subseteq I(R)$ then $d \in I(R)$, because $I(R)$ is R-closed. Then, because $I(R) = T_S(I(R))$, there exists $Z \in S_d$ such that $Z \subseteq I(R)$. Thus, we have that $I(R) \models R_d \rightarrow S_d$.

If $Z \in S_d$ and $Z \subseteq I(R)$ then $d \in I(R)$, because $I(R) = T_S(I(R))$. Since $I(R) = T_R(I(R))$, there exists $X \in R_d$ such that $X \subseteq I(R)$. Thus, we have that $I(R) \models S_d \rightarrow R_d$. $\square$

We end this section by proving that reverse-implication-based rule replacements are partially correct.

Theorem 3 (Partial Correctness) *If $I(R) \models R \Leftarrow S$ then $I(R) \supseteq I(S)$.*

Proof. If $d \in T_S(I(R))$ then, by definition of T_S, there exists $(Z/d) \in S$ (i.e., $Z \in S_d$) and $Z \subseteq I(R)$. Since $I(R) \models R \Leftarrow S$, there exists $(X/d) \in R$ (i.e., $X \in R_d$) such that $X \subseteq I(R)$. By the fact that $I(R)$ is R-closed, it follows that $d \in I(R)$. Thus, $T_S(I(R)) \subseteq I(R)$, that is, $I(R)$ is a prefixpoint of T_S and, since $lfp(T_S)$ is the *least* prefixpoint of T_S (see Theorem 1), we have that $I(R) \supseteq lfp(T_S) = I(S)$. $\square$

4   The Unique Fixpoint Method

In this section we study a method for proving that a rule replacement $\rho : R \mapsto S$ is increasing, that is $I(R) \subseteq I(S)$. This method is based on the fact that, when a rule set R is *terminating* in the sense specified below, its corresponding immediate consequence operator T_R has a unique fixpoint. By combining the method for proving that $\rho : R \mapsto S$ is increasing, with the Partial Correctness Theorem 3, we have a method for for showing that $I(R) = I(S)$, that is, the *total correctness* of the rule replacement.

Other sufficient conditions for showing the total correctness of rule replacements, based on the notion of *proof*, will be considered in the subsequent sections.

Definition 6 A rule set R over D is *terminating* iff for all d_0 in D there is no infinite sequence $s = \langle d_0, d_1, \ldots, d_i, d_{i+1}, \ldots \rangle$ of elements of D, such that for all d_i and d_{i+1} in s, there exists a rule (X/d_i) in R and d_{i+1} in X.

A well-founded relation is a binary relation $\succ$ on a set D such that there is no infinite sequence $d_0 \succ d_1 \succ \ldots \succ d_i \succ d_{i+1} \succ \ldots$ of elements of D.

Theorem 4 (Characterization of Terminating Rule Sets) *A rule set R over D is terminating iff there exists a well-founded relation $\succ$ on D such that for all rules (X/y) in R and for all x in X we have that $y \succ x$.*

Proof. (If part.) Let s be a sequence $\langle d_0, d_1, \ldots, d_i, d_{i+1}, \ldots \rangle$ of elements of D. Then for all d_i and d_{i+1} in s we have that $d_i \succ d_{i+1}$ and thus, by the hypothesis that $\succ$ is well-founded, we have that s is finite.
(Only if part.) Let us consider the relation $\succ$ on D such that $y \succ x$ iff there exists a rule $(X/y) \in R$ and $x \in X$. If R is terminating then $\succ$ is a well-founded relation. $\square$

Bezem [2] gives a characterization of terminating definite logic programs which is similar to our characterization of terminating rule sets. In [2] a program P is said to be terminating iff for all ground goals G, all SLD-derivations of P starting from G are finite. Bezem's result says that a definite logic program P is terminating iff there exists a function $|.|$ from the set B_P of all ground atoms in the Herbrand universe to the set of natural numbers such that, for all ground instances $A \leftarrow B_1, \ldots, B_n$ of clauses in P, and for all $i \in \{1, \ldots, n\}$, we have that $|A| > |B_i|$, where $>$ is the *greater than* relation on natural numbers.

However, it may happen that a program P has an infinite SLD-derivation for some ground goal and, at the same time, there exists a well-founded relation, say $\succ$, on B_P such that for each ground instance of a clause in P the head is in the $\succ$ relation with each atom of the body. This means that in Bezem's characterization the $>$ ordering on natural numbers cannot be replaced by an arbitrary well-founded relation.

Consider, for instance, the program Q:

$p(a) \leftarrow q(X)$
$q(f(X)) \leftarrow q(X)$

For this program there exists the following infinite SLD-derivation:

$p(a), \ q(X1), \ q(X2), \ \ldots$

and there exists also a well-founded relation $\succ$ on B_Q such that for each ground instance $h \leftarrow b$ of a clause in Q, it is the case that $h \succ b$. Indeed, such a well-founded relation $\succ$ is defined as follows:

for all ground terms t and u in the Herbrand universe,
$p(t) \succ q(u) \quad \text{and} \quad q(f(t)) \succ q(t).$ $\qquad\qquad$ □

Theorem 5 *If R is a terminating rule set, then $I(R)$ is the unique fixpoint of T_R.*

Proof. By Theorem 4 there exists a well-founded relation $\succ$ such that, for all rules $(X/y) \in R$ and for all $x \in X$, we have that $y \succ x$. We now prove that T_R has a unique fixpoint. Let us assume that there are two fixpoints A and B of T_R and we prove by well-founded induction w.r.t. $\succ$ that $y \in A$ iff $y \in B$.

The inductive hypothesis is: for all $x \in D$, if $y \succ x$ then $(x \in A$ iff $x \in B)$.

If $y \in A$ then there exists a rule $(X/y) \in R$ with $X \subseteq A$, because A is a fixpoint of T_R. We also have that for all $x' \in X$, $y \succ x'$ and therefore, by the inductive hypothesis, $x' \in B$. Thus, $X \subseteq B$ and, since B is a fixpoint of T_R and $(X/y) \in R$, we have that $y \in B$. Similarly, we can prove that if $y \in B$ then $y \in A$.

Thus, $I(R)$, which is the least fixpoint of T_R (see Theorem 1), is also the unique fixpoint of T_R. $\qquad\qquad$ □

Theorem 5 is related to a result of Bezem [2], which states that if a definite logic program P is terminating then $T_P^\omega(\emptyset) = T_P^\omega(B_P)$. Indeed, from $T_P^\omega(\emptyset) = lfp(T_P) \subseteq gfp(T_P) \subseteq T_P^\omega(B_P)$ and $T_P^\omega(\emptyset) = T_P^\omega(B_P)$, we have that $lfp(T_P) = gfp(T_P)$ and thus, T_P has a unique fixpoint.

In order to prove that a rule replacement is increasing we may use the following lemma.

Lemma 1 *If $I(R) \models R \Rightarrow S$ then $I(R) \subseteq gfp(T_S)$.*

Proof. Take any $d \in I(R)$. Then there exists $(X/d) \in R$ (i.e., $X \in R_d$) and $X \subseteq I(R)$, because $I(R) = T_R(I(R))$. Since $I(R) \models R \Rightarrow S$, there exists $(Z/d) \in S$ (i.e., $Z \in S_d$) such that $Z \subseteq I(R)$. By the definition of T_S, from $Z \subseteq I(R)$ we have that $d \in T_S(I(R))$. Thus, $T_S(I(R)) \supseteq I(R)$, that is, $I(R)$ is a postfixpoint of T_S and, since $gfp(T_S)$ is the *greatest* postfixpoint of T_S (see Theorem 1), we have that $I(R) \subseteq gfp(T_S)$. $\qquad\qquad$ □

We now present our sufficient condition for a rule replacement to be increasing. This condition is based on the assumption that the rule set derived by rule replacement is terminating.

Lemma 2 (Unique Fixpoint Lemma) *If $I(R) \models R \Rightarrow S$ and S is terminating, then $I(R) \subseteq I(S)$.*

Proof. By Lemma 1 and Theorem 5, we have that $I(R) \subseteq gfp(T_S) = lfp(T_S) = I(S)$. $\qquad\qquad$ □

By combining Theorem 3 and Lemma 2 we have the following result.

494

Theorem 6 (Total Correctness: Unique Fixpoint Method) *If $\rho : R \mapsto S$ is a rule replacement such that $I(R) \models R \Leftrightarrow S$ and S is terminating, then $I(R) = I(S)$.*

5 The Improvement Method

The Unique Fixpoint Method (that is, Theorem 6) cannot be used to prove the total correctness of an equivalence-based rule replacement $\rho : R \mapsto S$ when the rule set S is not terminating. In this section we consider a different method, called *Improvement Method* for proving the total correctness of $\rho : R \mapsto S$, which is applicable also in the case where S is not terminating. The Improvement Method relies on the notion of *R-proofs* (that is, proofs which use the rules of R) and it ensures the total correctness of $\rho : R \mapsto S$ when the premises of S have smaller R-proofs than the corresponding premises of R.

Our Improvement Method is named after Sands' method for proving the total correctness of some transformations of higher-order functional programs [11]. Sands' Improvement Method can be derived from our Improvement Method by defining the semantics of higher-order functional programs by means of rule sets (see, for instance, the 'big step' operational semantics of higher-order functional languages in [16]).

Also the method based on the size of the smallest proof of an atom used in [13] to prove the correctness of the unfolding, folding, and goal replacement transformations of logic programs can be derived by the Improvement Method presented here.

In this section we consider *finitary* rule sets, that is, we assume that the set of premises of each rule is finite.

Definition 7 (Finitary R-Proofs) Let R be a finitary rule set over D and $d \in D$. A *finitary R-proof of d* is a finite tree π_d whose nodes are labeled by elements of D such that:

(i) the root of π_d is labeled by d,

(ii) if a leaf of π_d is labeled by y, then $(\emptyset/y) \in R$, and

(iii) if a node N of π_d is labeled by y and the sons of N are labeled by $x_1, \ldots, x_n$, then $(\{x_1, \ldots, x_n\}/y) \in R$.

Given a finite subset A of D, a *finitary R-proof of A* is the set $\pi_A = \{\pi_d \mid d \in A\}$. The *size* of π_A is the number $\sigma(\pi_A)$ of nodes in π_A.

We denote by $\Pi(R)$ the union of the set of all finitary R-proofs of elements of D and the set of all finitary R-proofs of finite subsets of D.

When understood from the context, we will simply say R-proof, instead of finitary R-proof.

Definition 8 Let R be a finitary rule set over D. For any finite set $A \subseteq D$, we say that A is *R-provable*, written $R \vdash A$, iff there exists an R-proof of A.

We have the following characterization of the inductive set defined by a finitary rule set (see, for instance, [1, 16]).

Theorem 7 *Given a finitary rule set R over D and a finite subset A of D, we have that $A \subseteq I(R)$ iff $R \vdash A$.*

Definition 9 Let R be a finitary rule set over D and $\rho : R \mapsto S$ be a rule replacement.

(i) For $\mathbf{X}, \mathbf{Z} \subseteq \wp(D)$, $\mathbf{X}$ *is* $\geq$-*improved by* $\mathbf{Z}$ *in* R, written $\Pi(R) \models \mathbf{X} \geq \mathbf{Z}$, iff for all $X \in \mathbf{X}$, if there exists an R-proof π_X of X then there exist $Z \in \mathbf{Z}$ and $\pi_Z \in \Pi(R)$ such that $\sigma(\pi_X) \geq \sigma(\pi_Z)$.

(ii) We write $\Pi(R) \models R \geq S$ iff for all $d \in D$, $\Pi(R) \models R_d \geq S_d$.

From Theorem 7 it follows that $\Pi(R) \models \mathbf{X} \geq \mathbf{Z}$ implies $I(R) \models \mathbf{X} \to \mathbf{Z}$ and, thus, $\Pi(R) \models R \geq S$ implies $I(R) \models R \Rightarrow S$.

Lemma 3 (Improvement) *Let R be a finitary rule set over D and $\rho : R \mapsto S$ be a rule replacement such that $\Pi(R) \models R \geq S$. Then $I(R) \subseteq I(S)$.*

Proof. By Theorem 7 it is enough to prove that for all $\pi_d \in \Pi(R)$ with $d \in D$, we have that $d \in I(S)$. We will prove this fact by well-founded induction w.r.t. $>$.

Take $\pi_d \in \Pi(R)$ with $d \in D$. Assume that for all R-proofs π_y with $y \in D$, if $\sigma(\pi_d) > \sigma(\pi_y)$ then $y \in I(S)$.

If the root of π_d has $m \geq 0$ sons, labeled by $x_1, \dots, x_m$, then by the definition of R-proof (see Definition 7), $\{x_1, \dots, x_m\} \in R_d$ and there exists an R-proof $\pi_{\{x_1,\dots,x_m\}}$ of $\{x_1, \dots, x_m\}$ such that $\sigma(\pi_d) > \sigma(\pi_{\{x_1,\dots,x_m\}})$. Now, since $\Pi(R) \models R \geq S$, there exist $\{z_1, \dots, z_n\} \in S_d$ and an R-proof $\pi_{\{z_1,\dots,z_n\}}$ of $\{z_1, \dots, z_n\}$ such that $\sigma(\pi_{\{x_1,\dots,x_m\}}) \geq \sigma(\pi_{\{z_1,\dots,z_n\}})$.

Thus, for $i = 1, \dots, n$, we have that $\sigma(\pi_d) > \sigma(\pi_{\{x_1,\dots,x_m\}}) \geq \sigma(\pi_{\{z_1,\dots,z_n\}}) \geq \sigma(\pi_{z_i})$. Then, by the induction hypothesis, we have that for $i = 1, \dots, n$, $z_i \in I(S)$ and, since $\{z_1, \dots, z_n\} \in S_d$ and $I(S)$ is S-closed, we have that $d \in I(S)$. $\square$

By combining Theorem 3 and Lemma 3 we have the following result.

Theorem 8 (Total Correctness: Improvement Method) *Let R be a finitary rule set. If $\rho : R \mapsto S$ is a rule replacement such that $I(R) \models R \Leftarrow S$ and $\Pi(R) \models R \geq S$, then $I(R) = I(S)$.*

6   The Well-Founded Improvement Method

In this section we generalize the Improvement Method in two ways: (i) we consider rule sets that are possibly not finitary, that is, rule sets with a possibly infinite number of premises, such that their associated immediate consequence operators are *continuous* (notice that for any *finitary* rule set R, the operator T_R is continuous), and (ii) we replace the concept of *size* of a proof by that of a function into an arbitrary well-founded set. The resulting method will be called *Well-Founded Improvement Method.*

Definition 10 (Finite Depth R-Proofs) Let R be a (possibly not finitary) rule set over D and $d \in D$. A *finite depth R-proof* of d is a tree φ_d whose nodes are labeled by elements of D such that:

(i) the root of φ_d is labeled by d,

(ii) if a leaf of φ_d is labeled by y, then $(\emptyset/y) \in R$,

(iii) if a node N of φ_d is labeled by y and $X = \{x \mid x \text{ is the label of a son of } N\}$, then $(X/y) \in R$, and

(iv) each branch of φ_d has finite length.

Given a (finite or infinite) subset A of D, a *finite depth R-proof of A* is the set $\varphi_A = \{\varphi_d \mid d \in A\}$.

Notice that a finite depth R-proof is a tree with possibly infinite branching. When understood from the context we will simply say R-proof, instead of finite depth R-proof.

As in the case of finitary rule sets, for a finite or infinite A, we write $R \vdash A$ iff there exists a finite depth R-proof of A.

We denote by $\Phi(R)$ the union of the set of all finite depth R-proofs of elements of D and the set of all finite depth R-proofs of subsets of D.

Obviously, we have that for every A, if $R \vdash A$ then $A \subseteq I(R)$. The reader may verify that the converse does not hold for rule sets which are not finitary. However, we have the following result.

A rule set R whose immediate consequence operator T_R is continuous, is said to be a *continuous rule set*.

Theorem 9 *Let R be a continuous rule set over D. For every (finite or infinite) $A \subseteq D$, we have that: $A \subseteq I(R)$ iff $R \vdash A$.*

Let $\succ$ be a transitive well-founded relation on a set W and let $\succeq$ be the partial order $(\succ \cup =)$. Let R be a rule set over D and $\mu : \Phi(R) \to W$ be a function such that the following two properties hold:

- *(Father-Son Monotonicity)* for all $\varphi_d \in \Phi(R)$, with $d \in D$, such that X is the set of elements of D labeling the sons of the root of φ_d, there exists $\varphi_X \in \Phi(R)$ such that $\mu(\varphi_d) \succ \mu(\varphi_X)$, and

- *(Membership Monotonicity)* for all $\varphi_Z \in \Phi(R)$, with $Z \subseteq D$, and for all $z \in Z$, there exists φ_z such that $\mu(\varphi_Z) \succeq \mu(\varphi_z)$.

Definition 11 Let R be a rule set over D and $\rho : R \mapsto S$ be a rule replacement.
(i) For $\mathbf{X}, \mathbf{Z} \subseteq \wp(D)$, $\mathbf{X}$ *is $\succeq$-improved by $\mathbf{Z}$ in R*, written $\Phi(R) \models \mathbf{X} \succeq \mathbf{Z}$, iff for all $X \in \mathbf{X}$, if there exists an R-proof φ_X of X then there exist $Z \in \mathbf{Z}$ and $\varphi_Z \in \Phi(R)$ such that $\mu(\varphi_X) \succeq \mu(\varphi_Z)$.
(ii) We write $\Phi(R) \models R \succeq S$ iff for all $d \in D$, $\Phi(R) \models R_d \succeq S_d$.

Similarly to Section 5, for a *continuous* rule set R, we have that $\Phi(R) \models \mathbf{X} \succeq \mathbf{Z}$ implies $I(R) \models \mathbf{X} \to \mathbf{Z}$ and, thus, $\Phi(R) \models R \succeq S$ implies $I(R) \models R{\Rightarrow}S$.

Lemma 4 (Well-Founded Improvement) *Let R be a continuous rule set over D and $\rho : R \mapsto S$ be a rule replacement such that $\Phi(R) \models R \succeq S$. Then $I(R) \subseteq I(S)$.*

Proof. Similarly to the proof of Theorem 3, we show, by well-founded induction w.r.t. $\succ$, that for all R-proofs φ_d with $d \in D$, we have that $d \in I(S)$. This property implies the thesis because R is continuous and, by Theorem 9, d has an R-proof iff $d \in I(R)$.

Take $\varphi_d \in \Phi(R)$ with $d \in D$. Suppose that for all R-proofs φ_y with $y \in D$, if $\mu(\varphi_d) \succ \mu(\varphi_y)$ then $y \in I(S)$.

Let X be the set of elements of D that label the sons of the root of φ_d. Then by the definition of R-proof (see Definition 10), $X \in R_d$ and by the father-son monotonicity property there exists an R-proof φ_X of X such that $\mu(\varphi_d) \succ \mu(\varphi_X)$. Since $\Phi(R) \models R \succeq S$, there exist $Z \in S_d$ and an R-proof φ_Z of Z such that $\mu(\varphi_X) \succeq \mu(\varphi_Z)$.

By using the membership monotonicity property of μ, for all $z \in Z$, there exists φ_z such that $\mu(\varphi_Z) \succeq \mu(\varphi_z)$. Thus, for all $z \in Z$, we have that: $\mu(\varphi_d) \succ \mu(\varphi_X) \succeq \mu(\varphi_Z) \succeq \mu(\varphi_z)$. Then, by the induction hypothesis, for all $z \in Z$, we have that $z \in I(S)$ and thus, $Z \subseteq I(S)$. Since $Z \in S_d$ (i.e., $(Z/d) \in S$) and $I(S)$ is S-closed, we conclude that $d \in I(S)$. □

Thus, by combining Theorem 3 and Lemma 4 we have the following result.

Theorem 10 (Total Correctness: Well-Founded Improvement Method)
Let R be a continuous rule set and $\rho : R \mapsto S$ be a rule replacement. If $I(R) \models R \Leftarrow S$ and $\Phi(R) \models R \succeq S$, then $I(R) = I(S)$.

7 Related Work and Conclusions

We have presented a theory of *transformations of inductive definitions* which provides a common foundation for the theories of *transformations of programs* developed within various programming languages.

The methods for proving the correctness of the transformations of rule sets we have presented here, are generalizations of methods used in specific frameworks, mainly in the field of functional and logic programming. Our Unique Fixpoint Method is related to McCarthy's recursion induction principle for proving the equivalence of two continuous functions on flat cpo's [8]. The use of McCarthy's principle was also suggested as a technique for proving the correctness of the folding and unfolding transformations in the seminal paper by Burstall and Darlington [4]. A method for proving the equivalence of recursive applicative program schemata based on the existence of a unique fixpoint of a set of equations, was also studied by Courcelle [5].

The Improvement Method and the Well-Founded Improvement Method are generalizations of several methods used in functional and logic programming for proving that program transformations, such as folding, unfolding, and replacement, are correct. In particular, Sands [11] has proposed the so called *Local Improvement* Method, which consists in replacing an expression e_1 in the definition of a higher-order function by a new expression e_2 which is semantically equivalent to e_1 and, for each closing context $C[\_]$, $C[e_2]$ evaluates to weak head normal form in no more reduction steps than $C[e_1]$. This method can be derived from ours because: (i) the semantics of higher-order functional programs can be described in terms of inductive definitions (over the set of closed expressions), (ii) the replacement of semantically equivalent expressions can be viewed as a particular case of equivalence-based rule replacement, and (iii) the evaluation of an expression to weak head normal form can be viewed as a proof whose size corresponds to the number of reduction steps.

Various other methods which have been used for proving the correctness of the folding, unfolding, and goal replacement transformations of definite logic programs, can be derived by our Well-Founded Improvement Method. Among these methods we would like to mention the ones used in: (i) the landmark paper by Tamaki and Sato [13], where the authors prove a correctness result for the above mentioned transformations w.r.t. the least Herbrand model, (ii) the generalization of [13] that the same authors presented in [14], where a lexicographic ordering between atoms is adopted for proving the correctness of a more powerful folding transformation, and (iii) the papers [3, 6, 12] which extend the proofs of correctness of the folding and unfolding transformations w.r.t. universal termination, computed answer substitutions, and finite failure semantics.

For lack of space, we have not presented these special cases in detail. However, in all these cases one may: (i) describe the appropriate semantics for definite logic programs as an inductive set defined by a set of rules over a suitable domain, (ii) show that the folding, unfolding, and goal replacement transformations induce rule replacements of this set of rules, and (iii) derive the specific measure on proofs to be used for proving the correctness of the program transformations as an instance of our μ measure enjoying the father-son and membership monotonicity properties.

Finally, as work related to ours, we would like to mention a recent paper by Roychoudhury et al. [10], where the authors present a parametrized framework for proving correctness conditions w.r.t. the least Herbrand model for various extensions of the folding rule originally proposed in [13]. This framework is parametrized w.r.t. an abstract measure of atoms (not *proofs*, as we do). The properties of this abstract measure are more specific than the ones required here for the function μ used in our Well-Founded Improvement Method. In particular, the framework of [10] requires the existence of a 4-tuple $\langle \mathcal{M}, \oplus, \preceq, \mathcal{W} \rangle$ such that: (i) $\langle \mathcal{M}, \oplus \rangle$ is a *commutative group* with identity $0 \in \mathcal{M}$, (ii) $\preceq$ is a *linear order*, (iii) $\oplus$ is a *monotone* operation w.r.t. $\preceq$, and $\mathcal{W}$ is a subset of $\{x \in \mathcal{M} \mid 0 \preceq x\}$, over which $\preceq$ is *well-founded*. In contrast, we only require the existence of a function μ from the set of all proofs into a set with a well-founded, transitive relation, such that the *father-son monotonicity* and *membership monotonicity* properties hold (see Section 6).

Besides being parametric w.r.t. the well-founded relation used for the Well-Founded Improvement Method, our approach is also parametric w.r.t. other relevant aspects. Indeed, it is parametric w.r.t.: (1) *the programming language*, because it provides theoretical tools for proving the correctness of program transformations in all languages whose semantics can be defined by means of sets of inductive rules on arbitrary domains, (2) *the inductive rules* used for defining the semantics of the programming language of interest, and indeed, these rules are allowed to be either finitary or infinitary (as long as they are continuous), and finally, (3) *the program transformations*, because in our approach we can deal with a very general, in fact, complete, set of transformations.

Acknowledgements

We would like to thank C.R. Ramakrishnan for stimulating conversations on the issue of proving the correctness of logic program transformations. This work has been partially supported by MURST Progetto Cofinanziato 'Tecniche Formali per la Specifica, l'Analisi, la Verifica, la Sintesi e la Trasformazione di Sistemi Software' (Italy), Progetto Coordinato CNR 'Programmazione Logica' (Italy), and Progetto Coordinato CNR 'Verifica, Analisi e Trasformazione dei Programmi Logici' (Italy).

References

[1] P. Aczel. An introduction to inductive definitions. In J. Barwise, editor, *Handbook of Mathematical Logic*, chapter 7, pages 739–782. North-Holland, 1977.

[2] M. Bezem. Characterizing termination of logic programs with level mappings. In E.L. Lusk and R.A. Overbeek, editors, *Proceedings of the North American*

Conference on Logic Programming, Cleveland, Ohio (USA), pages 69–80. MIT Press, 1989.

[3] A. Bossi and N. Cocco. Preserving universal termination through unfold/fold. In *Proceedings ALP '94*, Lecture Notes in Computer Science 850, pages 269–286. Springer-Verlag, 1994.

[4] R. M. Burstall and J. Darlington. A transformation system for developing recursive programs. *Journal of the ACM*, 24(1):44–67, January 1977.

[5] B. Courcelle. Recursive applicative program schemes. In J. van Leuveen, editor, *Handbook of Theoretical Computer Science*, volume B, pages 459–492. Elsevier, 1990.

[6] T. Kawamura and T. Kanamori. Preservation of stronger equivalence in unfold/fold logic program transformation. *Theoretical Computer Science*, 75:139–156, 1990.

[7] J. W. Lloyd. *Foundations of Logic Programming*. Springer-Verlag, Berlin, 1987. Second Edition.

[8] J. McCarthy. Towards a mathematical science of computation. In C.M. Popplewell, editor, *Information Processing : Proceedings of IFIP 1962*, pages 21–28, Amsterdam, 1963. North Holland.

[9] A. Pettorossi and M. Proietti. Transformation of logic programs: Foundations and techniques. *Journal of Logic Programming*, 19,20:261–320, 1994.

[10] A. Roychoudhury, K.N. Kumar, C.R. Ramakrishnan, and I.V. Ramakrishnan. A generalized unfold/fold transformation system for definite logic programs. Technical report, Department of Computer Science, SUNY at Stony Brook, USA, 1998.

[11] D. Sands. Total correctness by local improvement in the transformation of functional programs. *ACM Toplas*, 18(2):175–234, 1996.

[12] H. Seki. Unfold/fold transformation of stratified programs. *Theoretical Computer Science*, 86:107–139, 1991.

[13] H. Tamaki and T. Sato. Unfold/fold transformation of logic programs. In S.-Å. Tärnlund, editor, *Proceedings of the Second International Conference on Logic Programming, Uppsala, Sweden*, pages 127–138. Uppsala University, 1984.

[14] H. Tamaki and T. Sato. A generalized correctness proof of the unfold/fold logic program transformation. Technical Report 86-4, Ibaraki University, Japan, 1986.

[15] M. H. van Emden and R. Kowalski. The semantics of predicate logic as a programming language. *Journal of the ACM*, 23(4):733–742, 1976.

[16] G. Winskel. *The Formal Semantics of Programming Languages: An Introduction*. The MIT Press, 1993.

Binding-Time Analysis for Mercury

Wim Vanhoof
Maurice Bruynooghe
Department of Computer Science,
K.U.Leuven, Belgium
{wimvh,maurice}@cs.kuleuven.ac.be

Abstract

In this paper, we describe a binding-time analysis (BTA) for a statically typed and strongly moded pure logic programming language, in casu Mercury. Binding-time analysis is the key concept in achieving off-line program specialisation: the analysis starts from a description of the program's input available for specialisation, and propagates this information throughout the program, deriving directives for when and how to perform specialisation. Exploiting the possibilities offered by Mercury's strong type and mode system, we present a completely automatic BTA dealing with partially static binding-times.

1 Introduction

Program specialisation is a well-studied source-to-source transformation, capable of optimising a program P with respect to a known part s of its input (s, d): Some (ideally all) program parts depending only on s are evaluated at specialisation-time, whereas the remaining operations are residualised in a new program P_s. In general, $P_s(d)$ will compute more efficiently than $P(s, d)$ since the former has less operations to perform.

In the *off-line* approach to specialisation, the program is analysed using a description of the input available for specialisation (e.g. [7, 2]). Such a description states, in its most rudimentary form, which of the program query's input arguments are bound to a value at specialisation-time. The task of *binding-time analysis* (BTA) is to propagate this information from the query throughout the whole program, deriving *binding times* for every variable in the program, stating whether or not it is bound to a value at a specific program point.

From the result of this BTA, a set of directives is produced, specifying for each operation whether it can be performed at specialisation-time (when concrete input will be available), or should be residualised. Actual specialisation is achieved afterwards, by merely following the generated directives, running parts of the program on the available concrete input. However, all control decisions for the specialiser are taken beforehand, during BTA.

In a logic programming setting, most attention has been paid to *on-line* specialisation: Without prior analysis, the program is run with the available input under the supervision of a control system that decides –

during specialisation – what operations to evaluate or to residualise while guaranteeing termination. In general, an on-line system can achieve more thorough specialisation results due to the availability of concrete input to the control system [10, 11].

However, the off-line approach offers a lot of advantages: While the division in two phases makes the process conceptually cleaner, the output of BTA is interesting in its own right: The results of BTA can be used by other analyses apart from specialisation, or may be inspected by the user – enabling a better understanding of the process and the obtained results. Moreover, off-line techniques are generally considered to be more efficient than their on-line counterparts, and seem to be better suited for self-application [7].

Despite the advantages offered, little work on BTA for logic programming languages exists [13, 8, 3]. Moreover, to the best of our knowledge, no *completely automatic* BTA for logic programming exists, since all such analyses rely on extra information supplied by the user.

Recently, Mercury was introduced as a logic programming language, specifically tuned towards the creation of large-scale applications [14]. To that extent, the language was provided with a type, mode and determinism system. In this work, we show how precisely this extra information can be fruitfully used in the construction of a completely automatic BTA for Mercury, providing the necessary means for off-line specialisation, suited for industrial application and hence fitting Mercury's design philosophy.

2 Binding-time Analysis

Typical input to a specialiser is a program P and a (partial) description of P's input. Traditionally, this information is described by specifying for each input argument of P whether it is *static* – that is, fully known at specialisation time, or *dynamic* – (possibly) fully unknown at specialisation-time. The primary task of BTA is to obtain such information for *every* program variable [7]. In the context of specialisation of logic programs, classifying program variables as either static or dynamic is in general too coarse-grained (e.g. [3]). We start by describing how Mercury's type system allows us to represent more detailed binding times, enabling the analysis to deal with variables that are *partially static* at specialisation time.

2.1 Describing Binding Times

Mercury is a statically typed language of which we consider a first-order subset. Let $\mathcal{T}_V$, $\mathcal{T}_C$, $\mathcal{T}_F$, Var denote the sets of respectively type variables, type constructors, type functors and program variables for a given program P. A type in Mercury ($\mathcal{M}T$) is either a type variable or a type constructor applied to a number of types:

$$\mathcal{M}T ::= V \in \mathcal{T}_V \mid \gamma(t_1, \ldots, t_n) \text{ with } \gamma/n \in \mathcal{T}_C \text{ and } t_i \in \mathcal{M}T, \forall i \in \{1 \ldots n\}$$

A type constructor $\gamma/n \in \mathcal{T}_C$ is defined by a type definition ($\mathcal{T}Def$), with the constraint that all type variables occurring in the right hand side also occur in the left hand side:

$$\mathcal{T}Def ::= \gamma(V_1, \ldots, V_n) \longrightarrow c_1(t_{1,1}, \ldots, t_{1,m_1}) ; \ldots ; c_l(t_{l,1}, \ldots, t_{l,m_l}).$$
$$\text{where } \gamma/n \in \mathcal{T}_C, c_i \in \mathcal{T}_F, V_i \in \mathcal{T}_V \text{ and } t_{i,j} \in \mathcal{M}\mathcal{T}$$

A *type substitution* is defined as a mapping $TSubst : \mathcal{T}_V \mapsto \mathcal{M}\mathcal{T}$. By definition, any $t \in \mathcal{M}\mathcal{T}$ corresponds with a type tree in the usual way: a type variable $V \in \mathcal{T}_V$ is represented by a single *type node* labelled V, whereas a type $t = \gamma(V_1, \ldots, V_n)\theta$ ($\theta \in TSubst$) is represented by a type node labelled t, which has a *constructor* node labelled c_i as child for each constructor application $c_i(t_{i,1}, \ldots, t_{i,n_i})$ in γ's definition. This constructor node in turn has n_i children: the type trees for $t_{i,1}\theta, \ldots, t_{i,n_i}\theta$. Conceptually, a recursive type corresponds to an infinite type tree. However, any type can be represented by a finite *type graph* by imposing an equivalence relation on the type nodes of its type tree: two type nodes on a branch from the root of a type tree are equivalent if they are labelled with the same type. For such a type graph t, $\mathcal{OR}(t)$ represents the (finite) set of type nodes of t.

Example 2.1 The type `list(T)` $\in \mathcal{M}\mathcal{T}$ is defined through a type definition `list(T) ---> []  ;  [T|list(T)]`, where $T \in \mathcal{T}_V$ and `[]`$/0$ and $./2 \in \mathcal{T}_F$. See Figure 1 for its type graph.

Given a type graph for $t = \gamma(V_1, \ldots, V_n)\theta$ ($\theta \in TSubst$), $t^{[c_i/k]}$ selects the k-th child of the constructor node labelled c_i among the children of t in the graph. $[c_i/k]$ is called a *selector*, with `[]` being the empty one: $t^{[]} = t$. In Example 2.1, $list(T)^{[./1]}$ equals T and $list(T)^{[./2]}$ equals $list(T)$ (see Figure 1). Now, we are able to define the notion of an *instantiatedness tree*.

Definition 2.2
An *instantiatedness tree* is a function $\tau : \mathcal{OR}(t) \mapsto \{free, bound\}$ for a given $t \in \mathcal{M}\mathcal{T}$ such that $\tau(\eta) = free$ implies that $\tau(\eta') = free$ for all $\eta' \in \mathcal{OR}(t)$ descending from η. The set of all instantiatedness trees over a given type t is denoted by $\mathcal{IT}(t)$; the set of all instantiatedness trees (regardless their type) is denoted by $\mathcal{IT}$.

Any $\tau \in \mathcal{IT}(t)$ represents a set of partial values of type t in which the position corresponding to $\eta \in \mathcal{OR}(t)$ is bound to a functor in case $\tau(\eta) = bound$, and a free variable in case $\tau(\eta) = free$. Figure 1 shows two instantiatedness trees for the type `list(int)`: τ_{il1} denoting a *free* (unbound) value, and τ_{il2}, denoting a list-skeleton: the list constructor is bound, but the elements are free. The domain of instantiatedness trees is partially ordered by the *covers* relation:

Definition 2.3 For any types t_1, t_2 such that $t_1 = t_2\theta$ or $t_2 = t_1\theta$, let $\tau_1 \in \mathcal{IT}(t_1), \tau_2 \in \mathcal{IT}(t_2)$. τ_1 *covers* τ_2, $\tau_1 \succeq \tau_2$ iff $\forall \eta \in \mathcal{OR}(t_1) \cap \mathcal{OR}(t_2), \tau_2(\eta) =$

503

free implies $\tau_1(\eta) = free$. That is, if $\bar{\tau}_1$, $\bar{\tau}_2$ denote τ_1, respectively τ_2 restricted to $\mathcal{OR}(t_1) \cap \mathcal{OR}(t_2)$, than $\bar{\tau}_1$ can be obtained from $\bar{\tau}_2$ by changing some nodes from *bound* to *free*.

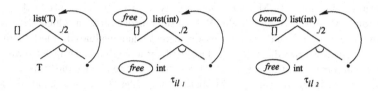

Figure 1: Type graph for list(T) and instantiatedness trees for list(int), where $\tau_{il1} \succeq \tau_{il2}$

$\top_t$ (all nodes *free*) and $\bot_t$ (all nodes *bound*) denote the top, respectively bottom elements of $(\mathcal{IT}(t), \succeq)$. In case the type is obvious, we also simply write $\top$ and $\bot$. For $\tau \in \mathcal{IT}(t)$, $\tau^{[c_i/k]}$ denotes an instantiatedness tree $\in \mathcal{IT}(t^{[c_i/k]})$: the subtree of τ consisting of the nodes of $t^{[c_i/k]}$.

Instantiatedness trees are traditionally used in Mercury to define a predicate *mode*: with each argument, say X of type t, a function: $\mathcal{IT}(t) \mapsto \mathcal{IT}(t)$ is associated defining the change in X's instantiatedness state between the predicate's entry and exit points.

In this paper, we adopt the notion of an instantiatedness tree to denote a variable's state of instantiation *during specialisation*. To that extent, we define the notion of a *binding-time environment*:

Definition 2.4 A *binding-time environment* is a mapping $Var \mapsto \mathcal{IT}$. The set of all binding-time environments is denoted by $BTEnv$.

A binding-time environment is thus a set of pairs, associating an instantiatedness tree to a program variable. We use such a set to represent, at a given program point, the instantiatedness state of each of these variables during specialisation.

Example 2.5 Let τ_{il1} and τ_{il2} denote the instantiatedness trees depicted in Figure 1. $\pi = \{(X, \tau_{il1}), (Y, \tau_{il2})\}$ is a binding-time environment stating that the variable X is free during specialisation, whereas the variable Y is bound to a list skeleton.

To ease notation, we allow an element (X, τ) of $\pi \in BTEnv$ to be partially defined, that is, the set $\{(X^{f,1}, \tau_1), \ldots, (X^{f,n}, \tau_n)\}$ defines a single pair (X, τ), where τ is obtained from $\bot_t$ by replacing $\bot_t^{[f/i]}$ by τ_i for $\tau \in \mathcal{IT}(t)$ for all $1 \le i \le n$.

2.2 Binding-time Analysis for Mercury

2.2.1 Mercury

A well-typed, well-moded Mercury program [14] consists of a number of procedure definitions. In Mercury terminology, a procedure is a predicate definition with precisely one mode. We consider procedures in which the goals are reordered such that they are mode-correct when evaluated in left-to-right order. Such a procedure can be described by a single clause in *superhomogeneous form* [14]: the arguments in the head of the clause and in predicate calls in the body are replaced by distinct variables, explicit unifications are generated for these variables in the body, and complex unifications are broken down into several simpler ones. Let *Proc* denote the set of procedures in a given program P.

Definition 2.6 (Superhomogeneous form)

$$
\begin{aligned}
PCall &::= \ p(Y_1, \ldots, Y_n) \\
Unif &::= \ X \Rightarrow f(Y_1, \ldots, Y_n) \ \text{(deconstruction)} \\
&\quad \mid X \Leftarrow f(Y_1 \ldots, Y_n) \ \text{(construction)} \mid X == Y \ \text{(test)} \\
&\quad \mid X := Y \ \text{(assignment)} \\
Atom &::= \ PCall \mid Unif \\
Goal &::= \ Atom \mid G, A \mid G_1; G_2 \mid if \ G \ then \ A \ else \ A' \mid not \ G
\end{aligned}
$$

where $G, G_1, G_2 \in Goal$, $A, A' \in Atom$,[1] $p \in Proc$, $X, Y, Y_1, \ldots, Y_n \in Var$.

Due to the mode correctness, there are a number of additional constraints: the arguments of a predicate call are classified as either input (ground at the time of the call), or output (free at the time of the call, ground at exit). Both variables in a test are of atomic type and input to the test. For the deconstruction defined above, X is input, and all Y_i output, whereas in the construction it is the other way round. To the assignment, X is output and Y input.

A program P consists of N procedure definitions, where each procedure is defined as $p_k(F_1, \ldots, F_{n_k})\text{:-}G_k$ with $G_k \in Goal$ and $F_1, \ldots, F_{n_k} \in Var$. For each such procedure definition, $\mathcal{F}_{in}^k$ and $\mathcal{F}_{out}^k$ denotes the set of input, respectively output arguments of p_k.

Example 2.7 Consider the definition of $append(list(T) :: in, list(T) :: in, list(T) :: out)$ where for each argument position $t :: in$ or $t :: out$ denotes that the corresponding argument is of type t and is an input, respectively output argument.

$$
\begin{aligned}
append(X, Y, Z)\text{:-} \ &X \Rightarrow [], Z := Y; \\
&X \Rightarrow [E \mid E_s], append(E_s, Y, R), Z \Leftarrow [E|R].
\end{aligned}
$$

---

[1]The goals (G, A) and *if G then A else A'* (Definition 2.6) are syntactically more restricted than in Mercury (due to the presence of the atoms). The form of Definition 2.6 can, however, be syntactically derived from the more general one, and enables a more elegant exposition of the analysis.

2.2.2 Basic Binding-Time Analysis

The task of binding-time analysis is, given an instantiatedness state of a main procedure's input arguments, to compute the instantiatedness state of each program variable in a specific atom. Therefore, we need to analyse each procedure's body goal with respect to the binding times for its input arguments. Our analysis is *polyvariant*, that is, different analyses of the same body goal are performed with respect to a different binding-time environment for the procedure's input arguments. Before presenting the actual analysis functions, we define the necessary environments.

Definition 2.8 A *procedure environment* is a mapping $BTEnv \mapsto BTEnv$. The set of all such procedure environments is denoted by $ProcEnv$.

A procedure environment Ψ_k maps, for a procedure p_k, a binding-time environment π_{call} – representing an instantiatedness state for each input argument – to another binding-time environment π_{exit} – representing the corresponding instantiatedness states for the output arguments: $\Psi_k(\pi_{call}) = \pi_{exit}$. In case $\Psi_k(\pi)$ is undefined for $\pi \in BTEnv$, $\Psi_k(\pi) = \{(F, \bot) \mid F \in \mathcal{F}_{out}^k\}$. Reconsider Example 2.7 and τ_{il2} as defined in Figure 1; The procedure environment $\{(\{(X, \tau_{il2}), (Y, \tau_{il2})\}, \{(Z, \tau_{il2})\})\}$ denotes that when *append* is called with both input arguments instantiated to a list skeleton, its output argument will be bound to a list skeleton.

During BTA, we will construct such a procedure environment for every procedure, and collect these in a program environment:

Definition 2.9 A *program environment*, the domain of which is denoted by $ProgEnv$, is an N-tuple of $ProcEnv$, with N the number of procedures in a program P. If $\Psi \in ProgEnv$, Ψ_k denotes the k-th element of Ψ and $\Psi[\Psi_k/\phi]$ denotes Ψ in which Ψ_k is replaced by ϕ: $< \Psi_1, \ldots, \Psi_{k-1}, \phi, \Psi_{k+1}, \ldots, \Psi_N >$ for $\phi \in ProcEnv$.

Starting from the covers relation, we define the following *greater than* relations on the newly introduced environments: $\forall \pi, \pi' \in BTEnv : \pi' \sqsupseteq \pi \Leftrightarrow \forall (X, \tau) \in \pi, (X, \tau') \in \pi'$ and $\tau' \succeq \tau$. For all $\phi, \phi' \in ProcEnv$: $\phi' \sqsupseteq \phi \Leftrightarrow \forall (\pi_i, \pi_o) \in \phi, (\pi_i, \pi_o') \in \phi'$ and $\pi_o' \sqsupseteq \pi_o$ and $\forall < \Psi_1, \ldots, \Psi_N >$, $< \Psi_1', \ldots, \Psi_N' > \in ProgEnv$: $< \Psi_1', \ldots, \Psi_N' > \sqsupseteq < \Psi_1, \ldots, \Psi_N > \Leftrightarrow \forall i \in \{1 \ldots N\} : \Psi_i' \sqsupseteq \Psi_i$. An essential operator is the *least upperbound* of two mappings: When a partial order exists on $\mathcal{R}$, we define for all mappings $f, g : \mathcal{D} \mapsto \mathcal{R}$, $f \sqcup g = \{(d, r_1 \sqcup r_2) \mid (d, r_1) \in f$ and $(d, r_2) \in g\} \cup \{(d, r) \mid$ either $(d, r) \in f$ and $\nexists (d, r') \in g$ or $(d, r) \in g$ and $\nexists (d, r') \in f\}$, where $\sqcup$ denotes the least upperbound on $\mathcal{R}$. For any set S, $\{e :: S_s\}$ denotes the deconstruction of S such that $S = \{e\} \cup S_s$ and $e \notin S_s$.

We will now introduce the analysis step by step, starting from a first function α which analyses a single atom A, taking the current program environment as input together with a binding-time environment (consisting of binding-times for the variables that are input to A). α updates this binding-time environment with the binding-times for A's output arguments, and possibly adds a new call pattern to the program environment (in case A is a procedure call).

Definition 2.10 $\alpha : Atom \times BTEnv \times ProgEnv \mapsto BTEnv \times ProgEnv$ is defined as

$$\alpha(X \Rightarrow f(Y_1, \ldots, Y_n), \pi, \Psi) = (\pi \sqcup \{(Y_1, \tau_X^{[f/1]}), \ldots, (Y_n, \tau_X^{[f/n]})\}, \Psi)$$
$$\text{where } (X, \tau_X) \in \pi$$

$$\alpha(X == Y, \pi, \Psi) = (\pi, \Psi)$$

$$\alpha(X := Y, \pi, \Psi) = (\pi \sqcup \{(X, \tau_Y)\}, \Psi) \text{ where } (Y, \tau_Y) \in \pi$$

$$\alpha(X \Leftarrow f(Y_1, \ldots, Y_n)\pi, \Psi) = (\pi \sqcup \{(X^{f,1}, \tau_{Y_1}), \ldots, (X^{f,n}, \tau_{Y_n})\}, \Psi)$$
$$\text{where } \forall i : (Y_i, \tau_{Y_i}) \in \pi$$

$$\alpha(p_k(X_1, \ldots, X_n), \pi, \Psi) = (\pi \sqcup \pi_{out}, \Psi') \text{ where}$$
$$\pi_{out} = \{(X_i, \tau_{F_i}) \mid F_i \in \mathcal{F}_{out}^k, (F_i, \tau_{F_i}) \in \Psi_k(\pi_{in})\}$$
$$\pi_{in} = \{(F_i, \tau_{X_i}) \mid F_i \in \mathcal{F}_{in}^k \text{ and } (X_i, \tau_{X_i}) \in \pi\}$$
$$\Psi' = \Psi[\Psi_k/\Psi_k \sqcup \{(\pi_{in}, \{(F_i, \bot) \mid F_i \in \mathcal{F}_{out}^k\})\}]$$

Handling unification is straightforward: the binding-time environment π is updated with binding times for the unification's output argument(s), derived from the input binding-times contained in π. Since no new calls are encountered, the program environment Ψ remains unchanged. When analysing a procedure call to p_k, the binding times of p_k's output arguments, given the binding times of its input arguments, are found in Ψ_k, the procedure environment for p_k. The new program environment Ψ' is the old one updated with the procedure environment $(\pi_{in}, \{(F_i, \bot) \mid F_i \in \mathcal{F}_{out}^k\})$ of the new call to p_k. The use of $\sqcup$ in the update ensures that if p_k was already analysed with call pattern π_{in}, the resulting exit pattern (already registered in Ψ_k), is preserved and used in the construction of the binding times for the call's actual output arguments. If it was not, the call's output arguments are initialised to $\bot$. The definitions of π_{in} and π_{out} provide the mapping between the formal procedure arguments $(\mathcal{F}_{in}^k \cup \mathcal{F}_{out}^k)$ and the actual arguments of the call.

2.2.3 Incorporating Specialisation Control

The binding times produced by BTA reflect a variable's state of instantiatedness during specialisation. Therefore, the bindings for the output variables of an atom A, as produced by $\alpha(A, \pi, \Psi)$, are valid only when A is actually reduced during specialisation and values for A's output variables are computed. When A is residualised, on the other hand, the atom is not evaluated, and no output at all is computed during specialisation. In the latter case, A's output variables – denoted by $out(A)$ – need to be bound to $\top$ during BTA, reflecting their instantiatedness state ($free$) during specialisation.

To that extent, we introduce a control aspect in the BTA: Our analysis models a rather conservative specialisation control strategy, in the sense that during specialisation, no atoms are reduced that are under dynamic control.

An atom is under dynamic control, when it is not certain to be evaluated at run-time, since it depends on the success or failure of another goal, of which the result is unknown at specialisation-time.

This control strategy is reflected in BTA: The binding times for A's output arguments are made $\top$ (regardless of the result of α) in case A is under dynamic control of a goal G, and reducing G results in residual code of which success or failure at run-time is unknown at specialisation-time.

To model the reducibility of a goal, we introduce the domain $(\mathcal{R}ed, >) = \{\mathbf{RD}, \mathbf{NF}, \mathbf{RS}\}$ on which the ordering $\mathbf{RS} > \mathbf{NF} > \mathbf{RD}$ is imposed. To any goal $G \in Goal$, we associate a value in $\mathcal{R}ed$, denoted by $\mathcal{A}(G, \pi, \Psi)$ specifying the effect of specialising G w.r.t. a binding-time environment π and program environment Ψ: $\mathcal{A}(G, \pi, \Psi) = \mathbf{RD}$ means that G is completely reduced to $true$ or $fail$ at specialisation-time. $\mathcal{A}(G, \pi, \Psi) = \mathbf{RS}$ denotes that specialising the goal results in some residualised code, and $\mathcal{A}(G, \pi, \Psi) = \mathbf{NF}$ denotes a specialisation result that is either $true$ or some residual code, but which is certain not to fail when evaluated at run-time.

Given such a function $\mathcal{A}$, we can define an analysis function β which analyses a goal given a binding-time environment (consisting of binding times for the variables of the goal) and a program environment representing the BTA so far. The result is an updated binding-time environment and an updated program environment.

Definition 2.11 $\beta : Goal \times BTEnv \times ProgEnv \mapsto BTEnv \times ProgEnv$

$\beta(A, \pi, \Psi) = \alpha(A, \pi, \Psi)$

$\beta(not\ G, \pi, \Psi) = \beta(G, \pi, \Psi)$

$$\beta((G, A), \pi, \Psi) = \begin{cases} (\pi^A, \Psi^A) & \text{if } \mathcal{A}(G, \pi, \Psi) \in \{\mathbf{RD}, \mathbf{NF}\}, \text{ or} \\ (\pi^G \cup \{(V, \top) \mid V \in out(A)\}, \Psi^A) & \text{otherwise} \end{cases}$$
$$\text{where } (\pi^G, \Psi^G) = \beta(G, \pi, \Psi) \text{ and } (\pi^A, \Psi^A) = \alpha(A, \pi^G, \Psi^G)$$

$$\beta((G_1; G_2), \pi, \Psi) = (\pi^{G_1} \sqcup \pi^{G_2}, \Psi^{G_2}) \text{ where } (\pi^{G_1}, \Psi^{G_1}) = \beta(G_1, \pi, \Psi)$$
$$\text{and } (\pi^{G_2}, \Psi^{G_2}) = \beta(G_2, \pi, \Psi^{G_1})$$

$$\beta(if\ G\ then\ A_1\ else\ A_2, \pi, \Psi) = \begin{cases} (\pi^{A_1}, \Psi^{A_1}) & \text{if } \mathcal{A}(G, \pi, \Psi) = \mathbf{NF}, \text{ or} \\ (\pi^{A_1} \sqcup \pi^{A_2}, \Psi^{A_2}) & \text{if } \mathcal{A}(G, \pi, \Psi) = \mathbf{RD}, \text{ or} \\ (\pi^G \sqcup \{(V, \top) \mid V \in out(A_1) \cup out(A_2)\}, \Psi^{A_2}) \end{cases}$$
$$\text{where } (\pi^G, \Psi^G) = \beta(G, \pi, \Psi), (\pi^{A_1}, \Psi^{A_1}) = \alpha(A_1, \pi^G, \Psi^G)$$
$$\text{and } (\pi^{A_2}, \Psi^{A_2}) = \alpha(A_2, \pi, \Psi^{A_1})$$

β evaluates a non atomic goal by evaluating its subgoals and combining the resulting binding-time environments, taking the described control strategy into account: When reducing a subgoal G may result in residual code which can possibly fail at run-time, the output variables of an atom A in a conjunction (G, A) are bound to $\top$, since A is under dynamic control of G. Note that code is needed to execute the residual call to A, hence $\alpha(A, \pi^G, \Psi^G)$ is to be computed, and Ψ^A is always the new program environment. The same holds for the atoms A_1 and A_2 in an $if - then - else$ if G reduces to code at specialisation-time. If, on the other hand, G reduces to $true$ or to code which is certain not to fail at run-time, only A_1's output binding times are taken into account. If G reduces to *true* or *fail* (implying that the *if* will be reduced at specialisation-time), the output binding times of A_1 and A_2 are combined using $\sqcup$. The result of analysing $not(G)$ is simply the result of analysing G, since in Mercury, a goal $not(G)$ may not bind variables occurring outside G.

Example 2.12 Let G denote the body of the *append* procedure in Example 2.7 and consider the instantiatedness tree τ_{il2} of Figure 1. Let $\pi = \{(X, \tau_{il2}), (Y, \tau_{il2})\}$ be a binding-time environment and Ψ a program environment (with only one entry for *append*), $\Psi =< \emptyset >$. If $(\pi', \Psi') = \beta(G, \pi, \Psi)$, then

$$\pi' = \{(X, \tau_{il2}), (Y, \tau_{il2}), (E, \tau_{il2}^{[./1]}), (E_s, \tau_{il2}), (R, \bot), (Z, \tau_{il2})\}$$
$$\Psi' =< \{(\{(X, \tau_{il2}), (Y, \tau_{il2})\}, \{(Z, \bot)\})\} >$$

Given a goal G, β returns the binding-time environment as computed at the exit of G. In what follows, we sometimes need the binding-time environments computed by β at the entry and exit points of a specific subgoal G' in G, while computing a binding-time environment for G. Therefore, we introduce a variant of β, β': Given $G, G' \in Goal$ with G' a subgoal of G. Let $\beta'(G, G', \pi, \Psi)$ denote a function: $Goal \times Goal \times BTEnv \times ProgEnv \mapsto BTEnv \times BTEnv$ performing exactly the same analysis as β, but returning the binding time environments as computed by β on entry and exit points of G' during analysis of G. Remains the definition of $\mathcal{A}$:

Definition 2.13 $\mathcal{A} : Goal \times BTEnv \times ProgEnv \mapsto \mathcal{R}ed$
$\mathcal{A}(X \Rightarrow f(\ldots), \pi, \Psi) = \mathbf{RS}$ if $(X, \top) \in BTEnv$, or $\mathbf{RD}$ otherwise.
$\mathcal{A}(X == Y, \pi, \Psi) = \mathbf{RS}$ if $(X, \top) \in \pi$ or $(Y, \top) \in \pi$, or $\mathbf{RD}$ otherwise.
$\mathcal{A}(X := Y, \pi, \Psi) = \mathbf{NF}$ if $(Y, \top) \in \pi$, or $\mathbf{RD}$ otherwise.
$\mathcal{A}(X \Leftarrow f(\ldots), \pi, \Psi) = \mathbf{RD}$.
$\mathcal{A}(if\ G\ then\ A_1\ else\ A_2, \pi, \Psi) =$
$\left\{ \begin{array}{l} \mathbf{NF} \sqcup \mathcal{A}(A_1, \pi, \Psi) \text{ if } \mathcal{A}(G, \pi, \Psi) = \mathbf{NF}, \text{ or} \\ \mathcal{A}(G, \pi, \Psi) \sqcup \mathcal{A}(A_1, \pi', \Psi) \sqcup \mathcal{A}(A_2, \pi, \Psi) \text{ where}(\pi', \Psi') = \beta(G, \pi, \Psi) \end{array} \right.$
$\mathcal{A}(not\ G, \pi, \Psi) = \mathbf{RD}$ if $\mathcal{A}(G, \pi, \Psi) \in \{\mathbf{RD}, \mathbf{NF}\}$, or $\mathbf{RS}$ otherwise.
$\mathcal{A}((G_1\ ;\ G_2), \pi, \Psi) = \mathcal{A}(G_1, \pi, \Psi) \sqcup \mathcal{A}(G_2, \pi, \Psi)$.
$\mathcal{A}((G, A), \pi, \Psi) = \mathcal{A}(G, \pi, \Psi) \sqcup \mathcal{A}(A, \pi', \Psi)$ where$(\pi', \Psi') = \beta(G, \pi, \Psi)$.
$\mathcal{A}(p_k(X_1, \ldots, X_n), \pi, \Psi) = \mathcal{A}(G_k, \pi', \Psi) \sqcap det(p_k)$
where $\pi' = \{(F_i, \tau_{X_i}) \mid F_i \in \mathcal{F}_{in}^k \text{ and } (X_i, \tau_{X_i}) \in \pi\}$
and G_k the body of p_k's definition.

Whether or not a unification is reducible (**RD**) or should be residualised (**RS**) depends on the binding times of the input variables. Note that an assignment may be residualised, in which case it is classified as non-failing. The reducibility of a composed goal depends on the reducibility of the different subgoals. The reducibility of a procedure call depends on the reducibility for its body goal. In case the body goal is classified as **RS**, the call may be classified **NF** in case the procedure is declared (or inferred) as a non-failing procedure. The determinism declaration of a procedure is formalised by a function $det : Proc \mapsto \mathcal{R}ed$, where $det(p_k) = \mathbf{NF}$ expresses that no call to p_k will fail, whereas $det(p_k) = \mathbf{RS}$ denotes possible failure.

We now return to the basic operation of our BTA: analysing the body of a procedure, with respect to a set of binding times, namely the binding times of the procedure's input arguments for every call pattern collected during analysis. The result is a binding-time environment for the procedure's output arguments, which is recorded in an updated program environment.

Definition 2.14 For any procedure p_i:-G_i with ϕ a procedure environment for p_i and $\Psi \in ProgEnv$, $\delta(G_i, \phi, \Psi) : Goal \times ProcEnv \times ProgEnv \mapsto ProgEnv$ is defined as:

$$\delta(G_i, \phi, \Psi) = \begin{cases} \Psi & \text{if } \phi = \emptyset \\ \delta(G_i, S_s, \Psi'[\Psi_i'/\Psi_i' \sqcup \{(\pi_{in}, \pi'_{out})\}]) & \text{if } \phi = \{(\pi_{in}, \pi_{out}) :: S_s\} \\ & \text{and } (\pi'_{out}, \Psi') = \beta(G_i, \pi_{in}, \Psi) \end{cases}$$

To analyse a program, its set of procedure bodies needs to be analysed, for which purpose we define Δ, as an extension of δ defined above.

Definition 2.15 For a program p_1:-$G_1, \ldots, p_N$:-G_N, let $S \subseteq \{G_1, \ldots, G_n\}$ and $\Psi \in ProgEnv$. Then $\Delta : 2^{Goal} \times ProgEnv \mapsto ProgEnv$ is defined as:

$$\Delta(S, \Psi) = \begin{cases} \Psi & \text{if } S = \emptyset \\ \Delta(S_s, \delta(G_i, \Psi_i, \Psi)) & \text{if } S = \{G_i :: S_s\} \end{cases}$$

The result of binding-time analysis for a program p_1:-$G_1, \ldots, p_N$:-G_N is the least solution Ψ to the equation $\Psi = \Delta(\{G_1, \ldots, G_N\}, \Psi)$ (1). Starting from an initial program environment Ψ^0, this least solution can be found by repeatedly computing, for all $i > 0$, $\Psi^i = \Delta(\{G_1, \ldots, G_N\}, \Psi^{i-1})$ (2) until a fixpoint is reached. If we assume that p_1 is the program's main procedure and π_{in}^1 represents the initial binding-time environment for this procedure's input arguments, $\Psi^0 =< \{(\pi_{in}^1, \{(F, \bot) \mid F \in \mathcal{F}_{out}^1\}), \emptyset, \ldots, \emptyset >$.

2.3 Congruence

The result of BTA, Ψ, represents a complete data flow analysis in terms of the program variables' binding times. In order to be useful, Ψ must be *congruent*: For a variable X of type t and a selector δ, let X^δ denote the part of X's value corresponding to t^δ. If there is a data flow path in P such that $X^{\delta_X} := Y^{\delta_Y}$ (through matching or parameter binding), this path must be represented in Ψ by binding times for X and Y, say τ_X and τ_Y such that $\tau_X^{\delta_X} \succeq \tau_Y^{\delta_Y}$.

Definition 2.16 Given a program p_1:-$G_1, \ldots, p_N$:-G_N, a program environment $\Psi \in ProgEnv$ is *congruent* when for each atomic subgoal A of any G_i and $\forall(\pi_{in}^i, \pi_{out}^i) \in \Psi_i$ the following holds: If $(\pi_{call}, \pi_{exit}) = \beta'(G_i, A, \pi_{in}^i, \Psi)$ and

- $A = (Y \Rightarrow f(X_1, \ldots, X_n))$ then $\forall i \in \{1 \ldots n\} : \tau_{X_i} \succeq \tau_Y^{[f/i]}$ where (X_i, τ_{X_i}) and $(Y, \tau_Y) \in \pi_{exit}$.
- $A = (Y \Leftarrow f(X_1, \ldots, X_n))$ then $\forall i \in \{1 \ldots n\} : \tau_Y^{[f/i]} \succeq \tau_{X_i}$ where (X_i, τ_{X_i}) and $(Y, \tau_Y) \in \pi_{exit}$.

- $A = (X := Y)$ then $\tau_X \succeq \tau_Y$ where $(X, \tau_X), (Y, \tau_Y) \in \pi_{exit}$.
- $A = p_k(X_1, \ldots, X_n)$ then $\exists(\pi_{in}^k, \pi_{out}^k) \in \Psi_k$ such that
  - $\forall F_i \in \mathcal{F}_{in}^k : \tau_{F_i} \succeq \tau_{X_i}$ where $(F_i, \tau_{F_i}) \in \pi_{in}^k$ and $(X_i, \tau_{X_i}) \in \pi_{call}$.
  - $\forall F_i \in \mathcal{F}_{out}^k : \tau_{X_i} \succeq \tau_{F_i}$ where $(F_i, \tau_{F_i}) \in \pi_{out}^k$ and $(X_i, \tau_{X_i}) \in \pi_{exit}$.

Given this definition of congruence, we can state the following important result:

Theorem 2.17 For a program $p_1{:-}G_1,\ldots,p_N{:-}G_N$, let p_1 be the main procedure and π_{in}^1 an initial binding time environment for p_1's input arguments. If $\Psi^0 = < \{(\pi_{in}^1, \{(F, \bot) \mid F \in \mathcal{F}_{out}^1\}), \emptyset, \ldots, \emptyset >$, the fixpoint Ψ^n, $n \in I\!N$, of $\Psi^i = \Delta(\{G_1,\ldots,G_N\}, \Psi^{i-1}), \forall i > 0$ exists and is the least congruent solution to $\Psi = \Delta(\{G_1,\ldots,G_N\}, \Psi)$.

Proof For any update of $\Psi \in ProgEnv$ into Ψ' in α and δ holds that $\Psi \sqsubseteq \Psi'$. By the way the program environment is threaded through Δ via δ, β and α, $\Psi^i \sqsubseteq \Psi^{i+1}$, $\forall i > 0$ in (2). As such, repeated applications of Δ yield a monotonic sequence of program environments, implying the existence of $\Psi \in ProgEnv$ satisfying (1). This fixpoint is finite ($\exists n \in I\!N : \Psi^n = \Psi$): Since for any finite type tree t, $\mathcal{IT}(t)$ is finite, and hence the number of possible program environments for a program P is finite. By definition, α constructs a congruent binding-time environment, and the use of $\sqcup$ in β to combine binding-time environments preserves congruence. So Ψ is a congruent solution. Moreover, it is the least congruent solution, since all exit patterns recorded in Ψ start from $\bot$ and are changed to a higher value (using $\sqcup$) only when congruence so requires. □

3 From Binding Times to Specialisation

3.1 From Binding Times to Annotations

From the program environment resulting from BTA, instructions whether to reduce or residualise a goal can be derived. A suitable way of representing these instructions, is through an annotated version of the source program. To that purpose, we introduce a two-level syntax, as in e.g. [7]: The syntactic domains $2PCall, 2Unif, 2Atom$ and $2Goal$ are defined as in Definition 2.6, except that each construct appears in a *static* as well as *dynamic* variant: For a goal $G \in Goal$, G^s and G^d denote the static, respectively dynamic variant of G in $2Goal$. A static annotation is a directive to the specialiser to reduce this goal, a dynamic one the instruction to residualise it. Reducing a statically annotated atom involves either performing unification or unfolding a procedure call – replacing it by a renamed version of the body goal in which parameters have been substituted. Reduction of a static *if then else* consists of evaluating the test goal, and depending on success or failure of the latter, reducing or residualising either the *then* or *else* atom. Reducing a static *not G* involves reducing G, and then either succeeding or failing, depending on the success or failure of G. Conjunctions and disjunctions are not explicitly annotated, since the specialiser treats them as connectives, and always considers both their subgoals for reduction. The two-level versions of procedures (*Proc*) and programs (*Prog*) are denoted by 2*Proc* and 2*Prog*.

Definition 3.1 shows how to derive a version of a program P that is annotated with respect to a congruent program environment Ψ. A rule like $\pi \vdash G \vartriangleright_a G'$ should be read as follows: G' is a version of G, annotated w.r.t. Ψ, given de binding-time environment π. Given two such rules, ρ_1 and ρ_2, $\frac{\rho_1}{\rho_2}$ denotes that ρ_2 holds if ρ_1 holds. We also introduce the following notation: Given a binding-time environment π, π_G denotes a binding-time environment π_{in} where $(\pi_{in}, \pi_{out}) = \beta'(G_k, G, \pi, \Psi)$ if G_k is the procedure body of which G is a subgoal.

Definition 3.1

$$\vartriangleright_a : Goal \mapsto 2Goal, \quad \vartriangleright_a^p : Procedure \mapsto 2Procedure, \quad \vartriangleright_a^P : Prog \mapsto 2Prog$$

$$\frac{\pi \vdash G_1 \vartriangleright_a G_1', G_2 \vartriangleright_a G_2'}{\pi \vdash (G_1 ; G_2) \vartriangleright_a (G_1' ; G_2')} \qquad \frac{\pi \vdash A \in Unif, \mathcal{A}(A, \pi, \Psi) = \mathbf{RD}}{\pi \vdash A \vartriangleright_a A^s} \qquad \frac{\pi \vdash A \in Unif, \mathcal{A}(A, \pi, \Psi) \in \{\mathbf{NF}, \mathbf{RS}\}}{\pi \vdash A \vartriangleright_a A^d}$$

$$\frac{\pi \vdash G \vartriangleright_a G', \pi_A \vdash A \vartriangleright_a A' \text{ and } \mathcal{A}(G, \pi, \Psi) \in \{\mathbf{RD}, \mathbf{NF}\}}{(G, A) \vartriangleright_a (G', A')} \qquad \frac{\pi \vdash G \vartriangleright_a G' \text{ and } \mathcal{A}(G, \pi, \Psi) = \mathbf{RS}}{(G, A) \vartriangleright_a (G', A^d)}$$

$$\frac{\pi \vdash G \vartriangleright_a G' \text{ and } \mathcal{A}(G, \pi, \Psi) = \mathbf{RD}}{\pi \vdash not\ G \vartriangleright_a not^s\ G'} \qquad \frac{\pi \vdash G \vartriangleright_a G' \text{ and } \mathcal{A}(G, \pi, \Psi) = \mathbf{RS}}{\pi \vdash not\ G \vartriangleright_a not^d\ G'} \qquad \frac{\pi \vdash G \vartriangleright_a G' \text{ and } \mathcal{A}(G, \pi, \Psi) = \mathbf{NF}}{\pi \vdash not\ G \vartriangleright_a fail}$$

$$\frac{\pi \vdash G \vartriangleright_a G' \text{ and } \mathcal{A}(G, \pi, \Psi) = \mathbf{RS}}{\pi \vdash if\ G\ then\ A_1\ else\ A_2 \vartriangleright_a if^d\ G'\ then\ A_1^d\ else\ A_2^d} \qquad \frac{\pi \vdash G \vartriangleright_a G', \pi_{A_1} \vdash A_1 \vartriangleright_a A_1' \text{ and } \mathcal{A}(G, \pi, \Psi) = \mathbf{NF}}{\pi \vdash if\ G\ then\ A_1\ else\ A_2 \vartriangleright_a (G', A_1')}$$

$$\frac{\pi \vdash G \vartriangleright_a G', \pi_{A_1} \vdash A_1 \vartriangleright_a A_1', \pi_{A_2} \vdash A_2 \vartriangleright_a A_2' \text{ and } \mathcal{A}(G, \pi, \Psi) = \mathbf{RD}}{\pi \vdash if\ G\ then\ A_1\ else\ A_2 \vartriangleright_a if^s\ G'\ then\ A_1'\ else\ A_2'}$$

$$\frac{\pi \vdash p_k(X_1, ..., X_n) \in PCall, \exists F_i \in \mathcal{F}_{out}^k : (X_i, \tau) \in \pi \text{ and } \tau \neq \mathsf{T}}{\pi \vdash p_k(X_1, ..., X_n) \vartriangleright_a p_k^c(X_1, ..., X_n)^s} \text{ where } c = \{\tau_i \mid (X_i, \tau_i) \in \pi \text{ and } F_i \in \mathcal{F}_{in}^k\}$$

$$\frac{\pi \vdash p_k(X_1, ..., X_n) \in PCall, \forall F_i \in \mathcal{F}_{out}^k : (X_i, \mathsf{T}) \in \pi}{\pi \vdash p_k(X_1, ..., X_n) \vartriangleright_a p_k^c(X_1, ..., X_n)^d} \text{ where } c = \{\tau_i \mid (X_i, \tau_i) \in \pi \text{ and } F_i \in \mathcal{F}_{in}^k\}$$

$$\frac{\pi \vdash G_i \vartriangleright_a G_i'}{\pi \vdash p_i(F_1, ..., F_n) :- G_i \vartriangleright_a^p p_i^c(F_1, ..., F_n) :- G_i'} \text{ where } c = \{\tau_i \mid (F_i, \tau_i) \in \pi \text{ and } F_i \in \mathcal{F}_{in}^i\}$$

$$\frac{\forall p_i(F_1, ..., F_n) : -G_i \in P \text{ and } \forall (\pi_c, \pi_e) \in \Psi_i :}{\pi_c \vdash p_i(F_1, ..., F_n) : -G_i \vartriangleright_a^p p_i^c(F_1, ..., F_n) : -G_i' \text{ and } p_i^c(F_1, ..., F_n) : -G_i' \in P'}}{P \vartriangleright_a^P P'}$$

Given the result of BTA, Ψ, for every procedure $p_i(F_1, ..., F_{n_i}):-G_i \in P$ and for all $(\pi_{call}, \pi_{exit}) \in \Psi_i$, a procedure $p_i^{call}(F_1, ..., F_{n_i}):-G_i^a$ is created, where p_i^{call} denotes a renaming of p_i w.r.t. π_{call} and G^a is an annotated version of G_i in which every procedure call is renamed according to its call pattern.

3.2 Safeness and Termination of the Specialiser

The rules of Definition 3.1 define a *well-annotated* program [7], which can be shown to be safe: if an atom A is annotated static, the variables that are input to A will be sufficiently instantiated at specialisation-time (as predicted by BTA) in order for A to be reducible. If a *not G* or *if G then A_1 else A_2* construct is annotated static, G will reduce completely to true or fail at specialisation-time, and hence the construct itself can be evaluated.

Starting from an annotated program and an initial procedure call, say $p_k(t_1, \ldots, t_n)$ with $t_1, \ldots, t_n$ valid Mercury terms, the program is specialised in the usual way: a new procedure $p_k(t_1, \ldots, t_n) : -G'_k$ is created, where G'_k denotes the result of reducing the annotated body of p_k in an environment where p_k's input arguments are bound to the appropriate terms. When during this reduction, code is residualised, the variables in the residualised code are substituted by their value obtained from reduction (if no value for a variable was obtained, it is left as a variable in the residual code). For every procedure call in G'_k, a new procedure is created in the same way, unless it is a variant of a previously encountered call.

Two aspects play a crucial role in termination of this specialisation process: Firstly, the process of reducing a goal should be finite. The defined BTA ensures finiteness of reduction: procedure calls are only unfolded when they are not under dynamic control. As such, termination of the process is guaranteed unless there is a static loop in the program [7]: a static loop meaning that a procedure call is specialised of which an instance does not terminate when evaluated under Mercury. This kind of termination can be compared to the so-called *local* termination in the context of on-line specialisation (e.g. [10]).

Secondly, one must ensure that there is no infinite number of different residual procedure calls to be specialised. This kind of *global* termination is not guaranteed by BTA alone. Consider the following annotated procedure $p(list(T) :: in, T :: in, list(T) :: in, list(T) :: out)$ that deconstructs a list L, and builds a new list R of the same length, but in which all elements are initialised to the value E. The procedure uses an accumulator.

Example 3.2

$p(L, E, Acc, R)\text{:-}Acc2 \Leftarrow^s [E|Acc],$
$\qquad\qquad if^d \ L \Rightarrow^d [X|Xs] \ then \ p(Xs, E, Acc2, R)^d \ else \ R :=^d Acc2.$

This procedure is well-annotated given as binding-times that L is *free* and the other input arguments are completely static. Specialising the call $p(L, a, [], R)$ results in an infinite number of residual calls $p(L, a, [], R)$, $p(L, a, [a], R)$, $p(L, a, [a, a], R), \ldots$ to be specialised.

Global termination can be achieved by specialising appropriate *generalisations* of residualised calls, mapping several residualised calls to the same (specialised) procedure. Since often, this global termination problem arises due to the concrete input to the specialiser, it seems natural to guarantee global termination on the level of the specialiser, when concrete input is available. A wealth of generalisation techniques do exist (see e.g. [10]).

4 Conclusion and Further Work

Performing BTA by abstract interpretation is well studied in the context of functional (e.g. [7, 6, 2]) and imperative languages (e.g. [1]). In [12] for example, a BTA for polymorphically typed languages is presented that is based on *projections* [9], capable of dealing with *partially static* values.

Initial efforts to produce a BTA for logic programming include [13, 8, 3]. These analyses, however, are not completely automatic or lack a general notion of partially static, and are often unable to handle terms that are less instantiated at specialisation-time than they will be at run-time. Much of the encountered difficulties are due to the lack of a type system or the presence of extra-logical features.

In this work, we present a polymorphic and polyvariant BTA for Mercury that, contrary to e.g. [8, 3], exploits the notion of partially static binding-times. We show that the classic framework of BTA by abstract interpretation is applicable to Mercury, but needs to be extended in order to deal correctly with unification and predicates – instead of functions – which can either fail or succeed with multiple output values. The resulting BTA is completely automatic and does not require any more user input than the type and mode information already required by Mercury (except for the initial binding times of the main predicate's input arguments).

The described BTA was implemented in Mercury, and produces, apart from a set of directions for the specialiser, an annotated program encoded in HTML. The use of different colors makes the binding times and the annotations visible for human inspection, illustrating a clear advantage of BTA for specialisation over on-line techniques lacking such a pre-analysis.

Topics of further research include extending the analysis to handle more involved mode declarations and higher-order features of Mercury. A less conservative control strategy – propagating binding-time information over dynamic control structures – may provide better specialisation opportunities at the cost of a specialiser that will have to perform more checks at specialisation-time (becoming more on-line) if it is to guarantee termination. When no strategy at all is incorporated, the resulting analysis is instantiatedness analysis, denoting for every variable its instantiatedness at run-time, given the instantiatedness of the main predicate's input arguments.

Specialisation, combined with other optimisation techniques like structure filtering [4], can change the determinism of a predicate and possibly requires the derivation of new type definitions. Exactly when and how to do this, is also a topic for further research.

Acknowledgments

The authors thank Bern Martens for fruitful discussions, and anonymous referees for valuable comments which helped to improve the paper. Wim Vanhoof is supported by a grant of the IWT, Belgium. Maurice Bruynooghe is supported by "FWO Vlaanderen". This research was partially supported by the ESPRIT ARGo and GOA LP+ projects.

References

[1] L. O. Andersen. Binding-time analysis and the taming of C pointers. In *Proceedings of the ACM SIGPLAN Symposium on Partial Evaluation and Semantics-Based Program Manipulation. PEPM'93*, pages 47–58, New York, NY, USA, 1993. ACM Press.

[2] A. Bondorf and J. Jørgensen. Efficient analyses for realistic off-line partial evaluation. *Journal of Functional Programming*, 3(3):315–346, July 93.

[3] Maurice Bruynooghe, Michael Leuschel, and Kostis Sagonas. A polyvariant binding-time analysis for off-line partial deduction. In C. Hankin, editor, *Programming Languages and Systems, Proc. of ESOP'98, part of ETAPS'98*, pages 27–41, Lisbon, Portugal, 1998. Springer-Verlag. LNCS 1381.

[4] J. Gallagher and M. Bruynooghe. Some low-level source transformations for logic programs. In M. Bruynooghe, editor, *Proceedings Meta'90*, pages 229–244, Leuven, April 1990.

[5] J. Gallagher and M. Bruynooghe. The derivation of an algorithm for program specialisation. *New Generation Computing*, 9(3&4):305–333, 1991.

[6] F. Henglein and C. Mossin. Polymorphic binding-time analysis. *Lecture Notes in Computer Science*, 788, 1994.

[7] N. D. Jones, C. K. Gomard, and P. Sestoft. *Partial Evaluation and Automatic Program Generation*. Prentice Hall, 1993.

[8] J. Jørgensen and M. Leuschel. Efficiently generating efficient generating extensions in Prolog. In O. Danvy, R. Glück, and P. Thiemann, editors, *Proceedings Dagstuhl Seminar on Partial Evaluation*, pages 238–262, Schloss Dagstuhl, Germany, 1996. Springer-Verlag, LNCS 1110.

[9] J. Launchbury. Dependent sums express separation of binding times. In K. Davis and J. Hughes, editors, *Functional Programming*, pages 238 – 253. Springer-Verlag, 1989.

[10] M. Leuschel, B. Martens, and D. De Schreye. Controlling generalisation and polyvariance in partial deduction of normal logic programs. *ACM Transactions on Programming Languages and Systems*, 20(1), 1998.

[11] B. Martens and D. De Schreye. Automatic finite unfolding using well-founded measures. *Journal of Logic Programming*, 28(2):89–146, 1996.

[12] T Mogensen. Binding Time Analysis for Polymorphically Typed Higher Order Languages. In J Diaz and F Orejas, editors, *TAPSOFT'89, Barcelona, Spain*, volume 352 of *LNCS*, pages 298–312. Springer-Verlag, March 1989.

[13] T. Mogensen and A. Bondorf. Logimix: A self-applicable partial evaluator for Prolog. In K.-K. Lau and T. Clement, editors, *Proceedings LOPSTR'92*, pages 214–227. Springer-Verlag, Workshops in Computing Series, 1993.

[14] Zoltan Somogyi, Fergus Henderson, and Thomas Conway. The execution algorithm of Mercury, an efficient purely declarative logic programming language. *Journal of Logic Programming*, 29(1–3):17–64, October–November 1996.

Solving TSP with Time Windows with Constraints

Filippo Focacci, Michela Milano
Dip. Ingegneria - University of Ferrara
Via Saragat, 1
Ferrara, 41100 Italy
{ffocacci, mmilano}@deis.unibo.it

Andrea Lodi
DEIS - University of Bologna
V.le Risorgimento, 2
Bologna 40136 Italy
alodi@deis.unibo.it

Abstract

This paper presents a set of techniques for solving the Travelling Salesman Problems (TSP) with Time Windows (TSPTW) with constraints. These techniques are based on two views of the TSPTW, i.e., TSP and a scheduling problem. From the scheduling perspective, we use powerful propagation schemes, that cope with feasibility issues due to the presence of time windows. On the other hand, the TSP model involving costs on arcs takes into account the optimization aspect of the problem. For *optimization reasoning*, Operations Research (OR) branch and bound and reduced cost fixing techniques have been extensively studied. In this paper, we propose: (*i*) propagation schemes deriving from the formulation of the TSPTW exploiting routing and scheduling models; (*ii*) the use of OR algorithms for lower bound calculation and reduced cost fixing for performing domain filtering; (*iii*) branching strategies exploiting information on costs and problem structure. The interesting point is that these techniques interact and exchange results through shared variables in the constraint store. The cooperation of pruning techniques with OR algorithms taking into account information on costs leads to excellent performances and increases the flexibility of OR approaches. We evaluate the use of these techniques on several sets of problems from the literature; computational results show that we achieve better results than previous Constraint Logic Programming algorithms and we are competitive with state of the art OR techniques. Moreover, we are able to find the optimal solution for instances which have never been solved to optimality before.

1   Introduction

In this paper, we study the Travelling Salesman Problem with Time Windows (TSPTW), which is the problem of finding a minimum cost tour visiting a set of cities where each city is visited exactly once. In addition, each city must be visited within a given time window even if early arrivals are allowed. In general, the cost is computed as the sum of travel costs from each couple of cities in the path. The problem is NP-hard, and Savelsberg [31] showed that even finding a feasible solution of TSPTW is NP-complete. TSPTW has important applications in routing and scheduling. For this reason, it has been extensively studied in the OR field [16], and also previously faced via Constraint Logic Programming [27].

The TSPTW can be seen as the union of two combinatorial optimization problems, i.e., the Travelling Salesman Problem (TSP) and a scheduling problem. In TSPs *optimization* usually results to be the most difficult issue. In fact, although the feasibility problem of finding an hamiltonian cycle in a graph is also NP-hard [20], it is usually easy to find a feasible solution for a TSP, while the optimal solution is very hard to find. TSPs have been efficiently solved by using OR methods such as Branch and Cut [1] and Local Search [31]. Some OR Branch and Bound approaches have also been proposed, see for instance [24]. All the OR exact methods (i.e. Branch and Cut, and Branch and Bound) for TSP optimally solve a relaxation of the original problem.

On the other hand, scheduling problems with release dates and due dates may contain difficult feasibility issues involving disjunctive, precedence and resource capacity constraints. The solution of scheduling problems is probably one of the most promising CP areas of application to date [6, 10, 11]. This is due to the definition of powerful propagation techniques, such as the *edge finding* [7], in global constraints.

In this setting, we propose a set of techniques for solving the TSPTW with constraints that merges OR techniques for coping with the optimization perspective, and CLP propagation algorithms for the feasibility viewpoint. We show a set of constraint propagation algorithms deriving from the field of scheduling and routing problems. One important contribution of this paper concerns the use of *cost-based* propagation, previously used for solving pure TSPs [19], matching and scheduling problems with set up times [18]. We have implemented a filtering algorithm that prunes variable domains on the basis of lower bound calculation and reduced cost fixing. The idea is to remove from variable domains values which cannot lead to better solution than the best one found so far. Moreover, using the information on costs we have developed effective branching strategies, such as a variant of the well known *sub-tour elimination* used for TSPs [5].

The integration of cost-based filtering algorithms in CLP leads to fundamental advantages both from the CLP and OR perspectives. From the CLP viewpoint, the use of OR algorithms allows to: (*i*) substantially reduce the search space, thus leading to performance improvements with respect to pure CLP algorithms; (ii) better cope with information deriving from objective function, which are, in general, not effectively handled by CLP tools; (iii) define new search strategies deriving from information on costs.

From the OR side, the advantages of using CLP tools are that: (i) the OR techniques used, i.e., lower bound calculation and reduced cost fixing, not only interact with each other, but interact also with other problem constraints, since domain filtering deriving from considerations on costs may trigger other propagation on shared variables and vice-versa; (ii) when embedded in a CLP framework, OR techniques benefit from the flexibility of CLP models and can be easily adapted to variants of the same problem without additional effort.

We will show that the synergy between OR optimization techniques embedded in global constraints, and CLP constraint solving techniques makes the resulting framework a technique of choice for the TSPTW. In fact, the algorithm proposed outperforms previous CLP approaches and is competitive with state of the art OR approaches, and can be easily adapted to variants of the problem, e.g., TSPTW with precedence constraints, with pickup and delivery, with multiple time windows.

2 TSPTW: definition and previous approaches

The Travelling Salesman Problem with Time Windows is a time constrained variant of the Travelling Salesman Problem. It consists of finding the minimum cost path to be travelled by a vehicle, starting and returning at the same depot, which must visit a set of n cities exactly once. Each couple of cities has an associated travel time. The service at a node i should begin within a time window $[a_i, b_i]$ associated to the node. Early arrivals are allowed, in the sense that the vehicle can arrive before the time window lower bound. However, in this case the vehicle has to wait until the node is ready for the beginning of service. This problem can be found in a variety of real life applications such as routing, scheduling, manufacturing and delivery problems. For this reason, the problem has been studied both in the Operations Research and Constraint Programming fields.

Within the OR community, despite to the difficulty of the problem (as mentioned even finding a feasible tour to the TSPTW is NP-complete), many exact algorithms have been presented.

The first approaches are due to Christofides, Mingozzi and Toth [13] and Baker [3] and consider a variant of the problem where the total schedule time has to be minimized (MPTW). The first paper presents a branch-and-bound algorithm based on a state space relaxation approach, whereas the second one is again a branch-and-bound algorithm exploiting a time constrained critical path formulation. Langevin et al. [24] addressed both MPTW and TSPTW by using a two-commodity flow formulation within a branch-and-bound scheme. Dumas, Desrosiers, Gélinas and Solomon [17] proposed a dynamic programming approach for the TSPTW that extensively exploits elimination tests to reduce the state space. More recently, a dynamic programming algorithm has been recently presented by Mingozzi, Bianco and Ricciardelli [25]. The algorithm embeds bounding functions able to reduce the state space (derived by a generalization of the state space relaxation technique [13]) and can be also applied to TSPTW problems with precedence constraints.

The most recent approaches are due to Ascheuer, Fischetti and Grötschel [2] and to Balas and Simonetti [4]. The first paper considers several formulations for the asymmetric version of the problem and compares them within a branch-and-cut scheme, whereas the second one is again a dynamic programming framework.

Quite surprisingly, despite the importance of the problem, few efforts have been devoted to the study of the TSPTW in the Constraint Programming community. Caseau and Koppstein [9] have faced a large task assignment problem where a set of small TSPTW instances are solved with a good average performance. The combination of scheduling and routing models allows to benefit from the advantages of each formalization when one view of the problem dominates the other.

More recently, TSPTW has been faced by enriching a simple CLP model with redundant constraints [27]. These additional constraints embed arc-elimination and time window reduction algorithms previously proposed in the OR field in [24] and [15] respectively.

A variant of the TSPTW, called TSP with Multiple Time Windows, has been solved in [28]. The authors underline the CLP flexibility by showing that this variant of the TSPTW can be solved with exactly the same algorithm used for the original problem by slightly changing the model.

In the Constraint Programming community, some work has been done concerning pure TSPs. Caseau and Laburthe [12] have solved small TSP instances with constraints by using a set of simple, but effective, propagation algorithms, and cost based reasoning deriving from the use of the Lagrangian relaxation of the problem.

Following that paper, we have previously tackled pure TSPs in [19], by exploiting lower bound calculation and reduced costs fixing. On pure TSPs, we have achieved the best known results which are, however, far to be comparable with state-of-the-art OR branch and cut approaches to the problem. In this paper, we have adopted the same techniques for performing cost-based domain filtering for the time-constrained variant of the problem. We achieve results comparable, in some cases even better, than those found via sophisticated Branch and Cut approaches. This comes from the flexibility of Constraint Logic Programming models that allow to cope with variants of the same problem in an easy way, while traditional OR approaches require much effort if the problem specifications slightly change. Moreover, we are able to find the optimal solution for instances which have never been solved to optimality before.

3 CLP Model of the TSPTW

A CLP model of the TSPTW has been previously described in [27]; in this section, we will recall the model, and the set of constraints used to enforce feasibility. Let $V = 0, 1, 2, \ldots, n, n + 1$ be a set of nodes, where nodes $1, \ldots, n$ represent the cities to be visited, and nodes 0 and $n + 1$ represent the origin and destination depots. Each node has an associated time window $TW_i = [a_i, b_i]$ representing the time frame during which the service at city i must be executed. Also, each node has an associated duration dur_i, which represents the duration of the service to be performed at city i. For each couple of cities i and j, $t_{i,j}$ is the travel cost from i to j.

We define four domain variables per node. Domain variables $Next_i$ and $Prev_i$ identify cities visited after and before node i respectively. The domain of variables $Next_i$ contains values $[1..n + 1]$, except for $Next_{n+1}$ which is set to 0, while the domain of each $Prev_i$ contains values $[0, .., n]$, except for $Prev_0$ which is set to $n + 1$. Domain variable $Cost_i$ identifies the cost to be paid to go from node i to node $Next_i$, i.e., $t_{i,Next_i}$. Finally, domain variable $Start_i$ identifies the time at which the service begins at node i. With no loss of generality, we can impose $Start_0 = 0$, and $Cost_{n+1} = 0$.

A feasible solution of the TSPTW is an assignment of a different value to each variable (a successor in the path) by avoiding sub-tours and respecting time windows constraints. An optimal solution of the problem is the one minimizing the sum of the travel costs $t_{i,Next_i}$.

Using the introduced variables, a CLP model for TSPTW is the following:

$$Z(TSPTW) \quad = \min \sum_{i \in V} Cost_i \tag{1}$$

$$\text{subject to} \tag{2}$$

$$alldifferent([Next_0, ..., Next_{n+1}]) \tag{3}$$

$$nocycle([Next_0, ..., Next_n]) \tag{4}$$

$$Next_i = j \Leftrightarrow Prev_j = i \; \forall i, j \in V \tag{5}$$

$$Next_i = j \Rightarrow Cost_i = t_{i,j} \; \forall i, j \in V \tag{6}$$

$$Next_i = j \Rightarrow Start_i + dur_i + Cost_i \leq Start_j \; \forall i, j \in V \tag{7}$$

$$a_i \leq Start_i \leq b_i \; \forall i \in V \tag{8}$$

The *alldifferent* constraint imposes that each node has exactly one outgoing and exactly one incoming arc, i.e., each city is visited exactly once. The *nocycle* constraint forbids sub-tours. Equations (5) create the link between the $Next$ and $Prev$ variables; equations (6) create a link between the travel cost matrix and variables $Cost$. More interesting are equations (7) that define a connection between the TSP model (variables $Next$ and $Prev$) and the scheduling model (variables $Start$) with sequence dependent set up times

$(t_{i,j})$. Equations (8) simply define the bounds of variables $Start$ by imposing that the service in a node should start within the node time window.

4 Propagation Techniques

In this section we define the propagation scheme used for solving the TSPTW. We have exploited both well known CLP filtering algorithms and propagation techniques built from scratch for the problem. Concerning the constraint of difference, we have used the J.C. Régin [29] filtering algorithm.

For the *nocycle* constraint, we have implemented the simple, but effective, propagation described in [12] and [27]. As soon as a variable $Next_i$ (resp. $Prev_j$) is instantiated to value j (resp. i), we remove from the variable representing the end of the partial path starting in j the value representing the start of the partial path ending in i.

The set of equations (5) are propagated by considering the counterpart of the constraint: whenever a value j is removed from the domain of variable $Next_i$, the value i is removed from the domain of variable $Prev_j$, and viceversa.

The set of equations (6) is maintained by forcing

$$Cost_i \geq \min_{k \in Dom(Next_i)} t_{i,k} \; \forall i \in V \tag{9}$$

$$Cost_i \leq \max_{k \in Dom(Next_i)} t_{i,k} \; \forall i \in V \tag{10}$$

where $Dom(V)$ identifies the domain of variable V.

Analogous propagation is performed for (7):

$$Start_i \geq \min_{k \in Dom(Prev_i)} \{Start_{Min_k} + dur_k + t_{k,i}\} \; \forall i \in V \tag{11}$$

$$Start_i \leq \max_{k \in Dom(Next_i)} \{Start_{Max_k} - t_{i,k} - dur_i\} \; \forall i \in V \tag{12}$$

where $Start_{Min}$ and $Start_{Max}$ identify the lower and upper bounds of variable $Start$ respectively.

In addition, under certain conditions some values can be removed from the domain of variable $Next_i$. In fact, if

$$Start_{Min_i} + dur_i + t_{i,j} > Start_{Max_j} \Rightarrow Next_i \neq j \; \forall i,j \in V \tag{13}$$

As proposed in [24], if for each node i we maintain the set of all nodes $\mathcal{B}_i$ which must precede and the set of all nodes $\mathcal{A}_i$ which must follow i, we are able to perform a more powerful propagation. In fact, if for a given couple of nodes i and j, the set of successors of i and the set of predecessors of j have non empty intersection, this implies that at least a third node k must be between i and j, and therefore we can remove j from the domain of $Next_i$.

The sets $\mathcal{B}_i$ and $\mathcal{A}_i$ can be calculated as follows:

$$\mathcal{B}_i = \{k \in V | Start_{Min_i} + sp_{i,k} > Start_{Max_k}\} \qquad (14)$$

$$\mathcal{A}_i = \{k \in V | Start_{Min_k} + sp_{k,i} > Start_{Max_i}\} \qquad (15)$$

where $sp_{i,j}$ is the shortest path from i to j. The computation of the shortest path from any node to any other has an $O(n^3)$ complexity. We have experimentally tested this propagation algorithm where the shortest path was recalculated at each node of the search tree, and found disappointing results, since the shortest path calculation is computationally too expensive w.r.t. the performed pruning. We have therefore used the sets $\mathcal{B}_i$ and $\mathcal{A}_i$ defined by the *Precedence Graph Constraint* of ILOG Scheduler [22]. The Precedence Graph Constraint of ILOG Scheduler maintains, for each activity, its relative position with respect to all the other activities on a given resource. For example, for an activity A we can ask for the set of all activities which surely precede (resp. succeed) A in the resource, or all activities which are still unranked with respect to A (i.e., may precede or succeed). The relative position is gathered by joining the temporal information obtained by time bounds of activities, temporal constraints, disjunctive constraints, and temporal closure.

Finally, additional rules based on predecessor and successor sets to possibly reduce the domain of *Start* variables have been proposed in [15]:

$$Start_i \geq \max_{k \in \mathcal{B}_i}(Start_k + sp_{k,i}) \qquad (16)$$

$$Start_i \leq \min_{k \in \mathcal{A}_i}(Start_k - sp_{i,k}) \qquad (17)$$

As for the previous case, we have tested this reduction rule, but decided not to use it in our propagation scheme because the pruning obtained did not pay off the computational complexity of the shortest path matrix computation.

We have implemented and tested the above mentioned filtering algorithms by using ILOG Solver and Scheduler [23, 22], after creating a mapping between TSPTW and a scheduling problem with a single unary resource and sequence dependent setup times. In the mapping, each visit corresponds to an activity. The start time variable of activity i corresponds to $Start_i$ in the TSPTW, and its duration is equal to dur_i. A transition time matrix is defined based on matrix $t_{i,j}$ which enforces that the beginning of activity j is after the end of activity i plus $t_{i,j}$ if activity j is scheduled immediately after activity i.

The flexibility of Constraint Programming allowed us to smoothly merge the routing and scheduling models propagation techniques.

5 Cost-based Domain Filtering

In this section, we describe the cost-based domain filtering algorithms previously used in [19] and [18] for TSPs, Matching and Scheduling Problems with set up times, and proposed as a general technique in [18].

The idea is to create a global constraint embedding a propagation algorithm aimed at removing from variable domains those assignments which do not improve the best solution found so far. Domain filtering is achieved by optimally solving a problem which is a relaxation of the original problem. In this paper, we consider the Assignment Problem (AP) [14] as a relaxation of the TSP (and consequently of the TSPTW). The AP is the graph theory problem of finding a set of *disjoint* sub-tours such that all the vertices in V are visited and the overall cost is a minimum. AP provides an optimal integer solution, and, if such a solution is composed by a single tour, is then optimal for TSP. The AP optimal solution is obtained through a *primal-dual* algorithm described in [8].

The AP relaxation provides: the optimal AP solution, i.e., a variable assignment; the value of the optimal AP solution which is a lower bound LB on the original problem; a reduced cost matrix $\bar{c}$. Each $\bar{c}_{ij}$ estimates the additional cost to be added to LB if variable $Next_i$ is assigned to j.

We have used these results for performing domain filtering and for defining branching strategies, that will be described in Section 6. The lower bound value LB is trivially linked to the variable representing the objective function Z through the constraint $LB \leq Z$. More interesting is the propagation based on reduced costs. Given the reduced cost matrix $\bar{c}$ of element $\bar{c}_{ij}$, it is known that $LB_{Next_i=j} = LB + \bar{c}_{ij}$ is a valid lower bound for the problem where $Next_i$ is assigned to j. Therefore we can impose:

$$\forall i, j \text{ if } LB_{Next_i=j} > Z_{max} \text{ then } Next_i \neq j \tag{18}$$

An improvement to the use of the reduced costs can be exploited as follows: we want to evaluate if value j could be removed from the domain of variable $Next_i$. Let $Next_i = k$ and $Next_l = j$ in the optimal AP solution. In order to assign $Next_i = j$, a minimum augmenting path, say PTH, from l to k has to be determined since l and k should be re-assigned. Thus, the cost of the optimal AP solution where $Next_i = j$ is $LB + \bar{c}_{ij} + cost(PTH)$, where $cost(PTH)$ is clearly the cost of path PTH. Two bounds on this cost have been proposed in [19] and used in this paper.

The events triggering this propagation are changes in the upper bound of the objective function variable Z and each change in the problem variable domains. Note that the AP solution is re-computed only if the removed value j belongs to the solution of the assignment problem. The solution of the AP relaxation at the root node requires in the worst case $O(n^3)$, whereas each following AP re-computation due to domain reduction can be efficiently computed in $O(n^2)$ time through a single augmenting path step (see [8] for details). The reduced cost matrix is obtained without extra computational effort during the AP solution, while the bounds on $cost(PTH)$ are computed in $O(n^2)$. Thus, the total time complexity of the filtering algorithm is $O(n^2)$.

Reduced cost fixing appeared to be particularly suited for Constraint Programming. In fact, while reduced cost fixing is extensively used in OR frameworks, it is usually not exploited to trigger other constraints, but only in the following lower bound computation, i.e., the following branching node. When embedded in a CP framework, the reduced cost fixing produces domain reduction which usually triggers other problem constraints through shared variables.

For this reason, the AP lower bound that is not used in OR for solving TSPTWs, since it is not a tight bound, becomes, as shown in Section 7 extremely effective when used in combination with other propagation algorithms, and gives results comparable with state of the art OR algorithms.

6   Branching Schemes

We have already mentioned that the TSPTW can be seen as a mix of TSP and Scheduling Problem. For this reason we have tested different branching strategies suited for one or the other aspect of the problem. In this section, we present two branching techniques: the first is more suitable for the TSP model, while the second is a branching strategy often used in scheduling problems, thus being more focused on time windows feasibility.

The most commonly used branching scheme for Branch and Bound algorithms for TSP which uses the AP as relaxation is the *sub-tour elimination strategy* [5]. At any stage of the search tree, we consider the solution of the AP, and we choose a tour identified by arcs $(i_1, i_2), (i_2, i_3), \ldots, (i_s, i_1)$. The *sub-tour elimination* strategy imposes the following disjunction:
$(Next_{i_1} \neq i_2) | (Next_{i_1} = i_2 \wedge Next_{i_2} \neq i_3) | \ldots | (Next_{i_1} = i_2 \wedge \ldots Next_{i_{s-1}} = i_s \wedge Next_{i_s} \neq i_1)$

The tour chosen $(i_1, i_2), (i_2, i_3), \ldots, (i_s, i_1)$, infeasible for the TSP, will not appear in any of the generated branches. This search strategy has an important drawback when applied to TSPTW: the branching decision $(Next_{i_k} \neq i_{k+1})$ has often no influence on the *Start* variables, i.e., on the scheduling view of the problem. The use of CLP allowed us to easily obtain a variant of the sub-tour elimination strategy for the TSPTW. In fact, instead of partitioning the search space by fixing and removing values, we can use constraints. Again, in any stage of the search tree, we consider the solution of the AP, and we choose a tour identified by arcs $(i_1, i_2), (i_2, i_3), \ldots, (i_s, i_1)$. We impose the following disjunction:
$(i_1 \succ i_2) | (i_1 \prec i_2 \wedge i_2 \succ i_3) | \ldots | (i_1 \prec i_2 \wedge \ldots i_{s-1} \prec i_s \wedge i_s \succ i_1)$

Where $(i_h \succ i_k)$ introduces a temporal constraint between the visits at nodes h and k. Also in this case the tour chosen $(i_1, i_2), (i_2, i_3), \ldots, (i_s, i_1)$, infeasible for the TSP, will not appear in any of the generated branches, since the temporal constraint will propagate both on the *Next* variables and on the *Start* variables. This search strategy appeared to be very effective for TSPTW with large time windows since in this case the TSP view dominates the scheduling one.

The second heuristics tested is a typical scheduling branching strategy. When dealing with scheduling problems, very often a solution is built in chronological order. At each node of the search tree the activity with the minimum earliest start time is chosen and scheduled. In our case, we sequence all nodes starting assigning a node to the initial depot (we fix its variable *Next*), until the last node which will be assigned to the final depot. For each given node, we choose the value to be assigned as follows: among all values having zero reduced cost (we know that there exists at least one of such values), we select the one corresponding to the node with the smallest latest start time. This strategy is always able to quickly find solutions for the TSPTW (maybe of not very good quality), and it is therefore particularly suited when the scheduling part is dominant.

7 Computational results

The overall approach has been implemented using ILOG Solver and Scheduler, and runs on a Pentium II 200 MHz. We tested the algorithm on three different sets of problems from the literature in order to obtain a strong indication of the effectiveness of the proposed approach with respect to both OR and CP literature.

The first set of problems considered was proposed in [24]. In particular, Langevin et al. solved randomly-generated symmetric instances with up to 60 cities (see [24] for a detailed description of the problem generation method).

n	w	subtour		sequence		Langevin [24]
		time	fails	time	fails	time
40	20	0.05	3.2	0.066	3.2	1.7
	30	0.078	7.4	0.078	8.4	4.4
	40	0.08	12	0.122	15.6	7.3
	60	0.186	26	0.22	31.6	-
60	20	0.22	7.75	0.19	7.25	7.9
	30	0.27	15.75	0.2075	15.25	15.0
	40	0.412	30	0.465	51.5	17.6
	60	0.78	63.75	2.0475	195	-
80	20	0.538	14.6	0.45	15.8	-
	30	0.912	47.2	1.43	71.4	-
	40	1.846	86	17.04	1247	-
	60	93.822	4682.6	4/5 in 15 mins		-

Table 1: Results on instances from Langevin et al. [24]

Results are shown in Table 1 where n is the number of cities and w the size of the time windows. We report computing times (in seconds) and number of fails of the sub-tour elimination strategy and the chronological scheduling strategy on an average of 5 randomly generated problems. Since the problems do not present feasibility issues, the sub-tour elimination strategy outperforms the sequence one. The results reported in the last column are taken from [24] and were obtained on a SUN Sparc Station 2. Note that the solved instances are obviously not the same from [24], but the same generation policy has been maintained. Also Mingozzi et al. [25] solved instances from the same set by Dynamic Programming and claim to obtain computing times on average five times smaller than those achieved by Langevin et al..

The second set of problems is derived from the RC instances of Solomon [32] for the Vehicle Routing Problem with Time Windows (VRPTW). In particular, the TSPTW instances are obtained by considering the single-vehicle decomposition deriving from VRPTW solutions in the literature (i.e., Rochat and Taillard [30] and Taillard et al. [33]). This decomposition generates instances with up to 40 cities and has been solved by Pesant et al. [27]. It is easy to see that the optimization of the route of a single vehicle is in general very interesting because directly leads to an improvement of the overall VRPTW solution.

The results (reported in Table 2) for these instances in terms of computing times, number of failures and quality of the solution are compared with the ones of the CLP approach by Pesant et al. [27] (where the CPU time is given with respect to a SUN SS1000). Note that our results are obtained by solving the problem from scratch, while [27] solves the problems by imposing as objective function upper bound, the best solution for the problem taken from Taillard et al. [30] (reported in column VRP) which is always very close to the optimal one.

Inst.	n	Subtour			Sequence			Pesant et al. [27]			VRP
		best	time	fails	best	time	fails	best	time	fails	best
rc201.0	25	378.62	0.1	19	378.62	0.15	25	378.62	51	607	378.7
rc201.1	28	374.70	3.21	778	374.70	51.5	13.5k	374.7	311	4.03k	376.6
rc201.3	19	232.54	0.09	25	232.54	0.11	35	232.54	6.5	77	232.6
rc202.0	25	246.23	9.81	2.96k	246.22	5.9	1.83k	246.22	4.16k	32.2k	246.3
rc202.1	22	206.54	1.77	553	206.53	3.4	1.07k	206.53	1.80k	19.5k	206.6
rc202.2	27	341.77	1.11	257	341.77	0.93	265	341.77	696	5.15k	345.1
rc202.3	26	367.85	33.35	8.06k	367.85	325	111k	367.85	11.1k	65.3k	369.8
rc205.0	26	251.65	6.88	1.74k	251.65	4.4	1.45k	251.65	652	4.77k	251.7
rc205.1	22	271.22	0.09	17	271.22	0.16	54	271.22	128	1.32k	271.3
rc205.2	28	434.69	847	237k	434.69	1.21k	375k	436.64	24h	-	442.5
rc205.3	24	361.24	3.81	1.04k	361.24	6.78	2.27k	361.24	7.02k	90.9k	362.9
rc207.0	37	-	2h	-	436.69	757	112k	436.69	24h	-	439.6
rc207.1	33	396.39	2.7k	484k	396.36	1.70k	332k	396.36	24h	-	396.4
rc207.2	30	246.41	284	62k	246.41	160	40k	246.41	6.79k	62.9k	246.5

Table 2: Results on rc2 instances from Solomon et al. [32]

We find the optimal solution for each instance and prove optimality, while Pesant et al. [27] are not able to prove optimality of instances rc205.2, rc207.0 and rc207.1 in 24h. Moreover, we are able to find the optimal solution which has never been found before to problem rc205.2. From Table 2 we can see that, while the sub-tour elimination strategy for random instances (Table 1) always outperforms the chronological one, in this case, depending from the problem structure, the chronological strategy can lead to better results. For example, in the rc207.0 instance, the sub-tour elimination strategy fails to find any feasible solution in 2 hours.

The third set of instances derives from real-world problems with up to 233 cities originally proposed by Ascheuer et al. [2]. These instances are asymmetric and derive from stacker crane routing applications [1].

The results for a subset of these asymmetric instances are reported in Table 3 and are compared with the ones obtained by the branch-and-cut approach of Ascheuer et al. [2] (on a Sun Sparc Station 10). In the second column, we report either the value of the optimal solution (when known) or the lower and upper bounds of the objective function from Ascheuer et al.. Numbers in round brackets refer to results obtained by the dynamic programming approach by Balas and Simonetti [4].

Instance	Ascheuer et al. [2]		Sequence			Sequence LDS		
	best	time	best	time	fails	best	time	fails
rbg010a	149	0.12	149	0.03	11	149	0.02	11
rbg016a	179	0.2	179	0.04	12	179	0.03	12
rbg020a	210	0.2	210	0.03	10	210	0.04	10
rbg027a	268	2.25	268	0.19	33	268	0.18	33
rbg031a	328	1.7	328	279	99.5k	328	318	89.2k
rbg048a	[456-527]	5h	503	2h	-	487	2h	-
rbg049a	[420-501] (486)*	5h	505	2h	-	497	2h	-
rbg050b	[453-542] (518)*	5h	546	2h	-	548	2h	-
rbg050c	[508-536]	5h	573	2h	-	542	2h	-

Table 3: Results on rbg instances from Ascheuer et al. [2]

In this set of instances, the search strategy that gave best results is the chronological heuristics, while we could not achieve good results by using the sub-tour elimination strategy. In addition, since in rbg instances the scheduling component dominates the TSP one, we have tested the *Limited Discrepancy Search (LDS)* [26], previously proved to be effective in scheduling problems. LDS was first defined in [21] and is based on the assumption that the left branches are more likely to be successful than right ones. In particular, with the LDS strategy we obtain the best known solution for the rbg048a instance.

A final remark concerns the use of a pure CP approach with ILOG Solver and Scheduler. We did not report results in detail, since they are disappointing. For the 14 instances of Table 2, for example, this approach is able to prove optimality only in 8 cases within 30 minutes, and the computing times are at least 10 times larger than those obtained by our approach.

8 Conclusions and Future Work

We have proposed a set of techniques for solving the TSPTW with constraints. Starting from a TSPTW model combining a TSP and a Scheduling

---

[1]The complete set can be downloaded from the web page: http://www.zib.de/ascheuer/ATSPTWinstances.html along with the best known solutions.

Problem, we use a set of propagation techniques based on feasibility reasoning and exploiting information on costs. We incorporate in global constraints OR bounding and reduced cost fixing techniques. In addition, we proposed two branching strategies that can be used to solve TSPTW and are more or less effective w.r.t. the problem topology (small or large time windows). In particular, we proposed a variant of the sub-tour elimination strategy of TSP adapted to TSPTW.

We achieved remarkable results w.r.t. both previous CLP approaches and OR algorithms. In particular, we are able to find one new best known solutions for real life instances of ATSPTW and one best known solution for an instance deriving from VRPTW. The problem sets analyzed strongly differ each other, and a search strategy may be more effective for one or the other set due to the different problem structure. The quality of the results obtained on a variety of problems considered allows us to claim that our approach can be seen as a technique of choice for solving TSPTW. Unfortunately, there not exist a standard library (such as the TSPLIB) for TSPTW, and approaches which seem to perform the best, based on Dynamic Programming [25], to our knowledge were only tested on randomly generated problems.

Although we did not explicitly compare our results with the ones obtained in [17, 25], the preliminary tests run show that we are still a little behind their performances. Nevertheless, a Dynamic Programming (DP) approach heavily depends on the time discretization used. In fact, in a DP formulation the number of different states to be considered (the memory space) for each node is proportional to the number of time points in the time windows and this limits the applicability of a DP approach. Further investigation and more detailed comparisons are subject of current work.

Acknowledgments

This work has been partially supported by ILOG S.A. (France). The authors are grateful to F. Laburthe, U. Junker, W. Nuijten, J. Pommier, J.F. Puget, P. Refalo, P. Toth and D. Vigo for fruitful discussions and suggestions. Thanks are also due to anonymous referees for useful comments on an earlier version of this paper.

References

[1] D. Applegate, R.E. Bixby, V. Chvátal, and W. Cook. Finding cuts in tsp. unpublished, 1994.

[2] N. Ascheuer, M. Fischetti, and M. Grötschel. Solving atsp with time windows by branch-and-cut. unpublished, 1999.

[3] E. Backer. An exact algorithm for the timed constrained travelling salesman problem. *Operations Research*, 31:938–945, 1983.

[4] E. Balas and N. Simonetti. Linear time dynamic programming algorithms for some classes of restricted tsp's. unpublished, 1996.

[5] E. Balas and P. Toth. Branch and bound methods. In E.L. Lawler, J.K. Lenstra, A.H.G. Rinnooy Kan, and D.B. Shmoys, editors, *The Travelling Salesman Problem*. John Wiley and Sons, 1985.

[6] P. Baptiste, C. Le Pape, and W. Nuijten. Efficient operations research algorithms in constraint-based scheduling. In *Proceedings of IJCAI'95*, 1995.

[7] J. Carlier and E. Pinson. An algorithm for solving job shop scheduling. *Management Science*, 35:164–176, 1995.

[8] G. Carpaneto, S. Martello, and P. Toth. Algorithms and codes for the assignment problem. *Annals of Operations Research*, 13:193–223, 1988.

[9] Y. Caseau and P. Koppstein. A Rule-based approach to a Time-Constrainted Traveling Salesman Problem. In *Proceedings of Symposium of Artificial Intelligence and Mathematics*, 1992.

[10] Y. Caseau and F. Laburte. Cumulative scheduling with task intervals. In *Proceedings of the JICSLP96*. MIT Press, 1996.

[11] Y. Caseau and F. Laburthe. Improved CLP scheduling with task intervals. In *Proceedings of ICLP'94*, 1994.

[12] Y. Caseau and F. Laburthe. Solving small TSPs with constraints. In *Proceedings of ICLP'97*, 1997.

[13] N. Christofides, A. Mingozzi, and P. Toth. State space relaxation procedures for the computation of bounds to routing problems. *Networks*, 11:145–164, 1981.

[14] M. Dell'Amico and S. Martello. Linear assignment. In M. Dell'Amico, F. Maffioli, and S. Martello, editors, *Annotated Bibliographies in Combinatorial Optimization*. Wiley, 1997.

[15] M. Desrochers, J. Desrosiers, and M.M. Solomon. A new Optimization Algorithm for the Vehicle Routing problem with Time Windows. *Operations Research*, 40:342–354, 1992.

[16] J. Desrosiers, Y. Dumas, M.M. Solomon, and F. Soumis. Time constrained routing and scheduling. In M.O. Ball, T.L. Magnanti, C.L. Monma, and G.L. Nemhauser, editors, *Network Routing*. Elsevier, 1995.

[17] Y. Dumas, J. Desrosiers, E. Gelinas, and M.M. Solomon. An optimal algorithm for the travelling salesman problem with the time windows. *Operations Research*, 43:367–371, 1995.

[18] F. Focacci, A. Lodi, and M. Milano. Cost-based domain filtering. *Proc. International Conference on Principles and Practice of Constraint Programming CP99*, 1999.

[19] F. Focacci, A. Lodi, M. Milano, and D. Vigo. Solving TSP through the integration of OR and CP techniques. *Proc. CP98 Workshop on Large Scale Combinatorial Optimisation and Constraints*, 1998.

[20] M.R. Garey and D.S. Johnson. *Computers and Intractability: a Guide to the Theory of NP-Completeness*. Freeman, San Francisco, 1979.

529

[21] W.D. Harvey and M.L. Ginsberg. Limited discrepancy search. *Proc. IJCAI95*, 1995.

[22] ILOG. *ILOG Scheduler 4.4 Reference Manual.*

[23] ILOG. *ILOG Solver 4.4 Reference Manual.*

[24] A. Langevin, M. Desrochers, J. Desrosiers, and F. Soumis. A two-commodity flow formulation for the Traveling Salesman and Makespan Problem with Time Windows. *Networks*, 23:631–640, 1993.

[25] A. Mingozzi, L. Bianco, and S. Ricciardelli. Dynamic programming strategies for the travelling salesman problem with time windows and precedence constraints. *Operations Research*, 45:365–377, 1997.

[26] L. Perron. Integration into constraint programming and parallelization of or/ai search methods. In *CP-AI-OR'99 Workshop on Integration of AI and OR techniques in Constraint Programming for Combinatorial Optimization Problems*, 1999.

[27] G. Pesant, M. Gendreau, J.Y. Potvin, and J.M. Rousseau. An exact constraint logic programming algorithm for the travelling salesman problem with time windows. *Transportation Science*, 32(1):12–29, 1998.

[28] G. Pesant, M. Gendreau, J.Y. Potvin, and J.M. Rousseau. On the flexibility of Constraint Programming models: From Single to Multiple Time Windows for the Travelling Salesman Problem. *European Journal of Operational Research*, 117(2):253–263, 1999.

[29] J.C. Régin. A filtering algorithm for constraints of difference in CSPs. In *Proceedings of AAAI'94*, 1994.

[30] Y. Rochat and E.D. Taillard. Probabilistic diversification and intensification in local search for vehicle routing. *Journal of Heuristics*, 1:147–167, 1995.

[31] M.W.P. Savelsberg. Local search in Routing Poblem with Time Windows. *Annals of Operations Research*, 4:285–305, 1985.

[32] M.M. Solomon. Algorithms for the vehicle routing and scheduling problem with time window constraints. *Operations Research*, 35:254–265, 1987.

[33] E.D. Taillard, P. Badeau, M. Gendreau, F. Guertin, and J.-Y. Potvin. A new neighborhood structure for the vehicle routing problems with time windows. unpublished, 1995.

Finding Fair Allocations for the Coalition Problem with Constraints

Evan Tick
CDC North America, 9W 57th Street,
New York, NY 10019, USA
ticke@cdcna.cdcc.com

Roland H. C. Yap
School of Computing, National University of Singapore,
Singapore 119260, Republic of Singapore
ryap@comp.nus.edu.sg

Michael J. Maher
School of Computing & Information Technology, Griffith University,
Nathan, Queensland 4111, Australia
M.Maher@cit.gu.edu.au

Abstract

Fair allocation of payoffs among cooperating players who can form various coalitions of differing utilities is the classic game theoretic "coalition problem." Shapley's value is perhaps the most famous fairness criterion. In this paper, a new allocation principle is proposed based on constraints. Initially constraints are defined by the coalition payoffs, in the standard way. The algorithm proceeds by "tightening" the constraints in a fair manner until the solution space is sufficiently small. An arbitrary boundary point is then chosen as the "fair" allocation. Our technique has been implemented in the constraint programming language $CLP(\mathcal{R})$ and evaluated against Shapley values for various benchmark problems. We show how our method is related to Shapley values, some empirical tests and describe an application to bond swaps.

1 Introduction

This paper investigates a constraint approach to the standard *coalition problem* in game theory. Consider a scenario with two companies, A and B. If A markets a product on his own, a return of \$1M is feasible. Similarly for B, a return of \$2M is feasible. If however both A and B join forces, then a return of \$4M is feasible due to synergistic effects and economies of scale. The question then is given that the best strategy is for A and B to cooperate, how should the payoff be distributed between A and B. This simple example illustrates a 2 player cooperative game which is a special case of the more general problem. In general, the coalition problem deals with n players who can cooperate with each other to form coalitions. An assumption is that cooperation requires negotiation between the players and such bargaining can be enforced. The problem is formalized by assigning to each coalition (subset of cooperating players) a utility which represents the value of the coalition. Normally, the (grand) coalition comprising the entire group has the greatest utility. In this case, we assume that all players cooperate, receiving the highest payment. The problem is to divide this payment among the players in a "fair" way.

For instance Raiffa [4] shows, for the three-party coalition problem, how to convert the utilities into a linear program where the variables correspond to the fair payment to the corresponding player. An n-player game defines at most $2^n - 1$ constraints with n variables. Each constraint defines the payoff bound of a unique potential coalition. The $2^n - 1$ constraints derive from the $2^n - 1$ subsets within a set of n elements. Each subset defines a potential coalition.

If the resulting constraints have no solution, i.e., is inconsistent, it indicates that the individual coalition constraints are too restrictive to allow any fair allocation. Certain allocation techniques, including our own and Shapley values can produce a solution even if the constraints are inconsistent. In this paper, however, we focus on consistent problems.

If the constraint set is consistent, then it represents the convex hull of a multi-dimensional solution space to the problem. In other words, all points *within* and *on* the hull represent feasible allocations of the group payment among the cooperating players. One linear programming approach would be to specify an objective function which can optimize over the perimeter of the space. Unfortunately, it is highly likely that perimeter values are "unfair" in the sense that certain players feel cheated because of the gap between what they are receiving and what they could receive if they joined a smaller coalition. Such players might drop out of the union, leaving the Pareto frontier. Intuitively, fair solutions are *within* the space, and therefore not the perimeter solutions obtained with optimizing the linear program.

Raiffa [4] and Shapley [3] suggest heuristics for finding a fair internal point. In fact, their algorithms do not involve the constraint space per se: they compute the fair solution from the original data, i.e., the coalition payoffs. Thus, as mentioned above, they can produce an allocation even for an inconsistent problem with no rational agreement point.

In this paper we present some alternative techniques for a fair allocation. This is accomplished by first formulating the linear constraints as previously described. The algorithm here, implemented in CLP($\mathcal{R}$) [2] then artificially tightens the constraints in an incremental, "fair" manner. Intuitively, we assume that each coalition payoff is worth *more* than it actually is, slowly reducing the size of the solution space. The tightening process itself is a parameter of the algorithm, and we propose three possibilities: absolute, relative and hybrid tightening. As we tighten the constraints, we eventually produce a very small solution space that contains acceptable solutions. We then arbitrarily choose a solution to present as the answer.[1]

This technique is practical with constraint programming languages which allow easy manipulations of complex constraints. The advantage of the technique is that it can potentially be extended to produce solutions where Shapley values and other techniques based on average marginal utility cannot.

This paper is organized as follows. The constraint based algorithm is formally defined in Section 2. Section 4 reviews Shapley's axioms and discusses fairness issues. A CLP($\mathcal{R}$) implementation is summarized in Section 3. Section 5 illustrates the technique for the Scandinavian Cement Problem from Raiffa [4]. Section 6 presents empirical benchmark analysis comparing the proposed technique to Shapley values. Section 7 describes a financial bond swapping application of our work. Conclusions and future work are summarized in Section 8.

2 A Constraint-based Coalition Allocation Algorithm

First we will briefly review the game theoretic setting for the coalition problems addressed here (see [3, 4]). Consider an n-player game where variable X_i denotes the allocated payoff to player $1 \leq i \leq n$ from the (cooperative) group payoff. We require $X_i \geq 0$, i.e., we don't allow negative shares. We will use N to denote the set of all players $\{1, \ldots, n\}$. A coalition C_i is a subset of N. The coalition composed of all players, N, is the *grand coalition*. For each coalition, we define a payoff function $p()$ which gives the value of that coalition where $p(\emptyset) = 0$. We require that $p()$ is non-negative. In addition, we will assume that $p()$ is *superadditive*, i.e. $p(U) + p(V) \leq p(U \cup V)$ for all $U, V \subseteq N$ and $U \cap V = \emptyset$. We will assume that the grand coalition gives the highest payoff and is the optimal strategy.

The problem then is then how to allocate $p(N)$ to X_i such that

$$\sum_{i=1}^{n} X_i = p(N).$$

This coalition problem can be formulated as a linear program (see [4]) as follows:

- The grand coalition gives the constraint $\sum_{i=1}^{n} X_i = p(N)$. This being the maximum cooperative group payoff.

- For each coalition which is smaller than the the grand coalition, $\sum_{i \in C_i} X_i \geq p(C_i)$, so that each coalition is happy. This is the proper-subset coalition payoffs. There are at most $2^n - 2$ such inequalities.

---

[1] The definition of "small space" is made indirectly with a parameter ϵ that defines the termination condition of the tightening procedure, as discussed in Section 2.

This system of constraints is also called the *core*.

The algorithm inputs are a set T of inequalities describing the proper-subset coalition payoffs, and an equality G describing the cooperative group payoff. Assume that constraints in T are normalized in the form $\sum_{k \in C_j} X_k \geq$ RHS_j, where RHS_j is some real, nonnegative constant, for $1 \leq j \leq |T|$.

We define a tightening vector $\overline{K}$ of constants, and

$$T(\overline{K}) = \{ \sum_{k \in C_j} X_k \geq \gamma(\text{RHS}_j, K_j) \mid 1 \leq j \leq |T| \}$$

where $\gamma()$ is called the fair tightening function. The definition of $\gamma()$ will be deferred until Section 4. Let $S(\overline{K}) = T(\overline{K}) \cup G$.

Figure 1 gives the pseudo-code of the algorithm. The arguments of the algorithm are the parameterized constraints $S()$, a termination granularity ϵ, and an increment Δ_{max}. Important local variables are the tightening vector $\overline{K}$ and a bit vector $\overline{F}$. Δ_{max} is chosen as a sufficiently large real number. We used $(\Delta_{max}, \epsilon) = (1000, 0.0001)$ in the tests conducted in Section 6.

```
search( S(), ε, Δ_max ) {
    initialize K̄ =< 0, 0, ..., 0 >
              F̄ =< 1, 1, ...1 >
    while (F̄ ≠ 0̄) do {
        Δ = Δ_max
        while (Δ > ε) do {                                    (I)
            K̄ = K̄ + ΔF̄
            if ¬SAT(S(K̄)) then
                K̄ = K̄ − ΔF̄
            Δ = Δ/2
        }
        for { ∀ j | 1 ≤ j ≤ |S| } do {                        (II)
            R̄ = K̄
            R_j = K_j + 2ε
            F_j = { 1  if SAT(S(R̄))
                  { 0  otherwise
        }
    }
    for { ∀ j | 1 ≤ j ≤ |S| } do {                            (III)
        R(K̄) = S(K̄) \ ∑_{k∈C_j} X_k ≥ γ(RHS_j, K_j)
                      ∪ ∑_{k∈C_j} X_k = γ(RHS_j, K_j)
        if SAT( R(K̄) ) then
            S(K̄) = R(K̄)
    }
    return S(K̄)
}
```

Figure 1: Constraint Tightening Algorithm

The bit vector $\overline{F}$ uses a '1' to represent that the corresponding tightening parameter is non-fixed, a '0' to represent that it is fixed. The outer loop of the algorithm finds the tightest $\overline{K}$ such that $S(\overline{K})$ is satisfied. Phase I finds the largest consistent increment for all non-fixed tightening parameters. Phase II then fixes critical parameters that previously limited the tightening search. This loop (containing phases I and II) iterates until all parameters are fixed. Phase III then finds an arbitrary solution within this space by conditional conversion of inequalities to equalities.

Some clarifications about the algorithm in Figure 1 are in order.

- We assume that the grand coalition is the only pareto-efficient solution. This can be generalized to deal with other definitions of optimal coalitions, but we show this simpler case for clarity.

- The ratio ϵ/Δ is the percentage variation that is acceptable. Furthermore, note that arbitrary solutions are at most $2\epsilon\sqrt{n}$ apart in the space, the usual Euclidean distance. Thus we can tune the search with ϵ.

- The reassignment of $\Delta = \Delta_{max}$ within the main loop is conservative. However, the phase I loop is sufficiently simple to quickly reduce Δ each time through.

- One way of computing a minimum initial Δ_{max} is the maximum K over all inequalities i such that $\gamma(RHS_i, K) = RHS_G$, where RHS_G is the bound of the grand coalition, assumed to be the largest bound.

- The algorithm can easily be extended with negative Δ so as to *relax* an initially unsatisfiable constraint system, i.e. an empty core, to permit a solution.

- The algorithm makes use of a constraint solver, SAT() which determines if the constraints are satisfiable. A side-effect of SAT() is the instantiation of variables if they are ground. Thus phase III generates a specific solution by converting the inequalities to equations.

Considering the time complexity of the proposed algorithm, let m be the number of legal coalitions (including the grand coalition). Input size m is bounded by $2^n - 1$ for an n-player game. In the worst case, we need to iterate m times, wherein each iteration only one coalition is tightened. Within each iteration, we need to make $log_2(\Delta/\epsilon)$ search steps. Each search step we need to solve m linear inequalities. Let's call this cost $P(m)$ which is polynomial for some solution algorithms, and exponential worst-case for the Simplex method, but polynomial average case. Thus the worst-case time complexity order is $O(mP(m)log_2(\Delta_{max}/\epsilon))$.

The complexity is exponential in the number of players because of the combinatorial explosion in the number of coalitions that can be formed.

```
search1( _, _, Delta, Epsilon, Final, Final ) :-
  Delta < Epsilon, !.

search1( Id, Prev, Delta, Epsilon, K0, Final ) :-
  Next = Prev + Delta,
  update( K0, Next, K1 ),
  const( Id, K1 ), !,
  search1( Id, Next, Delta/2, Epsilon, K1, Final ).

search1( Id, Prev, Delta, Epsilon, K, Final ) :-
  search1( Id, Prev, Delta/2, Epsilon, K, Final ).

update( [], _, [] ).
update( [ f(fix,K) | Ks ], New, [ f(fix,K) | Vs ] ) :-
  update( Ks, New, Vs ).
update( [ f(float,_) | Ks ], New, [ f(float,New) | Vs ] ) :-
  update( Ks, New, Vs ).
```

Figure 2: Binary Search for Tightening Parameters in CLP($\mathcal{R}$)

A naive implementation of Shapley's algorithm has a complexity $O(n \cdot n!)$ because it requires computing the marginal utility for each player for each permutation of the n player coalitions. See Owen [3] for discussion of special cases where Shapley values can be computed more efficiently.

3 Implementation

The previously described algorithm was implemented in 184 lines of CLP($\mathcal{R}$) [1, 2]. In this section only the kernel of the implementation is described: the binary search for the tightening parameters.

Figure 2 shows the CLP($\mathcal{R}$) implementation of the search procedure. The main procedure, **search1/6** is passed the payoff data (**Id**), the tightest bounds known to keep the space solvable (**Prev**), the current increment to attempt on the bounds (**Delta**), the minimum granularity for termination (**Epsilon**), and the current tightening vector (**K0**). The last argument (**Final**) is the output tightening vector.

Clause (1) of **search1/6** terminates the search when the increment is smaller than the desired granularity. Clause (2) increments the current tightening vector and tries the new constraint set and tightening vector with **const/2**. If the space is still nonempty, the search recurses with half the increment. If the space is empty, the clause (3) is executed which retains the old tightening vector, but also halves the increment.

Procedure **update/3** updates the tightening vector. Any K_i is implemented by the data structure f(Type,Value) where Type is either fix (the parameter is fixed) or float (the parameter has not yet been fixed). Only non-fixed parameters are incremented.

All parameters are initialized as float, and if sufficiently iterated, all parameters eventually become fix. The test to convert a non-fixed to a fixed parameter is not shown here. Essentially, each non-fixed parameter is separately incremented by 2ϵ. For each such trial where the space becomes empty, the parameter becomes fixed.

4 Fairness and the Constraint Tightening Function

All non-fixed parameters are increased in step during an iteration. Once the space becomes unsatisfiable, critical parameters are fixed, and another iteration is executed. However, the tightening algorithm is only as "fair"[2] as the γ function which defines how the constraints are inflated. To further understand how fairness relates to γ, we first review the Shapley axioms [3].

Shapley stipulated that n-person coalition games must satisfy the following three criteria to be considered fair. He went on to prove that Shapley values are the only technique that can make this guarantee.

1. A *carrier* of a game must split the entire group payoff: none must go to *slackers*. For example, consider a 3-player game where $p(\{X\}) = 0$, $p(\{Y\}) = 5$, $p(\{Z\}) = 5$, $p(\{X,Y\}) = 5$, $p(\{X,Z\}) = 5$, $p(\{Y,Z\}) = 10$, and $p(\{X,Y,Z\}) = 10$. The $p()$ function gives the payoff of a coalition. Here X is the slacker and $\{Y,Z\}$ is the carrier. A fair solution will pay X nothing.

2. Fair solutions are invariant under relabeling the players. In other words, the search strategy or solution method does not depend on the order that players are considered.

3. Fair solutions are linearly composable. For example, consider two n-player games G_1 and G_2 with solutions S_1 and S_2. If we sum corresponding coalition payoffs in both games into G_3, then the fair solution to G_3 should be $S_1 + S_2$. The implications of this axiom are far reaching. It means that fair solutions are insensitive to *translation* or *scaling* of payoffs. For example given a game denominated in dollars or yen, the solution is identical. Less intuitively, if we offer an extra $100 to each player in a game, a fair solution gives each player his original cut (before the bonus) plus the $100. In other words, the bonus cannot affect a fair solution.

It is arguable if these axioms are necessary or sufficient to define fairness. Certainly there are alternatives to Shapley values that have been proposed,

---

[2]What is fair will depend on the assumptions made.

type	function	Shapley axioms
absolute	$\gamma(\text{RHS}, K) = \text{RHS} + f(K)$	2 & 3
relative	$\gamma(\text{RHS}, K) = \text{RHS}(1 + g(K))$	1 & 2
hybrid	$\gamma(\text{RHS}, K) = \text{RHS}(1 + g(K)) + f(K)$	2

Table 1: Families of Partially Fair γ Functions ($f(0) = g(0) = 0$)

e.g., Raiffa's "offers that cannot readily be refused" method ([4] pg. 270). Raiffa claims:

> "It is not easy to suggest a compelling set of 'fairness principles' that deserve to be universally accepted as *the* arbitrated solution."

Without taking sides in this dispute, it is enlightening to evaluate the fairness of the tightening method with respect to these axioms. For the $\gamma(\text{RHS}, K)$ function to make sense, it must necessarily obey:

1. monotonicity in K to ensure that the bounds get tighter.

2. $\gamma(\text{RHS}, 0) = \text{RHS}$ to ensure consistency with the original problem.

In addition to these, J. Larson[3] conjectured that if γ also obeys the following two axioms in addition to those above, it will necessarily obey Shapley's axioms:

3. $\gamma(0, K) = 0$ to ensure that slackers don't get paid!

4. $\gamma(R + S, K) = \gamma(R, K) + \gamma(S, K)$.

We also hypothesize that in fact no γ can satisfy all four of the previous tightening axioms. However, we offer three families of γ functions that achieve partial success, summarized in Table 1 where f and g are any monotonic functions in K such that $f(0) = g(0) = 0$.

Intuitively, absolute tightening shrinks the space without regard to its displacement from the origin. Thus slackers eventually get some payoff, making the family less fair. Relative tightening is less intuitive: it doesn't suffer from the fair carrier problem, but rather it is not linearly composable.

To visualize relative tightening, consider a rectangle in two-space defined by four inequalities such that each side is parallel to an axis, as shown in Figure 3. Each side of the rectangle will travel inwards towards the solution space, *in proportion to its distance from its parallel axis*. Thus the space will be shrinking as shown (the tightening vectors are not drawn to scale).

---

[3]Personal communication.

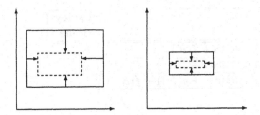

Figure 3: Illustrating Tightening Procedure

At some point during the binary search, two opposite sides of the rectangle will *cross*, making the space empty. The tightening parameters (corresponding to these two sides) allowing the smallest nonempty space will then be fixed. During the next iteration, the remaining two sides will continue to travel towards each other until they also cross. It is important to note that the final small rectangle will *not* lie in the center of mass of the original rectangle. Since the sides moved in proportion to their distances from the axes, the final space will be biased towards the origin.

The relative tightening procedure strongly resembles Raiffa's "balanced increments" method ([4], pg. 243). Furthermore, the families of tightening functions have an economics interpretation. Consider the coalitions as processes that convert inputs into utility. Then $\overline{K}$ are additional inputs that we feed the system, and $\partial\gamma/\partial K$ is the rate as which inputs are converted into utility. Absolute tightening presupposes that $\partial\gamma/\partial K = \partial f(K)/\partial K$ so there is no "economy of scale" associated with the original value of a coalition. Relative tightening presupposes that $\partial\gamma/\partial K = RHS(\partial g(K)/\partial K)$. Thus utility production is amplified by the original coalition value.

The hybrid family loses both Shapley axioms 1 and 3, but offers the flexibility to perhaps moderate the tightening process through judicious selection of f and g. From an economic standpoint, coalition "production" is modeled as a combination of fixed and variable effects, as in any realistic process. Heuristic experimentation with the hybrid family is a topic of future research. In the remainder of the paper, we focus on absolute and relative tightening functions where $f(K) = g(K) = K$.

5 Examples

Raiffa [4] presents a 3-player game called the Scandinavian Cement Problem. Consider players X, Y, and Z with the following coalition payoffs: $p(\{X\}) = 30$, $p(\{Y\}) = 22$, $p(\{Z\}) = 5$, $p(\{X, Y\}) = 59$, $p(\{X, Z\}) = 45$, $p(\{Y, Z\}) = 39$, and $p(\{X, Y, Z\}) = 77$. Raiffa presents this as a linear programming problem in which he immediately eliminates one of the variables in order to plot the solution space in two dimensions. Here we plot the constraints in three dimensions because it better illustrates how the constraint tightening

Iteration	K1	K2	K3	K4	K5	K6
0	1000	1000	1000	1000	1000	1000
1	0.07689	0.07689	0.07689	0.07689	0.07689*	0.07689*
2	0.166655*	0.166655	0.166655	0.07689	0.07689*	0.07689*
3	0.166655*	0.297189*	0.297189	0.07689*	0.07689*	0.07689*
4	0.166655*	0.297189*	1.69241*	0.07689*	0.07689*	0.07689*

Table 2: Scandinavian Cement: Relative Tightening

behaves.

The linear constraints can be formulated in CLP($\mathcal{R}$) as follows:

```
const( [ X, Y, Z ] ) :-
    X           >= 30,   Y           >= 22,
    Z           >= 5,    X + Y       >= 59,
    X + Z       >= 45,   Y + Z       >= 39,
    X + Y + Z   = 77.
```

Since const/1 succeeds, it indicates that the solution space is nonempty. Const can be extended with tightening factors K_i (here we show relative tightening):

```
const( [ X,Y,Z ], [ K1,K2,K3,K4,K5,K6 ] ) :-
    X           >= 30*(1 + K1),
    Y           >= 22*(1 + K2),
    Z           >= 5*(1 + K3),
    X + Y       >= 59*(1 + K4),
    X + Z       >= 45*(1 + K5),
    Y + Z       >= 39*(1 + K6),
    X + Y + Z   = 77.
```

In relative tightening, the factors are implemented as a percentage of the original lower bound. Thus for instance if K1 = 0.2, the singleton X coalition is being "tightened" by 20% over its original value of 30 to 36. Table 2 shows the six parameters for successive iterations of the relative tightening algorithm. Initially parameters are set very high (1000%), but the binary search algorithm rapidly focuses the space in the first iteration to 7.6%. Parameters labeled "*" have been fixed by the search, i.e., no further tightening is possible for that constraint, given the minimal granularity ϵ. In this problem, the second iteration almost doubles parameters K1, K2, and K3 to 17%. The third iteration doubles parameters K2 and K3 to 30%. Finally, the widest constraint, for coalition $\{Z\}$, is tightened down in the final iteration with K3 = 169%.

Figure 4 (not drawn to scale) illustrates the 3-dimensional solution space of the problem. The $X + Y + Z = 77$ plane is shown, as are the projections of $X \geq 30$, $Y \geq 22$, and $Z \geq 5$. These projections on the plane define an asymmetric triangle from the larger equilateral triangle. The 2-player coalition constraints are not shown in this figure.

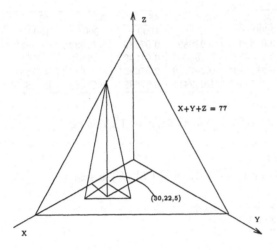

Figure 4: Scandinavian Solution Space: 3D View

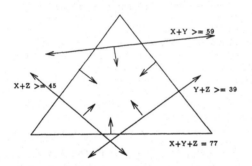

Figure 5: Shrinking the Scandinavian Solution Space

Figure 5 (not drawn to scale) illustrates the problem in a 2-space defined by the plane $X + Y + Z = 77$. The asymmetric triangle is intersected by the three inequality constraints representing the 2-player coalition payoffs. As the RHS bounds of 2-player coalitions are increased during tightening, these three constraints move towards the center of the solution space. As the RHS bounds of 1-player coalitions are increased during tightening, the three edges of the triangle move towards the center of the solution space.

The primary advantage of our method over others is not in its more refined definition of fairness, but rather in its ability to solve ad hoc problems. These become important when coalition payoffs are not precise: lower bounds or ranges may be known. In addition, we may desire to model dependencies among different coalitions' payoffs. We illustrate this by considering alternative versions of the Scandinavian Cement problem. Conventional techniques do not address these extended problems.

Suppose we know that $p(\{X\}) > 30$ and $p(\{Y\}) > 22$ (other information is as previously stated). Player X and Y have dependent payoffs such that if $p(\{X\}) > 32$ then $p(\{Y\}) > 25$. This can be modeled (before the tightening transformation) as:

```
const( [ X, Y, Z ] ) :-
    X           >= 30,
    Y           >= 22,   dep( X, Y ),
    Z           >=  5,
    X + Y       >= 59,
    X + Z       >= 45,
    Y + Z       >= 39,
    X + Y + Z    = 77.

dep( X, _ ) :- X =< 32.
dep( X, Y ) :- X > 32, Y > 25.
```

More complex relationships between X and Y can be similarly modeled in $CLP(\mathcal{R})$, an arbitrary example is,

```
dep( X, _ ) :- X =< 32.
dep( X, Y ) :- X >  32, X < 35, Y >  25, Y < 30.
dep( X, Y ) :- X >= 35, X < 40, Y >= 30, Y < 33.
dep( X, Y ) :- X >= 40, Y = 33.
```

6   Empirical Analysis

Table 3 shows eight benchmark games of 3 and 4 players used to evaluate the proposed allocation technique. Note that the games do *not* all have the same total payoff. Cement is the Scandinavian Cement problem. Tweak1 is a slight variant of cement used to illustrate some shortcomings of proposed algorithm. The next five games were randomly generated. The final game tweak5 is a slight variant of rand5, again illustrating how our solutions diverge from Shapley values when the space is irregular. For each game, the Shapley values, relative and absolute tightened values are given. The mean squared differences with respect to the Shapley values are given.

Obviously how accurately the tightening methods approximate Shapley values is highly variable. Neither relative nor absolute tightening appears to be superior. To illustrate the discrepancies with Shapley values, consider tweak1 which takes the original Scandinavian Cement problem and modifies the payoff to coalition $\{X, Z\}$ from 45 to 53. The resulting relative mean squared difference increases by a factor of 31 times. Notice that the effect of boosting the $\{X, Z\}$ payoff relative to all others is the same in all techniques: Y's side payment decreases, subsidizing X and Z. The relative tightening scheme however more significantly penalizes Y (by 20%) than do the Shapley values, which penalizes Y by only 10%. Absolute tightening gets MSE = 5 for tweak1, and approximates Shapley slightly better than does the relative scheme. However, it also breaks down for tweak5.

game	N	Shapley Values	Tightening Scheme	
			relative	absolute
cement		{35.5,28.5,13}	{35.0,28.5,13.5}	{34.4,28.3,14.3}
tweak1	3	{36.8,25.8,14.3}	{37.2,23.0,16.8}	{37,23,17}
rand1		{29.5,41,49.5}	{31.4,38.8,49.7}	{27.5,42,50.5}
rand2		{22.5,35,39.5}	{20.1,36.8,40.1}	{21.3,36.3,39.3}
rand3		{46.5,38.5,28.3,36.7}	{47.7,36.4,23.8,42.1}	{48,40,32,30}
rand4	4	{39.3,44.2,46.8,39.7}	{43.7,21.4,64.7,40.2}	{37.5,30.25,53.5,48.75}
rand5		{31.3,51.8,54.2,62.7}	{34.3,55.3,51.0,59.4}	{34,59,52,55}
tweak5		{37.2,46,48.3,68.5}	{49.4,35.7,28.1,86.8}	{60.5,38,31,70.5}
mean squared differences				
cement		0	0.155	1.06
tweak1	3	0	4.88	5.06
rand1		0	2.86	2.00
rand2		0	3.18	1.06
rand3		0	13.5	15.8
rand4	4	0	215	81.2
rand5		0	10.5	30.8
tweak5		0	249	228

Table 3: Benchmark Allocations: Shapley vs. Tightening

7 Application

Due to space constraints, we can only sketch an application of our technique in some financial optimization applications at Morgan Stanley. The problem is one of determining the swap of securities among a pool of participant portfolios to optimize an objective under various constraints (for a basic text, see [6]). At Morgan Stanley, such applications were developed within the context of the BondSwap system [5]. Various objectives included maximizing tax benefits and minimizing capital convexity charges. Engaging many participants is critical to the overall optimization because only with critical mass, can the universe of bonds reach sufficient size to enable profitable transactions even when highly constrained.

One very practical problem with conducting such a swap is for the participants to cooperate. On their own, it would be highly unlike for them to join forces. Individual firms are tempted to swap with the market, thereby facing higher overheads. An intermediary can be effective in convincing parties to join a coalition by *optimizing* and executing their swap at guaranteed prices. However, even with an intermediary, negotiation is needed to convince parties to join. For instance, participants can drop out if they perceive inequity in the division of gains.

The coalition technique described in this paper can be used to compute a fair division. First, the intermediary optimizes a set of portfolios of various coalitions, recording a total realizable gain with each experiment. These are the bounds for the coalitions. In practice, not all coalitions are needed because subgroups of subsidiary portfolios will only be included if their parent participates. The fair division can then be solved with our algorithm.

There are two main advantages to using our constraint approach for solving the fairness problem. First, we can model "special deals" made by the intermediary with individual firms. Secondly, we can integrate some of the general portfolio constraints up from the optimizer, into the fairness algorithm. For example, a typical portfolio constraint is a bound on the required *duration* of the portfolio. A constraint could be added in the fairness algorithm to compensate a firm more if their duration constraint is active.

8 Conclusions

This paper described a technique for determining a fair allocation for the classic n-player coalition problem. The solution exploits the use of a constraint programming language like $CLP(\mathcal{R})$ which provides the ability to easily manipulate and solve arithmetic constraints. It is well known how to model the coalition problem in terms of linear constraints. However fair allocation value methods like Shapley do not make use of the constraints at all. In this paper, we propose a computational approach based on constraint manipulation where any number of (multi-dimensional) linear constraints are tightened by iterative scaling. The tightening shrinks the solution space in a "fair" manner based on a parameterized γ function. One can continue shrinking the space until the final space is reduced to be arbitrarily small, from which any boundary point can be chosen as an allocation. The advantage of this approach compared with more direct approaches such as Shapley values or pure linear programming, is that the computational nature allows flexibility and incorporation of other considerations into the determination of fair allocation.

We demonstrate the technique for relative and absolute γ tightening functions, and discussed the properties of γ which relate to Shapley-fairness. Our empirical results for simple γ functions show differing approximations to Shapley values: some were close, some were not.

Interesting future research directions include: 1) experimentation with the family of γ functions to better approach Shapley-fairness; 2) derive a formal relationship between our scheme are two types of Raiffa-fairness: "balanced increments" and "offers that cannot readily be refused" [4], and 3) determine how to model, in constraints, uncertain coalition payoffs and a related attribute: risk preferences among players.

Acknowledgments

We thank Bob Clemen and James Larson for their comments and criticisms.

References

[1] N. C. Heintz, J. Jaffar, S. Michaylov, P. J. Stuckey, and R. H. C. Yap. *The CLP(R) Programmer's Manual Version 1.2*, September 1992.

[2] J. Jaffar, S. Michaylov, P. Stuckey, and R. H. C. Yap. The CLP($\mathcal{R}$) Language and System. *ACM Transactions on Programming Languages and Systems*, 14(3):339–395, 1992.

[3] G. Owen. *Game Theory*. Academic Press, Orlando, second edition, 1982.

[4] H. Raiffa. *The Art and Sciene of Negotiation*. Harvard University Press, Cambridge, 1982.

[5] E. Tick and A.R. Young. Optimizing Multi-Party Bond Portfolios for Tax Purposes. Technical report, Morgan Stanley & Co. Incorporated, June 1997.

[6] P. Wilmott. *Derivatives: the theory and practice of financial engineering*. John Wiley, 1998.

Constraint-based Round Robin Tournament Planning

Martin Henz
School of Computing
National University of Singapore
Singapore 117543
henz@comp.nus.edu.sg

Abstract

Sport tournament planning becomes a complex task in the presence of heterogeneous requirements from teams, media, fans and other parties. Existing approaches to sport tournament planning often rely on precomputed tournament schemes which may be too rigid to cater for these requirements. Existing work on sport tournaments suggests a separation of the planning process into three phases. In this work, it is shown that all three phases can be solved using finite-domain constraint programming. The design of Friar Tuck, a generic constraint-based round robin planning tool, is outlined. New numerical results on round robin tournaments obtained with Friar Tuck underline the potential of constraints over finite domains in this area.

1 Introduction

In a sport competition, n given teams play against each other over a period of time according to a certain scheme. The round robin scheme is popular in many team sports like football and basketball. It determines that every team t plays against every other team a fixed number of times r during the competition. If r is 1, the scheme is called single round robin, and if r is 2, it is called double round robin. The matches take place at one of the opponents' facilities. If a team uses its own facilities in a match, it is said to have a home match, otherwise it has an away match.

This paper focuses on temporally dense round robin tournaments (abbreviated as RR throughout the paper), in which the $rn(n-1)/2$ matches are distributed over a minimal number d of dates such that every team plays at most one match per date. If n is even, d is $r(n-1)$. A RR with an odd number of teams consists of rn dates in each of which $n-1$ teams play and one team does not. This team is said to have a bye.

Table 1 shows a RR for $n = 5$ and $r = 1$. The integral value in row t and column j tells the team against which team t plays in date j; the $+$ or $-$ symbol indicates that the match is a home match or an away match, respectively, for team t; and b indicates a bye. A similar notation is used by Schreuder [16] and Russell and Leung [14].

This basic setup can be refined by additional requirements in various ways. The following list contains common requirements in tournament planning practice.

- A match between two given teams may be fixed to a certain date. We shall refer to such constraints as FIX-AGAINST.

		dates				
		1	2	3	4	5
teams	1	+2	−4	b	+3	−5
	2	−1	+3	−5	b	+4
	3	+5	−2	+4	−1	b
	4	b	+1	−3	+5	−2
	5	−3	b	+2	−4	+1

Table 1: A Single Round Robin with 5 Teams

- A team may be required to play home, or to play away, or to have a bye at a certain date (FIX-HAB).

- The number of home and away games that a team plays at certain dates may be fixed (EXACT-HAB). For example, in Table 1, every team plays twice at home and twice bye, making for a balanced tournament.

- The number of home matches (or away matches or byes) that a team plays at certain dates may be limited (ATMOST-HAB). For example, in Table 1, every team plays at least once home in the first two dates.

- The number of home matches (or away matches or byes, or certain combinations of these) that a team plays in sequence may be limited (ATMOST-HAB-SEQUENCE). For example, in Table 1, no team plays more than one away match in a row. Furthermore, there are no occurrences of sequences of more than two away games or byes in a row.

- There may be a limit on the number of times in which a team plays in sequence against one of a specified set of (supposedly strong) teams (ATMOST-AGAINST-SEQUENCE). For example, in Table 1, no team plays in a row against team 1 and team 2.

Double round robin tournaments—particularly popular in many sports—often have to fulfill additional constraints like the following.

- If the first match between two teams t_1 and t_2 is is a home match for t_1, then the second match is a home match for t_2 and vice versa (EVEN-HAB).

- The tournament may be split into two halves, requiring that each team play against the other teams in the same order in both halves (MIRROR). Such a perfectly mirrored RR can be obtained from Table 1 by simply repeating it once.

Commercial products that support round robin timetabling typically have a fixed set of timetables up to some n preloaded. The timetabling process then consists of assigning the right teams to the rows of this timetable. For professional sports leagues, where fans, media and teams pose highly irregular constraints (for an interesting collection of such constraints, consider [12]) these timetables typically do not lead to acceptable solutions.

Existing systematic approaches to round robin planning [3, 1, 2, 16, 14, 15, 12] proceed in two main stages. In the first stage, feasible sets of n patterns are generated. A pattern is a sequence of d home/away/bye tokens that indicates home matches, away matches or byes for a team throughout the tournament. In the second stage, timetables are generated based on pattern sets from the first stage.

The combination of the following properties makes pattern sets attractive as an intermediate step towards timetables. On one hand, a pattern set characterizes a significant aspect of a timetable, namely in which way teams may alternate between home and away matches and byes. On the other hand, pattern sets are generic in a sense that they fix neither the teams that play according to its element patterns, nor the opponent teams. Often many timetables can be constructed from a given pattern set.

The author showed in [6] that using constraint programming for all phases of a complex problem provides a vast improvement over techniques reported in [12]. The aim of this paper is to explain the constraint programming approach to all phases of the timetabling process. To this goal, a number of common constraints are given and corresponding constraints for constraint programming models of the solution phases are outlined.

Whereas in this work, all phases are handled with constraint programming, Schaerf [15] provides a constraint-based solution only to the second phase. McAloon, Tretkoff and Wetzel [10] deal with a related problem in which the concept of home and away games is replaced by resources called periods.

Existing models of the subproblems are described in more detail in the next section. In Section 3, a brief introduction to the basic ideas of finite domain constraint programming is given before constraint programming models of pattern generation, pattern set generation and timetable generation are outlined in Sections 4, 5 and 6, respectively. Section 7 presents Friar Tuck, a constraint-based tool for RR planning in which these models are accessible through a graphical user interface which also allows the user to enter a variety of specialized constraints. Section 8 gives the results of computational experiments conducted with Friar Tuck.

2 Solution Phases

2.1 Patterns

A pattern is a sequence of values from the set of symbols $\{+, -, b\}$ that fulfills the given constraints. Each symbol indicates either a home match $(+)$, an away match $(-)$ or a bye (b) in the date that corresponds to the position of the symbol in the sequence. For example, the following pattern for $n = 5$ indicates an away match in date 4.

	dates				
	1	2	3	4	5
pattern	−	+	b	−	+

All possible patterns are generated that meet the required constraints among EXACT-HAB, ATMOST-HAB, ATMOST-HAB-SEQUENCE, EVEN-HAB and MIRROR.

2.2 Pattern Sets

From these patterns, sets of n patterns are generated that have the right number of occurrences of $+$, $-$ and b per date. For even n, there must be

$n/2$ occurrences of $+$ and $-$ each, and for odd n, there must be $(n-1)/2$ occurrences of $+$ and $-$ each and one b. Such sets are called pattern sets.

2.3 Timetables

This step generates complete timetables from a given pattern set. Two distinct ways to decompose the problem have been taken for this step.

The first decomposition—sketched by Cain [2]—assigns teams to pattern sets first. This assignment is subject to the constraints FIX-HAB. Finally, opponent teams are assigned to the entries of the pattern set such that the result is a RR that fulfills all other constraints.

For the second problem decomposition—described by Schreuder [16] and used by Nemhauser and Trick [12]—it is convenient to introduce the notion of a team placeholder. Each of n team placeholders stands for a team, but the assignment of teams to team placeholders is not fixed. The idea is that a timetable of team placeholders can stand for as many different actual timetables as there are such assignments. Now matches between team placeholders are assigned to the entries of the pattern sets such that the result is a RR of placeholders. Finally, every team is assigned to a different placeholder such that all relevant constraints are fulfilled.

3 Finite Domain Constraint Programming

For solving the various combinatorial search problems that arise in these phases, we use finite domain constraint programming. A central notion is the constraint store that contains basic constraints on the possible values of integer (finite domain) variables. During computation, these constraints become stronger as integer values are excluded from the domain of variables. More complex constraints cannot be expressed in general by the constraint store and thus are operationalized by propagators instead. Propagators observe the constraint store and amplify it whenever possible by adding basic constraints to it, implementing a certain notion of consistency. After exhaustive propagation, typically not all finite domain variables are fixed to unique values. The operational notion of search explores a tree of possible constraint stores by adding new constraints or propagators according to a search strategy. Before branching, exhaustive propagation is performed. The constraint programming approach is described in detail in [9].

4 Patterns

With the usual problem sizes and constraints in tournament planning, pattern generation is a straightforward task. Nemhauser and Trick [12] show that for the problem they study (double round robin for 9 teams), exhaustive enumeration of all patterns is computationally feasible. In that case, a declarative description of the constraints can be used for filtering out admissible patterns. For bigger n, a more algorithmic approach would be needed.

The advantage of constraint programming here is that a declarative formulation of the constraints on patterns can be used for bigger n. A straightforward model consists of 0/1 variables h_j, a_j (and b_j, if n odd), $1 \le j \le d$. A team that plays according to the pattern represented by these variables plays home (away, bye) at date j if and only if $h_j = 1$ ($a_j = 1$, $b_j = 1$). An obvious constraint is that for every j, the sum of h_j, a_j and b_j must be 1. The constraints EXACT-HAB, ATMOST-HAB, ATMOST-HAB-SEQUENCE, EVEN-HAB and MIRROR can be represented with the summation propagator and combinations of 0/1 propagators like conjunction and disjunction. For example, an ATMOST-HAB constraint that expresses that there must be at least one home game in the first two dates is represented by a propagator for the disequation $h_1 + h_2 \geq 1$. An ATMOST-HAB-SEQUENCE constraint that expresses that all sequences of home matches should be shorter than s is expressed by propagators corresponding to constraints of the form

$$h_1 + \cdots + h_s < s \wedge \cdots h_{n-s+1} + \cdots h_n < s$$

This approach to such sequence constraints in the context of finite domain constraint programming is present in [17]. It seems to be adequate with the problem sizes at hand; more powerful propagation algorithms are presented in [13].

In the presence of sequence constraints, the most effective search strategy seems to be to enumerate the h, a and b variables date-wise, i.e. in the order $h_1, a_1, b_1, h_2, a_2, b_2, \ldots, b_d$.

5 Pattern Sets

Graph-theoretical results cover the existence and generation of pattern sets with useful properties. A well-studied property of pattern sets concerns the presence of breaks, which are sequences of two home matches or two away matches in a row or separated only with a bye. Minimizing the number of breaks in the schedule is a specialization of the constraint ATMOST-HAB-SEQUENCE. De Werra [4] and Schreuder [16] show that for odd n, there are pattern sets with no breaks, and for even n, the minimal number of breaks is $n - 2$.

In the presence of irregular constraints on patterns, pattern set generation degenerates to a combinatorial search problem and can be formulated as a variant of graph coloring. Nemhauser and Trick [12] employ integer programming to solve this problem, using the following model. Let P be the set of all feasible patterns. The 0/1 variables for home, away and bye of a pattern in P with index i for date j are denoted by $h_{i,j}$, $a_{i,j}$ and $b_{i,j}$, respectively. For each pattern index i, a 0/1 variable x_i indicates whether this pattern occurs in the desired pattern set. For odd n, the constraints are as follows.

$$\sum_i h_{i,j} x_i = (n-1)/2, \sum_i a_{i,j} x_i = (n-1)/2, \sum_i b_{i,j} x_i = 1, \text{for all dates } j.$$

For even n the constraints are

$$\sum_i h_{i,j} x_i = n/2, \sum_i a_{i,j} x_i = n/2, \text{for all dates } j.$$

Nemhauser and Trick reformulate this model as an optimization problem and solve it with integer programming.

In [6], the author shows that constraint programming exhibits better performance for pattern set generation on the problem studied by Nemhauser and Trick. Constraint programming systems provide summation propagators for such linear equations.

Trick [18] suggests excluding pairs of patterns in which there is no possible meeting date for corresponding teams. More formally, for every pair i, i' s.t. $i \neq i'$, $\forall_j (h_{i,j} = 0 \vee a_{i',j} = 0)$ and $\forall_j (a_{i,j} = 0 \vee h_{i',j} = 0)$ the equation $x_i + x_{i'} \leq 1$ must hold.

Adding corresponding propagators is often crucial for a good performance. In the example reported in [6], an overall speedup of the scheduling process by a factor of three is achieved.

When it is not necessary to generate all feasible pattern sets, performance is greatly improved if not all feasible patterns are used, but a small number $s \geq n$ of patterns is randomly selected as input for pattern set generation. If no pattern set is found, the process is repeated with a new selection. As enumeration strategy, the most naive one, enumerating x in the order $x_1, x_2, \ldots, x_s$ was found to be most effective.

6 Timetables

The two models for timetable generation mentioned in Section 2.3 are described in detail here. Given is a pattern set in form of $n \times d$ matrices H, A and B of 0/1 variables whose entries $H_{i,j}$ ($A_{i,j}$, $B_{i,j}$) indicate home matches (away matches, byes) for pattern i in date j.

Furthermore, common to both approaches is a target timetable, represented by

- an $n \times d$ matrix α, whose entries variables $\alpha_{t,j}$ range over $0, \ldots, n$ and tell the opponent team against which team t plays in date j (0 stands for a bye), and

- matrices $\mathcal{H}$, $\mathcal{A}$ and $\mathcal{B}$ of 0/1 variables whose entries $\mathcal{H}_{t,j}$ ($\mathcal{A}_{t,j}$, $\mathcal{B}_{t,j}$) tell if team t plays home (plays away, has a bye) in date j.

The constraints FIX-HAB and FIX-AGAINST are represented by basic constraints on variables of α, $\mathcal{H}$, $\mathcal{A}$ and $\mathcal{B}$ in an obvious way. Constraints ATMOST-AGAINST-SEQUENCE can be expressed by sets of propagators over α similar to the constraints ATMOST-HAB-SEQUENCE in Section 4.

6.1 Cain's Method

Cain's method first assigns teams to patterns of the given pattern set. Accordingly, we introduce n finite domain variables p_i, $1 \leq i \leq n$. Each team t plays according to the pattern in row p_t of H, A and B. The constraints on the vector p and the matrix α are listed in Table 2.

These constraints can be easily implemented by propagators. Of particular importance is the last one, which links the given pattern set with the desired timetable, using the variables p_i as indices. It is expressible with the so-called element propagator [5]. The element propagator takes as arguments a finite domain variable k, a vector of integers v and a finite domain variable w.

$$element(k, v, w)$$

The semantics is $v_k = w$. Propagation can restrict the possible values for k, if a value in v is eliminated from w, and it can eliminate a number x from w,

1. For all dates j and teams t, at most one of the values $\alpha_{1,j}, \ldots, \alpha_{n,j}$ is t.

2. For all dates j and teams t_1 and t_2, $\alpha_{t_1,j} = t_2$ if and only if $\alpha_{t_2,j} = t_1$.

3. For all teams t_1 and t_2, the number of dates r for which $\alpha_{t_1,j} = t_2$ is r.

4. For all dates j and teams t_1, t_2, if $\alpha_{t_1,j} = t_2$, then

$$((\mathcal{H}_{t_1,j} = 1) \wedge (\mathcal{A}_{t_2,j} = 1)) \ \vee \ ((\mathcal{A}_{t_1,j} = 1) \wedge (\mathcal{H}_{t_2,j} = 1))$$

5. If n is odd, for all dates j and teams t, $\alpha_{t,j} = 0$ if and only if $\mathcal{B}_{t,j} = 1$.

6. For all dates j and all teams t : $H_{p_t,j} = \mathcal{H}_{t,j}$, $A_{p_t,j} = \mathcal{A}_{t,j}$; and $B_{p_t,j} = \mathcal{B}_{t,j}$ for odd n.

Table 2: Constraints on α

if the last index that pointed to an x in v is eliminated from k. The following propagator implements one of the desired constraints, namely $H_{p_1,2} = \mathcal{H}_{1,2}$.

$$element(p_1, H_2, \mathcal{H}_{1,2})$$

where H_2 stands for the second column of matrix H.

The search strategy of Cain's method first assigns patterns to teams by enumerating the variables in p. Note that in the presence of FIX-HAB constraints, the just-mentioned element propagators can prune the search tree in this process. Next, the variables in α are enumerated. Here, the propagators corresponding to the first three constraints in 2 may be able to prune the remaining search tree. Apparently, the best strategy is to enumerate date-wise, i.e. in the order $\alpha_{1,1}, \alpha_{2,1}, \ldots, \alpha_{n,1}, \alpha_{1,2}, \ldots, \alpha_{n,d}$.

6.2 Schreuder's Method

Schreuder proposes to construct a timetable of team placeholders first. For this purpose, a matrix β similar to α is introduced. Its entries $\beta_{i,j}$ fix the team placeholder against which team placeholder i "plays" in date j. The first three constraints on α given in Table 2 must hold correspondingly for β. Date-wise enumeration of β constructs a timetable of team placeholders. The patterns described by H, A, and B are associated with the team placeholders in sequential order, i.e. team placeholder 1 "plays" at date j according to $H_{1,j}$, $A_{1,j}$ and $B_{1,j}$.

The last step assigns teams to team placeholders. For this assignment, we introduce n finite domain variables q_i, $1 \le i \le n$. The constraints that link the given pattern set represented by H, A and B, q and $\mathcal{H}$, $\mathcal{A}$ and $\mathcal{B}$ are similar to the last constraint in Table 2. The relationship between α and β is a little more complicated. For all dates j and all teams t:

$$\beta_{q_t,j} = q_{\alpha_{t,j}}$$

Consider the following instance of this constraint.

$$\beta_{q_1,2} = q_{\alpha_{1,2}}$$

This instance can be expressed by two element propagators, introducing an auxiliary finite domain variable *against*, ranging from 1 to n.

$$element(q_1, \beta_2, against), element(\alpha_{1,2}, q, against).$$

where β_2 stands for the second column of matrix β. The element propagator as described in [5] takes as second argument a list of integers. Initially the second argument in both element propagators are vectors of finite domain variables. A standard implementation of the element propagator as provided for example by the Mozart system [11] will wait until all components of the second argument vector are determined. Thus these propagators become able to prune the search tree at a relatively late stage. A more powerful version of the element propagator that is able to propagate even if the vector is not determined, would doubtless improve the performance of this implementation of Schreuder's approach to timetable generation.

7 Friar Tuck

Crucial for planning an irregular RR tournament is a careful design of the constraints. It seems that a basic understanding of the solution process is necessary. The user needs to fine-tune the constraints as well as the solution process in order come to a satisfactory timetable. Thus, a useful tool should provide interactive access to all phases and allow fine-tuning of the solution process and constraints.

For this purpose, the tool Friar Tuck was designed. Friar Tuck is available at http://www.comp.nus.edu.sg/~henz/projects/FriarTuck/ in binary and source form. Friar Tuck is implemented using the finite domain constraint programming system Mozart 1.0 [11].

7.1 Structure

The user interface displays a graph representing the solution process as shown in Figure 1. Clicking on the nodes in this graph results in the display of a control panel for the corresponding phase on the right. In Figure 1, the user chose the control panel for timetable generation. Cain's method of assigning teams to patterns was selected.

7.2 Entry of Constraints

The interface for entering and editing tasks is displayed on the right after clicking on phase "Task" on the left. All constraints described in Section 1 can be entered by mouse-click, stored to and retrieved from files. The interface for the constraints FIX-HAB and FIX-AGAINST performs constraint propagation and consistency checking and thus supports semi-automatic timetable construction. Figure 2 shows the corresponding dialog window.

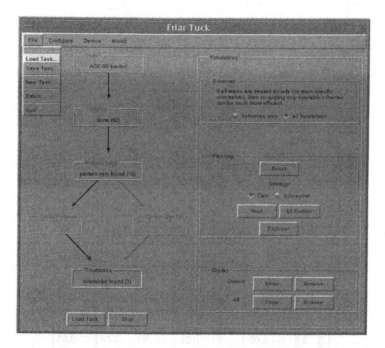

Figure 1: Friar Tuck (timetable interface)

7.3 Solution Process

After loading a task, asking for the "Next" timetable in the "Timetable" panel results in asking the pattern set phase for a pattern set. The pattern set phase in turn triggers the computation of all feasible patterns by the pattern phase. Based on a selection of these patterns, the pattern set phase computes the first pattern set which is sent to the timetable phase. The timetable phase now tries to construct a timetable based on this pattern set. If it succeeds, this timetable is provided to the user, and if it fails, it asks the pattern set phase for the next pattern set, etc.

In addition to this automatic mode, the user can interact with the first two phases separately and thus conduct experiments on pattern and pattern set generation. A batch mode supports automation of experiments such as the ones reported in the next section.

This interactive access is possible, since each of the phases' "Patterns", "Pattern Sets", and "Timetables" are implemented by instances of the class Search.object, which is provided by the Oz Standard Modules [7]. Search objects encapsulate constraint-based search and provide an interface to search from a more conventional programming environment. Newer versions of the C++ constraint programming library Ilog Solver [8] are based on the same idea of encapsulation.

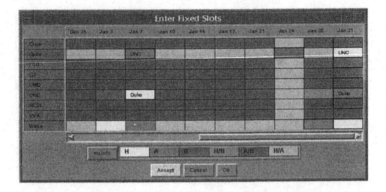

Figure 2: Friar Tuck (task interface)

		P		PS		T		Total
		S	R	S	R	S	R	R
	2	2	0.05	1	0.05	8	0.50	0.60
	4	8	0.05	8	0.12	16	0.07	0.24
	6	32	0.06	3824	77.6	32768	2134.0	2211.0
	8	128	0.14	?	.	?	.	.
# teams	3	12	0.05	8	0.50	8	0.10	0.65
	5	80	0.11	7776	246.2	6144	1654.5	1900.8
	7	448	2.31	?	.	?	.	.

Table 3: Single round robin, no restrictions; P: pattern generation; PS: pattern set generation; T: timetable generation; S: number of solutions; R: runtime in seconds.

8 Computational Results

In most examples that we encountered, Cain's method performs better than Schreuder's, including the ACC example reported in detail in [6]. All experiments reported in this section are run using Cain's method on a PC with a 223 MHz Pentium processor and 64 MBytes main memory running Mozart 1.0 under Windows 95.

8.1 No Restriction

In the unrestricted case, there are no closed formulae known to compute the number of pattern sets and timetables for a given n. The numbers grow very quickly with n as shown in Table 3. With no team-specific constraints, one given timetable can be used to generate $n!$ timetables which are identical up to team permutation. To generate only timetables that are different modulo team permutation, Friar Tuck allows the fixing of the vectors p (Cain's method) and q (Schreuder's method). In this section, only timetables that are different modulo team permutation are counted.

		P		PS		T		Total
		S	R	S	R	S	R	R
# teams	2	2	0.05	1	0.01	1	0.01	0.07
	4	6	0.05	1	0.11	2	0.02	0.18
	6	10	0.06	1	0.21	8	1.76	2.03
	8	14	0.07	1	3.8	320	17.1	20.9
	10	18	0.07	1	5.0	61440	344.1	349.1

Table 4: Single round robin, minimal number of breaks for even n; P: pattern generation; PS: pattern set generation; T: timetable generation; S: number of solutions; R: runtime in seconds.

8.2 Minimal Number of Breaks

For odd n, the timetables with no breaks are unique (up to switching home and away throughout the timetable) and have a very regular structure. They can be computed by Friar Tuck up to about $n = 35$.

For even n, the situation is more interesting. De Werra [4] and Schreuder [16] show that the minimal number of breaks in this case is $n - 2$. Table 4 shows the number of possible pattern sets and timetables with minimal number of breaks for even $n \leq 10$. The number of timetables forms an interesting sequence, although a conjecture for a closed formula is not obvious.

9 Conclusion

Constraint programming proves to be an effective solution technique for various known models of subproblems of round robin tournament planning.

The tool Friar Tuck provides a user interface to the planning process, from problem definition to fully automatic generation of timetables. Furthermore, Friar Tuck supports experimentation on subproblems such as pattern and pattern set generation. Friar Tuck is an example for a hierarchical problem solver whose implementation benefits from an object-oriented encapsulation of constraint-based search.

New experimental results regarding the number of patterns, pattern sets and timetables with regular constraints were presented. Such numbers may provide new insights into the algebraic and graph-theoretical structure of the underlying problems.

A separate study provides evidence that constraint programming is competitive with integer programming for pattern set and timetable generation [6]. More such studies and experiments are needed to assess the relative merits of competing approaches in this field.

Concerning the constraint programming approach, round robin tournaments provide a rich application field for specialized propagation techniques.

- More powerful sequence constraints for pattern generation may be considered [13].

- Pattern set generation may benefit from a specialized global propagator.

- The implementation of Schreuder's method may benefit from a generalized element propagator that allows the argument vector to contain finite domain variables instead of insisting on a vector of fixed integers.

Experience with challenging timetabling problems is needed to assess the relative efficiency of the described constraint-based and other approaches. Optimization criteria such as minimization of travel distance [3] should be supported.

References

[1] B. C. Ball and D. B. Webster. Optimal scheduling for even-numbered team athletic conferences. *AIIE Transactions*, 9:161–169, 1977.

[2] William O. Cain, Jr. The computer-assisted heuristic approach used to schedule the major league baseball clubs. In Shaul P. Ladany and Robert E. Machol, editors, *Optimal Strategies in Sports*, number 5 in Studies in Management Science and Systems, pages 32–41. North-Holland Publishing Co., Amsterdam, New York, Oxford, 1977.

[3] Robert T. Campbell and Der-San Chen. A minimum distance basketball scheduling problem. In Shaul P. Ladany; under the general supervision of Donald G.Morrison Robert E. Machol, editor, *Management Science in Sports*, number 4 in Studies in Management Sciences, pages 15–25. North-Holland Publishing Co., Amsterdam, New York, Oxford, 1976. Special issue of the journal Management Science.

[4] D. de Werra. Some models of graphs for scheduling sports competitions. *Discrete Applied Mathematics*, 21:47–65, 1988.

[5] Mehmet Dincbas, Helmut Simonis, and Pascal Van Hentenryck. Solving the car-sequencing problem in constraint logic programming. In Yves Kodratoff, editor, *Proceedings of the European Conference on Artificial Intelligence*, pages 290–295, Munich, Germany, August 1988. Pitman Publishers, London.

[6] Martin Henz. Scheduling a major college basketball conference—revisited. *Operations Research*, 2000. to appear.

[7] Martin Henz, Martin Müller, Christian Schulte, and Jörg Würtz. The Oz standard modules. DFKI Oz documentation series, German Research Center for Artificial Intelligence (DFKI), Stuhlsatzenhausweg 3, D-66123 Saarbrücken, Germany, 1997.

[8] ILOG Inc., Mountain View, CA 94043, USA, http://www.ilog.com. *ILOG Solver 4.0, Reference Manual*, 1997.

[9] Kim Marriott and Peter J. Stuckey. *Programming with Constraints*. The MIT Press, Cambridge, MA, 1998.

[10] Ken McAloon, Carol Tretkoff, and Gerhard Wetzel. Sports league scheduling. In *Proceedings of the 1997 ILOG Optimization Suite International Users' Conference*, Paris, July 1997.

[11] Mozart Consortium. The Mozart Programming System. Documentation and system available from http://www.mozart-oz.org, Programming Systems Lab, Saarbrücken, Swedish Institute of Computer Science, Stockholm, and Université catholique de Louvain, 1999.

[12] George L. Nemhauser and Michael A. Trick. Scheduling a major college basketball conference. *Operations Research*, 46(1), 1998.

[13] Jean-Charles Régin and Jean-François Puget. A filtering algorithm for global sequencing constraints. In Gert Smolka, editor, *Principles and Practice of Constraint Programming—CP97, Proceedings of the Third International Conference*, Lecture Notes in Computer Science 1330, pages 32–46, Schloss Hagenberg, Linz, Austria, October/November 1997. Springer-Verlag, Berlin.

[14] Robert A. Russell and Janny M. Y. Leung. Devising a cost effective schedule for a baseball league. *Operations Research*, 42(4):614–625, 1994.

[15] Andrea Schaerf. Scheduling sport tournaments using constraint logic programming. In *Proceedings of the European Conference on Artificial Intelligence*, pages 634–639, Budapest, Hungary, 1996. John Wiley & Sons.

[16] Jan A. M. Schreuder. Combinatorial aspects of construction of competition dutch professional football leagues. *Discrete Applied Mathematics*, 35:301–312, 1992.

[17] Barbara Smith. Succeed-first or fail-first: A case study in variable and value ordering. In *Proceedings of the 1996 ILOG Solver and ILOG Scheduler International Users' Conference*, Paris, July 1996.

[18] Michael Trick. Modifications to the problem description of "scheduling a major college basketball conference". WWW at http://mat.gsia.cmu.edu/acc_mod.html, 1998.

Logic Programming with Requests

Sandro Etalle
Department of Computer Science, Universiteit Maastricht
P.O. Box 616, 6200 MD Maastricht, The Netherlands
etalle@cs.unimaas.nl

Femke van Raamsdonk
Department of Theoretical Computer Science, Vrije Universiteit,
De Boelelaan 1081a, 1081 HV Amsterdam, The Netherlands
femke@cs.vu.nl
CWI, P.O. Box 94079, 1090 GB Amsterdam, The Netherlands.

Abstract

We propose an extension of logic programming where the user can specify, together with the initial query, the information he is interested in by means of a request. This allows one to extract a result from an incomplete computation, such as the prefix of an infinite derivation. The classical property of independence of the selection rule doesn't hold anymore. It is shown that under mild conditions a class of selection rules can be identified for which independence holds. A model-theoretic semantics for the language is given.

1 Introduction

The purpose of this paper is to present an extension of logic programming where it is possible to express a form of partial result. This is done by considering instead of the traditional successful derivations, where all subgoals are resolved, so-called adequate derivations, where possibly some subgoals remain. The intuition is that an adequate derivation is similar to a derivation in a lazy functional language, like for instance Haskell, where an expression is evaluated to a head-normal form. Adequacy is defined in terms of two new features that we add to logic programming, namely requests and strictness annotations.

Requests allow the user to specify the information (partial result) he is interested in. The definition is inspired by the definition of head normal form in functional programming: it is possible to specify that one wishes to compute the head-symbol of the value of a certain variable, or the complete value of a specific variable. Consider for instance the program

$$from(x, y) \leftarrow x' \text{ is } x + 1, \; from(x', z), \; y = [x|z].$$

that can be used to generate the list of natural numbers as follows:

$$from(0, y_0) \;\; \Rightarrow \;\; from(1, y_1), y_0 = [0|y_1]$$

$$\Rightarrow \quad from(2, y_2), y_1 = [1|y_2], y_0 = [0|y_1]$$
$$\Rightarrow \quad from(2, y_2), y_0 = [0, 1|y_2]$$
$$\Rightarrow \quad \ldots.$$

If the partial result is specified to be the value of the second natural number,

$$from(0, [x_0, x_1|z]) \quad \Rightarrow \quad from(1, y_1), [x_0, x_1|z] = [0|y_1]$$
$$\Rightarrow \quad from(2, y_2), y_1 = [1|y_2], [x_0, x_1|z] = [0|y_1]$$
$$\Rightarrow \quad from(2, y_2), [x_0, x_1|z] = [0, 1|y_2]$$

is a computation that is sufficient. We say that the last query satisfies the request expressing that we wish to compute the value of the variable x_1.

A strictness annotation, the second feature we add to logic programming, can be used by the programmer to specify which atoms can be left unsolved. As illustrated in the previous example, a query that satisfies the request specified by the user is not necessarily the empty one. Atoms that are annotated as *strict* need to be resolved. Intuitively, these atoms stand for tests that need to be performed in order to select the right branch of an SLD-tree. Atoms that are annotated as *lazy* may remain unresolved. Intuitively, these atoms stand for a calculation that may or may not be performed.

So, we take here a more concrete approach than in [7], where adequacy is a parameter with the intended use to extract a result from a partial computation. Another difference is that in [7] failure is replaced by a predicate for inadequacy, with the intended use to constrain the search space, whereas in the present paper failure is failure in the traditional sense.

Now the dynamics of our language is as follows. The computation proceeds until a point where the request specified by the user is satisfied, and where no strict atoms remain. If the computation fails, then the backtracking mechanism is used to explore alternatives, if any (in a Prolog-like implementation). In case deadlock is reached, the computation stops without providing any answer. No expressive power of the traditional approach is lost: successful derivations correspond to adequate derivations with the trivial request and all predicates declared to be strict.

A well-known result in the classical approach to logic programming is independence of the selection rule. This result doesn't hold anymore in the present setting, because not all atoms need to be selected. An obviously important question is then which selection rule should be applied. The idea is that only atoms that contribute to the desired result should be selected. We prove that under suitable conditions a class of selection rules can be identified that are correct in the sense that they yield adequate derivations whenever possible, and that are optimal in the sense that they yield adequate derivations with a minimal number of steps.

Further, we present a declarative semantics of logic programming with requests. Its definition makes use of a recombination of ideas of the s-semantics as defined in [6] and the Ω-semantics as defined in [5] (see also [6]). It is shown that under mild (necessary) restrictions the operational semantics is sound and complete with respect to the declarative one.

2 Programming with Requests

Delay Declarations. Logic programming languages which employ a dynamic selection rule need a mechanism for determining when an atom is selectable. Here we use delay declarations as introduced by Naish in [17]. We roughly follow the approach described by Apt and Luitjes in [4]. A *delay condition* is a conjunction built from delay base conditions of the form:

- *nonvar*(s), which holds if s is a non-variable term.

- *ground*(s), which holds if s is a ground term,

A difference with [4] is that we do not consider delay conditions that are disjunctions; this restriction is necessary for the main result (Theorem 3.5) to hold. A *delay declaration for a predicate symbol p* is defined as

> *delay A until c*

with A an atom with predicate symbol p and c a delay condition. We admit the possibility that there is more than one delay declaration for a relation symbol; this is a second difference with the approach of [4].

Derivations. A *program* is specified by a set of clauses and a set of delay declarations. An atom B is *selectable* in a program $\mathcal{P}$ if for every delay declaration *delay A until c* in $\mathcal{P}$ we have the following: if $B = A\sigma$ for some substitution σ, then $c\sigma$ holds. Note that an instance of a selectable atom is selectable. A *selection rule* is a mapping that given a state $\langle Q; \sigma \rangle$ returns a selectable atom in Q whenever Q contains a selectable atom, and returns a fresh symbol δ otherwise. A state not containing a selectable atom is said to be *in deadlock*. A difference with the standard approach is that instead of queries we consider *states*, which are pairs of the form $\langle Q; \sigma \rangle$ consisting of a query and a substitution. For a selection rule S, we have an S-derivation step $\langle Q; \sigma \rangle \overset{\tau}{\underset{C}{\Rightarrow}} \langle Q'; \sigma\tau \rangle$ if the clause C can be applied to the atom selected by S using most general unifier τ. We omit specifying the selection rule, the clause, the most general unifier whenever possible. Further, we usually specify only the relevant part of a substitution in a state. A (finite or infinite) sequence of S-derivation steps is called a *S-derivation*. We write $\Rightarrow^+$ for the transitive closure of $\Rightarrow$ and $\Rightarrow^*$ for its reflexive-transitive closure.

Requests. The key feature of the language we propose is that the user can specify which information he is interested in, and that a computation stops if it is observable that this information has been found. Expressing the desired information is done by means of so-called *requests*. We consider as an example the program *sieve* that implements the sieve of Eratosthenes:

$$
\begin{array}{lll}
primes(x) & \leftarrow & from(2, y), sieve(y, x). \\
from(x, [x|z]) & \leftarrow & x' \text{ is } x + 1, from(x', z). \\
sieve([x|y], [x|z]) & \leftarrow & filter(x, y, w), sieve(w, z). \\
filter(x, [y|z], w) & \leftarrow & div(x, y), filter(x, z, w). \\
filter(x, [y|z], [y|w]) & \leftarrow & nondiv(x, y), filter(x, z, w).
\end{array}
$$

We omit the clauses for the predicates *div* and *nondiv*. The following delay declarations are assumed:

> *delay filter*(x, y, w) *until nonvar*(y).
> *delay filter*$(x, [y|z], w)$ *until ground*$(x) \wedge$ *ground*(y).
> *delay sieve*(x, y) *until nonvar*(x).

We consider two examples where the information we are interested in is provided by a derivation that is not successful in the traditional sense of the word. First, suppose that we wish to find out whether the list of prime numbers is empty or not. The following derivation shows that the list of prime numbers is not empty, but of the form $[2|x']$ for some list x':

$$
\begin{aligned}
\langle primes(x); \epsilon\rangle \; &\Rightarrow \; \langle from(2, y), sieve(y, x); \epsilon\rangle \\
&\Rightarrow \; \langle from(3, z), sieve([2|z], x); \epsilon\rangle \\
&\Rightarrow \; \langle from(3, z), filter(2, z, u), sieve(u, x'); x \mapsto [2|x']\rangle.
\end{aligned}
$$

Second, suppose that our purpose is to compute the value of the second prime number. This is done in the following computation, which shows that value of the second prime number is 3:

$$
\begin{aligned}
\langle primes([x_1, x_2|l]); \epsilon\rangle \; &\Rightarrow \; \langle from(2, y), sieve(y, [x_1, x_2|l]); \epsilon\rangle \\
&\Rightarrow \; \langle from(3, z), y = [2|z], sieve(y, [x_1, x_2|l]); \epsilon\rangle \\
&\Rightarrow^* \; \langle from(3, z), filter(2, z, u), sieve(u, l); x_1 \mapsto 2\rangle \\
&\Rightarrow^* \; \langle from(4, z'), filter(2, [3|z'], u), sieve(u, [x_2|l]); x_1 \mapsto 2\rangle \\
&\Rightarrow^* \; \langle \ldots, filter(2, z', u'), sieve([3|u'], [x_2|l]); \ldots\rangle \\
&\Rightarrow \; \langle \ldots, filter(3, u', w), sieve(w, l); \ldots, x_2 \mapsto 3\rangle.
\end{aligned}
$$

In the first example, the derivation reveals as information the constructor at the top of the data-structure that is computed. This is like a head-normal form in functional programming. The second example is concerned with a variation on this theme: here the aim of the computation is to calculate the value of one of the variables that occur in the initial state. Both forms of partial information can be expressed by means of requests. Requests are built from two basic expressions that capture the two typical cases of the examples above: $Root(x)$, expressing that we aim at finding the constructor at the top of the value of x, and $Val(x)$, expressing that we aim at finding the value of x. The formal definition of requests is as follows.

Definition 2.1 A *request condition* or shortly a *request* is a conjunction (denoted using $\wedge$) built from the following request base conditions:

- $Root(x)$, which holds in a state $\langle Q; \sigma\rangle$ if $x\sigma \notin Var(Q)$,

- $Val(x)$, which holds in a state $\langle Q; \sigma\rangle$ if $Var(x\sigma) \cap Var(Q) = \emptyset$.

The empty conjunction is written as *True* and holds in any state $\langle Q; \sigma\rangle$. □

If a request r holds in a state $\langle Q; \sigma\rangle$, then we also say that the state $\langle Q; \sigma\rangle$ *satisfies* the request r. Going back to the two derivations in the program *sieve* above, we have that the request $Root(x)$ holds in the state

$$
\langle from(3, z), filter(2, z, u), sieve(u, x'); x \mapsto [2|x']\rangle,
$$

and we have that the request $Val(x_2)$ holds in the state

$$\langle \ldots, filter(3, u', w), sieve(w, l); x_1 \mapsto 2, x_2 \mapsto 3 \rangle.$$

Requests seem similar to delay declarations. There are however important differences. First, it depends on the substitution of a state whether a request holds or not. Further, the difference between $Root(x)$ and $nonvar(x)$ is that $Root(x)$ not only holds in $\langle Q; \sigma \rangle$ if $x\sigma$ is a non-variable term, but also if $x\sigma$ is a variable that will never be instantiated further; then it serves as a constant. There is a similar difference between $Val(x)$ and $ground(x)$.

One can easily imagine variations and extensions of the definition of requests as given above. Our choice for requests built using $Val(x)$ and $Root(x)$ is motivated by the correspondence with head-normal forms in functional programming and is, we feel, a natural one.

Note that if Q is ground, then we have that $\langle Q; \sigma \rangle$ satisfies r, for every substitution σ and for every request r. In particular, we have that $\langle \Box; \sigma \rangle$ satisfies r for every σ and r. So in a successful state any request is satisfied.

Strict and Lazy Predicates. The request conditions provide the user with a form of control in the sense that a computation can, as far as the user is concerned, stop once a state is reached where the specified request is satisfied. The language provides the programmer with an additional form of control: he can specify which atoms have to be evaluated and which ones may remain unselected. This is done by means of a partitioning of the predicates into *strict* and *lazy* ones. An atom is then strict (lazy) if its predicate is. The intuition is that strict atoms are meant to test and that a computation should not stop at a point where a test is not performed yet. Lazy atoms are meant to compute, and no harm is done if a derivation is stopped at a point where a(n unnecessary) part of the computation remains to be done.

Consider for example the program defined by the clause $p(x, a) \leftarrow x = 0..$ In one step $\langle p(1, y); \epsilon \rangle \Rightarrow \langle 1 = 0; y \mapsto a \rangle$ a state is reached in which the request $Val(y)$ holds. However, this state is intuitively speaking not safe since a next step would yield failure (as we will see below in Definition 2.3, our language inherits from logic programming the following notion of failure: a derivation fails if it ends in a state with a query that is not empty and no clause can be applied to the selected atom). Now the derivation does not stop in $\langle 1 = 0; y \mapsto a \rangle$ if the programmer has specified the predicate $=$ as strict; in that case every atom of the form $s = t$ needs to be selected eventually. The intuition is that $=$ is used as a test.

Dynamics. The operational semantics of our language makes use of the notion of request and of the partitioning of the predicates into strict and lazy ones. It is a refinement of the usual operational semantics of logic programming. The expressions that are transformed in a derivation are request conditions, consisting of a request and a state.

Definition 2.2

- A *request configuration* is an expression $r : \langle Q; \sigma \rangle$ with r a request and $\langle Q; \sigma \rangle$ a state.

- The definition of a derivation step is extended to request configurations as follows: if $\langle Q; \sigma \rangle \Rightarrow \langle Q'; \sigma' \rangle$, then $r : \langle Q; \sigma \rangle \Rightarrow r : \langle Q'; \sigma' \rangle$. □

The following definition is crucial.

Definition 2.3 Let $\mathcal{P}$ be a program. A request configuration $r : \langle Q; \sigma \rangle$ is

1. *adequate* if $\langle Q; \sigma \rangle$ satisfies r and Q doesn't contain strict atoms,

2. *failing* if $Q \neq \square$ and no clause from $\mathcal{P}$ can be applied to the selected atom in $\langle Q; \sigma \rangle$,

3. *deadlocked* if $Q \neq \square$ and $\langle Q; \sigma \rangle$ contains no selectable atom. □

In a derivation step, we assume that a suitable renaming of the clause is used, that is, one that has no variables in common with the request configuration. These notions carry over to derivations in the natural way: a finite derivation is adequate (failing, deadlocked) if its last request configuration is. Note that the notion of failing depends on the selection rule, which we let unspecified.

The implementation we imagine of our language is similar to the one of Prolog: if an adequate request configuration is reached, the computation stops and the desired information is communicated to the user. If a failing request configuration is reached, the computation stops and starts backtracking whenever this is possible.

We define the equivalence of two substitutions with respect to a request.

Definition 2.4 We define when two substitutions σ and τ are *equivalent with respect to a request* r, notation $\sigma \sim_r \tau$, by induction on the structure of r as follows:

1. $\sigma \sim_{True} \tau$ for every σ and τ,

2. $\sigma \sim_{Val(x)} \tau$ if $x\sigma$ is a renaming of $x\tau$,

3. $\sigma \sim_{Root(x)} \tau$ if $x\sigma$ and $x\tau$ have the same outermost function symbol or if $x\sigma$ and $x\tau$ are both variables,

4. $\sigma \sim_{r \wedge r'} \tau$ if $\sigma \sim_r \tau$ and $\sigma \sim_{r'} \tau$. □

For instance the substitutions $\{x \mapsto a, y \mapsto b\}$ and $\{x \mapsto a, y \mapsto c\}$ are equivalent with respect to the request $Val(x)$. It can be shown that if a computation has reached a state which satisfies a request r, then continuing the computation only yields states that satisfy r and that are equivalent to each other with respect to r.

Example. We consider the program for *quicksort* with accumulator:

$$
\begin{aligned}
q(xs, ys) &\leftarrow qa(xs, ys, [\,]).\\
qa([x|xs], ys, zs) &\leftarrow p(x, xs, ls, bs), qa(bs, ws, zs), qa(ls, ys, [x|ws]).\\
qa([\,], xs, xs) &\leftarrow .\\
p(x, [y|xs], [y|ls], bs) &\leftarrow x > y, p(x, xs, ls, bs).\\
p(x, [y|xs], ls, [y|bs]) &\leftarrow x \le y, p(x, xs, ls, bs).\\
p(x, [\,], [\,], [\,]) &\leftarrow .
\end{aligned}
$$

Let the only strict predicates be $>$ and $\le$. Suppose we are interested in knowing the smallest element of the list $[2, 1, 3]$. In order to compute it, we can use the request configuration $Val(y) : \langle qa([2, 1, 3], [y|ys], [\,]); \epsilon\rangle$. The computation proceeds as follows. In each step, the selected atom is written in **boldface**. Further, we omit the request, and write only a part of the substitution. The underlining of variables is to illustrate the definition of demanded atom in Section 3.

$$
\begin{aligned}
&\langle \mathbf{qa}([\mathbf{2}, \mathbf{1}, \mathbf{3}], [\underline{y}|\mathbf{ys}], [\,]); \ \epsilon\rangle\\
\Rightarrow\ &\langle \mathbf{p}(\mathbf{2}, [\mathbf{1}, \mathbf{3}], \underline{\mathbf{ls}}, \mathbf{bs}), qa(bs, ws, [\,]), qa(ls, [\underline{y}|ys], [2|ws]); \ \epsilon\rangle\\
\Rightarrow\ &\langle p(2, [3], ls', bs), qa(bs, ws, [\,]), \mathbf{qa}([\mathbf{1}|\mathbf{ls'}], [\underline{y}|\mathbf{ys}], [\mathbf{2}|\mathbf{ws}]); \ ls \mapsto [1|ls']\rangle\\
\Rightarrow\ &\langle \mathbf{p}(\mathbf{2}, [\mathbf{3}], \underline{\mathbf{ls'}}, \mathbf{bs}), qa(bs, ws, [\,]), p(1, ls', \underline{ls}'', bs''),\\
&\quad qa(bs'', ws'', [2|ws]), qa(ls'', [\underline{y}|ys], [1|ws'']); \ \epsilon\rangle\\
\Rightarrow\ &\langle \mathbf{p}(\mathbf{2}, [\,], \underline{\mathbf{ls'}}, \mathbf{bs'}), qa([3|bs'], ws, [\,]), p(1, ls', \underline{ls}'', bs''),\\
&\quad qa(bs'', ws'', [2|ws]), qa(ls'', [\underline{y}|ys], [1|ws'']); \ bs \mapsto [3|bs']\rangle\\
\Rightarrow\ &\langle qa([3], ws, [\,]), \mathbf{p}(\mathbf{1}, [\,], \underline{\mathbf{ls}}'', \mathbf{bs}''),\\
&\quad qa(bs'', ws'', [2|ws]), qa(ls'', [\underline{y}|ys], [1|ws'']); \ ls' \mapsto [\,], bs' \mapsto [\,]\rangle\\
\Rightarrow\ &\langle qa([3], ws, [\,]), qa([\,], ws'', [2|ws]), \mathbf{qa}([\,], [\underline{y}|\mathbf{ys}], [\mathbf{1}|\mathbf{ws}'']); ls'' \mapsto [\,], bs'' \mapsto [\,]\rangle\\
\Rightarrow\ &\langle qa([3], ws, [\,]), qa([\,], ws'', [2|ws]); \ y \mapsto 1, ys \mapsto ws''\rangle
\end{aligned}
$$

This derivation is adequate. It satisfies the initial request and has no strict predicates which still need to be resolved. Notice that in order to obtain the desired answer it was not necessary to order the whole list, as it would be the case with a classical SLD-derivation ending in success.

3 An Optimal Strategy

In this section we first explain why in the present framework independence of the selection rule does not hold. Then we show that under reasonable conditions it is possible to define selection rules that are *correct* in the sense that they yield an adequate state whenever possible, and that are *optimal* in the sense that they do so in the least possible number of derivation steps.

Independence. A well-known result for the classical approach to logic programming is the independence of the selection rule ([2, Theorem 3.33]). In the present setting this result does not hold anymore. Consider for instance the program consisting of the rules $p \leftarrow .$ and $q \leftarrow q..$ with p strict and q lazy. Starting in *True* : $\langle p, q; \epsilon\rangle$ we find, using the leftmost selection rule, the adequate derivation *True* : $\langle p, q; \epsilon\rangle \Rightarrow$ *True* : $\langle q; \epsilon\rangle$. There is however no adequate derivation using the rightmost selection rule. This is not really surprising: Whereas in order to reach the empty query all atoms have to be selected eventually, it is not necessarily the case that all atoms have to be selected in order to reach an adequate request configuration.

Our Approach. The question arises which selection rule should be used in order to find an adequate derivation, or more precisely, an adequate SLD-tree, whenever possible. Possible answers are to use a fair selection rule, then every atom has to be selected eventually, or to restrict attention to programs and queries for which it doesn't matter which selection rule is used. The first approach is a quite inefficient one, and the second one is completely unsuitable to deal with potentially infinite data-structures and computations, since it means in particular that non-termination is excluded.

What we do instead is the following. We define for each request configuration the set of *demanded atoms*. If the programs and queries we consider are restricted to the ones that have, intuitively speaking, a functional and sequential character, then it is possible to show that in order to reach an adequate request configuration (if there is one), it is necessary and sufficient to select all demanded atoms. As a consequence, it can be shown that for the class of *demand-driven selection rules*, that are defined as the selection rules selecting demanded atoms only the following form of independence holds: if a request configuration admits an adequate derivation then it admits an adequate derivation via any demand-driven selection rule, yielding a computed answer substitution that is equivalent as far as the request under consideration is concerned.

We first define demanded atoms and the demand-driven selection rules. Then we formulate restrictions on the programs and queries that we consider.

Demanded Atoms. The aim is now to identify a set of atoms, called the demanded atoms, such that every atom in the set has to be selected eventually in order to reach an adequate request configuration whenever possible. For the definition we need to consider *moded* programs and queries, where modes are used to indicate whether an argument of a predicate is used as input or as output. A mode of a predicate symbol p is defined as a function that assigns to every argument of p either *in* or *out*. In the first case the argument is said to be *input* and in the second case it is said to be *output*. Reasonable modes for the predicates used in the programs *sieve* and *quicksort* are as follows:

primes :	*out*	*q* :	*in* × *out*
from :	*in* × *out*	*qa* :	*in* × *out* × *in*
sieve :	*in* × *out*	*p* :	*in* × *in* × *out* × *out*
filter :	*in* × *in* × *out*	>:	*in* × *in*
div :	*in* × *in*	≤:	*in* × *in*
nondiv :	*in* × *in*		

Henceforth it is assumed that every predicate has a unique mode; in case of multiple modes the predicates are renamed.

Now demanded atoms come in three sorts. First, it is clear that every strict atom needs to be selected eventually, since a request configuration in which strict atoms are present cannot be adequate. Second, some atoms need to be selected in order to satisfy the request under consideration. For instance, in order to satisfy a request of the form $Val(x)$, an atom that produces a value of x, that is, an atom having an occurrence of x in its output position, needs to be selected. Third, it might be the case that an atom that needs to be selected in order to reach an adequate request configuration cannot be selected yet because it is not sufficiently instantiated, and as a consequence does not satisfy its delay declarations. In that case there is at least one variable that needs to be bound to a value. Then an atom having this variable in an output position needs to be selected. This intuition is now formalized in the following definition.

Definition 3.1

- Let $r : \langle Q; \sigma \rangle$ be a request configuration. We define when r *demands* a variable of Q by induction on the definition of request as follows:

    1. *True* does not demand any variable,
    2. $Val(x)$ demands all variables in $x\sigma \cap Var(Q)$,
    3. $Root(x)$ demands $x\sigma$ if it is a variable of Q, and does not demand any variable otherwise,
    4. $(r \wedge r')$ demands all variables demanded by r and all variables demanded by r'.

- An atom A in Q *demands* a variable x if for every substitution σ such that $A\tau$ is selectable, $x\sigma$ is a non-variable term.

- The set of *demanded atoms of level n* of a request configuration $r : \langle Q; \sigma \rangle$, denoted by $\mathcal{D}_n(r : \langle Q; \sigma \rangle)$, is defined as follows:

    1. if A is strict, then $A \in \mathcal{D}_0(r : \langle Q; \sigma \rangle)$,
    2. if there is a variable demanded by r that occurs in an output position of A, then $A \in \mathcal{D}_0(r : \langle Q; \sigma \rangle)$,
    3. if there is a variable demanded by an atom in $\mathcal{D}_{n-1}(r : \langle Q; \sigma \rangle)$ that occurs in an output position of A, then $A \in \mathcal{D}_n(r : \langle Q; \sigma \rangle)$.

- The set of *demanded atoms* of a request configuration $r : \langle Q; \sigma \rangle$, denoted by $\mathcal{D}(r : \langle Q; \sigma \rangle)$, is defined as $\bigcup_0^\infty \mathcal{D}_n(r : \langle Q; \sigma \rangle)$. $\quad\square$

We have that the variable x is demanded in the request configuration $Val(x) : \langle primes([x|l]); \epsilon \rangle$. Hence the atom $primes([x|l])$ is demanded. Performing a derivation step yields $Val(x) : \langle from(2, y), sieve(y, [x|l]); \epsilon \rangle$. Here x is still demanded by the request $Val(x)$, so the atom $sieve(y, [x|l])$ is demanded. Moreover, the atom $sieve(y, [x|l])$ demands the variable y, and therefore the atom $from(2, y)$ is demanded as well. In the example *quicksort*, the demanded variables in the derivation are underlined.

The notion of demanded atom is used to define the demand-driven selection rules are follows.

Definition 3.2 A *demand-driven selection rule* is a mapping that given a request configuration $r : \langle Q; \sigma \rangle$ that is not adequate returns an atom in Q that is selectable and demanded, and returns δ otherwise. □

In fact the terminology is a bit sloppy here, since a demand-driven selection may return δ in a request configuration that contains selectable atoms (but no atoms that are both selectable and demanded), and as a consequence it is strictly speaking not a selection rule.

Main Result. The aim is now to show that independence of the selection rule holds for the class of demand-driven selection rules. To that end we need to impose some restriction on the programs and queries that are considered.

The first restriction, ws-modedness, concerns the data-flow in a program. It is equivalent to the combination of well-modedness and simply modedness as defined in [3].

Definition 3.3 A clause $p_0(\vec{t_0}, \vec{s}_{n+1}) \leftarrow p_1(\vec{s_1}, \vec{t_1}), \ldots, p_n(\vec{s_n}, \vec{t_n})$ is said to be *ws-moded* if

- $Var(\vec{s_i}) \subseteq \bigcup_{j=1}^{j=i-1} Var(\vec{t_j})$,

- $\vec{t_1}, \ldots, \vec{t_n}$ are distinct variables not occurring in t_0. □

A query Q is said to be *ws-moded* if the clause $q \leftarrow Q$ with q a dummy symbol is ws-moded. These definitions carry over to programs, states and request configurations in the usual way. The set of ws-moded queries is closed under computation with ws-moded clauses. Further, well-moded programs (queries) can be transformed into ws-moded ones; this transformation does not necessarily preserve termination.

The second restriction, mode-drivenness, concerns the interaction between data-flow and delay-declarations. It states that the data-flow taking place in the input position of an atom must proceed from the selected atom to the resolving clause, and not vice-versa, and that the selectability of an atom should depend uniquely on how his input arguments are instantiated.

Definition 3.4 A program $\mathcal{P}$ is said to be *mode-driven* if the following two requirements hold:

1. for every delay declaration *delay A until c* of $\mathcal{P}$ we have that all variables of c occur in input positions of A,

2. if B is a selectable atom and H is the head of a clause of $\mathcal{P}$ that can be applied to B, then B restricted to its input positions is an instance of H restricted to its input positions. $\qquad\Box$

Observe that the program *sieve* is mode-driven. In the language moded GHC [21], using guarded Horn clauses, an atom is selectable if requirements similar to the ones of mode-drivenness hold.

These restrictions imply some properties that are used to prove the main result. If in a request configuration the request is not satisfied, then there is a demanded atom. Moreover, if a request configuration is not adequate but admits an adequate derivation, then there is an atom that is demanded and selectable. This means that a demand-driven selection rule doesn't deadlock prematurely. Further, every demanded atom has to be selected eventually in order to obtain an adequate derivation.

Theorem 3.5 *Let $\mathcal{P}$ be a ws-moded and mode-driven program and let S be a demand-driven selection rule. Let $r : \langle Q; \sigma \rangle$ be a ws-moded request configuration. If there is an adequate derivation*

$$r : \langle Q; \sigma \rangle \Rightarrow^* r : \langle Q'; \sigma' \rangle$$

consisting of n derivation steps, then there is an adequate S-derivation

$$r : \langle Q; \sigma \rangle \Rightarrow^* r : \langle Q''; \sigma'' \rangle$$

consisting of not more than n derivation steps. Moreover, $\sigma' \sim_r \sigma''$. $\qquad\Box$

4 Declarative Semantics

A declarative semantics for logic programming with requests is defined. The definition is a recombination of ideas present in the s-semantics defined in [6] and the Ω-semantics defined in [5], and also reported in [6]. The aim of the s-semantics approach is to model the observable behaviour of logic programming. The Ω-semantics is defined to provide a compositional semantics for definite logic programs. We will use notation and terminology as in [6].

The Immediate Consequence Operator. Let $\mathcal{P}$ be a program. The set of atoms of $\mathcal{P}$ modulo variable renaming is denoted by $\mathcal{B}$. A subset of $\mathcal{B}$ is called an *interpretation* (in [6] this is called a π-interpretation). The application of the immediate consequence operator, or bottom-up operator, denoted by $T_{\mathcal{P}}^l$, to an interpretation I is defined as follows:

$$T_{\mathcal{P}}^l(I) = I \cup \{A \in \mathcal{B} \mid \quad \exists A' \leftarrow B_1, \ldots, B_n \in \mathcal{P}, \\ \exists B_1', \ldots, B_n' \text{ variants of atoms in } I, \\ \exists \theta = mgu((B_1, \ldots, B_n), (B_1', \ldots, B_n')), \\ A = A'\theta \qquad \}$$

The variants $B_1', \ldots, B_n'$ are supposed to be renamed apart. This definition differs from the usual one in two respects. First, it deals with non-ground interpretations as is also the case in the s-semantics. Second, it adds I to its output, which is needed to properly deal with lazy atoms. We define

$$
\begin{aligned}
T_{\mathcal{P}}^l \!\uparrow 0(I) &= I, \\
T_{\mathcal{P}}^l \!\uparrow i+1(I) &= T_{\mathcal{P}}^l(T_{\mathcal{P}}^l \!\uparrow i(I)), \\
T_{\mathcal{P}}^l \!\uparrow \omega(I) &= \bigcup_{i \geq 0} T_{\mathcal{P}}^l \!\uparrow i(I).
\end{aligned}
$$

By well-known results, $T_{\mathcal{P}}^l \!\uparrow \omega(I)$ is the least fixpoint of $T_{\mathcal{P}}^l$ containing I.

The Model. The *lazy base* of a program $\mathcal{P}$, denoted by $LB_{\mathcal{P}}$, is defined as the set that contains for every lazy predicate p an atom of the form $p(x_1, \ldots, x_n)$ with $x_1, \ldots, x_n$ different variables. So $LB_{\mathcal{P}}$ contains exactly one representative for each lazy predicate in the language of $\mathcal{P}$. We write LB instead of $LB_{\mathcal{P}}$ if $\mathcal{P}$ is clear from the context.

Definition 4.1 The *lazy model* of a program $\mathcal{P}$, denoted by $\mathcal{L}(\mathcal{P})$, is defined as $T_{\mathcal{P}}^l \!\uparrow \omega(LB)$. $\qquad\qquad\square$

The lazy model of a program is related to the π-*model* as defined in [6] and the *s-model* as defined in [8] as follows. First, $\mathcal{L}(\mathcal{P})$ is a π-*model* of $\mathcal{P}$. Second, $Ground(\mathcal{L}(\mathcal{P}))$ is the least Herbrand model containing $Ground(LB_{\mathcal{P}})$, and finally, $\mathcal{L}(\mathcal{P})$ is the least *s-model* (with respect to $\subseteq$) of $\mathcal{P}$ containing $LB_{\mathcal{P}}$.

Soundness and Completeness. In order to show soundness and completeness of the operational semantics with respect to the declarative one we need to impose two restrictions on the programs. The first is that for every clause of the program we have that all variables occurring in the head occur in the body as well. These programs are said to be *allowed* (see [14]). The second restriction is that there are no delay declarations. Under these restrictions we have the following result.

Theorem 4.2 *Let $\mathcal{P}$ be an allowed program without delay declarations. Let θ be a substitution and let $r : \langle A; \epsilon \rangle$ be a request configuration. Suppose that $Var(r) \subseteq Var(A)$. Then the following two statements are equivalent:*

1. *There exist a derivation $r : \langle A; \epsilon \rangle \Rightarrow^* r : \langle B_1, \ldots, B_m; \sigma \rangle$ such that*

   - *$r : \langle B_1, \ldots, B_m; \sigma \rangle$ is adequate,*
   - *$A\sigma = A\theta$ (modulo variable renaming).*

2. *There exist $A' \in \mathcal{L}(\mathcal{P})$, and a substitution $\sigma' = mgu(A, A')$ such that*

   - *$\langle A\sigma'; \sigma' \rangle$ satisfies r,*
   - *$A\sigma' = A\theta$ (modulo variable renaming). $\qquad\qquad\square$*

The restriction to allowed programs is necessary for the implication 1 implies 2 to hold. Consider for instance the program defined by the clause $p(x) \leftarrow q.$. Its lazy base is the empty set and its lazy model is $\{p(x)\}$. We have an adequate derivation $Val(x) : \langle p(x); \epsilon \rangle \Rightarrow Val(x) : \langle q; \epsilon \rangle$, but the request $Val(x)$ is not satisfied in the state $\langle p(x); \epsilon \rangle$. With the definition of the immediate consequence operator as considered here, the restriction to programs without delay declarations is for the implication 2 implies 1 to hold. Consider the same program as above, now extended with the delay declaration $delay\ p(x)\ until\ ground(x)$. In the state $\langle p(x); \epsilon \rangle$ the empty request is satisfied, but there is no adequate derivation starting in the request configuration $\langle p(x); \epsilon \rangle$.

5 Concluding Remarks

In [7], we studied a generalization of logic programming where success and failure are replaced by predicates for adequacy and inadequacy. In that general setting we defined, inspired by [12], needed atoms as atoms that have to be selected eventually in order to reach an adequate state, and we showed that under certain conditions adequate SLD-trees are obtained by repeatedly selecting needed atoms. The setting of the present paper is much more concrete. In particular, whereas needed atoms cannot be computed, demanded atoms as considered here can be effectively found. We remark that demanded atoms are needed in the sense of [7].

An important underlying idea in the framework we propose is that the more specific an answer substitution is, the more is the information it carries. This is similar to what happens in concurrent constraint languages such as in Oz [20] and ccp [19], where information can be added by further instantiating logical variables. Yet, this is in contrast with the classical logic programming approach. In particular it is in contrast with the S-semantics [6] of a program, where the empty answer substitution is considered the most general one, hence the one holding the most information.

A difference with the approach as in ccp and Oz is that there a thread (agent) carries its computation out as long as it has a sufficient input for doing so, even if the output is not needed by any other agent. So the computation mechanism of ccp and Oz can be called *input driven*. The computational mechanism of the language proposed in the present paper is *output driven*, and as such more related to the call-by-need evaluation mechanism of lazy functional programming languages as Haskell. The analogy with such functional programming languages stops here; our proposal is an strict extension of logic programming, enjoying the presence of logical variables, unification and nondeterminism (implemented via backtracking).

The papers [17] and [15] have in common that they propose a system in which the selection rule is dynamic and guided by a mechanism similar to the delay declarations we use here as well (those constructs were actually introduced by Naish in [17]). In both cases the term 'lazy evaluation' is used to indicate that the selection rule is dynamic; the computational mechanism is the standard one of logic programming, so there is no generalization of the notion of successful derivation as in the present paper.

A different yet related area of research is that of the integration of functional and logic programming. Several functional-logic languages such as Kernel-LEAF [9], Babel [16], Curry [11], Escher [13] have been the subject of extensive research. For an overview of the subject see [10]. The present work is not meant to integrate the two programming paradigms, but only to enrich the expressive power of the logic programming.

Finally, the papers [1] and [18] concern methods to translate lazy functional programs into Prolog; the logical computational mechanism they refer to is also the standard one of Prolog. So although the titles seem to indicate otherwise, they are not related to the work presented here.

Acknowledgments. We are grateful to Krzysztof Apt and Vincent van Oostrom for helpful and inspiring discussions. The anonymous referees provided comments that were very useful in improving the presentation of the paper. This research was supported by NWO/SION project number 612-33-003, entitled 'Parallel declarative programming: transforming logic programs to lazy functional programs'.

References

[1] S. Antoy. Lazy evaluation in logic. In Maluszynski and M. Wirsing, editors, *Proceedings of PLILP '91*, volume 528 of LNCS, pages 371–382, Passau, Germany, 1991.

[2] K. R. Apt. *From Logic Programming to Prolog.* Prentice Hall, 1997.

[3] K. R. Apt and S. Etalle. On the unification free Prolog programs. In A. Borzyszkowski and S. Sokolowski, editors, *Proceedings of the Conference on Mathematical Foundations of Computer Science (MFCS '93)*, volume 711 of LNCS, pages 1–19, 1993.

[4] K. R. Apt and I. Luitjes. Verification of logic programs with delay declarations. In A. Borzyszkowski and S. Sokolowski, editors, *Proceedings of the Fourth International Conference on Algebraic Methodology and Software Technology, (AMAST '95)*, volume 936 of LNCS, 1995.

[5] A. Bossi, M. Gabbrielli, G. Levi, and M. C. Meo. A compositional semantics for logic programs. *Theoretical Computer Science*, 122(1-2):3–47, 1994.

[6] A. Bossi, M. Gabbrielli, G. Levi, and M. Martelli. The S-semantics approach: Theory and applications. *Journal of Logic Programming*, 19 & 20:149–198, May 1994.

[7] S. Etalle and F. van Raamsdonk. Beyond success and failure. In J. Jaffar, editor, *Joint International Conference and Symposium on Logic Programming*, pages 190–204, MIT Press, 1998.

[8] M. Falaschi, G. Levi, M. Martelli, and C. Palamidessi. Declarative modeling of the operational behavior of logic languages. *Theoretical Computer Science*, 69(3):289–318, 1989.

[9] E. Giovannetti, G. Levi, C. Moiso, and C. Palamidessi. Kernel-leaf: A logic plus functional language. *Journal of Computer and System Sciences*, 42(2):139–185, April 1991.

[10] M. Hanus. The integration of functions into logic programming: From theory to practice. *Journal of Logic Programming*, 19&20:583–628, 1994.

[11] M. Hanus, H. Kuchen, and J.J. Moreno-Navarro. Curry: A truly functional logic language. In *Proc. ILPS'95 Workshop on Visions for the Future of Logic Programming*, pages 95–107, 1995.

[12] G. Huet and J.-J. Lévy. Computations in orthogonal rewriting systems, I and II. In Jean-Louis Lassez and Gordon Plotkin, editors, *Computational Logic: Essays in honor of Alan Robinson*, pages 395–443. MIT Press, 1991.

[13] J. Lloyd. Combining functional and logic programming languages. In M. Bruynooghe, editor, *Proceedings ILPS'94*, MIT Press, 1994.

[14] J. Lloyd. *Foundations of Logic Programming*. Symbolic Computation – Artificial Intelligence. Springer-Verlag, Berlin, 1987. Second edition.

[15] S. Lüttringhaus. An interpreter with lazy evaluation for Prolog with functions. In E. Börger, H. Kleine Büning, and M. M. Richter, editors, *Proceedings of the 2nd Workshop on Computer Science Logic*, volume 385 of *LNCS*, pages 199–225, Berlin, October 1989. Springer.

[16] J. J. Moreno-Navarro and M. Rodríguez-Artalejo. Logic programming with functions and predicates: The language babel. *Journal of Logic Programming*, 12(3&4):191–223, 1992.

[17] L. Naish. An introduction to mu-prolog. Technical Report 82/2, The University of Melbourne, 1982.

[18] S. Narain. A technique for doing lazy evaluation in Prolog. *Journal of Logic Programming*, 3(3):259–276, 1986.

[19] V.A. Saraswat, M. Rinard, and P. Panangaden. Semantics foundations of concurrent constraint programming. In *Proc. Eighteenth Annual ACM Symp. on Principles of Programming Languages*. ACM Press, 1991.

[20] G. Smolka. The Oz programming model. In Jan van Leeuwen, editor, *Computer Science Today*, volume 1000 of LNCS. Springer-Verlag, 1995.

[21] K. Ueda and M. Morita. Moded flat GHC and its message-oriented implementation technique. *New Generation Computing*, 13(1):3–43, 1994.

$ACI1$ constraints

Agostino Dovier
Università di Verona, Italy
dovier@sci.univr.it

Carla Piazza
Università di Udine, Italy,
piazza@dimi.uniud.it

Enrico Pontelli
New Mexico State University, USA
epontell@cs.nmsu.edu

Gianfranco Rossi
Università di Parma, Italy
gianfr@prmat.math.unipr.it

Abstract

Disunification is the problem of deciding satisfiability of a system of equations and disequations w.r.t. a given equational theory. In this paper we study the disunification problem in the context of $ACI1$ equational theories. We provide a characterization of the interpretation structures suitable to model the axioms in $ACI1$ theories. The satisfiability problem is solved using known techniques for the equality constraints and novel methodologies to transform disequation constraints into solved forms. We propose three solved forms, offering an increasingly more precise characterization of the set of solutions. Two of them can be computed and tested in polynomial time. The novel results achieved open new possibilities in the practical and efficient manipulation of $ACI1$ constraints.

1   Introduction

Equational theories are first-order theories whose axioms are universally quantified equations between first-order terms [21]. A (non-empty) equational theory E forces certain classes of syntactically different terms to be interpreted as the same object in any model of E. For example, if E contains the axiom $X + Y = Y + X$, then the terms $a + b$ and $b + a$ will be interpreted in the same way in any model of E. However, an equational theory is generally not strong enough to state when two terms *must* be distinguished. As a matter of fact, a 1-element structure $\underline{1}$ is a model of *any* equational theory. In $\underline{1}$ any constraint of the form $s \neq t$ is unsatisfiable! If a "wider" structure is chosen, then the satisfiability problem for a set of positive (equations) and negative (disequations) constraints—a.k.a. *disunification problem*—becomes meaningful and complex.

In this paper we tackle this problem in the context of equational theories describing the *associative* (A), *commutative* (C), and *idempotent* (I) nature of a function symbol. Constraints in the context of ACI theories (or similar theories for set-like structures) have been shown to be very important from the theoretical as well as the practical point of view [18, 14, 13, 7]. The ultimate goal of our effort is to develop a framework for handling ACI constraints which can be used in *Constraint Logic Programming (CLP)*.

The problem of handling positive and negative constraints under equational theories has been explored in the literature. In [8] a general solution to the disunification problem is presented; unfortunately such solution is valid only for *compact* equational theories, and *ACI*—as discussed later— does not meet this requirement. The general problem of solving disequations w.r.t. a given equational theory is also addressed in [4]. Here the technique employed to solve the problem is that of transforming disequations into unification problems, whose solution sets—that, for finitary theories can be finitely represented—are exactly the negation of the solution set for the starting problem. The answer to the satisfiability problem is represented as a pair σ, Ψ, called *substitution with exceptions*: θ is a solution of the initial constraints if and only if θ is an instance of the substitution σ and θ is not an instance of any of the substitutions in the set Ψ. This test, as well as the test to verify whether σ, Ψ is non-empty, can be not trivial. Moreover, substitutions with exceptions correspond to solved form constraints containing universally quantified variables, which makes them unsuitable to be used in the context of a CLP system. Recently Baader and Schulz [2] developed a general technique capable of combining satisfiability algorithms for disunification in disjoint equational theories. The approach is very general and can be adapted to work for *ACI* theories on general signatures. However, the method leads to an exponential explosion of alternatives and there seems to be no practical way to obtain "partial" efficient solutions from such scheme.

In this paper we present constraint solving techniques to handle equation and disequation constraints under $ACI1$[1] in CLP languages. The presentation starts with a characterization of the structures which are suitable to model the axioms in $ACI1$—the *join-semilattices with bottom*. This is used to explore the issue of satisfiability of positive (Sect. 3) and negative (Sect. 4) constraints with respect to the different possible signatures of the language. This analysis captures the relationship between the satisfiability of negative constraints and the "shape" of the interpretation structure.

In the context of a CLP system, uninterpreted function symbols are typically manipulated as finite trees [19]. We develop a first-order theory which extends (general) $ACI1$ and corresponds to $T(\Sigma)/ =_{ACI1}$—i.e., the Herbrand Universe modulo the congruence relation imposed by $ACI1$—on the class of conjunctions of positive and negative constraints. This allows us to focus on the canonical domain of Herbrand terms. In this context we present three solved forms for disunification problems, as well as the algorithms which allow arbitrary $ACI1$ constraints to be transformed into any of these three forms (Sect. 5). These solved forms meet the general requirements for solved form constraints—e.g., deciding their satisfiability is trivial and efficient. Furthermore, all these solved forms are adequate to be efficiently used in the context of a CLP system—a property which was missing from some of the solved forms proposed by other researchers [2, 4]. Two of these solved forms (called *implicit* and *intermediate*) can be obtained in polynomial time from any conjunction of disequations. Finally, we show how the results have a direct application to solve set-based constraints, taking advantage of the polynomial nature of the implicit solved form proposed. The results achieved open new possibilities in the *practical* manipulation of

---

[1] $ACI1$ is ACI with an additional axiom requiring the existence of an identity element for the ACI operator.

$ACI1$ constraints, thus overcoming limitations and inefficiencies present in the existing CLP languages over set structures [10]. Sections 6 and 7 summarize our results and relate them to analogous problems in the literature.[2]

2 Preliminaries

Throughout the paper we assume the standard notions and notation used in first-order logic, unification theory, and constraint logic programming (e.g., [12, 21, 16]). In particular, let Σ be a first-order signature with arity function ar, Π be a collection of *predicate symbols*, and $\mathcal{V}$ a denumerable collection of variables. $T(\Sigma, \mathcal{V})$ $(T(\Sigma))$ denotes the set of first-order terms (resp. ground terms) built from Σ and $\mathcal{V}$ (resp. Σ). Moreover, we will call *admissible constraints* (Adm) a given set of first-order formulae over $\langle \Pi, \Sigma, \mathcal{V} \rangle$. Given a first-order theory T over $\langle \Pi, \Sigma, \mathcal{V} \rangle$ and a model $\mathcal{A}$ of T, T and $\mathcal{A}$ *correspond on* Adm [16] if, for each $c \in Adm$, we have that ($T \models \exists(c)$ iff $\mathcal{A} \models \exists(c)$). A *valuation* of a constraint c is an assignment of values from A to the free variables of c—where A is the domain of $\mathcal{A}$.

If $s, t \in T(\Sigma, \mathcal{V})$, then $s = t$ is a Σ-*equation* and $s \neq t$ is a Σ-*disequation*. An *equational theory* is a first-order theory whose axioms are universally quantified Σ-equations. Given an equational theory E, we can define the concept of E-*equality* $(=_E)$ as the *least congruence relation* over $T(\Sigma, \mathcal{V})$ which contains E and which is closed under substitution [3]. The relation $=_E$ induces a partition of $T(\Sigma)$ into congruence classes. The set of these classes will be denoted by $T(\Sigma)/ =_E$. $T(\Sigma)/ =_E$, together with a mapping (the interpretation function) which assigns the equivalence class $[t]$ to each term t is a model of the theory E.

Given a conjunction $C \equiv (s_1 = t_1 \wedge \ldots \wedge s_n = t_n)$ of Σ-equations, the *(decision) E-unification problem* is the problem of deciding whether $E \models \exists C$. If E is an equational theory, Birkoff's completeness theorem [21] ensures that $E \models \exists C$ if and only if $T(\Sigma)/ =_E \models \exists C$. From a constraint point of view, Σ-equations can be chosen as admissible constraints. The theory E and the model identified by $T(\Sigma)/ =_E$ correspond on the class containing all possible conjunctions of equations [16].

Given a conjunction $C \equiv (s_1 \neq t_1 \wedge \ldots \wedge s_n \neq t_n)$ of Σ-disequations (i.e., a disequation constraint), we call *(decision) E-disequation problem* the problem of establishing whether $E \models \exists C$. For an equational theory E, this test has always a negative answer, since, for instance, the structure $\mathbf{1} = \langle \{\bot\}, (\cdot)^{\mathbf{1}} \rangle$, with $(\cdot)^{\mathbf{1}}$ the interpretation of all terms in the unique element $\bot$, is a model of any equational theory, and in $\mathbf{1}$ any constraint of the form $s \neq t$ is unsatisfiable. This problem originates from the fact that any (non-empty) equational theory E forces certain distinct terms to be interpreted in the same way in any model of E—however, it is not strong enough to state when two terms *must* be distinguished in each model of E. As a consequence, the disequation problem is typically stated as the problem of verifying satisfiability of $\exists C$ w.r.t. a given interpretation structure $\mathcal{A}$ (usually, $T(\Sigma)/ =_E$)—i.e., $\mathcal{A} \models \exists C$. A related problem is that of finding the structures $\mathcal{A}$ fulfilling such property.

---

[2]Complete proofs available at www.cs.nmsu.edu/lldap/prj_lp/papers/dppr99.html

Example 2.1 *Let E consist of the unique axiom $X = Y$ and let* Adm *contain all Σ-equations and Σ-disequations. Then E corresponds with $\underline{1}$—in particular, E is the complete theory of $\underline{1}$.*

If E corresponds with $\underline{1}$, then E is said to be *trivial*. In particular:

Proposition 2.2 *Given a non-trivial equational theory E such that* Adm *contains all Σ-equations and Σ-disequations, there is no structure corresponding to E.*

A theory E is *satisfaction complete* [16] if for each admissible constraint c either $E \models \vec{\exists}c$ or $E \models \neg\vec{\exists}c$. In terms of satisfaction completeness of non-trivial theories, Proposition 2.2 leads to the following result:

Corollary 2.3 *Given a non-trivial equational theory E such that* Adm *contains all Σ-equations and Σ-disequations, E is not satisfaction complete.*

As mentioned in Sect. 1, our ultimate goal is to handle constraints composed by arbitrary conjunctions C of Σ-equations and Σ-disequations. This class of problems has been typically referred to as *E-disunification problems* [8, 4]. An *E-solution* σ of C in a structure $\mathcal{A}$—denoted $\mathcal{A} \models C\sigma$—is a valuation $\sigma : \mathcal{V} \longrightarrow A$, extended as usual to terms, such that $s\sigma =_A t\sigma$ for all $s = t$ in C and $s\sigma \neq_A t\sigma$ for all $s \neq t$ in C.

The technique for handling equations and disequations presented in this paper provides us with a methodology to tackle disunification problems. In fact, if E is a finitary theory—i.e., every unification problem admits a finite complete collection of most general unifiers—then a disunification problem C can be simply solved by computing a complete set of unifiers for the equations in C and then verifying whether, given any of these unifiers σ, there is a solution for the disequations of C^σ [2].

Let $\Sigma \supseteq \{\emptyset, \cup\}$ be a signature containing the binary function symbol $\cup$ and the constant symbol $\emptyset$. Let us also define a one-to-one function $\# : \Sigma \cup \mathcal{V} \longrightarrow \mathbb{N}$, which will be used to obtain an order over $T(\Sigma, \mathcal{V})$. Observe that $\emptyset$ and $\cup$ can be replaced by any other pair of function symbols fulfilling the same axioms. A signature Σ is *general* if it contains at least one function symbol of arity > 0 and different from $\cup$.

Let us also recall some standard definitions from lattice theory [15]. A relation $\leq \subseteq L \times L$ is a *partial order* on L if $\leq$ is reflexive, antisymmetric, and transitive. Let us denote with $\perp$ the *bottom* of the partial order, when it exists—i.e., $(\forall x \in L)(\perp \leq x)$. $\langle L, \leq \rangle$ is a *join-semilattice* if the element $x \bigvee y \in L$ exists for each $x, y \in L$, where $x \bigvee y$ (read "x join y") is the unique element satisfying $x \leq x \bigvee y, y \leq x \bigvee y$ and for all $z \in L$ such that $x \leq z$ and $y \leq z$ it holds that $x \bigvee y \leq z$. If $\langle L, \leq \rangle$ is a partial order with bottom $\perp$, then $a \in L$ is an *atom* if $(\forall x \in L)((x \leq a \wedge x \neq a) \to x = \perp)$.

The following equations describe the theory $ACI1$:

(A)	$(X \cup Y) \cup Z = X \cup (Y \cup Z)$		(I)	$X \cup X = X$
(C)	$X \cup Y = Y \cup X$		(1)	$\emptyset \cup X = X$

Let us analyze the structures $\mathcal{A} = \langle A, (\cdot)^{\mathcal{A}} \rangle$ for $\Sigma = \{\emptyset, \cup\}$ that are models of $ACI1$. By definition of structure, the domain A is not empty. We indicate $(\emptyset)^{\mathcal{A}} \in A$ as $\perp$. A relation $\leq$ is induced by $(\cup)^{\mathcal{A}}$ (simply denoted by $\cup^{\mathcal{A}}$) on A: $x \leq y \leftrightarrow x \cup^{\mathcal{A}} y = y$.

Proposition 2.4 *Let $\mathcal{A} = \langle A, (\cdot)^{\mathcal{A}} \rangle$ be a model of ACI. Then $\leq$ is a partial order on A. If $\mathcal{A}$ is a model of ACI1, then $\bot = (\emptyset)^{\mathcal{A}}$ is the bottom of A.*

It is easy to observe that if $\mathcal{A}$ is not a model of *ACI*, then $\leq$ is not guaranteed to be a partial order. Given a structure $\mathcal{A}$ for $\{\emptyset, \cup\}$ that is a model of *ACI*1, we denote with $\langle A, \leq \rangle$ the partial order defined above [15].

Proposition 2.5 *Let $\mathcal{A} = \langle A, (\cdot)^{\mathcal{A}} \rangle$ be a structure for $\{\emptyset, \cup\}$ with $\bot = (\emptyset)^{\mathcal{A}} \in A$. $\mathcal{A}$ is a model of ACI1 iff $\langle A, \leq \rangle$ is a join-semilattice with bottom $\bot$.*

The *ACI*1 axioms allow us to design a normalization function for $T(\Sigma, \mathcal{V})$-terms, $\rho : T(\Sigma, \mathcal{V}) \longrightarrow T(\Sigma, \mathcal{V})$. Intuitively, the effect of ρ is to remove repeated elements and occurrences of $\emptyset$ from unions and reorder the elements of a union according to the ordering induced by $\#$. For example, given a term $t \in T(\{\emptyset, \cup\}, \mathcal{V})$, then $\rho(t)$ is always of the form: $\emptyset$ or $X_1 \cup \ldots \cup X_m$ where $\#(X_1) < \cdots < \#(X_m)$. Observe that the result of $\rho(t)$ is not properly a term, but the associativity of $\cup$ allows us to use these entities as terms.

Theorem 2.6 *Let $S = \Sigma \setminus \{\emptyset, \cup\}$. If $t \in T(\Sigma, \mathcal{V})$, vars$(t) = \bar{X}$, $|t| = n$, then ACI1 $\models \forall \bar{X} (\rho(t) = t)$ and (1) if S is a set of constant symbols, then $\rho(t)$ can be performed in time $O(n \log n)$, (2) if S contains a function symbol of arity greater than 0, then $\rho(t)$ can be performed in time $O(n^2)$.*

Thus, $\rho(t)$ can be chosen as the canonical representative of the *ACI*1-congruence class $[t]$ in $T(\Sigma)$ or $T(\Sigma, \mathcal{V})$ to which t belongs. Given a conjunction $C \equiv (s_1 \pi_1 t_1 \wedge \ldots \wedge s_h \pi_h t_h)$ where $\pi_i \in \{=, \neq\}$, its *canonical form* is the formula $\rho(C) \equiv \rho(s_1) \pi_1 \rho(t_1) \wedge \ldots \wedge \rho(s_h) \pi_h \rho(t_h)$. The worst-case time complexity for the computation of the canonical form of C is $O(n^2)$, where $n = |C|$. In particular, ρ is an idempotent operation, thus $\rho(t) \equiv \rho(\rho(t))$ for all terms t.

Corollary 2.7 *If $C \equiv (s_1 \pi_1 t_1 \wedge \ldots \wedge s_h \pi_h t_h)$, where $\pi_i \in \{=, \neq\}$, then ACI1 $\models \vec{\forall}(C \leftrightarrow \rho(C))$.*

3 $ACI1$ Equation Constraints - Unification

Given two terms s, t, we are interested in the decision problem $ACI1 \models \vec{\exists}(s = t)$ and in computing a complete set of $ACI1$ unifiers. An overview of the general decision and unification problems in presence of $ACI1$ operators can be found in [11]. Thanks to Corollary 2.7, we can concentrate on the problem $\rho(s) = \rho(t)$. The problem can be classified in three possible classes, according to the form of the signature Σ:

Elementary Unification: $\Sigma = \{\emptyset, \cup\}$. $\rho(s) = \rho(t)$ is of the form:[3]
$$X_1 \cup \ldots \cup X_m = Y_1 \cup \ldots \cup Y_n$$

The *decision* problem in this case admits always an affirmative answer—i.e., the valuation $[V/\emptyset : V \in vars(s,t)]$. A unique most general solution always exists and it can be easily computed using the technique of [1].

---

[3]When $m = 0$ the l.h.s. is simply $\emptyset$ and, similarly, if $n = 0$ then the r.h.s. is $\emptyset$.

Unification with Constants: $\Sigma = \{\cup, \emptyset, c_1, \ldots, c_n\}$, where $\{c_1, \ldots, c_n\}$ is a finite collection of constants distinct from $\emptyset$. $\rho(s) = \rho(t)$ is of the form:

$$X_1 \cup \ldots \cup X_k \cup b_1 \cup \ldots \cup b_h = Y_1 \cup \ldots \cup Y_q \cup d_1 \cup \ldots \cup d_p$$

The decision problem $ACI1 \models \exists(\rho(s) = \rho(t))$ can be solved in time $O(n)$ where $n = |\rho(s)| + |\rho(t)|$. In [1] it is shown how to compute the (minimal) complete set of most general unifiers for this problem. Uniqueness of the most general unifier is lost, due to the presence of constants, but the problem remains *finitary*—i.e., it is possible to describe the complete set of solutions through a finite number of unifiers.

General Unification: $\Sigma = \{\cup, \emptyset, f_1, f_2, \ldots\}$ (a general signature). The general unification problem has the following format:

$$X_1 \cup \ldots \cup X_h \cup s_1 \cup \ldots \cup s_k = Y_1 \cup \ldots \cup Y_p \cup t_1 \cup \ldots \cup t_q$$

where s_i, t_j are terms whose main functor is different from $\cup$. The decision problem is NP-complete [17, 9]. Algorithms to compute complete collections of unifiers for this class of problems have been presented in the literature—either as combination of simpler unification procedures [3] or as ad-hoc unification algorithms [11].

4 $ACI1$ Disequation Constraints - Disunification

In this section we will concentrate on the problem of handling conjunctions of disequations. The whole disunification problem (conjunctions of equations and disequations) can be solved in two stages. First, unification techniques from the previous section are used on the equations. Then, after applying the resulting substitutions, we can safely remove all equations and concentrate on the problems $\rho(s) \neq \rho(t)$. While in the unification case each equation is satisfiable in at least one model of $ACI1$, the same does not hold in the case of disequations: a negative constraint can be unsatisfiable in all models (e.g., $\emptyset \neq \emptyset$). Other constraints (e.g., $X_1 \neq X_2$) are satisfiable in some structures and unsatisfiable in others. Thus, the study of $ACI1$ disequations requires an analysis of the possible structures for the given theory.

The case of *elementary* disequation constraints (i.e., when $\Sigma = \{\emptyset, \cup\}$) can be viewed just as a simpler subcase of $ACI1$ disequation constraints with constants. Thus we prefer to skip it here, due to space limitations.

4.1 $ACI1$ Disequation Constraints with Constants

Let $\Sigma = \{\emptyset \equiv c_0, \cup, c_1, \ldots, c_m\}$. Let us analyze the structures over such Σ. All models $\mathcal{A}$ for elementary $ACI1$ (thus, all join-semilattices with bottom— Prop. 2.5) are also models of $ACI1$ with constants, provided an interpretation for the constant symbols in Σ is given. However, it is natural to focus on structures in which the m constants are interpreted as distinct objects, each of them different from $\bot$. This can be forced by introducing an additional (non-equational) axiom in the theory $ACI1$:

$$(F_2') \quad c_i \neq c_j \quad i, j \in \{0, \ldots, m\}, i \neq j$$

Such structures are exactly all the join-semilattices with bottom with a domain of at least $m + 1$ objects. (F_2') is actually an instance of the *freeness axiom scheme* (F_2) of *Clark's Equational Theory* [6] (introduced first by Mal'cev in [20]). For example, if $m = 4$, all the structures below are models of such extended theory.

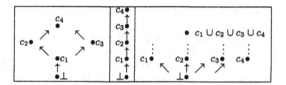

Among the possible models, we are interested in those fulfilling the axiom

$$(D_c) \quad (\forall I, J \subseteq \{1, \ldots, m\}) \left(I \neq J \to \bigcup_{i \in I} c_i \neq \bigcup_{j \in J} c_j \right)$$

(D stands for *Domain* and c for *constants*), where, if $A = \{a_1, \ldots, a_n\} \subseteq \{1, \ldots, m\}$, then $\bigcup_{i \in A} c_i$ represents the term $c_{a_1} \cup \cdots \cup c_{a_n}$. For instance, when $m = 2$, (D_c) becomes:

$$\emptyset \neq c_1 \wedge \emptyset \neq c_2 \wedge \emptyset \neq c_1 \cup c_2 \wedge c_1 \neq c_2 \wedge c_1 \neq c_1 \cup c_2 \wedge c_2 \neq c_1 \cup c_2$$

Among the structures satisfying these requirements, we can find the Boolean lattices, isomorphical to $\langle \wp(\{c_1, \ldots, c_m\}), \subseteq \rangle$, i.e., those having $\{c_1\}, \ldots, \{c_m\}$ as atoms. Assuming (D_c) we can also ignore (F_2'), since (D_c) implies (F_2').

Let us assume that $\#(\emptyset) = 0$ and $\#(c_i) = i$ for $i = 1, \ldots, m$; using ρ we can focus on the terms of the form $\emptyset$ or

$$X_1 \cup \cdots \cup X_k \cup c_{i_1} \cup \cdots \cup c_{i_h}$$

where $h + k > 0$ and $i_j < i_{j+1}$ for $j = 1, \ldots, h - 1$. The disequation $\rho(s) \neq \rho(t)$ gives rise to the following possible cases:
1. $r \neq r$
2. $c_{i_1} \cup \cdots \cup c_{i_h} \neq c_{j_1} \cup \cdots \cup c_{j_k}$ and $\{i_1, \ldots, i_h\} \neq \{j_1, \ldots, j_k\}$
3. $X_1 \cup \cdots \cup X_m \cup c_{i_1} \cup \cdots \cup c_{i_h} \neq Y_1 \cup \cdots \cup Y_n \cup c_{j_1} \cup \cdots \cup c_{j_k}$, $m > 0$.

Disequations of the first form are false in any model of $ACI1$. Disequations of the second kind are true (and therefore can be removed) in any model of $ACI1 + (D_c)$. In particular, given any join-semilattice with bottom different from $\underline{1}$, it is possible to build a structure which is a model of $ACI1$ and in which a given disequation of type 2 is satisfied. Similarly, satisfiability of disequations of the 3rd kind depends on the domain. In particular, a disequation of type 3 is:
- unsatisfiable in $\underline{1}$
- satisfiable in any model of $ACI1 + (D_c)$ if there is a constant which occurs on one side and not on the other, or if there is a constant in Σ which does not occur in the disequation.

The following theorem holds independently from the presence of (D_c):

Theorem 4.1 *If C is a disequation constraint in canonical form and it contains r disequations (of type 2 or 3), then C is satisfiable in any structure which contains a substructure isomorphical to $\langle \wp(\{a_1, \ldots, a_r\}), \subseteq \rangle$.*

Corollary 4.2 *If the structure is wide enough, then the decision problem for a disequation constraint C can be solved in $O(n \log n)$, where $n = |C|$. For a given fixed structure, the problem is NP-complete.*

4.2 General $ACI1$ Disequation Constraints

Let us assume that the signature Σ can contain any constant and function symbols. From Sect. 2 we know that when $\leq$ is induced by the interpretation of $\cup$, the models of $ACI1$ are the join-semilattices with bottom. However, in presence of a domain A and an interpretation $\cup^A$, the interpretation of the functions in Σ introduces a variety of possibilities for building models.

The most common interpretation of the constant and function symbols different from $\cup$ is the one induced by the structure $T(\Sigma)/ =_{ACI_1}$, denoted by $\mathcal{H}$. In this section we prove some results about this model. We also define a theory T such that $\mathcal{H}$ and T correspond on the class of formulae we are interested in, namely conjunctions of equations and disequations.

Example 4.3 *The figure below shows a representation of $\mathcal{H} = T(\Sigma)/=_{ACI_1}$ when $\Sigma = \{\emptyset, \cup, \{\cdot\}\}$ where $\{\cdot\}$ is a function symbol of arity 1. With a slight abuse of notation, we denote with $\{s, t\}$ the congruence class of $\{s\} \cup \{t\}$. This allows one to interpret $\mathcal{H}$ as the set of hereditarily finite and well-founded sets. Sets at level i contain exactly i elements.*

Let us start by observing that the atoms of $\langle \mathcal{H}, \leq \rangle$ are all and only the congruence classes containing terms with a main functor different from $\cup$. This is stated by the following lemma:

Lemma 4.4 *The atoms of $\langle \mathcal{H}, \leq \rangle$ are exactly the classes $[t]$, for some ground term $t \equiv f(t_1, \ldots, t_n)$, $f \not\equiv \cup$.*

Thus, with slight abuse of notation, from now on we will call *atom* any term whose main (outermost) function symbol is different from $\cup$. Observe that this property is not guaranteed to hold in other structures. For example, in any structure $\mathcal{A}$ in which $\mathcal{A} \models f(t_1, \ldots, t_n) \cup a = f(t_1, \ldots, t_n)$, for some $a \in \Sigma$, the term $f(t_1, \ldots, t_n)$ is not an atom. $\mathcal{H}$ also properly models the extensionality principle for equality between sets denoted by ACI terms:

Lemma 4.5 *Let s, t be two terms and $\mathcal{H} \models \exists (s \neq t)$. For all solutions σ, if $s_1 \cup \cdots \cup s_m \in \sigma(s)$ and $t_1 \cup \cdots \cup t_n \in \sigma(t)$, where all the s_i, t_j are atoms, then there are an atom a and an index i such that $s_i = a$ and for all t_j $t_j \neq a$ or, vice versa, $t_i = a$ and for all s_j $s_j \neq a$.*

The structure $\mathcal{H}$ is also a model of the freeness equational axioms:

(F_1) $\quad f(X_1, \ldots, X_n) = f(Y_1, \ldots, Y_n) \rightarrow \bigwedge_{i=1}^n X_i = Y_i \quad f \in \Sigma, f \not\equiv \cup$

(F_2) $\quad f(X_1, \ldots, X_m) \neq g(Y_1, \ldots, Y_n) \qquad\qquad\qquad f \not\equiv g, f, g \not\equiv \cup$

(F_3) $\quad (X \neq t_1 \cup \cdots \cup f(\cdots X \cdots) \cup \cdots \cup t_n) \qquad\quad f \not\equiv \cup$

The freeness axioms [6] have been refined to capture the behavior of $\cup$.

Similarly to what we did for (D_c), we need to enforce the property that unions of distinct atoms return distinct objects of the domain. Instead of extending (D_c)—which would be quite cumbersome in this context—we introduce the following axiom scheme (D_f): for all $f \in \Sigma$, $f \not\equiv \cup$, $ar(f) = n$:

$$f(X_1, \ldots, X_n) \cup X = Y_1 \cup Y_2 \rightarrow$$
$$\exists Z_1 Z_2 \left(\begin{array}{l} (Y_1 = f(X_1, \ldots, X_n) \cup Z_1 \wedge X = Z_1 \cup Y_2) \ \vee \\ (Y_2 = f(X_1, \ldots, X_n) \cup Z_2 \wedge X = Y_1 \cup Z_2) \ \vee \\ (Y_1 = f(X_1, \ldots, X_n) \cup Z_1 \wedge Y_2 = f(X_1, \ldots, X_n) \cup Z_2 \wedge X = Z_1 \cup Z_2) \end{array} \right)$$

Note that the ← direction is a simple consequence of the ACI axioms. This axiom scheme captures the intuitive notion of atoms in the context of ∪, and subsumes (D_c). Thus, axiom (D_c) can be safely removed:

Lemma 4.6 $ACI1D_fF_2 \models (D_c).$[4]

Hereafter we will use T_{ACI} to denote $ACI1F_1F_2F_3D_f$.

Theorem 4.7 $\mathcal{H}$ and T_{ACI} correspond on the class of all the conjunctions of equations and disequations.

The following theorem is fundamental for the satisfiability test of all the solved forms presented in this paper.

Theorem 4.8 Let Σ be a general signature. Given a disequation constraint $C \equiv (s_1 \neq t_1 \wedge \cdots \wedge s_n \neq t_n)$ such that $\rho(s_i) \not\equiv \rho(t_i)$ for all $i = 1, \ldots, n$, then C is satisfiable in $\mathcal{H}$, and in every model of T_{ACI}.

Corollary 4.9 If Σ is a general signature, then the satisfiability of a disequation constraint in $\mathcal{H}$ can be decided in polynomial time.

5   Solved forms

Most constraint systems rely on the availability of *constraints simplifiers* to transform constraints into equivalent "simpler" formulae. In particular, it is common to identify a class of formulae, called *solved forms*, which are the target of this simplification. As described in [8], solved forms should be:

- **solvable:** each solved form is either false or it admits at least one solution;
- **simple:** satisfiability of a solved form should be *trivially* decidable;
- **complete:** every constraint is equivalent to a finite (possibly empty) disjunction of solved forms.

We propose three solved forms for the $ACI1$-constraints considered in this paper. Each form can be computed from the previous ones. The first form (*implicit*) implicitly represents its set of solutions. Given a constraint C, a unique implicit solved form constraint can be computed from it in polynomial (quadratic) time with respect to the number $|C|$ of occurrences of symbols in C. The second solved form (*intermediate*) further simplifies a constraint in implicit solved form. In polynomial (cubic) time it is possible to compute a formula containing a collection of intermediate solved form constraints. Each component of the collection can be computed in polynomial time, but the number of components might be exponential (exponentiality arises due to the application of distributivity). The third solved form (*explicit*) represents explicitly its solutions. It can be computed from the first one on demand, and determining each disjunct requires exponential time.

All the solved forms are instances of the *compact formulae* defined in [8]. If the theory $ACI1$ were *compact*, the ability to reach a solved form would automatically ensure satisfiability of these constraints over $\mathcal{H}$ [8]. Unfortunately (see Sect. 6), $ACI1$ is not compact; thus, a direct proof of satisfiability of the different solved forms is required.

In the following subsections we precisely characterize the three solved forms. However, we anticipate that all of them fulfill the hypothesis of Theorem 4.8.

---

[4]The converse is not true. Consider $\Sigma = \{\emptyset, \cup, c\}$ and the lattice $\bot < a_1, \bot < a_2, a_1 < c, a_2 < c^A$. It fulfills (D_c) but not (D_f) (consider $c \cup \underbrace{\bot}_{X} = \underbrace{a_1}_{Y_1} \cup \underbrace{a_2}_{Y_2}$).

Corollary 5.1 *An implicit/intermediate/explicit solved form constraint C different from* false *is satisfiable in $\mathcal{H}$, and hence $T_{ACI} \models \exists C$.*

5.1 Implicit solved form

A variable X occurs *nested* in a term t if t is of the form: $t_1 \cup \cdots \cup f(\cdots X \cdots) \cup \cdots \cup t_n$, with $f \not\equiv \cup$. A constraint C is in *implicit solved form* if it is false, true, or $C \equiv (s_1 \neq t_1 \wedge \cdots \wedge s_n \neq t_n)$ and for all $i = 1, \ldots, n$

- $vars(s_i) \cup vars(t_i) \neq \emptyset$, and
- $s_i \equiv \rho(s_i)$ and $t_i \equiv \rho(t_i)$, and
- $s_i \not\equiv t_i$, and
- if t_i is a variable, then s_i is also a variable, and
- if s_i is a variable, then it does not occur nested in t_i.

Given a constraint $C \equiv (s_1 \neq t_1 \wedge \cdots \wedge s_n \neq t_n)$, we can obtain an equivalent constraint in implicit solved form, starting from $\rho(C)$ and applying the function impl_simpl of Fig. 1. Occurrences of true and false can be easily handled in linear time at the end of the rewriting process—we assume that the function tfsimpl performs this task. Clearly, tfsimpl(impl_simpl($\rho(t)$)) is in implicit solved form.

function impl_simpl(φ):			
while there is a disequation c in φ not in implicit s.f. do			
case c of			
(1)	$r \neq r$	$\mapsto$	false
(2)	$\left.\begin{array}{c} s \neq t \\ s \neq t, vars(s) = \emptyset \wedge vars(t) = \emptyset \end{array}\right\}$	$\mapsto$	true
(3)	$\left.\begin{array}{c} t \neq X, \\ t \text{ is not a variable} \end{array}\right\}$	$\mapsto$	$X \neq t$
(4)	$\left.\begin{array}{c} X \neq t_1 \cup \cdots \cup f(\cdots X \cdots) \cup \cdots \cup t_n, \\ f \not\equiv \cup \end{array}\right\}$	$\mapsto$	true
(5)	$\left.\begin{array}{c} f(\cdots) \neq g(\cdots), \\ f \not\equiv g, f \not\equiv \cup, g \not\equiv \cup \end{array}\right\}$	$\mapsto$	true

Figure 1: Rewriting procedure for implicit solved form

Proposition 5.2 *Given a constraint C, tfsimpl(impl_simpl($\rho(C)$)) can be computed in time $O(n^2)$ where $n = |C|$. Moreover, if $\bar{X} = vars(C)$, then $ACI1F_1F_2F_3 \models \forall \bar{X}(C \leftrightarrow \text{impl\_simpl}(\rho(C)))$.*

5.2 Intermediate solved form

A constraint in implicit solved form C is in *intermediate solved form* if it is false or $C \equiv (s_1 \neq t_1 \wedge \cdots \wedge s_n \neq t_n)$ and for all $i = 1, \ldots, n$

- s_i is a variable and s_i does not occur nested in t_i, or
- $s_i \equiv r_1 \cup \cdots \cup r_h$ and $t_i \equiv v_1 \cup \cdots \cup v_k$, $h, k \geq 2$.

The procedure described in Fig. 2 produces a formula containing only disequations in intermediate solved form. Moreover, the formula is equivalent to the original constraint.

Proposition 5.3 *Given a constraint C, the formula int_simpl($\rho(C)$) can be computed in time $O(n^3)$ ($n = |C|$). Moreover, $T_{ACI} \models \vec{\forall}(C \leftrightarrow \text{int\_simpl}(\rho(C)))$.*

```
function int_simpl(φ):
    while there is a disequation c in φ not in intermediate s.f. do
    case c of
```

(1)–(5)	as in impl_simpl		
(6)	$\left.\begin{array}{c} s_1 \cup s_2, \neq f(t_1,\ldots,t_n), \\ f \not\equiv \cup \end{array}\right\}$	$\mapsto$	$f(t_1,\ldots,t_n) \neq s_1 \cup s_2$
(7)	$f(s_1,\ldots,s_n) \neq f(t_1,\ldots,t_n)$	$\mapsto$	$\bigvee_{i=1}^{n} s_i \neq t_i$
(8)	$f(s_1,\ldots,s_n) \neq t_1 \cup t_2$	$\mapsto$	$\bigvee_{i=1}^{2}(f(s_1,\ldots,s_n) \neq t_i \wedge t_i \neq \emptyset) \vee$ $(f(s_1,\ldots,s_n) \neq t_1 \wedge f(s_1,\ldots,s_n) \neq t_2)$

Figure 2: Rewriting procedure for intermediate solved form

```
function expl_simpl(φ):
    while there is a disequation c in φ not in explicit s.f. do
    if c ≡ r ∪ s ≠ t ∪ u
        then replace c by ν(c)
        else replace c by int_simpl(c)
```

Figure 3: Rewriting procedure for explicit solved form

Nevertheless, a successive application of the distributivity can generate an exponential number of disjuncts. This consideration holds in any general equational theory E. For example, given a binary function symbol f and the constraint $f(X_1, Y_1) \neq f(V_1, Z_1) \wedge \cdots \wedge f(X_n, Y_n) \neq f(V_n, Z_n)$, after the application of the simplification rules in Fig. 2, we obtain (in time $O(n)$): $(X_1 \neq V_1 \vee Y_1 \neq Z_1) \wedge \cdots \wedge (X_n \neq V_n \vee Y_n \neq Z_n)$. The corresponding disjunctive normal form contains 2^n disjuncts. On the other hand, the presence of an exponential number of disjuncts generated by the int_simpl procedure implies that an explicit enumeration of the whole set of solutions requires exponential amount of time:

Corollary 5.4 *Given a constraint C, an intermediate solved form constraint C' that implies C can be computed in time $O(n^3)$, where $n = |C|$. Moreover, the disjunction of all the intermediate solved form constraints equivalent to C can be computed in time $2^{O(n)}$.*

Adopting a structure-sharing technique to implement int_simpl it should be possible to lower the complexity to $O(n^2)$ (instead of $O(n^3)$).

5.3 Explicit solved form

In this section we show how a disequation $r \cup s \neq t \cup u$ occurring in a constraint in intermediate solved form can be further simplified.

An intermediate solved form constraint C is in *explicit solved form* if it is false or $C \equiv (s_1 \neq t_1 \wedge \cdots \wedge s_n \neq t_n)$ and, for all $i = 1, \ldots, n$, the following holds: if s_i is not a variable, then $s_i \neq t_i$ is of the form:

$$X \cup Y_1 \cup \cdots \cup Y_h \neq Y_1 \cup \cdots \cup Y_h \cup r_1 \cup \cdots \cup r_k$$

The rewriting of a constraint C in intermediate solved form, different from false, into an equivalent constraint in explicit form (see Fig. 3) is based on the recursive replacement of each conjunct of the form

$$c \equiv \underbrace{X_1 \cup \ldots \cup X_m \cup t_1 \cup \ldots \cup t_h}_{\ell} \neq \underbrace{Y_1 \cup \ldots \cup Y_n \cup s_1 \cup \ldots \cup s_k}_{r},$$

with the formula $\nu(c) \equiv \varphi_\ell \vee \varphi_r$ where $\varphi_\ell \equiv \bigvee_{i=1}^{h} \varphi^i_{term} \vee \bigvee_{i=1}^{m} \varphi^i_{var}$ and

$$\varphi^i_{term} \equiv \bigwedge_{j=1}^{k}(t_i \neq s_j) \wedge \bigwedge_{j=1}^{n}(Y_j \neq Y_j \cup t_i)$$
$$\varphi^i_{var} \equiv \bigwedge_{J \subseteq \{1,\ldots,k\}}(X_i \cup Y_1 \cup \ldots \cup Y_n \neq Y_1 \cup \ldots \cup Y_n \cup \bigcup_{r \in J} s_r)$$

The definition of φ_r is perfectly symmetrical. Intuitively, φ^i_{term} asserts the fact that t_i does not belong to the set described by the r.h.s., while φ^i_{var} states that X_i is not a subset of the r.h.s.

The replacement of c with $\nu(c)$ can generate a number of new disequations (e.g., $s_1 \neq t_1$ with $s_1 \equiv f(\bar{t}_1)$ and $s_1 \equiv g(\bar{t}_2)$) that can be rewritten by the function int_simpl of Fig. 2. However, all the subproblems generated are of *smaller* size and the function expl_simpl will eventually terminate.

Proposition 5.5 *For a canonical disequation c of the form $X_1 \cup \ldots \cup X_m \cup t_1 \cup \ldots \cup t_h \neq Y_1 \cup \ldots \cup Y_n \cup s_1 \cup \ldots \cup s_k$ we have that $T_{ACI} \models \vec{\forall}(c \leftrightarrow \nu(c))$.*

Proposition 5.6 *Given an implicit solved form constraint C,*
$$T_{ACI} \models \vec{\forall}(C \leftrightarrow \mathsf{expl\_simpl}(C)).$$

Theorem 5.7 *Given an implicit solved form constraint C, expl_simpl(C) terminates.*

Observe that every disequation of the form $t_i \neq s_j$ occurs twice in $\nu(c)$. Adopting a structure-sharing technique, however, it is possible to keep the complexity of expl_simpl within $O(n^3)$. Moreover, $\nu(c)$ generates an exponential number of disequations. So, even if the number of steps is polynomial, the real complexity of the algorithm is exponential: $O(n^3 2^n)$.

Example 5.8 *Let us consider the constraint $f(X \cup a \cup g(Y), a) \neq f(X \cup Y \cup b, X)$ and assume that $\#(X) < \#(Y) < \#(a) < \#(b) < \#(g)$. The constraint is in implicit solved form; the corresponding disjunction of constraints in intermediate solved form is*

$$X \neq a \vee X \cup a \cup g(Y) \neq X \cup Y \cup b$$

and the corresponding disjunction of constraints in explicit solved form is

$X \neq a \vee \quad X \neq X \cup a \wedge Y \neq Y \cup a \vee$
$X \neq X \cup g(Y) \wedge Y \neq Y \cup g(Y) \vee X \neq X \cup b \vee$
$X \neq X \cup Y \wedge X \cup Y \neq X \cup a \wedge X \cup Y \neq X \cup g(Y) \wedge X \cup Y \neq X \cup a \cup g(Y)$

Observe that the components of the explicit solved form precisely identify the set of possible solutions. For instance, the second disjunct forces X and Y to be not of the form $a \cup s$ for any term s.

6 Discussion and Related Work

In [8] Comon studies the problem of determining adequate solved forms for disunification problems in the context of quotient algebras $T(\Sigma)/=_E$ for various classes of equational theories E. Comon identifies a class of formulae, called *compact formulae*. All the three solved forms presented in this paper fulfill the requirement of being compact formulae. Comon proves also that *compact* equational theories, i.e., theories for which:

- E-unification is finitary and decidable
- each equation $s = t$, $vars(s,t) = \{X\}$ and such that $s \neq_E t$ admits a finite number of solutions in $\mathcal{H}$

guarantee that every compact formula distinct from false is satisfiable in $T(\Sigma)/ =_E$ [8].

However, $ACI1$ is not compact, since equations of the type $X = X \cup a$ do not admit a finite set of solutions if $T(\Sigma)/ =_{ACI1}$ is infinite—which is the case when Σ is general. Nevertheless, we have demonstrated in the previous sections how to reduce an arbitrary disunification problem to a compact form, as well as the fact that the specific compact forms considered in our context are always satisfiable (Corollary 5.1). Thus, $ACI1$ represents a good example to indicate that compactness of the equational theory is a sufficient but *not necessary* condition for the satisfiability of formulae in compact form.

Bückert [4] introduces a general scheme for solving disunification problems in the context of an arbitrary equational theory E. Solutions of disunification problems are described through the use of *substitutions with exceptions*, i.e., entities of the form σ, Ψ where σ is a substitution and Ψ a set of substitutions. An actual solution to the disunification problem is represented by any instantiation of σ which is not an instantiation of any of the substitutions in Ψ. In the context of a theory E which is finitary w.r.t. unification, the set of all solutions to a disunification problem can be represented using a finite set of substitutions with exceptions—additionally, the Ψ component of each of them is guaranteed to be finite. Substitutions with exceptions can be obtained from the solutions of a set of unification problems.

Nevertheless, this approach is not suitable to be used in a CLP language. Each substitution with exceptions is equivalent to a formula of the type:

$$\exists \bar{W} \forall \bar{Y}(X_1 = t_1 \wedge \ldots \wedge X_n = t_n \wedge W_1 \neq s_1 \wedge \ldots \wedge W_m \neq s_m)$$

where $vars(s_1, \ldots, s_m) = \bar{Y}$, $vars(t_1, \ldots, t_n) \cap \bar{Y} = \emptyset$ and $W_1, \ldots, W_m \in \bar{W}$. This leads to the generation of formulae with arbitrary quantifications, that are inadequate to a CLP framework. Moreover, to guarantee the existence of solutions it is necessary to verify if σ is an E-instance of any substitution in Ψ—as in the *Inconsistency Lemma* in [4]. This requires solving additional E-unification problems as well as having an *explicit* representation of Ψ.

In [2] Baader and Schulz develop a general technique capable of combining the satisfiability algorithms (based on substitutions with exceptions) for disjoint equational theories. The approach is general and can be applied to $ACI1$ as well. However, it provides a unique solved form that can be reached in exponential time. The solution of [2] introduces a great variety of new variables and opens a large number of alternatives. In particular, with this method one has to guess: the partition of the m variables present in the problem ($m \leq n$) into equivalence classes, a *linear ordering* over the variables (among the possible $m!$), and a *type information* for each variable, specifying to which theory E_0, E_1 the variable belongs to (2^m possible choices). This leads to an overall complexity—modulo the usual combinatorial approximations—of $\approx \sqrt{2} \left(n^{\frac{3n-2}{2}} \right) \left(\left(\frac{2}{e} \right)^{\frac{n-2}{2}} \right)$. Thus, in a particular case as that presented in this paper, it is reasonable to improve their constraint solver, developed for a universal framework. We do not introduce new variables to solve inequations and, using the implicit solved form we do not introduce disjunctions. Starting from a constraint made of disequations, the complexity of our approach seems to be more promising (e.g., $O(n^2)$ for the implicit solved form) and practical.

In the context of CLP with sets, three major proposals have been presented in the literature. In [14], Gervet presents a language, called *Conjunto*, which incorporates a constraint solver over boolean lattices built from (flat) set intervals. The constraints can be more complex (e.g., boolean constraints) than those considered in this paper, but the domain isless general. In particular, the simulation of nested sets is not possible—which prevents the direct encoding of many interesting problems.

In CLPS [18] the authors use a solved form similar to the implicit one presented in this paper. On the other hand, their constraint solving mechanisms appear to be based on reducing the problem to standard forward-checking and lookahead techniques. The limited literature on the topic prevents us from a deeper comparison with the capabilities of CLPS.

{log} [9, 10] is a constraint logic programming language over hybrid and hereditarily finite sets. Sets in {log} are represented using a more restricted construction, based on the use of the constant $\emptyset$ and the binary function symbol *with* (interpreted as the set element insertion operation). The function symbol $\cup$, instead, is not available. The union operation, however, is provided in the extended version presented in [10] as a primitive constraint based on the ternary predicate symbol $\cup_3$. Unification in this context is still NP-complete and can be seen as an instance of the cases analyzed in this paper (see [11]). Disunification is relatively simpler: the constraint solvers developed for {log} [9] are capable of handling both equalities and disequalities, leading to a solved form containing only primitive constraints of the form $X = t$ and $Y \neq s$, where X, Y are variables, X occurs only once in the resulting constraint, and Y does not appear in s.

7 Conclusions

In this paper we have studied the problem of verifying the satisfiability of conjunctions of equations and disequations w.r.t. an $ACI1$ theory. The ability to efficiently verify the satisfiability of this class of formulae is vital to the development of more general and effective CLP languages embedding sets. Existing results in the area of E-disunification (e.g., [8, 4, 2]) present general techniques which are either inadequate to the needs of a CLP framework (e.g., [4, 2]) or unsuitable to the characteristics of $ACI1$ equational theories (e.g., [8]). The contributions of this paper are:

- we have characterized the structures suitable to model $ACI1$-like theories
- we have provided complexity results for the problem of verifying satisfiability of elementary disunification and disunification with constants
- in the general disunification case, we have characterized the axiomatization which captures the desired properties, and which corresponds to the "standard" $T(\Sigma)/ =_{ACI1}$ model
- we have proposed three solved forms, increasingly more precise in the characterization of the solutions set, and developed algorithms to compute the equivalent solved form for arbitrary conjunctions of disequations. Each solved form can be trivially tested for satisfiability. Furthermore two of the three solved forms can be computed and tested in polynomial time.

As future work, we will continue exploring the issue of solved forms for $ACI1$ constraints, e.g., to achieve even more precise representation of the solutions set. We will also explore the use of structure-sharing as a term representation technique to contain the size explosion during the unification phase of constraint solving.

Acknowledgments

The authors wish to thank R. Giacobazzi and D. Ranjan. A. Dovier and C. Piazza are partially supported by MURST. E. Pontelli is partially supported by NSF grants CDA9729848, EIA9810732, CCR9875279, and the US-Spain Research Program.

References

[1] F. Baader and W. Büttner. Unification in Commutative and Idempotent Monoids. *TCS*, 56:345–352, 1988.

[2] F. Baader and K. U. Schulz. Combination Techniques and Decision Problems for Disunification. *TCS*, 142:229–255, 1995.

[3] F. Baader and K. U. Schulz. Unification in the Union of Disjoint Equational Theories: Combining Decision Procedures. *JSC*, 21:211–243, 1996.

[4] H.-J. Bückert. Solving Disequations in Equational Theories. In *CADE 1988*, vol. 310 of *LNCS*, pages 517–526. Springer-Verlag, 1988.

[5] D. Cantone, A. Ferro, and E. G. Omodeo. *Computable Set Theory, Vol. 1*. Int. Series of Monographs on Computer Science. Clarendon Press, Oxford, 1989.

[6] K. L. Clark. Negation as Failure. In H. Gallaire and J. Minker, eds., *Logic and Databases*, pages 293–321. Plenum Press, 1978.

[7] M. Codish and V. Lagoon. Type Dependencies for Logic Programs using ACI-unification. *Israeli Symp. on Theory of Computing and Systems*, IEEE, 1996.

[8] H. Comon. Disunification: a Survey. In *Computational Logic: Essays in Honor of Alan Robinson*. MIT Press, 1991.

[9] A. Dovier, E. G. Omodeo, E. Pontelli, and G. Rossi. {log}: A Language for Programming in Logic with Finite Sets. *JLP*, 28(1):1–44, 1996.

[10] A. Dovier, C. Piazza, E. Pontelli, and G. Rossi. On the Representation and Management of Finite Sets in CLP-languages. *Proc. JICSLP*, MIT Press, 1998.

[11] A. Dovier, E. Pontelli, and G. Rossi. Set Unification Revisited. NMSU-CSTR-9817, Dept. of Computer Science, New Mexico State Univ., USA, Oct. 1998.

[12] H. B. Enderton. *A Mathematical Introduction to Logic*. Academic Press, 1972.

[13] C. Fidge et al. A Set-theoretic Model for Real-Time Specification and Reasoning. In *Mathematics of Program Construction*, Springer-Verlag, 1998.

[14] C. Gervet. Interval Propagation to Reason about Sets: Definition and Implementation of a Practical Language. *Constraints*, 1:191–246, 1997.

[15] G. Grätzer. *General Lattice Theory*. Birkhäuser-Verlag, 1978.

[16] J. Jaffar, M. Maher, K. Marriot, and P. Stuckey. The Semantics of Constraint Logic Programs. *JLP*, 37:1–46, 1998.

[17] D. Kapur and P. Narendran. NP-Completeness of the Set Unification and Matching Problems, In J. H. Siekmann ed., 8th CADE, Springer-Verlag, 1986.

[18] B. Legeard and E. Legros. Short Overview of the CLPS System. In *Proc. PLILP*, Vol. 528 of LNCS, pp. 431–433. Springer-Verlag, 1991.

[19] M. J. Maher. Complete Axiomatizations of the Algebras of Finite, Rational and Infinite Trees. In *Proc. 3rd Symp. LICS* (1988), 349–357.

[20] A. Mal'cev. Axiomatizable Classes of Locally Free Algebras of Various Types. In *The Metamathematics of Algebraic Systems*, North Holland, 1971, ch. 23.

[21] J. H. Siekmann. Unification Theory. In C. Kirchner, editor, *Unification*. Academic Press, 1990.

Declarative Pruning in a Functional Query Language

Mauricio Osorio
Universidad de las Americas
Departamento de Ingenieria en Sistemas Computacionales
Catarina Martir, Cholula, Puebla
72820 Mexico

Bharat Jayaraman
Department of Computer Science and Engineering
State University of New York at Buffalo
Buffalo, NY 14260, U.S.A.
bharat@cse.buffalo.edu

Juan Carlos Nieves
Benemerita Universidad Autonoma de Puebla
Facultad de Ciencias de la Computacion
72570 Puebla, Mexico

Abstract

We consider the problem of improving the computational efficiency of a functional query language. Our focus is on aggregate operations which have proven to be of practical interest in database querying. Since aggregate operations are typically non-monotonic in nature, recursive programs making use of aggregate operations must be suitably restricted in order that they have a well-defined meaning. In a recent paper we showed that partial-order clauses provide a well-structured means of formulating such queries. The present paper extends earlier work in exploring the notion of declarative pruning. By "declarative pruning" we mean that the programmer can specify declarative information about certain functions in the program without altering the meanings of these functions. Using this information, our proposed execution model provides for more efficient program execution. Essentially we require that certain domains must be totally-ordered (as opposed to being partially-ordered). Given this information, we show how the search space of solutions can be pruned efficiently. The paper presents examples illustrating the language and its computation model, and also presents a formal operational semantics.

1 Introduction

We use the term *functional query language* to refer to a functional language for querying a database, which is assumed to be given as a set of ground unit

589

predicate clauses. There are several benefits of a *functional* query language:
In comparison with approaches where a declarative query language such as
SQL is embedded in an imperative host languages such as C or C++, our
approach of a functional query language offers the advantage that the query
language is both general-purpose and declarative. In comparison with the
relational query languages recently described in the literature on deductive
databases [6, 11], the benefit of a *functional* language is that it offers a more
natural and declarative approach for recursive aggregate operations.

An aggregate operation is a function that maps a set to some value, e.g.,
the largest or smallest value in the set[1]. Aggregate operations are often non-
monotonic in nature, e.g., the largest or smallest value of a set can change if
the underlying database is enhanced with additional facts. Hence recursive
programs making use of aggregate operations must be restricted in order that
they have a well-defined meaning. The fact that aggregate operations are
functions, rather than predicates, suggests that a query language supporting
functions would be a natural framework for expressing aggregate operations.
Such an approach also permits a more natural means of stating monotonicity
requirements on aggregate operations.

In two recent papers we formulated a functional query language based
upon *partial-order clauses* [5, 9], and we refer the reader to these papers for
a full account of the paradigm. In comparison with traditional equational
clauses for defining functions, partial-order clauses offer better support for
defining recursive aggregate operations. We illustrate with an example from
[9]: Suppose that a graph is defined by a predicate edge(X,Y,C), where C is
the non-negative distance associated with a directed edge from a node X to
node Y, then the shortest distance from X to Y can be declaratively specified
through partial-order clauses as follows:

    short(X,Y) $\leq$ C :- edge(X,Y,C)
    short(X,Y) $\leq$ C+short(Z,Y) :- edge(X,Z,C)

The meaning of a ground expression (such as short(a,b)) is the *greatest
lower bound* (smallest number in the above example) of the results defined
by the different partial-order clauses. In order to have a well-defined function using partial-order clauses, whenever a function is circularly defined (as
could happen in the above example when the underlying graph is cyclic), it
is necessary that the constituent functions be monotonic. We refer to this
paradigm as *partial-order programming*, and we have found that it offers
conciseness, clarity, and flexibility in programing problems in graph theory,
optimization, program analysis, etc. Partial-order program clauses are actually a generalization of subset program clauses [2, 4] which allow one to
elegantly and efficiently program set-oriented computations.

The declarative semantics of partial-order programs is model-theoretic
in nature and follows the intuitions from fixed-point theory: a function definition has a well-defined semantics if it makes use of monotonic functions

---

[1]An axiomatization of aggregation constraints is given in [12]

with respect to the appropriate partial-orders. However, the requirement of using *only* monotonic functions is too severe, and therefore we seek a more liberal condition for a well-defined semantics. We have shown in [9] that a program has a unique least model if we can stratify, or partition, all program clauses into several levels such that all function calls at any given level depend upon others at the same level through *monotonic* functions, but may depend upon calls at lower levels through non-monotonic functions. In contrast with equational programs, for partial-order programs the least model is not obtained by a classical intersection of models (classical least fixed point), but by taking the *glb* of the denoted terms in the different models for some ground atom *f(terms)*.

In order to support this new notion of a least model, we developed an operational semantics that combines top-down goal reduction with *memo-tables*. Memo tables have been used in traditional functional languages (or equational programs) to detect dynamic common subexpressions. In the partial-order programming framework, however, memoization is primarily needed in order to detect circular constraints, or circular function calls. In general we need more than simple memoization when functions are defined circularly in terms of one another through *monotonic* functions. In such cases, we need to accumulate a set of *functional-constraints* and solve them by an iterative procedure for computing their least/greatest fixed-point.

The present paper extends earlier work in exploring the notion of declarative pruning. By "declarative pruning" we mean that the programmer can specify declarative information about certain functions in the program in a purely additive manner. Using this information, our proposed operational semantics will improve the efficiency of program execution. Essentially we require that certain domains must be totally-ordered (as opposed to being partially-ordered). Given this information, we show how the search space of solutions can be pruned efficiently.

Let us consider the *shortest distance* example again. Assume that the codomain of short is the set of natural numbers (non-negative numbers), which is totally-ordered under the numeric $\leq$ relation. The idea behind declarative pruning can be illustrated using the following database of edges.

```
edge(a,b,10).
edge(a,m,12).
edge(b,m,5).
edge(m,x,5).
edge(x,z,20).
```

Suppose we wanted to compute the value of short(a,z). We can reduce this expression in two possible ways: 10+short(b,z) and 12+short(m,z). Since 10 < 12, we reduce 10+short(b,z) first and obtain 10+5+short(m,z). Now we compare 12+short(m,z) and 10+5+short(m,z), and since 12 < 10+5, we eliminate the subexpression 10+5+short(m,z) from further consideration. That is, the final answer is obtainable by reducing 12+short(m,z). This form of pruning is called *monotonic pruning*.

Another form of pruning is also possible. To illustrate, suppose we added edge(m,z,3) to the above database of edges. Then, in reducing 12+short(m,z), we have two possible choices: 12+3 and 12+5+short(x,z). Since 12+3 < 12+5, the subexpression 12+5+short(x,z) is eliminated from further consideration. This form of pruning is called *inflationary pruning*.

It is possible to perform this kind of pruning since we know that the domain is totally-ordered and also that the domain is non-negative. When the domain is only partially-ordered, as is the case with the domain of sets under $\subseteq$, this kind of pruning is not possible. In general, the more order that we have in our lattice, the greater the possibility for pruning. Thus the paradigm of *total-order programming* can be seen as a special case of partial-order programming that improves the efficiency of program execution. It is useful for solving problems requiring search over a large data domain that can be totally ordered, e.g., database operations, approximation algorithms, optimization problems and others.

The rest of this paper is organized as follows: Section 2 provides some basic background on partial-order programming. We also define our class of well-defined programs and explain the basis of declarative pruning. Section 3 defines the operational semantics for our programs. The last section presents our conclusions and future work. We assume familiarity with basic concepts in the semantics of logic programs[2].

2   Partial-Order Clauses: Background

We first discuss conditional partial-order clauses, which have the form

$f(terms) \geq expression :- p_1(terms), \ldots, p_k(term)$
$f(terms) \leq expression :- p_1(terms), \ldots, p_k(term)$

where each variable in *expression* also occurs in *f(terms)* or in the body of the clause, $p_1(terms), \ldots, p_k(term)$ where $k \geq 0$; and each predicate p_i is an *extensional database predicate*, i.e., one that is defined by ground unit clauses. The syntax of *terms* and *expression* is given below:

term ::= *variable* | *constant* | *c(terms)*
terms ::= *term* | *term , terms*
expression ::= *term* | *c(exprs)* | *f(exprs)*
exprs ::= *expression* | *expression , exprs*

Our lexical convention in this paper is to begin constants with lowercase letters and variables with uppercase letters. The symbol *c* stands for a constructor symbol whereas *f* stands for a non-constructor function symbol, also called user-defined function symbol.

Before presenting some examples, we informally describe the operational semantics of partial-order clauses, as it will provide the reader some intuition about the language. First, it should be remembered that partial-order

---

[2]A good introductory treatment of the relevant concepts can be found in the text by Lloyd [7]

clauses essentially constitute a functional programming paradigm, and hence all functions will be called with *ground* terms as arguments. We will also use the term *query* to refer to the top-level function call, and its syntax is:

$f(ground\text{-}terms)$.

In the general case, multiple partial-order clauses will be used to define a function. Each match of a function call *f(terms)* against the left-hand side of any clause defining f will be used in instantiating the corresponding right-hand side expression; and, depending upon whether the partial-order clauses are $\geq$ or $\leq$, the *lub* or the *glb* respectively of all the resulting terms is taken as the result. In case none of the clauses match the call, the result will respectively be $\perp$ or $\top$ of the lattice. We refer to this as the $\perp$-as-failure (or $\top$-as-failure) assumption.

In order to simplify the presentation in the rest of the paper, we assume (unless stated otherwise) that every function is of one argument and that our programs use only $\leq$ clauses. Since we assume complete lattices, the $\geq$ case is dual and all the results hold immediately. The generalization to functions of several arguments is almost direct, assuming some minor technicalities that we discuss informally. We present examples to clarify these details.

We present below another well-known example where pruning is possible because of total-ordering of the domains.

Example 2.1 (Matrix Chain Product) *[13]*

Suppose that we are multiplying n matrices $M_1, ... M_n$. Let ch(J,K) denote the minimum number of scalar multiplications required to multiply $M_j, ... M_k$. Then, ch *is defined by the following inequalities:*

```
ch(I,I) ≤ 0 :- size(N), 1≤I, I≤ N
ch(J,K) ≤ ch(J,I)+ch(I+1,K) + r(J)*c(I)*c(K) :- J≤I, I≤ K-1
```

where we encode the size of matrix M_i by r(I), *number of rows, and* c(I), *number of columns, and we suppose that* c(I)=r(I+1). *The functions* r *and* c *have been omitted in the above code. The logic of the matrix chain product problem is very clearly specified in the above program. The program is well-defined because the condition* $J \leq I \leq K-1$ *prevents any circularity. Our operational semantics exploits the knowledge that + is inflationary to perform (in many cases) a substantial amount of pruning.*

In order to capture the $\top$-as-failure assumption, we assume that, for every function symbol f, the program is augmented by the clause: $f(X) \leq \top$.

Definition 2.1 *A function f is monotonic if $X \leq Y$ implies that $f(X) \leq f(Y)$. A function f is inflationary if $X \leq f(X)$. A function f is deflationary if $f(X) \leq X$.*

In preparation for the operational semantics, we first explain the notion of *reducing a program with respect to the extensional database.* Consider the function short of section 1 and the following edges:

```
edge(a,b,2)
edge(a,c,3)
```

Then the reduction short with respect to edge becomes:

```
short(a,b) ≤ 2
short(a,c) ≤ 3
short(a,Y) ≤ 2+short(b,Y)
short(a,Y) ≤ 3+short(c,Y)
```

We now define our class of legal programs. We suppose that our programs have already been reduced by the extensional database. Below we permit the definition of one function in terms of another function at the same level using *monotonic* functions. In the following definitions, as before, we assume functions with one argument.

Definition 2.2 *A program P is general stratified if there exists a mapping function, level : $F \to \mathcal{N}$, from the set F of user-defined (i.e., non-constructor) function symbols in P to (a finite subset of) the natural numbers $\mathcal{N}$ such that:*

(i) All clauses of the form $f(term_1) \le term_2$ are permitted.

(ii) For a clause of the form

   $f(term) \le g(expr)$

where f and g are user-defined functions, $level(f)$ is greater or equal to $level(g)$ and $level(f)$ is greater than $level(h)$, where h is any user-defined function symbol that occurs in expr.

(iii) For a clause of the form

   $f(terms) \le m(g(expr))$

where m is a monotonic function, $level(f)$ is greater than $level(m)$, $level(f)$ is greater or equal to $level(g)$ and $level(f)$ is greater than $level(h)$, where h is any function symbol that occurs in expr. A clause of this form is called a G-S clause (G-S stands for general-stratified).

(iv) No other form of clause is permitted.

Although a program can have different level mappings we select an image set consisting of consecutive natural numbers from 1. In the above definition, note that f and g are not necessarily different. Also, non-monotonic "dependence" occurs only with respect to lower-level functions. We can in fact have a more liberal definition than the one above: Since a composition of monotonic functions is monotonic, the function m in the above syntax can also be replaced by a composition of monotonic functions. except that we are working with functions rather than predicates.

3 Operational Semantics

We assume that all programs have been reduced by the extensional database. Our next step is to *flatten* the functional expressions on the right-hand sides of partial-order clauses [1, 3]. We illustrate flattening by a simple example: Assuming that f, g, h, and k are user-defined functions and the remaining function symbols are constructors, the flattened form of a clause

```
f(c(X,Y)) ≥ c1(k(d1(h(d2(Y,1)))))
```

is as follows:

```
f(c(X,Y)) ≥ c1(Y2) :- h(d2(Y,1)) = Y1, k(d1(Y1)) = Y2.
```

In the above flattened clause, we follow Prolog convention and use the notation :- for 'if' and commas for 'and'. The order in which the basic goals are listed on the right-hand side of a flattened clause is the *leftmost-innermost* order for reducing expressions.

Let *glb* a binary functional symbol with its intended interpretation. By abuse of language we use it with a variable number of arguments. For our operational semantics we need to extend the language by allowing terms including the *glb* symbol. However, our program as well as our queries disallow the use of *glb* in their terms.

The following definition gives the foundation of our notion of declarative pruning. When we have certain knowledge of the behavior of our functions, we may easily conclude for two expressions e_1 and e_2 that, for instance, $e_1 \leq e_2$, which we write as $e_1 \preceq e_2$. If in addition we need to compute $lub\{e_1, e_2\}$ we get e_2 without having to compute the value of e_1.

Definition 3.1 *Given a lattice L with partial order $\leq$, and two expressions e_1 and e_2, we write $e_1 \preceq e_2$ iff the following cases hold:*

1. $e_1 = f(\bar{t}_1, a, \bar{t}_2)$, $e_2 = f(\bar{t}_1, b, \bar{t}_2)$, a *and* b *are ground terms and* $a \leq b$ *is true, where* f *is a monotonic function and* $\bar{t}_1, \bar{t}_2$ *are vectors of terms.*

2. $e_1 = f(\bar{t}_1, a, \bar{t}_2)$, $e_2 = b$, a *and* b *are ground terms and* $a \leq b$ *is true, where* f *is a deflationary function and* $\bar{t}_1, \bar{t}_2$ *are vectors of terms.*

3. $e_1 = a$, $e_2 = f(\bar{t}_1, b, \bar{t}_2)$, a *and* b *are ground terms and* $a \leq b$ *is true, where* f *is an inflationary function and* $\bar{t}_1, \bar{t}_2$ *are vectors of terms.*

To illustrate this definition, we use the following example: let $f(X, Y) := X + Y$ and consider the lattice of integer numbers. Clearly f is monotonic (on both arguments) and $f(3, X) \leq f(5, X)$ no matter the value of X. Thus, we can state that $f(3, X) \preceq f(5, X)$, $f(3, 4) \preceq f(5, 4)$, etc. Moreover, if we consider the lattice of natural numbers then f is inflationary and $3 \leq f(3, X)$ no matter the value of X, so we can state that $3 \preceq f(3, X)$, $3 \preceq f(3, 2)$, etc.

Proposition 3.1 *Given a lattice and two expressions such that $e_1 \preceq e_2$ then $lub\{e_1, e_2\} = e_2$ and $glb\{e_1, e_2\} = e_1$.*

We first define the *lub-reduction* of a ground query expression G with respect to a *general stratified* program P starting from its flattened form. Note that the leftmost-order of reducing expressions in the flattened form ensures that all arguments of function calls will be ground when reduced.

The next several definitions are adapted from [9] for the present paper.

Definition 3.2 *A goal-sequence is a set of basic goals, $[f_1(u_1) = X_1, \cdots,$ $f_n(u_n) = X_n]$, where each f_i is a user-defined funtion symbol, each X_i is a variable and u_i is a term.*

Definition 3.3 *Given a general stratified program P and a ground query $f(t_1)$, where t_1 is a ground term, we define the glb-reduction of $f(t_1)$ with respect to P as the quadruple $< G, C, V, s >$, as follows (we assume as usual that the variables in distinct clause-variants are different). Let*
$P_1 := \{f(t\theta) \le Y :\text{-} B\theta \mid f(t_1) \le Y :\text{-} B$ *is a S-S clause-variant $\wedge$ θ matches[3] t and $t_1\}$*
$P_2 := \{f(t\theta) \le Y :\text{-} B\theta \mid f(t_1) \le Y :\text{-} B$ *is a G-S clause-variant $\wedge$ θ matches t and $t_1\}$*
Then
$\quad G := CAT(\{B \mid A :\text{-} B \in P_1\} \cup \{B_1 \mid A :\text{-} B \in P_2$ *and* $B = B_1 \cdot [last(B)]\})$
$\quad C := \{last(B) \mid A :\text{-} B \in P_2\}$
$\quad V := \{Y \mid f(t) \le Y :\text{-} B \in P_1 \cup P_2\}$
$\quad s := glb(\{u \mid f(t_1) \le u$ *is a ground instance of a unit clause}*$)$
where
$\quad CAT(\{B_1, \ldots, B_n\}) := [B_1, \ldots, B_n]$, *i.e., collecting all B_i in a list (order is immaterial)*
$\quad last([E_1, \ldots, E_n]) := E_n$
If there are no clauses with head $f(t) \le u$ such that $t\theta = t_1$ for any θ, then $s = \top$, and G, C, and V are all empty.

We separate G, the goal-sequence, from C, the equality constraints involving monotonic functions, since different operational strategies are used to solve them.

Example 3.1 *Let P be the following program in flattened form:*

$$h(X) \le \{10, 40\}$$
$$h(X) \le \{20, 40\}$$
$$h(X) \le Z_1 :\text{-} h(X) = Y_1, p(Y_1) = Z_1$$
$$h(X) \le Z_2 :\text{-} g(X) = Z_2 \; p(\{X\backslash\_\}) \le \{X, 30\}$$

Then the lub-reduction of $h(100)$ wrt P is $< G, C, V, s >$, where:
$$G := [[h(100) = Y_1], [g(100) = Z_2]] \quad C := \{p(Y_1) = Z_1\}$$
$$V := \{Z_1, Z_2\} \quad\quad\quad s := \{40\}$$

Definition 3.4 *A memo-table is a set of assertions of the form $f(t) = u$, where f is a user-defined function, t is a ground term, and u is any term.*

---

[3] Note that Y is not affected by θ.

Definition 3.5 *A functional-constraint is a set of basic goals* $\{f_1(u_1) = X_1, \cdots, f_n(u_n) = X_n\}$, *where each* f_i *is monotonic and every* u_i *is a term of the form* $glb\{t_i, X_{j1}, ..., X_{jm}\}$ *of some variables and possibly a ground term. Furthermore, if every* u_i, *where* $\{X_{j1}, ..., X_{jm}\} \subseteq \{X_1, ..., X_n\}$ *and* t_i *a ground term, and every* X_i *occurs in some* u_j *then we say that the functional-constraint is simple. If* $\{X_{j1}, ..., X_{jm}\}$ *is empty then* u_i *is just* t_i. *An element* $f_i(u_i) = X_i$ *of a functional constraint is said to be easy if* u_i *is ground.*

Definition 3.6 *Given a functional-constraint* $C := \{f_1(u_1) = X_1, \cdots, f_n(u_n) = X_n\}$, *we define* $level(C)=min\{i \mid P_i$ *defines all* $f_j, j = 1, ..., n\}$.

Definition 3.7 *An extended goal* G^e *is a tuple of the form* $< G, C, T, L >$ *where* G *is a list of goal-sequences,* C *is a functional-constraint,* T *is a memo-table, and* L *is a natural number. An initial extended goal has the form* $< [[f(t) = X]], \phi, \phi, L >$, *where* f *is a user-defined function of level* L, t *is a ground term, and* X *is a variable. A final extended goal has the form* $< [\,], \phi, T, L >$, *i.e., the goal-sequence and the functional constraint are both empty at the end.*

Note that there is no loss of generality in assuming that an initial extended goal consists of a single function call $f(t)$. In order to model a query expression e that had more than one user-defined function in it, we simply make expression e the body of a new function, say g, whose definition is $g(0) \leq e$, and the initial extended goal then becomes $< [[g(0) = X]], \phi, \phi, level(g) >$.

Definition 3.8 *Let* $G_1^e = < G_1, C_1, T_1, L_1 >$ *and let* $c \in C_1$, *we define the associated goal sequence of* c *as follows: Suppose* V_1 *are the variables that appear in the left hand side of* c. *Let* S *the goal sequence* $[f(t_1) = X_1, ..., f(t_n) = X_n]$ *(*$n \geq 1$*) such that* $V_1 \subseteq \{X_1, ..., X_n\}$. *Then* S *is called the associated goal sequence of* c, *or* $S = AGS(c)$. *Notice that it is possible that* c *has no goal sequence associated with it.*

Example 3.2 [4] *Let us consider the* **shortest distance** *program example with the following extensional database:*
edge(a,b,2), edge(a,b,3), edge(a,d,7), edge(b,c,5), edge(d,b,6)
The program reduced by the above extensional database in its flattened form becomes:

---

[4] More examples can be found in http://gente.pue.udlap.mx/josorio.

```
short(a,b) ≤ 2.    short(a,b) ≤ 3.    short(a,d) ≤ 7.
short(b,c) ≤ 5.    short(d,b) ≤ 6.
short(a,Y) ≤ D1 :- short(b,Y) = C1, 2 + C1 = D1.
short(a,Y) ≤ D2 :- short(b,Y) = C2, 3 + C2 = D2.
short(a,Y) ≤ D3 :- short(d,Y) = C3, 7 + C3 = D3.
short(b,Y) ≤ D4 :- short(c,Y) = C4, 5 + C4 = D4.
short(d,Y) ≤ D5 :- short(b,Y) = C5, 6 + C5 = D5.
```

The table below illustrates a derivation for the query short(a,c)=Ans. Since short is of level 2 and + is of level 1, the initial extended goal is $< [[short(a,c) = Ans]], \phi, \phi, 2 >$. We will now explain the 6 steps in the table. Keep in mind that an extended goal is defined by the list of goal sequences, the functional-constraint, the memo table, and the level. This information is in the table but we omit the level to save space.

1. The Red code in the S-T column means that we are in a reduction case of a function. This *reduce* operation is explained in [5]. The monotonic function is saved in the functional-constraint part.

2. The P-m code identifies a pruning step due to a monotonic function. Observe that $2 + C1 \preceq 3 + C1$ and so $glb\{D1, D2, D3\} = glb\{D1, D3\}$. We therefore delete the 3+C1=D2 entry in the functional constraint and update the short(a,c) entry of the table.

3. We found again a reduction case of a function but there is something interesting to point out. Do we reduce short(b,c) or short(d,c)? The best-first strategy selects the first option since $2 < 7$.

4. The P-i code identifies a pruning step due to an inflationary function. Since $D4 = 5 + C4$, $glb\{5, D4\}=5$.

5. The C-e means that we have a constraint case of an easy form (just a basic goal with a ground argument). This basic goal must be of a lower level respect to the original query in the table and so we can solve by recursion. Formally, we need to solve the extended goal $< 2 + 5 = D1, \phi, \phi, 1 >$. The solution $D1 \leftarrow 7$ is then applied to the table. We also save 2+5=7 in the table for a future reference.

6. We applied a pruning step and we arrive to a final extended goal. The solution of the original query is in the table, that is, short(a,c)=7 and therefore $Ans \leftarrow 7$ is the computed answer which is correct.

S-T	Goal Sequence	Constraint	Substitution	Memo Table
	[[short(a, c) = Ans]]	ϕ		ϕ
Red	[short(b, c) = C1] [short(d, c) = C3]]	{2 + C1 = D1, 3 + C1 = D2, 7 + C3 = D3}	{Ans ← glb{D1, D2, D3}, Y ← c}	{short(a, c) = glb{D1, D2, D3}}
P-m	[[short(b, c) = C1] [short(d, c) = C3]]	{2 + C1 = D1, 7 + C3 = D3}		{short(a, c) = glb{D1, D3}}
Red	[short(c, c) = C4] [short(d, c) = C3]]	{5 + C4 = D4, 2 + glb{5, D4} = D1, 7 + C3 = D3}	{C1 ← glb{5, D4}, Y ← c}	{short(a, c) = glb{D1, D3}, short(b, c) = glb{5, D4}}
P-i	[[short(d, c) = C3]]	{2 + 5 = D1, 7 + C3 = D3}		{short(a, c) = glb{D1, D3}, short(b, c) = 5}
C-s	[[short(d, c) = C3]]	{7 + C3 = D3}	{D1 ← 7}	{short(a, c) = glb{7, D3}, short(b, c) = 5, 2 + 5 = 7}
P-i	[]	ϕ		{short(a, c) = 7, short(b, c) = 5, 2 + 5 = 7}

Definition 3.9 *A substitution θ is a finite mapping from variables to terms and is written as: $\theta = \{X_1 \leftarrow t_1, ..., X_n \leftarrow t_n\}$. The pair $X_i \leftarrow t_i$ is called a binding. The variables $X_1, ..., X_2$ become bound to the terms $t_1, ..., t_n$ respectively. The $X_i's$ are all distinct variables and each t_i is a term distinct from X_i. If $t_i, .., t_n$ are distinct variables then θ is called a renaming substitution.*

Proposition 3.2 ([9]) *Every simple functional-constraint has a least correct answer.*

In the above definition, the least fixed point can be computed by an iterative procedure given bellow. It is clear that such a procedure could loop forever. We will return to this topic later.

Definition 3.10 ([9]) *For a simple functional-constraint $C := \{f_1(u_1) = X_1, \cdots, f_n(u_n) = X_n\}$ the computed answer, θ, for C is given by the following procedure:*

$\sigma := \{X_1 \leftarrow \top, ..., X_n \leftarrow \top\};$
repeat
  $\theta := \sigma;$
  $\sigma := \bigcup_{i=1,n}\{X_i \leftarrow s\}$ *where s is the computed answer for $f_i(u_i\theta)$ as per definition 3.13*
until $\theta = \sigma;$
return θ

In the above definition, we need to obtain the computed answer for a basic goal $f_i(u_i\theta) = X_i$, which is given in definition 3.13 below. Definitions 3.10 through 3.13 are thus mutually recursive, but the recursion is well-founded because the monotonic functions in the constraints are from strictly lower levels.

We define the notion of term substitution that is slightly more general than the standard definition as this is needed in our main definition (3.12).

Definition 3.11 *A term substitution θ is a pair of terms t_1 and t_2 that we denote by $\theta = \{t_1 \rightarrow t_2\}$. Let E be a set of basic goals or a list of goal-sequences, we define $E\theta$ as follows: Let z be a variable that does not occurs* in E; if exists E' such that t_1 does not appears in E' and $E = E'\theta_1$ where $\theta_1 := \{z \to t_1\}$, then $E\theta := E'\theta_2$ where $\theta_2 := \{z \to t_2\}$. If the given E' does not exists then $E\theta := E$.

Definition 3.12 *[9] Given a general-stratified program P, we define the reduction relation $G_1^e \to G_2^e$ as follows: Let $G_1^e = < G_1, C_1, T_1, L >$, where $G_1 = [S_1, \ldots, S_{i-1}, [E|R_1]|O]$ and $[E|R_1]$ is some element of G_1 and $R := [S_1, \ldots, S_{i-1}|O]$ is the remaining goal-sequence list of G_1. Then $G_2^e :=< G_2, C_2, T_2, L >$ is defined as follows:*

P-m) Monotonic Pruning: Suppose $e \in T_1$ is of the form $f(t) = glb\{t_1, \ldots, t_n\}$ and there exist goal sequences S and S' appearing in G_1:

Case 1: *If $f(a) = t_i$ appears in S or $f(a) = t_i \in C_1$ and $f(b) = t_j$ appear in S', where a and b are ground terms and $a \leq b$ is true, and f is a monotonic function. Then $G_2 := (G_1 \setminus S')\theta$, and $C_2 := C_1\theta$, and $T_2 := T_1\theta$ where θ is the term substitution $\{glb\{t_1, \ldots, t_n\} \leftarrow glb\{t_1, \ldots t_{j-1}, t_{j+1}, \ldots, t_n\}\}$[5]*

Case 2: *If $f(a) = t_i$ appears in S or $f(a) = t_i \in C_1$ and $f(b) = t_j \in C_1$, where a and b are ground terms and $a \leq b$ is true and f is a monotonic function. Then $G_2 := G_1\theta$, and $C_2 := (C_1 \setminus \{f(b) = t_j\})\theta$, and $T_2 := T_1\theta$ where θ is the term substitution $\{glb\{t_1, \ldots, t_n\} \leftarrow glb\{t_1, \ldots t_{j-1}, t_{j+1}, \ldots, t_n\}\}$*

P-i) Inflationary Pruning: Suppose $e \in T_1$ is of the form $f(t) = glb\{t_1, \ldots, t_n\}$ and exists S that is a goal sequence such that it appears in G_1 and t_i is the constant a:

Case 1: *If $f(b) = t_j$ appears in S where b is ground term and f is a inflationary function and $a \leq b$ is true. Then $G_2 := (G_1 \setminus S)\theta$, and $C_2 := C_1\theta$, and $T_2 := T_1\theta$ where θ is the term substitution $\{glb\{t_1, \ldots, t_n\} \leftarrow glb\{t_1, \ldots t_{j-1}, t_{j+1}, \ldots, t_n\}\}$*

Case 2: *If $f(b) = t_j \in C_1$, where b is ground term and f is a inflationary function and $a \leq b$ is true. Then $G_2 := (G_1 \setminus AGS(f(b) = t_j))\theta$ (definition 3.8), and $C_2 := (C_1 \setminus \{f(b) = t_j\})\theta$, and $T_2 := T_1\theta$ where θ is the term substitution $\{glb\{t_1, \ldots, t_n\} \leftarrow glb\{t_1, \ldots t_{j-1}, t_{j+1}, \ldots, t_n\}\}$*

C-e) Solve Easy Constraint: If $e \in C_1$ is an easy constraint then let θ be the computed answer of $< [[e]], \phi, \phi, level(e) >$. Moreover, assume that $< [], \phi, T_3, level(e) >$ is the final extended goal obtained in computing θ. Then $G_2 := G_1\theta$, $C_2 := (C_1 \setminus \{e\})\theta$, and $T_2 := (T_1\theta \cup T_3)$.

Rec) Recursion: If E is of the form $g(t_1) = X_1$, $level(g) < L$, t_1 is a ground term and the extended goal $< [[g(t_1) = X_1]], \phi, \phi, level(g) >$ has a

---

[5]$G_1 \setminus S'$ means to remove S' from G_1

computed answer θ where T_3 is the memo-table in the final extended goal, then $G_2 := R\theta$, $C_2 := C_1\theta$, $T_2 := T_1\theta \cup T_3$.

TLu) Table Lookup: If E is of the form $g(t_1) = X_1$ and $g(t_1) = w \in T_1$ for some w, then define $G_2 := G_1\theta$, $C_2 := C_1\theta$, and $T_2 := T_1\theta$, where $\theta := \{X_1 \leftarrow w\}$ if X_1 does not occur in w; otherwise, $\theta := \{X_1 \leftarrow glb\{s, Y_1, ..., Y_{i-1}, Y_{i+1}, ..., Y_m\}\}$, assuming that w is of the form $glb\{s, Y_1, ..., Y_{i-1}, X_1, Y_{i+1}, ..., Y_m\}$.

Red) Reduce: If E is of the form $g(t_1) = X_1$, $level(g) = L$, and $g(t_1)$ is not in table T_1, R_1 is $[]$, then let the glb-reduction of $g(t_1)$ wrt P be the quadruple $< G, C, \{Y_1, \cdots, Y_n\}, s >$ (definition 3.3). Define $\theta := \{X_1 \leftarrow glb\{s, Y_1, ..., Y_n\}\}$, and $G_2 := (G \cdot R)\theta$, and $C_2 := (C_1 \cup C)\theta$, and $T_2 := (T_1 \cup \{g(t_1) = X_1\})\theta$.

C-s) Solve Simple Constraint: If C_1 is a simple functional-constraint, then $G_2 := G_1\theta$, $C_2 := \phi$ and $T_2 := (T_1 \cup C_1)\theta$, where θ is the computed answer for C_1 (definition 3.10).

The order of the selection does not affect the soundness of the operational semantics, but only the efficiency. Our experimental results suggest the given order. A *reduce* step takes place only when we can not find any goal sequence where we could apply *pruning, solve easy constraint, recursion,* or *table lookup*. In addition if several goal sequences can be reduced, we select with respect to the best-first strategy explained in example 3.2.

Definition 3.13 *Let $\rightarrow^*$ denoted the reflexive transitive closure of the $\rightarrow$ relation. Let G_1^e be an extended initial goal that terminates with final extended goal $G_2^e := < [\,], \phi, T_2, L >$, i.e., $G_1^e \rightarrow^* G_2^e$. We define the computed answer for G_1^e as follows: If $G_1^e := < [[f(t) = X]], \phi, \phi, L >$, where t is ground, then the computed answer for G_1^e is $\{X \leftarrow s\}$, where $f(t) = s \in T_2$ for some s.*

Definition 3.14 *Given a list of goal sequences G and a functional-constraint C, $conj(G, C)$ denotes the goal sequence formed by goals from G or C.*

We are now ready to state the soundness of the operational semantics for general stratified programs. To fully understand the following, the reader needs to know the concepts involved in the definition of the declarative semantics [9], which we omitted for lack of space.

Definition 3.15 *Let P be a general stratified program and $G^e := < G, C, T, L >$ an extended goal where $conj(G, C)$ has the greatest correct answer θ. Then G^e is said to be table invariant if the following condition holds: Every entry E of T is of the form $f(t) = glb\{s_1, ..., s_m, X_1, ..., X_n\}$ where $n \geq 0$, t and every s_j are ground, every X_i occurs in G or C, and $\mathcal{M}(P) \models E\theta$.*

Theorem 3.1 (Soundness of General Stratified Programs)
*Let P be a general stratified program and $G^e := < [[f(t) = X]], \phi, \phi,$
$level(f) >$ an extended initial goal that terminates, with final extended goal
$G_2^e :=< [\,], \phi, T_2, level(f) >$, formally $G^e \to^* G_2^e$. Then the computed answer
for G^e is correct.*

The basic idea is to prove by induction on the well-founded order imposed
by the level of the program that every G_1^e such that $G^e \to^* G_1^e$ is invariant.
The base case is immediate, and for the induction case we need to check
each case of the $\to$ relation. The pruning cases follow by proposition 3.1
and the other cases are considered in [9]. Thus G_2^e is invariant, and hence
every entry in T_2 is ground and true.

4   Conclusions and Further Work

The main contribution of this paper lies in showing how the efficiency of
a functional query language can be enhanced through the notion of declarative pruning. We developed our approach starting from the paradigm of
partial-order programming, which provides good support for a functional
query language. The key idea underlying this paper is that more efficient
computations are possible when the resulting domain is totally ordered. This
information speeds up the search for a solution, by allowing one to prune
the search space for which no optimal solution can exist. This approach offers a significant improvement over top-down strategies in that infinite loops
are avoided, and expanding the same subgoal again requires only a table
look-up. The search strategy used here is a form of best-first search. In the
shortest-distance example, the search strategy essentially mimics Dijkstra's
algorithm. An interesting research issue would be to determine what other
search strategies can be used, and how the user might specify them.

The paradigm can be extended to implement *relaxation* in a straightforward manner. An example of a relaxation problem is to find the second-
shortest distance between a pair of nodes in a graph. Since we are working
with total orders, relaxing the constraints of a program to get the next
best solution is a simple modification. In addition, the paradigm can also
be extended to perform incremental recomputation. Making use of previously computed solutions, we can update solutions stored in a memo table
by recomputing only the sub-solutions of the problem that may have been
outdated by some change in the extensional database. The current step
in our research is the implementation of the paradigm. Here, memoization
and fixed-point iteration can be further explored for their usefulness in the
total-order domain, as well as in the extensions of relaxation and incremental
recomputation.

Acknowledgments

We thank the anonymous referees for their comments and suggestions. This research was supported in part by grants from CONACyT (C065-E9605) and the National Science Foundation (CCR 9613703).

References

[1] Brand, D. "Proving Theorems with the Modification Method," *SIAM Journal*, 4:412–430, 1975.

[2] B. Jayaraman, "Implementation of Subset-Equational Programs," *JLP*, 12(4):299-324, 1992.

[3] B. Jayaraman and D. Jana, "Set Constructors, Finite Sets, and Logical Semantics," *JLP*, 38(1):55–77, 1999.

[4] B. Jayaraman and K. Moon, "Subset logic programs and their implementation," *JLP*, to appear

[5] B. Jayaraman, M. Osorio and K. Moon, "Partial Order Programming (revisited)," *Proc. Algebraic Methodology and Software Technology*, pp. 561-575. Springer-Verlag, July 1995.

[6] Lefebvre, A. "Towards an Efficient Evaluation of Recursive Aggregates in Deductive Databases," *New Generation Comp.* 12:131-160, 1994.

[7] J.W. Lloyd, *Foundations of Logic Programming* (2 ed.), Springer-Verlag, 1987.

[8] M. Osorio and B. Jayaraman, "Aggregation and Well-Founded Semantics$^+$," *Proc. 5th Intl. Workshop on Non-Monotonic Extensions of Logic Programming*, pp. 71-90, LNAI 1216, J. Dix, L. Pereira and T. Przymusinski (eds.), Springer-Verlag, 1997.

[9] M. Osorio, B. Jayaraman, D. Plaisted "Theory of Partial-Order Programming," *Science of Computer Programming*, 34(3):207–238, 1999.

[10] M. Osorio and B. Jayaraman, "Aggregation and Negation as Failure," *New Generation Computing*, 17(3):255–284, 1999.

[11] K.A. Ross and Y. Sagiv, "Monotonic Aggregation in Deductive Databases," *Proc. 11th ACM Symp. on Principles of Database Systems*, pp. 114-126, San Diego, 1992.

[12] K.A. Ross, D. Srivastava, P.J. Stuckey, S. Sudarshan, "Foundations of Aggregation Constraints," *TCS* 193(1-2): 149–179, 1998.

[13] D.R. Stinson, "An introduction to the Design and Analysis of Algorithms," Winnipeg, Canada, 1987.

Poster Abstracts

Adding Functions to SICStus Prolog

Tibor Ásványi
Dept. of Comp. Sci., Eötvös Loránd Univ.
Budapest, Pázmány Péter sétány 1/d, H-1117
asvanyi@ludens.elte.hu

This product [3] allows user-defined functions and general evaluable expressions in SICStus Prolog 3. For this purpose, we generalize Prolog arithmetic. Therefore, according to [2] we believe the extension follows the spirit of the standardization of Prolog. The evaluation of our *nar-expressions* is defined by the standard arithmetic of SICStus, and by our *nar-functions* using the innermost narrowing method [1]. A nar-function is defined as an ordered set of (conditional) equations applied only in left-to-right direction. This extension is integrated with the *full* Prolog language, while maintaining *backward compatibility*, supporting *structured programming*, and keeping *run-time efficiency*. *Nar-Prolog* is the name of the extended language.

Goals may be *parameterized* by nar-expressions using special syntax. The extension is *constructor-based*. As a consequence of the integration of nar-expressions and meta-predicates (like setof/3) it introduces *meta-functions* parameterized by goals and *goal-expressions* allowing goals that perform subcomputations inside nar-expressions. *Higher order* nar-expressions may calculate goals or other nar-expressions. The nar-expressions can raise and handle *exceptions* inside the expressions. They may be indeterministic. The nar-functions inherit indexing from predicates. They may be static or dynamic like those. A nice integration of nar-functions, nar-expressions and data-constructors with the *module* system of SICStus is given.

The main characteristics of Nar-Prolog are dicussed in the *full paper*. Other features are described in comments at the beginning of the self-documenting *code* [3].

References

[1] Hanus M., *The Integration of Functions into Logic Programming*, The Journal of Logic Programming, Elsevier Science Publishing Co., Inc., New York 1994.

[2] Hodgson J., *WG17 Open Meèting at PACLP 99*, in: The ALP Newsleter Volume 12/2, May 1999.

[3] Ásványi T., *The Implementation of Nar-Prolog in a SICStus Prolog module* (source code + full paper)
http://valerie.inf.elte.hu/~asvanyi/pl/nar/narpl.pl
http://valerie.inf.elte.hu/~asvanyi/pl/nar/narpl_paper.ps.gz

Symbolic Execution for the Derivation of Meaningful Properties of Hybrid Systems [1]

Angelo E. M. Ciarlini
The Laboratory of Formal Methods, Departamento de Informática
Pontifícia Universidade Católica do R.J.
Rua Marquês de S.Vicente 225, 22.453-900 - Rio de Janeiro, Brazil
angelo@inf.puc-rio.br

Thom Frühwirth
Computer Science Institute
University of Munich
Oettingenstr. 67, D-80538 München, Germany
fruehwir@informatik.uni-muenchen.de

Several authors have recently suggested the use of constraint logic programming (CLP) for the verification of hybrid systems. The results of our research offer evidence that CLP can also be used for the derivation of essential properties of software specified by hybrid systems. The derived properties can be used to find meaningful test cases. In our approach, hybrid automata are automatically translated into a CLP program. The user can then study the behaviour of his system by specifying conditions under which the execution should be performed. The conditions are specified declaratively in a fragment of first order temporal logic relating variables' values at different times. Such a specification is translated automatically into conjunctions and disjunctions of constraints, which are taken into account during the symbolic execution of the CLP program. As a result, all possible paths that satisfy the conditions given initially are obtained, together with the corresponding necessary and sufficient constraints. Such constraints are translated and informed to the user who can then create reliable test plans by extracting good input values for testing the final code of his system. In order to avoid non-termination problems we use a depth-first iterative deepening search.

Our ideas have been used to implement the DExVal tool (Derivation of Meaningful Experiments for Validation). We have tried to incorporate the following features: independence between the specification of the system and the testing task; support for continuous variables; expressiveness of the query language; projection of the remaining constraints on the values of specific variables at specific times; and support for linear and non-linear expressions.

---

[1]This work is partially supported by the CNPq/BMBF Brazilian-German Programme on Scientific and Technological Cooperation

It Is Declarative
On Reasoning about Logic Programs

Włodzimierz Drabent
IPI PAN, Ordona 21, Pl – 01-237 Warszawa, Poland, and
IDA, Linköpings universitet, S – 581 83 Linköping, Sweden
wdr@ida.liu.se, http://www.ipipan.waw.pl/~drabent

A main advantage of logic programming is its declarativeness. For many purposes one can abstract from the "control" of programs and consider only their "logic". The latter means treating programs as sets of logical axioms. Such *declarative reading* of programs is sufficient for reasoning about (most) properties of the answers of programs.

This fact seems however to be forgotten in some texts concerning logic programming. They advocate reasoning in terms of operational semantics, also for cases for which a declarative semantics is sufficient. For instance, to prove properties of program answers a method is suggested, which refers to procedure calls and successes under LD-resolution. As a result, one is forced to think about logic programs in an almost imperative way. The advantage of declarativeness is lost.

We advocate using the declarative reading of logic programs in proving their properties, whenever the properties of interest are declarative. We present a straightforward proof method for partial correctness. It is based solely on the property that "whatever is computed is a logical consequence of the program". It boils down to the fact that $S \models P$ implies $S \models Q$, where S is a specification, P a program and Q a computed instance of a query. Thus $S \models P$ is the verification condition to be checked.

The approach is not new and can be traced back to the work of Clark in 1979. However it seems that the logic programming community is not sufficiently familiar with it. The approach is simpler and not less general than methods based on operational semantics.

We complement the proof method for partial correctness by a corresponding method for proving completeness. (Completeness means, speaking informally, that all the required answers are produced).

The author believes that both methods closely correspond to natural informal ways of declarative reasoning about logic programs, which are actually used by at least some logic programmers. The author believes that these methods (possibly treated informally) are a valuable tool for programmers in their every-day reasoning about programs. They should be included in teaching the basics of logic programming.

If it were necessary to resort to operational semantics in order to prove simple program properties then logic programming would not deserve to be called a declarative programming paradigm. This work shows that this is not the case.

Domains as First Class Objects in CLP(FD)

Marco Gavanelli
Dip. di Ingegneria - University of Ferrara
Via Saragat, 1 - 44100 Ferrara, Italy
mgavanelli@ing.unife.it

Evelina Lamma, Paola Mello, Michela Milano
DEIS - University of Bologna
Viale Risorgimento, 2 - 40136 Bologna, Italy
{elamma, pmello, mmilano}@deis.unibo.it

Constraint Logic Programming on Finite Domains (CLP(FD)) is an effective framework for modelling and solving Constraint Satisfaction Problems (CSPs). CSP solving requires that variable domains are known at the beginning of the computation while, in some cases, they result from some intermediate processing. Domains could be specified by means of constraints stating their properties, or asserted by a third-party system acquiring knowledge from the outer world. For these reasons, in [1] we defined an extension of the CSP framework called Interactive Constraint Satisfaction Problem (ICSP), where variable domains can be partially or completely unknown at the beginning of the computation and interactively acquired on demand. In this paper, we propose the corresponding CLP(FD) language extension, which allows to leave domains partially specified or even completely unspecified.

In the proposed extension, domains are first class objects representing collections ranging on the powerset of the intended domain of discourse. The resulting framework is a two sorted language: the first is the traditional finite domain sort, the second is the *domain sort*. We define operations and constraints on the two sorts and a constraint linking the two. In the resulting language, domains can be variables subject to operations and constraints. Since constraint propagation results in an imperative elimination of values, we propose a double domain representation: each variable has a *definition domain* and a *current domain*. The advantages of the proposed extension concern both efficiency (see [1]) and increased expressive power.

References

[1] R. Cucchiara, M. Gavanelli, E. Lamma, P. Mello, M. Milano and M. Piccardi. Constraint Propagation and Value Acquisition: why we should do it Interactively. *IJCAI*, 1999.

A Characterization of Acceptability

Pascal Hitzler[2] and **Anthony Karel Seda**
Department of Mathematics,
National University of Ireland - Cork, Ireland

Acceptable logic programs have been studied extensively in the context of proving termination of Prolog programs. It is difficult, however, to establish acceptability from the definition since this depends on finding a suitable model together with a suitable level mapping that one can use to check the conditions which characterize acceptability. We show that when working over a fixed but arbitrary preinterpretation, a method can be provided for obtaining both a suitable model M_P (P being an acceptable program) and a canonical level mapping which are sufficient for this purpose.

The model M_P is in fact the unique supported model of the acceptable program P, the existence of which was established by Apt and Pedreschi 1993 when they introduced acceptable programs. We derive two alternative characterizations of this model.

Let T_P be the single-step operator associated with P. Then the following statements hold. (1) M_P is the limit of the iterates $T_P^n(\emptyset)$, where $\emptyset$ denotes the valuation with respect to which every atom is false. The limit is taken in the Cantor topology on the space of all valuations. (2) M_P is the smallest model, under set-inclusion, with respect to which acceptability of P can be established.

Given an arbitrary program P and a model M we will give a construction of a partial level mapping $l_{P,M}$ for P and obtain the following results.

If P is acceptable with respect to some model M then the following statements hold. (1) $l_{P,M}$ is a total mapping. (2) P is acceptable with respect to M_P and l_{P,M_P}. (3) l_{P,M_P} is the pointwise least level mapping with respect to which acceptability of P can be established.

Acceptability is then characterized as follows.

A program P is acceptable iff all of the following conditions hold. (1) $T_P^n(\emptyset)$ converges in the Cantor topology. The limit is called M_P. (2) l_{P,M_P} is total. (3) For every ground clause $A \leftarrow L_1, \ldots, L_n$ of P and for all $i < n$ with $M_P \models L_1 \wedge \ldots \wedge L_i$ we have $l_{P,M_P}(A) > l_{P,M_P}(L_{i+1})$.

Finally, we show that l_{P,M_P} and M_P are also sufficient for discussing termination of non-ground queries.

---
[2]The first named author acknowledges financial support under grant SC/98/621 from Enterprise Ireland.

A Static Analysis for Classical Linear Logic Programming Language

Kyoung-Sun Kang and **Naoyuki Tamura**
Department of Computer and Systems Engineering,
Kobe University
1-1 Rokkodai, Nada, Kobe 657-8501, Japan
kang@pascal.seg.kobe-u.ac.jp, tamura@kobe-u.ac.jp

Since linear logic was proposed by J.-Y.Girard in 1987, several classical linear logic programming languages have been proposed. But, the proof search of the most of these languages is highly non-deterministic. Therefore, it is very important to find unprovable sequents before the execution of programs by a static analysis.

Andreoli et al. proposed a static analysis method for a classical linear logic programming language LO. But, their method can not handle multiplicative conjunctions, which is an important connective for a resource-sensitive feature of linear logic.

In this paper, we propose a new static analysis method applicable for a fragment of classical linear logic programming language including multiplicative conjunctions in addition to multiplicative disjunctions and linear implications. Abstract proof graph, which is an AND-OR graph representing all possible sequent proofs, is constructed from a given program and goal sequent. The graph can be repeatedly refined by propagating information to eliminate unprovable nodes from the graph, where the method of refinement is based on the idea of data-flow analysis for the optimization.

We applied our prototype analyzer for a sorting program written in Forum. The sorting program was improved about 1000 times faster for sorting 6 elements by using the analysis result.

References

[1] J.-M. Andreoli, R. Pareschi and T. Castagnetti. Static Analysis of Linear Logic Programming. *New Generation Computing*, 15:449–481, 1997.

[2] J. S. Hodas and J. Polakow. Forum as a Logic Programming Language: Preliminary Results and Observations. *Proceedings of the Linear Logic '96 Meeting*, Tokyo, Japan, 1996.

[3] J. S. Hodas, K. Watkins, N. Tamura and K. S. Kang. Efficient Implementation of a Linear Logic Programming. *Proceedings of the Joint International Conference and Symposium on Logic Programming*, 145–159, 1998

[4] D. Miller. Forum:A Multiple-Conclusion Specification Logic. *Theoretical Computer Science*, 165(1):201–232, 1996.

Isoinitial Models for Logic Programs: Some Preliminary Results

Kung-Kiu Lau

Department of Computer Science, University of Manchester
Oxford Road, Manchester M13 9PL, United Kingdom
kung-kiu@cs.man.ac.uk

Mario Ornaghi

Dipartimento di Scienze dell'Informazione
Universita' degli studi di Milano, Via Comelico 39/41, Milano, Italy
ornaghi@dsi.unimi.it

The traditional view of a definite logic program treats it as an initial theory. The intended model of a definite (Horn clause) logic program P is its Herbrand model H. It interprets P under the Closed World Assumption. Considering the class of all the models of P, H interprets P as an initial (Horn) theory. A distinguishing feature of an initial theory P is that, in general, it proves (computes) only positive literals (atoms) in P, so it does not deal with *negation*. This in our opinion is too restrictive because it does not provide a uniform semantics for negation and open programs, or parametricity. This view is therefore very much one of *programming-in-the-small*.

We believe that it is desirable to have a uniform semantics for both *programming-in-the-large* and *programming-in-the-small*, and to this end, we have been studying *isoinitial* models of logic programs. Our preliminary results suggest that isoinitial semantics fits the bill since it can provide a unifying semantics for definite and normal programs, and for closed and open programs. Isoinitial semantics handles not only negation but also parametricity in a uniform manner with respect to both closed and open programs. Moreover, constructive formal systems can help prove isoinitiality.

Clearly such a uniform semantics is important if logic programming is to be used for large-scale software development. Indeed we believe isoinitial semantics is a unique feature and a great advantage of the logic programming paradigm. We have already used isoinitial semantics in our work in formal program development and more recently in component-based software development, in computational logic [1, 2]. It is within this context that we plan to continue our study of isoinitial theories and models.

References

[1] K.-K. Lau and M. Ornaghi. OOD Frameworks in Component-based Software Development in Computational Logic. *LOPSTR'98, LNCS* 1559:101-123, 1999.
[2] J. Küster Filipe, K.-K. Lau, M. Ornaghi, and H. Yatsu. On Dynamic Aspects of OOD in Component-based Software Development in Computational Logic. Extended abstract for LOPSTR'99, 1999.

Implementing Prolog with Chronological Garbage Collection

Xining Li
Lakehead University
Thunder Bay, ON, Canada
xli@flash.lakeheadu.ca

Traditional Prolog implementations are based on the stack/heap memory architecture: stack holds local variables and control information, whereas the heap stores data objects which outlive procedure activations. A stack frame can be deallocated when an activation ends while heap space can only be reclaimed on backtracking or by garbage collection. Conventional garbage collection methods may yield poor performance. A reason for using stack/heap architecture is that deallocating stack frames is, in fact, cheap, incremental garbage collection. In this paper, I present a novel memory management approach which can be used in various logical/functional programming language implementations. This scheme uses a single stack for all dynamical memory requirements, embedding an efficient garbage collection algorithm, the Chronological Garbage Collection (CGC), to reclaim useless memory cells. CGC combines the advantages of copying, mark-compact, generational, and incremental algorithms. In brief, at some stage of execution, memory usage is checked. Two generations are divided by a dynamic generation line. The most important measurements to determine the invocation of collector are *generation-gap* and *cache-limit*. Generation-gap is defined as the distance from the youngest stack frame to some old frame. Cache-limit is a machine-dependent constant. The collector is invoked only if the generation-gap is greater than the cache-limit. The algorithm consists of two phases. The collection phase traverses from an initial root set, and creates copies of all root-reachable objects onto a free space. During collection, new roots might be added to the root set. This phase stops when the root set becomes empty. Then the compact phase will move copied objects back to the young area and the remaining space in young area will be returned to the free pool as a whole. An experimental interpreter of Logic Virtual Machine (LVM) has been implemented. The LVM adopts a hybrid of program sharing and structure copying to represent Prolog terms and introduces special instructions for garbage collection. Our benchmarks show that this approach has low runtime overhead, good virtual memory and cache performance, and very short, evenly distributed pause times. Some benchmarks even revealed that the CGC not only improves the program's cache performance by more than enough to pay its own cost, but also improves the execution performance which is competitive with the SICStus fast-code.

A Regular Type Analysis of Logic Programs

Lunjin Lu and **John G. Cleary**
Department of Computer Science
The University of Waikato

We present a new type analysis for logic programs. It is *prescriptive* in that type definitions for function symbols are provided by the programmer. Previous prescriptive type analyses are not precise enough for the following reasons. Firstly, they do not allow set operators in type expressions, forcing an over approximation when the least upper bound of types is needed. Secondly, they infer deterministic regular types by disallowing non-deterministic type definitions. Thirdly, they describe type information in a set of program states (substitutions) by a single *variable typing* that is a mapping from variables to types, severing type dependency between variables.

The new type analysis is designed as a specialization of an abstract interpretation framework for logic programs. It aims to remove the above three sources of imprecision. It uses a type language that consists of unrestricted regular types and allows set union and set intersection operators. It represents type information in a set of substitutions by a set of variable typings. The core operation of the new type analysis, called abstract unification, closely simulates concrete unification. The abstract unification is reduced to computing a set of variable typings that describes the set of those substitutions that satisfy both a set of equations in solved form and an initial set of variable typings. This is done by propagating type information in the initial set of variable typings via the equations in two steps. The first step uses type information about the variables on the lefthand sides of the equations to derive more type information about the variables occurring on the righthand sides. The derived type information is then used to strengthen the initial set of variable typings. The second step uses type information about the variables occurring in the terms on the righthand sides to derive more type information about the variables on the lefthand sides. The derived type information is used to strengthen the result of the first step.

The use of regular types and sets of variable typings makes the new type analysis more precise than those found in the literature. On the other hand, the fundamental problem of checking the emptiness of types is more complex in the new analysis. Experimental results, however, show that careful use of tabling reduces the increase of execution time to an average of 15%.

Using Static Analysis to Compile non-Sequential Functional Logic Programs

Julio Mariño and **Juan José Moreno-Navarro**
Universidad Politécnica de Madrid
{jmarino, jjmoreno}@fi.upm.es

The compilation of pattern matching in functional programming and unification in Prolog is one of the strongest points of declarative languages as it relieves the programmer from specifying a lot of control. The first implementations of the functional logic language Curry are appearing now but impose a number of restrictions to programs (such as overlapping rules) that we try to relax in this paper.

Some of these restrictions are related to the sequentiality of program rules, i.e. finding a safe and a (possibly) optimal evaluation order for the arguments of functions. Sequentiality is essential in the implementation of lazy functional logic programs because logic variables make parallel strategies as difficult to implement as dependent and-parallelism in logic programming. The issue of sequentiality in functional logic languages differs from the functional case in two other aspects. On one hand, textual order is no longer significant, as nondeterminism is allowed, so optimizations used in functional languages no longer apply. The other difference is that any program transformation used to make the rules sequential should preserve output substitutions.

We claim that for the vast majority of programs, the information obtained from type inference and strictness analysis can help a compiler to (i) derive an efficient evaluation order, and (ii) generate sequential code from most programs. This means taking into account the bodies of the rules, not only the left hand sides.

Our approach is the following: first, a purely syntactic analysis of the left hand sides of non-sequential definitions is used to find those positions that are responsible for the lack of sequentiality. Second, global analysis is used to study the strictness of the defined function at those points. If strictness is found at enough places, sequential code will be generated. We propose two methods for code generation. The first is a source code transformation and has the advantage that can be used with existing compilation techniques based on sequential definitional trees. The problem is that this transformation can affect computed answers.

Our second method preserves output substitutions and introduces a generalisation of sequential definitional trees that allows overlapping while being operationally sequential (*extended definitional trees*). We also introduce a new kind of parallel definitional trees (*or-checked definitional trees*) to manage run-time tests for those cases where strictness information is not strong enough to ensure a sequential computation at compile time.

The paper contains a denotational semantics with respect to which the proposed transformations are correct. A higher order strictness analyzer is defined abstracting that semantics and used to compile some higher order Curry functions. The full paper can be found at http://lml.ls.fi.upm.es/~labman/papers/sequentia.ps

Acknowledgements: This research was supported in part by the Spanish CICYT project TIC96.1012-C02-02.

Practical Investigation of Constraints with Graph Views

Tobias Müller
Programming Systems Lab, Universität des Saarlandes
Postfach 15 11 50, D-66041 Saarbrücken, Germany
tmueller@ps.uni-sb.de

Combinatorial problems can be efficiently tackled with constraint solving. The development of a constraint-based application requires modelling the problem and then implementing this model correctly. Typically, erroneous behavior of a constraint-based application is caused by either the model or the implementation (or both of them). Current constraint programming systems provide limited debugging support for these kinds of bugs.

We propose a debugging methodology and derive an interactive tool, called the *Constraint Investigator*, for debugging the model and the implementation of a constraint-based application. In particular, the Investigator is targeted at problems like wrong, void, or partial solu-

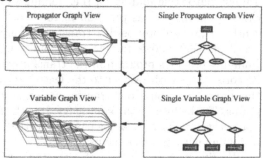

tions. A graph metaphor is used to reflect the constraints in the solver and to present them to the user in different views (see the Figure). We show that this metaphor is intuitive and that it scales up to real-life problem sizes.

The Constraint Investigator has been implemented in Mozart Oz [1]. It complements other constraint debugging tools as an interactive search tree visualizer, forming the base for an integrated constraint debugging environment.

A comprehensive presentation and discussion of the proposed debugging methodology and of the Constraint Investigator can be in [2].

References

[1] The Mozart Consortium. *The Mozart Programming System.* http://www.mozart-oz.org/.

[2] T. Müller. Practical investigation of constraints with graph views. http://www.ps.uni-sb.de/~tmueller/papers/iclp99_invest.ps.gz.

Generalized Unfold/fold Transformation Systems for Normal Logic Programs

Abhik Roychoudhury[1], K. Narayan Kumar[1,2] and I.V. Ramakrishnan[1]
[1] Dept. of Computer Science, SUNY Stony Brook, NY 11794, USA.
{abhik,kumar,ram}@cs.sunysb.edu
[2] Chennai Mathematical Institute, Chennai, India.
kumar@smi.ernet.in

Unfold/fold transformation systems for logic programs have been extensively investigated. Existing unfold/fold transformation systems for normal logic programs either allow only reversible folding [1] (i.e. folding only from the current program in the transformation sequence) or Tamaki-Sato style folding [3] (i.e. folding using a single non-recursive clause from a previous program in the transformation sequence). Recently in [2], we proposed a transformation system for definite logic programs that allows folding using multiple recursive clauses drawn from any previous program in the transformation sequence and proved its correctness with respect to the least Herbrand model semantics. In this paper we extend our transformation system to normal logic programs. To the best of our knowledge, it is the first unfold/fold transformation system for normal logic programs that allows disjunctive folding or folding with recursive clauses.

We give a uniform proof of correctness with respect to various semantics of negation including the well-founded model and stable model semantics by using Aravindan and Dung's notion of semantic kernel of normal logic programs. We also show how our transformation system subsumes existing Tamaki-Sato style systems for normal logic programs (in terms of transformation sequences allowed). Generalized unfold/fold transformation systems such as this one, facilitate development of techniques for verifying parameterized concurrent systems through logic program transformations.

References

[1] M. J. Maher. A transformation system for deductive database modules with perfect model semantics. *Theoretical Computer Science*, 110:377–403, 1993.

[2] A. Roychoudhury, K. Narayan Kumar, C.R. Ramakrishnan, and I.V. Ramakrishnan. A parameterized unfold/fold transformation framework for definite logic programs. In *Proceedings of Principles and Practice of Declarative Programming (PPDP)*, 1999.

[3] H. Seki. Unfold/fold transformation of general logic programs for well-founded semantics. *In Journal of Logic Programming*, pages 5–23, 1993.

Reactive Logic Programming by Reinforcement Learning

Taisuke Sato and **Satoshi Funada**
Graduate School of Information Science and Engineering
Tokyo Institute of Technology
Ookayama 2-12-2 Meguro-ku Tokyo
Japan 152

We combine logic programming with reinforcement learning in hopes that the proposed framework realizes a step toward reactive programming in which programs learn better behaviors reactively in response to the reward and penalty returned from an environment for the computed answer. We embed learning automatons in logic programs as primitive reinforcement learning [1] devices so that programs can learn how to make the most rewarding decisions through computational trials. We chose learning automatons because they do not presuppose the notion of states unlike MDP (Markov Decision Process)[1].

The behavior of a single learning automaton or hierarchically organized learning automatons has been analyzed quite extensively [3, 2], but when they are interwoven in a program, their connection forms a directed acyclic graph, for which not much has been analyzed. We therefore introduced the class of learning automaton networks, learning automatons organized as a directed acyclic network and proved that they asymptotically converge with probability one to the best choices when the learning rate is appropriately set [4].

We developed a special library of built-in predicates for manipulating learning automatons in logic programs, and applied our framework to solve a variant of TSP problem and the problem of Turing machine synthesis.

References

[1] Kaelbling,L.P. and Littman,M.L., Reinforcement Learning: A Survey, J. of Artificial Intelligence Research 4, pp237-285, 1996.

[2] Narendra,K.S. and Thathacher,M.A.L., Learning Automata: An Introduction, Prentice-Hall Inc., 1989.

[3] Poznyak,A.S. and Najim,K., Learning Automata and Stochastic Optimization, Lecture Notes in Control and Information Sciences 225, Springer, 1997.

[4] Sato,T., On Some Asymptotic Properties of Learning Automaton Networks, in preparation.

A Linear Tabling Mechanism

Neng-Fa Zhou
Brooklyn College, The City University of New York
zhou@sci.brooklyn.cuny.edu & zhou@mse.kyuech.ac.jp

Yi-Dong Shen, Li-Yan Yuan and **Jia-Huai You**
University of Alberta
{ydshen,yuan,you}@cs.ualberta.ca

Delaying-based tabling mechanisms, such as the one adopted in XSB, are non-linear in the sense that the computation state of delayed calls has to be preserved. When a call (consumer), which is a variant of a former call (producer), has used up the results in the table, it will be suspended. After the producer adds an answer to the table, the execution of the consumer will be resumed. The non-linearity of the suspend/resume mechanism considerably complicates the implementation. In SLG-WAM, the abstract machine adopted by XSB, the state of a consumer is preserved by freezing the stacks, i.e., by not allowing backtracking to reclaim the space on the stacks as is done in the WAM.

In this paper, we present the implementation of a linear tabling mechanism. The key idea is to let a call execute from the backtracking point of a former variant call if such a call exists. The mechanism works as follows: Each tabled call can be a producer and a consumer as well. When there are answers available in the table for the call, the call consumes the answers; otherwise, it, like a usual Prolog call, produces answers by using clauses until another variant call shows up. In this case, the later call steals the choice point from the former call and turns to produce answers by using the remaining clauses of the former call. After the call produces an answer, it also consumes one. Answers in a table are used in a *first-generated-first-used* fashion. Backtracking is strictly chronological. The later call will be re-executed to reach the fix-point. A failure occurs when the call has exhausted all the answers in its table and cannot produce any new answers by using the clauses.

The linear tabling mechanism has many advantages over the delaying-based ones: (1) it is relatively easy to implement; (2) it imposes no overhead on standard Prolog programs; and (3) it is easy to handle the cut operator. The weakness of the linear mechanism is the necessity of *re-computation* for computing fix-points. However, we have found that re-computation can be avoided for a large portion of calls of directly-recursive tabled predicates.

We have implemented the linear-tabling mechanism and made it available with B-Prolog. Experimental comparison shows that B-Prolog is close in performance to XSB and outperforms XSB when re-computation can be avoided.

Author Index

Logic Programming

Ehud Shapiro, editor
Koichi Furukawa, Jean-Louis Lassez, Fernando Pereira, and David H. D. Warren, associate editors

The Art of Prolog: Advanced Programming Techniques, Leon Sterling and Ehud Shapiro, 1986

Logic Programming: Proceedings of the Fourth International Conference (volumes 1 and 2), edited by Jean-Louis Lassez, 1987

Concurrent Prolog: Collected Papers (volumes 1 and 2), edited by Ehud Shapiro, 1987

Logic Programming: Proceedings of the Fifth International Conference and Symposium (volumes 1 and 2), edited by Robert A. Kowalski and Kenneth A. Bowen, 1988

Constraint Satisfaction in Logic Programming, Pascal Van Hentenryck, 1989

Logic-Based Knowledge Representation, edited by Peter Jackson, Han Reichgelt, and Frank van Harmelen, 1989

Logic Programming: Proceedings of the Sixth International Conference, edited by Giorgio Levi and Maurizio Martelli, 1989

Meta-Programming in Logic Programming, edited by Harvey Abramson and M. H. Rogers, 1989

Logic Programming: Proceedings of the North American Conference 1989 (volumes 1 and 2), edited by Ewing L. Lusk and Ross A. Overbeek, 1989

Logic Programming: Proceedings of the 1990 North American Conference, edited by Saumya Debray and Manuel Hermenegildo, 1990

Logic Programming: Proceedings of the Seventh International Conference, edited by David H. D. Warren and Peter Szeredi, 1990

The Craft of Prolog, Richard A. O'Keefe, 1990

The Practice of Prolog, edited by Leon S. Sterling, 1990

Eco-Logic: Logic-Based Approaches to Ecological Modelling, David Robertson, Alan Bundy, Robert Muetzelfeldt, Mandy Haggith, and Michael Uschold, 1991

Warren's Abstract Machine: A Tutorial Reconstruction, Hassan Aït-Kaci, 1991

Parallel Logic Programming, Evan Tick, 1991

Logic Programming: Proceedings of the Eighth International Conference, edited by Koichi Furukawa, 1991

Logic Programming: Proceedings of the 1991 International Symposium, edited by Vijay Saraswat and Kazunori Ueda, 1991

Foundations of Disjunctive Logic Programming, Jorge Lobo, Jack Minker, and Arcot Rajasekar, 1992

Types in Logic Programming, edited by Frank Pfenning, 1992

Logic Programming: Proceedings of the Joint International Conference and Symposium on Logic Programming, edited by Krzysztof Apt, 1992

Concurrent Constraint Programming, Vijay A. Saraswat, 1993

Logic Programming Languages: Constraints, Functions, and Objects, edited by K. R. Apt, J. W. de Bakker, and J. J. M. M. Rutten, 1993

Logic Programming: Proceedings of the Tenth International Conference on Logic Programming, edited by David S. Warren, 1993

Constraint Logic Programming: Selected Research, edited by Frédéric Benhamou and Alain Colmerauer, 1993

A Grammatical View of Logic Programming, Pierre Deransart and Jan Małuszyński, 1993

Logic Programming: Proceedings of the 1993 International Symposium, edited by Dale Miller, 1993

The Gödel Programming Language, Patricia Hill and John Lloyd, 1994

The Art of Prolog: Advanced Programming Techniques, second edition, Leon Sterling and Ehud Shapiro, 1994

Logic Programming: Proceedings of the Eleventh International Conference on Logic Programming, edited by Pascal Van Hentenryck, 1994

Logic Programming: Proceedings of the 1994 International Symposium, edited by Maurice Bruynooghe, 1994

Logic Programming: Proceedings of the Twelfth International Conference, edited by Leon Sterling, 1995

Logic Programming: Proceedings of the 1995 International Symposium, edited by John Lloyd, 1995

Inductive Logic Programming: From Machine Learning to Software Engineering, Francesco Bergadano and Daniele Gunetti, 1995

Meta-Logics and Logic Programming, Krzysztof Apt and Franco Turini, 1995

Logic Programming: Proceedings of the 1996 Joint International Conference and Symposium on Logic Programming, edited by Michael Maher, 1996

Logic Programming: Proceedings of the 14th International Conference on Logic Programming, edited by Lee Naish, 1997

Logic Programming: Proceedings of the 1997 International Symposium, edited by Jan Małuszyński, 1997

Logic Programming: Proceedings of the 1998 Joint International Conference and Symposium on Logic Programming, edited by Joxan Jaffar, 1998

Logic Programming: Proceedings of the 1999 International Conference on Logic Programming, edited by Danny De Schreye, 1999

Printed in the United States
by Baker & Taylor Publisher Services